HORNBY DUBLO TRAINS

Michael Foster

With a Compendium
compiled by Alan F. Ellis

FRANK HORNBY
1863–1936

GUILD PUBLISHING
LONDON

TELEPHONE: OLD SWAN 701 (6 LINES)

TELEGRAMS: MECCANO, LIVERPOOL.

LONDON OFFICE & WAREHOUSE,
WALNUT TREE WALK,
KENNINGTON ROAD, S.E.11.

HEAD OFFICE AND FACTORY,
BINNS ROAD, LIVERPOOL, 13.

MECCANO LTD.

LIVERPOOL

ALL CORRESPONDENCE SHOULD BE ADDRESSED
TO THE COMPANY AND NOT TO INDIVIDUALS

OUR REF.   YOUR REF.

LCN/BC.   :-

MECCANO AGENCIES:

MECCANO LTD TORONTO.
MECCANO (FRANCE), LTD PARIS.
MECCANO G.M.B.H. DÜSSELDORF.

AMSTERDAM.   HONG KONG.
ASUNCION.   IQUITOS.
AUCKLAND.   ISTANBUL.
BARCELONA.   JOHANNESBURG.
BASLE.   KARACHI.
BATAVIA.   MEXICO.
BOGOTA.   MONTE VIDEO.
BOMBAY.   NAIROBI.
BRUSSELS.   OSLO.
BUENOS AIRES.   RANGOON.
CALCUTTA.   RIO DE JANEIRO.
CAPE TOWN.   SAO PAULO.
CARACAS.   SHANGHAI.
COLOMBO.   STOCKHOLM.
DURBAN.   SYDNEY.
GENOA.   TRINIDAD.
GUAYAQUIL.   VALPARAISO.
HELSINGFORS.   VIENNA.

2nd May 1938.

Mr. D.G. Hanney, B.Sc.,
PINNER,
Middlesex.

Dear Sir,

We thank you for your letter and enquiries.

It is correct that we shall be introducing "OO" gauge railway
material later in the year.

In general our "OO" gauge material will be as
near to scale as possible. By this we mean that the locomotives
and rolling stock will be constructed practically to scale dimensions
or as close to them as the radius of the curves adopted and manufacturing considerations permit. The locomotives will have die-cast
bodies and die castings will be used extensively for the running
gear of the rolling stock. Rolling stock bodies will be of printed
tinplate.

The track scarcely falls within the tinplate
category, although it will incorporate a pressed metal base representing
the sleepers and ballast. The rails themselves will be of solid drawn metal.

The stations will be of wood , accurately in
proportion to the size of the trains, but with the platforms shortened
to some extent.

The general scale of the models will be 4 mm. to the foot, but the track will conform to the usual 16.5 mm gauge of the "HO" or 3.5 mm scale. The actual measurement between the rails will be .620 in. and the "between tyres", or back-to-back wheel dimension will be .560 in. The standard radius adopted for the curves will be 15 in. measured to the centre of the track.

Both clockwork and electric models will be available, electrification being carried out on the centre rail system. The locomotives will be fitted with permanent magnet motors arranged for a power supply of 12 volts D.C. For those who have an A.C. mains supply we intend to produce a transformer together with a rectifier and controller unit.

We hope that the foregoing will be useful to you and that if you require any further information you will not hesitate to write to us. Full information concerning our "OO" gauge trains will be included in our advertisements and in our literature , but this will not appear until the models are ready later in the year.

Yours faithfully,
MECCANO LIMITED.

W. H. McCormick.
ADVERTISING MANAGER.

This edition published 1987 by
Guild Publishing
by arrangement with
New Cavendish Books

To Barbara, Caroline and Andrew

The publishers thank Rovex Limited and Meccano Limited
for the use of the names 'Hornby Dublo' and 'Hornby',
and for the reproduction of their house material.

The author would particularly like to thank
Mr. Clifford Bowes, a mining colleague, who
rescued this manuscript when left in a
telephone box in the Lake District.

I would like to thank my publishers
for giving me such great latitude in the
presentation of the material.

The Hornby Companion Series

Design – John B. Cooper
Editorial direction – Allen Levy

Phototypeset by Western Printing Services Ltd, Bristol
Printed by Mandarin Offset

Please note:

The models and advertisments reproduced in this
book are period ones. The products shown have been
out of production at Meccano for at least 15 years.

Contents

Acknowledgements

Writing this book has not been a solo effort by any means. I was not born until three years after the system's introduction and indeed in my youth did not even have a Hornby Dublo layout. Instead an extensive Chad Valley layout graced my train room which was added to at Christmas and birthdays by my family in the way of extra coaches and model farm yard animals. The scenery was made from crepe paper and the wonderful models of Britains and other similar manufacturers littered the layout and remain with me still.

A team of five assisted with the compilation of this book namely Anthony Bianco, Alan Ellis, Dr. John Marr and John Callow. Without the work they have done, their enthusiasm for the subject, support and friendship the following work would never have appeared.

One thing that has surprised me on many occasions is the incredible way so many people have rallied round to help in showing me models, photographs, records and giving me reminiscences of years gone by.

A popular song in 1975 went. . . . 'There are more questions than answers, and the more I find out the less I know . . .' Such is the case in doing the research for this book. I have tried very hard to make it accurate but there are bound to be mistakes. I do hope that such models or drawings or photographs which have been missed out can be described to me so they can be put into the bulletin of the Hornby Railway Collectors Association for the benefit of all. This Club has some 700 members at present whose aim is the restoration, repair, running and showing of their models. As a diluter of the old social and age differences, railways in both full size and miniature must lead the field. From backstreet school kids to Bishops, from engineers to accountants they all share the enthusiasm the railway locomotive creates. I did not personally design, make and produce the Hornby Dublo range of railways and have naturally had to rely on the information given to me by so many people with direct experience and draw my own conclusions to fill the gaps. It is only right that I should record the names of those from my correspondence files here as what I have tried to do is compile into one book the information they have given me. I make no claim for this to be the definitive book on the subject as so much information has been lost or forgotten, but purely to act as the base, the skeleton of what was and was not produced in the Hornby Dublo range.

We no doubt will see in the future, books on the Triang 00 range, the Trix and Marklin H0 products, as well as a book on all the smaller private companies showing the models of Stewart Reidpath, Bonds, Beeson, City Model Company, George E. Mellor, Keysers, Wills Finecast, etc., while there is still time. Believe me, daily, models and information are disposed of and the number of shops and people I have visited who have said: 'Oh, if only you had come last month/week – we had the whole lot but needed the space and have thrown it out!'.

Here then is the list of people who have knowingly (or unknowingly) contributed greatly to the contents of this book. To those not mentioned my deepest thanks and sincere apologies for overlooking them.

Mr. Bob Albutt of Bobs Models, Birmingham
Mr. Stan Anderson, Founder of Hornby Dublo Circle
Mr. Lennart Anstrom of Sweden
Mr. Tim Armitage of Huddersfield
Mr. Neil Atkinson of R.B.S. Long Eaton, Nottingham
Mr. Bruce Baxter of New Zealand
Mr. Stewart Bean
Mr. David Benjamin
Mr. Leslie Bevis-Smith of the S-gauge Model Railway Society
Mrs. Judy Brettle of Wyatt and Tizard, Birmingham
Mr. Roger Bristow
Mr. Michael Bucher of Meccano France
Mr. Sam and Mr. David Burns
Mr. Mike Butler of B.I.P. Plastics Ltd.
Mrs. Joyce Buttigieg of Engine 'n Tender, South London
Mr. Royston Carss – retired editor of H.R.C.A. Collector Magazine
Mr. Ian Chisholm
Mr. Ron Collins
Count Coluzzi of Switzerland
Mr. Ian Cosens
Mr. Derek Crowson
Mr. Alan Daniels
Mr. Richard Davis
Mr. Pierre Delfeld of Meccano France
Mr. Bob Denny of Long Eaton, Nottingham
Mr. Dudley Dimmock for writing my foreword

Mr. Ted Doyle
Mr. Bob Dunning
Mr. Don Ellis
Mr. Andrew Emerson
Mr. Dick Fawcett
Mr. Cyril Freezer editor of Model Railways
Mr. Jack Gahan – ex Meccano Ltd.
Mr. Jim Gamble
Mr. Charles Gent
Mr. David Gilbert
Mr. Dick Goddard of Rastusout Warehousement Ltd.
Mr. Peter Gomm. Co-founder of Hornby Railway Collectors Association
Mr. Simon Goodyear
Mr. Humphrey Gore of J. Walter Thompson – Publicity Agents
Mr. John Griffiths
Mr. Bob Grossmith – Meccano Ltd.
Mr. Douglas Hanney
Mr. Norman Hatton of Hattons Model Shop, Liverpool
Messrs Ian and Darrell Hayman of the Train Shop, Warwick
Mr. Peter Hemy of the Great Western Railway Society
Mr. John Hicks – of the Parade, Sutton Coldfield
Mr. Ted Higgs
Mr. J. L. Holbrook
Mr. Peter Holmes of the Gresley Society
Mr. N. P. Hughes of Rigby Metal Components Ltd.

Mr. Bob Issott
Mr. David Jamieson – Hornby Dublo sub-editor H.R.C.A. Collector Magazine
Mr. Chris Jelley – ex Meccano Ltd.
Mr. Clifford Jones – ex Meccano Ltd.
Mr. Jim Joyce – author of many excellent articles on small scale railways
Mr. Colin Judge of Oxford Publishing Co.
Mr. John Kermode
Mr. Melvin Keyser of K's Kits i.e. N. & K. C. Keyser Ltd., of Banbury
Mr. Peter King – ex Meccano Ltd.
Mr. Roger Lassere of Meccano France
Mr. Martin Levy of Mega Models, London
Mr. Richard Lines of Rovex Hornby Ltd.
Mr. Lawson Little
Mr. Eduardo Lozano of Argentina
Mr. Barry Makey
Mr. Geoffrey Masterson
Mr. Peter Matthews of the Meccano Museum, South Africa
Mr. George Mellor of G. E. Mellor (GEM) Products Ltd.
Mr. Piers Milne of Bobs Models Ltd., Birmingham
Mr. Albert Montserrad of Meccano France
Mr. George Moon
Mr. Bob Moy – ex Meccano Ltd.
Mr. Vic Mumby – Meccano Ltd.
Mr. Bob Murray

Mr. Doug McHard – ex Meccano Ltd.
Mr. Archie Napier-Ewing
Mr. David Nathan – editor of H.R.C.A. Collector Magazine
Mr. J. H. Newman of Birmingham Aluminium Co. Ltd.
Mrs. Sheila Owen
Mr. Colin Parker
Mr. Seighart Pobel of Berlin, West Germany
Mr. Bert Pollard
Mr. George Porter of G. & R. Wrenn Ltd.
Mr. S. C. Pritchard of Peco Ltd.
Mr. John Procter of Brighton
Mr. Peter Randall. Co-founder of Hornby Railway Collectors Association
Mike & Sue Richardson of Modellers World Publications Ltd.
Mr. John Ridley
Mr. Ray Riisnaes. Co-founder of Hornby Railway Collectors Association
Roy and Joyce Salmen of J. & R. Models, Sandiacre, Notts.
Mr. John Shimwell of Platform 2, Wimbledon, South London
Mr. Colin Sparrow of Beatties Ltd.
Mr. Peter Spencer
Mr. Frank Steele of Ontario, Canada
Mr. S. W. Stevens-Stratten Editor of Model Railway Constructor Magazine
Mr. Cliff Stossel
Mr. Bill Stott of Nu-Cast Model Engineering Co., Hartlepool

Mr. Joe Swain
Mr. Eric Taft, Meccano Ltd.
Mr. Alan Taylor
Mr. Eddie Templeman of Meks Models
Mr. Paul Topple
The late Eric Treacy, Revd. Bishop of Wakefield
Mr. Ron Truin
Mr. Cyril Vincent of Adur Models Ltd.
Mr. Albert Walsh of Canada
Mr. Bert Warncken – ex Meccano Ltd. employee
Mr. Don White
Mr. Chris Willis
Mr. Bob Wills of Wills Finecast Scale Model Kits., Ltd.
Mr. Peter Winchester of the Southern Railway Group
Mr. Ken Winfindale. Hon. Secretary of the H.R.C.A.
Mr. George and Mr. Cedric Wrenn of G. & R. Wrenn Ltd.
Mr. Geoff Wright of M. W. Models Ltd., Henley on Thames. Oxon.
Mr. Bob Wyatt of Wyatt and Tizard Ltd., Birmingham
Mr. Ronald Wyborn – ex Meccano Ltd.

and all those authors of articles in the model railway press, the Hornby Dublo Circle and the Hornby Railway Collectors Association Bulletin.

Preface

It was in May 1973 that I first had letters published in the model railway press explaining I was undertaking the research of this book and hoped to have it completed by 1975. The reasons that it did not appear are the usual ones of time, lack of knowledge, cowardice and finance: research is expensive.

Because my profession as a drilling engineer in mineral exploration has taken me to many countries of the world, no sooner had I published this letter than I found that I was spending at least three to four months each year overseas. There were too many unanswered questions which, I felt, had to be traced and problems to be solved before putting pen to paper.

Finally, I must be honest and admit outright cowardice. I have never written a book before and am a normal sensitive human being. It was Geoffrey Masterson of Hampshire in one of his splendid letters to me, who said . . . 'it is a sad fact that people seem more anxious to find fault with a finished product than to contribute usefully to its accurate production'. The people I have formally acknowledged in this book and indeed many others, have helped, encouraged and supported me beyond measure to the extent that I now feel – publish and be damned! I hope you, my reader, have as much pleasure in reading this book as I have had in putting it together.

Michael Foster
Oxon

Foreword

BY DUDLEY DIMMOCK

My first view of the Hornby Dublo system was in a toy shop in Palmers Green, North London, in the years before the last war. It was just one set comprising an 0-6-2 Tank loco, some goods stock and the 3-rail track so reminiscent of the Marklin track of that period.

What was remarkable about this set lay in the fact that the rest of the window was given over to the then predominating '0' gauge Hornby system, and this Hornby Dublo set was in one corner, almost overshadowed by its big brothers. But my interest was aroused, and I found an excuse to go inside and have a look at the set at close quarters.

At that time I was modelling in '00' making my own locos from sheet metal and buying the minimum of parts to create my models. Track and rolling stock were also made by myself from parts, and as most modellers at that time used the 3-rail system with outside third rail, I realised it would not be difficult to convert the centre rail pickup method used by the Hornby Dublo, to the outside third rail system. But there was a snag, the accepted working voltage on all British DC models at that time was 6 volt, and here were the Hornby people using 12 volt. My electrical training and background made me realise instantly that the designers of these new Hornby Dublo loco mechanisms knew what they were doing. The greater pressure of 12 volt helped to overcome the 'dirt' and corrosion problem on the track and enabled finer wire and more turns on the armature windings, giving a better magnetic field, thus using smaller currents which in turn gave better control and smaller transformers and rectifiers thus reducing the costs of these items.

It could be said that the Hornby Dublo system really opened up the model railway hobby to the countless thousands who had had this privilege denied them. In the past the battle for the markets had been between Hornby '0' gauge and the '0' gauge and larger gauges of Bassett-Lowke. Mr. W. J. Bassett-Lowke can be said to have foreseen that there would be a great potential for model railways in Britain if that demand could be met. Unfortunately there were few factories in Britain that could meet that need, and so he turned to the factories of Gebr. Bing and Marklin in Germany. Under his guidance, British prototypes in '0' gauge and larger were produced in relatively low quantities, which resulted in high unit prices and these were available to the British public in the Bassett-Lowke shops in Holborn, London, Manchester and Northampton. A splendid trade ensued with the so called 'upper classes', the 'County' people who could afford (in the years between the wars), the £25 or thereabouts for a gauge '0' loco with track and accessories in proportional price rates.

As a lad, I recall gazing with awe at those marvellous models, realising they were out of my reach financially, but determined that one day I should satisfy my desire to own one of these treasures.

Little did I know that one day I should pass through the portals of this famous shop in Holborn as manager to Mr. Bassett-Lowke. I was not alone in my desire for these models, there were thousands who felt as I did and Mr. Hornby met that desire on a plane we could all afford with an ever increasing range of '0' gauge models. But this increasing range was matched with the ever decreasing size of the houses. It was becoming apparent that something smaller than '0' gauge was needed.

Mr. Bassett-Lowke had already once more turned

to the Germans, and the Twin Train System – later to be known as Trix – was introduced into this country with British liveries and an ingenious system to enable two trains to run on the same track independently controlled. Unfortunately, in the opinion of many, the Trix train models did not have the realism of the '0' gauge models. To begin with only 0–4–0 locos were available, not even resembling the prototype and these fell very short of what was required with their protruding brush caps and toylike appearance. Even the express type locos did not look all that much better, and the large 'steam roller' tyres with their huge treads and flanges did much to destroy the image of the real thing.

Mr. Hornby must have been aware of these shortcomings because the Hornby Dublo system had near scale wheels, had scale proportional bodywork on the locos and rolling stock, and looked like the prototype. The control was superior and real shunting and other real life train movements could be simulated. The early Hornby Dublo had a very ingenious coupling based on spring steel which gave positive coupling, but uncoupling was not so easy. However, I devised a modification to this coupling which gave perfect coupling and uncoupling, but it was not taken up by Hornby when I submitted the idea to them.

The word Hornby Dublo, of course, is coined from the phonetic pronunciation of '00'. The early Trix trains were really 'H0' and to understand how these symbols came to be used one must delve into the history of model railways. To differentiate between the various big gauges of the past, the trade gave the symbol '0' to trains that ran on $1\frac{1}{4}''$ gauge track and '1' to those that ran on $1\frac{3}{4}''$ gauge track, and so on. As the measurement of the gauge '0' track was then 33 mm,

when Trix started their small gauge they called it 'Half 0' which became abbreviated to 'H0' and the trains ran on a track of 16.5 mm (half the gauge '0' track). As an early modeller and builder of small locos, I found as did countless others that 'H0' used a scale measurement of $3\frac{1}{2}$ mm to the foot which made it very difficult to get small motors of that period into the body of the loco. Because of this and other reasons of wheel clearance and bogie swing on locos, we decided to model in 4 mm to the foot whilst still retaining the same gauge of 16.5 mm which was used on the 'H0' $3\frac{1}{2}$ mm scale system. This gave us bigger loco bodies and answered nearly all our problems and saved us making and creating a separate track system for the 4 mm scale which would have entailed expensive jigs and tools. To differentiate between the $3\frac{1}{2}$ mm H0 scale and the 4 mm scale with their larger bodies, it was decided to call the new 4 mm system '00' gauge or phonetically 'Double 0 gauge' and Hornby seized upon the idea because of the increased body size which enabled them to fit in their motor and coined their own name of 'Dublo'.

The coming of the war in 1939 prevented a great development of the Hornby Dublo system. However, it was obvious that Hornby's knew that it would be all Hornby Dublo after the war, the pre-war sales had already convinced them of its great potential. Gradually, as Hornby's recovered from the war effort and could turn to post-war expansion, the great variety of locos, track, signals, buildings and rolling stock became more and more apparent and developed into the huge system that we all remember today.

Looking back over the years, it is interesting to realise that a small band of enthusiasts which included myself were striving to make working models of

locos, rolling stock and accessories half the size of the then popular '0' gauge – '0' gauge enthusiasts mockingly referred to our efforts as 'Mice' and thought that we must be mad to try and make such small models. Nearly everything had to be made by hand, until stalwarts like Arthur Hambling came along and produced the manufactured parts we so badly needed. Bonds of Euston Road produced a splendid 0–6–2 Tank loco in '00' scale and it was the basic design of their motor unit that Hornby's used for their own '00' loco, except they modified the brush gear and used 12 volts instead of the established 6 volt system. Following Continental practice, Hornby's used Mazac, which is a zinc based alloy for the loco body, chassis and wheels and this gave the weight and adhesion required. Overnight, the hobby in the small scale of '00' was suddenly opened up to thousands of ordinary people at prices they could afford and it was no longer the prerogative of the wealthy few or of those who had had the skill and patience to make their own models which even then were more costly than the 'manufactured' Hornby Dublo.

Mr. Michael Foster, our Author or Compiler as he prefers to call himself, is to be congratulated in bringing together the Hornby Dublo Story for posterity, to enable people to learn about a marvellous system and to bring to the forefront the facts and figures of history which otherwise would have remained buried and forgotten as the years sped by.

A Historical Survey 1938-1964

One should call this piece the Preface but I find I am inclined to wander on occasions in a similar manner to that of my favourite comedian, Francis Howard, Esq. In an hilarious television series in England some years back called 'Up Pompeii' he commenced the introduction to each episode with a long discourse, punctuated with disconnected ramblings – 'Ah, yes, where was I?. . . . The Prologue'.

There were models of railway locomotives before there were full sized locomotives themselves as pioneers tried out their various ideas before putting them into full size practice. Engineers amateur and professional throughout the industrialised countries in the middle of the 19th Century, laboriously constructed static and working models of either their favourite prototype or what they considered a locomotive should look like.

It was not until 1891 that Gebr. Marklin produced a standard set of gauges in the smaller ranges and at the Leipzig Spring Fair introduced the 48 mm gauge which became known as gauge 1. By 1895 their catalogue listed as well as gauge 1, gauge 2 at 54 mm and gauge 3 at 75 mm. They also introduced a smaller gauge at 35 mm which could really have had no other name but gauge 0. The toy manufacturers of Nuremberg recognised this and started manufacturing to suit although it was some time before all the other major manufacturers of the period, such as Bing, Planck and Carette followed.

Up till now the models had been either clockwork or live steam and it was at the Paris Exhibition, 1900 that electric model railways were first properly introduced to the public (although earlier commercial examples are known). Naturally, all models of the day were expensive and could only be afforded by the more affluent elements of society who, apart from finance, had the space both indoors and outdoors for setting up their railways. There were minor variations in the early gauges and in 1901 the *Model Engineer* magazine reproduced a letter on proposed standardisation. The renowned Mr. Henry Greenly eventually set the new standards – now measured between the rails as opposed to the centres of the rails.

The famous Bing company were the first to start investigating the possibilities of smaller model railways than gauge 0 and in 1912 had advertised what they called Lilliputbahnen running on 28 mm gauge track but this was not repeated after the First World War. At this time I understand they also produced as a sales advertising gimmick for the Premier Line – the London North Western Railway Company, a 2 mm gauge tinplate train, non-powered – of a 'George V' class locomotive and a rake of five coaches. I recently purchased a complete set of this although three or four of the wheels on the coaches were missing. You can imagine my surprise and delight, therefore, when I went to my local train shop in Warwick and purchased new N gauge nylon railway wheels which fitted exactly into the holes on the coaches! Not bad service for a toy some 65 years old.

After the First World War the farsighted Wenman J. Bassett-Lowke, realising the trend of people moving into smaller houses, instructed Mr. Greenly again to visit Germany and the result was the introduction in 1921 of the famous Bing 00 gauge Table Railway running on 16 mm track and scaled at 4 mm to the foot. The object even at that early stage, was to provide a railway that was capable of being set up quickly and run satisfactorily on the ordinary dining room table. It was advertised in 1922 in this country in British liveries of the day. The locomotives had clockwork mechanisms and were followed in Autumn 1923 by the first electric versions. The centre rail was insulated with fibre washers and indeed was the direct descendant of not only Marklin, but also our Hornby Dublo track.

The effect was startling. The extremely cheap price brought model railways to the mass market for the first time and there was a complete range of accessories in the way of stations, engine sheds, turntables, coaches, tank engines, tender engines and goods wagons. Hopefully this fascinating system will be the subject of a complete book in the not too distant future.

Many manufacturers gave up the larger models in gauge 2 and 3 on recommencement of production after the First World War. Concentration was on gauge 0 which was primarily used indoors and gauge 1 which was considered the most satisfactory outdoor or garden railway.

In the mid 1920s another war occurred in this country – namely the scale war, with the pioneers blindly shouting out their chosen scale and decrying any other opinion. The results of an interesting vote on the subject were noted in the November 1926 issue of *Model Railway News*. On a total casting of only 123 votes one hundred and six votes were in favour of a 3.5 mm scale running on a 16 mm gauge. Fifteen votes were for a 4 mm scale × 19 mm gauge and only two votes for what was to be the successful 4 mm scale × 16 mm gauge. I must admit, reflecting on the scene some 50 years later looking at photographs and models, the most realistic of all was the 4 mm scale on 19 mm track, but I digress, where was I? Ah yes – the prologue . . .

The famous Walkers and Holtzapffel Company (now W & H Models Ltd., London) made the first real attempt to give the public a reasonably priced model in 4 mm scale of British outline. In the late 1920s there seems to have been a slight decline in the intensity of railway modelling and doubtless this was not only helped by the industrial slump but also by the confusion of scales and gauges. A Home Office scare on running electric railways on house mains voltage as many proprietary railways in 0 gauge were, created much adverse publicity. Indeed, such was the debate, that articles appeared in *The Times* and the then *Daily Sketch* newspapers. I shall leave it to my fellow author, Bruce Baxter, in his Hornby 0 gauge book, to go into fuller detail on the potentially lethal first electric locomotive produced by the Meccano Company under their Hornby trade name – namely the high voltage 'Metropolitan' locomotive.

However, the pioneers continued in 00, the Marshall Stewart Company was by now producing brass track and in 1927 Bonds of Euston Road were advertising point parts. Marshall Stewart became the Stewart Reidpath Company and were the originators in this country of H0 (Half 0 gauge: namely 3.5 mm). By 1930 Bonds Ltd. were also producing electric mechanisms. In 1929 George E. Mellor of GEM products started production of 00 gauge parts and slowly the embryonic form of small scale model railways emerged. Many enthusiasts were wanting something far superior in outline to the Bing Table Railway and were frantically constructing their own locomotives and rolling stock from the many parts available from specialist manufacturers with varying degrees of success and reliability.

On 24th August 1932 the great Bing empire collapsed, though the Table Railway was kept in production right up to the start of the Second World War by Karl Bub who took over some aspects of Bing's production. The Trix organisation was founded by Franz Bing and Stefan Kahn. Bassett-Lowke naturally kept in contact with the Bing family, having built up friendships over many visits to Germany from the turn of the century onwards and persuaded the new Trix company to standardise its scale at 3.5 mm to 1 foot, or 1:87 scale ratio which Trix rounded off at 1:90 once more launching a minor revolution onto the model railway scene. Trix trains were reviewed in the December 1935 *Model Railway News* and operated on an alternating current at 14 volts. A major leap forward had occurred in Trix's use of diecast locomotive

bodies although of a crude 0–4–0 design with tenders, tinplate coaches, etc. From their advertisement in February 1936, Bassett-Lowke stated that such was the demand and interest in their new Twin Train, that they had sold out all their available supplies well before Christmas. The engines cost 10s. 6d. each (55p today) with the coaches in SR colours only, (really continental green) at 2s. each (10p) and the wagons 8d. each (4p) only. On Easter Tuesday, in April 1936, Bassett-Lowke had further supplies on their stand at the Model Railway Club Exhibition and stated that they had concluded arrangements for the manufacture of these models in England and English outline and liveries would be on the market by the following October.

Their advertisement of November 1936 continues – 'There are English pattern locomotives and tenders in LNER and LMS colours, a compact little tank locomotive in black and goods rolling stock and bogie passenger coaches 6½″ long finished off in fine detail with cellophane windows and set out on a layout of the same smooth running track on bakelite base but "British Made".'

The development of this system was, to say the least, rapid and there followed up to the commencement of the Second World War in 1939, Pacific outline locomotives such as the 'Flying Scotsman' of the LNER and the 'Princess' Class and streamline 'Coronation' Class locomotives of the LMS, as well as the Southern Electric Set. Electrically controlled points, crossovers, signals, yardlamps, miniature passengers and railway personnel were available and by 1937 there were twenty-five different goods vehicles in British outline alone. The original buildings, footbridges, engine sheds etc., were in wood and there was a magnificent terminal building produced by Bassett-Lowke, written up in the November 1937 *Model Railway News*. In December 1937 the famous 'Many Ways' Station Complex (designed, I believe, by Mr. Twining) was introduced to the market. The Trix range had the same effect as the Bing Table Railway of a decade or so earlier and once again battle lines were drawn up, not only between scale and toy railway followers, but also as to whether railways in this size should be called H0 or 00. Letters promoting one or the other waxed and waned in the model railway press to the extent that even W. J. Bassett-Lowke

himself replied in the May 1937 *Model Railway News* issue as follows:

'Dear Sirs, May we as the originators of the small size in model railways on a commercial basis make our contribution to the discussion of H0 and 00 as symbols of this small gauge?

'During the year 1920 the writer thought the time had arrived for a smaller gauge in model railways especially in view of the limited amount of space available in modern houses and flats. In consultation with Mr. Henry Greenly it was decided that half 0 gauge should be adopted and the designs and samples were made to this size. As gauge 0 is 32 mm therefore the original size of this small gauge was fixed at 16 mm.

'The Table Railway as it was called was placed on the market in the Autumn of 1921 and consisted of a clockwork locomotive, passenger and goods rolling stock track, station building, signals, etc., and was later introduced fitted with electric motors (Autumn 1923). It was decided to call this gauge 00 and we have never departed from this standard symbol. In the first volume of the *Model Railway News* we notice Messrs. Stewart Reidpath in the March issue of 1925 refers to this size as 00 gauge as also do other writers in later editions. How the term H0 ever arose we have not been able to trace unless it came from America.

'In measuring up the rolling stock of this original railway we find that the models were to the scale dimensions of 3½ mm to the foot although, of course, shortened to enable them to negotiate the small radius curves. In introducing the new Trix train railway last year the same standard gauge and scale was adopted and all British models are to the scale loading gauge of 3½ mm to the foot. Continental models are also to the same scale but they are slightly larger in proportion owing to a larger loading gauge in use abroad. In our opinion 00 has always been the recognised symbol of this gauge and it is a pity the term has ever been departed from by later manufacturers. Yours faithfully, signed: W. J. Bassett-Lowke.'

The letter somewhat conflicted with an article on page 103 of Henry Greenly's wonderful book *Model Railways* published in 1924 where he states 'The actual gauge is 16 mm and the scale is 4 mm to the foot.'

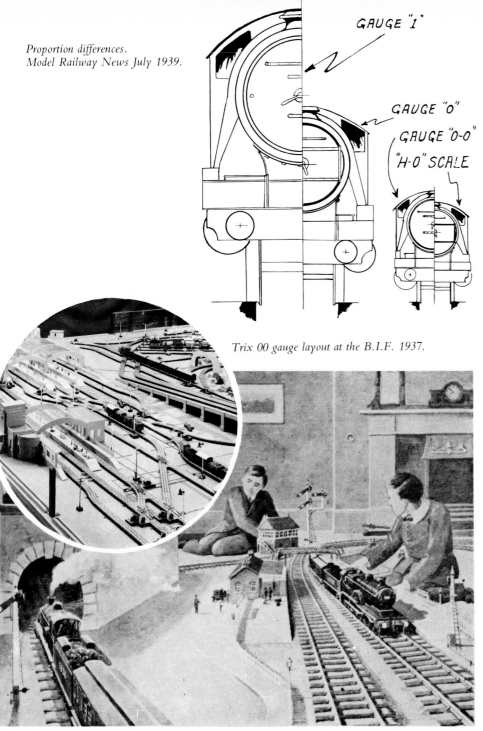

Proportion differences.
Model Railway News July 1939.

GAUGE "1"

GAUGE "O"

GAUGE "0-0"
"H-O" SCALE

Trix 00 gauge layout at the B.I.F. 1937.

'Could only be afforded by the more affluent elements of Society.'

BOYS! HERE'S THRILLING NEWS!

**Look out for the new Hornby-Dublo Trains, Gauge OO.
The perfect table-top railway at last!**

The Hornby-Dublo Trains are unique in their scale accuracy of design and beauty of finish. The tiny locomotives are fitted with motors, either clockwork or electric, of a power and reliability never before achieved in this gauge. The Remote Control of the electric locomotives is perfect—starting, stopping, reversing and speed regulation are all carried out by the movement of one lever. The control is positive. Move the lever to "Forward" and the train goes forward; move it to "Backward" and the train goes backward — *every time!*

The Hornby-Dublo Electric Trains operate on 12-volt direct current, and are intended to be run from mains alternating current through a Dublo Transformer connected to a Dublo Controller. Where mains alternating current is not available, the trains can be run satisfactorily from a 12-volt accumulator.

- ELECTRIC OR CLOCKWORK
- BUILT TO SCALE
- REALISTIC DETAIL
- PERFECT REMOTE CONTROL
- AUTOMATIC COUPLINGS
- SIMPLE AND SAFE

Here are two of the Hornby-Dublo Trains. The upper one has a splendid model of the famous L.N.E.R. streamlined locomotive "Sir Nigel Gresley," hauling a two-coach articulated unit. The tank engine hauling the goods train is available in the colours of all four groups.

HORNBY-DUBLO TRAINS

Ready in October

★ FULL DETAILS AND PRICES IN NEXT MONTH'S "M.M."

Manufactured by MECCANO LTD.   -   BINNS ROAD   -   LIVERPOOL 13

13

No. 00 CLOCKWORK TRAINS

(GAUGE 0)

Each No. 00 Clockwork Train Set is now supplied complete with set of Curved Rails to form a circle 2 ft. in diameter, and two Straight Rails. They form ideal commencing sets for the boy who wishes to build up a model railway gradually, and those fortunate boys who already possess more elaborate railways will find them admirably suitable for use as additional " suburban " rolling stock, etc. They are strongly built and fitted with reliable clockwork mechanism.

Each set contains Loco, Tender, and two Passenger Coaches, with set of Rails as described above. The Loco is fitted with brake and regulator, non-reversing. In colours to represent G.N., Midland, or L.N.W. Railway rolling stock.

No. 00 Clockwork Train, complete set, well boxed, Price **10/6**. Loco, Price **6/6**. Coach, Price **1/–**. Tender, Price **9d**.

ASK YOUR DEALER TO SHOW YOU SAMPLES

HORNBY CLOCK WORK TRAINS

THE TRAINS WITH THE GUARANTEE

Typical advertisement of the mid-1920s. This one November 1924.

14

The Lazy Boys of To-day

I see that a firm of engineers at Ilford (Essex) has been complaining that it cannot get enough boys to fill the vacant positions in their works. It seems that there are plenty of boys of a kind, but this firm's experience is that the boy of to-day is " lazy, ignorant, dirty and stupid."

" Many lads who have been sent to us," the firm states, " slouch up with both hands in their trousers pockets and lounge wearily against the door-post. They conduct an interview with the foreman with the inevitable ' fag-end ' in the corner of the mouth. Some are exceedingly dirty, others appear to be mentally deficient. Quite a good percentage obviously do not want work, and when not engaged, go away feeling quite relieved. One lad questioned as to the number of sixteenths in an inch, replied that he did not know, but on further consideration he thought there were fourteen ! "

I am sure that no Meccano boys have yet applied for a job with this particular firm whose indictment, I am certain, cannot be applied to any reader of the "*M.M.*" Their remarks show, however, that there is always an opening for a bright intelligent boy. In these days of trade depression and unemployment, when every one should be trying his hardest to " get on " either at school or at work, it is a matter for regret that it should be possible for any firm to find boys who are not eager to work and who do not want to " make good."

217

Extract from April 1926 Meccano Magazine. Nothing's changed!

So it is onto this scene of complete and utter chaos (or so it appears with hindsight) that the whole railway world split into strong camps of those followers of scale model railways and toy trains, of modelling in 00 scale and H0 scale, that the Meccano Company decided to launch its Hornby Dublo 00 trains with the first advertisement in the September 1938 issue of the *Meccano Magazine*. Mr. George Mellor put the case as well as he puts his excellent models together in the foreword to his 1938/39 catalogue:

'DOUBLE 0' GAUGE

'During the past few months a great deal of misunderstanding and difference of opinion has been aroused as to the correct scale and track gauge for Double 0. This has been caused through writers with no direct and personal knowledge of the manufacture of scale model railways and accessories in the smallest gauges rushing into print with their theoretical views on a subject which requires practical experience. A great deal of experiment was necessary before manufacturers in this country came to the conclusion that 4 mm scale 16.5 mm gauge was the only practical gauge for the amateur model railway enthusiast. The whole crux of the matter lies in the fact that it is impossible to employ exact scale wheel treads and flanges in a working model as these would be so small that the slightest error in aligning the track or the suspicion of a warp on the baseboard would be sufficient to cause derailments. If therefore, these dimensions are increased and the rest of the model made strictly to scale the proportions of the completed model are destroyed and the whole character of the prototype lost. If, however, all dimensions are made slightly oversize to the same extent as the wheels and bearings one has a model which is correctly proportioned and which appears correct to the eye. Hence 4 mm scale 16.5 mm gauge.

'We can supply to special order, models in H0 (3½ mm scale 16.5 mm gauge) and also in 4 mm scale 19 mm gauge (we refuse to label this "00") but cannot recommend their adoption. Certain manufacturers do cater for these scales and we hold agencies for most of their products which are listed within the pages of this catalogue. Goods of our own manufacture are ALL

built to 4 mm scale 16.5 mm gauge, the original and *only* practical "Double 0" Gauge.'

Ah yes . . . Hmm . . . The prologue . . .

THE HORNBY DUBLO STORY

'I well remember the excitement which the introduction of Dublo trains aroused and there is no doubt it was the finest system of that era, even better than Marklin which is saying a lot. It was a robust, simple system that was easy to develop and was set fair for a rosy future.'

from a letter from Mr. Jack Gahan
Ex-Meccano Company employee.

'whether Dublo is ever collected as Hornby "0" gauges remains to be seen!'

from Editorial of the *Hornby Railway Collector Magazine* Vol. 1. No. 1 in May 1969.

Gauge 0 Hornby railways closely followed in many ways the history of 00 as they too were conceived and introduced in 1920 following the introduction of the architrave Meccano part (although renamed 'corner gusset' in 1953 and still available as part no. 108 in the modern Meccano). This, together with the buffers and train coupling hooks, really launched the first locomotive and set Frank Hornby on the lines of producing his own reliable railways to fill the market in the aftermath of the First World War. The Meccano guarantee was the high symbol of quality and after sales service even then.

Mr. Hornby had already presented a train set at the 1915 British Industries Fair, almost certainly produced in Nuremberg and shipped prior to the commencement of hostilities. He was, in fact, in Germany in those fateful days immediately preceding the declaration in 1914 and by sheer chance caught one of the last trains out of the country, his English manager of Meccano Gmbh being 'interned for the duration'. This little known set – The Raylo train, ran on 22 mm (7/8″) track and was the original of what we call today 'S' gauge railway. The locomotive body being tin-printed in similar outline and style to the Table Railway which followed it.

A generation of British youth had been slaughtered and there was much hostility to the idea of buying German goods in this country. However, Germany's world famous toy companies soon recommenced production and items were imported in large numbers into the U.K. by such stores as Gamages Ltd., carefully stamped 'foreign made' only.

The Meccano Company did have extremely close contacts with Nuremberg. There has been much direct proof, such as a large Meccano clockwork motor which was carefully stamped 'Made in Nuremberg' and there are many items in the Hornby range, such as the electric lamps on signals and level crossing gates, etc., which are absolutely identical to those manufactured by Marklin or Bing. This leads me to believe that the many small manufacturing companies in Nuremberg would make a product and then sell it to the larger, now household names. However, these and other aspects of Anglo-German trade are probably best left to future historians, when and if verifiable evidence comes to light.

Frank Hornby was born in 1863 on the site of Lime Street Station, Liverpool. We know much of his early life from a fascinating book produced in America in 1916 by Mr. M. P. Gould and published by the Meccano Company Incorporated of New York. It is called *Frank Hornby – the Boy who Made $1,000,000 with a Toy*, which was reprinted by New Cavendish Books several years ago. It tells how one Christmas, on his way to join his wife and two sons staying with some relatives he was wondering what to give them for presents and as he looked outside he saw a crane in operation beside the railway track. From hand cut and drilled strips the whole Meccano empire emerged and has become a classic, not only of engineering skills, but also of successful sales and marketing techniques. These last ten to fifteen years have seen a lot of changes in the toy industry with many household names going either permanently or temporarily to the wall (including tragically the Meccano Company in 1964) only to be reborn. I am delighted to see the Meccano system going from strength to strength despite the problems of maintaining a quality product in an inflationary era. To me it is the finest, most satisfying 'toy' ever made – suitable for all from 8 to 80. I frequently curse inefficient shop assistants as they have rarely in the past seemed to stock the particular Meccano item I wanted. However, a letter or telephone call to perhaps the most famous Meccano shop of all, M.W. Models of Greys Road, Henley on Thames, Oxon, brings the required part by return of post. I digress. . . .

In 1925 the Meccano Company advertised No. 00 clockwork trains but these were literally in 0 gauge scale and absolutely identical to products manufactured by Bing. The only difference being the MML stamp on the smoke box door and underneath the tender and base of the coaches on the Meccano products and I would think it absolutely certain that these were either sub-contract manufactured items produced from Nuremberg or Meccano Ltd., purchased the dies. As you have already seen the 00 Table Railways as we call them, had only just appeared on the scene and those dictating policy in Binns Road, Liverpool doubtless kept a close eye on their success. However, they do not appear to have been very impressed as replying to Mr. E. Winn of London S.E.5 in the February 1927 *Meccano Magazine*, they stated 'We do not contemplate the introduction of a gauge 00 miniature railway as there is little demand for model railways built to this scale.' And again in August 1929 replying to Mr. V. Chancellor of Guildford . . . 'We specialise in 0 gauge and do not propose to adopt any other.' This was the time of the massive world wide industrial recession and in a press cutting of 1933 the Directors of the Company felt, in order to counteract any shrinkage in their business due to the difficult times in which they were living (we never seem to escape, do we?) new lines should be manufactured and marketed and these started off first of all with the aeroplane constructor kits and then the motor car kits. Modelled Miniatures came in 1934, stamped 'Hornby series' and were indeed the forerunners of the famous Dinky Toy range. Looking through the various press cuttings copied for me by Mr. Malcolm Unwin, the Librarian of *The Liverpool Echo* there are fascinating comments on the history of the Company which note that in October 1928 the Meccano Company took a court action against the Marklin Company which ended up in the Anglo-German mixed arbitration tribunal. Meccano were the holders of all the shares in the Company registered in Germany under the name Meccano Gmbh. The Company was registered as the proprietor in Germany of the trade mark Meccano

which, they claimed, naturally, was of great value. During the First World War the German Company was liquidated under the German War Liquidation scheme and all their assets, other than the trade mark were sold to the German Toy Traders Association on 8th August 1917. The liquidator had in effect informed the English Company that the trade mark was not included in the sale. However, the assets, *including the trade mark* Meccano, were resold by the German Toy Traders Association to Gebr. Marklin who applied to the Imperial Patenting Office to register the trade mark in their name and, the liquidator of the German Meccano Company assenting, this was done. A Dr. Isaa who appeared for the German Government in the respondence argued that as Meccano had no factory in Germany and no employees, and only ownership of the shares in the Gmbh they had no industrial rights in Germany, the latter being the rights of the German Company. Giving judgement the President of the Court, Baron von Heeckeren said the decision of the tribunal was that the name of the claimant should be removed from the register in Germany as the proprietors of the trade mark Meccano and that the respondents, i.e. Marklin should pay £100 towards the cost of the proceedings.

Enough of the commercial problems and on with the story:

'Dealers in toys woke up to the fact that a new era in toys had commenced. The boys were no longer contented to play with something which gave pleasure for an hour and was then thrown away or which broke even before it had ceased to have the power of giving pleasure; that boys had brains and could be interested in things which stimulated serious thought and which called forth powers of invention and ingenuity hitherto stifled for lack of an outlet. They commenced to study the hobby for themselves and with study came appreciation.'

How very true and as true today as when this was written in the second edition of the *Meccano Magazine* for November and December 1916 written by Frank Hornby himself. Mr. Hornby was in many ways years ahead of his time in management terms. Perhaps it is us who have stepped backwards as he goes on in

another article to say . . . 'if your work doesn't interest you and your mind is on other things, you will feel overworked, hard done by, unhappy and unsuccessful. If, on the other hand you take a real interest in your work . . . make it your hobby. Enjoyment, enthusiasm, and keenness are the keywords to success in everything but most of all business.' The art of management, of creating happiness, security and enthusiasm amongst one's employees and letting them share the rewards is as important today as it was 50 years ago and is all too often forgotten by modern day management, who may be technically competent but are walking disaster areas when it comes to personal relations and injecting enthusiasm. 'Leadership', wrote Sir Horatio Nelson, 'is not a mere matter of giving orders, but of evoking the will to serve.' There are born leaders and Frank Hornby was definitely one of them. The *Meccano Magazine* of December 1934 describes the incredible improvement in the toy trade in particular compared with those 34 years ago at the turn of the century and goes on:

'In those days the only locomotives available other than expensive scale models were either big wooden affairs that bore little resemblance to any engine ever seen on any real railway or crudely constructed clockwork affairs which often found their way to the junk heap in a few weeks owing to the failure of their mechanisms. The range of other toys also was extremely limited and boys thought themselves fortunate to possess toy swords, tin trumpets, wooden forts, pop guns, Noah's Arks and similar articles, the use of which called for a vigorous display of fancy and imagination. What a contrast the shop windows of to-day show. Meccano outfits have played a great part in brightening them and every boy revels in the opportunity these give him of building working models that have real engineering. Hornby trains bring realism into miniature railway working for thousands of enthusiasts and electricity, chemistry and other branches of knowledge all contribute their share to the wonderful array of working toys and experimental outfits. All these things are typical of the outlook of the modern boy. He is no longer content, as his predecessors were, to be taken into a shop to choose a toy but despises mere playthings and instead demands toys that appeal to his intellect and with which he can "do things".'

By 1938 most advertisements were now for the 00/H0 scale models and to my knowledge it was the old Gresham Model Railways Company of 79 Gresham Street, London who put out the first trade advertisement of Hornby Dublo showing a picture of the Great Western 0–6–2 Tank locomotive announcing an 00 gauge electric engine at 17s. 6d. and also a reversing clockwork engine at 12s. 6d.

It must have been incredible because here at last was the answer to the railway enthusiasts' dream. A railway system involving locomotives of far greater scale appearance, strength and reliability than any comparable model at a fraction of the price. Even in August 1934 Bonds of Euston were advertising an N2 type 0–6–2 Tank locomotive for 45s. Models by Beeson of Willesden, Cimco (City Model Company) 37 Drury Street, London, and others were between £5–£15 each. The great Meccano organisation was extremely active to the extent that their travellers were visiting toy shops and telling them, dependent on the quantity they had purchased previously, exactly which models they could and could not have and how many, such was the demand for their products across the board. Indeed, queues formed in shops as soon as the Dublo quota arrived. The design decisions to enter 00 scale were almost certainly taken at the New Products Committee meetings of the Meccano Company in 1937 as it was during the latter part of that year that the first drawings were made of the new system, one year after the death of Frank Hornby, on 21st September 1936. The first reference I have found outside the Company, of the intention to introduce an 00 gauge railway was in a letter dated 2/5/38 (reproduced earlier) by Mr. W. M. McCormack the then Advertising Manager to Mr. Douglas Hanney then of Pinner, Middlesex and I am deeply grateful to Mr. Hanney for allowing me to reproduce the letter and, incidentally, for the pleasant evenings spent with him in Farnham.

Mr. Ronald Wyborn ex-Chief Electrical Engineer of the Company tells in one of his fascinating letters to me:

'The Advent of Dublo

In 1937 it was decided an 00 gauge system should be introduced. The Board considered the best way to test the market was to initially introduce a tank loco in all liveries and the LNER passenger loco Sir Nigel Gresley. I was given the job of designing the motors and control units and co-ordinating all the electrical requirements for production.

Time was extremely short and track, rolling stock and accessory design was shared between the Chief Designer, Donald Smith and the Chief Draughtsman.

All on the technical side were determined from the start to ensure control of quality and special measures were taken to segregate all parts for Dublo from other work during production stages. The name Dublo was the brainchild of the Commercial Director, Mr. George Jones.

For my part, realising that quality of performance was to be achieved not only in terms of design but also in production technique, certain governing factors had been formulated from which in the course of development we hardly ever deviated.

Thus the motor would be integral with the loco diecast frame to give rigidity and a low centre of gravity. It would incorporate a vertical armature with worm drive running in adjustable bearings with ball end thrust. The armature would have a barrel commutator to allow skimming in situ. The magnet was a conventional horseshoe but with a high cobalt content to give high permanence (anisotropic magnets were not yet available).

On the production side new winding machines and a burnishing machine for the armature journals were installed. All movement of parts from one department to another was in special colour-coded containers to assist inspection and checking.

The mechanism assembly was done in "B" block using a slide assembly method. It was decided against conveyorisation and each mechanism was progressively assembled on a cradle which was pushed from one operator to another in a slide as each part of the assembly was completed. Each assembly line was 60 ft long and it was arranged that one half of the assembly was completed on one side of each line so that the cradles finished up at the same end where they started.

After assembly and testing the mechanisms were transported to the Train Room at the other end of the Works where the housings were attached and the locos finally tested.

I think it was a pity that 3-rail track was introduced at the beginning which was a direct influence of Marklin. Contrary to what has been suggested, neither this track nor later 2-rail track was ever made outside of Binns Road.

One year's production and then came the war, and we shortly thereafter went over entirely to war-time production. To meet and maintain the required standards additional test and inspection equipment was installed. For example X-ray and analytical apparatus, metalurgical and ageing-test equipment all of which became a unique advantage when hostilities ceased. Incidentally, I was able to add radiography to my previous technical experiences, also a lot of valuable knowledge was gained in the quality evaluation of zinc-based diecasting materials, and we developed the steam ageing test later to be adopted by British Standards.'

I have heard that in the old days Frank Hornby, himself, insisted on interviewing all new distributors to ensure they came up to his standard and he also carefully protected them by allowing only one distributor per town or ensuring in the larger cities that one distributor was at least half a mile away from another distributor. I have heard some complain of highhanded attitudes, but it is purely a question of supply and demand and I had a letter in November 1974 which stated: 'regarding opening new agencies we are completely unable to do so at the present time and we are turning down applications daily as until we are able to supply existing agents in full and not on a quota basis new outlets only aggravate the position and cause considerable ill feeling with existing retailers'. This letter being from Mr. Cedric Wrenn, Sales Director of G & R Wrenn Railways but more of these worthy gentlemen later! A model shop owner in the immediate post war period told me: 'They (Meccano) used to send round a list of printed items virtually telling you what you could and could not have. It seemed a very highhanded way of going on. . . .' When demand outsteps supply what else can one do?

Of course, the 0 gauge fraternity then, as now, frowned on the introduction of these 'Mice' and their followers and there was much lighthearted rivalry.

The first catalogue was inserted into the *1938/39 Hornby Book of Trains* despite its coding of 7/837/ 117/U.K.

A point here: almost all Meccano literature had, on the back page, a special printing code and taking the one I have just mentioned, the 7 refers to the code for the actual printer who prepared the pamphlet and could be anything from 1 to 16. The figure: 837 is August 1937. The next figure: 117 means 117,000 were printed. On some of the smaller instruction sheets you might just have 50 M: i.e. 50 mille or 50,000. The U.K. is obviously the United Kingdom edition as there were editions for the other major markets of the Meccano Company such as Australia, New Zealand, Canada, India, South Africa, etc. This is in many ways a classic case in point and doubtless confusing, because, you see, the 1938/9 *Hornby Book of Trains* was printed, according to this, in August 1937 and yet it was not advertised and released to the public until October 1938. Could it be a misprint – rare in Meccano circles?

The catalogue reproduced here shows how Hornby Dublo started in a big way with the clockwork and electric varieties of the 4–6–2 'Sir Nigel Gresley' A4 locomotive and the 0–6–2 Tank locomotive in the liveries of the four main companies. Indeed, there are 12 goods wagons available immediately as well as the standard LNER coach and the articulated version. Full descriptions of the various items naturally can be found in the respective chapters later in the book. Boys of my generation (born 1941) and younger can only imagine the impact on the hungry market. Never before had a mass produced scale locomotive been available in such detail at such a reasonable price and it was the first British outline 4–6–2 passenger locomotive on the market. Even the renowned Edward Beal, author of so many helpful scale model railway books commented in his book *Scale Railway Modelling Today*, published in 1939 on the new Dublo Models: 'There is very little that can be done in the way of improvement or embellishment.' Bassett-Lowke had brought out the Twin train 4–6–2 of continental design in March 1938 but it was not until three months after the introduction of the Hornby Dublo range that Trix advertised their LMS 'Princess' Class locomotive and LNER 'Flying Scotsman' in the December issue of the *Model Railway news*.

The price of the Trix Pacifics were £4. 7s. 6d. against the Hornby Dublo version at 29s. 6d.

The Meccano Company in keeping with their policy of the best, had really gone to town in perfecting over the preceding four or five years their diecasting techniques and they used the experience gained in assembling their Dinky Toys to obtain the incredible scale appearance of their locomotives. They not only looked right but ran superbly. Mention has already been made in the Foreword of the farsighted idea to concentrate on the 12v supply and use DC motors against the far more expensively constructed Trix 14v AC. As a rule the scale modellers were still struggling with 6v DC.

The models were pounced upon by young and old alike and many serious modellers purchased a locomotive to discard the body and use the mechanism. Many articles on the different locomotives and wheel arrangements that could be obtained from the chassis units were described in the model railway press of the period. Although never advertised, complete chassis units could be purchased by writing to Meccano enclosing a postal order for 10s. (50p) less than the price of the complete locomotive.

My original Bank Manager was normally far more interested in the up-dated collectors value of his own early Hornby Dublo train set than discussing such mundane matters as my overdraft (a view not always shared by his Head Office!) and I was extremely fortunate in that when I married and moved some 50 miles from Sutton Coldfield my new Bank Manager was also a railway enthusiast. He kindly gave me some figures showing how the purchasing value of the pound had shrunk over the years and it became so interesting that I have set out below some of the figures which I have worked out, the object being to adjust the price in the period catalogues, by a notional inflation factor. You will see how the hobby has grown and how mass production has kept the prices relatively stable. Take for example the Sir Nigel locomotive costing 30 shillings (£1.50). Multiply by 10 and you have £15, pretty well the current price.

Year	Value	Multiply Sales Price by:
1939	1,000p	10
1948	625	6.25
1951	500	5
1954	450	4.5
1956	425	4.25
1957	400	4
1961	380	3.8
1964	330	3.3

The table is based on taking the pound sterling as being worth 100p on the 1st January 1978. A further example is an item costing £1 in the catalogue in 1951 would now be worth an equivalent £5 at today's value. Not interested? Ah yes. The prologue. . . .

Of course, by this time the Meccano Company and their Hornby Trains trade mark had the most enviable reputation for reliability, quality and after-sales service. The competition had been looked at closely and their good and bad points analysed. Trix, Marklin and Bing used wound field motors and one of the 'customer benefits' plugged in the Hornby Dublo sales literature was that the operator could now guarantee the required direction of running every single time purely by changing the direction of the current by moving the lever on his controller.

As the Chief Engineer of the period said, it was a pity that Hornby did not commence with a 2-rail system instead of being closely influenced by the Marklin system. The track was not the usual pressed tinplate but correct rail section fitted to a tinplate base for strength and rigidity allowing a quick set-up and dismantling time when tea-time came.

The higher voltage 12v DC against the usual 6v then used by the majority of model railway enthusiasts was less affected by dirt and grease which invariably accumulated on the rails, considerably affecting performance.

As well as the electric locomotives there was also a range of clockwork motors in both the 0–6–2 Tank and the 'Sir Nigel Gresley' locomotive. These were beautiful little motors, if not a trifle delicate for the younger market at which they were aimed and it was a great shame that no trackside controls such as a brake stop were ever fitted. The chief enjoyment, reading from the Meccano magazines, seemed to be to not only try to arrange that the engine stopped at the station by

1938-1939

HORNBY-DUBLO TRAINS

THE PERFECT TABLE RAILWAY
Gauge OO

Manufactured by
MECCANO LIMITED
Binns Road, Liverpool, 13
7/938/185 U.K.

BUILT TO SCALE

REALISTIC DETAIL

PERFECT REMOTE CONTROL

LOOK OUT FOR DEVELOPMENTS!

The Hornby-Dublo system is to be developed and extended in every direction. There will be new Locomotives and Coaches, and new Vans and Wagons of almost every type. Points and Signals will be Electrically Operated; and best of all, there will be track of 17¼in. radius to form, in conjunction with the present track, a perfect double track on which, by means of the Dublo Transformer No. 2, two trains can be run at the same time, and started, stopped, reversed and controlled for speed entirely independently of one another!

Watch our announcements!

A complete scale miniature railway in small space.

Hornby-Dublo Trains are unique in their scale accuracy and beauty of finish. They have been designed with the co-operation of the railway companies, who supplied special photographs and scale drawings. The Locomotives are fitted with motors, either clockwork or electric, of a power and reliability never before achieved in this gauge. The Remote Control of the Electric Locomotives is perfect—starting, stopping, reversing and speed regulation are all carried out by the movement of a single lever on a special Controller at the lineside. The control is positive. Move the lever to "Forward" and the train goes forward; move it to "Backward" and the train goes backward—**no matter in what direction it was running previously.**

The track consists of solid drawn brass rail, giving the greatest electrical conductivity, mounted on a realistic metal base with holes for screwing down to a baseboard for permanent layouts.

The underframes of the Vans and Wagons, and the bogies of the Passenger Coaches, are pressure die-cast. All vehicles are fitted with pressure die-cast wheels, which ensure perfectly smooth running. Automatic couplings, designed to link at any point on the track, are fitted to all Coaches, Vans and Wagons.

The signals are realistic working models of the latest upper-quadrant type. The Buffer Stops have working heads.

The Main Line Station, which is constructed in wood, is a splendid model in the modern style that is becoming so popular. It will accommodate a three-coach train, and by means of the printed slips provided can be named "Berwick" (L.N.E.R.), "Penrith" (L.M.S.), "Truro" (G.W.R.) and "Ashford" (S.R.). There are also an Island Platform and a Goods Depot.

The Hornby-Dublo Electric Trains operate on 12-volt Direct Current and are intended to be run from mains Alternating Current through a Dublo Transformer connected to a Dublo Controller. Where the mains supply is Direct Current, or where there is no mains current at all, the trains can be run with perfect success from a 12-volt accumulator.

EDP1 HORNBY-DUBLO ELECTRIC AND DP1 CLOCKWORK PASSENGER TRAIN SETS. L.N.E.R.

ELECTRIC

EDP1 Hornby-Dublo Electric Passenger Train Set, L.N.E.R. Contains EDL1 Streamlined Six-coupled Locomotive "**Sir Nigel Gresley**" (Automatic Reversing), Tender D1, Two-Coach Articulated Unit D2, Dublo Controller No. 1, seven EDA Curved Rails, one EDAT Curved Terminal Rail and two EDB Straight Rails. (To be run from Dublo Transformers No. 1 or No. 2, not included in Set). Price 70/-
Where the mains supply is D.C., or there is no supply, the above Set is available with Dublo Controller No. 1a (for use with 12-volt accumulators) as follows:—
EDPA1 Electric Passenger Train Set, L.N.E.R. (with Dublo Controller No. 1a for use with 12-volt accumulators). Price 61/6

CLOCKWORK

DP1 Clockwork Passenger Train Set, L.N.E.R. Contains DL1 Streamlined Six-coupled Locomotive "**Sir Nigel Gresley**" (Reversing), Tender D1, Two-Coach Articulated Unit D2, eight DA Curved Rails and two DB Straight Rails. Price 39/6

The components of these Passenger Train Sets are obtainable separately at the following prices:—
EDL1 Electric Streamlined Six-coupled Locomotive (Automatic Reversing) with Tender L.N.E.R. Price 29/6
DL1 Clockwork Streamlined Six-coupled Locomotive (Reversing) with Tender L.N.E.R. Price 23/-
EDL1 Electric Streamlined Six-coupled Locomotive L.N.E.R. (Automatic Reversing) without Tender. Price 25/-
DL1 Clockwork Streamlined Six-coupled Locomotive L.N.E.R. (Reversing) without Tender. Price 18/6
Tender D1 L.N.E.R. Price 4/6
Two-Coach Articulated Unit D2 L.N.E.R. Price 6/6
Dublo Controller No. 1 (for use with Dublo Transformer No. 1 or No. 2). Price 21/-
Dublo Controller No. 1a (for use with 12-volt accumulators). Price 12/6

EDG7 HORNBY-DUBLO ELECTRIC AND DG7 CLOCKWORK TANK GOODS TRAIN SETS

ELECTRIC

EDG7 Electric Tank Goods Train Set, L.M.S., L.N.E.R., G.W.R., or S.R. Contains EDL7 Six-coupled Tank Locomotive (Automatic Reversing), Open Goods Wagon D1, Goods Van D1, Goods Brake Van D1, Dublo Controller No. 1, seven EDA Curved Rails, one EDAT Curved Terminal Rail and two EDB Straight Rails. (To be run from Dublo Transformers No. 1 or No. 2, not included in Set). Price 55/-

Where the mains supply is D.C., or there is no supply, the above Set is available with Dublo Controller No. 1a (for use with 12-volt accumulators) as follows:—
EDGA7 Electric Tank Goods Train Set. (With Dublo Controller No. 1a for use with 12-volt accumulators). Price 46/6

CLOCKWORK

DG7 Clockwork Tank Goods Train Set, L.M.S., L.N.E.R., G.W.R., or S.R. Contains DL7 Six-coupled Tank Locomotive (Reversing), Open Goods Wagon D1, Goods Van D1, Goods Brake Van D1, eight DA Curved Rails, and two DB Straight Rails. Price 27/6

The components of these Goods Train Sets are obtainable separately at the following prices:—
EDL7 Electric Six-coupled Tank Locomotive (Automatic Reversing). Price 17/6
DL7 Clockwork Six-coupled Tank Locomotive (Reversing) Price 12/6
Goods Brake Van D1 Price 2/6
Open Goods Wagon D1, Price 1/4   Goods Van D1, Price 1/6
Dublo Controller No. 1 (for use with Transformer No. 1 or No. 2). Price 21/-
Dublo Controller No. 1a (for use with 12-volt accumulators) Price 12/6

20

HORNBY-DUBLO ROLLING STOCK

GOODS BRAKE VAN D1 S.R.

The latest type of 25-ton Goods Brake Van operated by the Southern Railway. Price 2/6

GOODS BRAKE VAN D1 L.M.S.

This Van is coloured in the latest L.M.S. bauxite brown. Price 2/6

GOODS BRAKE VAN D1 G.W.

A fine model of the characteristic 20-ton long-bodied G.W.R. Goods Brake Van. Price 2/6

GOODS BRAKE VAN D1 L.N.E.R.

An accurate model of the standard L.N.E.R. 20-ton Goods Brake Van. Price 2/6

12-TON GOODS VAN D1 L.N.E.R.

The vertical boarding of standard N.E. vans is a feature of this vehicle; red-brown finish as used for N.E. express goods wagons. Price 1/6

12-TON GOODS VAN D1 S.R.

A modern 12-ton van for general goods; S.R. chocolate brown finish with white lettering. Price 1/6

12-TON GOODS VAN D1 L.M.S.

Typical of the latest vans for goods traffic; finished in L.M.S. Bauxite brown. Price 1/6

12-TON GOODS VAN D1 G.W.R.

Conforms to the latest G.W. standards in design and finish; grey with white lettering and white roof. Price 1/6

12-TON OPEN GOODS WAGON D1 S.R.

Model of standard 12-ton Open Goods Wagon, finished in S.R. chocolate brown with white lettering. Price 1/4

12-TON OPEN GOODS WAGON D1 G.W.R.

G.W.R. standard Open Goods Wagon, finished in grey with white lettering. Price 1/4

12-TON OPEN GOODS WAGON D1 L.M.S.

The standard L.M.S. Open Goods Wagon, finished in the company's characteristic Bauxite Brown. Price 1/4

12-TON OPEN GOODS WAGON D1 L.N.E.R.

L.N.E.R. Open Goods Wagon, finished in grey with white lettering. Price 1/4

CORRIDOR COACH D1 L.N.E.R.

An accurately detailed model of a standard L.N.E.R. teak-finished Corridor Coach. Price 3/6

TWO-COACH ARTICULATED UNIT D2 L.N.E.R.

A perfect representation of the teak-finished Corridor Articulated Unit used on the principal L.N.E.R. expresses. Price 6/6

HORNBY-DUBLO GAUGE OO TRACK

The track consists of solid drawn brass rails strongly mounted on a realistic metal base. 16½ mm. (approx. ⅝in.) measured between rails. 15in. Radius.

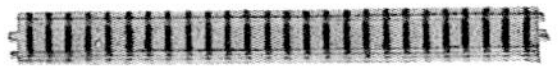

DB Straight Rail

EDPR Points (Electric)   *DA Curved Rail*

ELECTRIC
EDB Straight rails (length 11½in.)	per doz. 15/-
EDB½ Straight half-rails	per doz. 12/-
EDBS Short rails	per doz. 9/-
EDA Curved rails (8 to circle)	per doz. 15/-
EDA½ Curved half-rails	per doz. 12/-
EDAT Curved terminal rails	per doz. 21/-

POINTS (ELECTRIC)
EDPR Points right-hand	per pair 9/6
EDPL Points left-hand	

POINTS (CLOCKWORK)
DPR Points right-hand	per pair 6/6
DPL Points left-hand	

CLOCKWORK
DB Straight rails (length 11½in.)	per doz. 12/-
DB½ Straight half-rails	per doz. 9/-
DBS Short rails	per doz. 6/-
DA Curved rails (8 to circle)	per doz. 12/-
DA½ Curved half-rails	per doz. 9/-

HORNBY-DUBLO ACCESSORIES

MAIN LINE STATION D1

SIGNAL D1
SIGNAL D2

A particularly fine model in wood of a modern-style station. It is long enough to accommodate a three-coach train, and is supplied with printed gummed slips giving a choice of four names—"Berwick" (L.N.E.R.), "Penrith" (L.M.S.), "Truro" (G.W.R.) and "Ashford" (S.R.). Size: Length 24 in., width 4½in., height, 3 5/16in. Price 7/6

Latest type Upper Quadrant Signal. Single Arm "Home" or "Distant". Price 1/-

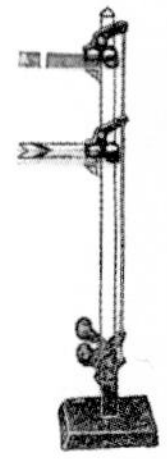

Latest type Upper Quadrant Signals. Double Arm "Home" and "Distant". Price 1/4

ISLAND PLATFORM D1

This platform can be used separately between two tracks, or in conjunction with the Main Line Station, which it resembles in design and construction. Size: Length 24in., width 2½in., height 2¼in. Price 4/9

GOODS DEPOT D1

TUNNEL D1 (SHORT)

This Tunnel is 5½in. long and is suitable for either curved or straight track. Price 1/3

A realistic depot for goods traffic in the same style as the Main Line Station and Island Platform. Size: Length 12in., width 4in., height 2½in. Price 4/11

TUNNEL D2 (LONG)

This Tunnel is 11½in. long. It cannot be used on curved track. Price 1/8

BUFFER STOP D1

A particularly realistic model of a type to be seen in the sidings in most goods yards. Fitted with working spring heads. Price 10d.

SIGNAL CABIN D1
A typical example in wood of a medium-sized Signal Cabin. Supplied with four gummed slips printed with the names "Berwick", "Penrith", "Truro" and "Ashford". Price 11d.

MINIATURE RAILWAY STAFF D1
This Set consists of six figures: Driver, Porter, Ticket Collector, Stationmaster, Guard and Shunter. These figures are strong, well finished and to scale. Price 1/-

MINIATURE PASSENGERS D2
The Set includes three men and three women passengers. They are to the same scale as all the other items in the Hornby-Dublo system and are attractively coloured. Price 1/-

DUBLO TRANSFORMERS
DUBLO TRANSFORMER No. 1 (Output 10 VA at 12 volts)
This Transformer has an output of 10 VA at 12 volts, and is available for the following Alternating Current supplies: 100/110 volts, 50 cycles, and 210/240 volts, 50 cycles. It can be specially wound for other supplies, if required. Price 9/6

DUBLO TRANSFORMER No. 2 (Output 20VA at 12 volts)
This Transformer has an output of 20VA at 12 volts for running two trains on separate tracks by means of two No. 1 Dublo Controllers. Available for the following Alternating Current supplies: 100/110 volts, 50 cycles, and 210/240 volts, 50 cycles. It can be specially wound for other supplies. Price 12/6

Dublo Transformer No. 1

DUBLO CONTROLLERS
DUBLO CONTROLLER No. 1 (for use with Dublo Transformer No. 1 or No. 2)
This Controller is fitted with a single handle by which a train can be started, stopped, reversed, and regulated for speed. A circuit breaker is incorporated. Price 21/-

DUBLO CONTROLLER No. 1a (for use with 12-volt accumulators)
This Controller, similar to No. 1 described above, is for use with 12-volt accumulators. Price 12/6

Dublo Controller No. 1

Ready for the "Right Away"!

counting the number of turns but also the number of 'clicks' in the turn. However, commercially they were not a success and even before the start of the hostilities in 1939, it had been decided to delete them. Chris McTaggart had close contact with Mr. E. G. Page, the Australian agent for Meccano and he reported in a letter to the *H.R.C.A. Collector Magazine* a few years ago that Mr. Page told him that he had understood the mechanisms were made in Holland by Van Rhylermeer but I have no further information on this. Incidentally, Van Rhylermeer is not be confused with Van Riemsdijk who made superb clockwork motors in this period in London. The latter (Van Riemsdijk) company continued their clockwork motor experience by developing a clockwork parking meter activated and regularly wound up by the weight of the fall of an old sixpence!

However, towards the end of the original Meccano Company in the early 1960s, against fierce competition from cheap clockwork train sets for the younger enthusiasts put out by both Playcraft and Triang, they retooled their clockwork mechanism from old parts and tested them. Consideration was given to introducing this in the yellow diesel shunter body of the 'Starter' sets, but it did not stand up favourably to the other motors and so clockwork remained a period piece. I must admit the reference to Van Rhylermeer is very interesting. The Meccano Company certainly did not lack skill in the manufacture of larger clockwork motors for their 0 gauge models or Meccano toys and I would love to have more information on this. Many a clockwork motor is considerably improved by being wound up and allowed to unwind in a bowl of 'Redex' lubricant. This frees all the old clogged oil and fluff – then a light sewing machine oil lubrication and away it goes – rejuvenated! D1 lubricating oil for clockwork motors Blue Seal. D2 lubricating oil for Electric motors Red Seal.

The prologue. . . .

The quality control and superior manufacturing techniques introduced by Mr. Wyborn certainly paid off and a letter to me from Mr. V. J. Bunn, Director of the Model Engineering and Construction Company then in Birmingham went on. . . .

'Hornby Dublo are reminders of the good old days of British made goods which were made to last a lifetime if well looked after, being robust in design, if not actually authentic scalewise. We have had many various aged Hornby Dublo models passing through our hands, either as a secondhand resale or sent in by customers for a face lift . . . scale wheeling and a repaint and line, making it into a poor man's scale model. Irrespective of age, very few were found below a very reasonable standard in running aspect.

'Compared to the modern cars costing at least 100 times more and considered scrap after around six or eight years, the old Hornby Dublo, if given the same amount of revered attention as most people give to their cars, will still be running superbly well into the year 2,000 AD and more.'

I believe that the models already considered as antiques and much sought after by collectors, will be running indefinitely. Demand always creates supply and when one looks at the variety of spare parts now available for the Hornby 0 gauge in the way of wheels, white metal castings, motor and body spares, etc., the enthusiast with access to manufacturing facilities will always be able to make the required parts for his own needs, his friends or enthusiast associations.

However, sadly, as with Dinky Toys, a lot of pre-war Hornby Dublo castings have failed and in particular the wheels and bogie/chassis units. Jim Whittaker investigated this problem and wrote: 'apparently the majority of zinc based castings are produced from mazac 5 for which the formula is. . . Aluminium 4 %   Magnesium 0.04 %   Copper 1.0 %   Zinc 94.86 per cent.

'Having got over the shock of realising that such fine limits can be achieved in respect of mixing metals I was even more surprised to learn that the zinc content has to have a purity level of at least 99.9 %. To achieve this high level a distilling process is involved (zinc boils at 907 °C), though I am told that an alternative is to refine it electrolytically (all sounds very expensive for a toy engine!). However, the 99.9 % purity level is almost certainly the key to the trouble. The accidental intrusion of only 0.1 % of lead in the metal mix is sufficient to produce a cracked or powdered wheel in due course of time and it seems likely that this degree of cleanliness was not consistently achieved. Although the trouble was most severe in the late '30s affecting, regrettably, many of the more superior Hornby type locos (0 gauge) like "Princess

VOL. XXIII. Nº 12.   DECEMBER 1938

MECCANO MAGAZINE

A MECCANO FACTORY PRECISION TOOL

6ᴰ

23

★ IMPORTANT ANNOUNCEMENT

TO READERS OF THE MODEL RAILWAY NEWS

The perfect Gauge "OO" railway!

HORNBY-DUBLO TRAINS

Hornby-Dublo Trains are unique in their scale accuracy and beauty of finish. The Locomotives are fitted with motors either clockwork or electric, of a power and reliability never before achieved in this gauge. The Remote Control of the Electric Locomotives is perfect—starting, stopping, reversing and speed regulation are all carried out by the movement of a single lever on a special Controller at the lineside.

The track consists of solid drawn brass rail, mounted on a realistic metal base with holes for screwing down to a baseboard for permanent layouts.

The underframes of the Vans and Wagons, and the bogies of the Passenger Coaches, are pressure die-cast. All vehicles are fitted with pressure die-cast wheels. Automatic couplings are fitted to all Coaches, Vans and Wagons.

The Main Line Station, which is constructed in wood, will accommodate a three-coach train, and by means of the printed slips provided can be named " Berwick " (L.N.E.R.), " Penrith " (L.M.S.), " Truro " (G.W.R.) and " Ashford " (S.R.). There are also an Island Platform and a Goods Depot.

The Hornby-Dublo Electric Trains operate on 12-volt Direct Current and are intended to be run from mains Alternating Current through a Dublo Transformer connected to a Dublo Controller. Where the mains supply is Direct Current, or where there is no mains current at all, the trains can be run from a 12-volt accumulator.

DO NOT MISS THIS!

● *A Special Folder, printed in colour, is available giving details and prices of the complete Hornby-Dublo range. Free from any Meccano dealer, or direct from Meccano Ltd., Dept. M.R., Binns Road, Liverpool 13.*

A CORNER OF A HORNBY-DUBLO RAILWAY LAYOUT SHOWING THE REMARKABLE REALISM OF THE NEW TRAINS.

PASSENGER TRAIN SETS (ELECTRIC OR CLOCKWORK) L.N.E.R.

The trains in these sets, both Clockwork and Electric, consist of a perfect scale model of the famous L.N.E.R. streamlined " Pacific " Locomotive " Sir Nigel Gresley," an eight-wheeled Tender, and a Two-Coach Articulated Unit of the standard L.N.E.R. type. Rails are included, and in the electric Sets there is a Controller that gives complete remote control, both of speed and reversing, and incorporates a circuit breaker.

ELECTRIC PASSENGER SET (L.N.E.R.) **Price 70s.**   CLOCKWORK PASSENGER SET (L.N.E.R.) **Price 39s. 6d.**

GOODS TRAIN SETS (ELECTRIC OR CLOCKWORK) L.M.S., L.N.E.R., G.W.R., S.R.

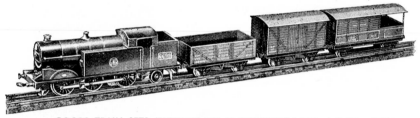

Each of these Sets includes a scale model of a six-coupled Tank Locomotive of the 0-6-2 type that is used by all four British groups. The trains consist of an Open Wagon, a Goods Van and a Brake Van. The Brake Vans are specially fine scale models of the latest types in use on the respective systems. Rails are included, and in the electric sets there is a Controller that gives complete remote control, both of speed and reversing and incorporates a circuit breaker.

ELECTRIC GOODS TRAIN SET. **Price 55s.**   CLOCKWORK GOODS TRAIN SET. **Price 27s. 6d.**
(L.M.S., L.N.E.R., G.W.R., S.R.)   (L.M.S., L.N.E.R., G.W.R., S.R.)

BRAKE VAN
True-to-type models of the latest Brake Vans used by the four main British railway groups. Long wheelbases with footboards.
Price 2s. 6d.

L.N.E.R. CORRIDOR COACH
A beautiful and accurate model of an L.N.E.R. First-Third corridor coach.
Price 3s. 6d.

SIGNALS — Splendid working models of the latest upperquadrant type. SINGLE ARM— " Home " (as illustrated) or " Distant." **Price 1s. each.**

DOUBLE ARM—" Home " and " Distant." **Price 1s. 4d. each.**

STATION

A model in wood of a station in modern style, attractively coloured, and long enough to accommodate a three-coach train. With it are packed printed gummed slips giving a choice of four names—" Berwick," L.N.E.R. ; " Penrith," L.M.S. ; " Truro," G.W.R. ; " Ashford," S.R. **Price 7s. 6d.**

MANUFACTURED BY MECCANO LIMITED, LIVERPOOL

Elizabeth", the "Eton" and "No 2 Specials" there is evidence that it existed much earlier, at least in spasms. In view of the close limits involved it is possible that even a change of foreman or workman in the casting shop was sufficient to produce a variation in quality and presumably it would take some time to become apparent. This only goes to show how much expertise is required even to produce a mechanical toy for sale at just a few shillings.'

From my own examination it seems a microscopic proportion of lead, tin or cadmium will all lead to failure of the casting and it seems to tie in with reports I have had from workmen in the factory saying that on occasions the wire binding the sack containing the zinc portions was thrown into the melting pot on another occasion the silver papers from a packet of cigarettes! However, as we have already read from Mr. Wyborn's letter that the large available production capacity for diecasting gave them very large orders for diecast parts for the war effort and consequently necessitated the very latest quality control and inspection equipment. Of course, this quality control problem was not purely confined to the Meccano Company. In a paper to the Metal Industry on 28th May 1937, Dr. A. C. Street reported that: 'The limitations of the alloys as produced 15 years earlier were still ingrained in many people's minds and one hears statements that the modern zinc based alloy is brittle or that it "grows" or disintegrates with time.' Modern zinc diecasting alloys are not prone to this type of deterioration as they are made from high purity (99.99 per cent) zinc and strictly controlled proportions of alloying elements viz:-

Aluminium (Al) 3.9 – 4.3 per cent
Copper (Cu) 0.975 – 1.25 per cent
Magnesium (Mg) 0.04 – 0.06 per cent

Impurities are limited to the following maxima:

Selenium (Se) 0.075 per cent
Lead (Pb) 0.0003 per cent
Cadmium (Cd) 0.0003 per cent
Tin (Sn) 0.0001 per cent

My profession is mineral exploration drilling, the object being to take core samples of the rock and subject them back in the laboratory to atomic absorption spectroscopy analysis and it was one lunchtime that the laboratories of the largest mineral analysts company in the United Kingdom were turned over to putting a disintegrated pre-war Hornby Dublo chassis unit and a post-war chassis unit through the system for analysis. To quote the final report:

'Nothing like this control was exercised over the composition of zinc alloys for diecasting in the 1930s particularly for application of lesser importance and hence the deterioration of the models.'

They went on to say that the cracks on the examples of the model railway chassis showed them were typical of metal fatigue – 'brought about by stress, vibration and intercrystalline corrosion!'

As such there is nothing to my knowledge that can be done to halt the corrosion on some of the pre-war models. I stress this as indeed there are in existence many superb models which will never disintegrate. It simply depends on whether your model is from one of the 'failure' batches of metal. Of course, the same happened to Dinky Toys and I heard that when the Meccano Company Museum display at Binns Road shut up entirely for the duration of the war and was re-opened in 1946, it was found that many of the Dinky Toys had collapsed or were belling to the extent that all those models, considered by the Meccano Company to be a poor advertisement to their skill, were scrapped. At an exhibition only a few months ago I shall always remember the expression of the owner of a rare early Dinky Toy who had just dropped it on the floor only to see this highly prized model disintegrate into a hundred pieces.

One of the most interesting points I have found in my researches is the fact that a lot of the pre-war and early post-war boxes had a quantity and date code printed on them. Let me give you an example. The Royal Daylight tank wagon box I have is coded BW5221–10M–3.39 which means that the works number would be 5221; 10 M (rather like the pamphlets and literature we have already mentioned) is short for a quantity of 10,000 and the date March 1939. Some other examples I have are a meat van BW1654 at 7.5M (7,500) dated October 1950 and an open wagon 25M or 25,000 dated April 1951. Even the wooden stations and buildings issued pre-war had such a code. The goods depot and island platform were produced as an initial batch of 3,250 in August 1938 whereas there were only 1,000 units of the city station. Like-wise the engine shed was a 1,000 run production and the box is dated 10.39 (October 1939). We have tried to include this information in the tabular section at the end of the book.

Despite the wagons introduced, people always wanted variety and especially so in passenger coaches. The 'Duchess of Atholl' locomotive and LMS coaches although advertised were just not available before the

00 track – pre-war designs (L. to R.)
by Bing, Marklin, Trix and Hornby.

war. It is interesting to see an advertisement by the Tyldesley & Holbrook Company of Deansgate, Manchester, advertising in 1939, litho papers to convert the teak coaches to LMS, GWR or SR as well as a range of private owner wagons. I had some correspondence with Mr. J. L. Holbrook who confirmed that these were the Merco series of papers distributed by the Hamblings Company and indeed are still available. Merco is short for the old Miniature Exhibition Railway Company of Watson Street, Dundee, who catered for those who enjoyed homebuilding from component parts. It was purely a question of sticking these excellent lithos to the sides of the coaches. Of course, they were not an exact fit but any Meccano boy could always cope with such improvisation.

This was 1938 and the interest of the public was agog at the incredible feats of speed produced by the railway companies and in particular the LMS and LNER. The introduction of the Coronation streamline trains, the running non-stop from London to Scotland ending in the world speed record for a steam locomotive of 126 miles per hour by the A4 'Mallard!' Railway locomotives seized the public's imagination to an even greater extent than that beautiful airliner Concorde does today. Reference was made to the fact that Meccano were very proud that their 00 model ('Sir Nigel Gresley') could also obtain in scale speed the same as its illustrious sister (so almost could the 0–6–2 tank!). The information book of the Hornby Railway Company states that to obtain scale speeds it is necessary to run the train over a distance measure in inches and time its run in seconds, then the scale speed per hour is the distance measured in inches divided by the time in seconds multiplied by 4.95 and this will equal the miles per hour required. (Incidentally, for 0 gauge it is exactly the same but multiply finally by 2.47 instead of 4.95.)

The speed with which new items were introduced was staggering particularly by modern day standards when one can frequently wait for twelve to eighteen months for items mentioned in a catalogue to appear today. As stated the initial advertisement was in the September 1938 *Meccano Magazine* and it is not sur-

prising that queues formed in the shops when the Dublo quota arrived. In March 1939 the new tank wagons were announced Royal Daylight, Esso (buff) and Power Ethyl as well as coal wagons which were the standard open wagons in the four regions with a plastic type coal load. The April 1939 *Meccano Magazine* as well as having an interesting write-up on anti-aircraft defence, carried an advertisement announcing many other new trucks including the cattle trucks in LMS and GWR liveries, the meat van in LMS and Southern Region together with the North Eastern fish van and horse box, although these were not generally available until later in the Spring. In June they hinted at a further range of buildings possibly later in the year and included Dublo in the part-exchange scheme which had been running for many years in 0 gauge. One was allowed 6s. credit on the 'Sir Nigel Gresley' clockwork locomotive and 8s. on the electric version. The Tank locomotive likewise was 4s. clockwork and 5s. 6d. electric. The July 1939 issue of the *Meccano Magazine* showed the first advertisement for the new city station and goods depot together with the buffer stop and the elusive wooden footbridge of which more is written in the building chapter later in this book. However, these items were not available until later in the year. September 1939 showed the highsided wagons (7 plank) with or without the imitation coal load in both the LMS and North Eastern liveries and the high capacity brick wagon and, of course, with September, came the declaration of the Second World War.

Month by month throughout the war the *Meccano Magazine* continued to be published and gave fascinating insights into the problems, successes and plans of the time. Publication was approximately 90,000 copies per month and almost matched the number of 'employees' (members) of the Hornby Railway Company. This was formed in October 1928 with Mr.

Ronnie Marshall Stead having the Number 1 membership. By 1929 it had risen to 12,000 members. By 1939 to 80,000. By 1949 to 120,000. By 1951 to 200,000. By 1956 to 270,000. The last membership number I have seen is 324,014 and in 1964, there were 585 branches.

Now this is the way to create interest and enjoyment from one's hobby and encourage demand for one's products and I am surprised that no magazine today can give the layman such a wide and interesting range of topics particularly on the mechanical side with emphasis on engineering and construction, ships and aircraft and the development of the steam locomotive. The month by month articles on the development of the aircraft from the post First World War period to present day is quite unique. But I digress . . . ah yes, the prologue. . . .

December 1939 showed in detail the new developments of the city station and engine shed together with the long awaited electrically operated points, signals and isolating rail switch. These items

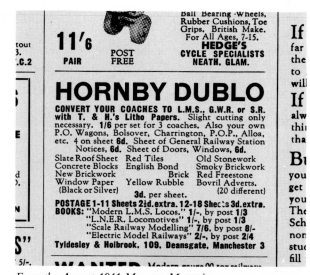

From the August 1941 Meccano Magazine.

Typical early box code. This one for the D304 'Royal Daylight' tank wagon. Ten thousand produced in March 1939.

A New Hornby-Dublo L.M.S. Express Passenger Train Set

This fine new Train Set comprises a perfect representation of the L.M.S. "Duchess of Atholl," one of the magnificent "Duchess" class express locomotives recently introduced, with tender, first-third and brake-third corridor coaches of standard L.M.S. type. *Ready Autumn.*

Extract from Hornby Dublo literature 1/239/10.

were produced before the war and were immediately snapped up. As the factory swung over to war-time production there was, of course, no hope of further supplies and many were the pleas in the wants columns of the model railway press. Of course, demand was far in excess of supply and so commenced the secondhand business which today must take a sizeable portion of the model railway trade. Most railway shops have shelves of secondhand or traded-in items today as do many specialist secondhand shops. Train and Dinky Toy swapmeets take place all over the country almost every weekend. Georges Ltd., of 11 Friar Street, Ipswich appear to be the first to advertise 'perfect used models' and I should think they must have done a roaring trade. In February 1940 the *Meccano Magazine* was oversubscribed and editorials started insisting that boys had to make sure of their copies by placing a regular order. By April 1940 six of the editorial staff of Meccano were on active service.

1940

Television was not widespread in those days. It was the time of food rationing which began in January 1940 and crowds gathered round the radio for such shows as ITMA (It's That Man Again) Tommy Handley with Jack 'Funf speaking' Train being hailed as the greatest comedy show of all time. Sandy McPherson with 'Sandy's Halfhour' and Sandy 'Can you hear me, Mother' Powell giving the country something to laugh about. It was also the time of air raids and blackouts and here was Meccano advertising Hornby Dublo on the basis that it brightened Blackout Nights! It was the end of the period of the phony war. There were incredible shortages and the belt tightened throughout the whole life of the country now fighting in earnest for its very survival. Looking through some old magazines of this period I see that the weekly supply for one adult was 4 oz bacon or ham, 8 oz sugar, 2 oz tea, 8 oz fats of which 2 oz could be butter, 2 oz preserves, 1 oz cheese and 1s. (5p) worth of meat which nowadays is hardly sufficient for one meal alone. Eggs were on allocation and in very short supply and one was lucky to have one a week and imported fruit such as oranges and bananas literally just vanished. I can remember with great excitement,

VOL. XXVI. Nº 1   JANUARY 1941

MECCANO
MAGAZINE

6ᵈ

IN ACTION!

27

my mother giving me my first banana, I think it was in 1946, having never seen them before.

Price lists continued to come out from the Company until November 1941, although it was interesting to see that in that particular price list the articulated coaches were listed as not being available – too much metal content perhaps? The shutters came down. The new projects announced were shelved. In July 1941, the repairs department closed; January 1942 saw the end of the exchange scheme and in this year there was a total freeze on distribution and all stocks were held in bond for the duration. Such was the influence and wide enjoyment of the Meccano system, however, that this appeared to be allowed to continue in production until the Government finally ordered sales to cease on 30th September 1943. Surprisingly the January 1942 *Meccano Magazine* showed an advertisement with the 'Duchess of Atholl' locomotive but this was deleted in the February issue as they were inundated with requests for this model.

Month by month articles kept coming out, not only on full size railway developments but on useful track systems and in particular servicing the model locomotives to keep them running. It is fascinating to read about the awaited invasion of the European fortress in the April 1944 issue of our magazine, especially as the invasion itself did not take place for a further two months!

The hostilities ceased on the European front on 8th May 1945 but the world was still very much at war in the Pacific Ocean and it was not until 2nd September, following the dropping of two atomic bombs that global peace dawned. I am not a pacifist as such and if ordered would doubtless fight like most other people, but I must record the sheer futility and stupidity of war. The present intrigue around the world with major nations split into camps egging on their factions and trying out their latest techniques and machines of slaughter maddens me. It has been my privilege to visit over 30 countries throughout Africa and the Middle East, not only to stay in their capital cities but to go way out into the deserts and jungles with my drilling rigs. I have met in villages, towns, bars, airports, hotels and mining camps, people of all colours,

races and religions and have found not the slightest difference in any. They bleed, they laugh, they cry, they try to make a living to look after their families whether they earn £16 per month or £600.

Advertisements towards the close of hostilities carried such headings as 'Soon we hope we can bring you these wonderful toys again' – and in the Autumn of 1945 the Meccano Company went to their store rooms and sorted out all the available items, made up allocation parcels and forwarded them to their dealers in early December. In November Mr. Tommy Hulse, the only traveller at that time, set about to see what accounts remained in existence. So many shops had been bombed or their owners lost in the war that he had to start from scratch, visiting everyone on the pre-war list. The allocation quantity was based entirely on the size of business the dealers had done before the war. However, it was not until April 1946 that the first new items appeared from the Meccano factory, namely Dinky Toys with the Lagonda (38C) and Jeep (153A). During 1946 the uncompleted components were assembled and again in December 1946 a further allocation of toys was made to eager hands. Many of the items not only in 00 but also in 0 gauge had interesting non-standard components which then would not have made the slightest difference but today are the much discussed variations so beloved by collectors. For a short time the beautiful No. 2 bogie suburban coaches were supplied in 0 gauge in LMS, LNER, SR and GWR liveries even a black Compound with British Railways on its tender was shown at the 1948 British Industries Fair. One can soon see from the many price lists of the Company how production slowly geared back up to its pre-war capacity. March 1946 saw Meccano sets up to the No. 5 set together with the magic motor and some Dinky Toys. By May they had gone up to the No. 6 set with spare parts for Meccano also being available. It was not, however, until March 1947 that Hornby 0 gauge trains in the shape of the M0, m1 and No. 20 sets were available and not until the December issue of the 1947 *Meccano Magazine* was it announced that Hornby Dublo was here again with a new coupling which is a story entirely on its own. . . .

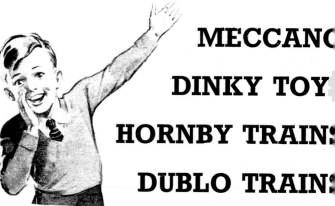

THE COUPLING

The pre-war coupling was of flat spring steel hardened and tempered. It was easily bent and broken. It had two small nibs pressed down, the front one at 35°

THE MECCANO MAGAZINE

MECCANO

DINKY TOY

HORNBY TRAIN

DUBLO TRAIN

VE Day has brought us nearer the time when we shall be able to supply these famous toys.

Our Works, which are still on war production, will change over to our own goods as rapidly as conditions permit—soon, we hope!

So keep looking out for our announcements.

MECCANO LIMITED · BINNS ROAD · LIVERPOOL 13

PUBLISHED BY MECCANO LTD., BINNS ROAD, LIVERPOOL 13, ENGLAND.
Printed by John Waddington Ltd., Leeds and London.

Meccano Magazine advertisement July 1945.

which was the coupling hook and the rear one set at 50° for shunting operations and indeed was scheduled for continued production on 4th March 1946. Mr. S. C. Pritchard, Managing Director of the Pritchard Engineering Company (Peco) then stepped onto the stage. In his letter to me on the coupling question, he wrote... 'In the days when Meccano was Meccano, it was a truly wonderful firm. It was a Company quite apart from the rest of the toy trade. I can truthfully state this in view of my own association with them over the coupling. They were an extremely honourable firm and honest to the extreme and they treated me very admirably. You ask about the coupling. The coupling was my own personal design and before Meccano got into production again with their Hornby trains after the war I approached them as many others have done to fit a new coupling, since their previous one left much to be desired, and was successful in interesting them in my design. They immediately went into production and showed the coupling as a new feature at the first toy fair after the war which in those days was part of the British Industries Fair. Patent applications had, of course, already been made but it takes several years to get a patent really granted. At the following fair a year later, Trix also had the coupling. They quite glibly copied it and told Meccano that the patent would never be granted. Meccano had every faith in the patent application and, of course, it was granted and at that stage they then proceeded against Trix. Naturally, I had many visits to their offices over this matter and as already stated, cannot speak too highly of the way I was treated. Needless to say they had the best legal advice and won the case. Having claimed all expenses from Trix, they then allowed them to go on manufacturing under licence to me and I really have to thank Meccano for our being in business today since I only sold the manufacturing rights to them covering the toy trade and retained the rights for the model trade. In those days there was a much bigger distinction between the two.'

Meeting Mr. Pritchard on 9th September 1975 he kindly went into further detail explaining that he started by manufacturing hair grips and the original Peco track chairs had been made on such machines. The Meccano Company had received at least 50 firm ideas on a new coupling and after having submitted his design he was informed that they were not interested

some three weeks later. Mr. Pritchard was not easily deterred and in the full tradition of determination took his coupling up to Liverpool. He was courteously received and the foreman of the train assembly room was called in and quite literally played with the coupling for three hours. After lunch Mr. Pritchard was called in to the office of the then Commercial Director, Mr. Hewitt, complete with butterfly collar and cravat and formally offered £1,000 in cash for his design. A princely sum indeed in those days. I think many a lesser man would have been swayed by this, but Mr. Pritchard stuck out for royalties and as he said, from the money received, launched his own extremely successful company.

To me it was quite wonderful to see almost exactly thirty years later, the same gentleman, and the same company, launching at the toy fair at the National Exhibition Centre, Birmingham in January 1978 a new version of this famous hook coupling. Quoting from the press handout. . . .

'Since it was incorporated by Meccano in reintroducing their Hornby Dublo system after the war, it has sold in many millions. It has now been upgraded by Peco to meet modern requirements so that the new version can not only be worked mechanically but also magnetically. The Peco Magni simplex auto coupler will, of course, operate the original type and retains all the advantages, especially the feature that enables it to be lifted straight from the train without fiddle or derailment.'

(I must admit that to me this is a superb feature. How many of us have tried to lift a wagon off a train of other makes and ended up holding virtually a line of sausages – I digress!)

'It now however incorporates a means of delayed uncoupling so that an item of rolling stock can be pushed along the track and left in any position desired. Special permanent magnets in addition to a mechanical decoupler will be available.'

I saw it in operation. It really is quite incredible.

Mr. A. Hunter wrote in the *H.R.C.A. Journal* on the coupling exchange scheme because the new coupling was totally inoperable with that of the pre-war type. He confirmed that Meccano sent complete replacement items. The costing is of interest as he lists the D2 high sided wagon at 10p, the D1 goods brake van 12½p, the D1 open wagon 8p, the D1 coach 17p

and the EDL7 Tank locomotive 92½p all of which included purchase tax but not postage for which 5p was requested. There was, however, considerable delay of anything up to nine months before the items were returned and basically they incorporated the new bases. The coupling was quite simple to install although it did necessitate on the castings, two 'udders' or stops which limited the radial action of the tail of the coupling. The drawing of the standard wagon bases dates the alteration, including the slots for the new axle brackets, to 15th August 1946.

The coupling remained in production for the next fifteen years and the super detailed Lowmac wagon introduced in November 1961 and the Southern Region utility van in December 1961, were the last items to be fitted with the metal coupling as standard. There was one important modification whereby the actual tongue of the hook unit itself was made much deeper on the introduction of the 2–6–4 Tank locomotive in November 1954. The reason for this was simple: the railway had originally been designed for a table top but all too frequently the layout was set up on the carpet and sometimes ran off the carpet onto the lino or wooden floor resulting in considerable unevenness of track to such an extent that the original hook couplings would lift off one another and give an unwanted slip coach effect as the train split.

These couplings were virtually unbreakable and could be easily bent back into shape if damaged.

The trade fairs of January 1961 introduced the super detail coaches with the hideous massively thick high density polythene coupling still to the existing design. This really was an ugly coupling which normally drooped and was totally impossible to bend back into correct shape. This development heralded the plastic era when plastic and its derivatives were king. Mr. Jack Wheeler for some twenty-three years secretary of the Railway Society at the City of London School, took the matter up with Mr. Parker the then manager of the Meccano London shop in Conduit Street. Apparently Mr. Parker was slightly affronted saying that they had a young man in their organisation who was an expert. . . .!

However, the cries were heard and according to the drawing, in June 1962 the design was changed to a much neater appearance altogether. In March 1963 the more suitable black Delrin was introduced on the

The pre-war coupling.

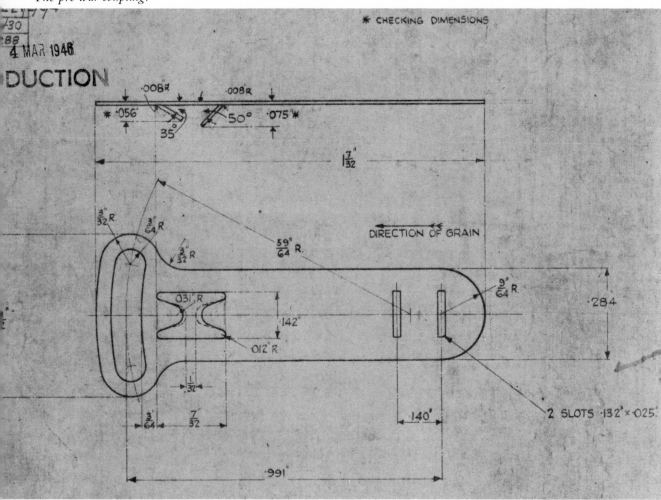

A pair of pre-war Hornby Dublo wagons with tin printed bodies to which handmade samples of the coupling had been fitted.

Underside view of one of the wagons again showing the coupling in position and also some rather unique wheels replacing the original. Each wheel had a ballrace inserted so that the wheels revolved around the axle which was fixed to the side members. This produced an extremely free running vehicle.

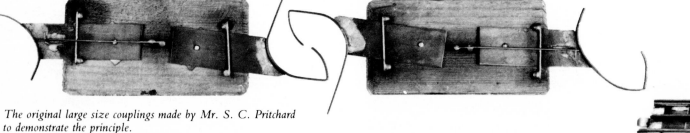

The original large size couplings made by Mr. S. C. Pritchard to demonstrate the principle.

The original handmade sample by S. C. Pritchard of the decoupling rail.

Special Service for Hornby-Dublo Owners

VEHICLES WITH THE NEW COUPLINGS

The automatic couplings fitted to post-war Hornby-Dublo Trains will not engage with the flat couplings fitted to trains of pre-war production. This means that many owners of Hornby-Dublo Trains who wish to add to their rolling stock find themselves unable to do so. "M.M." readers will know that the change in the design of the couplings has been made necessary to bring into use the new Uncoupling Rail, which has enormously increased the real railway operations that can be carried out on a Hornby-Dublo layout.

In the "M.M." for December 1947 we stated that a scheme was in preparation whereby owners of pre-war Hornby-Dublo Trains could return to Meccano Limited their rolling stock fitted with the old couplings, and obtain, on favourable terms, corresponding vehicles with new couplings. This scheme has now been put into operation. Those who wish to take advantage of it should write to Service Department, Meccano Limited, Binns Road, Liverpool 13, giving details of the vehicles they wish to exchange. They will then be told how much the transaction will cost them.

Two points should be noted. First, the scheme applies to the Hornby-Dublo Tank Locomotives, but not to the pre-war "Sir Nigel Gresley" Locomotive. It does apply to the tender (rear end) of the old "Sir Nigel." Second, as the Articulated Unit is not now in production, any Units of this kind will be replaced by two separate L.N.E.R. D1 Coaches.

Finally, for information about this new scheme write direct to Meccano Limited, not to Dealers.

A new PECO Wonderful Wagon in 00 gauge featuring the PECO Magni-Simplex Auto-coupler. The picture includes the permanent Magnet for fitting into the track.

(All photographs by courtesy of PECO Publications Ltd.)

From the May 1961 Model Railway Constructor.

NYLON COUPLINGS

Sir,—

I share the doubts which you express in the current issue regarding the new Hornby coupling. I recently bought a Hornby N2 and after only one month in use, one of the nylon couplings has failed to survive a minor accident which the old-type metal coupling would have taken in its stride. I feel that it should have been possible to design something better than this large, ugly and obtrusive piece of equipment. The hook supplied with the Peco conversion kits for Tri-ang vehicles is decidedly neater.

London, N.22.   H. E. PICKERING.

The couplings showing L. to R.:
Pre-war, early and later metal post-war type, coarse nylon type and final Delrin type.

The Pritchard Coupling fixed to one of the original tinplate Hornby Dublo coaches.

drawing. New products were completed introducing the new couplings although in the early 1960s such was the incredible stock of unsold items that it was totally impractical to up-date them. However, we are getting out of sequence. To my mind the late coupling, although good, was still not as good as the original steel type, but even that is not as good as the Magni Simplex coupling demonstrated to me on the Peco stand at Birmingham in January 1978. It is interesting to note that this special replacement service of the post-war coupling on pre-war items was not announced until December 1949! the Meccano Company advising these dealers that to keep the price down all models must be returned to Binns Road direct. Such was the restricted availability of models on the home market. I had great difficulty finding out exactly when the first British Industries Fair was after the war as Mr. Pritchard could not recall the precise year he went up to Meccano. It now transpires that he took his coupling idea to Meccano in late 1945, the Australian patent number reading No. 135121 for 4th December, 1945. The trade introduction at the British Industries Fair was at Earls Court in London in May 1947. It seems probable that the first post-war set available was the 0–6–2T set in December 1947. The shortages are hard for us to imagine today. Even in December 1948 the *Meccano Magazine* explained . . . 'extensions to the track are, for the time being, not possible as Hornby Dublo rails are not yet available separately, but certain items of goods rolling stock can be expected soon, so that a little more variety in train make-up becomes possible'. Stores limited each boy to one Dinky Toy and it was the devil's own job to persuade a friend who either did not want such a model or could not afford one to go in and buy it on your behalf. That is how one eager enthusiast described the situation to me. People were begging dealers to split up Hornby Dublo tank sets so they could get some extra rail or wagons but they seldom did. As I said the *Meccano Magazine* for December 1947 carried the first article reproduced here on the re-introduction of the Hornby Dublo railway system and looking through *Meccano Magazine* advertisements over the next two or three years a wide variation in prices is apparent:

BOXED SET PRICES

Date Year 'Sir Nigel Gresley' 'Duchess of Atholl' 0–6–2T Goods

Date Year	'Sir Nigel Gresley'	'Duchess of Atholl'	0–6–2T Goods
Dec 1947	157/6d. (£7.88)	177/6d. (£8.88)	135/–d. (£6.75)
Feb 1948	185/–d. (£9.25)	210/–d. (£10.50)	150/–d. (£7.50)
May 1948	167/6d. (£8.38)	190/–d. (£9.50)	135/–d. (£6.75)
May 1949	145/–d. (£7.25)	157/6d. (£7.88)	125/–d. (£6.25)

1948

Many a boy had to wait two years to get his first 'Duchess of Atholl' set as from the literature it appears that only the 0–6–2 goods sets were available for the time being. I have had many letters from enthusiasts recalling their original purchases and one tells how he ordered his 'Duchess' set in January 1948 having been promised one for his birthday in June. His mother went into the shop almost twice a week but June came and went and there was still no sign of his set at all. It was not until the morning of the 2nd November that they received a telephone call from the local dealer saying he had had some sets in the previous evening and that they had better come at once. He and his mother dashed round immediately and concluded their transaction. He recalled boys came from far and wide as his was the first set to arrive in that area. He pleaded for extra track and thought himself successful when he managed to obtain two extra straight lengths in March 1949 although by the Autumn of 1949 the supply situation began to improve on the home market. I have seen one or two 'Duchess' sets where the dealer has entered on the guarantee form the date of purchase and most of them seem to have been in November 1948. Another collector having had a set on order since pre-war days eventually took delivery of the first one to come into his shop on 2nd December. Of course, not only the models were in short supply but also the packaging and boxes and it appears that the original sets were supplied in the old Hornby M0 series boxes with a large drawing of the 'Royal Scot' locomotive on the top. It was not until June 1949 that the new Hornby Dublo boxes showing the pre-war advertisements of two boys controlling their layout appeared. This too shows the 'Duchess of Atholl' and the green-roofed later series pre-war buildings.

The first major production improvements after the war which were to become standard were the new split Alnico magnets. Work on these had been in progress for some time, particularly in Japan in pre-war years and there is a fascinating four page article by

The Meccano Showrooms at 4 Conduit Street, London W1.

Meccano Magazine article January 1948.

HORNBY DUBLO
ELECTRIC TRAINS
are here again!

Small supplies of these long-awaited trains are now becoming available. Here is your chance to get the Perfect Table Railway.

Complete sets ONLY will be available at first. Of the sets illustrated below the Tank Goods Set will be ready this month. The L.M.S. "Duchess of Atholl" Set and the L.N.E.R. "Sir Nigel Gresley" Set will follow early in the New Year.

Obtainable only from Meccano Dealers.

EDG7 Tank Goods Set, L.N.E.R., L.M.S., G.W.R., S.R.
Price 135/- (Including Tax)

EDP1 L.N.E.R. Passenger Set
Price 157/6 (Including Tax)

EDP2 L.M.S. Passenger Set
Price 177/6 (Including Tax)

Hornby-Dublo Trains are built to standard "00" Gauge. They are 12-volt Electric and power is obtained from A.C. mains through a Dublo Transformer and a Dublo Controller No. 1.

MADE IN ENGLAND BY MECCANO LIMITED

The Hornby-Dublo streamlined 4-6-2 locomotive "Sir Nigel Gresley."

The New Hornby-Dublo Trains

LAST month we were able to make a preliminary announcement regarding the long-awaited reappearance of Hornby-Dublo trains. We now give a few more details regarding the new train sets.

The upper illustration shows the handsome post-war Dublo version of the famous 4-6-2 streamliner *"Sir Nigel Gresley."* Like the prototype, it now carries the number "7," in accordance with the L.N.E.R. renumbering scheme recently carried out. The most striking change from the pre-war model, however, lies in the cutting away of the sideplates over the driving wheels. This gives quite a new interest to the engine, as the outside valve motion is reproduced very effectively and looks strikingly realistic when the engine is on the run. Return crank, eccentric rod, and expansion link are all provided, each with its characteristic movement, while the busy crosshead moves to and fro, with its attendant combination lever.

The L.N.E.R. Coaches are now separate vehicles, not articulated as formerly. Each vehicle therefore represents an 8-wheel bogie corridor coach of characteristic Doncaster outline and finish. One is a complete passenger coach and the other is a composite with guard's and luggage accommodation.

The engine of the L.M.S. Passenger Train was illustrated last month. This is the impressive 4-6-2 *"Duchess of Atholl,"* which captures completely the massive air of the real engine and is remarkably complete in detail. The characteristic double chimney is provided and the fittings at footplate level include the lubricators, sand-box fillers and steam-pipe covers that are found on the real thing. Below the footplate are the cylinders and valve chests with their fascinating rods and Walschaerts motion.

The Tender of the "Duchess" is a faithful reproduction of the modern L.M.S. high-sided tender. It is very fully detailed and the coal space has a load of "fuel."

The Coaches are modelled on the familiar L.M.S. standard corridor stock, one of them being a first-third and the other a brake-third with guard's and luggage accommodation. Actual cut-out windows "glazed" with celluloid are provided and there is a corridor partition inside each coach.

The Hornby-Dublo Tank Goods Train has not been changed.

The L.M.S. Brake-third vehicle of the Hornby-Dublo "Duchess of Atholl" Train Set.

A. G. Crawshaw in the October 1946 *Model Railway News* – writes . . .

POWER VERSUS SIZE

. . . 'Right at the beginning of these articles I mentioned that these new magnet materials could either be used to get more power in the same space or to get the same power in a smaller space and it cannot have escaped notice that the latter is the alternative I pinned my faith to. My reasons for this are twofold but which of them is the more important will be left to others to argue over. Firstly, the small engines. The motors for these were distinctly difficult as it was usually the magnet bulk that caused the trouble. The bad end of it could often be accommodated in the cab and bunker regions so long as the engine was a tank engine and so long as it did have a cab, but even then one sometimes had to grind lumps out of the magnet to clear axles and other untouchables and excuse the resulting loss in performance on the grounds that it was a small engine "and wouldn't anyway". Small magnets would certainly be a help here. The second reason is of a very different character but I am sure that it is sound nevertheless. It is that there is enough power in these mechanisms as they are, for all ordinary purposes provided they are properly designed and made. Doubters should remember some prewar efforts such as 16 bogie coaches being shot round by a Pacific to record just one of them.'

It is quite understandable that Meccano with their quality control and equipment and eager hungry market went over to the new magnets as soon as they were available and I put the changeover date to the Summer of 1949. Of the many Hornby Dublo instruction sheets issued by the Company, the first issue after the war was 16/947/25 (25,000 printed September 1947). A further 10,000 were printed in May 1949 showing the 4–6–2 chassis of the Gresley locomotive with the horseshoe magnet, yet three months later in August 1949 (16/849/25) a further 25,000 were printed, showing the new split magnet unit.

The next major development, in December 1949, introduced the uncoupling rail, one of the principal

features to attract Meccano to Mr. Pritchard's coupling and naturally the *Meccano Magazine* went to town on various shunting schemes. However, they were not out of the woods yet by any means and I really do now feel sorry for the designers in Binns Road as one problem after another attacked them. The next was the radio interference from model railways. Pretty well every home had a radio and it is with some pride that the engineers of the company recalled the fact that they led the field in the toy industry in achieving efficient suppression for their models. Of course, whilst it was most unpleasant to have a radio crackling from interference, the railways and electrical toys of the period completely obliterated the early television screens coming on to the mass market in the early 1950s.

1. Old type Horseshoe magnets.
   All these types i.e.   Sir Nigel Gresley
                           Duchess of Atholl
                           0-6-2 Tank
   220 turns per pole of 38 swg enamelled copper wire.

2. New Motors 1950 onwards
   Sir Nigel Gresley ⎫
   Duchess of Atholl ⎬ 120 turns per pole of 37 swg.
   0-6-2 Tank   100 turns per pole of 37 swg.

3. To re-energise magnet:
   Flux density is 20,000 gauss.
   Current consumption 0.65 amps approx. 8 watts max.

Extract from Hornby Railway Company Information Dept.

Pre-war and post-war chassis development.

Mr. Wyborn goes on . . .

'We had always attempted to be in the forefront in technical knowhow and application and an example of this is the suppression of radio and TV interference caused by the running of a loco. on a track layout.

'Insofar as model railways are concerned interference is the result not only of the action of the motor but also of the wheels or pick-up arrangement on the track. The latter also can behave as an efficient propagator of interference signals. The BBC had hardly resumed TV services after the War when we began to receive complaints of interference, particularly from fringe areas. Something had to be done and the way we set about it was to approach the P.O. Engineering Dept. suggesting a working liaison whereby we would do all the experimental work if they would help us by carrying out the testing because of course we were without the specialised equipment necessary for this. They co-operated fully and as the result we had full suppression of locos and track in months, and before any of our competitors had bothered to do anything about the problem.

'We were however not content to stop there and immediately began to set up our own testing apparatus which involved the building of a full size screened cage in which both operator and equipment were housed whilst testing was in progress. Later when we established a new laboratory we elaborated on this by building the cage into the roof space and by pushing a button the operator when ready could elevate a complete 14ft × 6ft track layout into the suspended floor of the cage, using standard P.O. test equipment. I think the foregoing illustrates the degree of effort which was bestowed in order to improve and maintain standards and to build into our product the technical qualities which we considered were the customers due.'

In September 1950 the new cast aluminium main line station, island platform and signal box were announced that it is a pity that they never introduced the goods shed. Indeed, one was drawn up but due to the shortage of metals, let alone the sales price, it was decided not to continue with this item. However, more of this in a later chapter.

From November 1955 Railway Modeller.

The real enthusiast solves the suppression problem !

Mr. R. Wyborn with G.P.O. Test apparatus checking a new prototype in 1956.

THE RAILWAY Modeller

Volume 1   No. 5
JUNE–JULY 1950

A FAR CRY, no doubt, from the usual model railway magazine frontispiece but in this issue we are specialising in the "beginner". Nevertheless most serious modellers start off with Hornby Dublo.

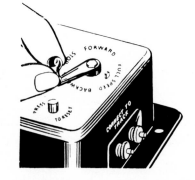

1951

The dark clouds of war again rolled across the sky. This time the Korean War. The Government had massive urgent rearmament plans to the extent that many of the principal materials such as brass were not available. Despite desperate pleas and the spectre of unemployment the Meccano factory at Speke faced shut down in March 1951 and was not to reopen again until October 1953. Indeed, metal shortage was so acute that the Company even considered returning to war time production of defence equipment and in December 1951 an advertisement warned all that replacements and spare parts may not be easy to obtain for some time. Not a single new product was introduced in 1951. Government stockpiling, the Korean War, and the rearmament programme were blamed for the restrictions on the use of zinc, copper and brass. These materials formed the basis – with scarce tinplate and various grades of steel – of most of the Meccano constructional sets, trains and other models and on 9th March the new Speke factory had to close.

1952

1952 was not much better and started off in January with a plea for all Hornby train boys to read fully the instructions. Naturally, I am concerned to keep my own Hornby Dublo trains running for another fifty years and so have instituted the identical tests to those used in the Meccano works – namely of checking and putting a tiny drop of oil on each of the axle units and then ensuring that the wagon or coach will, *from a standing start*, roll freely down a one in thirty degree slope. I just took a long strip of wood marked off 30 inches and then put a one inch block underneath the mark. It is quite surprising if all wagons do pass this test how freely your trains will run. Too much oil is another constant hazard and in my earlier ignorance (as opposed to present semi-ignorance) I used to use a standard tin of three-in-one which is a little heavy. I happily went into a local Wellington chemist to ask for a hyperdermic needle (ideal for oiling 00 trains) and suffered suspicious looks and was almost arrested as a

potential junkie! It does make sense though, because you will be surprised how much dust and dirt and bits of fluff jam into the works. February showed the fascinating little insulating tab details for blocking off sections of one's layout and on the inside front cover of the April issue of *Meccano Magazine* came the advertisement for miniature personnel in both 0 and 00 gauge. These were in 00 identical to the pre-war castings but very much inferior in paint detail. It also showed the loading gauge for the goods yard and then

we had to wait until September before the reintroduction of the electric points filtered through into the shops. The useful steel re-railer unit came in October and the electric signals returned in November. January 1953 showed a fascinating combined operation of electric signals and points and the inside cover of the February issue the introduction of the goods yard crane. An interesting story in many ways – it was a compromise as it was originally going to be a diecast goods depot!

Advertisement in November 1952 Railway Modeller.

Just a point here – I keep mentioning the *Meccano Magazine*. It is still in print at £4 per four issues a year. The back numbers are always difficult to find but MW Models Ltd., of 4 Greys Road, Henley on Thames, Oxon, usually have good stocks of most issues back to the 1930s.

April heralded the end of the pre-nationalisation liveries with the introduction of the new standard British Railways colours. Here came perhaps the most common locomotive of all, the EDL12 'Duchess of Montrose' in a beautiful gloss green livery together with the Eastern Region EDL11 'Silver King' locomotive and according to the advertisement the 0–6–2 Tank engine which would be following shortly. The D12 coach came in, crimson lake livery with cream panels lined in gold and black, which has on many occasions been degenerated to 'plum and spilt milk' or 'blood and custard'! This was for the main line corridor stock only as they do make reference in the following May issue to forthcoming suburban stock which is crimson lake, i.e. maroon only. The wagons shown on the initial advertisement were the D1 open wagon, the D2 (old high-sided wagon with coal load), the LMR brake van, the D1 high capacity wagon and the D1 cattle truck.

June saw the introduction of the isolating switch points which replaced the former units and eased a lot of the electrical control problems of the younger enthusiast. We must bear in mind that Hornby Dublo at this stage was very much considered for the toy market and younger enthusiast and it is interesting to read the notice inserted in the model railway press almost twelve months later in August 1954 by Faithful, Owen and Fraser, solicitors for Mr. Pritchard of Peco. It clearly states that the Meccano Company had the patent rights for toy railways whereas Mr. Pritchard retained the patent rights for the model railway industry. Of course, nowadays for all practical purposes they are merged.

June 1953 showed the 0–6–2 in its new livery finally arriving as well as the grey open wagon and brake van and on the rear page the introduction of the bogie bolster wagon, the drawings of which had been made pre-war, but were unable to be released. The

Hornby Dublo locomotives and rolling stock are now available in British Railways' colours. Our photograph shows the latest guise of these popular models.

Advertisement in May 1953 Meccano Magazine.

HORNBY DUBLO ELECTRIC TRAINS

1953 MODELS IN B.R. LIVERY

pent up energy and release of restriction of metal supply brought new models or accessories almost every month, while today we have to make do with these every year. July 1953 brought the junction signals in both hand operated and electric versions and August showed the first mention of the diecast mineral wagon. October saw the reintroduction of the EDA2 large radius curved rails and in November the introduction of the level crossing. It is sad to read in the December issue of *Meccano Magazine* the obituary to the father of commercial model railways in this country for over 50 years, W. J. Bassett-Lowke who died on 21st October, aged 76. I look forward to a book on his life and work, which I understand is in preparation.

The ever popular Hornby Dublo range of locomotives and rolling stock is now available in British Railways' liveries. At the same time Messrs. Meccano have taken the opportunity to bring these excellent models up to date, and to introduce new names and numbers.

The range of Dublo remote controlled accessories now includes uncoupler rails—a most useful fitting. Another recent addition to the range, the Dublo Re-railer, will be equally valuable for both Hornby Dublo and scale enthusiasts, as it eliminates the tedious fiddling needed to replace bogie stock and locomotives on the track.

Extract from April 1953 Railway Modeller.

The Winter of 1953/54 was spent in catching its breath although there were useful engineering and running articles, one quoting that 1 in 30 was the steepest recommended gradient for any Hornby Dublo layout. April 1954 showed the introduction of the low sided wagon and cable drum wagon and perhaps the answer to its never being fitted with an 'open' brake gear chassis as all the other models were in the later years, could be discovered from the box showing they had an initial production run of 25,000. I wondered at first if this was a misprint and it should be 2.5 thousand but then (although I believe that the quantity production figures have long since been lost), 85,000 units for the 'Duchess of Montrose' gleaned from a similar source does seem a realistic figure. An article in the popular weekly *Illustrated* magazine on 23rd November 1957 discusses the introduction of the 'Bristol Castle' locomotive and comment was made that a previous model – the 2–6–4 Tank locomotive? – had an initial production batch of 100,000 and Meccano were very proud of the fact that of this massive quantity only six locomotives came back under guarantee failure and were found to have serious defects. However, we go too fast for ourselves – the prologue – ah yes . . .

May 1954 showed the introduction of the lefthand and righthand diamond crossings and there followed many ingenious layout designs of crossings, sidings and loops. In October, some 12 months after the introduction of the level crossing a new road rail item was introduced as well as the now electrically operated uncoupling rail and on the back page the new 2–6–4 Tank locomotive. What a feast was in store as over the next few months the articles and write-ups on this magnificent and extremely well-chosen model were described in full with the D13 suburban maroon coaches with the tin printed windows.

The power units were improved upon and in the opinion of many the A2 and A3 types were the finest mass produced units at that time available. Mr. Wyborn explained . . .

'The A2 and A3 Power Units provide another example of our determination to produce a quality article. The transformers which formed part of these units were designed to be strictly in conformance with British Standards, and production testing was carried out on the most advanced equipment we could devise. Some idea of this is conveyed in photographs Nos. 2 and 3 which show transformer testing on the production line. No. 2 shows performance testing, and in No. 3 the operator is using an ionisation tester to check the quality of insulation between input and output windings. If this fell below the present standard it would be indicated on the instrument which she is observing and in addition an audio signal would sound from the speaker on the right of the instrument panel, which would also call the attention of the line inspector. To the extreme left of photo No. 3 can be seen a generator control panel which together with the controls behind the raised glass cover of the centre panel (also shown in photo. No. 2) enabled the characteristics of any supply in the world to be set up.

Awareness of this attitude towards quality must I think have gradually spread, because in the latter half of the 50s I was invited to represent the British toy industry on a permanent committee of British Standards. This was useful in allowing me to help provide a bastion against some of the shoddy products beginning to make their appearance from abroad. It also helped me later on to obtain acceptance into the appropriate standard for a short circuit proof transformer which I had devised and developed in an attempt to bring down cost by removing the necessity for any form of electrical protection. We had gone into production with this when later still I was also successful in getting it approved by the International Electrotechnical Commission on safety transformers at a specially convened meeting in Copenhagen. However it nearly backfired when the Australian Standards Commission decided to revise their national standard on safety transformers, which was mandatory, and which in the revised version by some mischance excluded this type of transformer by simple omission.

Now we had a very big export market in Australia, and it so happened that the revised standard made its appearance just after we had exported £20,000 worth of power units. Frantic

cables from our Australian agent followed by a copy of the offending document came to Binns Road. At a hurriedly called meeting the Board decided with simple judgement that since it was Wyborn that had got them into this mess it was equally up to him to get them out of it. Consequently I found myself on the next available flight to Sydney. Now everyone knows that the average Australian is a pretty rough fellow, and that he is not necessarily endowed with a natural love for the British, and here I was setting out to get them

to change one of their own recently issued Standards simply to allow us to import more of our goods into their country. Full realisation of the certain failure of my mission only dawned when I was already in flight heading east. By the time we landed at Sydney airport I had prepared a short list of firms to whom I could reasonably apply for a comparable job.

Imagine my surprise and relief when four days after landing I was invited to meet the chairman and two members of the committee involved

in order to present my case, and who turned out to be attentive and sympathetic. They invited me to present a thesis on the new transformer and within a fortnight of doing so they accepted it for inclusion in the next edition. You never can tell.'

Many would be the Hornby Dublo enthusiasts at this time who did not have AC mains supply and with the clockwork locomotives no longer available a battery operated controller was introduced in December far superior to the poor units often seen today.

Checking quality of insulation between input and output windings on A2 and A3 power units.

HORNBY RAILWAY COMPANY

By the Secretary

Hornby-Dublo Trains Driven by Battery

THIS month I have good news for those would-be Hornby-Dublo owners who have no A.C. mains supply. A popular question regarding Hornby-Dublo Trains has always been *"Can I run a Hornby-Dublo Train from a dry battery?"* The answer now is *"Yes,"* for a battery controller specially designed for the purpose has been introduced in the Hornby-Dublo system. This Battery Control Unit, to give it the correct title, is simple, neat and efficient, and it will be given a great welcome by all who are unable to make use of mains current, or who wish for any reason to employ the handy source of current that dry batteries provide.

It should be made quite clear straight away that the new Controller is not a cheap type with fixed resistance steps. On the contrary, the degree of control afforded is very smooth, so that those who run their Hornby-Dublo Trains with its aid can enjoy really good engine driving.

Simplicity in handling is the keynote, for the single handle mounted on top of the casing is used, not only to look after speed regulation, but also to reverse the direction of movement of the engine when required. A good feature of the Control Unit is that it tells the operator at once when there is a short circuit on the track, whether this is due to a derailment or to some other cause. This is done by means of a pilot or indicating lamp, which glows immediately

if there is any happening of this kind. The lamp goes out as soon as the trouble has been tracked down and put right, and normal working can be resumed without the operator doing anything more about it.

As the capacity of a dry battery is limited, it is only natural that some of you should wonder what particular type of battery it is best to use. A 12-volt supply is required, so we recommend that Hornby-Dublo owners should use three 4.5-volt dry batteries of Ever-Ready type 126 or Drydex type H30.

Extract from December 1954 Meccano Magazine.

1955

The electric uncoupling rail announced in the preceding October was finally introduced in January 1955 as well as an article on a turntable – why not indeed? There followed in the Summer the first mention of headboards and train name and destination boards although applying to full sized railways and it is wonderful how throughout the life of not only the Hornby Dublo system, but all Meccano products readers, young and old of the *Meccano Magazine* were given a first taste of delights to come.

It was in July 1955 that the end of steam locomotives on British Railways was announced to much dismay. However, Hornby Dublo was going from strength to strength and the first article by 'Tommy Dodd' (I believe Mr. Les Norman) appeared. At the same time new platform extensions for both the main line station and the island platform and two beautiful new tank wagons the Vacuum Oil in red with a Mobilgas motif and the yellow Shell Lubricating Oil were introduced. It was in this period – although I cannot be precise – that the letters 'L.F.' were printed on many wagon boxes. No reason was given though a theory voiced by an H.R.C.A. member writing in the magazine suggested it stood for 'Lead Free'. I recall a big scare at the time at the lead content of toys – with 'Little Johnny' chewing them to his detriment. Indeed, all metal toys came under review for sharp edges etc., and this must have had a detrimental effect on Meccano Construction sales – very unfairly in my opinion as such was the quality of the product that no such problems existed.

August 1955 *Meccano Magazine* contained a fascinating article on Mr. C. F. Blake's demonstration layout of operating post office trains. This layout was shown in Harrods store in London from 3rd to 15th January 1955 and it is interesting to note that with scale scenery and Exley T.P.O. coaches the Hornby Dublo 'Duchess of Atholl' locomotive on the layout was in continuous operation 8 hours a day without a single mishap of any kind except for one derailment caused by an unobserved vandal placing a piece of wood on the track and probably watching the result from a safe distance. To quote the article in the *Model Railway*

The Heart of the Engine

The Hornby-Dublo Locomotive Motor

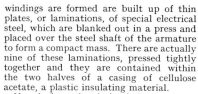

HAVE you ever wondered what makes a Hornby-Dublo locomotive run? Some of you may have had occasion to take off the housing of one of your own locomotives, and I am sure all of you have turned this over and peered in between the wheels. So that you will have some idea of the form of the small and powerful electric motor inside, which runs on current picked up from the centre rail of the track by the sprung shoes underneath it.

The heart of the motor is here pictured for you at the head of the page. It is the armature, the small part with electrical windings on it that rotates at speed and, through the worm on its shaft, drives the wheels of your locomotive through a skew gear mounted on the axle of the rear pair of coupled wheels. There is of course much

windings are formed are built up of thin plates, or laminations, of special electrical steel, which are blanked out in a press and placed over the steel shaft of the armature to form a compact mass. There are actually nine of these laminations, pressed tightly together and they are contained within the two halves of a casing of cellulose acetate, a plastic insulating material.

Now look at the shaft of the armature, as you see it in the little picture.

Below the laminations the shaft carries a two-start worm, that is a worm with two places where a gear wheel can begin to mesh with it. It is this worm that turns the skew gear through which the locomotive wheels are actually driven.

Above the laminations is a splined portion of the shaft. The purpose of this is to retain the

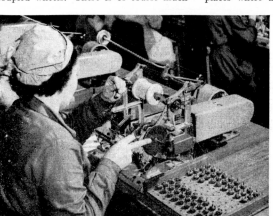

Winding the armature of a Hornby-Dublo locomotive motor.

commutator, through which current is supplied to the three windings of of the armature.

Now for the all important windings. In the illustration on this page is shown one of the winding machines used. An armature to be wound is held vertically in the machine by means of jaws that close over two of the three projecting arms of the laminations, leaving the third one free. It is on this arm that the winding is to be made. The holder is turned at speed when the machine is in operation, so that wire fed from the bobbin seen on the machine is wrapped round the

more to the motor than the armature, but what else there is we shall see as we run through the process by which the armature itself is completed.

In the illustration of the armature you can easily pick out the windings, of which you will see there are three, set at equal distances apart around the shaft of the motor. The parts around which the

---

laminations in the slots provided for it.

The wire must be laid evenly and compactly. So from the bobbin it is taken over pulleys mounted on spring-loaded arms to keep the tension on the wire constant throughout the operation. A counter on the machine tells the operator when a sufficient number of turns has been

A variable resistance for a train controller, with the former on which it is wound.

wound on, and the machine is then stopped the wire is cut and the end is temporarily secured. Then the jaws holding the armature in position are opened, and the part is moved round so that the second winding can be laid on, which of course is followed by the third.

The utmost care is taken in making the parts of the electric motor of a Hornby-Dublo locomotive, each of which is thoroughly examined before passing on for assembly. One example of the care taken in this respect is provided by the commutator already mentioned. This causes the current in each of the three armature windings to change its direction of flow twice every revolution of the armature, that is to "commute" the current in the windings. The face of this commutator, on which bear the two copper-carbon "brushes" that carry the current to it, is accurately machined after assembly to the armature to make sure that it is concentric with the armature shaft, so that the rotation will be perfectly smooth, without causing vibration of the brushes.

The ingenious machine on which the variable resistance is wound.

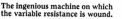

This very careful attention to ensure ~~rfect~~ "follow" of the brushes as they ~~ntact~~ the surface of the spinning ~~mmutator~~ is essential in view of the high ~~eed~~ which the latter will attain in service. ~~may~~ not be generally realised that the ~~eed~~ of the armature when the locomotive ~~flat~~ out will be in the region of 10,000 r.p.m.

The completed armature is mounted between the poles of a powerful permanent magnet. The actual magnet takes the form of a small rectangular block, which is made from an aluminium-nickel-iron alloy having special properties that make the magnet "anisotropic". This means simply that the magnet is capable of being magnetized fully along one axis only, but when this is done, the resulting magnetic force is many hundreds of times that previously obtained on the old type cobalt magnets.

The assembly of the locomotive ~~tor~~ is carried out with the magnet ~~magnetized~~. When assembly is ~~mpleted~~, the locomotive motor is placed ~~tween~~ the poles of a very powerful ~~gnetizer~~, which permanently magnetizes ~~block~~ in less than a second. ~~By~~ using this technique, the maximum ~~ssible~~ magnetic strength is obtained, but the magnet system is subsequently ~~turbed~~ by even partial disassembly, the ~~ength~~ will immediately fall by about ~~per~~ cent. That is why a warning is ~~ven~~ against dismantling in the instruction ~~oklet~~ issued with the train set.

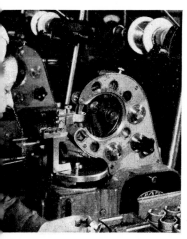

The final test of a newly-completed Hornby-Dublo 2-6-4 Tank locomotive.

Testing is no less painstaking and exact. The entire motor is fitted in a die-cast frame, to which the driving wheels of the locomotive are fitted, and with the aid of elaborate equipment testers make certain that the windings take the correct amount of current and that the motor is exactly as designed in other respects from an electrical point of view.

There is also a practical test in which the locomotive unit is run on a special track at this stage of assembly. This is by no means the end of testing. When the body or housing has been fitted over the unit the complete locomotive is again tested by running it on an oval track, first alone and then with a train of coaches, and only when it has proved itself to be up to the standard required is the label attached that indicates it to be a complete and perfect Hornby-Dublo electric locomotive.

As all the electrical requirements of the Hornby-Dublo railway system are actually made in the Works at Binns Road, there is a wide variety of intricate and ingenious winding machines in the Electrical Department. One of these is seen in the lower picture on the previous page; the

winding that it is designed for is shown above it. This is a variable resistance for a train controller, wound on a former of ceramic material, which is pictured separately.

The wire used for this variable resistance is constantan, a nickel copper alloy that is specially suitable. It is bare, and the successive windings, although very close together, do not touch each other. They must not, in fact, for if they did the resultant resistance value would be lowered, and the unit would be rejected.

Looking at the illustration on the previous page of the machine used for this winding, the ceramic former can readily be seen, held in position by a special fixture. This fixture rotates slowly while winding is in operation, the effect of this being that the former turns on its centre, so that each turn of wire is spaced away from the previous turn by the desired amount.

Wire for the winding comes from the spool at the top of the picture, and it is first wound on the vertical metal ring that passes through the former. This ring is known as the shuttle ring.

(Continued on page 692)

Testing a Hornby-Dublo Diamond Crossing.

Constructor this trouble free operation reflects great credit on the locomotive (Hornby Dublo) and rolling stock (Exley) which were used for the demonstration. November saw the introduction of the 40 ton bogie well wagon and a fascinating article in the December issue of the *Model Railway Constructor* reproduced here on the heart of the Hornby Dublo locomotive motor. Hornby Dublo was now beginning to overhaul Hornby 0 gauge and there were now 9 pages alone on Hornby Dublo matters in the *Meccano Magazine*, compared with two pages devoted to 0 gauge, the latter aimed principally at the junior railway modeller.

The Heart of the Engine—*(Continued from page 652)*

Needless to say, a gap can be created in it at the very beginning of the operation, so that the former can be placed in position, after which the ring is again closed. The end of the wire from the shuttle ring is threaded through a hole in the former, after which the ring is rotated rapidly, while of course the ceramic former itself turns more slowly. In this rotation the wire is carried up the outside of the former and down the inside as it is unwound from the ring, the result of course being the close and even winding seen in the illustration.

The machine is automatic. The length of wire wound on to the shuttle ring is determined by a special mechanism, and when the winding on the ceramic former is complete the machine stops automatically.

The shuttle ring can then be opened again and the completed winding removed. Nuts and screws are inserted in the two holes in the former, and the ends of the winding are looped under the heads of the screws before these are tightened. Then the resistance is ready, after testing and balancing the resistance into two electrical halves, for assembly into the controller for which it is intended.

Earlier on I pointed out that testing is of the greatest importance in the production of Hornby-Dublo locomotives, and this applies also to other electrical equipment of all kinds. A good example is illustrated in the lower picture on page 652. Here you will recognise the part under test as the Diamond Crossing, which for the purpose is fitted into a special rail layout.

There are two locomotives, each with a vehicle behind it, and these are run successively over the Crossing in both directions, journeys that they must complete smoothly and easily. A Diamond Crossing is regarded as suitable for Hornby-Dublo enthusiasts only when the operators are completely satisfied—and they are not only expert, from long practice, but also very critical of performance!

MECCANO LTD..

ARTICLE	TRANSFER FOR TENDERS - 2-8-0. FREIGHT LOCO. ETC.	MEMO Nº. 20053

USED ON		REFER ALSO TO		
14929.		MEMO	21051	
20774				
20627				

- 0-6-0 TANK
- CITY OF LONDON

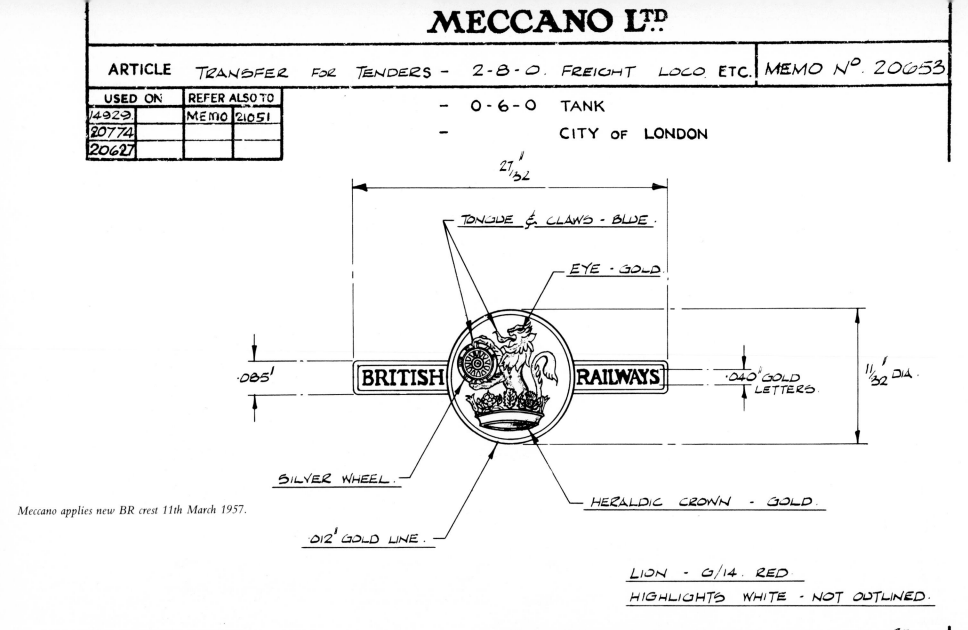

27/32"

TONGUE & CLAWS - BLUE.

EYE - GOLD.

·085'

BRITISH RAILWAYS

·040" GOLD LETTERS.

11/32" DIA.

SILVER WHEEL.

HERALDIC CROWN - GOLD.

Meccano applies new BR crest 11th March 1957.

·012' GOLD LINE.

LION - G/14. RED.

HIGHLIGHTS WHITE - NOT OUTLINED.

2	NOTE RE BACKGROUND DELETED				
	WAS LEFT & RIGHT HAND	571L	8-2-60	ER	
ISSUE	DESCRIPTION OF CHANGE	CO.No.	DATE	SIG.	
MATERIAL	....				

LIMITS ON DIMENSIONS   DRAWN RW

FRACTIONS — ± ·008"   TRACED

DECIMALS — ± ·003"   CHECKED

SPECIAL LIMITS AS SHOWN   APPROVED

DISTRIBUTION   SCALE 4/1.

DATE 11-3-57.

44

April 1956 saw the re-introduction of the Western Region goods brake van and it is strange to see that the platform extensions announced some ten months earlier had only now become available. May saw the introduction of the furniture van container to be followed in June by the insulated meat container. June 3rd also saw the final deletion of third class travel on British Railways. The crimson lake liveried Eastern Region coaches D11 were finally deleted from the 'Silver King' set in August and a new set EDP15 with the D12 coaches was introduced making it almost identical with the 'Duchess of Montrose' sets.

However, we once again go too fast. It was in June 1956 that the British Transport Commission announced that they were planning to adopt a new badge and indeed, new liveries for their main line coaches. The badge was designed by Dr. C. A. H. Franklyn, an eminent authority on heraldry, and showed the British Lion holding between its paws a silver locomotive wheel. The lion was derived from an heraldic crown of gold on which was arranged the rose (England) the thistle (Scotland) the leek (Wales) and the oakleaf for all of Great Britain and was indeed approved by the College of Arms in England and the Lyon Court in Scotland. It was first worn by the 'Britannia' Class locomotive 70016 'Ariel' on completion of an overhaul at Crewe Works. It did, I believe, latterly cause a lot of fun and games because it was British Railways practice at that time to have the lion always facing forward which necessitated a left and righthand badge to be fitted to their locomotives. However, only the one badge had been agreed and I am told that in March 1960 following pressure by the College of Heralds, the policy was revised whereby there would be just the one badge which is why, in the later Hornby Dublo models (drawing dates to 8th February 1960) it is possible to have locomotives with the lion facing forwards on both sides of the tender on one model and fore and aft on later examples. It appears it was not a mistake in the factory but the Meccano Company simply following their traditional policy of extreme accuracy with British Rail practice!

The new livery of full crimson lake for the 'Midlander', 'Merseyside Express', 'Mancunian' and 'Royal Scot' sets of coaches was very much praised at the time and the reason given for the change was that the earlier crimson lake and cream livery was so difficult to keep clean. The fact that at the same time, this permitted the Western Region main line trains, namely the 'Bristolian', 'Cornish Riviera' and 'Torbay Express' to revert to the GWR chocolate and cream livery made a slight nonsense of this reasoning. This was now the highlight of my era of train spotting, and living in Sutton Coldfield I used to spend my holidays

Right away!

HORNBY DUBLO ELECTRIC TRAINS

An advertisement from the November 1956 Railway Modeller.

45

cycling to Lichfield or Tamworth to watch all the LMR main line trains go through or go into Birmingham Snowhill Station and just gaze in awe and homage the GWR scene for hours on end. I am told my great grandfather worked for the Midland Railway Company in Derby and in earlier days I used to accompany my grandfather, who held a season ticket from Sutton Park Station to Birmingham New Street continuously for fifty years.

September saw the D14 transparent windowed maroon suburban coaches. The all tinprinted suburban coaches D13 had been in production less than two years and as they had gone to transparent windows with the LMS main line coaches on their introduction post-war, it has always surprised me that they did not have transparent windows in the suburban coaches from the outset.

October saw the new A2 controller unit and November the 20 ton tube wagon and ventilated van, the latter measuring over 5 inches in length and being a beautiful reproduction of the type of vehicle used for carrying perishable goods at express speeds. The last die-cast goods vehicle, was to my mind, the ugly double bolster wagon introduced in December. This is very much my ugly duckling of the range but nevertheless its capacity to carry logs, boilers and pipes, etc., made it a useful addition to freight operations.

It is amusing to see articles in the *Meccano Magazine* with such headlines as 'A Turntable . . . Why not Indeed'. Such an article appeared in the January 1955 issue and here we are in January 1957 with the introduction of the 3-rail turntable unit. They did indeed attempt to produce working electric turntables in both 2- and 3-rail but never got past the design stage and when one looks at the superb Marklin electric turntable still available today retailing at around £60 you can see what I mean! The back page of the January issue shows all the accessories including a first sight of the new girder bridge. March 1957 reports on the new Hornby Dublo travelling post office trains. Remember Mr. C. F. Blake's layout in Harrods in January 1955? June 1957 shows the introduction of the EDG16 goods set which to quote the introduction . . .

'The well tried and popular Hornby EDL 17 0–6–2 Tank locomotive is included in the set and there are two standard open wagons and a goods brake van. This simple make up together with a slight modification of the rail contents results in a favourable price and this I am sure will appeal to all those about to begin this splendid Hornby Dublo hobby.'

One can read considerably more into this simple statement. It shows they were already realising they were beginning to lose younger customers to such companies as Triang who had introduced their models some five years earlier, and in 2-rail and cheaper at that. I remember a model shop proprietor in Birmingham telling me that he always used to keep his Hornby Dublo models under a glass case or on a shelf at the back and have the cheaper sets from Triang and later Playcraft sets manufactured by Jouef on display at the full mercy of the 'compulsive' stock handlers (or 'ger-fingerpokers' as they are endearingly known in retail and collecting circles!) Model railways were such a unique indoor hobby and Scalextric and similar ranges of motor car racing had yet to appear. Steam was still king.

However, another rival appeared on the scene – TT model railways produced by Triang. They were certainly not the first as in September 1951 the Rokal Company marketed in England a very neat little train set with one foot radius curves. This system did not really progress in the absence of ready made British style locomotives, rolling stock and accessories, but now all this had been put to rights by Triang. The March *Railway Modeller* had a superb six page article on its introduction and it was heralded as 'the thing' and would do the same to 00 gauge scale model railways as 00 had some years earlier done to 0 gauge. It was to stay in production right up to 1964 when it too succumbed to the lack of interest in the modern full size diesel and electric locomotives. At that time, albeit briefly, the model racing car was king.

However, the 'ready to run' model railway hobby today is back with a vengeance, there being more major manufacturers and choice than at any time in the past. The total sales of model railways in the U.K. in 1975 was approximately £12 million and by the end of 1977 this had risen to £20 million and two new major British suppliers, namely Airfix models and the Mainline series by Palitoy as well as the superb and

very economical Lima range who have been producing British outline for two or three years now. Even Rivarossi announced the original 'Royal Scot' locomotive and coaches although in 3.5 mm scale.

One item which TT did kill before it was even born was the S gauge (standard) railway system which the Meccano Company was very definitely planning to bring out. The S gauge has a small but very enthusiastic following in the United Kingdom although its main home is in America. Basically it is a gauge between 0 gauge and 00 gauge with a track width of 22 mm. Around 1955 Meccano was planning to bring out a complete new railway system! They only got as far as making one coach and some pieces of track and I am much indebted to Mr. Bob Murray for allowing me to photograph what I understand to be the sole survivor. I do not know what locomotives were planned and information on this would be fascinating. However, TT railways were of a smaller scale, a larger layout in less space and must have hammered the idea flat. Let us return however to the Hornby Dublo development.

July 1957 evidenced the introduction of the EDG19 goods train set and in August the beautiful D22 maroon corridor coaches. These were immediately announced in the new EDP22 train set, i.e. the 'Duchess of Montrose', however they stated the crimson and cream D12 coaches would be retained for the time being.

It was considered by many at the time that the existing BR liveries were dull and the idea developed that if the models were dull, the boxes should be eye-catching. Packaging helps greatly to sell goods where impulse buying is concerned. Most enthusiasts made their choice, as now, from catalogues or seeing their model in a shop window. Look at the beautiful modern Hornby Catalogues today and their success. Definitely Hornby Books of Trains of the future. Hmm . . . the prologue . . .

The September issue of the *Meccano Magazine* introduced the 1957 Hornby Dublo folder and so the Company entered a phase that over the next four years was to achieve the highest levels of design achievement and sales. The 'Bristol Castle' locomotive created quite incredible interest and is by general agreement the finest mass produced commercial 00 gauge model locomotive ever produced to this day. With the locomotive came small WR tinplate corridor coaches and brake ends to be followed in November by restaurant cars in Western Region and the BR crimson lake and cream liveries. Both fitted now with nylon wheels! 2-rail?! The reason given was silent running, but who knows?

The advertisement for the 1957 catalogue (7/857/500) and indeed the catalogue itself both showed Mr. Harold Owen, the then Meccano Advertising Manager's classic mistake. There is the keen father pointing out details on the layout to his son and on a closer examination it will be seen that he has six fingers! As I have said, rare indeed were the mistakes and this went right the way through proof checking and was only discovered when a young boy wrote in to Meccano Limited just before Christmas. This instance is still referred to on many occasions in my talks with the Meccano employees although none of them could recall which particular catalogue it was featured in i.e. whether it was in Meccano, Dinky Toy or Hornby Trains. It was only by chance this Christmas, convalescing from an operation that I was able to have time to read through my catalogues and pinpoint it.

In December 1957 the Dublo Dinky Toys were introduced namely the 064 Austin Lorry, the 065 Morris Pickup and the 066 Bedford Flat Truck, the latter especially elongated to carry the standard Hornby Dublo container. Dinky Toys had been used for scenic effects on both 0 gauge and Dublo ever since pre-war years but only the following models were built to practically the same scale as Hornby Dublo and recommended for use by the Hornby Railway Company:

No. 22C Motor Truck
No. 25R Forward Control Lorry
No. 29B Streamlined Bus
No. 29C Double Decker Bus
No. 29E Single Deck Bus
No. 29G Luxury Coach
No. 35A Saloon Car
No. 35C MG Sports Car
No. 35D Austin Seven Car.

It was the double decker bus which had been the one produced on the identical scale to that of Hornby Dublo railway locomotives and I have dealt with Hornby Dublo Dinkies in a later chapter.

The Meccano S gauge prototype coach, shown between a standard Hornby Dublo and Bassett Lowke coach.

Harold Owen's Mistake! The six finger advert. 7/857/500.

Arguably the finest mass-produced model locomotive ever produced.

A new series–Dublo Dinky Toys...
scaled for Hornby-Dublo Trains

From the December 1957 Railway Modeller.

Now you can start to build up a model transport system with these new Dublo Dinky Toys, made to the scale of '00' gauge railways.

They are precision die-cast in metal, fitted with grey one-piece "non-scratch" moulded wheels and tyres, and finished in safe **lead free** enamel. Now's the time to start collecting. The first three models are shown below. Lookout for further models in this series.

With the new Dublo Dinky Toys you can make your Hornby-Dublo railway just as life-like and attractive as the road and rail layout shown in this picture.

The use of Dinky Toys with Hornby-Dublo layouts frequently leads to questions regarding the individual vehicles that are suitable. These no doubt will become fewer in number in view of the recent introduction of the series of Dublo Dinky Toys that were first announced last month. There are two of these vehicles in the picture below and you can see how well they fit in with the general scheme.

Of the older Dinky Toys the various Coaches, Nos. 281, 282, 283, also No. 290, Double Deck Bus, are suitable for 00 Gauge railways. In addition, No. 420 Leyland Forward Control Lorry, will do nicely.

No. 064—Austin Lorry
Length: 2½" 1/9 (inc. tax)

No. 065—Morris Pick-up
Length: 2 3/16" 1/9 (inc. tax)

You get more fun with

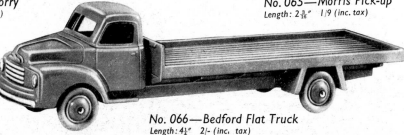

No. 066—Bedford Flat Truck
Length: 4¼" 2/- (inc. tax)

Dublo Dinky Toys vehicles are prominent in this scene. The Bedford Flat Truck carries a "case" made at home from a block of wood.

Excerpt from Meccano Magazine.

DUBLO *DINKY TOYS*

MADE IN ENGLAND BY MECCANO LTD.. BINNS ROAD, LIVERPOOL 13

PLEASE TELL YOUR FRIENDS ABOUT THE **RAILWAY MODELLER**

No sooner was Christmas and the Toy Fair of January 1958 over, than the super detail bulk grain wagon arrived creating as big a sensation in model railway circles as the 'Bristol Castle' some three months earlier.

The Meccano Company were by no means the first to use plastic (or to give it its correct title – Polystyrene) style rolling stock and indeed in many ways they lagged far behind their competitors in their changeover to this material. The Leeds Model Company had been producing (in 0 gauge) very good wagons and coaches before the Second World War and post-war both Triang and Leeds had standardised on plastic. However, despite their now acknowledged charm, they did not present the scale representation which the Meccano Company wanted for its enthusiasts and so they scoured the country looking for the best toolmakers available. Their sales were fantastic – they were making good money and naturally to our pleasure and benefit now they could afford to do it, and the best were at that time undoubtedly the B.I.P. Tools Company Division of British Industrial Plastics. B.I.P. had moved out to Streetly some 12 miles north of Birmingham but found difficulty in recruiting the skilled toolmakers required for the precision moulds their customers expected. Indeed, it was their customers' complaint that they could not get the detail from their existing mould makers that prompted B.I.P. to set up its own tool company and so it was decided they would move their toolroom back to where the best toolmakers in the U.K. could be found – at Tyburn Road, Erdington near Birmingham in 1936. To quote from their pamphlet. . . .

'Utilising the traditional sense of craftsmanship in the area and setting standards of workmanship that were a challenge to the best men, B.I.P. Tools Ltd., has built up a team of specialist toolmakers which is probably unmatched anywhere in the industry.'

It was indeed fortunate that I was able to contact them through their Press Information Manager, Mr. Mike Butler. It was just in time, because tragically a few months later that low investment in British industry had reduced their workload to the extent that instead of employing 15 draughtsmen they had 2, and

this particular division of the Company was finally shut down. The British Industrial Plastics Company is indeed older than Meccano having been formed in 1894 in the Black Country area to the north west of Birmingham.

The first order B.I.P. received for Hornby Dublo tooling was in September 1956 which in point of fact was for the refrigerator van although this was the fourth to be issued by the Company. Their record book showed that they produced over 90 moulds between 1956 and the latter part of 1960 and to give some idea of their complexity a letter from Mr. Butler stated:

'The bulk grain wagon tool alone had 17 separate drawings. The technicians at B.I.P. Tools from whom I have obtained this information still recall with surprising clarity some of the incidents during that four year period. Two particular points were mentioned: one was the fantastic concern shown by Meccano in ensuring that the coal looked "lifelike". The number of trial models that were made is beyond count and on the final tool drawing there was a stipulation that no straight line was to be more than 5/32 inch long! The second point refers to some 3,000 rivets which had to appear on one of the wagons. These were jig bored and measure 0.056 inches wide.'

I must admit I have not been able to find this particular wagon although the gunpowder van does have 500 rivets and the starter set – 0-4-0 Tank locomotive – a total of 700 and this for a cheap toy?

The moulds were fitted to machines which could produce up to 200 components per hour which in a normal 8 hour day gave a capacity of 1,600. Production runs from these superb moulds of a quarter of a million components was no problem at all and so perfectly did the tools bed together in all sections that they came away virtually clean and perfect every time with little or no flash. Once the tools had been machined they were liquid honed to avoid shine on the completed models resulting in the excellent matt finish. British Industrial Plastics Company tell their own story in an eight page article published in their house magazine, *Beetle Bulletin*, regrettably long since out of print and we reproduce extracts here.

The moulds and models were unrivalled in their time and, indeed, they are still in constant use with G

& R Wrenn Limited, who later acquired them. It was recalled for me that some collectors have a preference for the tinplate stock, but in any serious collection of Hornby Dublo the super detail plastic wagons *must* be included.

This is, of course, at the heart of the scale model argument but it became clear that for accuracy and detail metal could not compete with plastic. Today, however, with photo engraving techniques, etc. this argument does not hold per se. However, let us continue our story.

March 1958 brought three more Dublo Dinky Toys, the 063 Van, the 062 attractive Singer Roadster, and the 061 Ford Prefect as well as for the first time since the pre-war years, the new part exchange scheme and so, month by month, new sets and wagon models appeared and it was only natural that a superior freight locomotive should now be introduced to haul these new trains. August 1958 heralded the introduction of the 8F locomotive which received similar acclaim to the introduction of the Castle locomotives 10 months earlier. Not a bad year's work by any means! The September 1958 *Meccano Magazine* called the new 2-8-0 locomotive a triumph of design and indeed it was.

Of course, the Brighton Toy Fair in January 1958 had shown to the trade all the new models due out that year and indeed it must have been a vintage year, not only on the Hornby Dublo stand with its new 8F locomotive (which did receive some criticism in so much that the reviewer from the *Model Railway Constructor* commented . . . 'We hope the production model will have improved valve gear because the one we inspected was clumsy in the extreme!', but they went on full of praise for the Bo-Bo diesel locomotive and the colour light signals). Not far away the Trix stand displayed three newcomers too, the 'Britannia', a standard class 4-6-0 5MT and the Ruston & Hornsby 0-6-0 Diesel shunter complete with shunter's truck.

In October 1958, the headboards arrived with the beautiful stick-on labels for all the mainline expresses, including coach labels. Such is the quality of the embossed printing on the headboard labels that in many cases they look far more realistic than having specially engraved brass ones and I regret, that there are no such boards readily available today, but more of

From the March 1958 Meccano Magazine.

A New Part-Exchange Scheme

Allowances for Post-War Hornby Locomotives

A HORNBY-DUBLO electric railway is something for which every boy longs, whether he is new to the hobby or already has a Gauge 0 Hornby Clockwork line. And this is not surprising when we think of the wonderfully attractive Hornby-Dublo locomotives, two of which are shown on this page, and the delights of the easy remote control the Hornby-Dublo System provides, to mention only two of its many outstanding features.

No. 50 Hornby Locomotive and Tender.

No. 20 Hornby Locomotive and Tender.

For those who wish to make such a change a special part-exchange scheme is now available. In accordance with this, their post-war type old Gauge 0 Hornby locomotives can be handed in to their dealers, and allowances will be made for them on the purchase of a Hornby-Dublo Locomotive or Train Set.

Just how this scheme works can be seen from the details on the Hornby Locomotive Part-Exchange coupon, which is at the foot of the first column on page xxiv. To obtain the allowance for your own old locomotive as part payment towards the cost of the Hornby-Dublo Locomotive or Train Set you want, all that you have to do is to fill in the details on the coupon, and hand this to your dealer. Filling in the details simply means indicating by a cross which Hornby

Locomotive you are offering in part-exchange and stating which Hornby-Dublo Locomotive or Train Set you wish to purchase. Add your signature and address before giving the coupon to your dealer.

If for any reason you are unable to make this exchange through a dealer, all that is necessary is to fill in the coupon, as before, and then to send it direct to the Service Department, Meccano Ltd., Binns Road, Liverpool 13, along with your old Hornby Locomotive and a Postal Order or payment in some other form for the balance of the price of the new

Hornby-Dublo L18 2-6-4 Tank Locomotive.

Hornby-Dublo Locomotive or Train Set you want.

Now here is a fine plan that will enable every enthusiast to make a good start with a Hornby-Dublo railway. It does not matter whether the Locomotive that you wish to exchange is in working order or not. But only one old Hornby Gauge 0 Locomotive can be accepted in part-exchange payment. The scheme applies only in the United Kingdom.

Hornby-Dublo LT20 "Bristol Castle".

From the August 1958 Meccano Magazine.

A New SCALE-DETAILED 2-8-0 FREIGHT LOCOMOTIVE

for your Hornby-Dublo Railway

HORNBY-DUBLO LT25 L.M.R. 8F 2-8-0 FREIGHT LOCOMOTIVE AND TENDER

This fine new Locomotive is the first main line heavy goods engine in the Hornby-Dublo System. It represents the L.M.R. design of powerful 2-8-0 used for freight traffic. The Hornby-Dublo 2-8-0 captures the typical appearance of the real engines, with tapered boiler barrel, outside cylinders and motion, and a wealth of smaller detail finely reproduced.

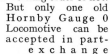

Overall Length 10¼ in.
U.K. Price **84/–** (inc. tax)

This fine new Locomotive has:

- ● **Eight-coupled Driving Wheels**
- ● **Typical semi-matt black finish**
- ● **Fully-detailed die-cast Tender**
- ● **Correct Walschaerts Valve Gear**

HORNBY DUBLO ELECTRIC TRAINS

Made and Guaranteed by Meccano Ltd., Binns Road, Liverpool.

Extract Meccano Newsletter of 27th December 1958.

HORNBY-DUBLO

WINDOW DISPLAY

COMPETITION

We are pleased to illustrate here the successful entry in the Hornby-Dublo Window Display competition that took place in October. Once again the entries included many excellent displays, and it was finally decided to award the first prize of £100 to Messrs. Hely's Ltd., 26/28, Dame Street, Dublin C.I.

The second prize of £50 was awarded to Midland Educational Co. Ltd., 17 & 21, Market Street, Leicester, and the third prize of £25 to Messrs. Fred Collinson & Son Ltd., 83, North Street, Ripon, Yorks. Consolation prizes of £5 each have been sent to a number of other successful entrants.

From the December 1958 Model Railway News.

Run a modern railway
- run diesel electric

SD6
COAL WAGON

ES7
COLOUR
LIGHT
SIGNAL
JUNCTION

HORNBY
DUBLO
ELECTRIC TRAINS

The new Bo - Bo Diesel Electric Locomotive

You've waited for it and it's worth it – the new Hornby-Dublo Bo-Bo Diesel Electric Locomotive is a superb model. Derived from the 1,000 h.p. British Railway type, that went into service only last year, it is a finely detailed model with moulded body and die-cast bogies, superbly finished in British Railways colours. An exciting modern locomotive – a must for every up-to-date model railway.

New too – the ES7 Colour Light Signal Junction For an up-to-the-minute model railway this colour light signal junction is another must. Exact in every detail and with special spring-loaded terminals.

A new 'Super-Detail' model Finely detailed, with moulded Polystyrene body and die-cast metal base, this coal wagon is a splendid addition to the 'Super-Detail' range and you'll want to make it an addition to your railway.

Ask your dealer for further details and prices

Made and guaranteed by

MECCANO LTD BINNS ROAD LIVERPOOL 13

51

this in a later chapter. October brought the Meccano T15 transformer unconditionally guaranteed for five years, such was the confidence and indeed quality of the system laid down by Mr. Ronald Wyborn and his colleagues. Further super detail wagons were appearing almost monthly and during this month the 16 ton mineral wagon and the grey LMR goods brake van were introduced. Also in October the Meccano Company revived their window display competition for their dealers. Messrs. Hely's Limited of 26/28 Dame Street, Dublin were judged the winners in December and awarded the first prize of £100. Such competitions were held frequently in the 1920s and 1930s but this is the first time, I believe, that Hornby Dublo was the star attraction.

In November 1958 the new two aspect colour light signals (shown earlier at the Toy Fair) both home and distant became available, as well as the United Glass bottle sand wagon. A further set also was the P15 the only difference it states from the earlier EDP5 set being that the A4 locomotive which was 'Silver King' is now the 'Mallard' complete with double chimney. There was also a most interesting three page write up on the prototype 1000 horse power Bo-Bo diesel locomotive D8000. Of course, no mention of the model at all although the inside front page of the December 1958 Meccano Magazine displayed a beautiful colour advertisement of this new Dublo locomotive.

The amount of argument and soul-searching in the planning stages of this locomotive is still remembered by those involved. It broke entirely new ground on several fronts. It has already been stated that the steam locomotive would be dead within a few years and Meccano were very much up to the minute following British Railways practice. Their advisers both official and unofficial in British Railways itself must have numbered hundreds. The typical trainspotter was a Hornby Dublo enthusiast and there were fears amongst the sales people that the trainspotter would decry the new diesel locomotives. I myself recall calling them 'powered carriages' having none of the appeal of the steam locomotive in action. It was thought that enthusiasts would be unlikely to buy such a model for their own layout. In the event, sales were not as bad as they imagined and the reason for its withdrawal from production four years later, was for

an entirely different reason, but more of that in its respective chapter.

The other main departure in this model was that this was the first plastic bodied locomotive ever in the Hornby Dublo range. The exquisite detail on the moulds was once more made by the Tool Division of British Industrial Plastics. Here the fears were that it would get damaged or crushed or would not have sufficient weight and adhesion to be a successful model and to a certain extent some of these fears have proved justified over the years. It is rare to find a Bo-Bo locomotive in good condition these days. Many of them appear to have lost their grey roof paint a result of frequent handling while this cannot be said to have happened on its diecast brethren. Still more wagons came on to the scene; this month the coal wagon No. 4635 and the Saxa Salt No. 4665.

Mr. Bob Moy, the Chief Model Maker of the Company who had sculpted in brass, the original 'Duchess of Atholl' locomotive and coaches before the war and had been in charge of the model display room ever since, had been very busy indeed. The photographs of the display models at the exhibitions and particularly some of the Meccano construction items had been unique but he did find time to make what has been described as the most impressive model railway display ever seen. The Meccano Company claimed that it was also the most extensive layout to be so used, involving 829 feet of track and I am indebted to the Model Railway News, January 1959 issue, for its description. The overall size of the layout was 12 feet × 5 feet × 7 feet and consisted of two spirals of gradients of 1 in 42 with viaducts connecting the tracks top and bottom. Double track was used as well as the new colour light signals controlling the trains. The Model Railway News Editor recalls that one morning before Christmas he had gone down Oxford Street to the Selfridges shop window where this model was displayed and was very disappointed to find it static. The Floor Manager at Selfridges was instructed to switch off the layout by the Metropolitan Police Force as it was causing so much interest that crowds were spreading across the pavement into

Oxford Street itself and quite literally blocking this famous road.

It was quite understandable that the next two months in 1959 should have a slight breather and the first new item of this year was the 00 Dinky Toy taxi No. 067 introduced in the March issue of the Meccano Magazine.

However, the lull before the storm.

THE HORNBY DUBLO 1959 MODERNISATION SCHEME

Modernisation was the word of the moment on the full size railways. Ever since nationalisation in 1948, strenuous attempts were made to standardise the railway system in this country but they were not wholly successful. A typical problem was the fact that there were 567,000 privately owned mineral wagons taken over at the time of nationalisation. A great number of these were of small carrying capacity and fitted with the old grease axle boxes. By 1953 over 200,000 of these had been broken up but it became totally apparent that a massive injection of capital was required and so in late 1954 the modernisation plan committed £1,200 million to re-equipping British Railways. This was revised to £1,600 million in 1957 and here too, on an almost parallel course, was Hornby Dublo. The massive investment that must have been necessary in tooling their new 'Castle' locomotive the 8F freight locomotive and the Bo-Bo, let alone the new super detail range of wagons culminated, in March, 1959 with their own modernisation programme totally redesigning their buildings and most important of all, commencing a parallel system of 2-rail operation.

As Ronald Wyborn said it was a great shame they did not start 2-rail, the possibility of which they had discussed in 1938, but instead had gone for the easier method of identically copying the Marklin system. (Mr. Warncken, Hornby Sales Director, observed that it was a great shame Dublo did not turn to 2-rail in 1956 as they could already assess the strength of the Triang system in the four years since its introduction.) It was in 1949 that a company called Rovex Plastics Limited, of Richmond Surrey, first turned their expertise to making reliable robust train sets in 2-rail. They were launched at Bentalls Store in Kingston-upon-Thames in December 1950 and within a few hours

Extract from January 1959 Model Railway News.

From the January 1959 Meccano Magazine.

Make 1959 'Modernisation Year' on your Railway!

Oxford Street, London.   A layout that stopped the public.

EYE-CATCHER

ONE of the most impressive window displays consisting of model railways that I have seen has been installed in an Oxford Street window of Selfridges. The design has been prepared by Meccano Limited. The claim is that it is the most extensive layout to be so used; with 829 ft of track, are there any counter-claims? Actually, it is in the formation, rather than the length of track, that the interest lies. The overall size of the layout is 12 ft × 5 ft × 7 ft tall! Two spirals with gradients of 1 in 42 are at the extremities, with viaducts carrying the connecting tracks at the top and the bottom. Double track is used. The new colour light signals "control" two further trains on the double track oval situated on the baseboard.

On a Saturday evening early in the Christmas month, I went along to see this display, and was disappointed to find it static. To tell the truth, I was curious to watch a descent from one of those spirals. From observation it would appear that they are not really helical, a slight rise in each turn moderating train speeds.

The reason given for the display being periodically switched off is congestion on the pavement. The interesting point is that the watching crowds more often than not consist of " big boys " rather than little 'uns.

HORNBY-DUBLO 2-RAIL NOW A FACT

From the March 1959 Railway Modeller.

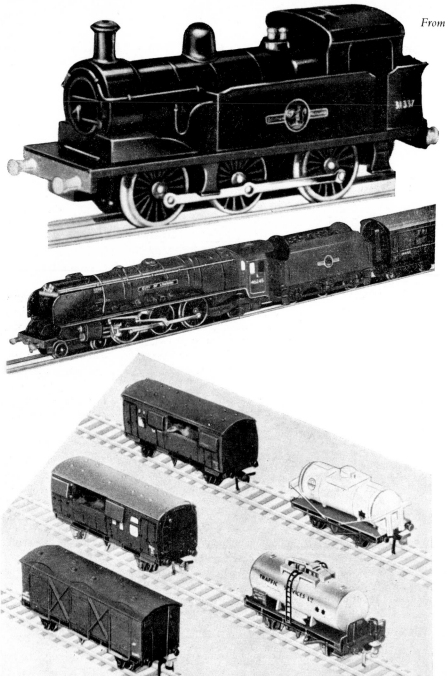

From the June 1959 Meccano Magazine.

OUT NOW!

... the book of the year on trains ...

HORNBY DUBLO BOOK OF TRAINS

54

were totally sold out. One can get a good idea of the quantity of components they were selling at that time by reading their book of 1961 entitled *Triang Railways – the First Ten Years*. However, Hornby Dublo were not alone in staying with 3-rail as Bassett-Lowke still manufactured 0 gauge in 3-rail though they were soon to offer a 2-rail version of their locomotives, as indeed did Trix. On the latter, to quote the *Model Railway Constructor*: 'What a pity Trix is committed to track which demands so much out of scale flanges.'

It normally takes well over twelve months to design, tool up and produce a new range of models and I cannot help thinking that the new products committee in Binns Road, Liverpool must have been somewhat influenced by the editorial in the February *Model Railway News* in 1957 which states:

'There is every indication that today the 2-rail system has become first favourite and is undoubtedly the system of the future.'

The first hint must have come with the nylon disc wheels on the Western Region tinplate restaurant car for the 'Bristol Castle'. Meccano started their system with two beautiful little 0-6-0 Tank locomotives based on the R1 Class of the South East and Chatham Railway long since merged into the Southern Railway. These were available in black and green livery, the latter having sweet little suburban coaches 4025 and 4026 in SR green. Also there was a complete new range of railway building kits including a suburban through station, island platform, engine shed with extension kits and a goods depot. With the exception of the island platform, all these were designed to include electric lighting kits to come out later in the year and there were platelayers huts, gradient posts and telegraph poles. As was to be expected, the Company had done their homework well and the problems of current collection from dirty rails were greatly eased by standardising on nickel silver track, the old diecast driving wheels being nickel plated. The second design 2-rail locomotive was announced as 'The City of London', an entirely new body casting of this popular class with a plastic sided tender. The trade reviews of the period go on to outline the changes in all the other locomotives in the range. The A4 'Silver King' locomotive would become 60030 'Golden Fleece', the 'Bristol Castle' would become 7032 'Denbigh Castle',

the 8F – 2–8–0 locomotive – would be 48109, the 4MT 2–6–4 Tank locomotive would become 80033 and the Bo-Bo diesel would become D8017. The 'Duchess of Montrose' would continue to be available in 3-rail only, as surprisingly also at this stage, would the 0-6-2 Tank locomotive.

Naturally, doubts were expressed on the future of the 3-rail range. They must have planned to change over completely to 2-rail as it would be the only sensible policy although with wisdom they told their followers that while there was still a demand for 3-rail, they would continue its manufacture. The fact that their stocks would, even on their sales at the time, last them for several years, is probably claiming the benefit of hindsight.

Slipping quietly into the April 1959 *Meccano Magazine*, is the Royal Mail Van 068 in the Dublo Dinky Toy range and then in May the superb *Hornby Dublo Book of Trains* – '48 picture packed pages of thrilling railway subjects in full colour giving a glamorous story of the railways of Britain', heralded the advertisement and it is the finest catalogue, I think, that they ever produced for their range. Many the father, elder brother or uncle who wistfully remembered the beautiful 0 gauge, *Hornby Books of Trains* which had been available practically every year from 1925 up to the outbreak of war in 1939.

With so much new material it is quite understandable that the copy writers of Meccano had a busy time in describing their new items and how they worked in real life. The articulated Bedford lorry in the Dublo Dinky Toy range came out in June to be followed by the platelayers hut in July and the 00 Dinky tractor in September.

I find many enthusiasts today looking for the August 1959 *Meccano Magazine* – it does not exist! Akin with almost all other trade magazines of the period it was hit by a nationwide printers' strike and so for the first time since the Summer of 1922 there was not a monthly issue of the *Meccano Magazine*. It is a sad fact of modern life that while a global total war had not once actually stopped a monthly issue however much it was delayed or reduced in content, a strike did succeed in shutting out this issue entirely.

Month by month, throughout the Summer and Autumn, the new products shown became available. September, the single track tunnel and engine shed,

the new AEC 00 Dinky Tanker No. 070 followed in October, together with the first write up on the Big Hook, the exquisite steam outline crane model which once again was designed with the younger enthusiast in mind with the strong handles for the jib and winch drums. November the new Marshall II power unit and in December the new 2-rail train sets were fully advertised together with the long awaited availability of the 2-rail 'Denbigh Castle' locomotive.

Naturally, it takes time with so many new products to build up a stock and despatch it to dealers and the reviewer of the *Railway Modeller* magazine stated . . . 'At all events they were well worth the small wait for here we have a "toy" system which is virtually in every respect a scale model railway. Moreover, we all know Meccano Limited's high standards which are fully maintained, indeed enhanced by these new products.'

1960

January had the new Marshall III power control unit as well as the new hand operated 2-rail points which had appeared just before Christmas. Despite the superb locomotive models and rolling stock the Hornby Dublo 2-rail system let down the younger enthusiast badly with its complicated track requirements, what with single and double isolating rails, etc. The Meccano Company had, as always, tried to provide the best and it must have overlooked the fact that the younger enthusiast, as today, regetfully tears open his box and pushes the pieces together without reading the detailed instructions. When he could not get his train set to work satisfactorily, he would then go and complain to his mother, who, understandably, could not do better, and would then complain to father when he came home from work with the cumulative effect that the Meccano dealers were inundated with requests for advice, complaints and hundreds of letters poured into Binns Road. If only the instructions had been read, the problems and bitter disappointments would, in the main, have been avoided and the general opinion today of the dealers I have spoken to, was that the 2-rail track system was simply too complicated. Handbooks appeared very quickly from Liverpool as did the redesigned Simplec points later but the damage had been done. The simpler, though cruder Triang track system did work and they must have had quite a boost to their sales at this period.

January 1960 saw the commencement of new wagons to the range with the ICI Chlorine tank wagon and the tinplate Esso black fuel oil tanker. The Chlorine tank wagon No. 4675 was advertised each month, but was not finally available until May but then to excellent reviews.

This was the first super detail wagon to have a super detail chassis. The original design for the standard wagon bases of a diecast unit, while perfectly satisfactory in 1938, and indeed immediately post war, was now becoming totally out of balance with its superior moulded bodywork and much was the criticism of the trade reviews on the standard diecast bases. Twelve months earlier, in March 1959 the *Model Railway Constructor* had an excellent three page article by Mr. A. M. Lawrence on 'improving proprietary rolling stock with particular reference to Hornby Dublo'. It involved drilling out the brake gear linkage rods, etc., of the diecast chassis and filing them down to an 'open appearance'. In common with other model railway magazines which adopt the peculiar practise of appearing some two to three weeks before the month they state, I wonder whether it was Lawrence who gave the final push to the new products committee at Binns Road to do something about this item of rolling stock in view of the fact that the chassis drawing for this wagon was commenced on the 22nd February 1959, a week after the article had appeared! The Meccano Company continued to use a diecast base and I believe very wisely as it gives considerable strength and low centre of gravity and consequent adhesion to the rails.

March 1960 had the British Railways maroon and Southern Region livery horseboxes as well as advertising the new traffic services tanker, although this would be available later. On 18th March, the naming ceremony of the last steam locomotive to be built for British Railways – 'Evening Star' – was held – the end of an era.

Many must have been the younger enthusiast who wanted to fit the 2-rail 'City of London' mechanism into the standard 3-rail 'Duchess of Montrose' body but the editor of the *Meccano Magazine* had to advise his readers that it was a different motor and would not fit into the casting.

This month also showed the Volkswagen Van with Hornby Dublo on the side and what an attractive little fellow it was. The Meccano Company were always very true to prototype and had never gone in for private owner wagons in Dublo even before the war. Unlike their 0 gauge elder brother and indeed Messrs. Trix, who apart from prototype private owner wagons such as Hinchcliffes and Charringtons, also listed two private owner wagons publicising Trix and Bassett-Lowke. In retrospect it was surprising that the Meccano Company did not increase their range of private owner models as it was indeed a competitor to the Matchbox range of road vehicles that had been introduced earlier. It is a fact that in later years the Meccano Company had planned a very extensive range of miniature model motor cars and had them made in Hong Kong but curiously enough exactly the same problems faced the new manufacturers there as had faced the Meccano Company some twenty-five years earlier – poor quality Mazak leading to disintegration and distortion of the models within 6 months! Perhaps the expense of the quality control equipment and indeed availability of materials made no other choice possible. However, I am beginning to encroach on the Dinky toy story and so will leave it to those more qualified in such matters.

In April the Southern Region horsebox became widely available although they stated the BR maroon version would follow shortly and there are photographs of the new 2-rail moulded wheels in both spoked and disc type. The May issue announced the final arrival of the traffic services wagon and this was promoted as the first vehicle of international character and indeed possibly the precursor of a whole range of such wagons, many of which sadly never appeared as the Meccano Company planned to go into export with Hornby Dublo model railways in a big way. The troublesome 2-rail Bo-Bo locomotive also made its appearance at the same time. I say troublesome because the comments from people involved with the production of this locomotive confirm that they would make 12 models and only 6 would pass the inspection test, they would then send them back to be checked over and perhaps get another 3 to pass the test but for some reason or other they could not get the remaining ones to work properly. Design problems, poor current pickup (in particular when you think that this was the first Dublo locomotive with rubber tyred traction) all went to create many headaches for its designers to the extent that by 1962 the locomotive had been withdrawn despite plans to use an alternative chassis unit including that of the French Hornby Acho.

June 1960 showed the arrival of the 00 Lansing Bagnall tractor and platform trailer units with, in July, a further assurance that as long as the demand lasted, 3-rail would always be available. Very strange to relate there was nothing at all to report in the August 1960 *Meccano Magazine* although September showed the Landrover and Horsebox Trailer. Still, they had somewhat flooded the market with wonderful new products over the past months and it was only natural that they should take a small break.

Take a break did I say? Not a chance! The *Railway Modeller* pulled a scoop by announcing in their September 1960 issue the new Ringfield motor unit which was without doubt to become one of the finest model railway motor units. The new locomotive into which they were fitted was the 8F 2-8-0 freight locomotive now to be numbered 48073 and, the famous 'Cardiff Castle'. The advertisement stated that the Castle locomotive would now pull many more coaches at a steady 130 m.p.h. in scale equivalent. Of course, as we all know, no such performance ever materialised in real life but these simple super efficient locomotives in full size had been timed up to 106 m.p.h.! Not a bad performance when one puts them alongside the mighty Pacific locomotives of the old LMS and LNER regions. Driver Gale of the Western Region officiated at the launch of this new motor. The object was for the locomotive to run sealed in its case for four days and four nights and re-enact the actual distance from London to Cardiff of 145 miles (approximately 11,000 scale miles). A group of celebrities including Mr. Roland G. Hornby, Chairman of Meccano Limited, and Mr. Donald Sinden the famous actor and his two sons witnessed the start and finish of this non-stop run. What a success it was. The engine achieved 11,663 scale miles and well fulfilled the manufacturers expectations. At the same time, it was announced that this new motor would be fitted into two new diesel style locomotive housings, the first

From the February 1960 Railway Modeller.

MECCANO DEMONSTRATE NEW PRODUCTS

THE managing director of Meccano Ltd., Mr. F. Dale, is seen here demonstrating the new Hornby-Dublo "City of London" two-rail Pacific to David Batey and his father, Mr. W. Batey, who is one of Newcastle's Meccano dealers. This occurred during the reception held last year by Tyne-Tees Television in connection with Meccano Ltd.'s extensive television advertising campaign in that area prior to Christmas.

From the July 1960 Meccano Magazine.

MECCANO
MAGAZINE

Editorial Office:
Binns Road
Liverpool 13
England

EDITOR: GEOFFREY BYROM
ASST. EDITOR: ERNEST MILLER

Vol. XLV
No. 7
July 1960

Hornby-Dublo Three-Rail: An Assurance

SINCE the advent of Hornby-Dublo Two-Rail Electric Trains, the Information Staff at Meccano headquarters have received a stream of letters asking about the future of Three-Rail equipment. These letters have been answered and the inquiries of the people concerned have been dealt with, or are in process of being dealt with, but I felt I should take this opportunity, in the *Meccano Magazine* itself, of disabusing the minds of our readers that the Hornby-Dublo Two-Rail system is, in the near future, to supersede Hornby-Dublo Three-Rail Electric Trains completely.

I want to make it clear to the thousands of Hornby-Dublo enthusiasts all over Great Britain and in countries abroad that there is no intention whatever of discarding Three-Rail in the foreseeable future. Indeed, there will be no attempt to cease Three-Rail production as long as the demand lasts, and that assurance I wish to give to all who have had any worries on this score.

Now, may I turn to another subject of immediate interest—the questionnaire in last month's issue. I have been delighted at the number of replies received so far; they have been pouring into the office every day, and sifting them is going to be a long and far from easy task. But I am sure the result of it all will be well worth while, and I want to thank all who have taken the trouble to complete the form and return it to this office. If for any reason you have not yet been able to complete your questionnaire, there is still time for you to post it to this office.

I think, perhaps, I should add this—so far, the bulk of the replies have been from our younger readers and I confess to being a little disappointed that the older generation (and there must be many, many readers over 21) have not responded in the same degree. Still, I am ever the optimist, and I wait hopefully for more completed questionnaires from the "Boys of the old brigade".

THE EDITOR.

Charles Boyes, a reader of the "Meccano Magazine" since he was 11, is here seen at work on one of the printing machines at John Waddington Ltd., Leeds, the printers of the "M.M."

321

57

From the November 1960 Meccano Magazine.

Hornby-Dublo "Castle's" Fine Endurance Run

TRAVELS 153 ACTUAL MILES IN FOUR DAYS

THE Hornby-Dublo Electric Locomotive fitted with the new Ring Field Motor, which formed the subject of the Editorial in last month's *Meccano Magazine*, has come through its endurance test in magnificent fashion.

You will doubtless remember that the locomotive, a Castle Class engine, travelling on a sealed layout in the Meccano Showrooms in Berkeley Square, London, was asked to haul six standard Corridor Coaches of the type regularly included in Hornby-Dublo Train Sets over a distance which, in actual mileage, is equal to that between London (Paddington) and Cardiff —just over **145** miles.

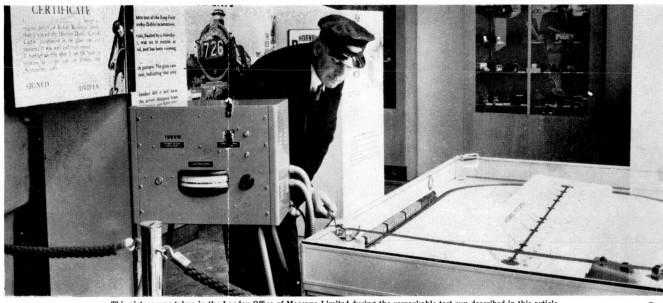

This picture was taken in the London Office of Meccano Limited during the remarkable test run described in this article.

HORNBY RAILWAY COMPANY

By the Secretary

It was expected that the train, a miniature representation of the famous *Red Dragon* which makes the actual journey, would have to run continually for about 100 hours to achieve this. In point of fact, this locomotive covered **153** miles, and the scale distance travelled was equal to 40 return trips between Paddington and Cardiff.

In hauling its load round and round a 6 ft. × 4 ft. test board, the Locomotive—*Cardiff Castle*— did, in

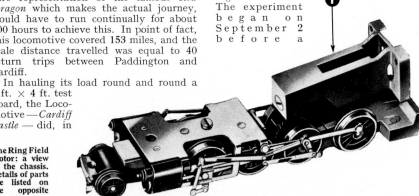

The Ring Field Motor: a view of the chassis. Details of parts are listed on the opposite page.

fact, make 46,000 circuits and the average scale speed over the entire run was 123·9 miles an hour.

In the whole of this four-day marathon of non-stop running the Ring Field Motor, which is to be fitted to several Hornby-Dublo Locomotives this season, did not falter nor did it require the slightest attention. The experiment began on September 2 before a

distinguished panel of witnesses including Mr. Roland G. Hornby, Chairman of Meccano Limited. Mr. Hornby was also present when the run terminated and with him were Mr. Donald Sinden, the well-known screen actor, and one of his two sons.

The train was set in motion at 11 a.m. by Driver John Gale of Acton, London, who was dressed in the blue overalls and black cap he wore as the driver of the famous *Red Dragon* from Paddington to Cardiff.

Driver Gale again visited the Meccano Showrooms on September 6 and, precisely at 11 a.m., brought the model to a halt.

When he was told that the Hornby-Dublo engine had, in scale terms, covered 11,600 miles Driver Gale, who had driven the Royal Train and many famous expresses,

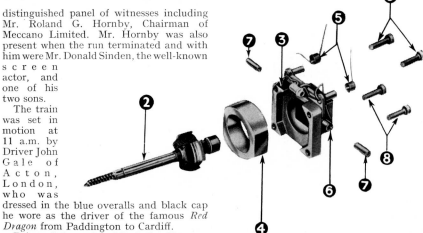

KEY TO PARTS:

1. Main casting	5. Brush springs
2. Armature and shaft	6. Brush holder
3. Commutator housing	7. Brushes
4. Ring Field magnet	8. Securing screws

being the English Electric type 5 Co-Co diesel locomotive with diecast housing and the 0–6–0 diesel shunter. The *Model Railway Constructor* review of November records the following:

'At low speeds the motor's high torque prevents magnetic locking. The speed/load curve is flat providing equivalent speed control on light or heavy loads. Under normal operating conditions the brushes are stated to have a life of over 200 hours. Housed in a solid diecast frame the motor is fully suppressed and runs quietly with minimum vibration.'

Commenting on the introduction of 2-rail Mr. Ronald Wyborn, then Chief Electrical Engineer at Binns Road wrote:

'I fail to recall the precise date when transition from Dublo 3- to 2-rail was first mooted but we were in part motivated by the increasing competition from other makers both at home and abroad. Marklin, Trix, Rivarossi, Lionel, Rovex were all breathing down our necks and it wasn't healthy. I would think it was early in 1957 when full development was finally under way. This new phase provided the opportunity to give consideration towards improving the design of the motor, and so the ring-field came into being.

'My reasons for using this form of magnet were several, chief among them was the attempt to reduce "Cogging" i.e.; the tendency for a tripolar armature to lock-in every third of a revolution when revolving slowly and at low power with the power unit controller resistance fully inserted. The ability to employ a completely closed ring magnet was made possible by the use of the comparatively new anisotropic material which would provide much higher magnetic strength through a preferred axis, but because of the ring format the poles would be less sharply defined. This was the theory which later proved to be correct. This type of magnetic material also gave much greater retentivity.

'I also decided to revert to a separate motor assembly making use of diecastings to give rigidity, and additionally to machine a 2-start worm drive integral with the armature shaft and to run the armature in adjustable oil-retaining bearings with ball endthrust. I consider it fitting to recall here the great help given to us by Messrs. Swift Levick & Sons in connection with the preparation of initial samples of magnets, and in particular to Dr. D. Hadfield their

Director of Research for his valuable technical assistance in the early stages of magnet development. I think the two final versions of the motor ($\frac{1}{2}''$ and $\frac{5}{8}''$ dia. armatures) fully justified the expectations which decided their introduction. Others thought so too, and it is probably not known that many were used in situations that had nothing to do with model locos. Harwell used them. The National Physical Laboratory used them to propel experimental scaled-down ship hulls in their tank testing equipment. They were also used commercially, and in one instance in connection with a fully automatic car parking and stacking model made by us and used by the Woolwich Borough Council to demonstrate the real thing on the occasion of its opening by royalty. The idea was that a motorist would drive his car into a lift at street level and getting out, would insert a key into a control box. The car, minus driver, would then be automatically conveyed to a point on any one of four storeys. By the same process he could later recover the car by returning it to the starting point. The model performed perfectly but the full scale version never did and I believe was later abandoned.'

Naturally, this redesigned motor necessitated further alterations to the body housing tooling of the locomotives into which it was fitted.

It is not at all surprising that such a performance should enter the model into the *Guinness Book of Records* and the October 1967 issue I have, records. . . . 'The record run for a model train was set at Berkeley Square, London on the 2nd to 6th September 1960 when the Hornby Dublo Engine "Cardiff Castle" ran 153 miles. The run was equivalent at scale to 11,600 miles averaging 123.9 m.p.h.'

Of course, records are meant to be broken although we had to wait a further 13 years till October 1973 when another Hornby locomotive, this time the Triang Hornby 'Black Five' Class 5 4–6–0 mixed traffic locomotive ran for 273 actual miles, the only maintenance needed being the replacement of worn brushes. An interesting coincidence here as this too was made with the Ringfield motor adapted to tender drive, a system which had already been investigated by Meccano in the early 1960s but once more we get out of step . . . the prologue . . .

The revised headboard and coach labels for the new train sets namely the 'Caledonian', the 'Talisman'

and the 'Red Dragon' were introduced in October 1960, and November saw the new 0–6–2 Tank goods set at last introduced as 2-rail. The passenger fruit van in the super detail rolling stock No. 4305 arrived, as well as a tragic report that Driver John Gale had died just after completion of the Ringfield endurance tests.

One would be excused for thinking that on looking at the innovations the Meccano Company had put into their Hornby Dublo Series since the introduction of their 'Bristol Castle' locomotive in October 1957, that there could be nothing more to come, but how wrong we were proved by the December issue. Of course, the trade had been in the know from the beginning of the year and if one reads the fine text of their reports on the show in the March and April model railway press issues, they do mention, not only the new diesel locomotives, but new passenger coaches. Page 1 of the December 1960 *Meccano Magazine* included a very modest initial advertisement which in my mind was to herald the finest range of passenger coaches ever available in 00 scale of British outline, even to this day. The trade was well used to the heavy moulding of the plastic coaches of their competitors and indeed, their reviews criticised the Meccano Company in retaining the tin printed sides but beauty is in the eye of the beholder and the Meccano Company had always strived to make their models look lifelike. I have to admit that I put my pen down here for a moment and went into my train room to look again at the sheer beauty and realism of these coaches and was quite simply wafted back a quarter of a century or more to my days of train spotting. However, the coaches did bring with them one unfortunate aspect in many peoples' eyes: the high density polythene coupling which we have already discussed. 'That great ugly monstrosity' as one friend described it. (At least I hope he was referring to the coupling!)

Inside the back page showed the new diesel locomotives as well as the first hint of the new plastic terminal/through station and passenger personnel – but more of these in their respective chapters. A belated write up on the passenger fruit van was followed in February by a write up on the 0–6–0 diesel shunter and featured photographs of a magnificent 60 ft 2-level Hornby Dublo 3-rail layout of Mr. R. J. B. Carruthers.

In March 1961, the beautiful new Pullman cars together with the super detail passenger sleeping cars and full brake van were announced. These were written up in detail in the April issue of *Meccano Magazine* and in May came the announcement that the two recently introduced diesel locomotives were now available in 3-rail and showed photographs of the 050 Hornby Dublo railway staff. Once more we accelerate too fast. Ronald Wyborn recalls:

'From time to time we were involved in odd assignments that relieved the humdrum of everyday work, but one that I look back upon with great pleasure was a little boy who was a polio victim, lying in an iron lung in Newcastle Royal Infirmary and pining for his Dublo train which he could no longer play with. All he could do was to move his chin and look through the mirror attached to the lung. In desperation his parents contacted us to see if there was anything we could do to help in the hope that it might at least relieve the little fellows boredom. Everybody pitched in immediately. I devised a pad switch which could be tied round the boys neck and which was operated by depressing the chin. This in turn motivated a series of sequence operating relays, so that one squeeze started the loco. The next squeeze stopped it. The third reversed it, etc. A series of coloured indicator lights in a special control box showed at any time which sequence was operating. Within a few days the whole contraption was on its way and everyone who had a hand in its preparation felt the happier.'

Many things had been happening on the Hornby Dublo side which, surprisingly did not have so much coverage in the *Meccano Magazine* as they did have in the model railway press and they came to the time that even they began to run out of superlatives.

Since the end of the British Industries Fair in the mid-fifties, the Meccano Company had taken to arranging their own personal exhibition of all their new products in their many ranges for their dealers and representatives. Before a group of amazed onlookers on a specially designed 18 ft long platform, the Hornby Dublo Co-Co diesel locomotive hauled a 2 st 7 lb young boy on a trolley which itself weighed half a stone (7 lb). This was followed by a similar demonstration, this time with a gross weight of $4\frac{1}{2}$ stone using two Co-Co units and finally a very attractive young lady, Miss Glenna Ferdinando, weighing with the trolley a modest 8 stone, was hauled along the track quite easily by three of these Ringfield powered model locomotives. The like had never been seen before and the feat almost completely overshadowed the trade introduction not only of the pullman coaches but also of the new Metropolitan Vickers Co-Bo locomotive and the rebuilt West Country Pacific 'Barnstaple'. The Company was now very much on the export trail and ably lead by Mr. Norman Craig, the Export Manager, had a highly successful fair at Nuremberg – the biggest international trade fair for toys. Many people of note visited their stand including Professor Ludwig Erhard, the then Minister of Economic Affairs for the Federal Republic of Germany as well as the British Ambassador to Bonn, Sir Christopher Steel and his wife and finally the Russian Ambassador to the Federal Republic. What went on at the Fair we shall never know in detail but it is hardly surprising that the Meccano Company with other leading British manufacturers exhibited in Moscow at the British Trade Fair which was held at the end of the following May. 'A children's paradise' was how Premier Krushchev described his visit to the Meccano display which included not only Meccano models and Dinky Toys but an attractive layout of Hornby Dublo electric trains. Indeed there is a very attractive photograph of Mr. Krushchev accompanied by Mr. Reginald Maudling, then President of the Board of Trade, inspecting the layout with Mr. Norman Craig. It bears out my point that one takes a model, and in particular a model of a railway locomotive, and immediately all the barriers of race, ideology and society are thrown out of the window, as they should be! In September 1961, the French Hornby-Acho Bo-Bo locomotive and coaches were being imported into the U.K. in limited quantities to test reaction. This wonderful railway system, indeed totally different to the Hornby Dublo range, was designed and built entirely in the French Meccano factories and I shall endeavour in their respective chapters not to get involved in the argument of which was the superior system. They were both good, in fact, quite exceptionally good, and many, on listening to the barely audible hum of the French Acho locomotive as it glides along the track could well lean towards them. However, they had the advantage and considerable access to all the experience gained not only by Hornby Dublo in England, but also by the many rapidly expanding European competitors. Unfortunately Meccano U.K. were tied, however unwillingly, for too long to their existing moulds and methods of operation.

There briefly came to the surface of the archives in Binns Road, reports of the New Products Committee of Binns Road and this gave a regular precis report each fortnight between 1961 and 1964, step by step plans, developments and ideas. It is indeed fortuitous that I made notes as the documentation has since disappeared. One of these meetings reported on the investigation carried out in Binns Road on the alternate bearings for their rolling stock and to quote the actual report. . . .

'Comment was made that the extensive test had been undertaken two years previously on both pinpoint and needle type bearings. Both types gave a lower friction co-efficient. Taking a standard D12 coach as a test vehicle, the standard Hornby Dublo axle gave a co-efficient of friction of 0.014 inches. Pinpoint bearing gave a reading of 0.005 inches and needle bearings a reading of 0.010 inches. It had been decided on the grounds of cost and production facilities at that time not to employ either. It was reported that Meccano France are using needle type bearings on their rolling stock.'

Later – at a meeting on 9th July 1963 it was reported that while the pinpoint axle had the lowest frictional losses, it was more prone to damage than the needle type. However, in view of the stock position the situation would be again reviewed in January 1964.

This comes back to my point about ensuring that your Hornby Dublo rolling stock passes its gradient test from a standing start. Interestingly too, it bears out the claim of Messrs. Wrenn when they introduced their own pullman coaches with the new pinpoint axles, at which time a locomotive could haul twice the number of Wrenn carriages to that of any other make (this proves the validity of Hornby's earlier thinking if not practise).

With the Company's rapidly climbing Hornby Dublo exports, it was deemed absolutely necessary to fit the NMRA couplings particularly for the American and Canadian markets which explains the change

A wonderful range from which to choose
HORNBY-DUBLO
2-RAIL LOCOMOTIVES

2217

2224

2207

2221

2231

2218

2232

The Hornby-Dublo system offers an excellent choice of precision-engineered locomotives, ranging from the old faithful 0-6-0 Tank to the large "Pacifics" and the latest Co-Co Diesel. They make an impressive collection. Seven from the range are illustrated here.

HORNBY DUBLO
ELECTRIC TRAINS

MADE BY MECCANO LIMITED, LIVERPOOL

HORNBY-DUBLO LOCOMOTIVES & TENDERS (2-RAIL)		
* 2206 0-6-0 Tank Locomotive B.R. (black)		1 16 0
2207 0-6-0 Tank Locomotive (green)		1 16 0
* 2211 "Golden Fleece" Locomotive and Tender E.R.		3 11 0
2217 0-6-2 Tank Locomotive		2 0 0
2218 2-6-4 Tank Locomotive B.R.		2 8 0
2221 "Cardiff Castle" Locomotive and Tender W.R.		4 4 0
2224 2-8-0 8F Goods Locomotive and Tender L.M.R.		4 4 0
* 2226 "City of London" Locomotive and Tender L.M.R.		4 4 0
2230 1,000 h.p. Co-Bo Diesel Electric Locomotive B.R.		3 5 0
2231 0-6-0 Diesel Electric Shunting Locomotive		1 15 0
2232 Co-Co Diesel-Electric Locomotive B.R.		4 4 0
* Not running		

MECCANO LTD. — 1961 TRADE FAIR

One of the highlights of this display of the latest and existing range of Meccano products was yet another remarkable test to show the capabilities of the Ring-Field motor.

Before a group of amazed onlookers and on a specially designed platform 18 ft long, a Hornby-Dublo Co-Co diesel hauled a 2 st. 7 lb. child on a trolley weighing ½ st. This was followed by a similar demonstration involving a gross weight of 4½ st. using two Co-Co units, as a finale a young lady weighing a modest 8 st. was hauled by three or these locomotives. Throughout the demonstration standard Marshal equipment was used, we were unable to obtain facts regarding power consumption, which was a pity, for they would have certainly been of interest. On each occasion the locomotives had no difficulty in overcoming the initial inertia, and accelerated to the extent provided by the run.

A number of new Hornby-Dublo models were on view and will become available during the year. The new steam outline model will delight all Southern fans, it is No 34005, *Barnstaple*, a member of the "West Country" class and the first S.R. express-passenger locomotive to be introduced into the Hornby-Dublo range—this long-felt want has at last been acknowledged. The model is fitted with a Ring-Field motor and from appearances should prove as popular as its full-size counterpart.

Another diesel outline locomotive was also on view, a Co-Bo diesel electric of the type introduced on British Railways in 1958 and manufactured by Metropolitan-Vickers. An interesting point about this model is that it will be available for 2- and 3-rail operation; it is also fitted with the Ring-Field motor.

A set of new Pullman cars looked extremely attractive and comprised 1st Class, 2nd Class and Brake 2nd Cars, fitted with interior details, seats, tables and lamps. The coaches are built predominantly of plastic; this includes the car sides—a variation from usual Meccano practice.

A number of new items of rolling stock were to be seen, S.R. four-wheeled utility van, E.R. Blue Spot fish van, "Lowmac" machine wagon, I.C.I. 20 ton Bulk Salt wagon and a "Presflo" Bulk Cement wagon.

The range of track parts will be extended to include a large radius curved half-rail, large radius curved half double isolating rail, left hand diamond crossing, 2-rail re-railer and a single track 2-rail level crossing.

A glimpse of things to come from Meccano Ltd. Top: 4-6-2 West Country class "Barnstaple." Centre: Co-Bo diesel-electric taken from prototype built by Metropolitan Vickers. Bottom: Pullman car brake/2nd "Aries," one of a set of three to be introduced shortly

Ronald Wyborn (left, kneeling) showing the power of his Ringfield Motors.

Co-Co Diesel with Ringfield Motor, from the Engineering Magazine.

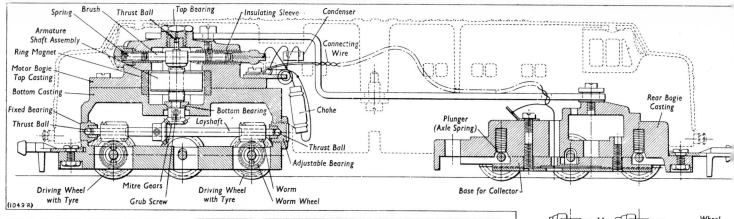

Spring · Brush · Thrust Ball · Top Bearing · Insulating Sleeve · Condenser
Armature Shaft Assembly · Connecting Wire
Ring Magnet
Motor Bogie Top Casting
Bottom Casting · Bottom Bearing · Choke · Rear Bogie Casting
Fixed Bearing · Layshaft · Plunger (Axle Spring)
Thrust Ball · Thrust Ball
Adjustable Bearing · Base for Collector
Driving Wheel with Tyre · Mitre Gears · Driving Wheel with Tyre · Worm
Grub Screw · Worm Wheel
(1049 R)

Wheel Coupling
Wheel Insulating Bush · Wire Current Collector
"ENGINEER"

MECCANO
MAGAZINE

Volume XLVI **No. 8** **August 1961**

At the British Trade Fair in Moscow Mr. Krushchev admires the exhibition by Meccano Limited which included Hornby-Dublo Electric Trains, Meccano and Dinky Toys. On Mr. Krushchev's right is Mr. Norman Craig, of Meccano Limited, and also in the picture are Mr. Mikoyan (extreme left) and Mr. Reginald Maudling, President of the Board of Trade (behind Mr. Krushchev).

Hornby-Dublo Enraptures Russia's Youth

WITH other leading British manufacturers, Meccano Limited made history a few weeks ago when the firm exhibited its products at the British Trade Fair in Moscow. Three members of the staff from Meccano Headquarters at Binns Road made the trip by air, travelling on the last leg of their outward journey direct from Amsterdam to Moscow in one of Russia's famous Tu.104 airliners. At the company's display stand at the exhibition, they demonstrated to admiring thousands Meccano itself, Hornby-Dublo Electric Trains, Dinky Toys, Hornby Speed Boats and Bayko. And a wonderful reception they got. Our editorial picture this month was taken at the exhibition and you can see the look of fascination on the faces of the Russian boys who pushed to the front of the Meccano stand to watch Hornby-Dublo Locomotives going through their paces. The display is described for you in this issue by Meccano's Export Manager.

from a rivet to a nut and bolt at this time. The initial plan was to launch this at the New York International Toy Fair in the new year. On 5th October 1961 a meeting of the New Products Committee reported that the tool cost for the NMRA coupling was only £130 and that all stock for the American market should have the American threaded screws. It may be of interest to note the other items recorded at this meeting.

2. *Two rail track* – the committee was investigating Jouef track.

3. *The Bo-Bo locomotive* – the shortcomings of the existing 2-rail locomotive were discussed and stemming from this the features to be avoided in future design were explained. Since the Southern Region electric suburban train bogie was under development the design problems had been overcome.

4. *Plastic type bases for rolling stock* – samples were successfully tried out and requirements for the necessary universal ballast plates for stability determined. Drawings being prepared.

5. *A Dublo 2-rail turntable* –it was decided not to proceed though the committee approved drawing office investigation into modifying the 3-rail.

6. *Further conversion to Ringfield motors* – discussion on converting the A4 'Golden Fleece' locomotive, the 'City of London' 2-6-4 Tank and the 0-6-2 Tank to Ringfield motors was made but it was decided to shelve the idea as the existing motors were already satisfactory and would make unnecessary the high re-tooling costs required.

Perseverance and the prologue . . .

September 1961 was indeed a big month. The new super detail coaches were now included in the 'Talisman' set and the new 3-rail 2-6-4 Tank locomotive 80059 was introduced. The comment was also made that the new moulded coupling was now to be standard.

The complicated 2-rail track, necessitating the use of single and double isolating rails because of the 'live' frog construction, was already taking its toll in poor sales. Many modellers chose the simpler 2-rail trackwork of competitors. The October issue of the *Meccano Magazine* brought 'Linesman' into action with the first of a new series on 2-rail schemes which continued to the takeover, attempting to clear up the enthusiasts circuit problems.

Also in October the 'Barnstaple' locomotive, the first of the rebuilt 'West Country' Class locomotives shown at the Meccano Exhibition earlier in the year appeared, coupled with a write up on the pullman coaches and the 'Bournemouth Belle' set.

November had the new terminal or through station kit as well as four new super detail goods wagons, the 4626 Presflo bulk cement, the 4627 ICI bulk salt, the 4652 machine wagon Lowmac and the 4300 blue spot fish van. Not to be outdone the 'City of Liverpool', the 3-rail version of the superior detailed 'Duchess' Class was announced as well as gradient and mile posts in box 5025, the curved double isolated rail, the 1521 aluminium wire cable drums and 60125 tube of graphite grease for the gears of the Co-Co style locomotives! If that wasn't enough, closer investigation of this particular issue also shows the introduction of the 1575 lighting kits and details of the 3-rail West Country locomotive – 34042 'Dorchester'. Re-reading this in the cold light of day the sheer problems of production and supply of this multitude of new products must have stretched the company's resources to the limit. Yet the flow continued for in December we were given details that the National Coal Board had included a tour of the Meccano factory in one of its publicity films *Mining Review*. The factory at Binns Road was heated by coal and the NCB had a highly successful film unit taking a monthy record of events connected with their industry which was now in its 15th year. They traced the progress of the new Hornby Dublo West Country locomotive 'Barnstaple' right from the drawing board through all the assembly and enamelling departments to its final test with a standard load of coaches round one of the assembly test tracks.

One would have thought that the days of the endurance test were almost over because what more could a locomotive achieve having not only hauled a boy but also in a triple set a fully grown young lady. However, once more the publicity and interest created by such events caused them to run yet a further test in their London Showroom at 22 Berkeley Square. This time it was again the Co-Co locomotive hauling 50 wagons. The locomotive weighing only 1 lb 6 oz was planned to haul a train over 17 feet in length and it was thought that it might be necessary to stop the locomotive once every 24 hours for the purpose of re-

oiling the armature bearings. However, as the run progressed it was obvious that this procedure was not going to be necessary. Indeed, when the locomotive was subsequently examined for wear on the brushes and commutator, it was found to be capable of running well in excess of the task set for it. Needless to say, the locomotive proved more than equal to its task although I wonder which bright spark had the task of calculating the tiny armature had completed more than 78 million revolutions!

If this wasn't enough no less than four new super detail coaches were announced: 4060 open coach first class Western Region, 4061 open coach second class Western Region, 4062 open coach first class BR, 4063 open coach second class BR. Continuing with an advertisement on the new 3-rail Ringfield Castle Class locomotive 5002 'Ludlow Castle' as well as the 3-rail Ringfield 2-8-0 8F locomotive 48094. An embarrassment of riches or a prelude to rags, for no other company in this field was actively marketing 2- and 3-rail systems.

There was also 4323 the Southern Region four wheel utility van, the 792 Dinky Toys packing cases, 2460 the 2-rail level crossing and a further selection of miniature passengers 052 and accessories, in addition to which the write up on the new Co-Bo diesel locomotive in both 2- and 3-rail and, if you look closely the introduction of the Wills finecast track-cleaning wagon! But more of this later.

The sheer technical design and reliability of the Hornby Dublo range of toy railways was not going without notice. The reliability of the product and after sales service of the Company and its many dealers were taken for granted by Hornby Dublo customers. It must have been with some pride though to the employees at Binns Road to have this one particular item in their range picked up and highlighted under the Product Profile in the *Engineering Magazine*. To quote the credit . . . 'This is the Design Council's magazine for engineers', and I am much indebted to Mr. A. A. H. Scott in 1975 acting Editor for allowing me to reproduce it here for you.

However, all was not well at home. It seems a saturation point had been reached and an excellent guide to the problems of the time can be found in the editorial of the March 1962 *Model Railway Constructor*. The then editor, Mr. G. M. Kichenside records that

Mr. Ray Riisnaes' (Co-Founder of the H.R.C.A.) Garden
Dublo Railway.

From the September 1961 Meccano Magazine.

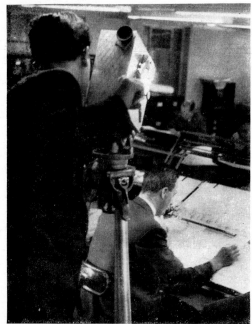

The camera records a scene in the Drawing Office.

L. to R.: The Mazac Wheel 1938–1951; the sintered iron
wheel of 1952–1959; the nylon disc and spoke wheel of
1959–1964; The French Hornby-Acho needle axle and the
present Hornby pinpoint axle assembly.

This month's picture stems from a visit paid to Binns Road, a few weeks ago, by a film unit from the National Coal Board. They are the team responsible for producing a monthly record, *Mining Review*, now in its fifteenth year. At these Works they traced the progress of the new Hornby-Dublo Rebuilt West Country Class Locomotive *Barnstaple* from the drawing board, through the assembly and enamelling departments, to its final test with a standard load of coaches round one of the Hornby test tracks. Shots taken by the film unit will be included in Issue Number 3 (15th year) of *Mining Review* which will have gone out to the circuits by the time these notes reach you. Although the Hornby-Dublo sequences form only a portion of this particular issue of *Mining Review*, I am sure that any of you who see them on the screen will find them absorbing.

Editorial from December 1961 Meccano Magazine.

some sections of the model railway trade were a little overburdened and that some manufacturers, particularly those producing models in large quantities at low prices, were easing their programmes. The Kitmaster Company (although in a slightly different field) had no new introductions at all planned for this year and nor were there any completely new locomotives in our Hornby Dublo range. The number of prospective model railway owners is not limitless and if the ranges of all the manufacturers added together provide more models than can be sold within a reasonable period, then either the retailers or the manufacturers were going to be left with too many unsold products on their hands and sadly this was exactly what was beginning to happen to Meccano. They were not clearing their shelves of stock to the extent that they could not update their products such as the axle units we have already discussed until they had had the room and, indeed, the financial return from the unsold stock. Of course, this was not happening to 00 gauge alone as the TT range heralded as the great newcomer a few years earlier was itself in trouble. It certainly had a following, but not to the extent that some manufacturers would have liked and certainly nowhere near challenging 00 in popularity. It seemed that many shop owners were not disposed to stock two complete ranges of models and kits one threequarters the size of the other even supposing that a very wide selection was available.

It seemed however that the situation was entirely different on the Continent with both German and French companies manufacturing their products direct to eagerly awaiting hands. Both Meccano and Trix had their respective companies and indeed the quality of these foreign products imported into the U.K. was generally considerably higher at that time than the home grown product.

January 1962 had details of the new 2-rail level crossing as well as introducing diamond crossings, lefthand and righthand, for the first time in 2-rail. Of course, there was some speculation, what with the recently introduced Hornby Acho range as well as the 'Barnstaple' locomotive and the Southern utility van

This Hornby Dublo Co-Co Diesel Electric locomotive completed 100 statute miles non-stop running, hauling a 17 ft 4 in long train of 51 wagons at 8.30 a.m., Thursday 5th October 1961.

that we were getting ready for a complete Channel tunnel style layout, the January 1962 *Railway Modeller* pointed out the now quite noticeable absence of Southern main line stock but as the *Meccano Magazine* has said many times, . . . 'Who knows – will this be a Toy Fair release?'.

The 1962 Meccano Trade Fair was again held at the Grosvenor Hotel in London and once more proved Mr. Cyril Freezer, then editor of the *Railway Modeller*, correct. Not only were there to be new Southern main line coaches, but a new range of suburban coaches and the Southern electric outline set. 1962 seems to have been a year of consolidation for there were not quite so many new products as previously which is really hardly surprising. The freight newcomers on show were the very attractive six wheeled United Dairies milk tanker 4657 and the ICI caustic liquor tank wagon 4685. Other new designs on show were the Prestwin Silo wagon 4658 and the gunpowder van 4313 the latter being a welcome return after an absence of 30 years or more since its famous Hornby 0 gauge counterpart. Another old favourite was the banana van 4301 and once more quoting Mr. Freezer's comments: 'Alas the gay pre-war Fyffes yellow must be replaced with the drab modern bauxite brown livery.' Finally two existing wagons in new colours: the 16 ton mineral wagon now in brown as a vacuum fitted wagon 4656 and the box van in red as the breakdown train packing van 4318. Three new train sets were heralded, two employing the new diesel locomotives the first the 'Royal Scot' set although it was pointed out that this should really be the 'Flying Scotsman' as the Deltics were only extensively used on the Eastern Region mainline and a fitted freight set headed by the 'Co-Bo'. The latter to simulate the recently introduced Condor freight trains and the subject of one of Mr. Cuneo's beautiful paintings, highlighted again in the 1972 18th edition Triang catalogue cover. The third set 2049 was the ever popular 0–6–2 Tank locomotive with breakdown crane, packing van and tinprinted suburban brake second. These sets were in the new style boxes.

The March issue of the *Meccano Magazine* reported naturally on the Fair which was opened by Lord Brabazon of Tara admiring advance models of the new Hornby Dublo Deltic locomotives modified in accordance with the prototype. This was the 2-rail version D9012 'Crepello' and the 3-rail D9001 'St. Paddy'. Of course, it takes time for all the items on show to be released. In March the 4313 gunpowder van and 4301 banana van became available as well as the new 4081–83 suburban coaches in Southern Region green and BR maroon liveries as both the standard coach and the brake/2nd. These really were perhaps the most attractive to me of all the Hornby Dublo coaches. One can well understand some 15 years later, why they are so highly prized by collectors.

April also brought out the breakdown train set while in May the Southern Region main line corridor coaches 4054 and 4055 together with the 4318 packing van appeared.

The magnificent feats of haulage demonstrated by the new Ringfield motor over recent months had had its effects on the shop retailer. Mr. and Mrs. T. J. Perry of 'Perrys' the famous model shop in Alum Rock, Birmingham, ran their 'Cardiff Castle' locomotive for no fewer than 570 actual miles on a large window layout. The locomotive hauled a train which often consisted of more than 20 items of rolling stock and yet apart from occasional brush changes and oiling it required no special maintenance. A further tribute, if tributes were needed, to the sheer reliability of this product range.

June 1962 heralded the introduction of the 5037 lineside notices which, though attractive, received quite considerable criticism owing to their being entirely out of scale. However, if they had been to scale, no one would have been able to read them so there had to be a compromise. June also brought in the 'Co-Bo' goods set 2033 with the now bauxite brown LMR brake van which was introduced specially for this set to indicate vacuum fitted for fast express freight trains. It raises the interesting point in enthusiast circles of why the 4312 Western Region brake van itself never seems to have been produced in the brown livery despite its appearing in the catalogues as such. But more of this in another chapter. July heralded the beautiful new Deltic locomotives in the eyecatching two-tone green. Surprisingly, this did not replace the initial standard BR green version which, to my mind, was really a most drab locomotive in appearance and both continued in production to the end.

August released the four new super detail wagons which we have discussed: 4656 mineral wagon, the six wheel United Dairies, the Prestwin Silo and the ICI caustic liquor as well as a write up on the wonderful performance Hornby Dublo Railway equipment put up at the Olympia Fair in London. This time it was linked with a £25,000 computer from the factory of the English Electric Company at Kidsgrove, Staffordshire. To quote – 'There, in 6 days from the 28th May to 2nd June they became stars at Olympia, showplace of the metropolis!'. The requirements of the English Electric Company meant that the models provided by Meccano Limited had to run continuously from nine in the morning to six at night, for the six days of the exhibition, that the points provided would have to be switched hundreds of times every day, that rolling stock would virtually not cease rolling from morning till night and the 'Crepello' Deltic chosen as the locomotive in charge would, likewise, be employed almost unceasingly. These were tremendous demands to make on a toy railway. The idea was to make up and dismantle goods trains of individually numbered wagons in any order required. In fact, so successful was this exhibition and so popular with the public, that the English Electric Company used the identical layout as the main attraction of their stand at the same trade fair two years later, with equal success. The object was to show in the clearest possible way, how control by computers such as their KDN2, was the answer to a wide variety of industrial and data processing problems. In operation every item of information received was infallibly registered in the computers main store and the course of action decided in accordance with the instruction given through the keyboard.

The Autumn seemed to pass peacefully although the September *Meccano Magazine* had a wonderful cartoon based on the Ringfield motor. The train enthusiast had to wait until October before the suburban electric train set was finally available in either 2-rail or 3-rail as well as the dummy trailer coach 4150. Naturally, these new items were written up and in December the year's progress in Hornby Dublo was reviewed, and two small changes put into effect.

Firstly, that the suburban electric sets now carried the yellow visual warning indication panel on the front of the locomotive. Once again copying main line practice, as these and the diesel railcars due to their almost imperceptible approach were known as 'silent deaths' to the railway employees.

Also there was an interesting change in the 050 railway personnel set insomuch that one of the two policemen (the one with his hands behind his back) was removed and replaced by a shunter with a pole, a similar though more attractive version of the earlier diecast unit.

Despite the attraction of the items introduced in the last years, matters were still not improving in Binns Road and the massive stocks were only partially depleted. The period leading up to Christmas 1962

HORNBY-DUBLO Electric Trains

The 2-rail locomotive stud in 1962.

An invitation to cover the visit of the Minister of State, Sir Keith Joseph, M.P., to the Binns Road Works of Meccano Limited recently came our way. The significance of Sir Keith's visit stems from the firm's fine record in the export field.

One of the direct consequences of the firm's importance in world trade (38 per cent. of Meccano's total trade went for the export market last year) is the £70,000 extension which is now under construction at Binns Road. A plaque to mark the occasion was unveiled by Sir Keith during his tour of the factory.

When completed the new building will house conveyors, approximately 100 ft long to handle the whole electrical network connected with the production of Hornby-Dublo trains.

Sir Keith Joseph, M.P., handling a "Marshall II"

Extract from the April 1962 Model Railway News.

Mr. Ronald Wyborn, Chief Electrical Engineer with L. to R. Mr. Chainey, Chief Inspector, Mr. Jones, Electrical Assembly Foreman and unknown lady check a 'Bristol Castle' loco in 1957.

67

had been disastrous. The big drop in sales hit the stock market and the ordinary Meccano Shares fell 3s. 1½d. to 6s. 3d. cutting £760,000 from the Company's market value. The Directors stated no interim dividend could be paid and it was unlikely a final dividend could be paid either! This was against the previous year when the Company had made a trading profit of £282,500 and paid a total dividend of 9 per cent.

The export sales for which they had planned and budgeted had not reaped the success they had hoped for as, although they had moderate sales in the old Commonwealth countries it was, I think a little naive to attempt to sell British outline models in the American and continental markets. In those countries they had their own suppliers and naturally wanted outlines of their own locomotives and it is not surprising that

on 2nd January 1963 a total marketing review of the Hornby Dublo range was undertaken. The Hornby Dublo owner was encouraged to try alternate train formations, such as using the new green Southern Region corridor coaches with the 'West Country' locomotive and using the A4 'Golden Fleece' locomotive with a rake of pullman coaches or the blue spot fish vans.

The trade too was heavily 'pushed' to make more sales and had fantastic prizes awaiting the winners of a further series of Hornby Dublo Window Display

HORNBY-DUBLO SHARES OLYMPIA TRIUMPH

£25,000 Computer Controls "Any Order" Shunt Sequence

A general view of the English Electric Company's stand showing clearly the outer track of the Hornby-Dublo layout, the raised inside portion (which is being traversed by the Type 5 Deltic coupled to four wagons) and the three sidings in which the trucks were marshalled. Several of the detectors can also be seen.

The KDN2 computer undergoing tests at the Kidsgrove Works of the English Electric Data Processing and Control Systems Division.

Mr. Wyborn wrote . . .

In 1962 we were approached by the English Electric Company who wanted to demonstrate their new computer in a popular way at a forthcoming exhibition. The idea was to use Dublo locos and wagons on a layout comprising an outer continuous running loop inside which were marshalling sidings fed from a gravity ramp,

with approach and take-off loops. Each wagon could be identified by a number, and the computer would be programmed to make up a train of any number of wagons in a pre-decided order. It would then move the train through electrically operated points onto the outer running track and then bring it back through the gravity ramp (having first moved onto the approach loop and reversed its

direction) to automatically uncouple and discharge the wagons into any one of three make-up sidings in predetermined order. We built the entire display with circuit controls under contract, and when finally coupled to the computer it was quite impressive. English Electric were so pleased with its performance they used it at successive exhibitions for two years.

Competitions. First prize was a fourteen day holiday for two in Miami U.S.A., via New York, with all normal expenses paid. Second was a Ford Consul Cortina motor car, fully taxed and insured for twelve months and the three third prizes were fortnight holidays for two on the French Riviera. I wish they could have published photographs of the winning displays. With so much being spent on this type of sales advertising, it is little wonder they only produced two postcard-size catalogues – one of eight pages 10/363/400 and one of twenty pages 7/363/400 showing the new E3000 electric locomotive. However, this latter model was not to appear for a further twelve months. Little wonder Meccano described their prizes as 'The best ever in the toy trade'. Desperation perhaps?

It was in the Spring of 1963 that Dr. Beeching, who had commenced his appointment with the British Transport Commission on 1st June 1961, put forward his long awaited plan on the reshaping of the whole railway structure and if ever there was a time for the Government of the day to grasp the clear information put into the report and act it was now. The incredible collection of data would to my layman's mind, quite easily have been used to decide which lines were to operate commercially and which lines were to have a total or percentage of subsidy. However, as we know, the opportunity was missed and many lines were shut for purely economic reasons. Many of those shut down could have been put to good use today although we are fortunate in having so many preservation societies with lines all round the country which enables us to recapture the rural railway. There were very few places in England and Wales which were more than at the most, half an hour's horse ride from a railway station and the longest distance between two railway stations was somewhere, I believe, in the home counties with a distance of no more than 8 miles.

However, the report was not entirely a long list of service cuts and foresaw a great expansion in long distance freight services worked on the now famous Liner Train principle of permanently coupled, air-braked, bogie flat wagons carrying containers from the main freight centres. The staff at Binns Road hoped dearly to follow this example as it would mean running trains with multiple use of particular wagons but unfortunately it came too late. Drawings were prepared of the various special container wagons but sadly were never put into production.

April 1963 brought the new 0–4–0 Starter goods sets and Hornby No. 1 controllers. This was a valiant attempt to regain the younger enthusiast as it had been found that once a boy had bought a cheap initial train set he invariably stayed with that particular product as he developed his layout – more often than not these were the cheaper Triang and Playcraft sets. Of course, starter sets had been shown at the Meccano Trade Fair earlier in the year and incorporated standard mouldings in the new colours of two common wagons with a new plastic sub-base. Without doubt the highlight of the show must have been the new 4070 and 4071 super detail restaurant cars and the Hornby Dublo 25KV AC electric locomotive E3000. Other now famous introductions were the hopper wagon 4644 and six wheel brake 4076 together with the new Simplec points with dead frogs. At once these eliminated the need for double isolating rails and removed one of the major criticisms of the Hornby Dublo 2-rail track. Bear in mind these criticisms were purely in the operation of the 2-rail track particularly by the younger enthusiast and were not levelled at its appearance, which, as one would expect from this company, was as good, if not superior, to anything available from the trade at that time. It was at this fair that Meccano also introduced the special bogie bolster wagon which was a standard coach sub-base with a timber trestle load. This was to check the appeal to the dealers, which couldn't have been very high because it was never put into production. The 'Co-Bo' locomotive, as in real life, had never caught the publics' imagination and to help clear the very large stock they had of this model, two crudely drilled holes were put into the Bo end and a lamp unit fitted inside. Many of the continental manufacturers had working headlights as did the new Hornby Acho locomotives. Twenty-four such locomotives were modified but the alteration was as crude almost as the physical appeal of the locomotive itself and never caught on.

I had a brief meeting once with Mr. Ferguson Smith, Manager of the Meccano Shop which used to be at 4 Conduit Street. He explained that many members of the public had called into their Berkeley Square showrooms and been disappointed at being unable to buy the items which were displayed there in the windows, being purely for trade callers only. It was decided to open a special display and retail shop in Conduit Street, and this came about in 1962. I suppose, understandably they had some criticism from Messrs. Lines Brothers, the then owners of Triang railways who at that time owned the world famous Hamley's Store. Here they sold Hornby Dublo in large quantities and did not want such local competition. The shop was shut on the takeover although commercially it had been a great success and there were plans to open similar shops in other centres throughout the country doubtless in a similar way to the famous Beatties Company over recent years. In the Meccano Shop, the Ian Allen Publishing Company arranged a large display stand of all their books under the control of Mr. John Kermode. Being himself a firm railway enthusiast, he used to repair and service customers' locomotives on the spot and ran a fascinating little Hornby Dublo display railway, which potential customers could operate. By sheer chance I met him at a toy shop in Exeter. He was kind enough to recall many fascinating aspects of the company and the system at this final stage of its life. One being that he thought that there were over 17,000 'Co-Bo' locomotives still in stock in Liverpool at the close of the retail shop in July 1964 but once more we are travelling too quickly.

Strenuous efforts were being made now to sell Hornby Dublo in increasingly competitive conditions and there was a special competition with prizes of £100, £75 and £50 worth of trains (or cash if preferred) open to any purchaser of a Hornby Dublo train set between then and November, who, in the judge's opinion could give the best three reasons for buying their set.

On 21st August 1963 the A.G.M. of the Meccano Company was held and Mr. Roland Hornby presented a dismal picture. The final loss of £164,534 was aggravated by a further £303,590 of reserves being needed to write down stocks and production tools. A massive reorganisation, he stated, was under way. Management and engineering consultants had been called in. Dinky Toy production would be increased to 20 million a year and in a stern answer to a suggestion that Meccano sets were dated said . . . 'Don't believe it. I cannot think the boy growing up in the

BOYS! HURRY TO YOUR HORNBY DEALER NOW

From the March 1963 Meccano Magazine.

Top: In this photograph by P. J. Lynch, A4 Pacific No. 60030 "Golden Fleece" is heading south from York on a train including low-sided plate and bolster wagons. Below: A Hornby-Dublo scene corresponding to that above, with a train of four-wheeled Double Bolster and Bogie Bolster Wagons hauled by the streamlined 4-6-2 "Golden Fleece." well-known to many miniature railway owners.

IN THE HORNBY DUBLO TRAINS COMPETITION

£575 WORTH OF PRIZES

10 MAGNIFICENT PRIZES TO BE WON

If you are the purchaser of any of the Hornby-Dublo Train Sets from now until the end of November, then you are automatically eligible to enter for this **free** competition. For full details ask your Hornby dealer for an entry form.

1st PRIZE
A stupendous 8 ft. × 4 ft. 6 in. working layout and Hornby-Dublo goods to a total value of £100 (or cash if preferred).

2nd PRIZE
A wonderful 6 ft. × 4 ft. working layout and Hornby-Dublo goods to a total value of £75 (or cash if preferred).

EIGHT 3rd PRIZES
Each of £50 value in Hornby-Dublo goods (or cash if preferred).

New
No. 4644
21-Ton Hopper Wagon

A finely detailed new item of rolling stock, this 21-ton Hopper Wagon has the characteristic sloping interior to take away the load of coal, ore or rock. Finished with grey body and standard black underframe this type of wagon is often made up in complete trains.

Length 4¼ in. (108 m.m.)

U.K. PRICE 6/6

HORNBY DUBLO

New
No. 4076
6-Wheeled Passenger Brake Van

Available at:
Gamages, Hamleys, Harrods, Selfridges and all good toy shops everywhere.

AVAILABLE LATER OVERSEAS

A new 6-wheeled Passenger Brake Van that can be used as an extra luggage van, or on fast freight trains. The van is made to match the coaches—with sturdy well-detailed black chassis, black ends and grey roof. An outstanding characteristic is the fact that this vehicle has no bogies, just 6 wheels and 3 axles equi-spaced on the chassis frame.

Length 5¹³⁄₁₆ in. (147 m.m.)

U.K. PRICE 13/-

HORNBY-DUBLO

THE Hornby-Dublo display at the Meccano Trade Fair at the Grosvenor Hotel, London, had three main developments of interest. The emphasis this year by Meccano is on the introduction of a complete (in so far as it contains the power unit) good-quality yet cheap starter set with the very sensible idea of attracting more and more people into the railway modelling hobby. With this we couldn't agree more. The foundation of the set is a new 0-4-0 side-tank locomotive which is of necessity free-lance but is based on an industrial design. Returning to the set, which is to retail at 89/6, it also contains a complete circle of two-rail track, two open wagons and a new short brake van. The power unit has a 12-volt D.C. 7VA rating with separate reverse and speed controls, and is double insulated for safety. This unit will be available separately at 35/-, but we understand the locomotive will not be available separately at least for some little time.

space age is any less imaginative than in the days of Jules Verne and H. G. Wells.'

A 20,000 square foot extension had been completed at Binns Road, now concentrating all production from their ancillary Speke and Fazakerley units under one roof and Mr. Hornby went on to say he was hopeful trading would be fully balanced in 1964.

Unhappily the turnover at home had not been maintained and the small increase in exports had not been enough to offset the business lost.

In October, the new Simplec electrically operated points appeared as well as the highly prized 4644 21 ton hopper wagons and 4076 six wheeled passenger brake van. A feature of these wagons being that the automatic couplings were no longer held in by pressed rivets or nuts and bolts, but by easily removable moulded plugs. Further evidence of the necessity to constantly review production costs. The effects of competition were being more strongly felt now and the New Products Committee were shown a model of the latest Triang 'Caledonian' locomotive which was much admired. Naturally discussion took place on the possibility of introducing a comparable historic range, but this was a non-starter. Ironic that some 15 years later, Ramsgate the home of Triang trains was to market a 3½″ live steam 'Rocket' under the name 'Hornby'.

Surprisingly the November 1963 *Meccano Magazine* had a full two page advertisement of the Trix railway system enjoying a further brief period of rebirth in the U.K. Once more the miniature train formations which seem to have been the theme of 1963 were heralded with an interesting article in the December issue on freight trains and their loads. In January 1964 a considerable effort was made to overcome the initial sales resistance to the Hornby Dublo 2-rail track by producing special track packs which added, dependent upon the set, a number of points and straight rails to augment the standard circle of track put in each train set box.

Extend your layout the 'Simplec' way . . .

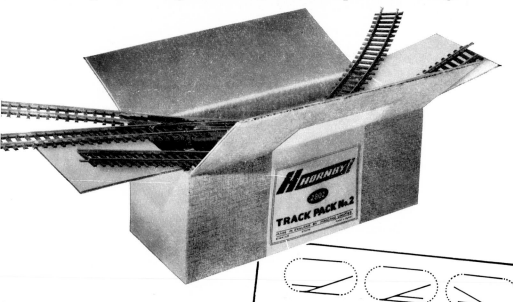

1964

The one lucky boy at this stage, was Robert Rogers of Aintree, Liverpool, whose father won a competition in the local *Liverpool Daily Post* newspaper out of 20,000 entries. Robert was made an honorary engine driver and apart from a special return trip to London as the guest of British Railways, taking in the sights and the now closed Clapham Transport Museum, he also won £100 worth of Hornby Dublo model railways, including every locomotive in the range.

However, all this hid the considerable activities going on backstage and it was finally announced on 14th February 1964 that the Lines Brothers toy empire

TRACK PACK No. 1 45/-

Contents:
10 FULL STRAIGHT RAILS 2701
6 2/3rds STRAIGHT RAILS 2702
3 1/3rd STRAIGHT RAILS 2703
1 SIMPLEC POINT R.H. 2750
1 SIMPLEC POINT L.H. 2751
2 TERMINAL CONNECTORS 2725
(Rails shown dotted are not supplied in the Track Pack)

TRACK PACK No. 2 65/-

Contents:
12 LARGE RADIUS FULL CURVED RAILS 2719
12 FULL STRAIGHT RAILS 2701
4 2/3rds STRAIGHT RAILS 2702
2 2/3rds STRAIGHT SINGLE ISOLATING RAILS 2738
2 SIMPLEC POINTS R.H. 2750
2 TERMINAL CONNECTORS 2725
(Rails shown dotted are not supplied in the Track Pack)

TRACK PACK No. 3 68/6

Contents:
4 FULL CURVED RAILS 2710
3 1/4 CURVED RAILS 2712
13 FULL STRAIGHT RAILS 2701
6 2/3rds STRAIGHT RAILS 2702
6 1/3rd STRAIGHT RAILS 2703
2 SIMPLEC POINTS R.H. 2750
1 SIMPLEC POINTS L.H. 2751
1 TERMINAL CONNECTOR 2725
(Rails shown dotted are not supplied in the Track Pack)

had purchased the full share capital of the Meccano Company for £781,000. As I have explained matters had not been well in Binns Road for the past two to three years not only on the Hornby Dublo front but on the Meccano constructional front and indeed, Dinky Toys, all three main product lines facing increasingly stiff competition which in the past had been practically non-existent. The press, both trade and national frequently allows itself to wallow in emotional nonsense, however there were two articles which to my mind put the case extremely accurately. The first was the editorial in the April 1964 *Model Railway Constructor* by the editor Alan Williams and the second a superb article in one of the newspapers by a Mr. Peter Wilsher (see page 80). They both make exceptionally interesting reading.

However, this was simply a total takeover and as most of us these days have experienced such, we understand that life goes on. Unlike most takeovers, though action was swift as here Lines Brothers had two very large model railway systems which in no way could be interchanged, without altering track and coupling units. The March 1964 *Meccano Magazine* announced finally that the production of all 3-rail items would be discontinued. At the toy fair earlier in the year Hornby had already stated that they planned to concentrate solely on 2-rail and had on show their new E3000 locomotive as well as the 'Red Rose' train set selling at £7. 15s. being the only three coach train set in the system and including the 4071 BR restaurant car. To the best of my knowledge the sets never materialised in the U.K. The E3000 locomotive was available in April together with details of the winners of the big competition in the Autumn. Andrew Farthing, then aged 13 of London NW1 was the winner and claimed the £100 selection of Hornby Dublo goods. The three short reasons why he preferred Hornby Dublo Trains to those of other makes were:

1. The best buys are Horn-buys.
2. I double my pleasure with Dublo treasures.
3. Their 'realistic railway replicas' are the three Rs for boys.

The advertisement claimed a very large volume of entries but did not give the actual figure.

Col. Beattie's famous Southgate Hobby Shop must have been very quick off the mark because he immediately bought 2,000 factory fresh now obsolete 3-rail locomotives and was offering them at less than half price and sold over 1,000 locomotives during April alone. In July 1964 the direct cash sales service the Meccano Company had carried on from Binns Road was discontinued, as there was a growing retail coverage there was much less call for this facility.

The takeover by Triang railways tied in very well in some respects for them as they themselves had announced at a trade fair at the beginning of the year that they were bringing out their own E3000 locomotive. However, with the new Hornby body and superb Ringfield motor it was put back in their range while the Hornby stocks were sold and then their own locomotive came out with the Hornby body moulding. An attempt was made to use the Triang catenary system with the Hornby Dublo track.

Many items seem to have found their way to Leather Lane, London to be sold off barrows at a price a quarter of market value – for instance £1. 10s. for a mint boxed 'Barnstaple'.

Beatties proudly announced in September that they had quite literally bought 'the lot'. So much success had they had in the quick sale of the 2,000 locomotives they had purchased earlier in the year, they now stated they had purchased all the 3-rail track and locomotives. By November their advertisements stated: 'At the moment we have plenty of track but the locomotives are selling fast!' Hattons of Liverpool were also heavily involved with the clearance of surplus stocks and a further irony was evidenced in the sale of many boxed sets through the Trix showroom in Great Portland Street, London.

An interesting article though in September, highlighted a complete reversal of earlier policy whereby Meccano were openly selling the Hornby Dublo chassis separately. We are now well into the era of the rapid rise in white metal kits fitting particularly onto the proprietary chassis of the time and many manufacturers designed their kits purely to fit direct onto the more readily available Triang chassis. There was quite understandably a limited range of locomotive bodies the Meccano Company could offer and it seemed the enthusiast of the day was becoming more concerned with the scale appearance of his model railway and wanting more regional locomotives. The clearance sale prices of the chassis being:

2-8-0	£3. 4s.	0-6-0 R1 Class	£1. 14s.
0-6-2 Tank	£2. 4s.	A4 Class Loco	£2. 12s.
Castle Class	£2. 18s.	West Country Class	£3. 18s.
2-6-4 Tank	£2. 18s.	City of London Class	£2. 18s.

New products continued to be released from Binns Road and October showed the new 2004 ready to run set with the 0-4-0 diesel shunter style with bright yellow body, this being made from the identical tooling as the 0-6-0 diesel shunter but approximately $\frac{1}{4}$ inch shorter with the front end metal steps removed. However, this was by no means the last product as finally in December 1964 came the rail cleaning wagon the last item to appear in the Hornby Dublo range. But the story by no means comes to an end. Mr. K. McMillar of Harrow, Middlesex also purchased a large quantity of 3-rail locomotives offering them at a 55 per cent final clearance offer and many were the offers in the advertisement pages of the model railway press for brand new Hornby Dublo products at these special clearance prices. The Winter of 1964/65 was spent with a lot of homework being done by the new Lines Brothers staff and much guessing on the part of the model railway trade and enthusiast. The February 1965 *Railway Modeller* states . . .

'The big question is, of course, what is going to happen to Hornby Dublo. We do know however that the 0 gauge is to be developed as a basic clockwork toy system primarily for the very young . . .'!

The Percy train set was already in production but was to enjoy a brief life as a true Hornby train. By May it was announced that a new policy governing the future of Triang and Hornby Dublo had been formulated and that the two systems were to be marketed under the name Triang Hornby. To overcome the major problem of two totally different couplings a converter wagon No. R577 was introduced with the Triang tension lock style coupling one end and the Hornby Dublo coupling the other. The track was to be the Triang super 4 and so it was also necessary to produce the R476 Triang Hornby piece of converter track to join the two differing permanent ways. Five locomotives were chosen to be retained in the Triang Hornby system and they were the West Country

GREAT CHANCE FOR
HORNBY 3-RAIL ENTHUSIASTS!

Hurry –

see your

stockist!

Soon production of 3-rail will be discontinued so 1964 is your last chance to build up your 3-rail layout with locomotives, rolling stock, track and accessories. Watch your dealer's window for special offers and announcements.

—MADE AND GUARANTEED BY MECCANO LIMITED.

POWERFUL NEW PANTOGRAPH LOCO

A mighty addition to the HORNBY DUBLO range!

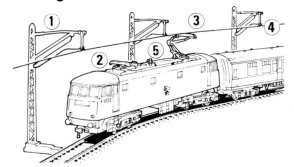

1 line masts

2 pantograph lowered

3 pantograph in contact with line

4 overhead line

5 plug converts from overhead to 2-track working

Overhead equipment available from most model railway stockists

4–6–2, the 0–6–0 South Eastern and Chatham Railway R1 Tank locomotive, the 0–6–2 N2 Tank locomotive, the Co-Bo diesel electric locomotive for fast freight trains and finally the 0–6–0 diesel electric shunting locomotive. Many of the station units were also retained though naturally these new products were marketed with the new Triang Hornby labels and boxes as soon as the existing stocks had run out. I keep mentioning this word 'stock' and I am indebted to Richard Lines for the considerable help and assistance he has given me over the years in my research, amongst which were the complete stock and sales figures for Hornby Dublo in 1964. 11,414 2-rail locomotives had been sold in 1964 but some 12,295 remained in stock. On the bogie passenger coaches, only 8,560 had been sold while there remained, blocking up the stores in Binns Road 107,950! The goods wagons were similar although they had certainly been popular as 45,574 that year had been sold but there still remained in stock 130,300 wagons! Despite strenuous efforts it was totally impracticable to afford the labour to alter all the couplings and yet if the Triang Company authorised the quick clearance of all these Hornby Dublo models, they would naturally totally extinguish their own market. They prepared stock sheets and allowed their salesmen to slowly dribble through quantities right up to 1970 when the entire remaining stock was sold to Mr. Dick Goddard of Rastasout Warehousemen Limited, down in the West Country. Part of his business was the purchasing of bankrupt or surplus or even damaged stock and covered practically everything from watches to furniture to electrical appliances. He advertised the stock in the newspapers and was inundated with letters and visitors, in fact some model railway clubs even ran buses down to his warehouse to purchase those goodies remaining. Soon all the locomotives, even the Co-Bo's, goods rolling stock and signals were sold and he was just left with some coaches and boxes of track and plastic 2-rail railer units. The final 250 cartons, 150 of which were the plastic railers, were finally purchased in the Summer of 1974 and sold at the Ratley Sale in early December.

There had been many Dinky Toy/diecast swap-meets around the country but never before a pure train meet here in the U.K. It must have started something as now they are held all over the country almost every weekend. No more Ratley Sales though – the village hall should only hold 120 and we had nearly 600! I and many others now know what a canned sardine feels like.

In March 1972 Mr. Stan Anderson formed the Hornby Dublo Circle – a collection of 40 enthusiasts who posted in sequence a whole series of lists of those models produced, questions etc. The object was to add such information as you could as each list passed around, naturally extracting the bits you wanted.

Unfortunately lists were lost in the post (poor excuse – some more likely retained) and the Circle eventually folded. Many members joined the Hornby Railway Collectors Association who, the same month had their own vote whether to include Dublo. Up until then they had been purely 0 gauge. The vote was two thirds in favour of Dublo being included.

And so ends the story of the Hornby Dublo range of model railways. The numerous models that still exist and are either run by collectors or stored up in

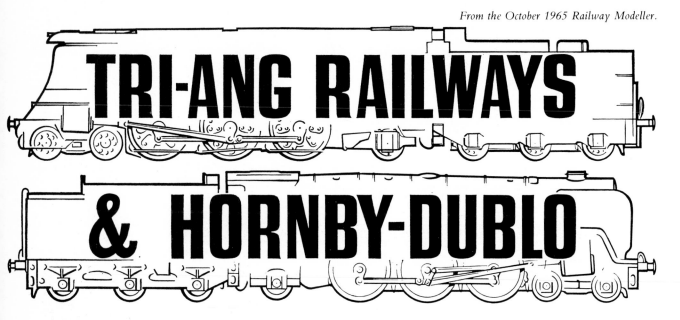

From the October 1965 Railway Modeller.

TRI-ANG RAILWAYS & HORNBY-DUBLO

THESE TWO FAMOUS MODEL RAILWAYS HAVE GOT TOGETHER FROM NOW ON, IT'S

Now that these two model railways have joined forces there is no end to the variety of exciting layouts that you can create. With Tri-ang Hornby you have the most wonderful choice in the world of locomotives, rolling stock, stations and accessories—don't wait till Christmas, see them now at your model railway shop. If you have a Hornby Dublo railway, remember you can easily add Tri-ang Hornby track and rolling stock to your layout with the specially created Converter Track and Converter Wagon.

Super detail Dublo wagons adapted to Triang Couplings.

boxes where they had been put away by their owners, turning sometimes mistakenly to more so called adult pursuits, are a credit to the skill of the employee of Meccano Limited.

It is however, by no means the end. The technical quality of these models will keep them running long past our lifetimes and they are already becoming antiques in their own right as a superb miniature reminder of the days when steam was king on British Railways.

I like to think that Hornby Dublo now has three children. The first born are the railway locomotives and wagons produced by the G & R Wrenn Company from the original tools, the products being updated as experience and techniques came to fruition. In 1966 they too were part of the Triang empire and Mr. George Wrenn approached the Triang directors with a request to assemble the Hornby Dublo tools and models and sell them under their own name (Wrenn). To his surprise the request was granted.

Secondly, you have the present Hornby Railways – the new generation of the old Triang Company whose improvements these last three to four years in the quality and appearance of their stock make them the leader by far of the present suppliers of British outline models and a fitting tribute to the quality of the name Hornby. Their yearly catalogue, I certainly feel, will be as much sought after in years to come as we today search after the old *Hornby Books of Trains*. Finally, and only recently born, there are the railways of the Airfix Company who themselves now own the Meccano Company. Many are the favourable comments I have received from both operators and retailers of this new system and at the time of going to press with their new 'Castle' Class locomotive displayed at the Toy Fair being described as the show stopper who knows what the future will bring silicon chips and all. It seems sad to me that these three systems should have to fight it out for survival and who knows what the future will bring. It is certainly not part of this story. This is purely the end of the beginning.

 &

Following the incorporation of Meccano Limited, the manufacturers of Hornby Dublo trains, into the Lines Bros. Group (Tri-ang), a careful analysis was undertaken to study the advantages and disadvantages of maintaining production of two entirely separate Model Railway Systems. The evidence showed clearly that there was excessive duplication of products in all fields and that since both systems operated on the 2-rail 12 volt D.C. standard, there were no fundamental obstacles to amalgamation.

The two railways will, therefore, be progressively brought together under the name TRI-ANG HORNBY and will use Tri-ang Super 4 Track and Tri-ang Couplings.

Existing owners of Hornby Dublo will continue to be able to purchase Hornby Dublo components while stocks last and can then go on to Tri-ang Hornby track by means of the special converter rail. A converter wagon with mixed couplings is also now available, so that no Hornby Dublo system will become obsolete. It must be recognised, however, that running trains with mixed couplings does not permit full remote uncoupling operations.

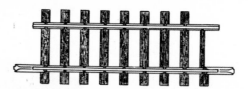

R.476 Tri-ang Hornby Converter Track. 2⅞" (7.2 cms.) long. U.K. Retail Price 1/-.

How a Converter Track connects Tri-ang Railways Super 4 with Hornby Dublo Track.

Hornby Dublo 2-rail Locomotives and Rolling Stock will operate satisfactorily on Tri-ang Railways Super 4 Track and most modern Tri-ang Railways Locomotives and Rolling Stock will operate on Hornby Dublo 2-rail Track.

It is not possible to fit Tri-ang Railways Uncoupling Ramps to Hornby Dublo Track, but if these exist on a Tri-ang Railways layout they do not interfere with Hornby Dublo couplings.

R.577 Tri-ang Hornby Converter Wagon. U.K. Retail Price 2/6.

Tri-ang Railways Tension-Lock Coupling

Hornby Dublo Coupling

The cover picture 'Night Scene at Crewe' was specially painted for Tri-ang Hornby by Terence Cuneo

COUPLINGS

Tri-ang Railways Tension-Lock Couplings operate vertically while Hornby Dublo Couplings operate horizontally. It is not, therefore, possible for the two types to connect together directly. The Converter Wagon is now introduced to enable users of either system to operate mixed Freight Trains.

This Wagon is now supplied, automatically, with the five ex-Hornby Dublo Locomotives listed under the name Tri-ang Hornby (see overleaf).

A Passenger Converter Vehicle will be introduced when Hornby Dublo Passenger Coaches cease to be available.

Tri-ang *HORNBY*

R.2235 4–6–2 West Country Class Locomotive 'Barnstaple' and Tender. U.K. Retail Price £5.15.0.

R.2233 Co–Bo Diesel-Electric Locomotive. U.K. Retail Price £4.6.0.

Each of these ex-Hornby Dublo Locomotives is now supplied complete with a Tri-ang Hornby Converter Wagon at no extra cost so that it can be used with Tri-ang Railways or Hornby Dublo Rolling Stock.

Hornby Dublo Locomotives have long been noted for their sturdy construction and their 12 Volt D.C. electric motors are built to last a lifetime.

The station buildings below may be used equally well with Tri-ang Railways and Hornby Dublo and the illustration overleaf shows what an exciting layout can now be created by the bringing together of these two marvellous Model Railways.

R.2217 0–6–2 Tank Locomotive. U.K. Retail Price *56/9.*

R.2207 0–6–0 Tank Locomotive. U.K. Retail Price *38/–.*

R.2231 0–6–0 Diesel-Electric Shunting Locomotive. U.K. Retail Price *64/–.*

R.5083 Terminus and Through Station Composite Kit. U.K. Retail Price *59/11.*

R.5084 Terminus Canopy Extension Kit (not illustrated). U.K. Retail Price *22/–.*

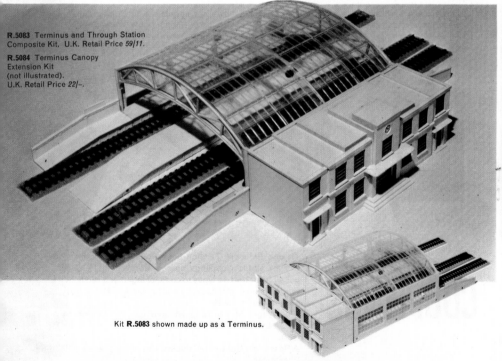

Kit **R.5083** shown made up as a Terminus.

R.5005

R.5020

R.5086

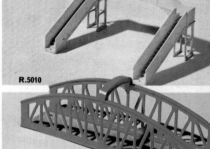

R.5010

R.5015

R.5030

R.5092

R.5005 Two-road Engine Shed Kit. U.K. Retail Price 19/6. **R.5006** (not illustrated). Engine Shed Extension Kit. Converts two-road shed into four-road. U.K. Retail Price 14/3. **R.5010** Footbridge. U.K. Retail Price 12/6. **R.5020** Goods Depot Kit with Working Crane. U.K. Retail Price 29/–. **R.5015** Girder Bridge. U.K. Retail Price 11/9. **R.5086** Platform Extension. U.K. Retail Price 2/11. **R.5087** Platform Fence (illustrated fitted to **R.5086**). U.K. Retail Price 1/7. **R.5089** Side Platform Extension (not illustrated). U.K. Retail Price 2/6. **R.5030** Island Platform Kit. U.K. Retail Price 11/3 **R.5092** Double Track Tunnel. U.K. Retail Price 25/6.

Derailment on the nursery floor

By PETER WILSHER

SIXTY-ODD years ago, a Liverpool metal-worker called Frank Hornby took home a sheet of copper, clamped it to the kitchen table and cut it into strips. His two young sons, Roland and Douglas, helped him to bore some holes: they bolted the bits together to make a rudimentary model crane and thus Meccano, one of the best and most ingenious toys invented this century, got itself born.

A good, cosy, rose-coloured success-story – carried on by Hornby trains after the First World War, Dinky Toys in the 'thirties; and trading profits nearing £1 million mark in 1956. But last week, in the middle of the biggest toy boom Britain has ever seen (£44 million net sales last year) the Meccano company ended its independent existence in a sour, unhappy mess of mounting losses, angry shareholders and un-met forecasts. The business, once valued in the market at over £3 million, is being absorbed into the vast Lines Brothers' nursery empire at an effective price around £800,000.

Roland Hornby, still chairman and joint managing director at 74, blames it all on the trains. "Everyone's gone off them—all over the world. Modern houses are too small for a decent layout and all the parents are spending their money on cars, washing machines and hire purchase. Trains were a third of our business, and last Christmas was a complete disaster." In fact, on top of the £250,000 pre-tax loss he expects for 1963-64 there is another £600,000 to be written off— almost entirely on 00 gauge locomotives, remotely controlled hopper trucks and lovingly-devised triple-point shunting systems which today's schoolboys (or fathers) no longer want.

But Hornby now gives the impression of a man bewildered by the downward rush of events. Certainly, at the meeting only last August, when the writing on the wall ought surely have been seen, he gave shareholders a most confident report ("trading fully balanced in 1964, and once more on a satisfactory and profitable basis") and no warning at all that the previous year's loss was to be almost doubled. And in fact Meccano's troubles go far deeper and farther back than a sudden collapse of the signal-and-guard's-van market. This is the picture of a once-great pioneering company fallen behind in almost every aspect of its activities.

"So many people climbed on our band-wagon," says Hornby passionately – and with some truth. But unfortunately that is no defence in a hard, cold commercial world.

In die-cast model motor-cars, Dinky Toys had the field to themselves for twenty years. But down in Swansea, Philip Ullman and Alfred Katz, of the fast-growing Mettoy company, saw gaps in the market and started putting opening doors, independent springing, and real windows on to their "Corgi" range. And in Hackney, Leslie Smith and John Odell, of Lesney Products, came up with their brilliantly successful "Matchbox" toys, which put Cortinas, and Minis, and Rolls-Royces on the nursery floor at a third, or even a quarter, of the Dinky price.

In constructional toys, Meccano remains, as Hornby told his shareholders last year, "a magical name" but not so uniquely magical as it once was. Every toy maker in the world has some kind of erector set nowadays – pop-together, prong-together, interlock or screw. And plastic is a lot cheaper than metal, if not always no durable – as Ralph Ehrmann's meteorically-expanding Airfix group has profitably demonstrated.

Even in trains, the view is not all-excusingly black. While Hornby flounders the Lines Brothers (who built up from a South London rocking-horse factory to the biggest toy company in the world) picked up the little Rovex business, then exclusively supplying rails and engines to Marks and Spencer. And as one of their admiring trade competitors says: "They found an acorn, and grew it into a tree" – a tree which, incidentally, now produces more than a third of their profits. More recently Mettoy acquired the agency for Jouet's fantastically cheap and successful French model railways, (cheapest set, fully electric, 35s.) which they sell under the "Playcraft" label through – among other outlets – Woolworth's 1,100 branches. After 18 months they claim "getting on for a quarter" of the market, by price, and a lot more by volume.

No-one can say Meccano haven't struggled to change, but their promotion and judgment seem to lack force these days. They went into house-building sets by acquiring "Bayco". But that was completely eclipsed by Courtaulds' "Lego" off-shoot, whose displays last Christmas seemed to fill every toy-shop window in the country. They sniffed for several years over the vastly popular electric road racing circuits ("there's nothing to it," Hornby still says wonderingly, "just cars and racing"). But seeing Lines' "Scalextric" and Airfix's "Motor Racing" make a packet they went in, belatedly, with a French import, "Circuit 24," and have just had to withdraw it as a total flop.

Other rather desperate sounding things are being test-marketed – adjustable roller skates; self-hardening Plastercine – but how much will survive the Lines merger remains to be seen. Already, in the past five years, the labour force in Liverpool has shrunk from 4,500 to something nearer 2,000.

Lines' offer, of one share for every eight Meccano, values the equity at 2s. 10½d – a sharp and sickening drop from Thursday's market price of 7s. 6d. for the ordinary and 5s. for the "A." which only carry a quarter of a vote. Quotations did not drop the whole way down to the offer level however – only 3s. 6d. This is mainly a reflection of doubt over the position of Mr Harold Drayton's British Electric Traction group, which holds roughly 30 per cent. of Meccano acquired in 1949.

As Mr Hornby, with his wife, fellow directors and the Meccano workers' trust, have accepted with over 52 per cent. of the votes, the deal is clearly a *fait accompli*. But the hope is that, with the powerful Drayton interest (now showing a £12,000 loss, after 14 years' patience), a better price might be negotiated for the outside holders.

Mr Drayton is in South Africa, and the B.E.T. board are holding their own counsel till they see the formal documents. Obviously no-one should sell or accept till their reaction is known. But even then there will be a further problem, as Lines itself has had a steep slump in profits (from £1.3 million after tax in 1960 to £411,000 last year). The shares yield 4.35 per cent. (against well under 3 per cent. for Mettoy, Lesney and Airfix) and the question is, how long it will take to get back to the 1961 dividend level. Chairman Mr W.M. Lines was only cautiously hopeful in his last report, and sorting out Meccano's troubles may delay the process even further. Cash in hand may well look more attractive than another long pull with the kiddiewinkies.

A contemporary newspaper cutting outlining the background to the financial problems of Meccano Ltd.

HORNBY-DUBLO TRAINS

THE PERFECT TABLE RAILWAY

Gauge OO

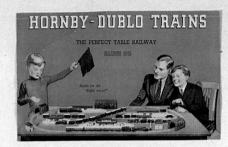

HORNBY-DUBLO TRAINS

THE PERFECT TABLE RAILWAY

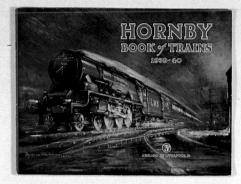

HORNBY
BOOK of TRAINS
1939-40

HORNBY
DUBLO
100% BRITISH

A REAL RAILWAY ON
YOUR OWN TABLE

Manufactured by
MECCANO LIMITED
BINNS ROAD
LIVERPOOL 13

HORNBY
DUBLO
ELECTRIC TRAINS

HORNBY
DUBLO
ELECTRIC TRAINS

HORNBY
DUBLO
ELECTRIC TRAINS

A Complete
Railway on
a Table

HORNBY
DUBLO
ELECTRIC TRAINS
GAUGE OO

HORNBY
DUBLO
ELECTRIC TRAINS

HORNBY
DUBLO
ELECTRIC TRAINS

NEW 2-RAIL
low-priced trains

HORNBY
DUBLO
ELECTRIC TRAINS

MADE AND GUARANTEED BY MECCANO LTD.

NEW 2-RAIL

HORNBY
DUBLO
ELECTRIC TRAINS

HORNBY
DUBLO
ELECTRIC TRAINS

3-RAIL
SYSTEM

The model railway
of superb detail and
super strength

HORNBY
DUBLO
BOOK OF TRAINS 1/6

HORNBY
DUBLO
ELECTRIC TRAINS

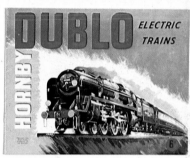

HORNBY
DUBLO
ELECTRIC TRAINS

HORNBY
DUBLO
3-RAIL SYSTEM

Hornby
DUBLO
3-RAIL SYSTEM

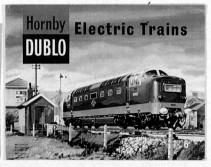

Hornby
DUBLO
Electric Trains

Hornby
DUBLO

2-RAIL
ELECTRIC TRAINS

HORNBY

LOCOMOTIVES · TRACK
ACCESSORIES · ROLLING STOCK

HORNBY TRAINS

HORNBY
DUBLO

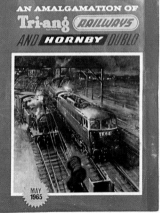

AN AMALGAMATION OF
Tri-ang RAILWAYS
AND HORNBY DUBLO

MAY 1965

The Models

'THE OBSESSED ARE IMMUNE
TO REASON'

I came upon the above expression on a recent visit to Iran. I thought how true a saying it was. You find such people throughout all walks of life, but the railway fraternity, and in particular the collectors, seem to have more than their fair share. Tolerance is one of my favourite words and I suppose this is really a defence mechanism which might have links with cowardice an emotion I am beginning to experience as I commence this second part of my book on the Hornby Dublo model railway system – the description of the models and main variations found to date.

You must remember that the Hornby Dublo Railways were manufactured as toys, primarily for children. As long as the model was technically competent such minor variations as metal or plastic couplings and different ends on the coaches, etc., against the standard were purely so they could complete the production runs. There are so many fascinating modifications although many I prefer to call 'production variations'.

In the following chapters I have endeavoured to give you the main variations one can encounter. I am bound to overlook some and I apologise now for their exclusion. I have, however, been able to locate, and have kindly been given permission by Meccano Ltd to reproduce many drawings of body housings, wagons, etc., which include dates and descriptions of actual and intended variations.

So many people have come up to me at exhibitions and swapmeets asking if I had heard about this or that variation. I try my best to write them down on backs of tickets and any other odd pieces of paper that are available. I do wish they had taken the time to write to me in order that I may have had a more precise record.

In this book you will find some tips on operation, servicing and oiling the locomotives and rolling stock to ensure smooth operation.

The fumes of burning oil, general dust and grime, let alone sticky fingermarks, which accumulate on all the Hornby Dublo locomotives and rolling stock can be very effectively cleaned I have found by using Johnson spray wax – 'Pledge'. This, in my experience is the best of all and I have used it on all my collection – both Dublo and 0 gauge. It not only takes off all the grime, but has an exceptionally mild abrasive effect unlike some other polishes which, after you have finished giving the model its final rub, discover you have gone right the way through the litho or enamel to the metal underneath!

I must admit the Hornby Dublo range is without doubt my favourite of all the 00 scale railways, but it is pointless to deny that there are some excellent models produced by their competitors. I would particularly refer readers to an article written by J. H. Russell in the June 1962 *Model Railway News* which describes the scale 4 mm modelling i.e. EM gauge with a track width of 19 mm. There are some photographs of the Hornby Dublo model locomotives converted to this scale and they show some of the most realistic scale railway modelling I have ever seen. A further compliment to the Hornby Dublo detail and an interesting insight of what might have been had a 19 mm gauge been chosen in those far off days of the 1920s.

The bulk of the research here has been from listing model variations and cross checking with fellow collectors directly or via the HRCA. Within the last six months I, and fellow members of the Meccano Archive Committee, have been given access to 5,000 odd drawings, etc., which show many of the variations by drawing amendment dates. This research will of course, continue over many years.

GENERAL STATISTICS OF BRITISH RAILWAYS

		1951	1964	1976
(1)	Number of locomotives	19,341	9,633	3,689
(2)	Passenger stations	6,214	4,145	2,361
(3)	Passengers carried	1,001,308,000	927,617,000	708,474,000
(4)	Total freight	284,803,000	239,647,000	176,209,000
(5)	Mineral content	169,388,000	147,425,000	97,001,000
(6)	BR staff	605,696	399,005	182,695
(7)	Total track miles	51,827	44,080	28,700
(8)	Total route miles	19,357	15,991	11,189

Showing the changes of the last twenty five years

THE N2 TANKS 0–6–2

This magnificent little locomotive has matched almost exactly its full size prototype, being fast, sturdy, reliable and in continuous use for 40 years. It was in 1907 that Mr. Ivatt, the Chief Mechanical Engineer of the Great Northern Railway introduced the N1 0–6–2 Tanks, but these were not a very successful design. In 1920 the renowned Mr. Gresley produced an initial batch of 60 locomotives to the N2 design which proved so successful that a total of 167 locomotives were eventually produced in batches through 1925, 1928 and 1929. The boiler was set above the steam chest and the squat chimney and dome were necessary to keep the locomotive inside the Metropolitan Railway loading gauges. They were principally used in suburban traffic which they handled with considerable success until British Railways converted to diesel some 40 years later. These locomotives were found not only working out of King's Cross (with condensing apparatus) but were scattered throughout the country operating in Scotland, the West Riding of Yorkshire and along the Great Eastern lines out of Liverpool Street Station, London.

Much information on the N2 Tank locos can be found in Mr. P. N. Townend's book *Top Shed*. The best on railway operation I have ever read. He relates. . . .

'The GN suburban service was operated with considerable enthusiasm and alacrity. Station work was prompt and it is on record that an empty train has been run into King's Cross Station, the inward engine

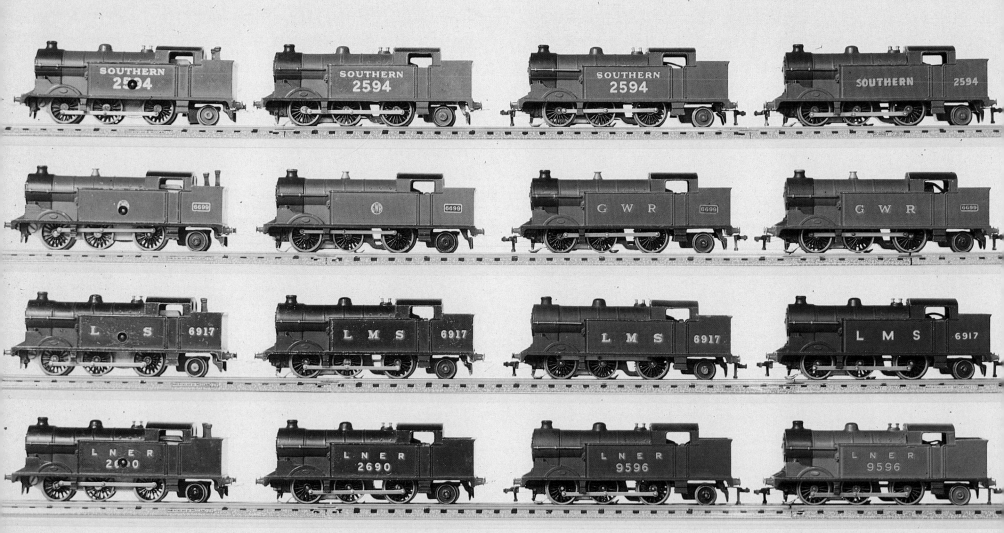

← *Page 84. The 0–6–2 Tank variations, showing in column 1 the pre-war clockwork, in column 2 the pre-war electric and columns 3 and 4 post-war prenationalisation variations.*

← *Page 85. Column 1 continuing final prenationalisation liveries. The top of column 2, Mr. Topple's interesting British Railways Tank. Top of column 3, the Pyramid Toys/Triang Loco and top of column 4 the Gaiety Loco. Finally, six of the British Railway nationalised livery variations and the post-war articulated LNER coach set.*

uncoupled, a fresh one shunted on at the other end and attached, brake re-created, heater pipes coupled, tail lamp fitted, destination boards on the locomotive and blinds on the stock changed, several hundred passengers embarked, and the train got away – all within 70 seconds!'

Some 55 N2 Tanks were based on 'Top Shed', King's Cross in the mid-1950s.

The locomotive's rectangular shape lent itself ideally to the model electric and clockwork mechanisms of the period and such companies as Bonds o' Euston produced commercial models in the early 1930s. The Hornby Dublo model, first drawn on 7th December 1937, appeared on the market 10 months later and I believe must hold the world record for being the longest model in continuous production – that is if one forgives the short interruption between the shut-down of the Hornby Dublo production lines in 1964 and the recommencement of manufacture using the original tools etc., by George Wrenn & Company.

The N2 Tank locomotive had a rare turn of speed and was often seen handling 8 coach suburban trains to and from Moorgate Station. In model form too those wonderful locomotives had an incredible turn of speed albeit not scale but out performing even the 'Duchess of Atholl'. The general information book used by the Hornby Railway Company lists the hauling capacity of the model at 12 goods vehicles on the level, 6 D1 coaches, or if working on a gradient 6 goods vehicles up a 1 in 20 gradient and 8 goods vehicles up a 1 in 30.

The models were produced pre-war in the four main group liveries in both clockwork and electric. The clockwork version was quickly observed to be a slow seller and it was already planned to stop produc-

tion of this version before the commencement of the Second World War. There are almost as many variations of this tank locomotive as that famous food company's 57 varieties! I shall attempt to list the principal variations, as follows:

PRE-WAR 0–6–2 TANKS

Common Features:
D shaped front coupling stud. Flat steel spring coupling. Straight edges to the front and rear buffer beams. Nickel plated buffer heads. A light pony truck in the rear with a split pin and washer connection and vertical play on the disc pony wheels. Large circular windows at the rear of the cabin. The word Hornby finely cast on top of the smoke box door.

SOUTHERN RAILWAY

The Southern Region version appeared in olive green with the letters 'Southern' and in large numbers '2594' on the tank sides, on the front buffer beam and at the top rear of the coal hopper, its disc trailing wheels and driving wheels were always painted the same green as the body. It was based on the Southern 0–6–2 Class E5 locomotive – a series of 30 tank locomotives. Three of this class existed in 1955.

GREAT WESTERN RAILWAY

In the beautiful Great Western green livery with the GWR circular monogram, which was introduced to the prototype in September 1934, mounted centrally on the tank sides. This was a loose interpretation of the 66 XX Class locomotive and one in real life – No. 6697 – can still be seen at Didcot, today.

LONDON MIDLAND & SCOTTISH RAILWAY

This model was in conventional gloss black livery with an LMS transfer on the tank side and the No. 6917 on the coal hopper side.

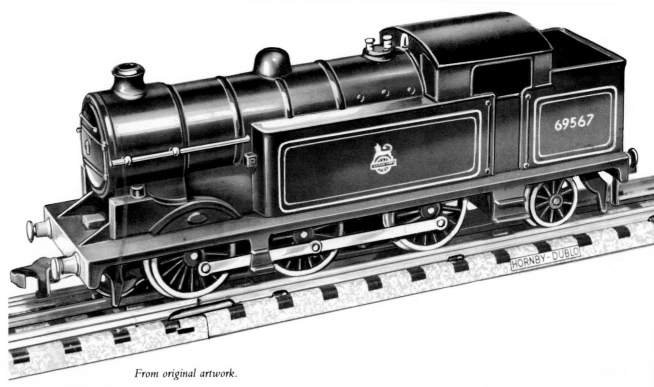

From original artwork.

LONDON NORTH EASTERN RAILWAY

Again in a standard gloss black livery with the No. 2690 on the tank sides and on the front and rear buffer beam as in real practise.

Edward Beal in his book *Scale Railway Modelling Today* published in 1939, stated that the 0–6–2 Tanks were painted dead black with lettering in gold for any of the four groups. As we have seen, this was not true, as both the Southern and the Great Western tanks only ever appeared in their respective green livery and indeed the *Meccano Magazine* a couple of months later published a correction.

IMMEDIATE POST-WAR (1947–1953)

With the re-introduction of the Hornby Dublo range of locomotives in December 1947, only the electric version was produced and although most followed their pre-war counterparts, there were numerous identification changes, obviously the principal one being the Peco hook coupling which we have already discussed in Part I. This meant that the front buffer beam had to have a slight recess cut away underneath in between the buffer units. One or two models are known to exist without this cutaway in the buffer beam. The drawing states the new coupling was drawn 9th March 1946, though surprisingly the cutaway is not clearly defined. The odd example may be a case of pre-war bodies on post-war chassis. Other changes from pre-war were the rear pony with a screw-fixing and no vertical play in the axles. Later versions had the heavier weighted pony axle base and smaller diameter spectacle windows at the rear of the cab. Also the buffer heads were painted silver as opposed to the pre-war nickel finish. As with the whole range of Hornby Dublo locomotives and rolling stock, they were constantly modified in the light of operating experience and customer comments and almost all the modifications were to improve either the running or the strength of the model.

SOUTHERN RAILWAY

Apart from the alterations we have mentioned, the first livery was identical to the pre-war model although as usual, following main line practice, a malachite green version came out in 1950 with the

'Rush hour' – July 1946 Meccano Magazine.

"Rush hour" scene at a Dublo terminus showing suburban arrivals each in charge of a Hornby-Dublo Tank Locomotive, an ideal type for local passenger traffic.

large letters 'Southern' on the tank sides and 2594 number on the hopper sides and the front and rear buffer beams. As the group illustration shows – there were two shades of malachite green and 'thick' bright yellow and 'thin' dull lettering and numbers. Some locomotives bore both the 'thick' and 'thin' lettering and some had silver and others gold Hornby Dublo labels on the rear of the coal bunker.

GREAT WESTERN RAILWAY

The principal difference here was the change to the GWR letters on the tank sides. It had been decided by the Great Western Railway in 1942 that instead of the circular GWR monogram their important locomotives would have the letter G and then the GWR crest and then the letter W on their tenders while the lesser locomotives just had a widely spaced GWR. There are many variations of transfers and letter sizes, especially the numbers on the hopper. A particularly rare version obviously a mistake (I know of four only) has the 'Duchess of Atholl' No. 6231 on the hopper. This never applied to a GWR 0–6–2 Tank in real life. All GWR locos had black painted disc pony wheels and drivers. Only the Southern and post-war green LNER locos had matching green painted wheels.

THE LONDON MIDLAND SCOTTISH RAILWAY

This locomotive appeared in black livery similar to the

pre-war model, although again there were various transfer alterations varying in colour from pale to bright yellow. The later models had the san serif lettering and semi-matt black finish, while the early post-war models had an overall matt black colour.

THE LONDON NORTH EASTERN RAILWAY

One must remember that these were, in fact, toys and with stocks and all production frozen during the war years, many items were released after the war with variations which confuse the collector today but, a little mystery adds to the enjoyment of a hobby and certainly keeps the correspondence columns busy. Although never advertised as such, the LNER locomotive (in black) did come out with the cutaway buffer beam and the pre-war lettering No. 2690 (frozen stock?) although its official lettering in the black matt version was 9596. The LNER had many of their tanks painted in that beautiful apple green livery and so Hornby Dublo, not to be outdone, introduced a green version of 9596 at the same time with transfer variations. (Note: with the change from the horseshoe magnet to the anlico half inch magnet, it seems to be the general rule that a silver decal was then used with the identical lettering. There have been so many body and chassis changes in servicing locomotives that one can only accept this as a general rule. Incidentally, the tank tops along the boiler on the green LNER and all the Southern versions, were painted black.)

EDG17 Tank Goods Set (from original artwork).

Hornby-Dublo Tanks

How to Keep Busy on Your Layouts

IT is probably correct to say that the Tank Locomotives are the busiest engines on any Hornby-Dublo layout. Indeed, there are some railways on which only tank engines are used, those that are in their simple early stages being excellent examples. Such railways are supplied by Hornby-Dublo Train Sets, either passenger or goods, that include one or other of the tank engines of the range and they make a splendid beginning.

As such railways develop, so invariably does the variety of rolling stock, and here the tank engine owner is fortunate because such an engine can deal with a very wide variety of traffic. Probably most Hornby-Dublo layouts have at least one EDL17 Tank Locomotive on the strength. This is the popular 0–6–2T, one of which appears in the picture above. It is equally at home on a local passenger or goods train and it is of course invaluable for shunting duties. On some layouts it is the custom to have one of these engines constantly on duty at the main station. There it can deal with yard shunting and it is at hand also to carry out any attaching or detaching movements that may be necessary when any long-distance train calls.

Operations of this kind are slick and enjoyable only when the layout is planned in advance with an eye on them. This means that Points, Signals, Uncoupling Rails and Isolating sections should be well placed. A few experiments may be necessary before the final arrangement can be determined, but this adds to the fun, and is of practical value to the Hornby-Dublo owner.

'The Busy Tanks' – December 1957 Meccano Magazine.

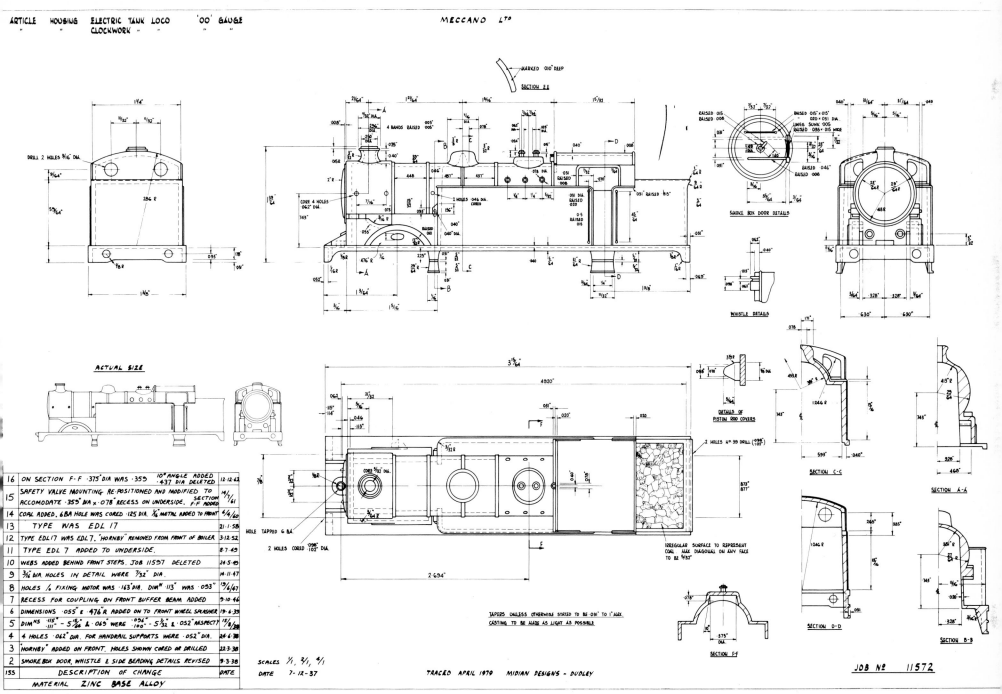

BRITISH RAILWAYS

According to the Meccano Dealers' leaflet of 29th May, Hornby Dublo followed the 1948 nationalisation of the four main groups with their version in June 1953. Our little friend came out in a new high gloss livery with No. 69567 on its cab side and the British Railways lion on the tank sides. Also the 'Hornby' name on the smoke box door was finally deleted and the number transfers added. The initial version had small fine numbers on the bunker sides and gloss black disc pony wheels. The chassis were also gloss black. Later issues had gloss black spoked disc wheels. The model soon changed to the common black livery, the small numbers on the bunker sides were increased in thickness and, the tail of the lion on the BR emblem increased in length. Next the type number cast on the underside of the body was changed to L17. Shortly afterwards the locomotive was issued with nickel silver plated wheels, plastic couplings, spoked plastic pony truck wheels, fine metal handrails and imitation coal in the bunker. Lastly the motif was changed to the BR totem in fore and aft format and the grey lining on the side panels changed to a darker grey.

In 1959 2-rail was introduced to the Hornby Dublo system and our Tank locomotive now appeared as No. 69550. The final variations came when alterations to the bearing on the top of the armature necessitated larger clearance so a larger safety valve cover had to be formed in the casting.

A very interesting model is owned by Mr. Paul Topple which is an LNER green liveried locomotive with 'British Railways' in full on top of the tank side and the No. E9560 underneath it. Many knowledgeable collectors have seen this model and can only conclude that it could well be a genuine prototype.

A drawing of the original steam locomotive body shell is illustrated and it is possible to read the list of variations and their dates.

On drawing No. 1576 there is reference to the housing assembly 1570 GWR being deleted on 4th December 1952 and at the same time housing No. 1571F. Could it be that a special French version was produced for the export market? I have no evidence of the existence of such a beast.

The Meccano Company enjoyed much success with the introduction of their Dublo system and soon realised that the whole future of their model railway production would eventually be in this scale. A competitor was the Trackmaster range introduced by Pyramid Toys Ltd. which had a creditable diecast N2 Tank body, with British Railways in yellow letters written on the tank sides and the number 69561 on the coal bunker. They produced this model from 1952 to 1954 when the Triang Railway Company brought it into their range and it became the only diecast-bodied locomotive the Triang Railway Company ever produced. However, at that stage it just had the then current BR emblem on the tank sides.

Surprisingly, at the same period the Kirdon Company marketed an identical body – identical at least from photographic comparison. They sold it as their 'famous 3/6 casting' and again as – 'the ultimate in locomotive construction kits'. A powerful motor, and scale wheels reported the Bradshaw Model products catalogue 1955/6 third edition. Even a driver and fireman were supplied. The kit sold for £1. 9s. 6d. against the 1954 Meccano price of 45s. So, whose was the original model? Kirdon Ltd. or Pyramid Toys Ltd.?

Perhaps Hornby's best competitor was the beautiful little model made in the 'Gaiety Range' by the Castle Art Products Company of Ward End, Birmingham and supplied through their sole selling agents – Dunn & Sutton then of Park Street, Birmingham 5. This was an excellent casting, with the embossed letters 'British Railways' on the tank sides and '46917' again embossed on the coal bunker, with imitation coal in the top. I have heard that privately the Meccano Company feverishly disclaimed what they called an imitation 0–6–2 Tank body as it was near identical to their own standard LMS Tank No. 6917. Nothing should improve a product or a service more than competition!

This same company also produced a very attractive GWR pannier Tank locomotive with an 0–6–0 wheel configuration. Trade topics of the *Model Railway News* for September 1940 show a similar model, in electric (although running on clockwork track) of an example by the famous Tyldesley & Holbrook of Manchester which had been supplied to one of their customers mounted straight onto a standard Hornby Dublo 0–6–2 chassis unit, suitably adapted.

The Walkers & Holtzapffel catalogue issued around 1955 shows a beautiful super detailed casting N2 Tank body – you have guessed! 'British Railways' cast on the tank side and '46917' on the bunker. It was fitted with the Riemsdijk clockwork mechanism and had such items as condenser pipes, coal and handrails etc. and sold for £3. 10s. 0d. plus 16s. purchase tax. A very pretty model – adding to the confusion of future historians. Fortunately the length over buffers differs. The Hornby Dublo model is 142 mm, the Trackmaster model 150 mm and the Gaeity 145 mm.

800 2-rail 69550 locos were sold in 1964, leaving 1,000 in stock.

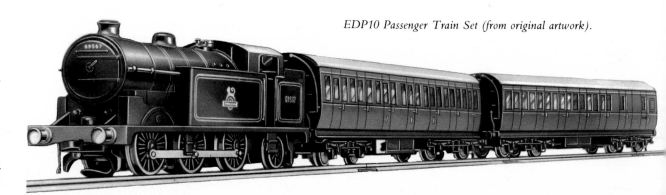

EDP10 Passenger Train Set (from original artwork).

THE A4 PACIFIC 4–6–2 LOCOMOTIVES

Sir Nigel Gresley was without doubt the hero of the hour in 1938. Almost exactly to the day, three years earlier than the introduction of the Hornby Dublo A4 locomotive, 'Sir Nigel Gresley', he had caught the imagination and enthusiasm of the whole of the country with his 'Silver Jubilee Express'. The trial run was held on 27th September 1935 and three days later the engine went into service on the new streamlined express. A remarkable achievement and saying much for the Doncaster workmanship and soundness of design. On the trial of the 'Silver Jubilee' train headed by 2509 'Silver Link', she averaged 100 m.p.h. for 43 miles and 91.8 m.p.h. for 70 miles, twice touching 112½ m.p.h. and creating an all time steam record. The LMS region, not to be outdone, ran its 'Coronation' locomotive 6220 on 29th June 1937 on a test run to 114 m.p.h. till an all too rapid approach to Crewe had to put the brakes on hard. Top Link driver Lawrence A. Earl of Campden Shed was quite convinced that he could have done 130 m.p.h. if the LMS had a similar racing track to that on the London North Eastern route. Unfortunately, it was never proved and on 3rd July 1938, heading 6 'Coronation' coaches and a dynamometer car, driver Joe Duddington, together with fireman Bray and inspector S. Jenkins, took the 'Mallard' locomotive to an all-time world record of 126 m.p.h.

On 26th November 1937, Mr. William Whitelaw, Chairman of the LNER, unveiled the plaque numbering the 100th LNER standard Pacific

locomotive as 'Sir Nigel Gresley', a fitting tribute to the designer and his design.

It was on St. Valentine's Day, 14th February 1938, that the drawing was completed in the Meccano Works for their own miniature A4 locomotive and it was the finest mass produced model to ever appear at that date. It heralded a new standard of excellence with a strong chassis, superb watchlike clockwork or electric motor and robust and detailed zinc-based casting.

The 'Silver King' locomotive was originally released in the special silver grey livery of the 'Silver Jubilee' train and I have never been able to fathom the exact story as to how a Hornby Dublo locomotive, painted in silver, frequently appeared in photographs in the early war years' *Meccano Magazine*. I have my own version, again with a repainted poor original condition valanced locomotive body and squeezing in a 'Silver King' chassis. The superb painting job being undertaken by Howell Dimmock Ltd. of Chantry, near Frome, Somerset.

THE 'SIR NIGEL GRESLEY' LOCOMOTIVE

The first model Hornby Dublo introduced was the 'Sir Nigel Gresley' locomotive equipped with the now famous corridor tender through which the crews could be changed without stopping the train on the long runs from London to Edinburgh. The model was complete in every detail, with black nameplate, tender lettering shaded in red (as per LNER practice at the time) and various other points such as the pre-war flat spring steel coupling on the tender, obviously the full valanced skirt over the simplified valve gear, the pony truck held by a split pin fixing and the original lightweight bogie chassis and rear pony casting. These being considerably strengthened on later models which appeared after the war.

The clockwork model, with the brake and control lever coming out through the roof of the cab, is a joy to behold and I note from one of the original drawings that the testing data of this locomotive was that it should run with one articulated coach for a minimum of 50 ft on one winding. The track circuit consisted of eight full curved and two full straight rails and had to be completed in a time of between 4.5 and 5.5 seconds per lap.

Page 47 of the February 1943 *Meccano Magazine*

shows one of the latest in this famous series of A4 Pacifics, No. 4901 'Capercaillie' (now renamed under the recently appointed Chief General Manager – 'Charles H. Newton'). The locomotive appears in wartime black livery, with reduced lettering and was one of the four Gresley streamliners to be fitted with the Kylchap arrangement of blast pipe with double chimney which proved so effective. To ease maintenance in wartime the valanced skirt was removed to allow ready access to the Walschaerts valve gear. The October 1944 *Model Railway News* showed a model so adapted from the pre-war Hornby Dublo locomotive by Mr. S. L. Newman and a modern equivalent can today be purchased from the George Wrenn Company, their model No. W2213 No. 4903 'Peregrine' the last real A4 to be built.

Although announced in December 1947 I conclude that it was not until the late Spring of 1948 that the post-war 'Sir Nigel Gresley' locomotive became available in electric only. She then carried a redbacked name plate and black shaded tender letters as in full size practice, although retained as the pre-war model, the red painted locomotive and tender wheels. As with Mr. Newman's model she now had the open valanced design and, like her cousin, 'Duchess of Atholl', the new full Walschaerts valve gear.

The difference between the pre-war and post-war blue 'Sir Nigel Gresley' tenders lay in the fact that the tender bogie carts were, on the pre-war and immediate post-war livery, in plain bright metal, whereas the later versions were painted black. Also there was a silver Hornby transfer set inside the corridor connec-

tion of the tender on the pre-war models and set underneath the chassis in between the two bogies, on the post-war models.

As with the 0–6–2 Tank locomotive, modifications such as heavier bogie units and screw fixing to the rear pony and different sizes of letter and nameplate transfers all came into being. There were smaller, rounder nameplates and then the EDL1 was stamped underneath the cab roof and then back again to square nameplates with the final versions having black wheels and more likely to be standard 'Silver King' chassis units.

The actual 'Sir Nigel Gresley' locomotive still had a kick in it when on 23rd May 1959 she was booked to haul a special train of eight coaches weighing 275 tons tare. This was to haul the Stephenson Locomotive Society special on its tour of Doncaster Works. Here she was, 22 years old, with well over 1 million miles already under her belt travelling for continuous stretches at well over 100 miles per hour and although there was some discussion as to the precise maximum it was agreed that it lay between 110 and 112 m.p.h. and so a compromise was agreed of 111 m.p.h.

THE 'SILVER KING' LOCOMOTIVE

I was very surprised that they named this first British Rail version of their A4 locomotive announced in

March 1953 as the 'Silver King'. This appeared to have been the least well known of the initial famous four 'Silver Jubilee' locomotives and spent most of her life as a back-up, stationed at Gateshead. She was originally fitted with a corridor tender, although a streamlined non-corridor tender was used from June 1948. Up to November 1963 she had completed 1,571,000 miles. I found it a curious coincidence that the majority of both main line and branchline locomotives seem to have completed mileages of between 1.3 to 1.6 million miles in their working lives.

The EDL11 locomotive and tender was announced as available in the dealers' leaflet 8/253/5 dated 25th February, but the complete train sets would not be ready till April.

Apart from the obvious green British Railways livery, one of the more noticeable modifications to the casting was the raised number plate on the boiler front, which was added, according to the drawing, on 6th August 1952. Indeed I have seen one or two of these new 'Silver King' castings finished but in blue and named 'Sir Nigel Gresley', making them the last of that particular series. The model appeared as all the original British Railways nationalisation green livery in a high gloss finish, although opinions vary as to when the more common matt finish came out. My own guess is towards the end of 1954 on the introduction of the 2–6–4 Tank locomotive.

THE 'MALLARD' LOCOMOTIVE

The next change in design occurred in October 1958, when the 3-rail 'Silver King' locomotive was replaced by the new 'Mallard' locomotive, complete with double chimney and a slot in the smoke box door to take one of the attractive new train headboard labels. The October date is taken from the *Meccano Magazine*, but dealers' leaflet of 23rd June 8/658/5000 announces the new P15 train set with L11 'Mallard' and two D12 coaches as well as the 'Mallard' separately at 65s. available in July. In real life the 'Mallard' was completed in March 1938 and was fitted as new with the double chimney and a streamlined non-corridor tender although it reverted to a corridor tender in March 1948. To the time of withdrawal, on 25th April 1963, she had completed 1,426,000 miles.

I must admit I am surprised that Hornby Dublo

did not go to the trouble in this instance of putting a small transfer on the centre, either side of the boiler casing, to copy the special plaques detailing the achievement of the world record for steam traction, fitted when she went on a routine works visit in March 1948. I am very glad to see today that the new Hornby Railway Company with their own A4 locomotive have corrected this oversight in their 1979 model.

I have seen one or two 'Silver King' locomotives sporting a double chimney obviously using the new casting and this is perfectly fair as the real locomotive was fitted with her own double chimney in June 1957. A coincidence – I wonder?

Only four A4 locomotives had been fitted new with the Kylchap double exhaust system and were always better runners and freer steamers than their single chimney sisters.

The 7 lbs of coal per mile saved by the double exhaust system finally persuaded the District Office to authorise the remaining A4's to be modified. The cost was £200 per loco and was carried out between May 1957 and November 1958. 19 A4 locomotives were at Top Shed in this period.

The 'Mallard' appeared initially with Mazac main driving wheels, the BR totem motif on the tender, coarse handrails and metal couplings, tender, leading bogie and trailing pony wheels. Later issues had fine handrails, nickel plated driving wheels, plastic tender, bogie and truck wheels and a plastic coupling.

THE 'GOLDEN FLEECE' LOCOMOTIVE

The 'Golden Fleece' locomotive was built in August 1937 in the LNER green livery of that period and was one of the locomotives used to haul the third and final LNER streamlined high speed train, the West Riding Limited, where indeed she worked for fourteen consecutive weeks on this train in 1939 with only three days break. She was fitted with her double chimney in May 1958 and had completed to the time of withdrawal on 29th December 1962, 1,420,000 miles. Her introduction to Hornby Dublo in December 1959 was in charge of the 'Talisman Express' set.

In her original form 'Golden Fleece' was No. 4495 and used to work the West Riding using a standard four articulated coach set i.e. eight coaches. I must admit it is an ambition of mine to repaint a badly scratched pre-war fully valanced body in the LNER green of the period and then attempt to locate some more articulated coaches to be able to recreate this express in model form.

The West Riding Limited train never had a beaver tail streamline observation coach as it was impractical to reverse the train at Leeds Central Station.

The *Model Railway Constructor* magazine had a very fair constructors review criticism of the new models and in particular in July 1960 they commented on the new 'Golden Fleece' locomotive that it was simply a 2-rail version of the existing 'Silver King'

locomotive and they went on. . . . 'The lining and handrails on the A4 are somewhat overscale as is the front end link coupling. Unfortunately no dummy cylinder detail has been included ahead of the cylinder proper rather spoiling the front view of the locomotive. The omission of the safety valves is equally regrettable since 00 gauge models are usually seen from above. The double chimney and whistle however are well proportioned and the semi-matt finish of the loco and tender is a great improvement on the glossier finish of the Silver King.' They go on complaining that both models sacrificed realism through

having six foot scale driving wheels, when in point of fact they should have been six foot eight inch and continue stating . . . 'It is hard to understand the reason for this feature since there appears to be adequate clearance between the wheels to permit greater accuracy in this respect.' They conclude that they found Hornby Dublo's 2-rail mechanism well nigh faultless and they felt that a little more attention to body detail would make the locomotives satisfactory in every respect.

At the time of the takeover 830 'Golden Fleece' locomotives were sold in 1964, leaving 120 in stock.

Hornby Dublo on a postage stamp!

From the March 1956 Meccano Magazine.

Mr. S. L. Newman's modified LNER Pacific, Model Railway News, October 1944.

A Modified " Dublo " 4-6-2

By S. L. NEWMAN

HEREWITH is a photograph of a model L.N.E.R. Pacific which I have recently finished, and, no doubt, will be of interest to other readers. It illustrates what can be done to modify a standard Hornby "Dublo" locomotive and tender to represent the prototype as now runnnig, i.e. with sidesheets removed and, therefore, exposing the Walschaerts valve-gear; also, the present wartime finish in black and new lettering.

Mr. Newman's modified " Dublo " 4-6-2 engine and tender.

VOL. XLI No. 3   MARCH 1956

MECCANO MAGAZINE

A KING'S CROSS DEPARTURE

Original Meccano drawings of the Housing.

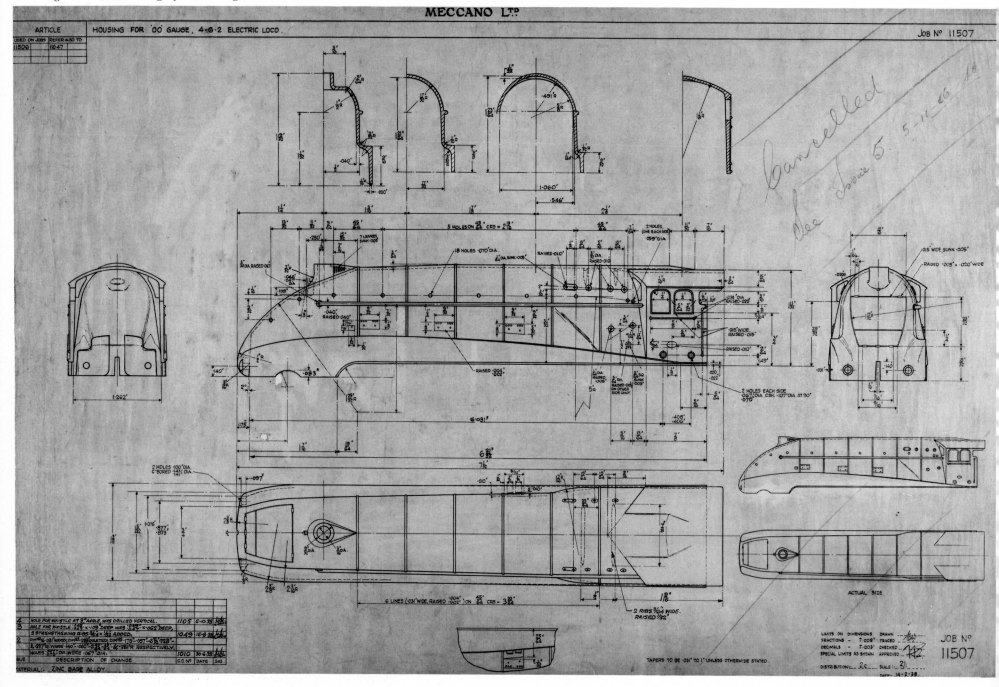

ARTICLE | HOUSING FOR OO GAUGE 4-6-2 ELECTRIC LOCO.

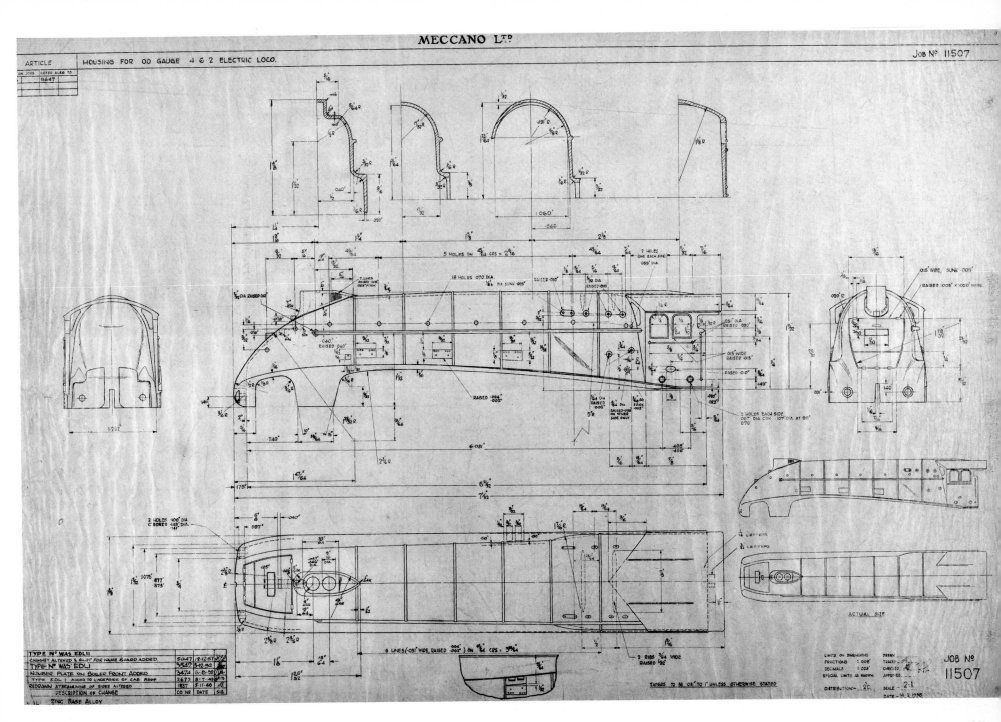

From the February 1938 Meccano Magazine.

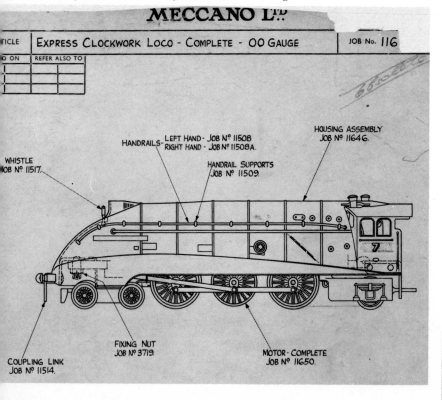

The Express clockwork loco, from a Meccano drawing.

	MECCANO LTD	
ARTICLE	EXPRESS CLOCKWORK LOCO - COMPLETE - OO GAUGE	JOB No. 116

WHISTLE
JOB No 11517

HANDRAILS — LEFT HAND - JOB No 11508
RIGHT HAND - JOB No 11508A.

HANDRAIL SUPPORTS
JOB No 11509.

HOUSING ASSEMBLY
JOB No 11646.

COUPLING LINK
JOB No 11514.

FIXING NUT
JOB No 3719.

MOTOR · COMPLETE
JOB No 11650.

98

Planned additional names – from a Meccano drawing.

MECCANO LTD

ARTICLE ADDITIONAL NAMES & NUMBERS for B.R. (STREAMLINED) LOCO - DUBLO			MEMO No 20760
USED ON	REFER ALSO TO		

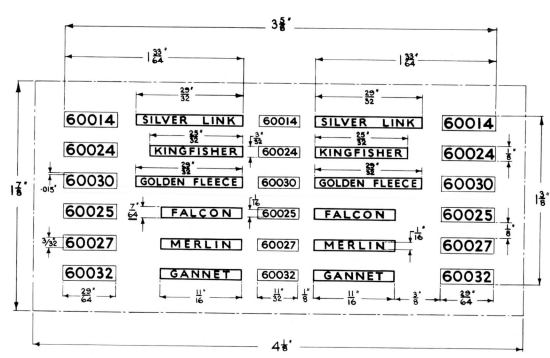

60014 — SILVER LINK — 60014 — SILVER LINK — 60014
60024 — KINGFISHER — 60024 — KINGFISHER — 60024
60030 — GOLDEN FLEECE — 60030 — GOLDEN FLEECE — 60030
60025 — FALCON — 60025 — FALCON — 60025
60027 — MERLIN — 60027 — MERLIN — 60027
60032 — GANNET — 60032 — GANNET — 60032

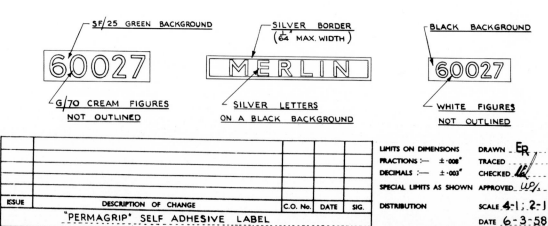

SF/25 GREEN BACKGROUND
G/70 CREAM FIGURES
NOT OUTLINED

SILVER BORDER
(1/64" MAX. WIDTH)
SILVER LETTERS
ON A BLACK BACKGROUND

BLACK BACKGROUND
WHITE FIGURES
NOT OUTLINED

					LIMITS ON DIMENSIONS	DRAWN ER
					FRACTIONS :— ± ·008"	TRACED
					DECIMALS :— ± ·003"	CHECKED
					SPECIAL LIMITS AS SHOWN	APPROVED
ISSUE	DESCRIPTION OF CHANGE		C.O. No.	DATE	SIG.	DISTRIBUTION	SCALE 4-1; 2-1
	"PERMAGRIP" SELF ADHESIVE LABEL						DATE 6-3-58

THE DUCHESSES
OF THE LONDON MIDLAND
& SCOTTISH REGION

No! Quite categorically the 'Duchess of Atholl' locomotive was not put into production before the commencement of the Second World War in late 1939. That should finally bring out any evidence to the contrary, but this is a very favourite topic of conversation amongst Hornby Dublo collectors and one I have been into at some length. Every single avenue I have followed reached the same conclusion. Oh indeed, the locomotive was planned. It was drawn on 25th January 1939. It is very rare to have a model in production and in the toy shops in less than 12 months and I believe that the model was planned for release by February 1940. I have been lucky to meet many people closely involved with the production of Hornby Dublo trains in the Meccano Factory at Binns Road and not least was Mr. Bob Moy, the Chief Toolmaker, who hand crafted the prototype model in brass and indeed, it is still in existence together with its two prototype LMS coaches and packed in a long red paper covered box not dissimilar in style to the box in which the 0 gauge 'Princess Elizabeth' locomotive was dispatched.

We have referred earlier to the fascinating way the Meccano Company through their *Meccano Magazine* and superb literature created the interest and demand and the whole programme of Summer 1939 was geared to whetting the palate of the enthusiasts with this new locomotive.

The locomotive was, as the 'Sir Nigel Gresley' locomotive, to have a zinc diecast body, with a tinplate tender and the single chimney.

Mr. Moy himself, and other colleagues who were in the Meccano factory at that time (as far as they can remember), confirm that no other preproduction models were released other than this prototype, although for many years there have been interesting rumours of two such models held by a collector in Australia, but they have yet to be revealed.

Having created the demand for this beautiful locomotive, the Meccano Company had a hard task to try and cool down the enthusiasm they had created. In a leaflet with their *1939/1940 Hornby Book of Trains* covering new developments in Dublo (reference 2/1239/20) they state. . . .

'We had planned to produce this year a beautiful Hornby Dublo reproduction of the LMS Princess Coronation Class locomotive "Duchess of Atholl" and indeed it is already very near completion. Unfortunately the war has compelled us to hold production and to turn our machines onto other work. In these uncertain days it is difficult to say when we shall be able to complete this fine production but announcement will be made as soon as possible in the *Meccano Magazine*.'

Naturally all their latest literature showed it as well as a complete price list dated September 1939. On 8th March 1940 Mr. W. H. McCormick the Advertising Manager of the Meccano Company wrote to Mr. S. Harriman at Easington Colliery in Co. Durham stating... 'Dear Sir, In reply to your letter production of the Hornby Dublo "Duchess of Atholl" locomotive has been postponed for the time being. It is hoped, however, that this engine, together with scale LMS corridor coaches will be on the market by October this year!'. In a copy of the dealers' leaflet reference 1/340/5 headed 'Our plans for 1940' the company go on to state . . . 'The outbreak of war prevented us from completing the LMS "Duchess of Atholl" train set. There is a good prospect of our being able to produce it this year however, and our travellers will take orders. We expect to have it ready September next and the price will be announced later in the year.' This was the period of the phoney war and shows how optimism determined that everything would be all right very quickly. Nothing further was heard until an

'Duchess of Atholl' at Carlisle Citadel Station.   Courtesy Eric Treacy.

The prototype.

advertisement again for the 'Duchess of Atholl' with the single chimney was shown on the back page of the January 1942 *Meccano Magazine*.

A March/April 1972 article in an Australian model railway magazine stated that a Mr. Jack Richardson of Traction Publications had visited the Meccano Factory in Liverpool during these troubled years where his attention was drawn to the prototype 'Duchess of Atholl' set. He remarked he had seen one in a toy shop in Liverpool earlier in the day, but the guide had replied that it must have been a Trix model as the set here was the only one assembled at that time

The original Bob Moys' model, circa 1938, used in pre-war artwork.
(See model as it exists today, pages 312 and 313). Photo from Meccano records.

and because of wartime conditions it would not appear until peacetime.

I have come across several references to a small model railway company who produced a mazac body of a Duchess locomotive at this time with the faults in the Hornby Dublo locomotive corrected. Someone suggested to me that Hamblings was the company, but I have never been able to trace this.

Collector Mr. Gordon Monks has in his possession a superb streamlined Hornby Dublo 'Coronation' locomotive, complete with pre-war tender, but this model has a wooden body and mock up tender

and further details will be found in a later chapter on models that might have been.

However, I do wonder if a Mr. Corbett of Burncross Road, Chapeltown, Sheffield, who advertised for a Hornby Dublo Duchess in the December 1944 *Model Railway Constructor* was ever successful?

THE 'DUCHESS OF ATHOLL' LOCOMOTIVE

In December 1947, the immensely successful Hornby Dublo range of model railways was once more released to Hornby enthusiasts, young and old, and the 'Duchess of Atholl' locomotive was available in Spring 1948, sporting a double chimney. The real No. 6234 'Duchess of Abercorn', the last of the 1938 series, was fitted with a double blast pipe and chimney and success was such that all subsequent Duchesses were so fitted, the existing engines modified on their next works visits. No. 6235 'City of Birmingham' was the first to be fitted with a double chimney as standard and indeed, the first to have her streamlined casings removed in 1946 and appear with her smoke deflectors. The real 'Duchess of Atholl' had her double

chimney fitted on 1st June 1940, although it was not until 7th September 1946, that she was equipped with smoke deflectors. This caused the Hornby Dublo engineers in the Meccano Factory a problem and the very first modification they made to their drawing of the 'Duchess of Atholl' was dated 8th January 1945 where it states that the chimney was circular (i.e. single). They hastily amended the tooling and as soon as materials were available, commenced production.

The second modification concerned the strengthening of the front steps which was dated on the drawing 2nd December 1948 and the third interesting modification was dated 23rd June 1949, when the six slots were drawn in the running plate to take the new smoke deflectors.

It must have been exceptionally confusing for the staff at Binns Road as the full size prototype which they tried so faithfully to copy changed so much. They probably attracted the highest criticism amongst young trainspotters and woe betide them if they made a mistake on standard practice as they would be inundated with letters until they were able to correct the fault. The real engine was painted initially in a special livery with gold colour lining instead of golden yellow with a thin vermilion strip each side. She was painted in wartime black livery in August 1945 and the British Railways experimental Oxford Blue with London North Western lining on 25th May 1948.

By now all the Mazac quality control problems had been corrected, but in common with the pre-war

'Sir Nigel Gresley' and 0–6–2 Tank locomotives, all the small items on the model such as the pony trucks etc., were of very fine construction and experience in running had shown that they needed to be made a lot stronger to avoid steps etc., breaking during the rough and tumble of table top operation.

The first production 'Duchess of Atholl' locomotives had a lightweight pony truck and front bogie constrained by a hooked vertical bar in a slot similar to that on 'Sir Nigel Gresley'. There was a large diameter head to the pony pivot bolt. They retained the horseshoe magnet motor and had fine lettering on the tender and large numbers on the smoke box door. The front buffer heads were very fine, so were the front steps and buffer beam. The tender chassis was not riveted, but only held on by two clips. These models became available as sets late in 1948 and locos boxed individually bore the date 6/1948 on their boxes. The body changes, mentioned earlier, were the stronger buffer heads and front steps and the tender chassis, whilst still not riveted, had a crimping between the wheel centres for increased strength. The letters EDL2 were cast on the underside of the cab roof and the drawing puts this date at 8th July 1949. It was at this period that the new Alinco magnet motor came into production and the heavier rear pony and front bogie, this time without the vertical bar. They seem to have done a lot of messing around with the size etc., of the nameplate pad and for some reason there was a raised rectangular pad on the offside of the boiler whereas the

earlier models had had a similar recess. I have never been able to find out what this was for. Numerous transfer changes, both to the LMS letters on the tender and on the numbers on the cabside now occurred as well as thicker and finer letters for the nameplate itself. One particular batch of models came out with an almost yellow lettering and maroon surround, instead of the standard silver lettering on black surround. However, on page 109 a copy of the original body housing drawing is illustrated.

In May 1948 the original locomotive was equipped with the experimental blue livery and it was understandable that in 1949 the Meccano Company should consider altering the colour of their locomotive and indeed one prototype was painted. Mr. Peter Randall on one of his visits to the Meccano Company, reported in 1972 that such a model was finished in blue as an experiment and that it once occupied a shelf in someone's office, but no one knows what has become of it. Another standard indentification of the early Atholl tenders was that the wheels were fully spoked whereas again for increased strength, the later 'Duchess of Montrose' tender wheels were filled in at the back, i.e. webbed. One of the last modifications was the addition of sandboxes to the running plate.

The success and accuracy of the model was legendary, but there were some mistakes, not the least being the fact that the wheels on the chassis do not line up with the wheel arches!

The original Hornby Dublo 'Duchess of Atholl' modified by S. C. Pritchard to bring it into line with the requirements of the scale enthusiast. Modifications included fine hand rails, re-wheeling throughout, engraved name plates, a tin roof rest by having a section added to the original and the roof extended forward to include the safety valves, close coupling between tender and locomotive.

Courtesy Mr. S. C. Pritchard of Peco.

The 'Duchess of Atholl' as supplied with smoke deflectors.

← *The 'Princess' Coronation Class Locomotives, with the rare Canadian Pacific Loco.*

Mr. S. C. Pritchard of the Peco Company made several visits to Meccano in the mid-1940s with his new coupling design and naturally he was very taken with the Duchess. He did produce a model to bring it into line with the requirements of the scale model railway enthusiasts and as we have already mentioned there was a big gap in this particular era between scale and toy enthusiasts. He wanted permission from Meccano to undertake alteration to 100 locomotives and the modifications he had in mind were to totally rewheel throughout with scale wheels, fit engraved nameplates, new handrails on either side of the boiler, a new tin roof rest by having a section added to the original and the roof extended forward to include the safety valves and finally close coupling between the locomotive and the tender. Apart from the wheels not being aligned, as we have already mentioned, perhaps the only major design fault was on the cab roof itself, but this was eventually corrected with the appearance of the new 'City of London' locomotive.

THE 'DUCHESS OF MONTROSE'

In November 1951 British Railways standardised on the new green livery and the 'Duchess of Montrose' locomotive was the first of the class to be so painted. These locomotives had all been running since the 1945/46 period with smoke deflectors and then, with all systems go, they introduced their new standard British Railways livery locomotives in a high gloss paint finish in February 1953, complete with the new smoke deflectors.

As with the 'Silver King' the EDL12 'Duchess' loco was ready in late February, complete with its D12 coaches according to dealers' leaflet 8/253/5.

However, I have seen several 'Duchess of Atholl' locomotives which appeared in their full maroon livery with what we call 'Duchess of Montrose' body, i.e. complete with smoke deflectors and this remains the only locomotive livery *never* publicised or advertised by the Meccano Company. One friend in the early 1950s sent his much used and battered 'Duchess of Atholl' locomotive back to Meccano for service and repair only to have it returned to him with a brand new maroon 'Duchess of Atholl' body with smoke deflectors and a most beautiful locomotive it looks.

Extract from Meccano Dealers' leaflet early 1940.

Although electrically-operated points and signals, large radius track, and isolating rails and switches were added to the Hornby-Dublo system very late last season, they helped considerably to strengthen this line and to increase sales. We have great faith in the Hornby-Dublo system. We believe it to be the most satisfactory and efficient Miniature Railway system ever introduced, and we are confident that if our dealers will demonstrate it to their customers, and encourage its sale, it will prove to be a valuable, permanent and profitable side to their business.

The outbreak of war prevented us from completing the L.M.S. **"Duchess of Atholl"** passenger train set. There is a good prospect of our being able to produce it this year, however, and our travellers will take orders. We expect to have it ready about September next, and the price will be announced later in the year.

Tragically the records of the quantity of 'Duchess of Montrose' locomotives sold have been lost, but my own personal estimate of the 'Duchess of Atholl' and 'Duchess of Montrose' models would be approximately 150,000.

In common with the other nationalisation liveries, the high gloss finish was changed for a matt finish and the model became perhaps the most common of the whole range. However, this should not detract from what is truly a magnificent souvenir of the beauty of the British steam locomotive at the end of its era. The last production run in 1958/9 of 'Montroses' appeared with nickel plated main driving wheels and black nylon bogie, pony and tender wheels. The later models had 'L12' cast on the underside of the cab roof as opposed to the earlier EDL12.

From the February 1939 Meccano Magazine.

The 'Duchess of Montrose' – from original artwork.

The 'City of Liverpool' – from original artwork. Note smokebox number mistake which should be 46247.

Extract from October 1961 Meccano Magazine.

A brilliant hill-climbing feat on the extremely difficult Carlisle main line with a special 10-coach, 350-ton train that had stopped at Hellifield, was the steady maintenance of nearly 60 m.p.h. right up the 15 miles at 1 in 100 from Settle to Blea Moor Tunnel by Princess Coronation 4–6–2, No. 46247, *City of Liverpool*. These big engines are seldom seen on that route, the occasion in question being by special arrangement for a railway enthusiasts' tour.

THE 'CITY OF LONDON'

The December 1959 *Meccano Magazine* announced the introduction of the new 'City of London' locomotive No. 46245 and the 'Caledonian' train set. It was a totally new casting with the cut away section in front of the framing in front of the smoke box and at long last correcting the cab roof and safety valves. I do not know why they went to a moulded form of tender. They record such items in their publicity as a well trimmed load of coal, the division plates and tank filler vents and pickup dome and, on the rear of the tender, lamp brackets etc.

Not only was the model an entirely new casting, but also an entirely new 2-rail motor and the Meccano Company had to point out that it was not possible to fit this motor into the standard 'Duchess of Montrose' body. The first issues had a metal tender coupling and the totem motifs both faced forwards.

The 'City of London's' introduction was not without fault – one of the first production samples on a test track in Binns Road inexplicably hurled itself off the rails at the first electric point it passed. The front steps by the smoke box had been produced to scale length – and fouled the casing of the point's solenoid. A hasty modification to the tool was made!

The 'City of London' locomotive in real life was the first of its class to be turned out in the wartime black livery on 26th June 1943, but more important she was the first of her class to be painted in the new British Railways standard red on 28th December 1957. On 20th July 1943 she was named by the Lord Mayor of London and in 1964 was the last of her class to work into a London terminus on a Crewe to Paddington enthusiasts' special. It is apt that she should be chosen to head the new Caledonian train, as in real life the 'Duchess of Montrose', still in green livery, had this honour and again strange that the May 1959 *Meccano Magazine* should show the next number down in her class 46244 'King George VI' hauling this new express. I leave it to the Secretary of the Hornby Railway Company who gives an official write-up in the March 1960 *Meccano Magazine* on this wonderful new locomotive. The April 1958 *Model Railway News* carried a note to the effect that the February issue of the Journal of the Stephenson Locomotive Society had announced that this locomotive was now painted in the old LMSR red livery. They said that this was probably to match up better with the new rolling stock, but it was a pointer to the fact that in spite of the many various styles that were adapted and discarded since 1948, nothing equalled, let alone surpassed, the standard liveries of the former 'Four Main Lines'.

580 'London's' were sold in 1964 leaving only 100 in stock.

THE 'CITY OF LIVERPOOL'

The 'Duchess of Montrose' locomotive continued to be the main LMR source of power in 3-rail for another few years and it was not until November 1961 that the 'City of Liverpool' No. 46247 was introduced by Hornby Dublo, and with the Meccano tradition in Liverpool it was a very pleasing choice. The model was in every way identical to the new castings etc. we have discussed on the 'City of London'.

The Meccano Company had a knack of introducing little articles etc., on their new models just a month or two before their official release announcement and only the month previously they had a report on a brilliant hill-climbing feat by the real locomotive over the extremely difficult Carlisle main line, with a special 10 coach, 350 ton train that had stopped at Hellifield. This was at the steady maintenance of nearly 60 m.p.h. right up the 15 miles at 1:100 from Settle to Blea Moor tunnel although it stated that these big engines were seldom seen on that route. They were created for the London–Glasgow expresses and were widely accepted as Stanier's masterpiece.

And so concludes the chapter on what for all my youth were my favourite locomotives. It is almost incredible the way both the commencement of the Hornby Dublo range with the highlight of British steam design in the late 1930s seemed to close with the decline of steam in the mid-1960s. Indeed anyone operating one of the Hornby Dublo Duchess models on a layout should ensure that there is a diagonal yellow stripe on the cabside running from top left to bottom right, which was applied to the 19 members of the class still in service on 1st September 1964 which were prohibited south of Crewe due to the height restrictions because of the new electrification construction.

THE 'CANADIAN PACIFIC' LOCOMOTIVE

Then as now the need to export was paramount for British industry immediately after the Second World War and frequent advertisements were put out by Meccano apologising for the shortage of materials and spare parts. One could not even buy extra rails let alone items of rolling stock. In 1952 the Meccano Company must have wondered what to do with the hundreds of 'Duchess' castings they still had on their hands. They were out of date with the new requirements for smoke deflectors and Hornby planners came up with the idea that they could adapt this model

for the Canadian market. This was exactly what they did and all the drawings were prepared in the late Spring and early Summer of 1952. This was not a new venture by any means as, as long ago as 1930, they had produced a standard 3C 0 gauge Hornby 4-4-2 locomotive as a 'Canadian Pacific' with pullman coaches in similar livery. (I would love to own one of these sets.) It was hard to explain why, with the drawings done at this time, it was not until September 1957 that the first announcement appeared that there were to be these Canadian train sets although it was not until February 1958 that the Canadian issue of the *Meccano Magazine* carried such an announcement. The

locomotive exists with No. 1215 on the smokebox door and a variation has the number above the door.

It was in many ways an attractive model and is highly sought after today complete with a dummy headlight and diecast cowcatcher unit riveted to the front buffer beam of the existing locomotive. The biggest mistake however, was to use the standard six wheel 'Duchess of Atholl' tender. Young boys were as keen in Canada as in any other industrial country that their models should be exact replicas of the real thing and any Canadian boy could tell you with scorn that none of their locomotives had six wheel tenders. If only they had used the eight wheel A4 locomotive

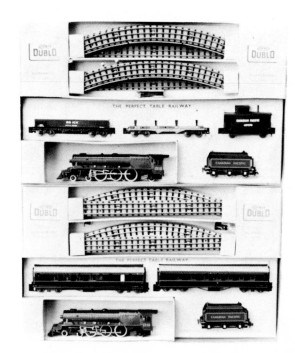
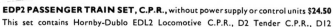

The only advertisement – a single sheet leaflet.

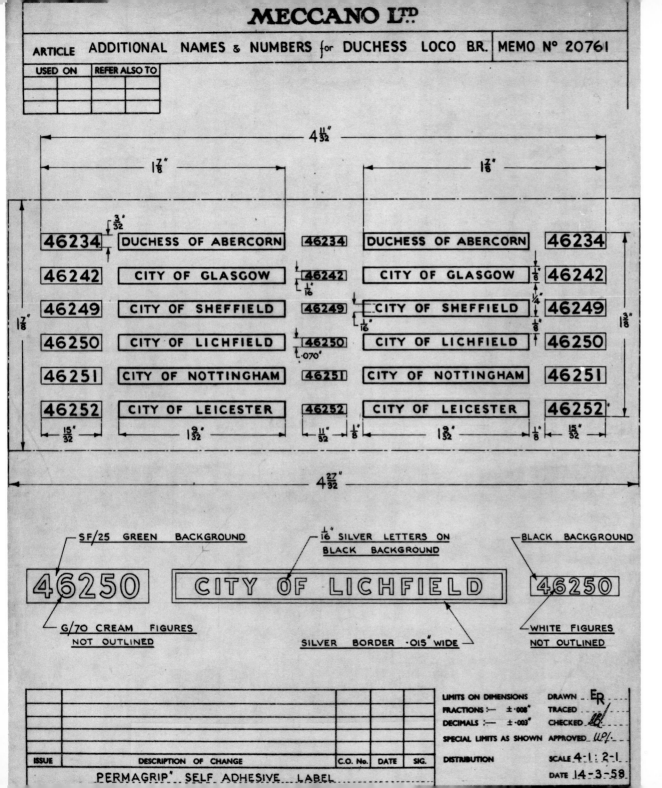

Planned additional names – from a Meccano drawing.

tender I think that the sales would have told a completely different story. One of my friends who was in the Meccano Company at that time wrote to me stating . . . 'The more I think about the ludicrous venture the more amazed I am at the optimism of the sales people. A full range of true to type Canadian locomotives and rolling stock was intended to follow up and I did all the research on them but the scheme was dropped. It was not until Triang took over that a wholehearted venture into the Canadian market was launched and with success!

The Triang Company did have considerable success with their own special models for the Canadian market and catalogues for a number of years. I have been unable to find out how many Dublo CPR locomotives were actually produced, but I imagine it would be in hundreds rather than thousands. The renowned Mr. John Markham, the well-known collector, wrote to me on 29th March 1974, confirming that these Hornby Dublo 'Canadian Pacific' locomotives were even scarce over in Canada and finished by saying – 'never made a proper Canadian tender!'

But, in a book of job numbers I have just received from Binns Road, 677 and 678 refer to 2- and 3-rail CNR locos – Canadian National Railways perhaps. It is dated 18/7/60. Who knows?

The passenger set was advertised initially with the standard D12 blood and custard livery coaches. The freight set was supplied with the English bogie brick wagon and the bogie bolster wagon, but there was one final alteration and that was to the brake van where the standard LMR unit was fitted with a tall chimney and cupola and called correctly a 'caboose' and finished in matt black. It certainly made a bit of a mess on my layout when I forgot about this extension to the roof and allowed a train which does look very effective with a quantity of bogie bolsters behind with a dummy timber load – to proceed with speed into a tunnel when it came to an all too sudden juddering stop.

I think the whole reason for the market failure of this basically good idea was purely using the wrong tender. They did make overtures to the Canadian market later by supplying special Bo-Bo diesel locomotives without buffers and with a non-powered unit to run double headed freight trains after Canadian practice. The only other body outline specially produced for an export market was the final 0–4–0 'Starter Set' locomotive with a light blue body and the outline of Australia printed on the tank sides with the words 'Commonwealth', but this was not until 1964.

I have heard rumours of many other models produced such as a maroon A4 locomotive or a 2–8–0 with a cowcatcher for the South African market, but none that have come physically to light.

Meccano Magazine cover from May 1959.

B.R. Photo.

MECCANO L^TD

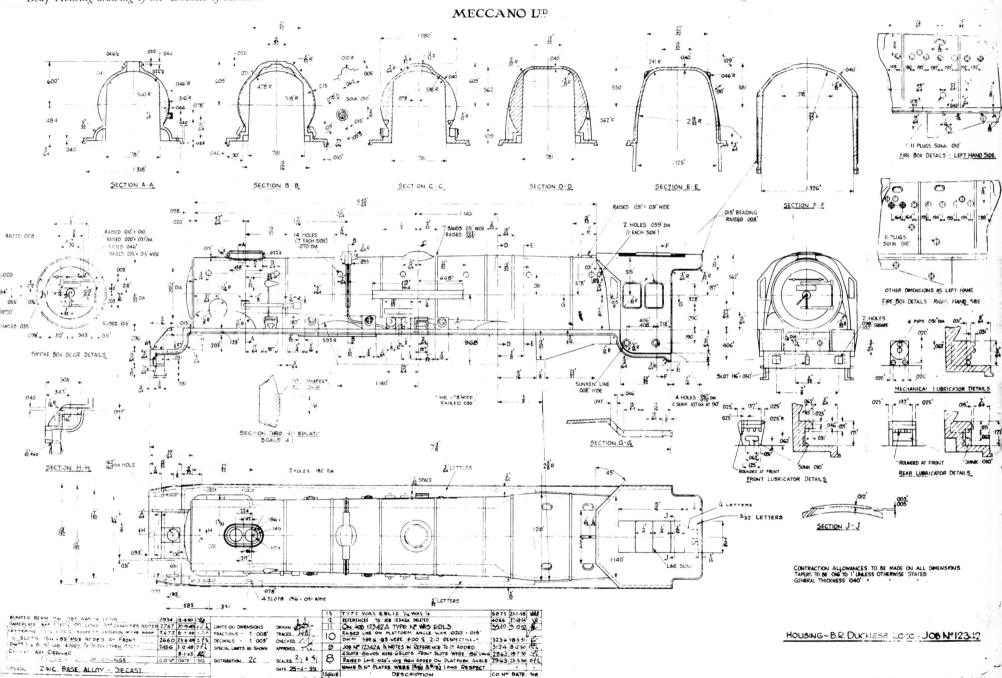

SECTION A·A

SECTION B·B

SECTION C·C

SECTION D·D

SECTION E·E

SECTION F·F

FIRE BOX DETAILS - LEFT HAND SIDE

SMOKE BOX DOOR DETAILS

OTHER DIMENSIONS AS LEFT HAND FIRE BOX DETAILS RIGHT HAND SIDE

SECTION THROUGH NAMEPLATE SCALE 4

SECTION G·G

MECHANICAL LUBRICATOR DETAILS

FRONT LUBRICATOR DETAILS

REAR LUBRICATOR DETAILS

SECTION H·H

SECTION J·J

CONTRACTION ALLOWANCES TO BE MADE ON ALL DIMENSIONS TAPERS TO BE ·016 TO 1" UNLESS OTHERWISE STATED GENERAL THICKNESS ·040"

HOUSING ~ B.R. DUCHESS LOCO · JOB N° 12342

MATERIAL ZINC BASE ALLOY - DIECAST.

THE 2–6–4 TANK LOCOMOTIVE

The nationalisation of British Railways in 1948 inaugurated the standardisation of designs for the new range of locomotives. A total of 54 Class 4 2–6–4 Tank locomotives were included in the 1951 programme, 44 of which were to be built at Brighton and 10 at Derby and they were to be allocated as follows: 21 to the Scottish Region, 10 to the Southern Region, 3 to the East and Northeast Region and 20 to the London Midland Region. The Drawing Office at Brighton carried out the designs concurrently with the Class 4 4–6–0 locomotives. The tank engine was intended for short distance working and to have almost universal availability over main and secondary lines throughout Great Britain.

Mr. R. W. G. Bryant made a plea to the model railway manufacturers in the April 1952 issue of the *Railway Modeller* stating that the trade was already well catered for by main line express locomotives and he would rather see a smaller and more universal locomotive and indeed he mentioned a Class 4 2–6–4 Tank as being highly desirable. The marketing and engineering departments took note of all letters and articles in the model press and indeed were in correspondence with thousands of boys all over the world and were then able to gauge quite closely the requirements of the market. The choice of the 2–6–4 Tank was logical and brilliant. They commenced their drawing on 25th February 1953.

They had their prototype on show at the Toy Fair in January 1954 with write-ups in the model trade press three months later. The model itself was avail-

able in the shops in November 1954 to be followed two months later by the tin printed suburban coaches. Meccano wrote in a dealers leaflet in August 1954 8/854/550 that they had hoped to produce the new locomotive before, but . . . 'this had not been possible because of the extremely heavy manufacturing programme necessitated by the demand for our products generally'. It was the very first production model of a BR standard locomotive and indeed the first post-war addition to the Hornby Dublo loco stud and naturally merited great interest. The *Railway Modeller* test report in December 1954 called it a magnificent production of a scale model that had been adapted to proprietary standards. The initial production batch was 100,000 and as I recorded earlier, Meccano were exceptionally proud that only six came back under guarantee with serious defects.

Many people had thought that the first model would be of the 'Britannia' which made her first appearance on 30th January 1951, but with a surfeit of 4–6–2 passenger locomotives and these tank locomotives spread throughout the country – the choice of the 2–6–4 class was all the more logical.

2-rail was already the system of the future, and within three months the *Model Railway News* in their February 1955 issue published a long article on how to convert the new tank locomotive for 2-rail operation.

Many people were confused by the novel arrangement of the magnetic shunt adjustment which was reached by adjusting the screw through a hole at the rear of the coal bunker. The Hornby Company general information book records 'that the magnetic shunt was provided for the purpose of varying within prescribed limits the flux available across the field pole tips. It will be fairly obvious that when the shunt is fully engaged a portion of the field flux is bypassed thus weakening the field strength in the air gaps between the armature and the field poles. Thus a very fine adjustment is provided which will enable the field and the armature fluxes to be balanced at starting i.e. when the armature torque is lowest to give a smooth start. The secondary effect is that with weakened field the armature current is increased, which increases the voltage drop across the armature and the motor runs slower. Withdrawing the shunt from the magnet of course has the opposite effect and the motor runs faster for a given voltage. Normally the strength of the field flux due to the magnet is more than actually

The prototype in Cathcart engine siding at Glasgow Central from Meccano records.

The prototype extract from the October 1951 Model Railway News.

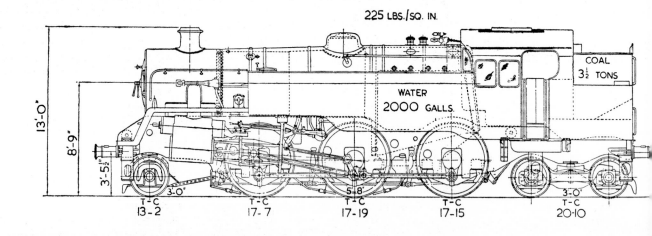

required to produce optimum useful power (the point where any increase in power is wasted due to the limit of track adhesion). The shunt does not therefore greatly affect top speeds of the locomotive.'

I was informed that the above system was necessary with the controllers then available, but within a few years the new range of Hornby Dublo controllers made such an adjustment unnecessary. At a product meeting on 29th December 1961 it was decided to delete the magnetic shunt unit to save on production costs, but it was not put into effect until 1963, due to the high stock position. Indeed the article stating that this was to be discontinued appeared in the February 1963 *Meccano Magazine*. That the hole at the rear end of the bunker was to be deleted appeared on the drawing on 19th February 1962, but again such was the high stock position that to my knowledge no Hornby Dublo produced model ever appeared without a hole in the back of the bunker.

The 2-rail version No. 80033 did not appear until November 1959, although it did have an interesting modification necessitated by having production problems with the original casting. They were principally concerned with the separate cast chimney unit (there had been some criticism of the original chimney) and indeed this relatively small item caused many of the production problems previously referred to. This chimney was drawn on 4th November 1957 although I still find it strange that there was such a long gap in producing the renewed 3-rail version, No. 80059, which did not appear until September 1961. This particular model was not produced in any great quantities, which naturally makes it a rare and highly desirable locomotive for the collector.

The 2-rail version had black plastic pony and bogie wheels and bush insulated driving wheels crank pins and valve gear on one side.

Perhaps one of the most interesting methods of dating was the fact that the hook of the coupling was extended top and bottom. The models produced prior to the introduction of 80054 suffered when running over bent rails where the young enthusiast had forced them together or the fact that the rails were on a carpet, or an uneven surface and many expresses and goods trains had frequent slip effects as they parted from their load on route. 80054 was the first to have this modified coupling.

In retrospect one thing which surprises me was the incredible size of these locomotives. I was at the Dart Valley at Buckfastleigh, Devon last year, standing beside locomotive 80064 which has been totally rebuilt by enthusiasts, and at rail level, it is a massive locomotive indeed. When we stand on platforms we are inclined to forget the size of these locomotives.

The 2–6–4 Tank locomotive was yet another winner for the Hornby Dublo stable. 850 of 80033 being sold in 1964 leaving 300 in stock.

The 80033 always worked on the Southern

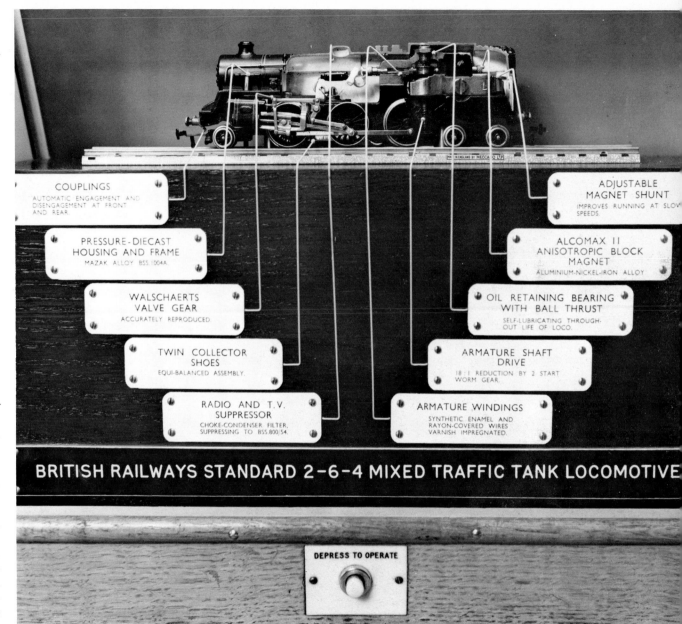

The cutaway display model.

Region, in fact, the class was the main power on the Oxted line, at peak hours hauling 8 or 9 coaches out of Victoria and London Bridge. 80054 was stationed in Scotland and 80059 was on the Somerset and Dorset Railway in 1965.

114

A MODEL RAILWAY
AT THE PACKAGING EXHIBITION

An exhibit which attracted a lot of attention at the recent Packaging Exhibition at Olympia was the model railway on the stand of the Flexile Metal Co., Ltd., collapsible tube manufacturers.

The layout 12 ft. × 6 ft. was a double oval with the far side rising 1 in 60 to reach the higher level and then falling 1 in 50 to pass under the high level, and back to the " Flexile factory " at the low level .

As will be seen from the photograph, the train appears out of the " Flexile factory," enters the tunnel on the opposite side, reappears from the tunnel behind " Flexile factory " and disappears into " Tube User's factory."

The locos were two Hornby Dublo 2-6-4 Tanks and the train consisted of three bogie bolster wagons each carrying one tube and two open flat trucks carrying three small tubes each, together with a goods brake, all Hornby Dublo.

The locos were used alternately and during the eleven days of the Exhibition covered approximately 255,000 feet between them, i.e., about twenty-four miles for each loco.

They were oiled before each day's run and gave no trouble, as long as the track was kept clean, particularly the curves and 1 in 60 rising gradient.

The model was designed and built by Messrs R. Wills of Coulsdon, Surrey, using Wrenn track. (Photo: Fox Photos. Ltd.)

Extract from the April 1955 Model Railway Constructor.

Running back to the shed. Meccano photograph.

THE GREAT WESTERN RAILWAY 'CASTLE' CLASS LOCOMOTIVES

As is evident, for almost twenty years there was a very wide gulf between the toy model railway used by children and the scale railway used by the enthusiast. Notwithstanding it has been shown that the scratch builder would be hard put to equal the preceding models such as the 'Sir Nigel Gresley' locomotive or the LMS Pacifics. With the introduction of the 'Bristol Castle' locomotive in October 1957 the gap closed even further between the toy and the scale model.

The 'Castle' was the finest mass-produced model railway locomotive to be manufactured of a British outline locomotive, and it was to take a further 20 years before its supremacy was challenged.

The surprise element was gone insomuch that it had been leaked to awaiting enthusiasts in the April 1957 *Railway Modeller* in their article 'Seen at the Brighton Toy Fair the previous January'. It comments . . . 'It is nice to see that the Castle has been chosen rather than the more obvious "King", for undoubtedly the "Castle" is more suitable for general purpose

work than the larger locomotive which is restricted to the principal main lines. Moreover as the "Castle's" wheelbase is identical to the "Hall", "Grange", "Star" and "Saint" classes many modifications seem possible for the enthusiast.'

I have never seen such universal acclaim at the introduction of a model railway locomotive than that that came with this beautiful model. It heralded the prime years of the Hornby Dublo range which commenced in 1957 with this model and closed some four years later with 2-rail, the super detail range of coaches and wagons and the Ringfield motor.

The Hornby Dublo design staff in Binns Road took a gamble that the railway enthusiasts would quickly adapt to the new diesel outline locomotives, but for the time being it was not to be – and so, as in real life, the temporary decline of rail and the decline of steam in particular in the early 1960s was reflected in the decline in the popularity of model railways generally. In addition the influence of new motorways and air travel coupled with the increased market share of the Triang Company, (the introduction of TT model railways which were claimed at the time to do to 00 scale what 00 scale had done to 0 gauge before the Second World War) all contributed to the specific decline of Hornby Dublo.

The *Model Railway Constructor* magazine in their superb 'Constructors Review' article commented . . . 'Quite frankly when we heard that Hornby Dublo were producing a Castle class locomotive we little thought that the finished item would be so excellent. Not only have they produced a superlative locomotive at a most modest price but they now bid fair to enter the scale model as well as the toy market.' They go on to praise the totally new design of motor and the smooth performance and indeed power perfectly capable of hauling ten bogie coaches without any slip. The *Model Railway News* of December 1957 'talking shop' article had probably the only noticeable criticism to quote . . . 'the flangeless wheels on the tender centre axle are horrible and are the only toylike touch to be found on the whole model, but a feature that can be easily remedied.'

Indeed so successful had the 'Castle' class locomotive been in real life in its performance, that the old London Midland and Scottish Railway back in 1926 tried to order 50 improved 'Castles' from Swindon, following trials with No. 5000 'Launceston Castle', but their request was refused. So successful too was the Hornby Dublo model and so accurate in its proportions that none other than Bassett-Lowke Limited, *the* kings of the model railway scene, even produced their own conversion of this basic model – exactly what Mr. Pritchard of Peco had wanted to do with the original 'Duchess of Atholl' locomotive ten years earlier.

It is a fitting tribute to this famous class of locomotive that, on 27th November 1965, 7029 the famous 'Clun Castle' locomotive, headed the last steam train to depart from the Great Western Padding-ton terminal in London. I played truant from work to stand on the platform and watch this last departure, only to find my picture in the national newspapers the next morning!

7013 'BRISTOL CASTLE' LOCOMOTIVE

In February 1952, the Western Region 'Royal' engine 4082 'Windsor Castle' was in Swindon Works undergoing overhaul when King George VI died. A much publicised photograph in April 1924 recalls not only His Majesty King George V and Queen Mary, but also Viscount Churchill, Chairman of the GWR, C. B. Collett, Chief Mechanical Engineer, Driver E. Rowe, Sir Felix Pole, General Manager GWR and Fireman A. Cooke, all squeezed onto the footplate of this famous locomotive.

The name, number and commemorative plates were fitted to 7013 'Bristol Castle' just ex works and 4082 received the plates ex 7013. This renaming was never rectified and I believe was not even admitted by the Western Region authorities. 'Windsor Castle' had not only been driven by His Majesty King George V, but had also hauled his funeral train to Windsor in 1936.

In a single page leaflet, reference 16/1057/100 M, covering the new 'Bristolian' Hornby Dublo passenger train, complete with Western Region tinplate coaches (to be covered in a later chapter) the reverse side shows a fine picture of the real prototype at speed between Paddington (London) and Temple Meads (Bristol), at Hullavington, in fact.

7032 'DENBIGH CASTLE'

Many of the famous toyshops, such as Eames of Reading, immediately produced 2-rail versions of the 'Bristol Castle' locomotives and it was not until two years

Railway Notes
By R. A. H. Weight

The Royal Funeral Trains

British Railways played their part fittingly when conveying the mortal remains of His late Majesty, King George VI, also members of the Royal Family from Sandringham to London, then a few days later from London to Windsor in February last.

The former L.N.E.R. Royal Train, still finished in varnished teak, was used for both journeys, the formation including a saloon fitted as a funeral car and painted black with white roof.

From Wolferton station in Norfolk, which has quite a distinctive style of architecture and carved timbering, the locomotive for the short journey along the Hunstanton branch to King's Lynn Junction, where reversal is necessary, was the "B2" 4-6-0 "Ford Castle." Thenceforward for the non-stop run to King's Cross, via Cambridge and Hitchin, the pioneer standard 4-6-2, No. 70000, "Britannia" was in charge. I understand that "B17" 4-6-0 No. 61619, "Welbeck Abbey" was stand-by engine at Cambridge.

After the impressive procession through London and following several special trains conveying mourners and guests from many parts of the world, the Funeral Train was hauled by No. 4082, "Windsor Castle," as depicted in our illustration. This is actually one of the modern "Castles" No. 7013, formerly "Bristol Castle," that has assumed the title and number plates, etc., of the famous 1924-built 4-6-0 which hauled the Funeral Train on the occasion of the passing of H.M. King George V in 1936, because the older engine was in Swindon Works during February last. Royal coats-of-arms on purple facings were carried on each side of the smoke-box during the journey to Windsor; the uppermost of the four headlamps was a special one surmounted by a Royal Crown.

The Royal Funeral Train of His late Majesty King George VI, en route for Windsor. Photograph by R. E. Vincent.

Extract from the May 1952 Meccano Magazine.

Building a 'Castle' locomotive – from Meccano records:

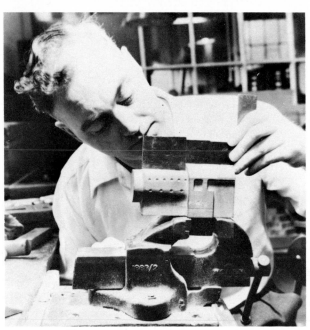

1. Mr. W. Ward Platt, chief draughtsman discusses a point with Mr. Vernon Rogers.

2. Mr. Ronald Low, pattern maker.

3. Mr. Brian Howard inspects the finished castings.

4. Mrs. Pat McMarton adds the paint.

5. Mr. Norman Jones and Olive check the motor assembly.

6. Mr. Bob Moy, Manager of the Display Department with one of his superb models.

The renowned 'Castle' Class Locomotives.→

119

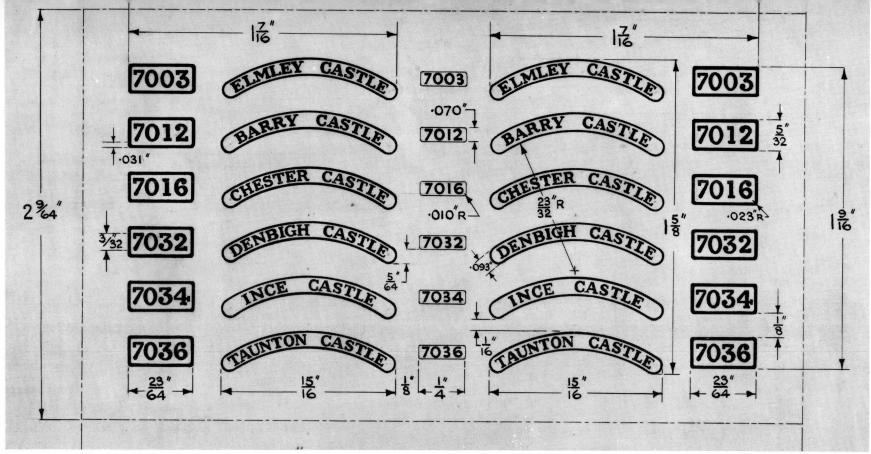

Planned additional names – from a Meccano drawing.

OUTSTANDING NEW HORNBY-DUBLO LOCO

Outstanding was the word – from the October 1957 Railway Modeller.

later, in October 1959, that the Hornby Dublo version 7032 'Denbigh Castle' appeared. Surprisingly they had still not corrected the centre tender wheels which remained flangeless perhaps due to derailing problems on points. Critics also commented that they were surprised that Meccano had never fitted the auto couplings to the front of their express engines as 'Castles' were known to haul coaches, tender first – did they? I suppose there must have been occasions when this practice has been adopted, but rarely and I must admit I agree with Hornby Dublo: heavy front couplings on their mainline expresses were not necessary.

Two months later, on 15th December 1959, the chassis of the Hornby Dublo 'Castle' Class locomotive was redrawn to accommodate the new 5/8" Ringfield motor.

4075 'CARDIFF CASTLE'

The new Ringfield motor was announced in the October 1960 *Meccano Magazine* and one can be forgiven for becoming accustomed to the claim that this *too* heralded the finest advance in model locomotive power plant design. Among the advantages, the advertisement quotes . . . '1. High torque particularly at low speeds with complete freedom from magnetic locking. 2. Flat speed/load curve providing equivalent speed control whether lightly or heavily loaded. 3. Protected motor commutator, armature and brush gear completely shrouded to keep out dirt and fluff. 4. Motor housed in solid diecast frame giving great rigidity of construction and ensuring quiet running with minimum of vibration. 5. Fully suppressed.'

To launch this new design, as we have mentioned in the earlier section, the famous actor Mr. Donald Sinden and his son, together with Engine Driver John

Meccano publicity photograph of 'Denbigh Castle'.

Gale of Acton, London (driver of the famous 'Red Dragon' express in real life) checked a magnificent endurance run where the locomotive did in fact make 46,000 circuits totalling 153 actual miles in four days. This feat exceeded the actual distance between London (Paddington) and Cardiff which is just over 145 miles. The new 2-rail Hornby Dublo locomotive, with the Ringfield motor, was 'Cardiff Castle' and headed the new passenger train set 2021 'The Red Dragon' at this stage complete with tinplate coaches. Much mileage was taken from the ensuing publicity and the feat even appeared in the *Guinness Book of Records* in 1967.

Mr. and Mrs. T. J. Perry of 'Perrys', a well-known Birmingham toy shop went one better in having a standard production model running round in their display window, hauling twenty items of rolling stock, which completed 570 statute miles and apart from occasional brush changes and oiling required no other maintenance. This record of 153 actual miles was not bettered until October 1973 by another Hornby engine (Hornby Railways) again with a tender drive Ringfield motor hauling six bogie coaches 273 miles.

600 'Cardiff Castles' were sold in 1964, and 225 remained in stock.

In fact, 'Cardiff Castle' nearly did not arrive at all. Collector Chris Willis reminded me of the fact that the real 'Cardiff Castle' was withdrawn on 24th March 1962, after 38 years of continuous service totalling 1,807,802 miles.

The drawing of the colour scheme – No. 21020 sheet 2 mentions the transfer change from memo 21046 to 40265 'Cardiff Castle' just three days after her withdrawal.

5002 'LUDLOW CASTLE'

We had to wait a further 12 months, until December 1961, before the 3-rail version, with Ringfield motor, appeared. However, it was not produced in very large quantities which accounts for its rarity and great popularity amongst collectors and thus its high price.

And so we conclude the four variations of the 'Castle' Class models which, to many, were the peers of the Hornby Dublo range.

Hornby-Dublo 4 mm. scale "Castle" Two-Rail.

Meccano, Ltd.   Price £3 19s. 0d.

The first two-rail Hornby-Dublo main line locomotive to reach us is "Denbigh Castle" which would appear to be identical to the three-rail version except for the method of current collection. The collectors are, of course, on the loco; they were under the tender in the three-rail version and for this reason the tender/loco coupling was semi-permanent, and this has been retained in the present version. Our praise and criticism of the earlier introduction apply to this one too. The mechanism is excellent giving steady and very powerful hauling. The engine starts infallibly at the touch of the controller. The body detail is good, both on the loco and tender; the handrails and slidebar/crosshead assembly are overscale, presumably to cope with juvenile handling. It is a pity that the centre tender wheels have to be flange-less; but Dublo radii are pretty tight. The paintwork and the finish generally is pretty good although the lining is a trifle heavy. We have always been mildly surprised that Meccano have not thought fit to put auto-couplings at the front of their express engines—"Castles" have been known to haul coaches tender-first, after all!

The "Cardiff Castle" locomotive and tender pictured above—a standard production from the assembly lines at the Meccano Factory in Liverpool—recently covered a total of no fewer than 570 statute miles while working on a large window layout at a Hornby dealer's shop in the Midlands. The locomotive hauled a train which often consisted of more than 20 items of rolling stock, yet, apart from occasional brush changes and oiling, it required no special maintenance. This is indeed a fine tribute to the efficiency of the Ring Field Motor which is fitted in this type of locomotive and the "Meccano Magazine" is indebted to the dealers concerned, Mr. and Mrs. T. J. Perry of "The Perrys", Alum Rock Road, Birmingham, for the loan of the locomotive and tender for photographic purposes.

Extract from May 1962 Meccano Magazine.

Extract from Constructor's Review – Model Railway Constructor October 1959.

Original Meccano drawing.

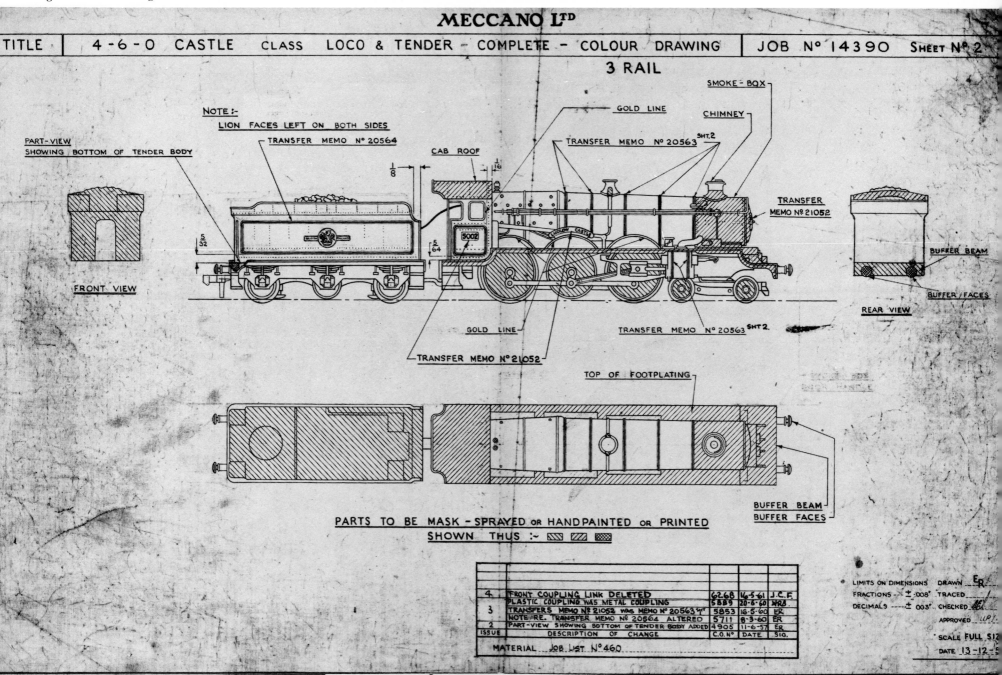

MECCANO LTD

| TITLE | 4-6-0 CASTLE CLASS LOCO & TENDER - COMPLETE - COLOUR DRAWING | JOB Nº 14390 | SHEET Nº 2 |

3 RAIL

PART-VIEW
SHOWING BOTTOM OF TENDER BODY

FRONT VIEW

NOTE :-
LION FACES LEFT ON BOTH SIDES
TRANSFER MEMO Nº 20564

CAB ROOF

SMOKE-BOX
GOLD LINE
CHIMNEY
TRANSFER MEMO Nº 20563 SHT.2

TRANSFER MEMO Nº 21052

BUFFER BEAM

BUFFER FACES

REAR VIEW

GOLD LINE

TRANSFER MEMO Nº 20563 SHT 2.

TRANSFER MEMO Nº 21052

TOP OF FOOTPLATING

BUFFER BEAM
BUFFER FACES

PARTS TO BE MASK-SPRAYED or HANDPAINTED or PRINTED
SHOWN THUS :-

4	FRONT COUPLING LINK DELETED	6268	14-5-61	J.C.F.
	PLASTIC COUPLING WAS METAL COUPLING	5889	20-5-60	WRB
3	TRANSFERS MEMO Nº 21052 WAS MEMO Nº 20563 4"	5853	16-5-60	ER
	NOTE RE. TRANSFER MEMO Nº 20564 ALTERED	5711	8-3-60	ER
2	PART-VIEW SHOWING BOTTOM OF TENDER BODY ADDED	4905	11-6-57	ER
ISSUE	DESCRIPTION OF CHANGE	C.O.Nº	DATE	SIG.
MATERIAL JOB LIST Nº 460				

LIMITS ON DIMENSIONS   DRAWN ER
FRACTIONS -- ± ·008"   TRACED
DECIMALS ---- ± ·003"   CHECKED

APPROVED

SCALE FULL SIZ

DATE 13-12-5

123

THE 2–8–0 8F
FREIGHT LOCOMOTIVE

The March 1958 *Railway Modeller* released the news of a Toy Fair sensation, three months after the first introduction of their 'Bristol Castle' locomotive and with the model railway world still ringing to its praises. They announced the impending release of two further locomotives, not only the new '8F' Freight locomotive, but also the new 1,000 horse power 'Bo-Bo diesel' locomotive and new super detailed rolling stock. The '8F' model was scheduled for delivery in the Autumn announced the August edition of *Railway Modeller* illustrating a press release photograph which even they said could not do this superb model justice. The locomotive choice filled a big gap, in that the famous prototype was in use on all regions of British Railways and indeed, used extensively by the War Department on overseas service. The only criticisms they could find were the over heavy handrails and the wide gap between the loco and tender which was not necessary on the large radius curves. One must remember that these models were designed to run on the standard Hornby Dublo 3-rail track and the fairly tight 15″ radius curves necessitated this gap, but could easily be rectified by the scale modeller with a far larger radius to work on. The *Model Railway Constructor* was quite ecstatic about this new model. They wrote in their August 1958 issue . . . 'We purposely made a guarded statement in our April issue knowing that the production model is often superior to the hand made prototype. We have been proved wise in our patience as the production model is superior, far

G25 LMR 2-8-0 Freight Train set – from original artwork.

Sensation! – from the March 1958 Railway Modeller.

superior, to the one we examined at Brighton. This really is a beautiful model and we have purposely devoted two photographs to it.'

The *Model Railway News* likewise in their August issue wrote . . . 'When Meccano Limited launches a new locomotive it usually arouses a great deal of interest in the model railway world; the Hornby Dublo Stanier 8F 2-8-0 we feel will be no exception. This splendid workmanlike model painted completely black looks very impressive indeed, nicely detailed while at the same time allowing for those few extra refinements to be added by the fastidious members of the hobby.

'The locomotive contains, in addition to the usual robust chassis, a wedge shaped block of lead screwed firmly inside the boiler and consequently giving the model extra adhesion for hauling power far in excess of that required for a train on the average layout. In real practice these locomotives can often be seen on shunting duties, apart from working on heavy long distance goods trains for which they were built and perhaps for this reason the leading axle frame on the model is so designed for the fitting of an automatic couping if desired. It is a very pleasing model, full of character and should prove immensely popular; it has already won our approval.'

The Meccano dealers' leaflet dated 26th August 1958 (1775/858/5000) reported . . . 'The demand for this new locomotive and tender has, however, been so considerable that some unavoidable delay in dealing with current orders . . . must be expected, we regret any inconvenience caused.'

TWO NEW HORNBY-DUBLO LOCOS

Photo, British Railways

A popular prototype, the ex-L.M.S. 8F 2-8-0, forms the first of the new Hornby-Dublo locos this year. The second up-to-the-minute choice will be the Vulcan Foundry BoBo diesel.

SO soon after the introduction of the "Castle" come two more first-class locomotives! Regrettably there is not time for us to publish a photograph of the models, but we show above the prototype of the first of the locos, the popular Stanier 8F 2-8-0. The need for a really heavy goods locomotive has been felt for some considerable time, and what finer prototype than this, for it has been used on all regions of British Railways and was one of the types chosen by the War Department for overseas service. Next comes the first diesel by Meccano. For their superb model they have chosen the Vulcan Foundry 1,000 h.p. BoBo diesel No. D8000, only just introduced on B.R.—they are certainly keeping pace with the Modernization Plan!

Either of these locomotives would be the appropriate motive power to haul a long train of the new range of super-detail wagons, vastly different from and superior to anything previously produced. The first of these, briefly mentioned last month, is the B.R. standard 20-ton bulk grain wagon, here illustrated. This attractive vehicle has a body moulded in high-impact plastic of the correct B.R. freight grey, finely detailed and possessing a delightful matt finish. The various angles and T sections are faithfully reproduced, and the side inspection doors are correctly finished, including the fixing bolts. The body is mounted on a new 11ft. 6in. wheelbase diecast chassis, which will doubtless be used for further vehicles in the range. It is vacuum fitted and clasp brakes are correctly located about the spoked plastic wheels, which are of finer standard than the original metal pattern and will run on scale track. This wagon is now available and retails at 6/9. An equally fine cattle truck with a similarly moulded body

is scheduled for release in April, while also to follow are a Western Region brake van, a six-ton refrigerator van and a high-sided open steel wagon—further brake vans are scheduled. To complete the modernization programme, two-aspect working colour light signals are now to be produced.

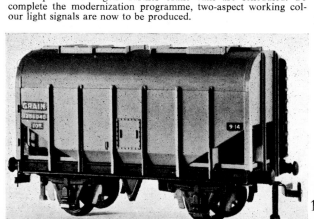

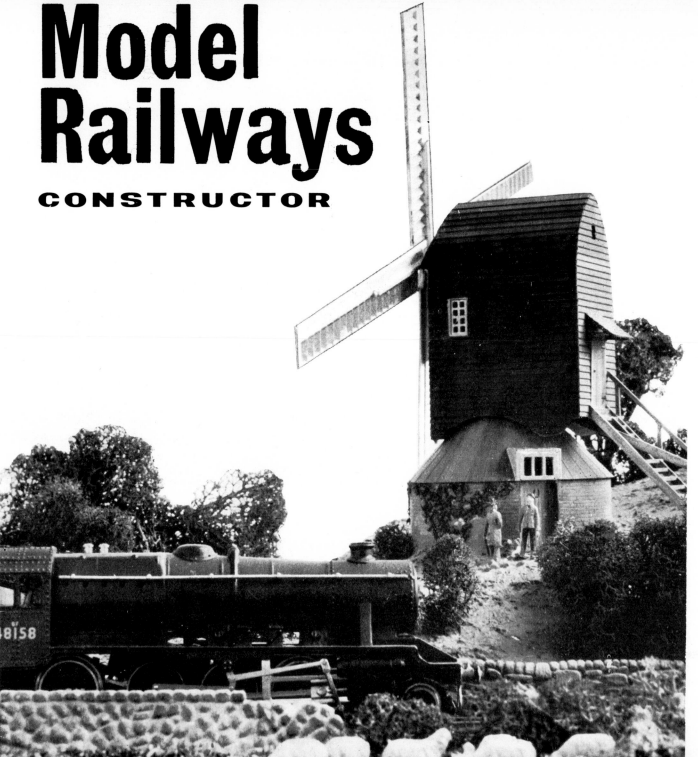

Model Railways

CONSTRUCTOR

The 2–8–0 8F Locomotives.–

MECCANO Lᵀᴰ 10 NOV 1960 PRODUCTION

| TITLE | LOCO & TENDER COMPLETE — 2-8-0 FREIGHT LOCO | JOB NO 1490 |

3 RAIL

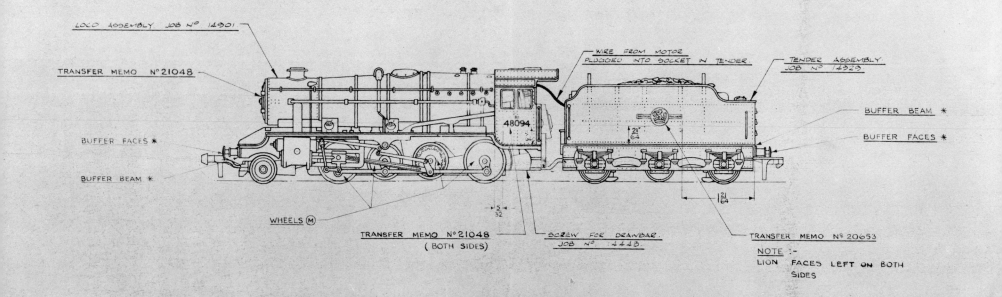

MASK - SPRAYED SHOWN THUS :- Ⓜ

HANDPAINTED " " :- ✳

3	COUPLING ADDED AT FRONT OF LOCO	6043	3-11-60	J.C.m.	
	PLASTIC COUPLING WAS METAL COUPLING.	5889	20-6-60	WRB	
2	MEMO Nº 21048 WAS MEMO Nº 20690	5816	27-4-60	ER	
	NOTE RE. TRANSFER MEMO Nº 20653 ALTERED	5711	4-4-60	ER	
ISSUE.	DESCRIPTION OF CHANGE	CO.Nº.	DATE.	SIG.	
MATERIAL	SEE JOB LIST Nº 282 SHT. 1.				

LIMITS ON DIMENSIONS.
FRACTIONS ± .008"
DECIMALS ± .003'

DRAWN. RT.
TRACED.
CHECKED
APPROVED WP
SCALE FULL SIZE
DATE 21.5.57

The original 3-rail model No. 48158 was commenced, according to the drawing, on 15th April 1957. The releases then paralleled the 'Castle' Class locomotive in that January 1959 heralded the release of the 2-rail version No. 48109 and while just under two years later, in October 1960, the Ringfield motor version in 2-rail came out, No. 48073.

The *Model Railway News* reported that on their test performance of this new motor 'it equalled all the superlatives used by the manufacturers. The new motor is slightly heavier than the previous one and by virtue of its shape occupies much more of the cab and the latter point is the only fault we can find and even this is superficial. The slow running performance of 48073 is remarkable. Using a Marshall 3 Power Control Unit set for pulse power, the first notch of the Controller moved the locomotive about half an inch in one minute!'

All the 8F locomotives modelled by Hornby Dublo appeared in the British Railways listings between 1948 and 1950 with the exception of 48094 which had returned from war service in the Middle East and was waiting to be demobilised. Frequently these primarily freight locomotives appeared on passenger, parcels and perishable produce trains and two of them 48309 and 48728 had the honour to work the Royal Train on 8th August 1955 during the Royal Tour of South Wales.

Some carried a five-pointed white star painted onto the cabside indicating that the wheels had been specially balanced to render them suitable for handling fast braked freight trains.

The introduction of the 8F locomotive, 48158 coincided with the new super detail rolling stock, the

---

OO gauge 2-8-0 " 8F " Locomotive and Tender for Two-Rail Running.

Meccano, Ltd.   **Price 81s. 6d. each.**

Continuing their two-rail programme, Meccano have now submitted their new version of the " 8F." This, like the 2-6-4T, has bush-insulated wheels and crank pins on one side and is a real hunk of freight motive power. Our sample ran smoothly and powerfully and made no bones about heavy goods trains. The body castings on both loco and tender were, unfortunately, a bit rough in places and the rivet detail, especially on the cab and tender sides, seems heavy. With this class of loco, the absence of a front auto-coupling is an omission which we hope Meccano will rectify; with a freight loco ability to haul tender-first is a necessity, not just a frill. But on performance and usefulness this loco cannot be faulted.

Extract from December 1959 Model Railway Constructor.

---

latter having amazing accuracy and proportion for their time and are certainly equal to anything produced since.

The last locomotive to appear in December 1961 was 48094 the 3-rail Ringfield version and again, as with 'Ludlow Castle' a small quantity only were produced making it, judging by the collectors' activity and price, the most desirable of the four models to many enthusiasts.

The drawings put the change from the metal to the plastic coupling as 20th June 1960. A front coupling was added some four months later on 3rd November. Ever since the model's introduction there had always been provision for a front coupling on the front pony just necessitating a rivet and a coupling. The heavy black nylon type coupling supplied on the front of some of the models was really a hideous contraption as I have already mentioned. It was sad that they ever changed from the simple metal coupling.

550 of No. 48073 – (2-rail Ringfield) locos were sold in 1964, leaving 200 in stock.

THE SOUTHERN 0–6–0
R1 TANK LOCOS

Mr. L. E. Carroll wrote in the readers' letters of the June 1954 *Railway Modeller* that he was trying to build up a set of models based on Southern practice, but 'to date my staunchest ally has been the old original Hornby Dublo – quiet, foolproof and powerful although alas too highly geared and of course not Southern. At the moment there is a great and absurd gulf between the excellent toy at £3 or so and the scale

model often indifferently produced at £15–£20.' He also reports that even so, followers of Southern practice needed an 0–6–0 or 0–6–2 Tank for shunting and pilot duties, say an R1 or an E5 . . . And indeed, what better model could Hornby introduce than the South East Chatham Railway's original class 'R1' 0–6–0 Tank locomotive. These were originally introduced in 1888 and by April 1960, when the last two were with-drawn – you guessed it 31337 and 31340 – the numbers of the two Hornby Dublo Tank locomotives which heralded the introduction of their 2-rail sets. The

Model Railway Constructor gave an excellent 'rigid test', as they called it, of this locomotive and stated it was one of the best proprietary models they had tested to date.

A lot of soul searching went on at Meccano as this was the first polystyrene steam outline body although it had been preceded by the polystyrene bodied 'Bo-Bo' locomotive enabling much detail to be included at the incredibly cheap price of 36s. The trade was once more ecstatic about the beautiful mechanism and one report stated that their only regret was that Hornby Dublo

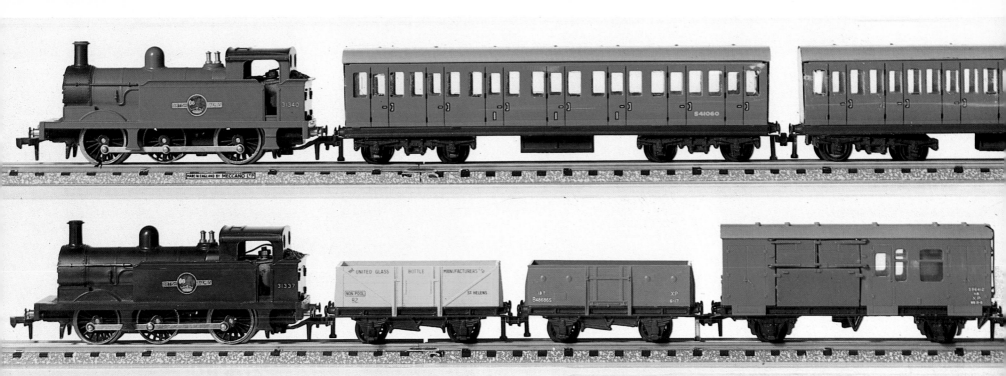

did not make separate components freely available. The motor is, to quote, 'a lovely unit which if sold separately for use in hand built jobs would add considerably to the prestige of the Hornby Company.'

Even at this late stage, the Hornby Dublo Company had never sold their components separately although two years later it was a different story and one could purchase separately whatever chassis was required. The *Railway Modeller* quoted in their write-up 'We have no doubt whatever that these lively locomotives will sell like hot cakes.' The last area of operation of these little tank locomotives was on the famous Folkestone Harbour incline, handling the heaviest boat trains weighing often more than 400 tons. Three of these little veterans would be seen in the front with another coupled in the rear, pushing hard. The whole performance in both sight and sound was tremendously impressive as it pushed its load up the mile-long harbour branch with gradients as much as one in thirty and it was here, too that the prototype

The Class R1 Tank locomotive.

'The Local' – extract from the August 1963 Meccano Magazine.

131

Extract from the November 1959 Meccano Magazine.

Two-Rail Talk

By the Secretary

SINCE I first mentioned the introduction of Hornby-Dublo Two-Rail in our talk last May, the first items of Hornby-Dublo Two-Rail equipment have begun to appear, and our advertisement pages in recent issues have given brief details of the train sets that include the new 0-6-0 Tank Locomotive shown in our picture above. Now I am able to say a little more about two-rail matters and you can be sure that the subject will be followed up in later issues.

You will already have admired Hornby-Dublo Two-Rail track, with its neat close-sleepered lengths of flat-bottomed rail. Good contact is essential for two-rail working, as the driving wheels alone are relied on for current collection, those on the right-hand side of the engine being insulated from their axles and from the wheels on the other side. So to be sure of this the rails are drawn in nickel silver, which has high conductivity, and indeed has the further good quality of not being prone to corrosion.

There are 12 curved rails to the circle in Hornby-Dublo Two-Rail, and the radius of the curves and points is 15 in. This last figure is already familiar to Hornby-Dublo three-rail owners, as their Curved Rails are of the same radius and it is interesting to note that as a result approximately the same amount of space is required for any given layout, whether two-rail or three-rail.

The Rails, Points and other components of the Hornby-Dublo Two-Rail system, and how to build up layouts of all kinds

with them will be explained in a special booklet to be issued shortly. In any case, the essential features for satisfactory operation will be known to those who have already obtained Hornby-Dublo Two-Rail Train Sets or Locomotives, as the instruction leaflets packed with them make matters clear so that I need not say a great deal about them here.

One point to note in considering two-rail working is that when we put an engine on the track, whichever way it is facing, the movement of the control handle governs whether the engine moves to the left or to the right, not necessarily forward or reverse. Wiring arrangements are right if the engine moves to the left, with the chimney leading, when the control handle is set for forward running.

The finely detailed appearance of the new engine above speaks for itself. It is a capable little engine with a friendly look, and is well built to deal with light local passenger or freight traffic, and in fact both a passenger and a goods train set including it are available. Those who have seen the Passenger Set will have noted that its appearance marks the introduction into the Hornby-Dublo range of Coaches in the smart and attractive green livery of the Southern Region of British Railways.

These vehicles, which are also available separately, are fitted with moulded wheels, as is all Hornby-Dublo rolling stock in current production, so they are suitable for either two-rail or three-rail running.

Extract from the April 1960 Meccano Magazine.

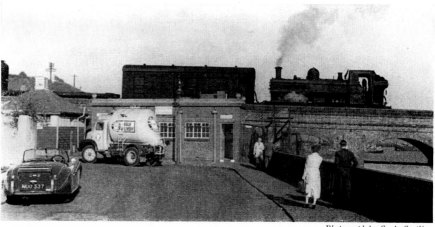

Photograph by C. A. Gostling

A Famous Folkestone Feature

Boat Train Climb from Harbour Station

By R. A. H. Weight

WHEN passing through Folkestone, on an embankment and then over a viaduct, travellers along the S.R. London–Dover main line, via Ashford, can see right over much of the town to the sea. To them the outer harbour and the protecting breakwaters, quayside sheds and station appear rather far off and decidedly "a long way down". It is to and from the Harbour Station that Folkestone boat trains run, for the town is the port for certain Anglo-French passenger, mail and cargo services.

Boat train handling at Folkestone is fraught with difficulties, and the line is somewhat exposed to the weather. The main problem is the difference in level, already referred to, between the main line and Folkestone Harbour Station. The two-track Harbour branch, about a mile long, includes an extremely steep 1-in-30 gradient, and on it there are level crossings, viaducts and a swing bridge over salt water. The ride is, indeed, an exceptional one over a section of railway normally traversed by Continental passengers only.

All the boat trains, whether empty or loaded, require the use of two or more engines up from the Harbour, according to weight. Only small, light types of tank locomotive are permissible. For many years until quite recently these duties

were in the hands of the R 0-6-0T class, built before the end of the last century by the former South Eastern Railway for shunting or short local freight duty, or of rebuilds classified as R1. In their original form these were domeless and had narrow, round cabs, and there were several variations. For the heaviest trains, weighing often more than 400 tons, three of those little veterans would be seen in front with another, coupled in rear to the last vehicle, pushing hard at the back. The whole performance, in both sight and sound, was tremendously impressive.

Their long service had to come to an end, however, and some have been scrapped. As there was no suitable S.R. replacement, G.W.R. type 0-6-0 pannier tank engines of entirely different appearance, squat and tough, are now in service there. They are more powerful than their predecessors, and not more than two ahead and one astern appear to meet heaviest requirements.

One locomotive takes these expresses down the incline, experienced drivers having the braking well in hand, and provision is made for train heating. The photograph above shows empty stock being assisted in rear from Folkestone on its way to Dover to connect with the inward steamer for the return working to Victoria, London, of the *Golden Arrow*.

of the track cleaning wagon was used, but more of this in its respective chapter. Two locomotives were produced namely 31337 in black and 31340 in green. The early versions of both the black and green models had the running number of the black version – 31337 – moulded on the smokebox door. This was corrected in later green versions by a transfer – 31340 – followed later by the black version with a similar transfer – 31337. All early models had nickel silver wheels, buffers, metal couplings and BR totem motifs pointing forward.

It was a great shame that these models could not have been produced in the original very attractive liveries of the South East Chatham Railway and the reason for the green coloured locomotive was an attempt to bring colour into a range which apart from the express passenger engines, was predominantly British Rail black.

Much to the sales peoples' surprise the green model was a poor seller although many were sent overseas where they sold well. Indeed in 1963/64 the green version was modified and wound for 6 volt working, again intended for the export market for battery operation.

The model was originally drawn on 23rd July 1958 and the drawing dates the deletion of the 31337 number moulding on the smoke box door, as 31st December 1960.

In the year 1964, 950 green 0–6–0 Tank locomotives were sold and the Triang Company took 800 into stock. However the black version sold 1,224 models and was out of stock at the takeover hence its relative rarity today.

The Hornby Dublo works were stuck with the dilemma of maintaining the quality achieved, particularly in the preceding few years whilst introducing a relatively cheap model in 2-rail to try to win back the increasing sales of the Triang Company with the junior enthusiast. As a model the R1 was an exceptionally good and popular choice.

No. 31340, built in 1889 in real life had completed 1,262,537 miles by the time of her withdrawal in 1956. Some of the class had special low chimneys and low cabs for working the Canterbury and Whitstable branch.

FIRST HORNBY 2-RAIL

OUR illustration above shows the first of the new Hornby-Dublo two-rail locos, the 0-6-0T based on the ex-S.E.C.R. R1 class tanks, famous for their work on the Folkestone Harbour incline.

The model has a solid diecast frame fitted with the new standard Hornby-Dublo tunnel magnet motor. The diecast wheels have plated tyres and are centre-insulated on one side, these being provided with a simple but effective spring pickup. The motor is fitted with television suppressors.

The body is moulded in polystyrene and is available in black or green, finished with B.R. crest and numbers. Turned brass safety valves and turned plated buffers are fitted. The body is retained with a screw through the chimney and the cap is quite separate; thus the manufacturers have been able to include even the fixing bolts around the base.

The total weight is 7¼oz., of which the chassis and motor provide 6½oz., and the motor is extremely powerful. The haulage powers are limited by this fact, but there is room to add lead to improve matters. However, the cost is also light, only 36/- for a locomotive which is quite definitely in the scale class. The flanges are a trifle thick for absolute B.R.M.S.B. requirements, but actually only a very slight adjustment to checkrails is needed on some points to enable these locomotives to pass.

While an attractive locomotive in its own right, it must not be forgotten that it also represents a very inexpensive two-rail six-coupled mechanism, on which one can construct one's own body. The wheels are 4ft. 9in. in diameter over the treads, and the coupled wheelbase is 6ft. 6in. + 7ft. 9in., front overhang to the end of the chassis is 6ft. and rear overhang 6ft. 6in. The fixing screw centre-line is 2ft. 6in. in front of the leading wheel centre. All dimensions are given in scale feet and inches for OO so that interested readers can see how closely the chassis corresponds with any prototype they may favour.

To sum up, this is an excellent light locomotive and would be ideal as the sole motive power for a small branch.

We have no doubt whatever that these lively locomotives will sell like hot cakes.

Extract from News Special in the July 1959 Railway Modeller.

THE REBUILT 4–6–2 WEST COUNTRY LOCOMOTIVES

It is funny, I was never very keen on Southern Railway steam locomotives as a boy, but as I worked on the research for this book I became very attracted to the air-smoothed casings and indeed managed to obtain (in beautiful condition) one of the early Graham Farish 'Merchant Navy' Class locomotives which is now amongst my favourites. There was an excellent article in the August 1945 *Meccano Magazine* that discusses the first three West Country Pacifics 'Exeter', 'Salisbury' and 'Plymouth'.

It was in February 1956 that Mr. J. N. Maskelyne announced in the *Model Railway News* that 3518 'British India Line' of the 'Merchant Navy' Class was to be rebuilt with three sets of Walschaerts valve gear, a new crank axle and cylinders and to have the air-smoothed casing removed.

Following the great success of these modifications, all the 'Merchant Navy' and 'West Country' Classes were subsequently rebuilt and the first 'West Country' to be modified was none other than our own 34005 'Barnstaple' in June 1957, fitted with the large 5,500 gallon tender. The locomotive received a lot of publicity at the time and it was doubtless helped by the superb eight page article in the *Model Railway News* in September 1960 on Mr. Jack Newton's complete scratch building project of this locomotive. Hornby

Dublo commenced their drawing on 21st June 1960, and were doubtless delighted to see the immense publicity for this class by Mr. Newton's article. Their model appeared in October 1961 following the much publicised luxury train set of the year – the 'Bournemouth Belle' – with the new super detailed pullman coaches. From the trade point of view it was not a great success and the *Constructor* 'Review' reported they were frankly a little disappointed. The criticisms they raised included an overscaled chimney rim, and

OUR FRONT COVER

Our cover picture this month, prepared from a B.R. Southern Region photograph, shows an express from Bournemouth bound for Waterloo. The Bournemouth services have long enjoyed a special reputation and they include such well-known trains as the **Royal Wessex** *and the all-Pullman* **Bournemouth Belle.** *The picture is of special interest to Hornby-Dublo enthusiasts as the engine, No. 34048* Crediton, *belongs to the 4–6–2 Rebuilt West Country class, represented in Hornby-Dublo by the Two-Rail Barnstaple model, referred to in last month's issue, and the Three-Rail Dorchester. West Country locomotives share the Bournemouth and other workings with the slightly larger, but less numerous, 4–6–2s of the powerful Merchant Navy class.*

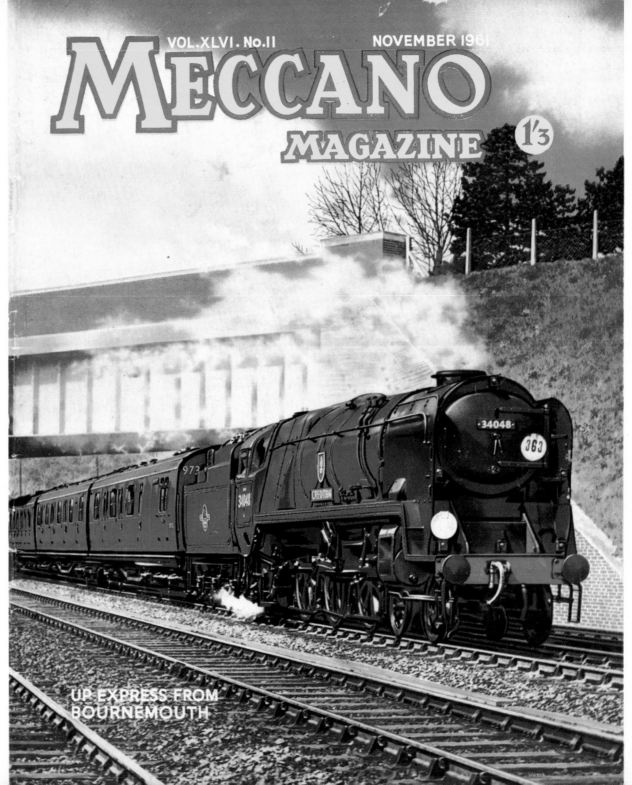

VOL. XLVI. No. 11   NOVEMBER 1961

MECCANO MAGAZINE

1/3

UP EXPRESS FROM BOURNEMOUTH

NEW

The Luxury Train Set of the Year

No. 2035 Pullman Train Set S.R. (2-rail)

A new luxury express for Hornby-Dublo railways. It consists of three Pullman Cars, First Class, Second Class and Brake/2nd respectively, and the Engine is 4–6–2 *Barnstaple*, of the S.R. rebuilt "West Country" Class. 2-Rail track requiring a space of 4 ft. by 3 ft. is included.

U.K. Price £9.18.1.

AVAILABLE SEPARATELY

No. 2235 2-Rail *Barnstaple* 4–6–2 "West Country" Class Locomotive and Tender.
U.K. Price £5.16.5.

NEW, TOO

A 3-Rail version is also available, sales No. 3235 *Dorchester* 4–6–2 "West Country" Locomotive and Tender (3-Rail)
U.K. Price £5.16.5.

HORNBY DUBLO

MADE IN ENGLAND BY MECCANO LTD.

the Ringfield motor protruding outside the cab which resulted in an unnecessarily long locomotive to tender coupling. The rear bogie and tender wheels all had standard spoked axles on the model instead of the special B.F.B. (Bullied, Firth-Brown) type. Although the tender is accurately modelled, this particular type was never fitted to 34005 in real life and there are other minor discrepancies such as one ladder only was fitted instead of the usual two. These and many other small criticisms made the trade suggest that much more attention should have been given to what was otherwise a reasonable model. The *Model Railway News* even recorded that the main driving wheels were 2.5 mm smaller than correct scale diameter. In conclusion it was a good model, but one which would have been much better had more attention been paid to detail. However, it was only poor when one considers the superlative models which had preceded it and many people welcomed the return of a diecast locomotive body and the fact that it filled the gap for the Southern enthusiast in having his own mainline express locomotive.

Advertisement from the November 1961 Meccano Magazine.

It was during the completion of the initial production run of this model that the National Coal Board sent their film unit to the Meccano Factory as the whole factory heating was by solid fuel.

The 3-rail version No. 34042 'Dorchester', came out at the same time. Likewise this model was fitted with the now world famous Ringfield motor and technically the model was equal to any of its cousins. It just seems a shame that these minor items had not been corrected from the start, and indeed some of model railway press were suggesting that the enthusiast should pick up his paint brush and a tin of light green paint and paint in the front steps of the running board by the smoke deflectors green as on the prototype as they had been masked black on the model.

I do not have figures for the sales of the 'Dorchester' locomotive or any 3-rail loco, all being sold to Beatties and such companies earlier, but in 1964 only 340 'Barnstaple' locomotives were sold leaving a stock to be taken over of 2,650.

Hornby-Dublo S.R. 'Barnstaple', with coaches – from a Meccano publicity photograph.

A Meccano publicity photograph.

The rebuilt West Country Class Locomotives.

Extracts from the July 1974 Model Railway Magazine.

THE 0-4-0 LOCOMOTIVE OF THE STARTER SETS

The Triang Company had been making inroads into the traditional Hornby Dublo market, as indeed had other model railway producers such as Playcraft and the white metal kit specialists. High stocks remained unsold and the Meccano Company realised they must do everything possible to try and recapture the younger enthusiast. With this in mind they brought out their new 'ready to run' train sets. The

New Products Committee met on 1st December 1961 and examined the Playcraft trains made by Jouef and launched an immediate investigation towards producing a cheap train set at a comparable price. At the following meeting, on 15th December, it was agreed to start immediately for production by 1963. The following design criteria were decided:-

(1) Sets would have a normal guarantee of 60 days.
(2) Reasonable life of loco to be 12 months (200 hours operations).

(3) No servicing outside guarantee period.
(4) Individual performance standards to be relaxed against the high Hornby Dublo requirements.
(5) loco housing need not be any set prototype but 0-4-0 type
(6) Two items of goods rolling stock would be included

By 15th March 1962 it was decided that a retail price of 50s. for the set was acceptable and this allowed the addition of a brake van.

Meccano Trade Exhibition in January 1963 introducing the starter set (far right).

From original Meccano artwork.

On the initial tests the brush life in phosphor bronze only lasted 10 hours. It was thus decided to use beryllium copper giving a minimum of 35 hours life. The commutator wore out after 120 hours so it was agreed to increase the thickness 0.003 inches which would cover this. The brush life was now 50 hours.

The Hornby Dublo 2-rail track was considered too expensive and fragile for the younger enthusiast, so a stronger track section eight to the circle against twelve, was prepared. It was suggested that use be made of surplus stock wagons in November 1963, but the problems of packaging made this impractical. The best introduction would obviously be from the *Meccano Magazine* itself and their April 1963 issue states . . . 'Of special interest to those youngsters who are anxious to obtain their first taste of the Hornby Dublo hobby is the news that we are introducing an efficient and inexpensive new train set under catalogue number 2001. A special point about this set is that it is complete with power control unit so the owner has available in one box everything he needs to start operations right away. The items for the new train set make up a goods train of simple character and the locomotive represents a tank engine of moderate size. It does not follow the lines of any particular prototype but has been designed to incorporate typical features of British practice. It possesses a motor of particular efficient character for its size, designed to ensure satisfactory life. The design of the motor has been kept as simple as possible so that the routine maintenance is kept to a minimum.

'Externally the engine is of pleasing outline and the outside cylinders provided help to give it an air of real purpose and capability. The housing is of plastic

moulding which has allowed the maximum detail to be incorporated. Such things as rivet heads, handrails and so on are all there together with the various items of piping that form such an intricate feature of many full sized engines. This new addition to the Hornby Dublo locomotive family looks very workmanlike in its black finish and I am sure it will appeal strongly to those who see it. To make up the train are two wagons of representative types with fully detailed moulded super detail bodywork finished in attractive colours. Constructionally the bodywork is standard with that of the 13 ton open wagon and the open wagon steel type respectively so that there is plenty of character even in such a small train. In addition there is a goods brake van of effective appearance with moulded bodywork that includes features found in BR standard practice. It does not incorporate the long wheel base characteristic of the existing goods brakes in the system but the bodywork is arranged very neatly on a short four wheel base giving a particularly attractive

The write-up in the August 1963 Railway Modeller.

HORNBY-DUBLO STARTER SET

THE Hornby-Dublo starter set breaks new ground by incorporating a power unit with controller, providing in the one box the basic essentials. A plain circle of standard Hornby-Dublo two-rail track is supplied, a power clip feeds the current. The two wagons and brake-van are standard bodies unrelieved by any lettering, fitted to a new plastic under-frame. The locomotive incorporates several novel design features. The wheels are just solid die-cast with raised spokes, with a stub axle integral with the wheel. Two such wheels are joined by an insulating tube, the pick-up being through the frames, which are individually clipped to a plastic spacer. The motor, which drives all four wheels through a spur and crown wheel train, has a large armature and simple metal brushes, bearing directly on the commutator. The plastic body is sprung on to the body for easy oiling. The power unit has a rated output of only 0.7 amp. The whole outfit costs £4/9/6.

appearance. The set includes curved rails to form a circle and these curves have the standard radius of 15 inches. A board measuring 3 ft square is necessary to accommodate the track comfortably and leave room in a convenient corner for the control unit.'

Understandably the set did not rate very highly with the model railway press who were geared to the older enthusiast. The moulded detail of the locomotive body was really far too good for the market, but to me the worst item was the way the locomotive just clipped to the chassis unit. I do not know whether it was supposed to be a quick release coupling to allow the motor unit to come away from the bodywork when little Willy dropped it and so avoid damage to the latter, but I have never yet seen one firmly fixed. However the set certainly had its appeal and successes, not only with the younger enthusiast, but also with the older using it for small industrial working schemes and sidings. It was well advertised and apart from an advertisement in November 1963, there were three magnificent colour advertisements in March, April and May 1964. There were 5,000 sets in stock at the beginning of 1964 and by the time of the takeover of the stock at the end of the year there were only 1,900 remaining.

I mentioned in the earlier section of this book that the Meccano Company had planned to bring out a small clockwork motor again for the young enthusiast

READY TO RUN

2 RAIL · 00 GAUGE

H HORNBY 2001

Complete with power/control unit for only

89/6

Here's your chance to start your own railway with a wonderful low-price set! The Hornby Tank Goods Set has 0-4-0 Tank Goods Loco, 2 open trucks, a guards van, a track over 8 feet in circumference, *PLUS a Hornby Power/Control Unit* which provides speed control and reversing!

—*MADE AND GUARANTEED BY MECCANO LIMITED.*

Enlarge your layout with these new Track Packs.

It's so easy to make exciting, larger layouts with these Track Packs which contain extra rails and Simplex Points. The dotted lines show the rails which are included in the Tank Goods Set, the other lines show the rails in the Track Packs which can be added to the Set,

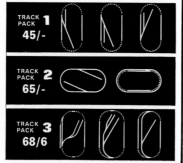

TRACK PACK **1** 45/-

TRACK PACK **2** 65/-

TRACK PACK **3** 68/6

H HORNBY 2001 2 RAIL·00 GAUGE

READY-TO-RUN electric train set

Start your own railway with this wonderful, low-price Tank Goods Set! The 2001 Set includes a track over 8 feet in circumference *PLUS a Hornby Power Control Unit* which provides speed control and reversing at no extra cost.

TRACK PACKS ENLARGE YOUR LAYOUT

Add to your fun and increase your layouts with Hornby Track Packs. There are three to choose from containing extra rails and Simplec Points—and you can make many different layouts with every Pack.

MADE AND GUARANTEED BY MECCANO LIMITED.

HORNBY

COMPLETE with power control unit for only **85/-**

The 0–4–0 Starter Set Locomotive in typical surroundings with the Yardmen's cabin, made up from a D14 Coach and TPO trackside base unit. The Dinky Toy set and the 'Bugbox' 4-wheel Coaches, using D14 Coaches and goods brake van chassis crossing a bridge made from a turntable girder.

THE already extensive range of Hornby-Dublo Train Sets has been still further enlarged by the introduction of a new ready-to-run train set, under sales no. 2004.

The new set is supplied complete with Hornby Power Unit, giving four different speeds, plus reverse, locomotive, rolling stock and track. It has sufficient track to form a circle 3 feet in diameter and a departure from other Hornby-Dublo train sets is that only eight sections of track are needed to form a circle, instead of twelve.

This new forty-five degree curved track will not change the geometry of existing layouts and no difficulty should be encountered with plans in Hornby-Dublo layout booklets. Full running instructions are provided with the set.

The new four-wheel diesel locomotive is finished in attractive yellow and, in keeping with other Hornby-Dublo locomotives, has a high standard of detail. An open wagon, a mineral wagon and a brake van are included in the set.

The 2004 Set forms an excellent introduction to the Hornby-Dublo track system and the circle of track supplied

The front of the box in which the 2004 Train Set is supplied.

The back of the train set box gives various layout formations.

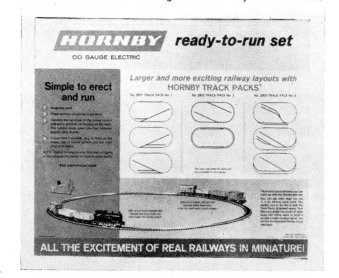

for their purpose, they thought that the metal ladder round the radiator would cause problems for the younger enthusiast.

Unbeknown obviously at the time, this particular model caused Mr. George Wrenn considerable headaches when he announced in one of his catalogues the reintroduction of the Hornby Dublo shunter locomotive. He could not find the toolwork for the body, as the original mould had been removed and adapted to make this particular starter set model. The cost of making another identical mould was astronomical and caused a considerable delay in his planned release of this model. However, the Hornby model did not have the appeal of the little 0–4–0 steam outline locomotive and while some 2,000 sets were sold in 1964, 3,500 remained in stock at the closure.

Surprisingly on 19th March 1964, the drawing of the 0–4–0 steam outline body was remoulded in a light blue polystyrene with the outline of Australia on the tankside and the word 'Commonwealth' written through the centre. The model certainly went into production although I have been unable to find out for how long and the reaction of the Australian enthusiast. (Released June 1964.)

With this the last steam outline locomotive manufactured by the Meccano Company the sad commercial affairs of the Company overtook it and it remained the last item produced in their range.

It was reborn as No. 8 in the Dinky catalogue for 1972. The locomotive reappeared as a non motorised Dinky Toy model 784. An identical casting, with royal blue livery and GER stickers on the tank sides and brass funnel. The model also appeared as a set with two wagons, again using old tools – that of the 13 ton standard wagon No. 4670 and the French Acho counterpart – 708 open goods wagon.

The set had plastic wheels capable of being pushed around big brothers 00 track and was greeted with considerable enthusiasm by the sales team. Further additions, coaches etc. were mooted but somehow they never caught on, and by the 1975 Dinky catalogue (No. 11) was finally deleted.

and indeed had drawn up the wheels and intended to have this particular range available both in clockwork and electric. From old parts they reassembled a pre-war 0–6–0 clockwork motor and tested it against the equivalent Triang model, but unfortunately it was not a success and the rebirth of the clockwork motor was stillborn.

In October 1964, the 0–4–0 locomotive stud was enlarged still further by the introduction of a new 2004 set using an identical motor, but this time without a connecting rod.

The locomotive body was the attractive diesel shunter body shortened some 3/16ths of an inch at the front end, as apart from being somewhat overlength

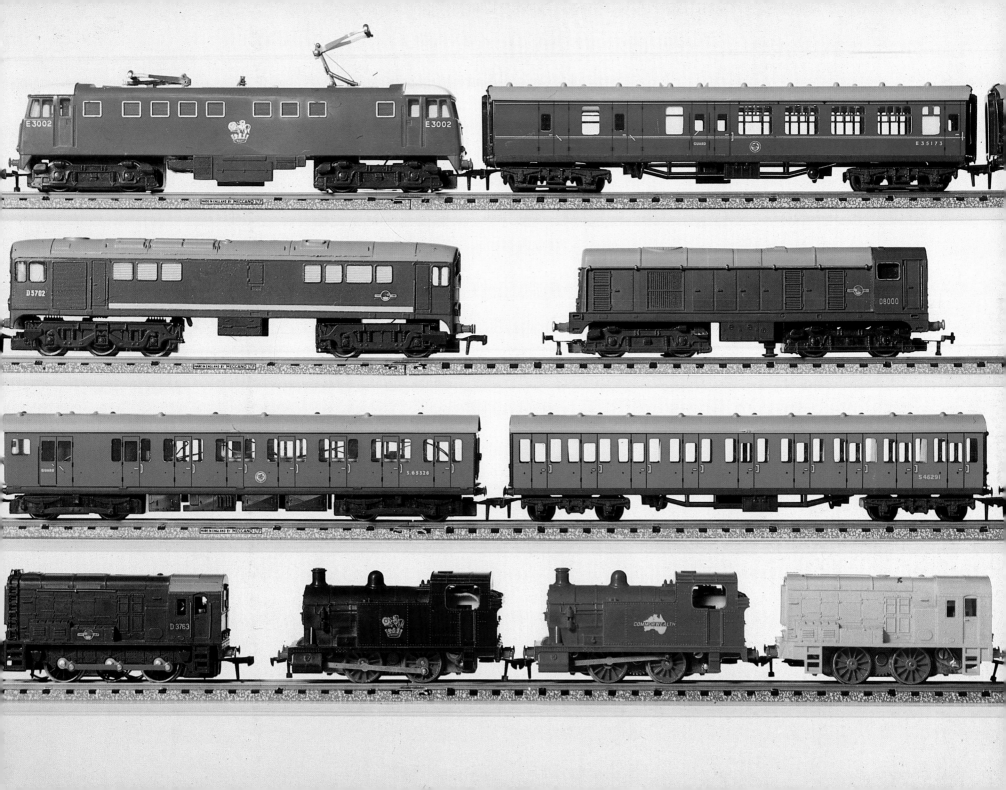

THE DIESEL & ELECTRIC OUTLINE LOCOMOTIVES

THE 1000 H.P. BO-BO LOCOMOTIVE

The first of British Railways 'pilot scheme' mainline diesel electric locomotives was handed over to the British Transport Commission at a ceremony held at the Vulcan Foundry, Newton-le-Willows on 2nd June 1957. It was numbered D8000 and introduced 20 type A, 1000 horse-power locomotives. They were described by the makers as mixed traffic locos, but they were primarily intended for freight power. They were not equipped with coach heating boilers, but they had train pipes to transmit heat from the boiler-fitted locomotives of the 'B' or 'C' type diesels that were to come if they were required to work as a multiple unit with this type on a passenger train. They were of course suitable to work passenger trains in the Summer when train heating was not required. The original locomotive underwent trials at Derby in the latter part of June that year and afterwards was allocated to Devons Road, Bow for cross London freight working. The driver's controls were very neatly built into duplicate pre-fabricated desks one at the left hand forward and the other at the left hand reverse driving position. A dead man's handle was provided and an additional pedal operated the sanding gear. Every consideration was given to the comfort of the locomotive crew, as in addition to well upholstered seats, up to four kilowatt of cab heating was available and a special heater had been built into each control desk to supply

warm air to the driver's feet! There was even the refinement of a cooker. The locomotive was designed for a maximum speed of 75 m.p.h. and with a maximum tractive force of 42,000 lbs and despite the famous Mr. J. N. Maskelyne's comments in 'Railway Topics' in the December 1957 *Model Railway News*, I personally do find this particular locomotive to have very attractive lines.

The Hornby Dublo diesel electric locomotive model was announced in December 1958 under the heading . . . 'Run a Modern Railway – Run Diesel Electric!'.

At this time Hornby Dublo had in production their super detail range of goods rolling stock for 12 months and considerable argument went on in the Design Office both for and against a plastic or diecast body. I am glad that the moulded body won because when one examines the incredible wealth of detail put into this model it comes into a class of its own. The super detailed goods wagons were appearing almost monthly and together with the new colour light signals, the whole impression was of a modern, beautifully produced miniature railway system.

The 'Constructors Review' of the *Model Railway Constructor* commented . . . 'We have nothing but praise for this very fine model', while the *Model Railway News* comments . . . 'The wealth and quality of detail included in the moulded body gives this model much more interest and character than would have been thought possible from the shapeless outline and boxlike appearance which diesel locomotives in general seem to possess. The D8000 is a very fine model and should prove a useful and hardworking addition to the "stud" unless one is strongly prejudiced against this form of locomotion.' Yes, indeed, diesel locomotives certainly lacked the main support of the railway enthusiast, whereas in real life their ability to work all round the clock, seven days a week was a considerable blessing. The only criticism came from the *Railway Modeller* with the justifiable comment of the heavy overscale handrails. It stated that this could easily be rectified.

In 3-rail, even with rubber tyred traction on one pair of main drivers, the locomotive was very successful and sold in its thousands, but come the 2-rail version No. D8017 in February 1959, Meccano had to admit the only failure in their range. In May 1960 the

The original – from Meccano records.

A NEW model of a NEW diesel

HORNBY-DUBLO L30 1000 b.h.p. Bo-Bo Diesel-Electric Locomotive

Here's the latest Hornby-Dublo Locomotive—a realistic model of the first B.R. standard design diesel-electric for main-line duties—the English Electric Type 1 (Series D8000).

This excellent model has a moulded body with a wealth of characteristic detail. A metal ladder is fitted on the offside. Bogie frames and wheels are die-cast. Powered by a highly efficient motor with worm reduction gear working on two axles, this new locomotive has phenomenal hauling power and acceleration. It is extremely smooth in operation. Include it in the programme of development for your Hornby-Dublo Railway.

Overall Length: 7¾ in.   U.K. Price: £3 2s. 6d. (inc. tax)

SEE this NEW Diesel at YOUR Dealers

HORNBY
DUBLO
ELECTRIC TRAINS

Secretary of the Hornby Railway Company wrote in the *Meccano Magazine* that it was absolutely essential to see that the rails and the wheels of the 2-rail locomotives were in a thoroughly clean condition and stressed that the instruction book should be read to the letter. He went on that it was particularly necessary that no oil found its way to the rubber tyres that were fitted to one pair of the driving wheels on the motor bogie as the tyres stretch in service and uneven running might result if sufficient attention was not given to this point. Also that any irregularity in the running surface caused by the tyres in this condition could affect the necessary contact between the rails and the wheels. The whole problem was the current collection. At a Products Meeting on 5th October 1961, the shortcomings were discussed with the result that these features were to be avoided in future designs. Although the Southern Electric train bogie was a similar design, the problems here had been overcome. The 2-rail locomotive was shown in the company's catalogues up to April 1962 (8/462/250 and 16/462/170) and the last reference we have found is a price sheet dated June 1962. (The next catalogue in January 1963 (16/163/50M) does not show it.) The main faults appear to be in the brush spring and also the characteristic of the model to pick up dirt on the commutator and with the usual over-oiling of most model railways and dirty track, coupled with the fact that one of the main driving wheels had rubber tyres, there was poor current collection on the straight and even worse, on the curves. This failure must have hurt the Meccano Company greatly and they continued discussing the possible reintroduction of the model up to 11th February 1963. They even considered adapting the French Hornby-Acho 'Bo-Bo' chassis. However, it was not to be and at a meeting on 24th April 1963, the possible reintroduction of the 2-rail 'Bo-Bo' locomotive was finally abandoned.

However, they obviously had large stocks of this model and the question was what to do with them. As with the surplus 'Duchess of Atholl' diecast bodies some years earlier, Binns Road thoughts once more turned to Canada and a novel arrangement.

Advertisement in the December 1958 Meccano Magazine.

HORNBY DIESEL A WINNER

The 2- and 3-rail locomotives were sold, without buffers, although in standard British Rail livery. Also as many Canadian freight trains were double headed, moreover with diesel locomotives, they supplied the bodies without buffers and even without a motor. This particular variation was made in order that they could use a powered version and a dummy (or indeed several dummies coupled throughout the train to simulate North American freight train practice). They were apparently made up by the Meccano agents in Canada as no one I have spoken to at Binns Road remembers them.

This was the first diesel outline locomotive the Hornby Dublo Company produced and it is sad that the 2-rail version should have ended in failure.

THE latest Hornby-Dublo diesel-electric locomotive is an excellent model of the Vulcan Foundry series of Class 1 Bo-Bo mixed traffic locomotives now in service on British Railways. Before describing the model we feel that a few words concerning prototype duties would not be out of place. At present these locomotives are confined to freight and shunting services, where their ability to work all round the clock seven days a week is of the greatest service. It is, however, probable that, following the pattern of transatlantic practice, they will appear on passenger services singly and in tandem when the regions are more intensively dieselized than at present. As a matter of interest the cab is, officially, at the back of the locomotive, but when it is desired to run two in tandem the cabs are located on the outside!

The model has a superbly detailed polystyrene body moulding with glazed windows in the cab, carried on heavy die-cast bogies linked by a stout flanged steel plate running the entire length of the body top. The auto coupling is mounted on the bogies, which are both of inside bearing pattern, with dummy outer frames simply attached by screws. Plunger type centre third collectors are arranged on each of the bogies.

The motor bogie is specially designed, and incorporates the standard British pattern drive, with the motor, located between the wheels, driving both axles direct through single stage worm gearing. The brushgear is thus readily accessible for eventual replacement, while the mechanical losses are reduced to the absolute minimum. The upper portion has been kept commendably slim, which permits the bogie a considerable degree of movement.

One pair of bogie wheels has been fitted with rubber tyres, and travelling forward the haulage power is excellent, but in reverse there is a tendency for these wheels to slip and the load is correspondingly reduced. Nevertheless the locomotive has hauled reasonable trains in both directions up a 1 in 25 grade and is in our opinion perfectly adequate for all normal model railway requirements. The motor is exceptionally silent—unlike the prototype—and operation is commendably smooth.

Apart from the handrails, which can be easily changed, the model is undoubtedly in the scale class and only needs conversion to run on any two-rail scale system. We would, incidentally, advise that this conversion be carried out professionally unless the enthusiast is extremely experienced and can use a lathe.

To sum up, the new locomotive is an

excellent one, superbly detailed and with adequate haulage capacity. It can be used on the model for all services from shunting up to intermediate passenger and will doubtless form the first step in many enthusiasts' modernization plans.

Extract from the February 1959 Railway Modeller.

The Chassis – 3-rail – of the Bo-Bo locomotive – from original artwork.

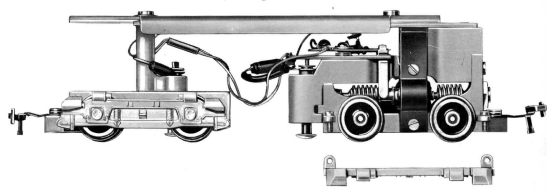

149

Set No. 3230 1,000 h.p. Diesel Electric Goods
From original Meccano artwork.

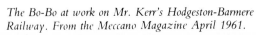

The Bo-Bo at work on Mr. Kerr's Hodgeston-Barmere
Railway. From the Meccano Magazine April 1961.

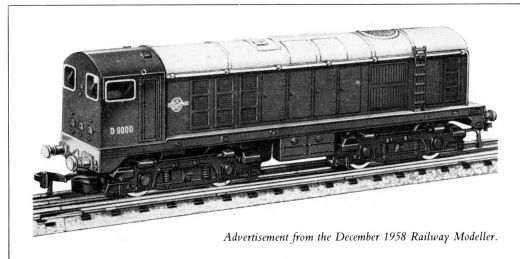

Advertisement from the December 1958 Railway Modeller.

THE DELTIC DIESEL ELECTRIC LOCOMOTIVES

On realising the East coast mainline could not be electrified for many years, British Rail found themselves in a crisis. The end of steam was rapidly approaching, there were no possibilities for immediate electrification, added to which the most powerful diesel locomotives at that time were achieving only 2,000 horse power. Their thoughts must have turned to the LMS diesel electric locomotive of 1600 horse power No. 10000, designed and built by H. G. Ivatt in 1947. This locomotive, with her sister 10001, hauled 545 ton trains with ease up Beattock Bank. At the same time D. Napier and Son had successfully developed a lightweight diesel engine, primarily for motor gunboats and the English Electric Company adapted this and built the prototype 'Deltic' as a private venture. The locomotive was offered for trial to British Railways and following a successful period in service from October 1955, an order was finally placed (as part of the railway's re-equipment and modernisation programme) for 22 production locomotives to be designated type '5'. With the total weight of only 106 tons and a rating of 3,300 horse power the 'Deltic' had the lowest weight/power ratio ever achieved in diesel locomotive design – 721 lbs per horse power. The axle load of 18 tons gave a wide range of route availability on British Railways' system and most sections of standard and broad gauge railway systems overseas. It was geared for a maximum speed of 105 m.p.h. The primary power came from two 1,650 h.p. 'Napier Deltic' high speed, lightweight, two stroke diesel

engines, each of which drove a 1,100 kw main generator and 45 kw auxiliary generator. The main generators supplied power to six axle hung traction motors, while current at a constant low voltage for the auxiliary generators was used for battery charging, main generator field excitation and the operation of all auxiliary machinery. The prototype locomotive was in service 17 hours each day, six days a week and for some months had achieved an average of approximately 4,000 miles per week.

The locomotive was not originally designed for use on British Railways, but was built by the English Electric Company in the hope of attracting buyers from overseas. Its completion coincided with the proposal to electrify the East coast route from King's Cross to Leeds, a proposal that was to fall through shortly thereafter. The 'Deltic' locomotive was by far the most expensive among the British Rail diesel fleet and compared to conventional locomotives their engines were extremely complex. Eventually it was agreed that 22 be built in a slightly modified form.

After seven years work the original 'Deltic' retired in July 1963 and can now be seen in the Science Museum in South Kensington, London. She completed 450,000 miles of revenue earning service and at the time of her construction was the most powerful single unit diesel electric locomotive in the world. It seemed that the cost of providing special spares for a one-off experimental locomotive was just not on.

The 'Deltic's' justification was surely seen in the fantastic acceleration shown in the current Eastern

← *The 'Deltic' locomotives, with, at the top, the Kitmaster 'Deltic', painted by D. J. Howell Ltd., for comparison.*

'The prototype' – from an English Electric photograph in Meccano records.

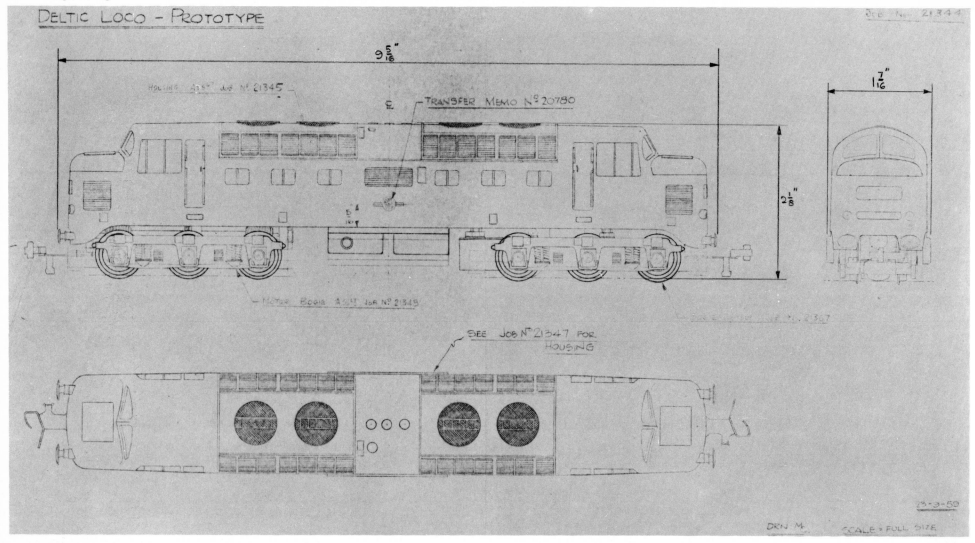

DELTIC LOCO - PROTOTYPE

Region timetable where schedules had been slashed in no uncertain manner. With steam off the road south of Peterborough by the Summer of 1963, the diesels were at last able to show the scoffers what they could do in the way of speed and performance. The Meccano Company obviously kept an ear very close to the ground on the future locomotive modernisation programme and Mr. J. H. Davis of the Traction Department, English Electric Company forwarded to them full copies of all the necessary drawings etc. The pro-

duction model was planned as early as 2nd July 1958, although he noted at that time two items that were apparent; the headlamp which was built into the prototype and seen to such effect on the superb Kitmaster model would obviously not appear on the British Railways version and nor would the moulded lines which extend the whole length of the locomotive. The final colour scheme of the prototype locomotives had still not been decided and on 7th January 1960, Meccano were again in correspondence with Mr. Davis on

the proposed colour scheme and to quote . . . 'at the moment we are assuming it will be similar to the type 1 locomotive you have already constructed i.e. light grey roof, olive green body and black bogie' but nothing had been decided upon.

The new diecast bodied locomotive was shown at both the Harrogate and Brighton Toy Fairs at the beginning of 1960, although it did not appear on the market until December 1960.

The incredible power of the Ringfield motor had already been proved earlier in 1960 by what many called the most astounding feat ever, in the history of model railway haulage power, namely the coupling of one of these locomotives hauling a 3 stone child on a special trolley and three of the locomotives coupled together hauling Miss Glenna Ferdinando who weighed 8 stone! The feat itself was not original as the *Model Railway News* of September 1932 showed a photograph of a Bing gauge 4 'King Edward' clockwork locomotive owned by Mr. S. F. Hepburn of Weybridge, hauling his three year old daughter, but the Hornby Dublo feat was a first for 00 gauge!

The *Model Railway Constructor* once more gave the finest critical write up of the new model because in point of fact the Hornby Dublo Company had beaten British Rail to the punch and produced their model before the final design details on the prototype production model had been completed. One of the major criticisms was the short length, a scale of 59 ft over the buffers on the Dublo Model against the 69 ft 6 ins of the real locomotive, itself some 2 ft longer than the original prototype. The other major discrepancy was lower body panels which have a considerable turn under effect although they do state that this is not a criticism of the Hornby locomotive for which the tools were presumably made before the design changes in the original were decided upon. Owing to the large demand for the 2-rail version it was not until May 1961 that the 3232 3-rail locomotive was available.

Some three months after the introduction of the Hornby Dublo locomotive, the real life production locomotives came out in their well-known two-tone green livery and very attractive they looked. The first to enter service was D9001 'St. Paddy' on 23rd February 1961, five days earlier than the numerically first loco D9000 'Royal Scots Grey'. The large rectangle head code panel was to contain a four character code, figure/letter/figure/figure, indicating respectively the class, destination area and two figure train or route number. The lower panel on the Hornby Dublo model was originally intended on the full size locomotives to display the train name, but later discarded.

It was doubtless to try and promote more sales, that a further major endurance test was held on 1st October 1961, starting at 9.30 a.m. on a Sunday morning. The locomotive, which weighed only 1 lb 6 ozs, actually hauled a train of 51 wagons measuring over 17 ft in length and covered a statute 100 miles at an average scale speed of more than 82 m.p.h. by 8.30 a.m. on Thursday, 5th October. The engine ran for 95¼ hours non-stop and as I have recorded earlier I wonder who had the task of working out how many times the armature had revolved? The answer came out as 78 million!

The Meccano Company planned to produce their model in the correct new British Rail livery at the end of that year and at their Trade Fairs early in 1962, showed an advance model of this. It must have had a

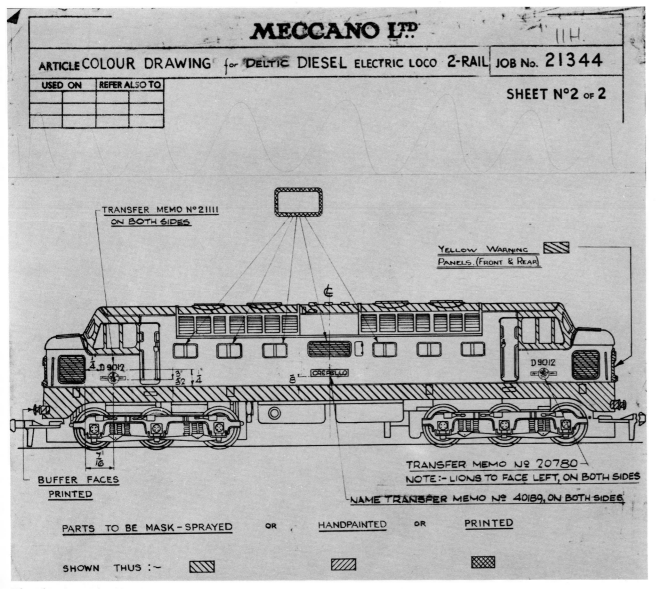

The colour instructions.

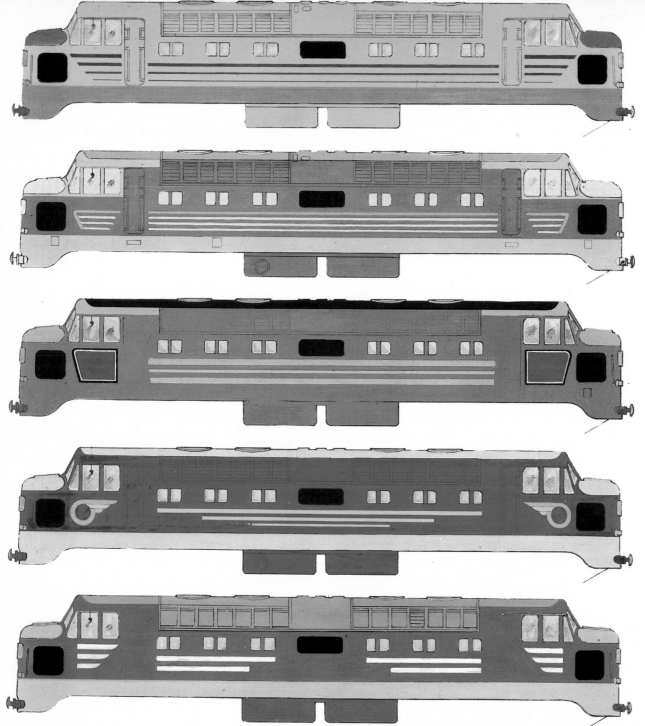

The export drive. Planned body liveries found in Binns Road. Do they relate to real life?

very good reception, as the drawings were duly altered and in July 1962, the 'Co-Co Deltic' locomotives, in authentic colours, were released.

The original advertisement showed the standard new livery, although the descriptive article showed the yellow warning panel which had now become standard on British Railways locomotives and this was added to the drawing on 17th April. I have never seen a two-tone named 'Deltic' loco without this yellow warning panel.

Following traditional LNER and Eastern Region practice, some of the class of locomotives were named after famous racehorses. The 2-rail version No. D9012 was named after 'Crepello' which won the 2,000 Guineas race and the Derby, while the 3-rail version,

'St. Paddy' approaching York with the up 'Flying Scotsman'
– another of Eric Treacy's superb photographs.

'Crepello' in modern livery leaving King's Cross. Photo Eric Treacy.

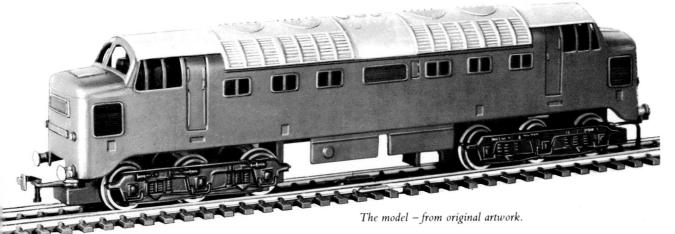

The model – from original artwork.

released at the same time No. D9001, 'St. Paddy' won both the Derby and the St. Leger. Both locomotives came from the same stud and it seems that some of the class were named after past Derby winners.

The January 1962 Trade Fair of the Meccano Company showed the new 2-rail 'Crepello' locomotive hauling no fewer than 28 super detail bogie coaches – with ease! – my platforms only take 16 coaches! (Well, slight exaggeration!). This feat is only two more coaches than the heaviest ever recorded in real life. A V2 loco hauled 26 carriages totalling 870 tons, with 1,300 passengers, from Peterborough to King's Cross (76 miles in 102 minutes) on 31st March 1940.

The new liveried Deltic 'Crepello' loco hauling 28 superdetail coaches at its trade launching January 1962.

Extract from the December 1960 Railway Modeller.

The obvious aims of export sales of the real life locomotive were matched also by the desire to export by the Meccano Company in order to counterbalance the very poor sales they experienced in the U.K. in the early 1960s. The 'Deltic' was the first locomotive to have threaded nut and bolt connectors for the front and rear couplings to allow rapid change to either continental or the NMRA American standards.

Amongst old drawing office papers, I found five distinct colour schemes of the body shell and I would love to hear from anyone who can confirm whether they were purely a designer's dream or whether they copied real life locomotive practice related to particular countries.

The original all-green body of the 'Co-Co' diesel electric locomotive continued right to the end of the Hornby Dublo production No. 2232 and 3232 and while the 2-rail sold 300 in 1964, 550 remained in stock

at the end of the year. These locomotives were called Class 3 in the *Meccano Magazine* whereas the 'Deltic Co-Co' was always called Class 5. One thousand of these latter locomotives were sold in 1964, but here too a further 600 remained unsold. Incidentally, a small slip of paper found on the floor of the drawing office in Binns Road refers to the recommended grease for the gears on the 'Co-Co' and 'Co-Bo' diesel electric locomotives which should be Rocol Molytone 380 or any Molybdenum disulphide grease. A further variation on these models was that the original ones had diecast outside axle frame units held by two screws, whereas the later versions had plastic side frames. I wonder what plans there were to have different side frames depending on the various export markets they were hoping to enter. A list of job numbers refers to 670 and 671 as 'Deltic' locomotives, 2- and 3-rail respectively – with headlamps! I can find no further

LATEST NEWS FROM HORNBY

AT a reception for leading toy buyers held recently by Meccano Ltd. one of the models prominently displayed was an advance sample of the Co-Co diesel being admired here by Mr. Handley of Gamages and Mr. Reynolds of Hanleys. At the time of writing we understand that it is practically ready and that it is a model of one of the very latest B.R. main-line diesels.

This model will, we understand, be fitted with the new ring field motor and the performance appears to be exceptionally good. Indeed, it is most unlikely that many model layouts could accommodate the maximum trains this locomotive will haul. Watch for our full test report. The retail price is 77/6.

VOL. XLVIII. No. I   JANUARY 1963

MECCANO
MAGAZINE

1/3

"CREPELLO" IN ACTION

information other than the Minutes of the New Product Committee 22nd October 1963, which notes the 24 'Co-Bo's' to be prepared and a sample of the 'Co-Co'. And so concludes the chapter on the most publicised and most powerful of all the Hornby Dublo locomotives ever produced.

Other manufacturers have since made 'Deltic' locomotives, but I am surprised that nobody has yet to my knowledge, copied the Edinburgh Haymarket shed's famous 9010 the 'Kings Own Scottish Borderer' as by January 1973 she had completed two million miles of revenue-earning service in just $11\frac{1}{2}$ years.

Extract from the January 1961 Model Railway Constructor.

THE 0–6–0 DIESEL SHUNTER

The Hornby Dublo diesel electric 350 horse power shunting locomotive was announced at the same time as the 'Deltic' model in the December 1960 *Meccano Magazine* and was based on the standard BR design found in large numbers in yard service all over the country. However, unlike the 'Deltic' body, but comparable with the earlier 'Bo-Bo' model, this was produced in high impact polystyrene, with the same wealth of body detail, a fitting tribute to the skill of the toolmakers of B.I.P. Tools Limited. The model had been planned to come out in the old LMS style (all black) and was shown as such in the Meccano export catalogue number 9/560/2.5, although from 1956 all shunting locomotives came out in the new standard BR green. I wonder if any model shunting locomotives were supplied in black livery? They continued to be nicknamed 'Donkeys' or 'Nags' as had their steam ancestors all going back to the days when shunting operations for the most part were undertaken by cart horses.

They were not the first standard diesel shunter model by any means. The Bradshaw model railway catalogue of 1955/6 shows one by Kirdon. It had a high impact polystyrene body in BR black, a heavy duty 3 pole 12 volt DC motor geared to four wheels and sold for £4. 18s. 0d.

The *Constructors* 'Review' about this model was not complimentary and to quote . . . 'quite frankly it

disappointed us considerably'. The model they tested had a haulage capacity much less than they had expected and its maximum comfortable load was no more than 6 bogie coaches and any increase produced considerable slipping. It had a maximum scale speed of 180 m.p.h. when running light, but could not maintain a satisfactory slow speed below 25 or 30 m.p.h.

They thought that the adhesion could be improved if the body had been in diecast metal

like that of the 'Deltic' and that a different gear ratio giving a much lower speed range could have been employed.

In May 1961, the 3-rail version was available, number D3763 (the 2-rail version, being D3302) and in general had a far better report in the June *Model Railway Constructor*. They state . . . 'We were able to achieve some realistically smooth starts and stops with this locomotive which in general ran far more

smoothly than its 2-rail twin. Its slow running potentialities were superior too; we were able to get it down to a mere crawl of 2 to 3 m.p.h., either light or with about a dozen wagons.' On the other hand despite its slightly increased weight (1 oz), it could handle no more than six Hornby Dublo super detail coaches without slipping. They do have the honesty to state that the difference in performance between the 2-rail and 3-rail shunters was a little surprising, but they can

Meccano Ltd

The Liverpool firm are again in prominence with four more new items in their Hornby-Dublo range.

A useful hard-working 0-6-0 diesel-electric shunting locomotive is now available for goods yard and freight train duties. The model is fitted with the smooth running and powerful Ring Field motor and is capable of hauling trains far in excess of those likely to be handled on most model railways.

A single screw, placed centrally on top of the body holds the motor and chassis unit in position under the body shell. Almost the whole interior of the plastic body is occupied, by the very substantial die-cast chassis housing and the Ring Field motor; the latter is located at the cab end with the armature mounted vertically and driving one axle through worm and pinion gears. Die-cast dummy outside frames showing spring details are attached separately and held in place by four bolts.

The plastic moulded body is convincingly detailed, on the model we examined, however, the vented doors at the " front " have sagged a little. Price **55s. 6d.**

only conclude that the 2-rail example was one of the 'black sheep' from the production line.

However, things were not all well with this locomotive. The totally enclosed plastic body had no real ventilators which meant that the motor itself became relatively hot. At this stage Meccano plastic was being used for everything, even the card on the armature winding. Up till now they had all been, or so I was told, fibre card, but now they were very thin, light plastic, with the result that the heat of the armature windings frequently melted this insulation, causing a short circuit and one or two shops have told me that they often replaced armatures on this particular model.

Another apparent cause of the heat was possibly the locking of the connecting rods which realistically had the outside cranks of their prototype. The original connecting rods were a single piece covering all three axles and this was drawn on 9th March 1960. By 19th

HORNBY-DUBLO   OO
B.R. Co-Co " Deltic " Diesel-electric locomotive   82s 6d
B.R. 0-6-0 Diesel-electric shunter   58s 6d
12V d.c. three-rail

DESPITE the present popularity, amounting almost to universal use, of two-rail electrification, Meccano Ltd have not forgotten their earlier followers who are still using three-rail equipment and have introduced three-rail versions of both the " Deltic " Co-Co main line diesel locomotive and the 0-6-0 diesel shunting locomotive. Both are fitted with ring-field motors and apart from the method of current collection and return are generally similar to their two-rail counterparts reviewed in our January (" Deltic ") and March (diesel shunter) issues. The " Deltic's " cast-metal body is again finished in plain green livery with no identifying marks other than the British Railways crest. The diesel shunter has the same plastic body but carries a different number, D3763 instead of the two-rail version's D3302. In performance there is little to choose between the two- and

August 1961, this had been altered to dual coupling rods just linking two axles although I have never heard the official reason fully explained.

In June 1961, the renowned *Trains Illustrated Magazine* reported that wasp black and yellow danger stripes were fitted fore and aft on the diesel shunters and were a most effective warning device.

The model trade tried to persuade the Meccano Company to reproduce the wasp warning lines on their own superb detailed model as they thought the cost of doing this would only be marginal, but it was too late. The fortunes of the Company were already sliding downhill and it was never put into practice. I have often been surprised that later model railway manufacturers producing six wheel shunter bodies, such as Messrs. Hornby, Wrenn and Lima can not produce an alternative body. In 1968 the famous Sentinal Company gained a design award in the capital goods section for a very attractive and simple shunter. This would make a welcome change.

750 2-rail shunters (2231) were sold in 1964, but 1100 remained in stock at the takeover.

The Hornby three-rail diesel-electric shunter at work in our marshalling yard. The character, though not the beauty, of this model would be improved if some diagonal black and yellow stripes were painted on the ends, as on the prototype.

Extract from the June 1961 Model Railway Constructor.

three-rail versions of the " Deltic." Both have the excellent high- and low-speed and hauling characteristics on which we commented several times recently, which must be attributed in part to their satisfactory adhesion weight, identical on each at 1lb 4¾oz.

Our three-rail shunter, which at 13¾oz was heavier than the two-rail version (12¾oz), was a better performer although the loads it would haul were no greater. We were able to achieve some realistically smooth starts and stops with this locomotive, which in general ran far more smoothly than its two-rail twin. Its slow-running potentialities were superior, too; we were able to get it down to a mere crawl of 2-3 m.p.h., either light or with about a dozen wagons. On the other hand, despite its slightly increased weight it could handle no more than six Hornby-Dublo

" super-detail " coaches without slipping and although this is adequate for most layouts there is not the reserve of hauling power found in the " Deltic " locomotive. The difference in performance between the two- and three-rail shunters is a little surprising and we can only conclude that our two-rail example was one of the " black sheep " from the production line which crop up occasionally.

THE 'CO-BO' DIESEL ELECTRIC LOCOMOTIVE

It is ironic that Chapter 13 should deal with the most unsuccessful locomotive in the whole Hornby Dublo range – the new 'Co-Bo' diesel electric locomotive. This was modelled on the type 2 1,200 h.p. locomotive, built by Metropolitan-Vickers for fast passenger freight duties on the London Midland region.

The bodywork was similar to the 'Deltics' with a well detailed diecast body and the Ringfield motor giving it almost 'Deltic' hauling power. The 2-rail version carried the running number D5702, while the 3-rail version was D5713 and they both arrived together in December 1961.

The *Model Railway Constructor* 'Review' again hit the nail on the head stating that they were a little disappointed when Meccano Limited first announced their new locomotive, for the prototype was one of

the very few which have not been perpetuated under the modernisation plan. Its 'box-on-wheels' design is by no means the most imposing and on this model this effect is exaggerated by an obviously hollow diecast metal body, unfortunately, in this instance, without the saving grace of fine detail well executed. The review ended by stating that British model manufacturers will only bring themselves into the same high class as their continental contemporaries by combining the excellence of such power units as the Hornby

TITLE	COMPLETE ASSEMBLY — CO-BO LOCO 3 RAIL.	JOB No 21788

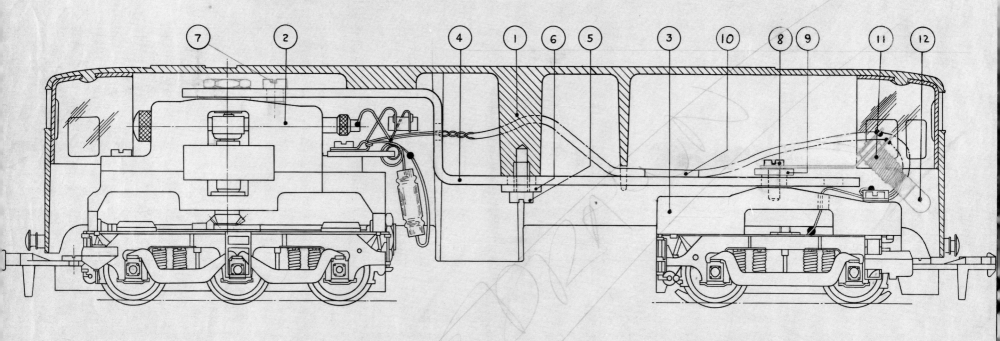

NOTE :- FOR DETAILS OF CONNECTING WIRES
SEE BOGIE ASSEMBLIES JOBS No 21790 & 21791

ITEM	DESCRIPTION	JOB No	No OFF
12	LAMP	21795	1
11	LAMP BRACKET . & HOLDER	21794	1
1	HOUSING ASSEMBLY	21771	1
2	MOTOR BOGIE ASSEMBLY — 3 RAIL	21790	1
3	REAR BOGIE ASSEMBLY — 3 RAIL	21791	1
4	MOUNTING PLATE	21365	1
5	SCREW (MOUNTING PLATE TO HOUSING)	27	1
6	WASHER (MOUNTING PLATE TO HOUSING)	39	1
7	SCREW (M/BOGIE TO MOUNTING PLATE)	21363	1
8	SCREW (R/BOGIE TO MOUNTING PLATE)	2954	1
9	INSULATING BUSH (R/BOGIE TO MOUNTING PLATE)	21397	1
10	SELF ADHESIVE ELECTRICAL CELLULOSE TAPE	11240	1

3.	JOBS 21794/95 (ITEMS 11&12) ADDED		7251	28·11·63	V.G.
2.	ON ITEM No 3, CASTING MODIFIED		6452	16·11·61	J.R.C.
ISSUE	DESCRIPTION OF CHANGE		C.O.No	DATE	SIG

MATERIAL :-   SEE JOB LIST No 675

DRAWN	I.S.
TRACED	E.M.
CHECKED	
APPROVED	
SCALE	2:1
DATE	26·9·60

← *The 'Co-Bo' headlight plan – only 24 made – from original Meccano drawings.*

The colour instructions.

Ringfield motor with the abundance of correct body detail found in the latest plastic-bodied models.

In June 1962, to try and boost sales, the 2-rail 'Co-Bo' was available in the new set which included the LMR super detail goods brake van now finished in bauxite brown livery for fast train working. It had previously appeared in standard light grey livery. The wagons included the refrigerator van, the bulk grain wagon and the 12 ton ventilated van.

Perhaps its principal claim to fame was for hauling the famous 'Condor Express' from London (Hendon) to Glasgow, a distance of 400 miles (then the fastest freight service in Europe). It was immortalised by Mr. Cuneo's magnificent painting and indeed was depicted on the cover of the No. 18 edition of the *Triang Model Railway Catalogue* in 1972.

It was definitely planned to have a headboard although this was never put into production.

On 27th April 1962, the yellow warning panels were added on the drawings of the 'Co-Bo' locomotive, but such were the stocks of this unpopular model, that until these were considerably reduced, production versions with this modification would not be put into being and I have not evidenced a 'Co-Bo' locomotive with a yellow warning panel.

In an effort to increase sales at the Product Development Committee meeting on 22nd October 1963, it was suggested to add headlight units as had been the practice on European model railways and 24 such locomotives were made with lights to check market reaction at the January Toy Fairs. The drawings were duly amended on 11th December 1963, but

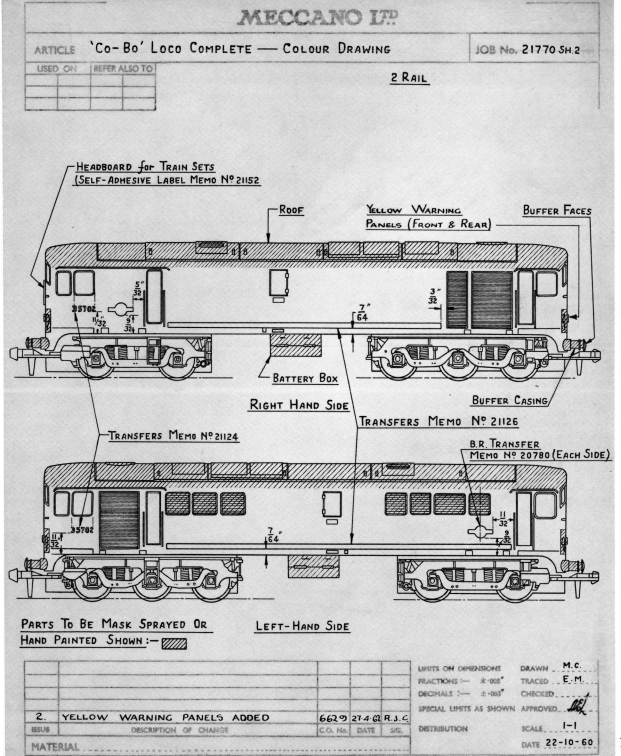

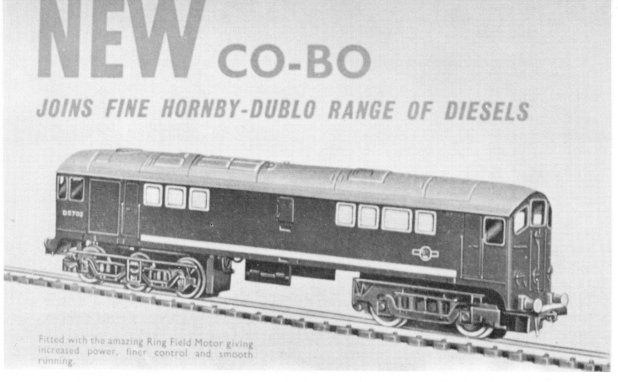

NEW CO-BO
JOINS FINE HORNBY-DUBLO RANGE OF DIESELS

Fitted with the amazing Ring Field Motor giving increased power, finer control and smooth running.

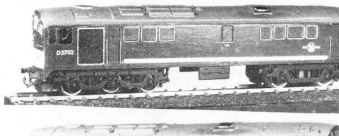

RAILWAY MODELLER

For the average enthusiast   May '79 45p

the general reaction was very poor and by 17th January 1964 the modification was deleted.

The alterations were crude to the extreme involving a central light bulb fitted to the chassis at the Bo end and two large holes drilled in the front plate. Several genuine models are known to exist, but I have deliberately left out the exact details, as in any other hobbies, we have our rogues who would very soon convert the standard model into a highly prized rarity on their kitchen table!

In 1964 only 130 of these models were sold and 3,150 2-rail 'Co-Bo' locomotives remained at the time of the takeover.

That wonderful west country character and train collector – Archie Napier Ewing – has a 'Co-Bo' loco, new in its box from Meccano, sporting a driver! A one-off attempt to create more sales – or a planned production variation – who knows? I had thought it was from the 050 Railway Staff set of figures but on examination it is a super detail style figure, but, totally different from any of the figures issued.

The driver, in a seated posture on a base had the number '2' moulded on the back and his left arm folded across his waist. Archie has a further figure, identical except the left arm is folded across his heart – and the number '3' moulded at the back.

Close examination of the photograph on page 456 of the December 1961 *Meccano Magazine*, introducing the 'Co-Bo' shows a driver at the controls, seated as in Archie's model at the Co end – near left hand side!

17 years later, with added warning panel – the Hornby Dublo model still makes headlines!

The Triang Catalogue for 1972 – note the headboard which was to be No. 1703 on the Hornby Dublo Model.

Tri-ang HORNBY
MODEL RAILWAYS EDITION 18

THE SOUTHERN REGION ELECTRIC SUBURBAN TRAINS

It was on 27th May 1957, that the first of the new 57 three car electric multiple units built at Eastleigh, with GEC electric equipment, went into operation for the Euston to Watford and Broad Street–Richmond services of the London Midland Region. As early as 28th September 1961, the New Product Committee at the Meccano Company had chosen a Southern electric set.

One gentleman raised a query about the possibility of redesigning the drive unit to give a four wheel drive, but was overruled as it was necessary to finalise the design to allow for early tooling.

With three coaches, the price of £7.00 was arrived at on 24th November 1961, but it was decided that this was far too high. It was planned to delete the centre coach and through modifications to the original design reduce the selling price to £5.19s. 6d. as this was thought the maximum permissible. There were clip-on side mouldings to symbolise the outside rail current collectors, which again were a further attempt at price cutting rather than a more secure fixing and sad to relate they do fall off and one frequently finds them missing. By 29th August 1962, 200 sample sets were in production and they were announced in the *Meccano Magazine* in October of that year, in both 2- and 3-rail versions, in the now familiar all green livery. The new model had been shown at the Toy Fair earlier in the year and was to be the only new locomotive to appear

in that year. The *Constructor* 'Review' gave an excellent write up pointing out that it was, despite its green livery and numbers, a fairly accurate model of the London Midland Region, London Area, suburban set. However, by the time the model went into full production the visual warning indicator panel – the yellow band on the front of the motor and rear car – had been introduced on the prototype and the December 1962 *Meccano Magazine* mentions a last minute change in production. However, I have seen one or two models without this yellow panel and can only assume that they were from the initial batch of 200. As sold, the unit is a two-car set with a powered brake second vehicle and dummy driving trailer brake second. To make the unit into a standard three car formation, the Southern Region super detail suburban second class coach (which had come out just a few months earlier) was used and it all goes to make a very attractive unit.

A sceptic at the Design Committee meeting some months earlier, was dubious about the hauling capacity of the powered motor coach when he noticed that the Ringfield motor drove one axle of the motor bogie only and so was pleasantly surprised to find that the

unit fairly romped away with two coaches in tow and in point of fact this was all the prototype car was asked to do. However, a further three car, non-motored set was added with no noticeable effect on performance and they went on until a train of twelve bogie passenger cars was made up before serious wheel slip set in. The Design Committee had no hesitation in recommending this as a most realistic unit.

Apart from the very early models with no visual warning indicator panel, one or two modifications appeared in so much as the non-driving ends of the motor and trailer coaches seemed to vary, at one stage having black inside faces and another a privet green.

As they used a photograph of the maroon Watford set to model from, I am surprised that they did not produce a standard LMR maroon version at the same time as they could have also used the maroon suburban centre coaches to good effect. Surprisingly, nil/nil figures are recorded for sale/stock 1964.

The prototype – BR photograph of New Euston–Watford electric stock, built at Eastleigh in 1957. Why did Meccano never introduce it in BR maroon using the S.D. suburban coaches.

A three coach train was planned but thought too expensive.

HORNBY-DUBLO OO
Suburban Electric unit Motor coach 81s 6d
Driving trailer 21s 0d

EVER since the Hornby multiple-unit was announced last March, we have been wondering how close to the prototype it would be in scale length, realistic appearance and accuracy of detail. The model has now gone into production, and we can report that, despite the coach numbers, it is a fairly accurate model of a London Midland Region London Area suburban set. Knowing the reluctance of Hornby to change from metal to plastic sides, we were not surprised to find that the printed tin sides had been perpetuated; we are pleased to see, however, that the outer ends of the driving vehicles are fitted with a most realistic moulded green plastic front end which, apart from the absence of a destination indicator, and with clear plastic in the headcode panel, is an almost exact reproduction of the somewhat austere Eastleigh front end fitted to these units. To bring the model right up to date, a yellow warning panel is painted on each front end below the cab windows; this feature has only appeared on the prototype units within the past few months. As sold, the unit is a two-car set, with a powered motor brake second, and a driving trailer brake second. This latter vehicle correctly has an identical body to the motor coach, but is not powered and is fitted with trailer bogies, with plastic dummy shoe-beams on the outer bogie. To bring the unit up to its correct three-car formation, an S.R. suburban second, as reviewed in our June issue, is used. The bodywork and finish of the new coaches follows the pattern established with the locomotive-hauled suburban stock; tin printed sides, plastic ends and roofs, plastic couplings and, on the unpowered vehicle, metal bogie frames and plastic wheels. If anything, the detail on the printed sides is slightly superior to that on the earlier coaches. The driving cab side windows have been modelled as one large opening, whereas in fact they are divided into two by a central vertical bar; this detail could easily be added with card or even silver paper. No seating unit is fitted to the motor coach, as the motor and associated wiring and weighting bar occupy most of the space; in the driving

trailer, a compartment-type seat unit, but with low intermediate partitions, is fitted; the prototype vehicles are of the saloon arrangement, so a central passageway should have been provided between the seats. For some reason, despite its obvious affinity to an L.M.R. unit, both coaches have been given Southern Region coach numbers which are, in fact, correct for B.R. standard 2-EPB unit number 5712; although also Eastleigh-built to the same overall design, all standard stock on the Southern Region is built on the longer 63ft 5in underframe, against the 56ft 11in frames of the L.M.R. units, and therefore have eight compartments against seven in the L.M.R. units. The driving trailers on the S.R. units are completely different as, apart from being longer, they have no guard's compartment, and therefore have nine compartments. Nor does the difference finish here, for the Southern units have a different frontal arrangement of jumper cables, buck-eye couplings and oval buffers.

We were inclined to be somewhat sceptical about the probable hauling capacity of the motor coach when we noticed that the ring field motor drove only one axle of the motor bogie, even allowing for the rubber treads on the wheels, and the considerable weight in the coach sub-frame. We were, therefore, surprised and pleased to find that the unit fairly romped away with two coaches in tow, when formed as a three-car unit; this is all that the prototype car would be asked to do, but the Hornby motor coach will pull a second three-car set without any noticeable effect on performance. Indeed, we formed the train up to twelve cars before serious wheelslip set in, and the motor began to get overheated. This performance is well in excess of all normal requirements on a model railway, and when one considers that a normal twelve-car formation on B.R. includes at least six motored bogies, the performance is very impressive. On the L.M.R. units, both bogies of the motor coach are powered, and accordingly Hornby have fitted correct plastic motor bogie side frames, complete with dummy shoe gear, to both bogies. A strong metal bar keeps the frame rigid; a plastic underframe detail moulding is bolted to the underside of this bar, and this moulding also incorporates a solid chunk of lead weight. Current is collected through both sets of wheels on the dummy

motor bogie, and through the wheels of the unpowered axle on the powered bogie. As all these wheels are nickel-silver plated, current collection is very good, and even at a scale walking pace, which the unit will maintain happily for long periods, the torque of the motor is steady, indicating a smooth and uninterrupted power supply. Maximum scale speed of the unit formed as a three-car train is over 120 m.p.h.—well in excess of the performance of the prototype, and certainly too fast for realistic suburban operation!

We have no hesitation in commending this as a most realistic unit, and despite its few blemishes it should satisfy most electric traction enthusiasts, although at nearly £6 for a three-car unit, a fleet of electric trains will be financially out of the question for most people. The motor coach and driving trailer are available as a two-car unit in an attractive set, complete with a circuit of track, for 118s.

Extract from Model Railway Constructor December 1962.

Whether this was because no figures were available, or all production was sold in 1963, we shall never know. It was a highly successful model and more than made up for the poor performance of the earlier 'Bo-Bo' locomotive. It was planned to use this power pack with suitably adapted side plates in a new version of the 'Bo-Bo', but the end was in sight and the project was never completed.

THE E3000 PANTOGRAPH ELECTRIC LOCOMOTIVE

Locomotive number E3001 was the first of the 25 KV AC locomotives to be supplied to British Railways by the Associated Electrical Industries Traction Division which combined the traction activities of the two famous companies, formerly known as the British Thomson-Houston Company and the Metropolitan-Vickers Electrical Company limited.

Of these 3,300 h.p. locomotives 35 were supplied to the general requirements of the British Transport Commission and 23 of them were type A units. The specification for type A locomotives required that they should be capable of hauling a 475 ton passenger train at 90 m.p.h. or a 950 ton mineral train at 55 m.p.h. The unit is a 'Bo-Bo' type with four series wound traction motors mounted onto two fabricated bogies and a nominal weight of 80 tons. The remaining units were type B, which were identical, but with an altered gear ratio arranged for a maximum speed of 80 m.p.h. The latter versions were capable of hauling mineral trains of 1,250 tons at 55 m.p.h. The first locomotive, E3001, was handed over to British Railways at a ceremony at Sandbach on Friday, 27th November 1959, to be used initially on the Manchester–Crewe electrification. A beautiful model had been produced by Lilliput and was advertised as early as October 1960.

It was felt at the Meccano Design Committee

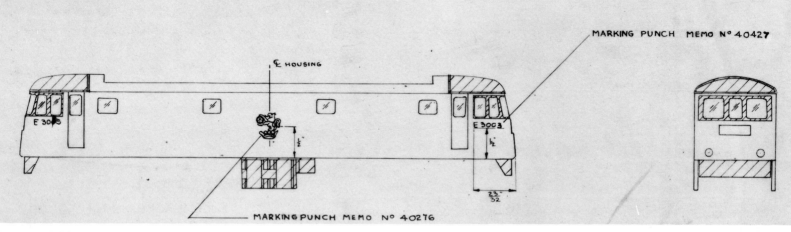

MECCANO LTD

HOUSING ASSEMBLY 3300 H.P. ELECTRIC LOCO – 3 RAIL   COLOUR DRAWING

MARKING PUNCH MEMO Nº 40427

€ HOUSING

E 3003

E 3003

MARKING PUNCH MEMO Nº 40276

meeting on 2nd February 1962, that a new locomotive with a working pantograph should be available in 1964. On 16th January 1963, it was agreed to proceed with the model although a price of 75s. was thought high in comparison with the proposed Triang model. The initial production run was to be 10,000 units and it was planned to include it in set No. 2254 (clearly shown in the last 1964 catalogue and including three coaches, the centre coach being the famous maroon super detail restaurant car No. 4071). It was planned to release the model in January 1964, and it was announced at the Toy Fairs that month although it was not available until the following September. The set was never issued.

These new locomotives were referred to in railway circles as 'Blue flash' not to be confused with 'Blue streak' which were the diesel pullman trains running primarily on the Western Region main lines.

A full page article on the 'striking new model' appeared in the April 1964 *Meccano Magazine* together with an article in the August issue on running this new locomotive to quote 'which is sure to prove a great favourite with model railway lovers'. It was designed to operate not only from 2-rail track, but also from overhead equipment; the Triang catenary provided a very suitable system. The planned model was to have the same number as the Lilliput's number – E3001, and this has caused a lot of confusion in model railway collecting circles as I feel convinced that the only model Hornby Dublo ever produced had the number E3002 on it. This was probably to avoid confusion with the Lilliput model, although it was planned and indeed drawn that the 3-rail version of this locomotive was to be E3003. This was never put into production,

The prototype supplied by AEI Traction Division to the London Midland Region of British Railways.

Meccano publicity photograph showing Triang catenary equipment. Note painted white cab windows and low slung loco number.

but indeed a 3-rail version was supplied to special order, primarily for export markets.

The model finally appeared in the October 1964 *Meccano Magazine* and again I have to fall back on the magnificent test report from the *Model Railway Constructor*. They stated that one example had been on the market for some time while another was listed in a proprietary catalogue in addition to the new Hornby

Dublo locomotive. They further point out that this new locomotive was the first to have emerged from the Hornby Dublo stable since the take over by Triang early in the year. They state that the numbers and crest are stamped and painted on the body sides, presumably for the sake of economy, but detract from the locomotive's appearance by being overscale. Likewise the plain blue ends are true to prototype, but are spoilt

by the small head code panel. Other minor details which could so easily have been rectified, and indeed appeared on the prototype models and on the original mock-ups, were the deletion of the white painted window surrounds and red buffer heads!

The motor unit supported a huge ring magnet and was the most powerful locomotive the *Model Railway Constructor* had tested. In the haulage test, they had to abandon their standard test circuit and lay a larger one for E3002 and its 16 coach train being whisked around at a scale 90 m.p.h.

The side frames to the bogies were loosely clip fitted and were a poor economy measure. The new, very neatly designed coupling unit which had been first introduced on the six-wheel brake and hopper wagons was now fitted to this locomotive and could be easily removed to allow another coupling to be fitted if required.

Typical of the cost cutting involved – the E3000 loco used the identical side frames as the 'Bo-Bo' locomotive but in plastic thus saving the tooling cost.

I wonder why they did not undertake the small detail painting indicated on the drawings for 1st August 1963. The cab windows should be spray painted white, but this had been deleted by 3rd June 1964. In the following month, November, the *Model Railway Constructor* reported that they had heard that the 3-rail version of the locomotive would not now proceed and also that the ineffective method of attaching the bogie side frames was receiving attention and that a modification was now in hand which would result in a more secure fitting. I don't think this ever came into being. The *Model Railway News* also had a magnificent report on the power of this locomotive. All tests through points and very tight reverse curves were passed with flying colours so they placed it on their 'kill or cure' gradient. This time it was a one in eight gradient and the locomotive (with an all metal wagon with a one pound weight on it), from a standing start on the gradient, pushed the loaded wagon to the top as though on level track. 'The loco was brought back to the starting point again and with the same load, but the controller switched to half wave we sent it on its way to the top once more and although it reached the top we could see that this was indeed its limit.' They concluded that it was a very satisfactory engine.

The *Railway Modeller* as well as commenting on the points we have already covered, also criticised the somewhat heavy pantograph appearance when compared with the far finer Hornby-Acho version, while the *Model Railway News* had a test load of 12 mainline

Hornby–Dublo 25kV a.c. Bo-Bo

THE prototype of this month's subject in *track test* is no stranger to the model railway enthusiast. One example has been on the market for some time, while another is listed in a proprietary catalogue, in addition to the Hornby-Dublo electric locomotive, No. E3002, which has recently appeared. In view of the constant demand for locomotives of all types to "fill the gaps" it is a pity that there should be duplication of this kind, simply to overcome the difference in standards and the difficulty of running proprietary locomotives and stock on other proprietary makes of track.

The Prototype

For the London Midland Region West Coast electrification scheme an initial order of 100 25kV a.c. Bo-Bo electric locomotives of 3,300 h.p. was placed with various manufacturers and by the time the first section was opened, between Manchester and Crewe on September 12, 1960, examples of several types were in service. The first to appear was the A.E.I. (British Thomson-Houston) version and No. E3001, built in 1959, was the first 25kV locomotive built for British Railways. The batch is now complete and numbers 23 locomotives, Nos.

E3001–23, while Nos. E3096/7 are externally similar. The latter were originally intended as freight locomotives (Type B) with different gear ratios but it was subsequently realised that the passenger locomotives (Type A) were suitable for freight working and the few Type B locomotives were completed with similar equipment to the Type As. The "first hundred" electric locomotives now handle nearly all locomotive-hauled traffic between Liverpool, Manchester and Crewe and their use on the main line is steadily increasing as the current is switched on in sections southwards from Crewe to Euston.

The Model

The first new locomotive to emerge from the Hornby-Dublo stable since the takeover by Tri-ang is, as may have been expected, a combination of the two manufacturers' characteristic features—Hornby chassis with Ringfield motor and Tri-ang-like plastic body. The body is a reasonably accurate model but is spoilt by detail faults; numbers and crest are stamped and painted on the body sides, presumably for the sake of economy, but detract from the locomotive's appearance by being overscale. The rather plain ends are true to prototype but are spoilt by the small headcode panel. Minor details on the ends which can easily be rectified are the colour of the window surrounds, which should be white, and

▲ *A.E.I. (B.T.H.) 25kV a.c. Bo-Bo electric locomotive No. E3019 at Stockport Edgeley in September 1961; photo by Alan H. Bryant.*

Extract from the October 1964 Model Railway Constructor.

The roof of No. E3002, like that of the prototype, is plain, but the pantographs on the model are rather overscale.

the red buffers. Roof detail is effective, although the letters "A" and "B", referring to the pantographs, are rather conspicuous. Current collection from the track or overhead catenary is determined by a changeover plug, neatly disguised as a circuit-breaker, which can be plugged into the respective socket in the roof. The pantographs are not as neat as those employed on the French-built Hornby-Acho S.N.C.F. electric locomotive, but work well and are robust enough to withstand a considerable amount of rough handling. Livery of No. E3002 is the rich blue of a freshly-painted locomotive.

The chassis employs the famous Ringfield motor and is one of the most powerful we have tested. During the haulage test, in fact, we had to abandon our standard test circuit and lay a larger one, as No. E3002 was in grave danger of catching up with the tail of its 16-coach train, which was being whisked around at a scale 90 m.p.h.! Unfortunately, the visible parts of the chassis fall below the standard of its performance. The plastic detachable bogie side frame is the same pattern as that used on the now withdrawn Type 1 Bo-Bo, which is a

similar design to that employed on the B.T.H. electric locomotives. The wheelbase of the prototype diesel, however, is only 8ft 6in, compared with the 10ft 9in of the electric, and the use of the Type 1's bogie sideframes gives No. E3002 a rather elongated appearance. The sideframes are very loosely clip-fitted, which we feel is a retrograde step in view of the fact that the screw-fitting on the Type 1 was completely successful. The neat coupler featured on the recent six-wheel brake and hopper wagon is employed and we are pleased to note that it can be removed, so that another type can be fitted if desired.

Current collection from the track is through nickel-silver contacts on the wheels of all three non-powered axles.

As previously mentioned, performance was exemplary, but an explanatory note is required regarding the haulage capacity. The results obtained with the motor bogie leading were far superior to those obtained with the non-powered bogie at the leading end. In the latter case, the 16-coach train mentioned above was about the maximum load started without slipping and maximum speed with this load was in the region

of a scale 40 m.p.h. In order to cause a momentary slip on starting with the powered bogie leading we had to increase the load to 14 Hornby and 10 Tri-ang coaches, while the heaviest train started by No. E3002 consisted of 18 Hornby (13 of which were propelled, to prevent the locomotive pulling the train off the track on the curves) and 10 Tri-ang coaches. This massive formation reduced the locomotive's speed to that of a pick-up goods and considerable slipping was evident.

With such a remarkable model as this, it is a pity that the body can be faulted, but the performance more than makes up for any deficiencies in this case. Hornby-Dublo locomotives have long been noted for their reliability, power and general high standard and it is fitting that the name should continue to be associated with excellent workmanship as the new motive power of British Railways gradually finds its way onto the model railways of this country. One cannot fail to be impressed by the power output of the Ringfield motor in this model and at such a reasonable price No. E3002 should become a firm favourite with the modellers of the present-day scene.

Performance and Specification
Type of motor: 3-pole Ringfield
Drive: Worm and gear on inner motor bogie axle
Gear ratio: 11 : 1
Maximum scale speed (light): 140 m.p.h.
  (with 5 Hornby-Dublo coaches): 140 m.p.h.
Minimum scale speed (light): 7½ m.p.h.
  (with 5 Hornby-Dublo coaches): 7½ m.p.h.
Maximum load started without slipping: see text
Maximum load: see text
Weight of chassis: 16½oz.
Body construction: Plastic moulding
Type of coupler: Hornby-Dublo standard
Wheels plated?: Yes
Wheel back-to-back: 14.5mm.
Flangeless wheels: None
TV suppression?: Yes
Livery: BR electric blue
Finish: Semi-gloss
Additional features: rubber-tyred wheels on driving axle. Also available for 3-rail.

coaches and 48 wagons which represented almost the whole Hornby Dublo catalogue. This was hauled with ease for a considerable time and a check showed that the temperature of the motor had not risen above the normal. Indeed the appearance of this model delayed the release of the Triang Railways version (which appeared in their catalogue earlier) and when it was issued, they used the excellent Hornby Dublo moulding, slightly modified. Their model, numbered E3001, appeared in November 1966, although for some reason with their own bogie power unit fitted with knurled wheels – rather noisy.

At the time of researching this particular chapter in the mid-seventies, the all electric London to Glasgow route had yet to be completed and I remember reading in Eric Treacy's first book *Steam Up* a remarkable paragraph under 'What's in a Name'!

He writes 'in one of Neville Cardus's matchless essays on cricket he tells of his horror in finding that a Worcestershire cricketer with the unmusical name of Gaukrodger had dared to make a big score against his beloved Lancashire. He had nothing against Mr. Gaukrodger but his name. "I decided," said Cardus, "that Gaukrodger was an impossible name for a cricketer!". That's how I feel when I see a great handsome rebuilt Royal Scot bearing the name "Girl Guide" or a London Midland Region Stanier Pacific bearing the name of that dainty and charming lady "Duchess of Kent". How much better if these monsters had received the names of our Cumberland hills – Great Gable, Skiddaw, Scafell, Blencathra, Hellvelyn, Langdale or even of our Yorkshire Fells – Pen-y-Ghent, Ingleborough, Whernside, Wild Boar and so on, names speak of power and majesty!'

I couldn't help feeling at the time that it would be marvellous to see the new electric locomotives gliding past with these names and indeed was overjoyed to see that British Railways were reverting to the practice of naming some of these beautiful locomotives. Digressing – even more so when I read in the *Daily Telegraph* on 30/9/79 that British Rail were to name one of their class 8600 locos after Bishop E. Treacy. In the end – only 4,000 models were produced, 2,500 being sold in 1964 and 1,500 remained in stock.

Manufacturer: Meccano Ltd., Binns Road, Liverpool, 13

Catalogue number: 2245

Price: 75s 0d

Scale: 4mm–1ft   Voltage: 12V d.c. (2-rail and overhead)

Principal Dimensions

Model	Scale Equivalent	Prototype
Locomotive: E3002		Number series: E3001-23
Weight: 18½oz	—	79 tons 12 cwt
Length over buffers: 220mm	55ft 0in	56ft 6in
Wheel diameter: 14mm	3ft 0in	4ft 0in
Wheel centres: 34mm	8ft 6in	10ft 9in
Bogie centres: 134mm	33ft 6in	31ft 6in

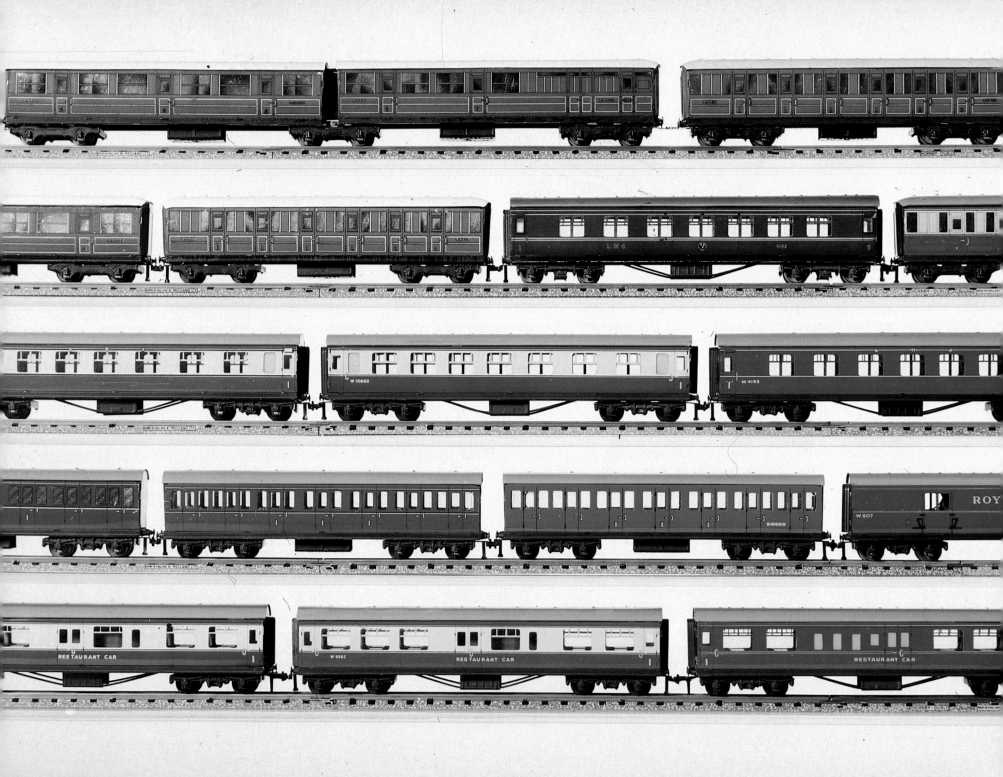

Rolling Stock

THE LNER COACHES

The first coaches produced in the Hornby Dublo system were the corridor teak tinplated coaches to go with the 'Sir Nigel Gresley' locomotive. There was the standard LNER first/third corridor coach number 42759 and the very attractive and understandably highly prized articulated set, incorporating an all third coach number 45401 and a matching brake end, number 45402.

The articulated coaches had been in use on the London North Eastern Railway for many years. The *Meccano Magazine* of February 1925 even showed a photograph of one of the first units to be built on the articulated system evolved by Mr. H. N. Gresley. The articulated principle was adopted in the quintuple, or five coach dining car trains between King's Cross and Leeds although by the mid-nineteen twenties had been successfully applied to the express trains on the London (King's Cross) and Edinburgh (Waverley) route. It was also announced that same year that the new LNER suburban rolling stock was also to be built on the articulated principle.

The Gresley twin articulated sets in real life remained in express service on British Railways until the early 1960s although no more were built after his death in 1941.

These remained the only Hornby Dublo coaches available before the war, although there were the much publicised LMS corridor coaches with transparent windows awaiting the end of the war for the

←*The Tinplate Coaches.*

The D2 articulated coach.

arrival of the 'Duchess of Atholl' locomotive. As mentioned in the first chapter, the company Tyldesley and Holbrook supplied litho papers in LMS, Southern and Great Western Region liveries which, although to scale length, could be suitably adapted to stick onto the sides of the tinplate coaches to give alternate trains to be used with the multi-region 0–6–2 Tank locomotive.

The Hornby Dublo coaches were of exceptionally sturdy design, made of 0.12 in tinplate, with zinc diecast bogie units and wheels. Sturdy, reliable, and realistic.

The articulated sets were certainly supplied after the war with the Peco hook couplings. A post-war box code is D2–BW 10199–2M–4/48, i.e. two thousand in April 1948. I believe them to be pre-war stock which had been frozen during the war and they were never promoted on the U.K. market. I have indeed seen a price list and catalogue listing them for the Indian market and the artwork in the December 1948 *Meccano Magazine* showed the 'Duchess of

Hornby-Dublo Suburban Train Working

ONE of the advantages of the smart and imposing Hornby-Dublo Standard Tank Locomotive is that its "mixed traffic" character allows it to be used equally well on passenger as on goods services. It is typical of the useful 0-6-2 tank of actual practice with medium-sized driving wheels, that does a great

A realistic suburban station formed of two Island Platforms. One train is held in the bay platform while the other gets ahead on the main line.

amount of work in local goods and passenger services. The Hornby-Dublo range does not as yet include suburban passenger coaches, but it is possible to conduct local passenger traffic by means of the standard Two-Coach Articulated Unit. Although this represents a main line corridor "twin," real corridor stock appears at times on local work, especially when filling in time between long-distance trips; so that the use of the Dublo Unit in miniature for suburban duties is quite reasonable.

With a single engine and train quite an interesting service can be run, even on the simplest layout. On a continuous track, an "all stations" train can make successive halts at the same station on each circuit in order to represent the conditions of making a journey from point to point. The actual methods of working will depend to some extent on the station layout. Thus if a loop line is provided at the station, forming in effect separate "up" and "down" tracks, the "running round" of the engine ready for the return trip when the end of a "journey" is reached can easily be carried out. During periods of heavy traffic the "turn round time" allowed at terminal points is usually very short, so that smart working is necessary if time is to be kept. On a Dublo system a single operator can amuse himself by seeing just how smartly the running round operation, and in fact the terminal work generally, can be divided up in a satisfactory manner.

If there is no loop line, "running round" cannot be done in the orthodox manner, but the engine can be got to the other end of the train ready for the return journey by uncoupling it at the end of a journey and running it right round the track until it reaches the train again. The train can then make another trip

and so be worked back to its original starting point.

This simple routine can be varied by imagining a "rush hour" period, when the train may require to be strengthened by the addition of another vehicle. The Corridor Coach D1 can be added to the Twin Unit for several journeys and then detached when traffic slackens off again. At other times a van or two can be conveyed by the train for some particular local traffic—a Horsebox perhaps, or one of the various vehicles suitable for the carriage of perishable or urgent goods.

With bigger layouts more involved operations become possible, and as a rule the larger systems have sufficient equipment to allow such working to be carried out. A terminus station, for instance, arranged perhaps with the components of the Hornby-Dublo City Station Outfit, can have a platform and tracks reserved for suburban traffic. If a running-round loop is provided, then a single engine can give very good service. It frequently happens however that the length available for a terminus station does not permit of the inclusion of crossover points, and the length of "draw ahead" track near to the Buffer Stops, necessary for running round facilities. Then we have to adopt the "turnover" system of engine working. This means that one engine brings the train in and is detached; another engine, which has been waiting in an engine siding or perhaps in an Engine Shed or yard outside

Two Main Line Stations and an Island Platform make up this four-track station. Traffic is evidently quiet at the moment as the "local" shown is using the main or "fast" line.

the terminus, comes on to the other end of the train ready for the return journey. Soon the train departs and the first engine is then released to stand by until it in its turn takes out another train that has arrived.

To carry out this scheme it is necessary to arrange for the platform lines in the terminus to be sectionalised by means of the Isolating Rail which we have dealt with previously in these pages.

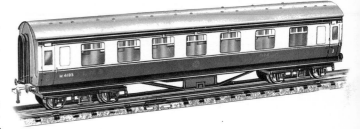

Atholl' locomotive with a double chimney, the new 'Sir Nigel Gresley' locomotive with full valve gear and open valances, and on closer inspection an artic. set behind the 'Sir Nigel Gresley' locomotive!

I have confirmation from three different sources of positive remembrance of a triple articulated set comprising two brake thirds and a centre all third coach. One source says they were specially made up in the Toronto factory of the Meccano Company and I was told recently by one of the employees in W. & H. Models' shop in London that a triple articulated Hornby Dublo set had passed through their hands some months earlier. Such a modification would be simple enough to make, although neither I nor any other collectors I have met or corresponded with have been able to examine one first hand.

After the war the first/third, all third and brake/third coaches were produced individually with the new couplings. The all third coach number 45401 usually had plain (all teak) ends – i.e. non-corridor for working suburban trains. However, the dummy sections in dark brown and black are also known as are plain teak ends on the first/third and brake/third coaches. The last production of all third coaches, before the introduction of British Rail liveries in April 1953 had grey roofs. They were available after 1953 in plain mid-blue boxes with stick-on end labels.

The first/third and brake/third coaches continued in British Rail plum and spilt milk colours referred to as D11 coaches although the numbers were now E42759E and E45402E. They were identical in body construction and outline but with grey roofs retaining the Gresley pattern bogies. The later versions had the standard Dublo British Rail bogie.

THE LMS COACHES

The LMS coaches to go with the 'Duchess of Atholl' set were in many ways superior to the London North Eastern teak models as they had transparent windows, interior corridor partitions and dummy end sections.

There are many shade variations of the coaches, some doubtless affected by sunlight, but in general the earlier coaches had a very dark brownish red colour with a silver roof simulating the galvanised roofs of the original coaches they depict. The later versions had a lighter shade of red with a grey roof.

I have seen one LMS coach with matt as opposed to the usual gloss finish in a distinctly brown shade. It was in a pale blue box, number DR363 code BW 9238–8M (8,000) – 4/40 (April 1940). This does tie in with the theory that the release of the 'Duchess of Atholl' locomotive would take place in late 1940 and I feel convinced that some coaches were indeed made pre-war although frozen and the new bogies and couplings fitted to them after the war. (The pressings for the coaches were certainly available pre-war as evidenced by the painted versions in the famous demonstration set, illustrated.) The LMS bogie for the coach itself did not have its drawing commenced until 29th March 1939 so although well advertised to create interest and demand, it would have been quite a rush to get it finished in that year.

THE STANDARD BRITISH RAILWAYS COACHES

These, the most common of all the Hornby Dublo coaches, appeared with the advertisement of British Rail livery in April 1953, though they had been ready since February. They were called type D12 and were basically the LMS coaches, but in the much brighter BR colours of 'plum and spilt milk', more usually called 'blood and custard' and the colours seem to show off the detail better than did the early LMS maroon livery. The *Model Railway News* in its 'Talking Shop' column of July 1953 also reported the interesting fact that the coaches were only slightly shorter in scale length compared with the new British Railways standard coach. These were 64 ft 6 ins in length, on a 9 ft width and designed to be used on all main lines throughout the country, being introduced in 1951. The Hornby Dublo coaches would need to be $10\frac{1}{8}$ inches in length to be scale, against $8\frac{1}{8}$ inches as manufactured.

These very attractive D12 coaches were primarily supplied with the 'Duchess of Montrose' as the Eastern Region locomotive, the 'Silver King' still used the D11 coaches right up until 1956, when this train, EDP11 changed to EDP15 and was supplied with the D12 coaches.

There are again many colour variations of the D12 coaches ranging from almost a bright orange to a deep plum colour. The records have long since been lost, but I do not think I am wrong in my estimate that at least 250,000 of both the standard coach and the brake/third, were produced.

The D3 LMS coaches.

THE D13/14 BR MAROON SUBURBAN COACHES

It was in November 1954 that the new British Rail standard 2–6–4 Tank locomotive was introduced and the following month came the write up on the new maroon suburban coaches for the 2–6–4 T designated type D13. These were almost identical in some respects to the earlier teak Eastern Region coaches, in that they had lithographed tinprinted windows and to many this was a retrograde step following the transparent windows of the LMS and British Rail coaches. The Meccano archive drawings, of Hornby 0 gauge and Hornby-Dublo on loan to the Hornby Railway Collectors Association for collation – has proved those suburban coaches were drawn before the war – in November 1937! They were for articulated suburban coach sets, presumably in teak livery and it would have been possible to have four coach sets as in real life. I wonder if they planned to do standard coaches in the other three liveries for the 0–6–2 Tank locomotives? All of which were passenger engines. The GWR

The D13 BR maroon suburban coach – from original artwork.

The new D14 coaches, from an advertisement in the September 1956 Meccano Magazine.

HORNBY DUBLO ELECTRIC TRAINS

EDP14

EDP10

Two additions to the range of Hornby-Dublo Train Sets

There is now a choice of six Hornby-Dublo Train Sets including EDP10 and EDP14 which are new in composition. Both these Sets are representative of trains used for local passenger services, and they contain improved Suburban Coaches D14 with transparent windows.

EDP10 0–6–2 Tank Passenger Train Set
This set contains Hornby-Dublo EDL17 Tank Locomotive 0–6–2, B.R., D14 Suburban Coach 1st/3rd, D14 Suburban Coach Brake/3rd, and Rails.

U.K. PRICE **£5.7.6** *including Tax*

EDP14 2–6–4 Tank Passenger Train Set
This set contains Hornby-Dublo EDL18 Tank Locomotive 2–6–4 B.R., D14 Suburban Coach 1st/3rd, two D14 Suburban Coaches Brake/3rd, and Rails.

U.K. PRICE **£6.13.6** *including Tax*

Suburban Coach D14 1st/3rd B.R.
(with transparent windows)
U.K. Price **10/–** *including Tax*

Suburban Coach D14 Brake/3rd B.R.
(with transparent windows)
U.K. Price **10/–** *including Tax*

MADE AND GUARANTEED BY MECCANO LTD.

The EDP22 'Royal Scot' train set – from original artwork.

could have been sweet! It took them two years to sell their production as it was not until September 1956 that, to quote the Meccano literature, the improved suburban coaches with transparent windows (D14) were introduced. These were the last third class coaches produced, although following British Rail practice third class was not put on the doors, only first class being indicated as such. Indeed it was in 1956 that third class seats and fares were officially abolished and second class seats became standard. One must remember that these were mass produced items for the younger enthusiast and toy trade as opposed to the scale modeller and it is not surprising that to complete production runs there were many production 'irregularities' which fascinate the collector today. There are a whole variety of suburban coaches with either unlithographed end pieces or brake end lithographs, with tinprinted windows at the end on standard suburban coaches when they should be on the brake/thirds, etc. These were purely to complete the toy and as rarities I personally do not rate them.

D22 BRITISH RAIL MAROON MAIN LINE COACHES

In the early Summer of 1956, British Railways decided to gradually replace their main line corridor stock with a one colour finish in maroon (easier to keep clean, they said) and some 14 months later, in August 1957, Hornby Dublo introduced their new D22 corridor coaches with a brake/second and first/second corridor coach. The *Meccano Magazine* of August 1957 goes on to record that these changes were being made gradually as was the actual practice. So, in Hornby Dublo, red and cream stock was retained for the time being. They do mention that the new train set, EDP22, with the 'Duchess of Montrose' locomotive would include these attractive D22 corridor coaches and for me (in mint condition) these coaches have a particular appeal. It is, however, hard to choose as I find there is considerable beauty and charm in all the

Hornby Dublo coaches and indeed in the whole system.

The *Meccano Magazine* states that one could also use these coaches on the 'Talisman' train running on the Eastern Region with the 'Silver King' locomotive. When they actually introduced this set in 1959, Hornby put it behind the 2-rail 'Golden Fleece' locomotive, but retained the suitably adapted D12 coaches (blood and custard).

The *Meccano Magazine* article continues, stating that for the Southern and Western Regions, these colours were not applicable, as they would retain the green for the Southern and the familiar brown and cream of the former Great Western Railway in respect of the new Western Region long distance expresses. It had not yet been possible to incorporate this change in Hornby Dublo.

The D14 Brake/3rd – from original artwork.

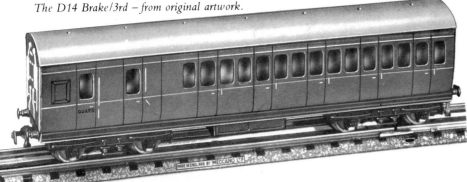

The D22 BR main line maroon coaches – from original artwork.

183

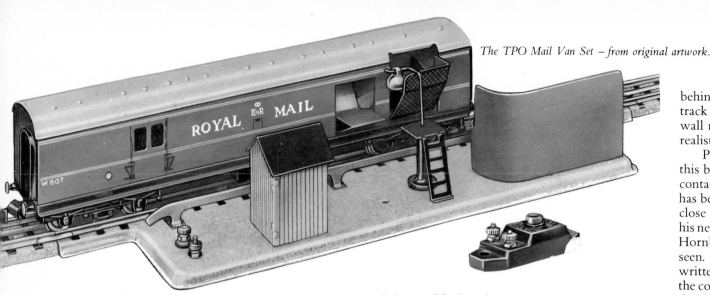

THE TPO MAIL VAN SET

Earlier in the year in March 1957 to be exact, Meccano introduced a truly magnificent travelling post office mail van set and as their advertisement stated it was real in everything but size! It had been shown a few weeks earlier on children's television, but this was the first advertisement.

The first travelling post office was run on 6th January 1838 between Birmingham and Liverpool and the last TPO coach apparatus to be used was on 4th October 1971, just north of Penrith, although the actual sorting of mail while a train was travelling was stopped in 1940. This beautiful article – of immense play value – could pick up and set down little metal pouches, literally at the press of a button. This item was available originally, in 3-rail, although later in 2-rail operation. The actual model had a number W807 on the side whereas the box in which it was packed showed the number as W795. I wonder if any of the latter were produced? It is best to let the official write ups on the model speak for themselves. The *Railway Modeller* in their 'Trade Window' review in April 1957 stated that – 'this latest addition to the Hornby Dublo range is a fascinating gimmick. Although intended primarily for the popular proprietary system it is apparent to us that this model has possibilities in the field of pure scale models.'

It is possible that there was an over supply, particularly on the 2-rail model as, with the demise of the steam locomotive and general decline in enthusiasm for miniature railways against the rapidly advancing model car racing circuits of the time, there were numerous TPO sets available on the market at very cheap prices. I once purchased a dozen base units for 10p each, removed the little cab and have fitted them on my layout with a variety of uses: as a little privy behind a country station, as a fog man's hut beside the track and even mounting them together behind a sea wall reminiscent of the early bathing huts, and very realistic they look too!

Perhaps the greatest pleasure I have had in putting this book together, apart from the close almost daily contact with the Hornby Dublo products themselves, has been meeting the many people who have become close friends. Charles Gent, of Liverpool, had above his newsagents shop, many years ago, one of the finest Hornby Dublo model railway layouts I have ever seen. Talking to him he explained that he had once written to the Meccano Company complaining that the collector shoe on the Mail Coach was too long and that he found that it frequently hit the casing of the electric point motors. Meccano wrote back stating that his track must be out of line as it was designed to miss the point casing by 1/64th of an inch! The mail van with two bags, lineside apparatus with switch and mail bags (per dozen) were available in a set or separately within one month of their introduction.

The Northbound Night Mail on the London, Newborough and Easthyde Railway – June 1963 Meccano Magazine.

The D20 composite restaurant cars – advertisement in the November 1957 Meccano Magazine.

THE WESTERN REGION COACHES AND TINPLATE RESTAURANT CARS

In October 1957, the 'Hornby Dublo Train Week' was held and commenced with the introduction of the famous 'Bristol Castle' locomotive. To match this beautiful engine, as had been hinted at earlier, new tinplate coaches came in similar styling to the D22 all maroon coach, but in the famous Western Region chocolate and cream livery as the D21 coach, again as first/second and brake/second. These were complete with sintered 3-rail wheels although the very next month, November 1957, Hornby Dublo advertised their new restaurant cars, the D20, initially in Western Region colours and the blood and custard livery of the earlier main line coaches. The Meccano write up in the December 1957 issue of *Meccano Magazine* stated that the D20 restaurant car followed standard Hornby Dublo practice in the bodywork and underframe, but had a striking new feature – its wheels were moulded in black plastic, in one piece with their axles so they were exceedingly smooth and quiet when running! The model trade soon picked this up; the *Railway Modeller* stated that it was possible to run this coach on scale 2-rail systems and the *Model Railway Constructor* confirmed the Meccano advertisement saying that in their opinion the coaches had a quieter, smoother ride with these new 2-rail wheels, the introduction of which caught the whole trade by surprise. They also commented that they liked the way the bogies had their pivots off-set towards the centre of the coach, a fact which reduces the overhang on the necessarily sharp curves. The very early D20 (4047 and 4048 only), D21 and D22 coaches had sintered metal wheels, but soon changed to the nylon moulded type.

It was not until 1959 that the all maroon 4049 Restaurant Car appeared. It was written up in the December 1959 *Model Railway Constructor*, but not in a very good light as they wrote . . . 'we feel that this coach shows up how "dated" rolling stock in lithographed tinplate really is. The makers have gone to immense trouble to produce something of high quality with quite incredibly complete fittings internally, and yet the total effect is contained in a perfectly flat (though superbly painted) shell of tinplate with detail painted on held together with bent over lugs. And the inside is good. The sides are double skinned so that the glass lies absolutely flush against the coach sides. The seats and tables are well produced as are the kitchen corridors and partitions dividing the coach. The two classes of dining saloons are clearly discernible in different colour schemes. The first class seats even have arm rests. Even the inside walls of the coach are properly painted. We feel that if the outside of the body came up to the high standard of the interior this coach would appeal to a much wider range of modellers than it can do at the moment.'

In collecting circles this coach appears to be quite rare. To me, the crime was in the choice of the maroon colour which was totally different to the D22 maroon coaches and spoilt the whole train when it was fitted to the centre. Why they could not have matched the colour to the D22 coaches heaven alone knows! However, they (4049) were relatively short-lived although I consider they have never been surpassed in commercial modelling even to this day.

The D21 WR Main Line coach – from original artwork.

THE SOUTHERN TINPLATE SUBURBAN COACHES

In April 1959, Hornby Dublo announced their modernisation programme with the obvious emphasis on 2-rail operation. They brought out two beautiful little 0–6–0 class 'R1' Southern Tank locomotives and with the green locomotive a 2-rail passenger train set, number 2207, in September of that year. The two coaches included were identical in their stampings to the D14 Suburban coaches, but they were finished in a very attractive green and part numbered 4025 and 4026.

Trains of these coaches (with nylon wheels capable of running on the old 3-rail track) were not only hauled by the 0–6–0 Tank locomotive but also by 2–6–4 Tank locomotives and even the old prenationalisation Southern livery 0–6–2 Tank locomotive. A veteran indeed and quite cheerfully copying real life practice!

Constructor's Review of the SR suburban coaches, and the BR→ maroon restaurant car – December 1959 Model Railway Constructor.

It was not until December 1960 that the super detail coaches were announced with their nylon couplings, although I have seen samples of these later versions of the tinplate coaches including the D22 maroon coach and the tinplate restaurant cars all sporting the nylon coupling as well as the metal, but that is another chapter.

OO gauge S.R. 1st/2nd Suburban Coach.
Meccano, Ltd.   **Price 10s. 3d. each.**

Whilst this new version of the Hornby-Dublo suburban coach is an improvement on their previous suburban stock in that the window openings are now cut out and glazed, our remarks on the exterior of the B.R. Composite Restaurant Car apply equally well here. Hornby-Dublo fans will welcome this extension of the range available to them, but we cannot see it having a much wider appeal. A Brake/2nd is also available at the same price.

'Southern Scene' – from the March 1961 Meccano Magazine.

TINPLATE AND DIECAST GOODS WAGONS

I must admit this chapter scares me, there are so many models and variations that I am hard put to cover them in sufficient detail to please every collector while still making it interesting for the casual reader. Alan Ellis in his compilation at the end of this book sets out lists of the full variations identified to date. So I shall content myself with the main points.

The principle of construction was to have a diecast zinc base alloy chassis unit with a very simple pressed axle carrier, held on by two flat staples and the same zinc cast wheel units with square profiles. Both the wheels and the chassis units of the pre-war models were subject to considerable distortion due to the poor quality control then available in the metal. So many pre-war wagons I have seen are so distorted that from a collector's point of view, it would be unwise to run them too much, vibration being one of the accelerators of the break-up process.

The system started with two basic chassis units, the goods wagon chassis being drawn on 18th October 1937 followed by the slightly longer chassis used for the brake vans. These bases gave a low centre of gravity and stability to the models and they carried on top, pressed tin outlines of all the various bodies. The detail on them was quite superb. With a slide-on roof, identical in principle to their 0 gauge big brothers, the result was an extremely sturdy realistic unit.

The original introductory Hornby Dublo catalogue (reference 7/938/185) showed that from the inception there were twelve wagon variations – an open wagon, covered van and brake van for each of the four main line regions.

The open wagons were all identical in painting detail with the Southern Region in its famous chocolate brown colour with white lettering, the LMS in its characteristic bauxite brown livery and the Great Western and LNER wagons in grey both with white

The post-war, prenationalisation Tinplate Wagons, identical → except for the chassis to pre-war wagons. The BR maroon Horsebox, second from right, bottom row, just squaring things up!

lettering. The twelve ton goods vans, however, were all totally different from each other in their planking arrangements and closely followed their full size prototypes. The Southern Region in its chocolate brown livery with white lettering and roof, while the LMS bauxite brown van had a dark silver roof representing the galvanised finish they had on their roofs and indeed modelled on the 'Duchess of Atholl' coaches. The Great Western van sported a white roof as well, while the vertical boarding on the standard London North Eastern van was a feature of that particular vehicle, the red brown finish being used on North Eastern express goods wagons.

The brake vans again all copied the well known outlines of their forebears, all being referred to as 20 ton brake vans with the exception of the Southern Railway which was 25 tons. All again had the white roofs with the exception of the LMS region which were silver.

Once again the details of these vans can be found in Alan Ellis's superb compilation at the rear of this book. Each box again had its printed code giving not only the date, but the quantity produced; for instance the open wagons had 15M i.e. 15,000 produced, dated 8/38 i.e. August 1938, with a little region sticker on the box to denote whether LMS, SR, GWR etc.

An original Meccano drawing.

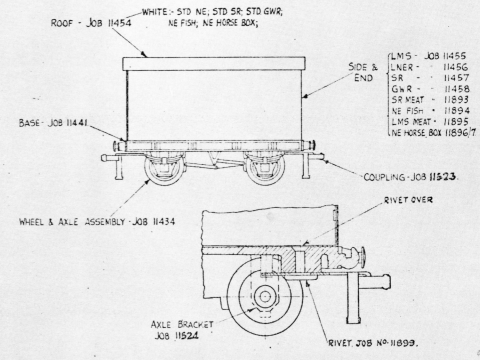

MECCANO LTD.

ARTICLE	VAN ASSEMBLY - ROLLING STOCK - LMS.	00 GAUGE	JOB Nº 11450.

USED ON JOBS				NE	11451.
	"	"	"	SR.	11452.
	"	"	"	GWR.	11453.
				SR MEAT	11885.
				NE FISH	11886.
				LMS MEAT	11887.
				NE HORSE BOX	11888.

2 0 AUG 1947
PRODUCTION

ROOF, JOB 11454A :- GREY :- STD LMS; SR MEAT;
LMS MEAT;

WHITE :- STD NE; STD SR; STD GWR;
ROOF - JOB 11454   NE FISH; NE HORSE BOX;

LMS - JOB 11455
LNER - " 11456
SIDE & END   SR - " 11457
GWR - " 11458
SR MEAT " 11893
NE FISH " 11894
LMS MEAT " 11895
NE HORSE BOX 11896/7

BASE - JOB 11441

COUPLING - JOB 11523.

WHEEL & AXLE ASSEMBLY - JOB 11434

RIVET OVER

AXLE BRACKET
JOB 11524

RIVET, JOB Nº 11899.

SECTION THROUGH CENTRE OF VAN.

TEST :- VANS TO START AND RUN
FREELY DOWN GRADIENT OF
1 IN 25 (2° 18')

5	ROOF, JOB Nº 11454A ADDED	2017	20 8	
4	JOB Nºs 11416/7/8 DELETED. JOB Nºs 11523/4 & 11899 ADDED	1782	19.9.46	RWM
3	SR MEAT, NE FISH, LMS MEAT & NE HORSE BOX ADDED	1172	6-1-39	
2	TEST INFORMATION ADDED	10964	2.6.38	
ISSUE	DESCRIPTION OF CHANGE	CON	DATE	SIG

DRAWN BY
TRACED BY
MATERIAL SEE JOB LIST Nº 551.   CHECKED BY
DISTRIBUTION 3A

MEMO Nº

Scales 1/1 & 2/1   Date 5-11-37.

The Southern 25 ton brake van was a most successful design in real life. They were introduced in 1929 and were still being manufactured with minor variations right up to nationalisation. They were not unlike the standard London North Eastern brake van which was the forerunner of the standard British Railways van. The most obvious difference was that on the SR vans the body planking ran horizontally and on the LNER vans the planks ran vertically. Obviously the most readily noticeable variation was the attractive red sandbox fitted either end of the body.

I have seen some Southern Region brake vans and indeed there may be others in other regions, carrying the wrong inner sections. For instance, the London North Eastern brake van had a door and two windows either side of the door, with vertical planking. The Southern brake van, as we mentioned earlier had horizontal planking with a single door and window whereas the LMS version, like the North Eastern, had a door in the centre with two windows, but again with horizontal planking. I am indebted to Sam Burns and his son David for bringing to my attention the Southern Region brake vans, but with the LMS interior end section. As with all the other minor variations, one must recall that these were toys and if they ran out of a particular end part the nearest equivalent was brought into action.

You will recall that the first advertisement for Hornby Dublo appeared in the September 1938 *Meccano Magazine*. The March 1939 *Meccano Magazine*

Extract from the Meccano leaflet reference 1/239/10.

NEW HORNBY-DUBLO
ROLLING STOCK

Petrol Tank Wagon D1 "Esso"	Ready March
Petrol Tank Wagon D1 "Power Ethyl"	" "
Oil Tank Wagon D1 "Royal Daylight"	" "
Coal Wagon D1 L.M.S., N.E. G.W. and S.R.	" "
Meat Van D1 L.M.S. and S.R.	Ready April
Fish Van D1 N.E.	" "
Horse Box D1 N.E.	" "
Cattle Truck D1 L.M.S. and G.W.R.	" "
High-sided Wagon D2 L.M.S. and N.E.	Ready May
High-sided Coal Wagon D2 L.M.S. and N.E.	" "
High Capacity Wagon D1 N.E.	Ready Autumn

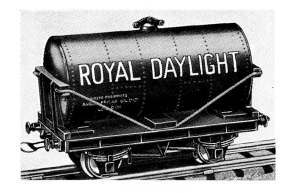

From the April 1939 Meccano Magazine.

heralded seven new wagons. They were the standard 12 ton open wagons in the four regions, but with dummy pressed in plastic coal outline and perhaps three of the most popular of all the Hornby Dublo wagons, the beautiful tankers. There was the buff Esso tanker, the red Royal Daylight and the green Power Ethyl. The Royal Daylight tanker had its counterpart in Hornby 0 gauge, but with nothing like the detail despite the fact that it was more than twice the size,

while the Power Ethyl tanker was almost an exact replica in reduced scale. An easy check is that all pre-war tankers had the diecast filling caps on top of them painted in the same colour as the tanker itself. All the post-war tankers had this filler dome painted in an uninteresting black.

These days a wagon announced by one of the major manufacturers frequently means a wait of ten months or more before it can be purchased at a local toy shop. Here however, was Meccano, literally months after introducing the first range of wagons,

announcing in April 1939, that they were introducing a further six. These were the cattle trucks in LMS and Great Western liveries with the four window apertures either side. For some reason the LMS version appears to be particularly rare and in common with the other LMS vans, sports the galvanised silver grey roof while the Great Western models retain the white roof. Next we had the meat vans, the LMS again had its silver grey roof, but surprisingly the Southern Region used the same roof, retaining as in real life, the peculiar shade of buff commonly used on SR vans. The two final vans were the fish van and the horse box for the North Eastern region. The fish van retained the red brown lettering and white roof of its sister wagon, whereas the horse box appeared in a teak brown finish. Concerning the horse box, I like the way the *Meccano Magazine* states: 'The detail on this van is perfect, the attendant's portion being correctly finished with windows "that can almost be seen through".' Despite the tinprinted sides, I do agree with them – they were most realistic.

189

The next wagons to be introduced were in September 1939 and they were the two high sided seven plank goods wagons in LMS and LNER livery which were either open for general mineral traffic or with the dummy plastic moulded coal load. Many advertisements showed the high sided wagon with a full diagonal white stripe, running from bottom left to top right. To my knowledge these never appeared, they denote the tipping/discharge end and only had a short white line on each side but not over the full length of

the wagon as shown in some immediate pre-war and post-war catalogues of the October 1939–1951 period. It is almost impossible to find these dummy coal loads today, although they can occasionally be found in secondhand shops. Either as wagons in railway sidings or for long coal trains they produce a most realistic effect. The other wagon is the famous bogie brick wagon. These brick wagons have quite a story in as much as they were designed by the LNER to haul, primarily to London (but throughout the country) 50

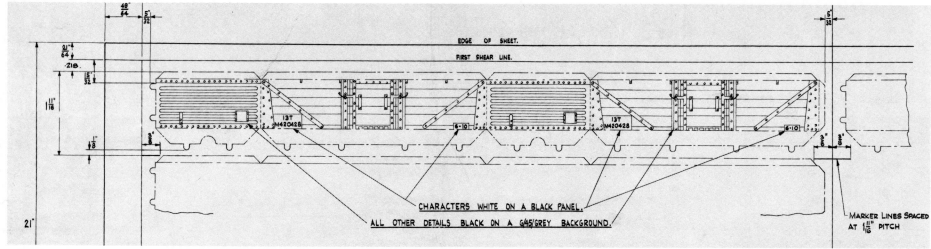

An original Meccano drawing.

From a Meccano publicity photograph. Note clockwork track.

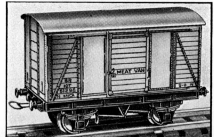

From the May 1939 Meccano Magazine.

From the September 1939 Meccano Magazine.

ton loads of twenty thousand bricks per wagon from the famous brick fields of the Peterborough district. They were finished in the correct colours of the prototype – a red brown shade used by the LNER for brake fitted and piped freight vehicles and were naturally capable of running at express speeds. From the collector's point of view, the many post-war variations of this particular model included a light brown and black chassis unit, the change after nationalisation from the North Eastern region letters to the BR letters and, finally, the alteration of words on the prototype from 'Return to Fletton' to 'Empty to Fletton'. From my own researches of liveries up to nationalisation, they were all North Eastern 'Return to Fletton' with the light brown chassis. It was the early BR example which had 'Empty to Fletton' with the brown chassis, but thereafter all with the black chassis. I have also seen two distinct colour variations on the tinprinted sides of the wagon between a standard brown and a darker brown. These had nothing to do with sunlight fading them. All these models had the diamond type bogie wheel arrangements and carried the number 163535 which was the first of the 2nd series of 25 built by the LNER in 1930. This particular body was also modelled in 0 gauge and the effort put into loading and unloading the real wagons must have been enormous. Eight of them were still in use in August 1966 although they were withdrawn soon afterwards as all deliveries were being containerised.

No further wagons were introduced before the start of the Second World War, although many were planned. All the models appeared again after the war, but with the new Peco couplings. The chassis were duly modified and instead of a one-off axle carrying unit there was a bright metal tab for each axle which was tucked out and under the axle box itself. The wagons still carried the mazac square profile wheel, but it too was subject to fatigue and distortion (pre-war), so a combination of this, metal shortages and desire for greater strength had Meccano draw a new rounded profile wheel – in sintered iron – on 31st January 1951.

A Southern brake van in real life.

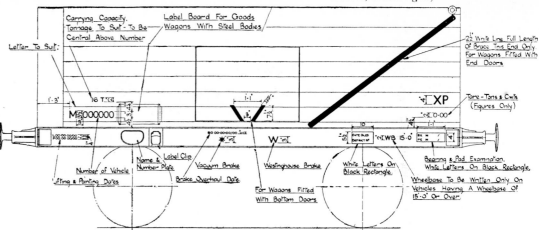

I could not find this drawing at all – until the ever helpful Mr. George Porter of Wrenn Railways suggested I contact Mr. M. P. Hughes, director of the Powder Metals Division of Rigby Metal Components of Yorkshire. In correspondence in February 1979, with the help of his employees who 'remembered the job well' he was able to find the original drawing. Rolling stock appeared with these new wheels in late 1951 or early 1952 and he records the average annual production at 7 million!

With the introduction of this wheel the axle tabs were finished in black. All the models produced before the war were continued after the war and the drawing dates show they were scheduled for production on 20th August 1947.

We have already mentioned the variations in the oil tankers with the black filling domes and the bogie brick wagon, but there are one or two other interesting items which came into being. I would stress at this stage to again check the vans against the standard test procedure, in that all were supposed to start and run freely down a gradient of 1 in 25. So many people do neglect this simple test and put a consequent greater strain on the locomotive and the armature. Of course, this problem does not apply on the new pinpoint axles, but all who regularly run early Hornby Dublo railways should check this point.

The post-war prenationalisation brake vans continued with their cream white roof although the LMS version had its original silver grey roof initially followed by gloss grey. One notable difference was the inclusion on the post-war brake van chassis of two vertical stays to the foot board. Apart from being to scale, they followed the concept of greater strength. There were distinct colour variations in several wagons, particularly those going from grey to a grey green finish. These included the North Eastern open wagon in both standard and high sided versions (both open and with coal load) as well as the Southern Region buff meat van which originally had silver grey roofs but later post-war prenationalisation issues had cream white roofs. The GWR cattle trucks are interesting in as much as that as well as grey and grey green livery the later prenationalisation issue had the standard British rail stamping i.e. three windows each side, as opposed to four and this is a fairly common variation. However, the LMS variation, with the three

windows per side is extremely rare and there is only one that I know of in existence. Mr. Cook, the collector concerned, kindly wrote to me when he saw I was querying whether this particular version ever existed and I would think it was a simple question of using up the old tinprinted sheets, but with the new stamp. The tank wagon variations appear to be distinct gold coloured and silver coloured lettering for the Royal Daylight and Power Ethyl wagons. It should be remembered that the Royal Daylight tanker was for carrying

oil whereas the Esso and the Power Ethyl were both petrol tankers.

The January 1940 *Meccano Magazine* heralded the Pool tanker Dinky Toy lorry and this was followed in August that year by the 0 gauge tanker version. It must seem strange to readers today that such new items appeared in the middle of war time, but this was the phony war when everybody thought it would be over in a matter of months. It also seems strange that they never produced such a model in Dublo scale

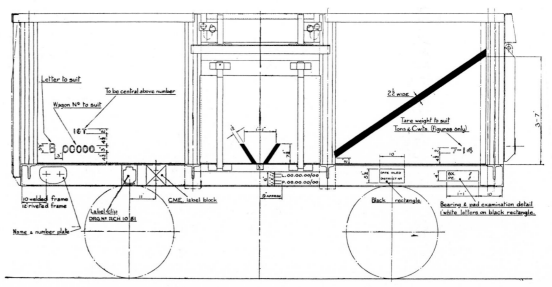

Extracts from the September and October 1949 Model Railway News.

– a similar reduction in size to the Power Ethyl wagon.

The reintroduction of the models after the war was slow and once more the open wagons and goods van were produced first, again only in sets. There were incredible shortages of raw materials in the immediate post-war years and even in 1951 – six years after the Second World War had ended – there was not a single new release from the Meccano factory of Hornby Dublo.

April 1953 heralded the nationalisation colours in British Railways, although it was not until June that there was an announcement on the new rolling stock. There were no less than fourteen goods vehicles immediately available and all prenationalisation wagons were deleted from the catalogues. There was the LMS brake van in grey and amongst the earlier variations were the smooth roof with no chimney followed by the more common version with the chimney and guttering above the verandah doors (the drawing date is 28/8/53). The Eastern Region brake van commenced with a white roof and then went to a

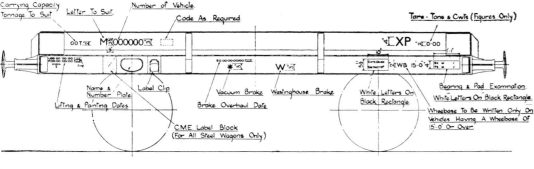

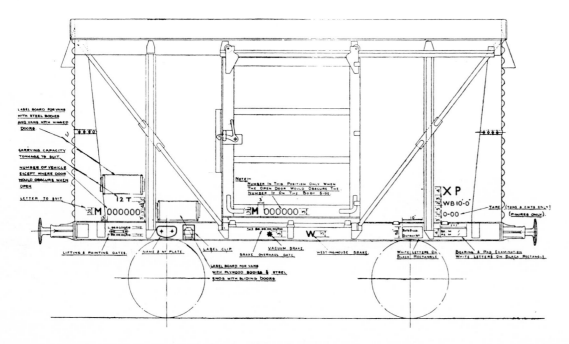

grey, then a grey roof with the chimney and finally a grey roof with a chimney and with the guttering ribs above the entry gangways shown in the 1953 (7/1053/250) catalogue. There was the D1 5 plank open wagon and coal wagon in grey livery as well as the bogie brick wagon with brown chassis, called the high capacity wagon still in the 7/1053/250 catalogue. There was the fish van with a grey roof, the grey high sided 7 plank mineral wagon and also a version with a dummy coal load. There was the all white insulated meat van, the cattle van in the new livery and sporting the three window aperture as well as a maroon horse box. The standard 12 ton covered van also appeared and there were two new tankers – the oil tank wagon Royal Daylight in red with the Esso badge above it and lettering 'paraffin' written underneath in black and the silver Esso petrol tanker with two Esso badges mounted each side of the tank.

June 1953 heralded the introduction of the bogie bolster wagon which had been drawn pre-war, but never issued. It had the normal diamond type axle frames, although these were replaced, as with other bogie goods vehicles stock, by the plate type bogie which was drawn on 11th October 1955 and introduced on 24th August 1956. More of this later.

Two months later the new diecast mineral wagon appeared in August and Ted Higgs reminds me that the first models had the diagonal white lines and number transfers put on the wrong way round. This mistake must have been discovered fairly quickly and from then all the transfers were correctly mounted.

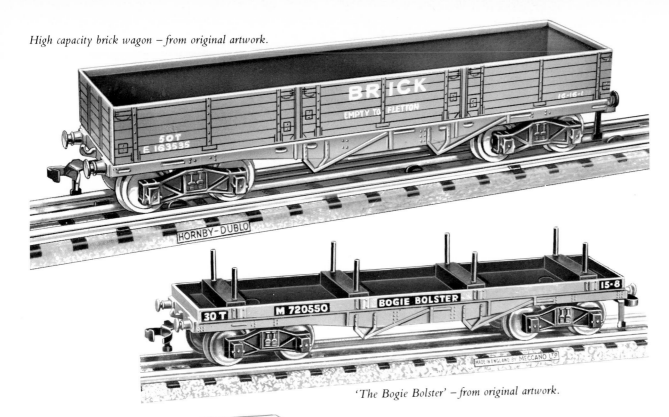

High capacity brick wagon – from original artwork.

'The Bogie Bolster' – from original artwork.

Low-sided wagon with cable drums – from original artwork.

Mineral wagon – from original artwork.

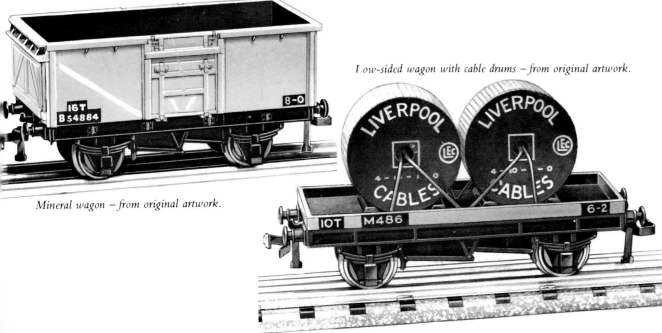

It was in April 1954 that the low sided wagons appeared, though shown as 'available later' in the 7/1053/250 catalogue. The first was the grey based wagon carrying two wooden lithographed cable drums. These had four diecast chocks in the base and holes through which were roped the cable drums in the correct position. Surprisingly it was not until the Meccano dealers' announcement leaflet dated 26th July 1956 that the D1 cable drums were available separately. The second wagon was bauxite brown in finish, denoting a vehicle fitted with automatic brakes and suitable for fast traffic and carried the 'XP' designation. Next came the rare green coloured Power petrol tank wagon no longer sporting the white hand of the pre-war and early post-war models and surprisingly with no announcement in the *Meccano Magazines*. It was shown in the 1954/55 catalogue, dated 7/754/200 and I would put the introduction as June 1954 with an end date of September 1956.

The *Meccano Magazine* for July 1955 heralded the Shell lubricating oil tanker and the Vacuum Oil Company tanker. The Shell tanker was in bright yellow with lettering in red and had been available a month earlier, while the Vacuum tanker with two Mobil Oil Pegasus badges either side, was in bright red with white lettering.

Four months later, in November 1955, the 40 ton bogie well wagon arrived with the report that the full size vehicles were employed for a variety of heavy loads like transformers, boilers, ships' propellers,

From the April 1954 Meccano Magazine.

Advertisement from the July 1955 Meccano Magazine.

HORNBY-DUBLO TANK WAGONS

Two additional models are now available in the colour finishes of famous oil companies.

HORNBY-DUBLO TANK WAGON D1 "SHELL LUBRICATING OIL"

Realistically finished in bright yellow with the lettering in red. The base is black.
PRICE **5/3** each
(inc. Tax)

HORNBY-DUBLO TANK WAGON D1 "VACUUM OIL CO. LTD."

Black base, bright red tank with lettering in white, and accurate reproductions of Mobiloil, Mobilgas trade marks.
PRICE **5/3** each
(inc. Tax)

HORNBY DUBLO
ELECTRIC TRAINS

THE PREMIER
NAME IN
00 GAUGE
TABLE RAILWAYS

MADE AND GUARANTEED BY MECCANO LIMITED

196

40 ton bogie well wagon – from original artwork.

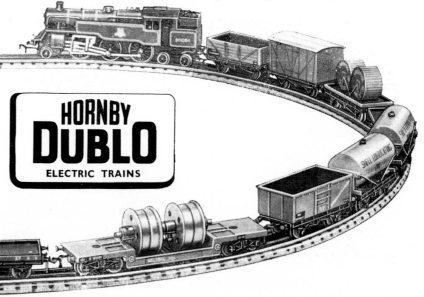

HORNBY DUBLO
ELECTRIC TRAINS

Extract from November 1955 Meccano Magazine.

granite blocks, etc. The bogie well wagon or as it is more commonly known, 'Weltrol', was the first to have the elongated hooks on the metal couplings which were introduced the year before on the 2–6–4 Tank locomotive. As with all the wagons which extended into the super detail era, they were available with the various plastic couplings and later issues had the plate type bogies. I personally cannot get too excited about the coupling variations, but each to his own and Alan Ellis has done a superb job in listing the variations in the compilation of those he has found to date.

April 1956 saw the reintroduction of the Western Region brake van in the familiar British Railways light grey livery sporting the Western Region running number W68796 and surprisingly labelled 14 tons. The identical van, but in pre-war and immediate post-war livery always showed this as a 20 ton van. It retained the name of 'Park Royal', but for the comfort of the guard had a chimney. The printed tinplate details of the bodywork were excellent, showing the usual WR details such as the longitudinal planking, the vertical 'T' strapping and the narrow windows of the guard's house. The lower body sides of the latter and a fence of the verandah have no planking shown because steel sheets form these parts in the original. This van would have looked superb with the 0–6–2 '56 XX' class locomotive which was planned, but more of this in a later chapter. Up to this point all the brake vans had used a common chassis, but in the overlap due to the arrival of the super detail series there was a considerable variation in the chassis. There are versions of all three brake vans with the standard short running boards and indeed with the later long running boards with the tab slots underneath. I know that the LMR and ER versions are original but the Great Western version I have has a question mark over it as I know its original parentage. The cardinal rule in all train collecting is that once a part has been 'got at' apply a degree of scepticism to the rest. The tabs have been got at. The super detail brake vans used a standard chassis with the long running boards and no tab slots.

The dealers' leaflet No. 8/685/500 of 23rd June 1958 announced the withdrawal of the tinplate brake vans – LMR, ER and GWR – from the pricelist in readiness for the introduction of the super detail models two months later.

★ *A Hornby-Dublo re-introduction in B.R. finish*

WR brake van – from original artwork.

Goods Brake Van
(Western Region)

This was always a popular model in its old G.W.R. finish, and will now be welcomed in its up-to-date style. It is a distinctive long-bodied W.R. Goods Brake Van with a deep verandah at one end. It is finished in grey and the finely-detailed body is mounted on a diecast base with long footboards.

PRICE **7/-** (inc. Tax)

HORNBY DUBLO

MADE BY MECCANO LTD. LIVERPOOL

Extract from April 1956 Meccano Magazine.

May 1956 showed the introduction of the flat truck carrying a furniture container. One must remember that these were pre-motorway days. Journeys took a considerable length of time by road and I remember in the late '40s and early '50s when, for seven years running, my parents took me down to St. Ives in Cornwall for holidays, it used to take two days by car from Sutton, staying overnight at a hotel near Taunton. I now go down and back in a day. If you wanted to move house, it was often a lot easier to move with the assistance of British Railways, as one was rarely more than half an hour's journey from a railway station and it was a relatively simple matter to have the delivery van come to the house and have everything loaded into a container which could then be moved lock, stock and barrel by road and rail to its new destination.

The following month, June, saw the introduction of the insulated meat container. Both these containers were made of wood with wrap round printed paper detailing looking extremely realistic. They had a little screw in eye on the top to enable the goods yard crane

to off load them onto the platform or onto the Dublo Dinky Bedford lorries. The Meccano Company was always extremely particular to copy in the minutest detail the practice of the real life railways (unlike with their 0 gauge and Dinky Toy ranges) and this is why they did not produce inhouse advertising rolling stock. In the drawing office at the close, however, there were two little wooden containers painted in yellow with a grey roof with the words 'Meccano' on them and I understand that these were mockups and that it was possible that they were planned for introduction. There is a picture of this in the colour plate of the super detail wagons. The correct wooden containers were available separately by June of that year.

Continuing with the policy of introducing virtually one new model per month when the Mobil Oil Company changed its trading name the old Vacuum Oil Company tanker was replaced by a similar unit sporting the Mobil Oil Company. The 1956/57 catalogue reference 7/556/500 (half a million catalogues printed!) shows both the Mobil and the Vacuum tanker.

November 1956 announced the introduction of the beautiful 20 ton tube wagon and the long type Western Region ventilated van. The write up in the Meccano article states: 'You, the reader, might have already seen these additions as the tube wagon actually made its appearance in October.' In a very good move to upgrade the realism of their models the write up records that the model had brackets specially formed so that they could represent brake blocks and hangers fore and aft of each wheel, and the Meccano Company took the opportunity to add representations of the brake cylinder and the V hangers that in real practice supported the brake shaft.

The long wheelbase ventilated van had not yet reached the shops, being due in November and was a remarkably attractive copy of the vehicle familiar under the old GWR code of 'mink D'. Both vehicles were in the bauxite colour and brake fitted enabling them to run on express freight passenger trains. Both had the 'XP' marking identification on them.

Advertisement from the July 1956 Meccano Magazine.

The up-to-date version of a popular model

HORNBY-DUBLO TANK WAGON D.1 "Mobil"

Following the recent change of trading name, road and rail vehicles of the Vacuum Oil Co. Ltd. have been altered to "Mobil Oil Co. Ltd." The Hornby-Dublo Tank Wagon D1 has been altered, too, and can now be obtained in the new finish. The tank is bright red with the name in white. Length over couplings, 3½ in. U.K. Price 5/9 (inc. tax).

MADE AND GUARANTEED BY MECCANO LTD.

HORNBY DUBLO ELECTRIC TRAINS

'Containers' – from the January 1937 Meccano Magazine.

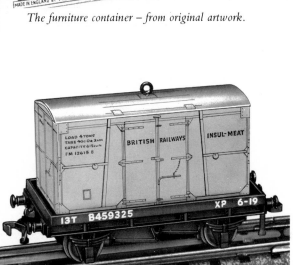

The furniture container – from original artwork.

The new Mobil tanker – from original artwork.

December 1956 showed the new four wheel double bolster wagon which was really an extended version of the low sided wagon. It did however sport a finely detailed diecast body and was used for the transportation of logs, timber, pipes and similar loads.

In July the revamped Mobil tanker appeared yet again. This was to be last and final variation at least for the upper part as it was still in its attractive red colour with a one piece Mobil badge on either side. It was first shown in the 1957 catalogue reference 7/857/500 and so makes it earlier brother – the Mobil Oil Company with the two badges – an exceptionally short production run. I would have thought it would have made it an exceptionally rare item, but I certainly seem to have seen plenty around. To me all the tinplate tankers are very attractive items particularly in long rakes of ten or more and all the more beautiful in good condition.

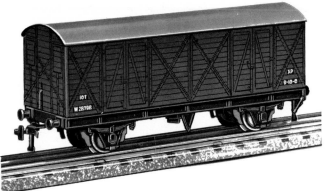

Long wheelbase ventilated van – from original artwork.

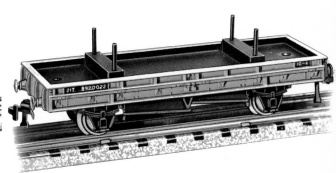

Double bolster wagon – from original artwork.

20 ton tube wagon – from original artwork.

logy, I decided to deal with it in the next chapter on super detail wagons.

Thirdly, the Dublo Dinky Toy tractor appeared in September 1959 and one month later, in the new Dublo catalogue heralding 2-rail, the old low-sided wagon appeared carrying a tractor No. 4649, and fitted with nylon wheels. The last three tinplate wagons (with the exception of the tankers), were the long wheelbase ventilated van, the tube wagon and the bogie brick wagon. These were all excluded from this 2-rail catalogue although the first two appeared one month later in the 3-rail catalogue 16/959/100.

Fourthly, the famous track cleaning wagon which was an applicaton of the diecast mineral wagon tool. This too is dealt with in the next chapter.

There are however, four notable exceptions. First the special Canadian Pacific caboose which used the LMR brake van body with a special long chimney and cupola on top. As in real life, the Canadian Railways had far larger loading gauges than British Rail. They were supplied in sets with the 'Canadian Pacific' locomotive and indeed in boxes on their own. I had thought they were never sold in this country, and I am indebted to Roger Bristow for informing me that they were on sale at Gamages, in the late 1950s.

Secondly, 'The Big Hook', the excellent breakdown crane unit which arrived in October 1959, and although it is diecast, in order to preserve the chrono-

The Canadian caboose – based on the LMR brake van.

THE SUPER DETAIL GOODS WAGONS

If I was asked to define the finest years of Hornby Dublo, I would state quite categorically the period was between October 1957 and the end of 1961. October 1957 heralded the introduction of the 'Bristol Castle' locomotive. The following month, with the Western Region tinplate coaches, came the tinplate restaurant cars 4047 and 4048 later with nylon wheels signalling the introduction of 2-rail some two years later. December 1957 heralded the introduction of the Dublo Dinky Toys, a range of vehicles to the correct scale for Hornby Dublo, and February 1958 the start of the new super detail range of goods wagons. I think super detail is an apt name for everything the Meccano Company produced from this period.

In my opinion the super detail of the goods rolling stock has never been surpassed either in quality or attention to detail. I even venture to submit that it will never be surpassed in the future, because the quality put into the model, right down to the liquid honing of the finished moulds to ensure a clean matt finish would, even at today's prices, be uneconomical to produce for what is basically a toy. Most of the super detail range of wagons are still in production in various liveries put out by Wrenn who took over the tools a couple of years or so after Meccano itself was taken over in 1964. Production runs of a quarter of a million units from each mould was considered a fair average before the quality would drop below that demanded. Of course, B.I.P. Tools Limited of Birmingham were considered to be the finest in the business, but the quality demanded by the Meccano Company tested them to their limits.

The first model, the 20 ton bulk grain wagon, as I mentioned arrived in February 1958 and involved no less than 17 major production drawings to produce the mould. The Meccano advertisement stated that it reproduced the special type of hopper vehicle used for the rail transport of grain. Accurately modelled features include dummy sliding roof hatches and side doors with bolt heads and handles and a ladder fitted at each end of the body. The dealers' leaflet, dated 22nd January 1958, reported that in recent weeks the demand for Hornby Dublo for many items of track and other accessories had been far greater than they had previously experienced and shortages were inevitable. They apologised for any inconvenience caused. In introducing this new super detail goods wagon, they quite rightly state: . . . 'it is considered the most fully detailed item of rolling stock in 00 gauge yet marketed.'

The *Model Railway Constructor* reported in their March 1958 issue . . . 'Following closely on their excellent Castle Class locomotive we have now received from Meccano their latest item of rolling stock – as revolutionary and as excellent in its way as the Castle. It is revolutionary because the old Hornby Dublo's lithographed tinplate for new stock is out and instead high quality moulded plastic bodies are the order of the day.' They continued . . . 'The underframe as in previous Hornby Dublo goods stock is a heavy diecasting and well detailed. We particularly liked the way the brake shoes are in line with the treads of the wheels (where, of course, they should be but seldom are in 16.5 mm gauge models. . . .). We heartily recommend this wagon to *all* 4 mm scale modellers and look forward eagerly to the other new items promised in the . . . extensive range of new stock . . . from Meccano.'

A word of caution – I have seen one dealer caught by buying what he thought was a hopper wagon which turned out to be a bulk grain with the roof neatly cut off. Comparing side by side there are many differences – but so rare are the hoppers these days such comparisons are seldom possible.

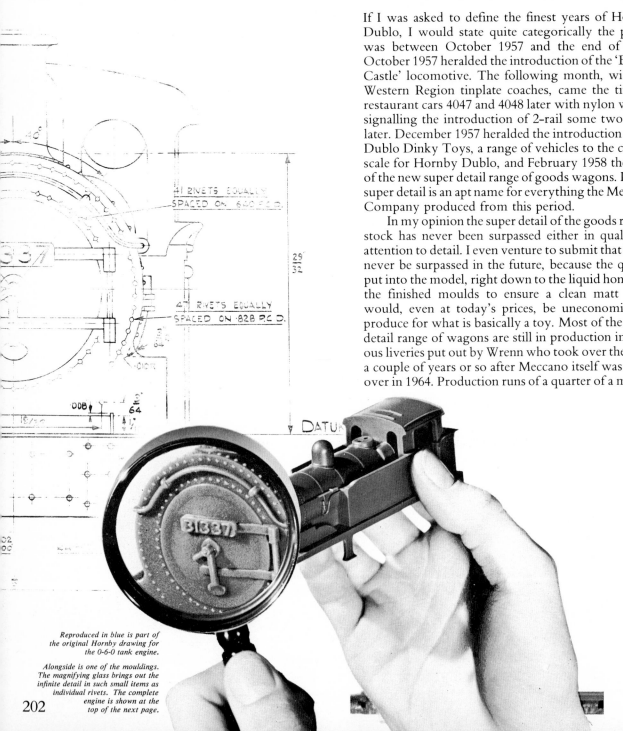

Reproduced in blue is part of the original Hornby drawing for the 0-6-0 tank engine.

Alongside is one of the mouldings. The magnifying glass brings out the infinite detail in such small items as individual rivets. The complete engine is shown at the top of the next page.

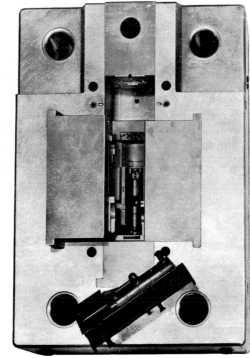

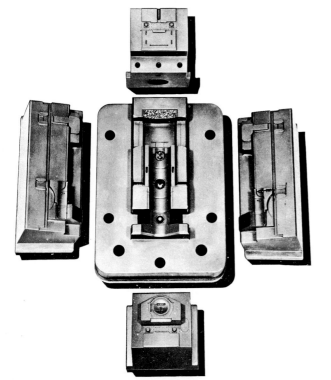

Extracts from the Beetle Bulletin, house magazine of British Industrial Plastics Ltd.

The hopper wagon has an undertaper on all four sides, and full brake gear detail on the chassis, while the 'grain' has a near standard chassis of the period and only tapering under either end. The 'hopper' is 86 mm long, the 'grain' 78 mm – be warned!

The following month, April, saw the new cattle wagons. This wagon came in for similar praise although the *Constructor* reported . . . 'The absence of bars is noticeable; one can only presume that considerations of price and durability decided Meccano on their omission.' The detail of the body moulding was superb and accurate. The *Meccano Magazine* stated that apart from the special open side construction that is a feature of the British Railways standard cattle wagons, in the original there is also an angle iron framework of various sections that in model form creates splendid opportunities for finely detailed relief work. These opportunities have been seized and in this new Hornby Dublo vehicle, the raised corner pillars, the door stanchions and the vertical and diagonal members on the sides and ends are reproduced in complete

detail and absolutely to scale, with minute bolt heads in all the right places. Just look at them through a magnifying glass and you will be astounded to see how completely right every little detail is.

As previously observed, model railway catalogues today advertise a new model and frequently the customer has to wait ten months or more before he can purchase it, or some cases even longer – yet here is the Meccano Company again introducing a new range of wagons and rolling them out of their production lines at the rate of one a month.

It must, however, be said that the former approach of long lead times has advantages in that production runs can be determined more accurately from advance sales.

In May the new wagon was the British Rail standard steel type 13 ton goods wagon with welded steel body designed for general goods work. The wagon was complete with all the detail even down to the planking on the floor as the *Meccano Magazine* stated . . . 'Wood can stand up to an enormous amount of

First of a range of moulded SUPER-DETAIL rolling stock

**SD6
20-TON
BULK
GRAIN
WAGON**

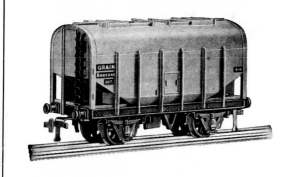

Here is the first of a new series of rolling stock with finely detailed bodywork of highest quality moulded construction. It reproduces the special type of hopper vehicle used for the rail transport of grain. Accurately modelled features include dummy sliding roof hatches and side doors with boltheads and handles. A ladder is fitted at each end of the body. The underframe is die-cast, and dummy clasp-type brake shoes are fitted on either side of the smooth-running, moulded spoked wheels. The finish is superb, with white lettering and numbers on black 'patches' transferred clearly on the body colour of B.R. grey. Length $3\frac{7}{8}$ in. (over couplings).
U.K. Price 6/9
(inc. tax)

Two of the new Hornby-Dublo Bulk Grain Wagons are prominent in this mixed freight train.

HORNBY DUBLO ELECTRIC TRAINS

Made in England
by Meccano Ltd.,
Binns Road, Liverpool 13

Advertisement from the March 1958 Meccano Magazine.

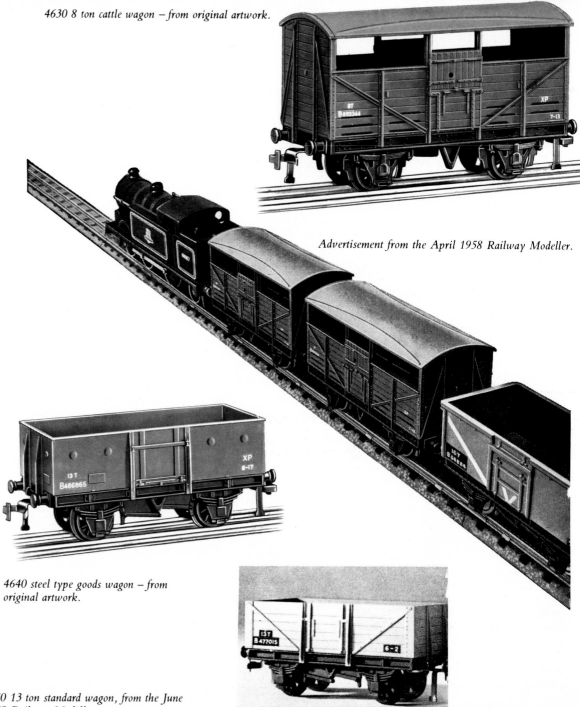

4630 8 ton cattle wagon – from original artwork.

Advertisement from the April 1958 Railway Modeller.

4640 steel type goods wagon – from original artwork.

4670 13 ton standard wagon, from the June 1958 Railway Modeller.

4320 Refrigerator van – from original artwork.

hard wear which is just as well because wagon floors undoubtedly have a rough time with loads and weather and a planked floor can be repaired more easily than a steel one.' It always seemed to me a fairly common vehicle, but the *Meccano Magazine* did implore its readers to examine it in even closer detail . . . 'for instance the former has steel tube capping around the upper edges of the sides and ends which prevent damage to the edges of the sheet steel ends and sides . . . this is neatly and accurately modelled. Again strengthening on the ends is looked after by a couple of vertical "T" section stanchions and these too are reproduced in remarkable fashion on the Hornby Dublo vehicle, even to the rather long taper that reduces the depth of the centre rib of the "Tees" towards the top. The four blisters which appear each side of the wagon represents the inner recesses that are embossed as it were in the body sides and ends to accommodate rings for use when loads have to be lashed in place. The housing of the rings in these recesses keep them neatly out of the way and they are not likely to interfere with loads or to be damaged themselves.' Once more the *Meccano Magazine* implores its readers . . . 'Don't be satisfied with reading about this new wagon and its recesses. See them for yourself and do this through a magnifying glass. You will then realise that there is the best of grounds for the claim that nothing as fine in their line has ever been made than the astonishing moulded vehicles of the Hornby SD6 series.

The next month, June, the standard 13 ton 5 planked goods wagon, was announced again with similar attention to detail. The 13 ton goods wagon

was drawn on 16th June 1956 although there is an amendment to the drawing stating that the floor planking detail was added on 22nd May 1957. As you see the wagon was introduced in June 1958 and I don't know if any wagons exist without this detail.

With the new model range coming off the production line like hot cakes and being released one per month, we have the arrival of the refrigerator wagon. The B.I.P. Tools Company bulletin stated that this was to be the first wagon to be released, but here it is listed as number 5. The *Railway Modeller* showed a preview of this in their new special article for the preceding month, June, and stated that this new van was a replica of the ex GWR 'Mica B' insulated van. They note . . . 'We feel there is little we can add to previous remarks about this fine series of vehicles – we have virtually exhausted our stock of superlatives.' I find the wire handrails to enable the yardman to climb up onto the roof to check the ice bunkers a weird feature as they can frequently be damaged by handling.

August 1958 listed the introductions already mentioned of the 2–8–0 8F locomotive, a fitting engine

indeed to haul this magnificent new product range.

Models continued to come thick and fast and in the same month the new 12 ton ventilated van arrived. The *Meccano Magazine* stated that there was now a splendid Hornby Dublo van for general freight traffic. The sides really look as though they are of planked construction, while the T-section stiffening members stand out as boldly as they do on the prototype. Several people must have queried the white roof as the article continues . . . 'There are BR standard vans about with a special white finish to their roofs. Obviously with the bauxite colour and the lettering XP this newcomer can be run on fast freight trains as well as the ordinary "pick up" goods.'

In September 1958 the new Western Region super detail brake van was available. It had indeed appeared a couple of months earlier, in June 1958, in the goods sets G19 and G16, but was only available separately at this time. The *Model Railway Constructor* in their September issue report . . . 'the detail is exquisite and complete and the neatness of the lettering will be the despair of all modellers who have to do their own by hand. 2-rail plastic wheels are of course fitted and the

HORNBY-DUBLO SD6 12-TON VENTILATED VAN

Here's the latest *super-detail* model in the new series of Hornby-Dublo moulded rolling stock with high-impact polystyrene bodies, die-cast metal frame and moulded spoked wheels.

It represents the B.R. van used extensively for general goods traffic. The high-quality body is finely detailed to show the planking, strappings, door details and the special ends of corrugated form. Finished in bauxite brown, it has a white roof.

Overall Length 3½ in.   **U.K. Price: 4/9** (inc. Tax)

Made by Meccano Limited, Binns Road, Liverpool 13

Super detail is scarcely a good enough description of the SD6 vehicles. Just look at this close-up of the new SD6 12-ton Goods Van as an example of their wonderful appearance. The doors seem ready to open!

Extract from the September 1958 Meccano Magazine.

4325 12 ton ventilated van from the August 1958 Meccano Magazine.

vehicle's running is particularly sweet.' Note too that it uses the long running board type wagon base although, as I reported earlier, I have seen models adapted to the old type short running base.

There is a fascinating story connected with this brake van although we have to jump ahead three years to fully appreciate it. In June 1962, the LMR brake van was issued in a bauxite brown livery for express train services with the 'Co-Bo' set. In the 1962 catalogue, reference 13/162/500 (half a million printed) a Western Region brake van is shown in bauxite brown livery and as part of the 0–6–0 set No. 2008. As drawn on 3rd October 1957, the Western Region brake van was to be moulded in the official description 'SF45 grey' but, there is a modification on the drawing dated 24th April 1961 when this was changed to 'SF16 red', i.e., the bauxite brown livery.

So, the drawing accurately shows this modification, but perhaps they had too big a stock and never got round to changing it as I have never met anyone who has seen a Western Region bauxite brake van. I would be rash to claim that they do not exist despite extensive contact with collectors all over the world.

Mr. Jack Gahan who worked in the Publicity Department of Hornby Dublo Railways at this period told me it was indeed planned, included in the

catalogue in error and to his knowledge never produced.

October 1958 brought in the superb printed head-board and coachboard labels, but more of these in their respective chapters. There was the T15 Meccano transformer which was unconditionally guaranteed for five years and two new super detail wagons, the 16 ton mineral wagon and the LMR goods brake van in grey livery. *Model Railway News* for November had a brief write-up on them stating that they live up to the

high standard set by the previous super detail series of rolling stock that has earned the acclaim of enthusiasts. Interestingly enough, underneath this is a photograph of Mr. Norman Hatton's new and larger premises at 180 Smithdown Road, Liverpool 15. I have been a customer of his for many years. It is without doubt one of the most fascinating shops in the whole country and models new and secondhand come and go with alarming rapidity. As I have already mentioned, the Midland Region bauxite brake van was reintroduced

Extract from the September 1958 Meccano Magazine.

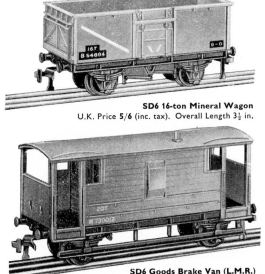

Advertisement from the October 1958 Meccano Magazine.

4312 goods brake van BR (WR) – from original artwork.

The prototype wagon. (Note canvas covers over the axle boxes.) From Meccano records.

4660 sand wagon – from original artwork.

'Problems were encountered in lettering the wagon' – Meccano drawing.

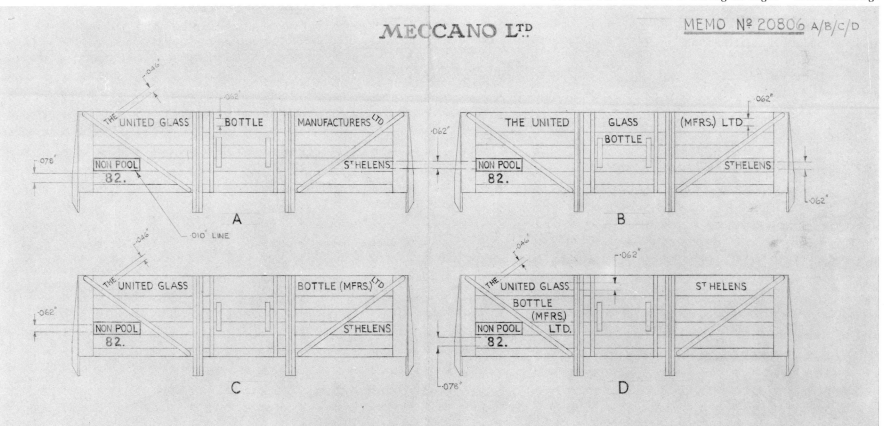

MECCANO L^TD

MEMO №20806 A/B/C/D

A

B

C

D

MARKINGS for THE UNITED GLASS BOTTLE MANUFACTURERS L^TD

DRAWN ER
SCALE 2-1
DATED 26-6-58
CHECKED

in June 1962 with the new 2033 diesel electric goods train set to represent the 'Condor' freight services.

In November 1958 the super detailed private owner wagon 'United Glass Bottle Manufacturers Limited' arrived. It used the same body as the earlier 13 ton wooden sided open wagon, but was finished in yellow with black lettering. There were several variations of this (like the Mobil tanker earlier), and I understand following a telephone call to their Publicity Manager, that at least five leading manufacturers towards the end of 1959 merged to become the United Glass Company Limited.

As the reproduced drawing shows the Meccano Company must have had a lot of fun trying to decide how to fit in all the wording of the original and the Drawing Office put up four proposals. Type A was chosen. The alteration to the tooling on changing the name was dated 20th October 1961 although I find it surprising that the original drawing for this was 25th July 1958 and here we are, only four months later, with its introduction.

The growing SUPER-DETAIL range

This new model is the thirteenth in the Hornby-Dublo series of SUPER-DETAIL rolling stock. It represents a standard B.R. Goods Brake Van. The finely-detailed body is moulded, and the frame is die-cast. Nylon wheels make it suitable for 2 or 3 rail running. Finished in bauxite brown for body with grey roof, and frame in matt black. Length over buffers 4 $\frac{8}{16}$ in.

U.K. Price: **6/-** (inc. tax)

SD6 Goods Brake Van B.R.

4311 BR brake van, advertisement from January 1959 Meccano Magazine.

Extract from the June 1959 Meccano Magazine.

While every praise continued the *Model Railway Constructor* 'Review' is the first reference I can find to publishing criticism of the old diecast chassis unit as they report in their December issue . . . 'the detailing on the body really is superb but again we feel that second thoughts should be given to the brake gear on these models. We realise that the wagon must be prepared for some rough handling but it should not be beyond the powers of the designers at Liverpool to improve this feature. Otherwise full marks.'

The *Railway Modeller* has alongside the write up on this wagon Bob Will's new Rail Cleaning Wagon but this occurs later in our story. Of course, to be

Advertisement from the December 1958 Meccano Magazine.

The prototype Saxa Salt wagon – from Meccano records.

really accurate, one should fit dummy canvas shields over the axle boxes on this sand wagon with the obvious intention of protecting the bearings from its dangerous load.

December 1958 heralded the 1,000 h.p. 'Bo-Bo' diesel locomotive as part of the new Hornby Dublo modernisation scheme and with it two further super detail wagons bringing the total to twelve – the SD 6 coal wagon and the Saxa Salt van. The coal wagon again used the standard five plank wooden open wagon which had an exact fit moulding of a coal load

while the Saxa Salt van was a very attractive copy of a real van as the photograph shows. It is equally attractive and indeed becoming rarer than its larger Hornby 0 gauge counterpart which preceded it.

January 1959 showed the new BR standard goods brake van modelled on the old Eastern Region van and finished in bauxite brown livery for express goods service. I thought I had found a new variation once when I found windows in the guards look-outs either side had been cut out but investigating the drawing showed no such modification and they had just been

done very accurately by an enthusiast. These look-outs are called 'duckets' in real life.

New models were usually notified to dealers one month before their advertised introduction. Like most items in the toy trade – then and now – there was a near 100 per cent markup. The trade price was 3s. 4d. for the ER goods brake van while the retail i.e. shop price was 6 shillings. By prior arrangement most leading dealers received a one off sample of all new products. Also by January 1959, the nylon wheels and axle assemblies could be purchased separately, both spoked and disc

'The Goods Depot', from a Meccano exhibition layout.

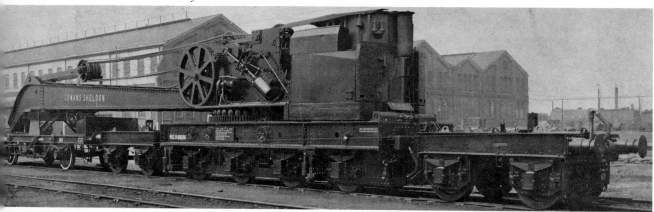

A real Cowans Sheldon crane – from Meccano records.

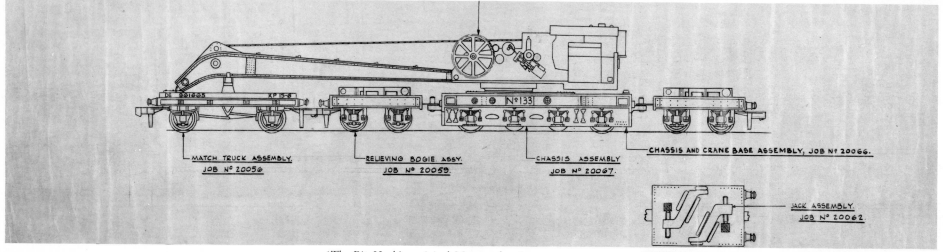

MATCH TRUCK ASSEMBLY.
JOB Nº 20056

RELIEVING BOGIE ASSY.
JOB Nº 20059.

CHASSIS ASSEMBLY
JOB Nº 20067.

CHASSIS AND CRANE BASE ASSEMBLY, JOB Nº 20066.

JACK ASSEMBLY.
JOB Nº 20062.

'The Big Hook' – original Meccano drawing.

type. This being announced in the Dealers' leaflet No. 2782/1258/5000 dated 27th December 1958.

There is almost a twelve month gap at this point which is quite understandable because they needed to catch their breath, issuing a wagon a month for the last nine months or more.

A rest? April 1959 announced their massive modernisation programme with 2-rail operation plus all the new sets and new polystyrene buildings. In May the very attractive Hornby Dublo *Book of Trains* appeared as well as the continuing releases of the Dublo Dinky Toy series. Behind the scenes though a lot must have been happening on the wagon front.

The March 1959 *Model Railway Constructor,* showed an excellent article by Mr. A. M. Lawrence on improving proprietary rolling stock with particular reference to Hornby Dublo. This basically entailed taking the present diecast base unit and drilling out the brake levers etc., to create a super detailed chassis. For reasons best known to themselves, it seems that most model railway magazines come out on approximately the 15th day of the preceding month. If this is the case, I wonder if it was Mr. Lawrence who finally tipped the scales in the Meccano Drawing Office, as the open diecast base unit for the standard four wheel wagons was drawn on 22nd February 1959, only one week after, I believe, the appearance of the article! Obvi-

Extract from the October 1963 Meccano Magazine.

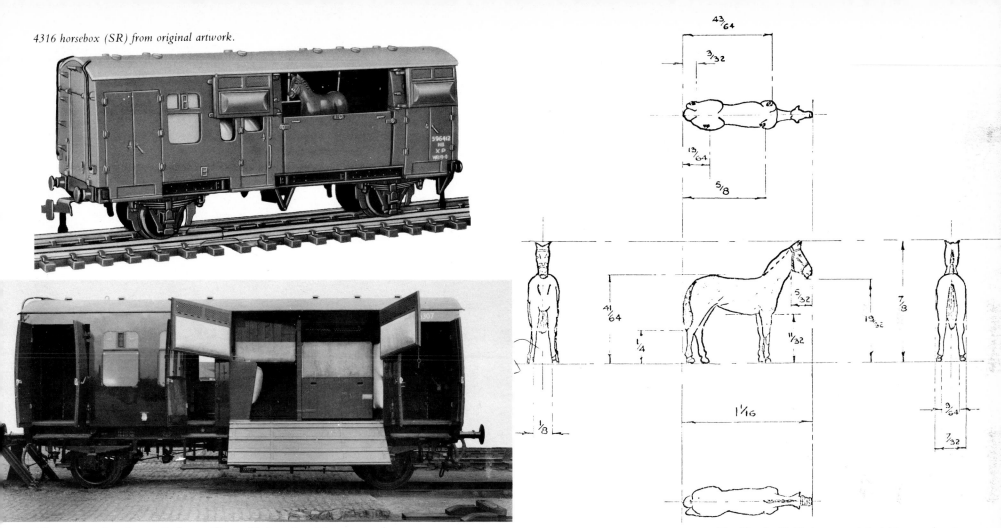

4316 horsebox (SR) from original artwork.

The prototype horsebox at Earlstown Wagon Works – from Meccano records.

The Hornby Dublo horse – original Meccano drawing.

ously the Company had their stocks to clear and so it was not until later that all (every single one) the models using this particular base appeared with the open brake gear version. All that is except for the flat container, cable drum and low sided wagon. I wonder if this has anything to do with the printing code on the box mentioned earlier – 80M – 80,000 units?! While on the question of quantities Mr. Richard Lines of Rovex gave me some stock and sales figures for 1964 at the time of the Triang takeover and I think they are of particular interest. I do stress that these figures are purely for the calendar year 1964, but they give an

interesting insight into what was in stock. Likewise it is impossible to date the exact introduction of the plate bogie. As I have mentioned this alteration to the weltrol wagon was dated 21st August 1956 on the drawing. It would depend so much on the stock position and its turnover.

THE BIG HOOK

October 1959 saw the introduction of the magnificent new breakdown set. It was heralded as 'that splendid new miniature of the most spectacular of all railway vehicle assemblies – a complete breakdown crane with

which vehicles can be restored to the track if they had been derailed'. The assembly includes the powerful crane itself, mounted on its own carriage, two relieving bogies each carrying two screw jacks and a match truck, the jib of the crane resting on the support on the match truck when the cavalcade is running. It was not only used for clearing the wreckage from the scene of a serious accident, but for more everyday purposes such as track laying and bridge work. The Hornby Dublo version really works and the jib can be used for hoisting a load and will rotate through a full circle.

The model was produced in two distinct finishes,

namely matt red and high gloss and was billed in advance publicity as one of the star introductions of the year for Hornby Dublo. The *Constructor* 'Review' reports that the accent was very much on the operating value. They went on to state that scale modellers must appreciate the market for which this introduction had been intended. Notwithstanding this some criticism must be made. The handles on each side are so excessively heavy that they are inclined to destroy the atmosphere of the whole train. The jacks (effective as they are in operation) are very heavy and stand out even more because they are finished in black, while their carrying trucks are painted entirely in red. In fact the entire breakdown train, with the exception of the cab roof and the top of the jib, is finished in the same unrelieved red. The match truck brake gear still has the old offending cast web on the brake details. They state that all these items can be corrected pretty easily by the modeller, the only job which calls for some thought being the winding gear. On the credit side the diecast detail of the whole model was good and the jib in particular was a really lovely casting. The crane worked well – there was plenty of weight in the casting and it rode well even over point work and tight curves. They concluded that it was certainly a spectacular piece of rolling stock, but – oh, those handles!

The *Railway Modeller* for November 1959 is less critical and states that while the bright red finish might be criticised, recent evidence to hand indicates that British Rail were using this particular shade for departmental vehicles. Yet again Hornby Dublo copying in exact detail the latest British Rail practice. Definitely a must for any layout they conclude.

4675 ICI Chlorine tank wagon – from the February 1960 *Meccano Magazine*.

The upper photograph shows three of the latest Hornby-Dublo "Traffic Services" tank wagons. The prototype shown in the lower photograph is specially designed to carry chemicals from British factories to places all over Europe except Russia and Spain. The wagons are finished in silver livery, this indicates inflammable contents, the anchor sign denotes that it goes by ferry, while the two stars show that the vehicle can travel by the fastest freight trains in the U.K.

The model measures 4½ in. in length and retails at 9s. 6d.

Extract from the June 1960 *Model Railway News*.

4679 *Traffic Services tank wagon – from original artwork.*

I am indebted to Mr. P. Tatlow of Guildford who wrote a fascinating letter in the November 1969 issue of the *Railway Modeller* on his researches into the origins of this particular crane. He wrote . . . 'I now know from information supplied by the Eastern Region of British Railways that number 133, the number carried by the Hornby Dublo Crane, is the Cambridge 45 ton Cowans Sheldon, but this time has the long jib as described in my article in the December 1960 *Railway Modeller* . . . I have therefore come to the conclusion that the original Hornby Dublo crane is a hybrid. Recently when running my long jibbed crane on a friend's layout which contained some 15 inch radius curves, we found that the end throw of the superstructure was positively enormous following which it had to be barred from the line. This led me to the thought that perhaps Hornby intended to model the Cambridge type but that in an effort to overcome the endthrow problems on their tight curves they used a shorter jib from another crane. Even so the relieving bogies are slightly too long which may have been to accommodate the couplings.'

On the same page Mr. Peter Wright wrote from Doncaster saying that they too had a 45 ton crane based there. His crane, SB1, in LNER days was an odd one being mounted on bogies and having no relieving trucks. It had a shorter reach than the later ones introduced in 1939. He continued . . . 'I wonder how many

owners of the Hornby model realise that it is a model of a crane which should be on an 8-wheel rigid frame with radial axle boxes at the end. Incidentally we thought our bogie crane was safer than the later pattern which was used by our neighbours – Peterborough gang – because ours gave a quicker indication of packings giving way rendering the cranes unstable. The livery of SB1 was originally engineer's blue with the bogie frames lined white. When I was with the gang in 1945 it was glossy black with the bogies lined red and white and a white jib head. Although withdrawn having a worn out boiler it was still in existence and is black lined white. Examples of the C and S cranes in LNER livery, such as the ill-fated King's Cross and Gorton cranes lost in the war on the way to the Middle East were glossy black with the water tanks bearing the legend "Chief Mechanical Engineer's Department" in white lined out with one thick red panel lining and a lower frame edge lined red.' It certainly was a very attractive item and even as late as 1964 1,800 units were sold leaving 300 in stock. April 1962 saw its introduction in the No. 2049 breakdown train set, a very rare and beautiful find these days.

The same month, October 1959, the Dublo Dinky Toy tractor appeared mounted on a low sided wagon as number 4649.

It was not until January 1960 that two new goods

wagons were released – the super detail ICI Chlorine tank wagon and 'Class B' black Esso Fuel Oil tinplate tanker. The *Constructor* 'Review' of April again records that it was a pity that Meccano still thought it necessary to retain the web behind the brake gear and to omit the brake levers on their wagons. Little did they know what had been going on behind the scenes these last twelve months. The Chlorine tanker itself had quite a history as although it was advertised in January, it did not come out for several months and continual apologies appeared in the *Meccano Magazine*. Of course, later versions of the Esso tanker, as with the other three tankers, all had the open brake gear chassis units.

The Airfix construction kit for this tanker records the background nicely in its assembly leaflet.

CLASS B TANK WAGON

Following publication of the British Railways Modernisation Plan in 1955, it became clear that future passenger and freight schedules would be revised and speeded up with the introduction of high-speed Diesel, Electro Diesel and all Electric Locomotives. Railway rolling stock would, therefore, be redesigned and constructed to operate within conditions envisaged under the new modernisation programme.

Whilst future Railway planning covered the design and construction of all stock, including passenger and freight, no general provision had been made for railway tank wagons carrying petroleum products which normally did not operate at speeds in excess of 45 m.p.h. and were subject to frequent examinations during transit.

In 1956 Esso Petroleum Co. Ltd., approached British Railways to design a new tank wagon capable of maximum capacity on four wheels within the 35 ton gross weight permitted under high-speed conditions.

Three prototype wagons were designed and constructed and, following certain trials and shunting tests, the Mark 1 was approved by British Railways. Subsequently over 800 of this type of wagon were ordered by the Esso Company from various builders. Two classes of vehicles were built, Class A for carrying Petrol and Highly Inflammable products, and Class B for carrying Fuel Oils, Diesel Oils and Kerosenes.

The tankers were divided into two types Class A and Class B. Class A was silver painted for inflammable liquids with a low flash point and had a capacity of 6,149 gallons while Class B was in black livery for heavy liquids and chemicals with a capacity of 5,370 gallons.

Extract from the February 1961 Model Railway Constructor.

HORNBY-DUBLO OO
G.W.R. Passenger Fruit Van
6s. 8d.

ALSO recently introduced by Meccano is a passenger fruit van, a model of the ex-Great Western "Fruit D." Although the prototype is not refrigerated, its wooden body was designed to give a continuous flow of cool air through the van. For this reason these vehicles have proved very useful for transporting freshly picked fruit rapidly from Western Region agricultural areas, particularly the Vale of Evesham, to the London markets and "Fruit Ds" are often to be seen at the rear of W.R. express trains. The Hornby model faithfully reproduces in semi-matt maroon plastic the prototype's planking, strapping and rivet detail as well as its multifarious door fastenings and end ventilator detail. The roof, which is finished in light grey, is complete with shell ventilators, gas-lamp tops and rain strips. To the uninformed eye, the long-wheelbase underframe looks devoid of detail, save for the vacuum brake cylinder and the brake hangers; in fact, all such long-wheelbase, fitted vehicles tend to look bare-framed. The only feature omitted on the Hornby model is the brake rigging, which would be very hard to reproduce in any detail on such a long-wheelbase vehicle. Fitted with the old-type coupling and the familiar nylon wheels, this vehicle should appeal not only to the Western Region modeller but also to the G.W.R. enthusiast.

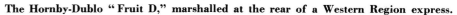

The Hornby-Dublo "Fruit D," marshalled at the rear of a Western Region express.

4305 'Fruit D' of the WR. It is a model!
Meccano publicity photograph.

The Class B tank barrel is fitted with steam coils to assist the off-loading of heavy fuel oils. Discharge of load is controlled by internal rod and plug, operated by the hand wheel located on top of the tank barrel. The Class B is painted black with two white stars to denote acceptance for high speed working.

The first true super detail items of rolling stock to reappear after almost twelve months absence, were the 4316 and 4315 horseboxes in SR green and BR maroon liveries, in March 1960 and these were advertised with the 4679 Traffic Services Ltd. tanker although the latter was marked available later. The horseboxes were exceptionally accurate models of the British Rail standard horsebox that were built at Earlestown. The handrails onto the roof, in fact, incorporate on the real wagon filler pipes for the water tank. The original drawings and photographs were loaned by the manufacturers to Meccano Limited with all the details for the serial numbers for the LMR, ER and WR which were produced in maroon. However, the Southern Region vehicles in SR green were numbers S96359 to S96414 – the Hornby Dublo model being S96412.

From the photograph of the original model the incredible detail which Meccano Company fitted into this even down to reproducing the padded interior sections is apparent. I must admit I find it difficult to open and close the doors and almost all the models for sale secondhand have these either missing or broken. Supplied with this wagon was a beautiful little polystyrene horse which was originally made in the SF16 red i.e. bauxite brown polystyrene but, on 25th January, the drawing states a change to polythene 95 brown – a lighter colour. This seems to indicate some problems in production or availability of materials. But all in all a very attractive model and much sought after. 18th March, 1960 also heralded a particular event in British Rail history with the naming ceremony of the last steam locomotive – 'Evening Star'.

There appears to have been some confusion between the arrival of the ICI Chlorine tanker and the traffic services vehicle and I believe the ICI tanker was the first to appear in April. In detail the model was not really that attractive, but it did have one saving grace. The first appearance of the open brake gear. The *Constructor* 'Review' of May 1960 recorded that . . . 'Ever since the introduction of the super detail series of

Extract from the November 1961 Model Railway Constructor.

"Presflo" bulk cement wagon 7s 1d

LATEST addition to the increasing range of Dublo Super Detail wagons is this "Presflo" bulk cement wagon. The body, moulded in correctly coloured bauxite plastic, carries a wealth of strapping and other detail. The 10ft 6in wheelbase and dummy vacuum brake gear allow this wagon to be correctly marshalled in fast, fitted freights. The body is secured to the chassis by plastic lugs and a single cheesehead screw. Full brake rigging and an access ladder at one end complete a sturdy and useful special traffic wagon.

rolling stock we have urged them to improve the appearance of the whole wagon by modifying the brake and running gear and we think the very satisfactory appearance of this latest wagon fully vindicates our view. The offending web in the brake gear has gone, the axle guards are vastly improved in detail.' In May the traffic services tanker appeared and this really was a most attractive vehicle. The real vehicles were specially designed to carry chemicals from British factories to all places over Europe except Russia and Spain. The wagon was finished in silver livery, indicating inflammable contents and the the the anchor sign denoted that it went by ferry. The two stars indicated that the vehicle could travel by the fastest freight trains in the U.K. I must admit I find a rake of these very attractive indeed and particularly with the brakeman's platform and dummy brake wheel.

Indeed this was the start of a whole European venture commencing with the Southern passenger coaches and around 1964 Meccano had open ferry wagons as part of a general plan to improve the export potential of Hornby Dublo on the Continent.

We had to wait until November 1960 for the introduction of the Western Region passenger fruit van – a model of the ex Great Western 'fruit D'. The

The bulk cement in operation. The lorry would have made a good Dublo Dinky Toy – from Meccano records.

HORNBY DUBLO   OO
Blue Spot Fish Van   **6s 9d**
Bulk Salt Wagon   **7s 1d**

THE latest Hornby-Dublo super-detail model is based on the Eastern Region "Blue Spot" insulated fish van. The design incorporates a 15ft wheelbase underframe, the minimum permissible length for vehicles running at unrestricted speed. The long wheelbase, compared with the body length, correctly gives the van a somewhat unusual aspect. The body is finished in white, as on refrigerated vehicles. The side panels carry the usual "XP" markings, the words "Insul-Fish" and a number prefixed E, since although these vehicles were built by British Railways, they are passenger-rated vehicles and are therefore numbered in the B.R. passenger stock series. The original batch of 500 vehicles were all allocated to the Eastern and North Eastern Regions for express fish traffic, either in complete trains or attached to ordinary passenger trains. The main departure from previous Hornby practice in this model is the use of a plastic underframe; this is a vast improvement on the previous cast metal underframe. The body is secured to this underframe by a single screw; it slots into a housing in the underframe which also carries a metal weight.

We have also received the new I.C.I. bulk salt wagon; this is identical to the "Presflo" cement wagon reviewed last month, save that the body is coloured dark bottle green. Like the "Presflo," it retails at 7s 1d.

"Blue Spot" Fish Van ER, No. 4300, price 6/9

Constructor reported that although the prototype was not refrigerated, its wooden body was designed to give a continuous flow of cool air through the van. For this reason these vehicles proved very useful for transporting freshly picked fruit rapidly from Western Region agricultural areas, particularly the Vale of Evesham, to the London Markets and the 'fruit Ds' were often seen at the rear of Western Region express trains. They continue . . . 'to the uninformed eye the long wheel base underframe looks devoid of detail save for the vacuum brake cylinder and brake hangers; in fact all such long wheel base fitted vehicles tend to look bare framed. The only feature omitted on the Hornby model is the brake rigging which would be very hard to reproduce in any detail on such a long wheel base vehicle. Fitted with the old type steel coupling and familiar nylon wheels this vehicle should appeal not only to the Western Region modeller but also to the GWR enthusiast.' Once again quite exquisite detail was put into the body shell.

January 1961 heralded the new super detail coaches with nylon couplings and the following September it was announced that these new couplings would be standard on all future wagons although we had to wait until November 1961 for four new super detail wagons to be issued simultaneously. They were the Prestflo bulk cement wagon, the ICI bulk salt wagon, the Lowmac machine wagon and the Blue Spot fish van. The Prestflo bulk cement wagon was first and in its correctly coloured bauxite livery, carried a wealth of strapping and other detail. These wagons were built by British Railways at Shildon in 1954, and between then and 1960 some 60 'Prestflo's of 20 ton capacity were built for the Cement Marketing Company by the Butterley Company. The

4652 The Lowmac wagon. Meccano publicity photograph.

cement was loaded by gravity and discharged by air pressure through a flexible pipe either to a storage silo or direct to a road vehicle. The 10 ft 6 in wheel base and dummy vacuum brake gear allowed this wagon to be correctly marshalled in fast fitted freights. December saw the introduction of its sister the ICI bulk salt wagon, which was an identical casting, but this time in the ICI transport blue as this very attractive blue green colour was called. These wagons were specially built to carry salt in bulk from Winsford in Cheshire to the Stoke works near Droitwich Spa. Together with the bulk salt wagon came the blue spot fish van. The *Meccano Magazine* for June 1958 reported that the increase in faster vacuum fitted freight trains which kept closely to schedule time and provided next day deliveries over long distances had a lot of problems in so much as the overheating of axle boxes fitted with the usual plain bearings and lubrication wrought havoc. Numerous wagons had new sets of wheels with roller bearing axle boxes fitted and all such wagons had a large blue circle or spot on a white background and ran, for example, on the 12.30 p.m. fish express from Aberdeen to King's Cross, reaching London at 2.30 a.m. the next morning in time for the early markets, Pacific locomotives often sharing the haulage of such super freight trains. Indeed there was an excellent article in the November 1958 *Meccano Magazine*. Investigation had shown that during one month alone 3 per cent of all Western Region freight trains had to be stopped en route to detach over 2,000 wagons; the result of individual wagons in freight trains having overheated axle boxes. However, another feature of this model wagon was that it was the first to have a moulded chassis frame with, as one had now come to expect, superb detailing.

Although advertised at the same time, the Low-mac wagon was first reviewed in January 1962. It did not have too much praise as it was, to quote 'a reasonable model of a common vehicle'. Obviously the detail was superb, although the *Constructor* did advise its readers to paint the buffers black with dirty silver heads. They suggested a load such as a piece of model machinery or a Dublo Dinky Toy could be used, although I find a Matchbox steamroller looks ideal. The April 1954 *Railway Modeller* also showed a photograph of the correct method of hitching cable drums to this wagon if so required.

The new plastic moulded cable drums on the low sided wagon No. 4646 received scant attention, although they were mentioned in an article in the November 1961 *Meccano Magazine*. These were moulded in yellow and labelled the Aluminium Wire and Cable Company, replacing the earlier wooden Liverpool cable drums. Naturally, the new cable drums, number 1521 were available separately.

The four wheel Southern utility van came in November 1961. It appeared in the shops just before Christmas and was officially known as a 'CCT' or covered carriage truck and had, in real life, end doors to facilitate the loading of motor vehicles or stage scenery. The *Constructor* 'Review' pointed out that these were dummy on the model and did not work. The *Constructor* went on to comment that the bodies general overall effect was convincing enough, despite the bright malachite livery on the body, which was rather unrealistic. At 12s. 8d. it was the most highly priced of all the super detail wagon range to date. Apart from the dummy end doors we have already mentioned, like the horsebox, the model did have four opening doors on either side and realistic scenes

of loading and unloading newspapers or parcels could be arranged. A very popular model with collectors.

April 1962 brought two more newcomers: number 4301 the banana van and 4313 the gunpowder van. The early 0 gauge gunpowder van has always been a popular item with collectors and the new super detail model captures exactly the low squat lines of the vehicles specially designed for the conveyance of explosives. Remember that when loaded the same rules applied to this van as to the loaded oil tanks – that at least two ordinary or empty vehicles were to be marshalled between the vehicle in question and the end of the train.

The banana van has always been a favourite of mine. It carries the yellow disc that distinguishes vans used for this particular traffic. Mr. R. W. Crawshaw of the London Midland Region of British Railways, wrote to the Meccano Company on 20th May 1960 stating that the model was basically identical to the BR standard 12 ton ventilated van – Hornby Dublo model 4325 – which was already in production. The extra vacuum pipe on the banana van was for steam heating

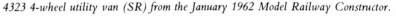

4323 4-wheel utility van (SR) from the January 1962 Model Railway Constructor.

Bananas, gunpowder and packing – sounds like a comedy trio! From the June 1962 Model Railway Constructor.

the vehicle. He pointed out that while the body was substantially the same, there were the following three variations. Plywood sides and doors instead of matchboarding, the small ventilator at the end of the ventilated van was not fitted on the banana van and, as we already mentioned, a yellow disc was painted on each side at opposite ends of the banana van.

Also written up in the April *Meccano Magazine* although not advertised until May, was the 4310 Hornby Dublo packing van. It represented the van that carried timbers, known as 'packing' for various purposes in breakdown work and at the same time was part of the new train set, the breakdown train number 2049. This was a very attractive item indeed, incorporating the 0–6–2 2-rail Tank locomotive, the big hook and a 'D14' brake end suburban coach with nylon wheels. The packing van made up the complement. The editor of the *Meccano Magazine* does point out, however, that it was a train set with a difference in so much that it was never issued with rails.

We have to wait until August 1962 when a further batch of four super detail vehicles were produced, all, bar one, highly desirable collector's items. These were the bauxite brown 16 ton mineral wagon number 4656, the 6-wheel United Dairies number 4657, 4658 the Prestwin Silo wagon and 4685 the bogie ICI Caustic Liquor tanker. The 16 ton mineral wagon was identical to the earlier grey finish model and showed

the wagon fitted for power braking. A rare model to find today.

The next model, the Prestwin Silo wagon, was usually run in block train formations and was a special purpose wagon designed to carry sand and other powdery loads. They never seem to have set the enthusiast on fire in collector terms, but the detail on them, particularly the valve gear at the top, is superb. In railway jargon, these particular wagons were known as 'Sabrinas' the name being purely coincidental with the remarkably well endowed starlet of the time. The Prestwin Silo wagon also has normal axle boxes despite the fact that the prototype had circular roller bearing axle boxes denoted by the red striped yellow axle boxes.

The next model was the United Dairies milk tanker, the first six-wheeled item of freight rolling stock in Hornby Dublo. These tankers were common sights being run in whole train loads on the Western Region by the United Dairies Company who supplied much of London and the Home Counties and were painted in their off-white colour. The tankers were glass lined and had a 3000 gallon capacity. I am surprised that they did not also bring out a model in the very smart Express Dairies livery of blue and white. There were three variations of this particular model and perhaps the chief one involved the chocks on which the main tank wagon sat. It really was rather

like a Chinese farce with all high, all low and high low, meaning that the initial production had all six chocks each side of a consistent length and there must have been problems in fitting the wire retaining bars as the next version had the second and fourth chock each side reduced in height. Another variation is in the colour of the polystyrene of the tank. As I mentioned, they were cream white, but I have seen one or two in distinct stone buff colours and this is not just painted, but it was also moulded right the way through. The same variation occurs on the blue spot fish vans which range from starch white to yellowy cream colour. At the bottom of each end of the tank was a representation of the fittings used for discharging purposes and for steam cleaning processes that all milk tanks had to undergo after they were emptied. Whether in train rakes or singly at suburban stations, these were without doubt, beautiful models and one could well understand the many liveried varieties which come on offer from the Wrenn Company.

The United Dairies tank wagon is based on the glass lined 6-wheel tanks used extensively by Western and Southern Regions. The last of the group is to me one of the most attractive: the bogie ICI Caustic Liquor tanker. This was modelled again in the ICI famous transport blue livery although it had been advertised and modelled as early as February 1954 by the Bradshaw model products Company in the Nucro

4658 Prestwin Silo wagon. From the February 1963 Meccano Magazine.

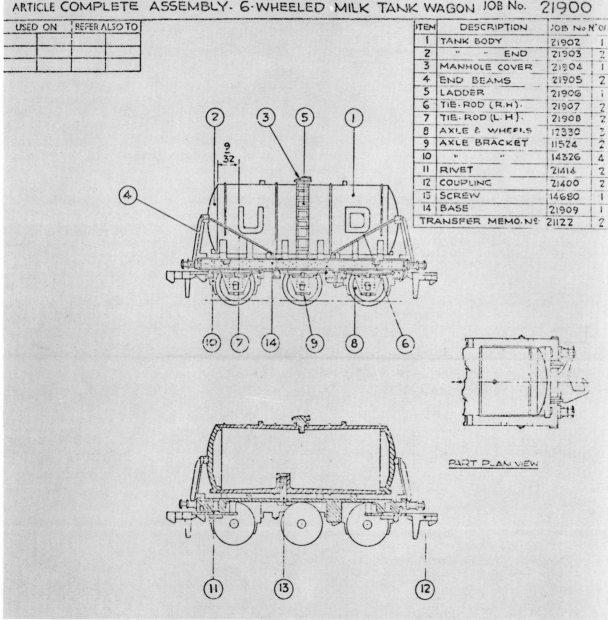

ARTICLE COMPLETE ASSEMBLY. 6·WHEELED MILK TANK WAGON JOB No. 21900

USED ON	REFER ALSO TO

ITEM	DESCRIPTION	JOB No	N° OFF
1	TANK BODY	21902	
2	" " END	21903	2
3	MANHOLE COVER	21904	1
4	END BEAMS	21905	2
5	LADDER	21906	1
6	TIE· ROD (R.H.)	21907	2
7	TIE. ROD (L.H.)	21908	2
8	AXLE & WHEELS	12330	3
9	AXLE BRACKET	11524	2
10	" "	14326	4
11	RIVET	21416	2
12	COUPLING	21400	2
13	SCREW	14680	1
14	BASE	21909	1
TRANSFER MEMO. N° 21122			2

PART PLAN VIEW

bogie tank wagon kit which retailed at 15s. 9d. There is a red version of this tanker by Triang in the bright post office red with white letters on a black base, but this is not to be confused with the Hornby Dublo model. The drawing, dated 2nd May 1961, refers to the altered position of transfers and puts the date as 9th April 1962. However, there are bogie tankers known to exist with the old diamond pattern bogie. Indeed the full size prototype had these as did the original drawings in Hornby Dublo and there is a photograph in the September 1962 issue of the *Model Railway News* showing this tanker with such bogies. There is even a special drawing dated 11th January 1961 relating to this bogie and I am uncertain whether they were moulded in plastic from the early diecast tools or whether they were in fact diecast. Perhaps they had problems in production because the 'Press Release' photographs in the *Constructor* show the standard plate bogie version and this is the more common item.

For some months at this time there had been considerable discussions in the Meccano Company about adapting the diecast standard 12 ton 4-wheel base to a plastic moulding with a more super detail effect. As far back as October 1961 sample plastic bases had been made and tried out successfully and the requirements for a universal ballast plate for stability determined. At a meeting on 28th February 1963, these moulded bases were again brought up with the possibility of using needle axles as the French Acho or pinpoint bearings. By April 1963 it had been decided that the plastic bases were to be used on the cheap 0–4–0 ready to run set which involved the 0–4–0 steam outline Tank locomotive and the 13 ton standard open wagon and steel wagon. These were in yellow and buff livery and, to complete the set, the main body of the Eastern Region brake van was moulded in a bright red colour and put on the same base. A very pretty little set, understandably successful and indeed much sought after by collectors today.

It was planned that these new lightweight, relatively simple outline moulded bases would be used on all 4-wheel goods rolling stock, but it was decided, quite rightly in Binns Road, that it would be a retrograde step in view of the continued improvement in

4657 6-wheeled milk tank wagon. From a Meccano drawing.

the quality of competitor's rolling stock. These models did have a first however, insomuch as they were the first to be fitted with the new fine scale moulded coupling. Far neater than the ugly large polythene coupling on the earlier models.

October 1963 saw the introduction of two of the most popular (and rare) items – the highly prized 6-wheel passenger brake van and the 21 ton hopper wagon. The *Model Railway Constructor* reported . . .

'The BR standard 21 ton mineral hopper is based on a design built in quantity for the Ministry of Supply and the LNER and now operated in large numbers by British Railways. These vehicles are very often in the news at the present time with the opening of bulk coal distribution centres in the London area fed by block trains, mainly from the Midlands. The Beeching Plan envisages more of these mechanised depots and this will, no doubt, one day change the typical coal train from a slowly plodding collection of assorted wooden and all steel vehicles which it has been up to the present

4685 ICI Caustic Liquor tanker – from the September 1962 Model Railway News.

WAGONS OF CHARACTER FROM HORNBY-DUBLO

TWO individual items of rolling stock have recently appeared from Meccano Limited and add further interest to goods train make-up and operation. The blue-green tankers as used by the I.C.I. for carrying caustic liquor has been faithfully copied in 4 mm. scale, a detailed die-cast underframe supports the high-capacity plastic tank and the latter features the correct markings. Price 12s. 6d.

time, to a faster, shorter train, of higher capacity hopper wagons running to an exacting schedule. With their latest wagon, therefore, Hornby Dublo are right up to the minute for although it is of the normal unfitted 21 ton hopper those employed on the NCB and Charringtons Bulk trains are of the same type. Some of the newer examples of this type of wagon are fitted with roller bearing axles boxes and those employed on the bulk coal trains are finished in a distinctive livery. The grey plastic body of the Hornby Dublo hopper carries the correct markings and we are pleased to see is correctly shaped inside. A 12 ft wheel base black metal chassis is employed and features of a modified coupler which is a less bulky "buck-eye" than formally used. The nylon pivot which has been introduced recently in place of the metal rivet does not seem to be as satisfactory in holding the coupler in the correct height especially with the greater flexibility of the coupler although it has the advantage of being removable if the coupler became damaged. The coupler on one end of our sample was very sloppy and enabled the wagon and the six wheel brake van which has a similar coupler to be pulled apart very easily. We would have much preferred to see the screw pivot as used on the Acho vehicles introduced on British models for this ensures stability and can also be removed if necessary. This apart we consider the hopper an excellent model and expect to see bulk coal trains on many modernised layouts of the future.'

Bulk trains of Hornby Dublo hopper wagons – at the price they are today?! The mind boggles. I am surprised they were not fitted with a dummy load but doubtless this would have been one of the improvements in the future.

A most peculiar modification for which I can find no reason or justification, is in the triangular gusset plates at the ends of the wagon. There is no modification shown on the drawing at all, but there are several wagons on the market at the moment which have a peculiar 'V' inserted in the middle of these gusset plates. I do not believe these originated from the Wrenn Factory although I would not be at all surprised to see the 'inventors' of our hobby substituting the new Wrenn bodies onto the diecast Hornby Dublo

The prototype – complete with diamond axle bogies.

219

chassis if the original bodies have been overpainted as many were. On all counts a beautiful wagon.

Finally we come to the Rail Cleaning Wagon – a mythical beast in many collectors' eyes as it is so scarce that few collectors own one. There is an interesting background in that a real Rail Cleaning Wagon did exist and was converted from an ex South Eastern ballast wagon and used at Folkestone Harbour. The rail cleaning apparatus was fitted above each rail and consisted of a brush forced down onto the rail by a screw acting through two coil springs. The wagon was fitted with Mansell wheels, wood faced, self-contained buffers and the Southern Eastern railway type grease axle boxes with springs screwed to them by long bolts and without the normal buckles. The original prototype body, sole bars, headstocks and buffer cases were red oxide with the running gear in black and white lettering. The mixture of oil and dirt on the model railway track had necessitated that a cleaning vehicle of some description be used for a number of years and it was Bob Wills of the Wills Finecast Company who had brought out his own track cleaning wagon, at the beginning of the 1960s, which was a replica of the real Southern Region wagon.

John Kermode wrote to me in March 1973 recalling his days in the Meccano Shop in London and stated . . . 'We also owned one item of Triang equipment! – the box car track cleaning wagon. This model made several circuits of the display in the window early in the morning before the shop was open as it was not intended that the public should see this operation. (Triang being the main competitor of the Company and we did not wish to advertise their products.)'

The story goes that a Meccano director came in early one morning, saw it and was distressed enough to call a hurried meeting in Liverpool when two competitor samples, the Wills track cleaning wagon and the Triang box car with the wide felt band were shown to the meeting with the idea of including such a vehicle in the Hornby Dublo range. One was hastily prepared and was basically our old friend the diecast mineral wagon body, adapted at the tipping end on a new special chassis unit, which by coincidence almost completely copied the Bob Wills design. It was painted in black with the letters 'Rail Cleaning Wagon' on the central doors either side. As with the

Bob Wills model, two cigarette filters completed the vehicle which was filled with fluid such as lighter fuel or 'Thawpit'. The choice of the mineral wagon was to try and overcome the necessity of a suitably heavy unit. The model was drawn on 27th November 1963 although it was not released until December the following year, long after the takeover of the Meccano Company. The write up in the December 1964 Meccano Magazine stated that for best results the vehicle should be propelled i.e. pushed rather than pulled and that it was important that methylated spirits and no other liquid be used since damage may result to the sleeper base.

However, the story does not end there, as according to the sales figures, 839 were sold in 1964, leaving a stock of 1,700! A total freeze was put on the sale of Hornby Dublo for the time being as, if the Triang Company released these models, in bulk, they would obviously affect to a great extent their own particular

range. However, strange to relate, they never ever appeared on the subsequent stock lists given to the Triang Salesmen and I have seen the figures from 1965, right the way through to 1970. What happened to these 1,700 track cleaning wagons? Rumours I heard from Binns Road were that they were inferior to the Triang model and so, together with lorry loads of unsold 3-rail track, were taken to be dumped in the Mersey. This is not literally true, but there was a big new dock extension project being undertaken at this time and an awful lot of fill material from the city was taken and so dumped. However, if one does want to complete the set of super detail wagons one must have this vehicle, hence its great demand and rarity.

The question was what the Triang Company should do with all the super detail wagons, as without doubt they were far superior in detail to their own models and yet they had been selling relatively slowly. Perhaps the Hornby Dublo Company, having had their peak years between 1957–61 latterly overestimated the demand. At the time of the takeover they had 128,200 wagons unsold. The July 1965 Meccano

4644 21 ton hopper wagons – Meccano publicity photograph.

MECCANO LTD

ARTICLE	DUBLO ROLLING STOCK WHEELS	MEMO № 20803

NOTE   DUBLO ROLLING STOCK HAS SPOKED WHEELS WITH THE FOLLOWING EXCEPTIONS

№	DESCRIPTION	TYPE of WHEEL	REMARKS
D1	HIGH CAPACITY WAGON	DISC	DIAMOND FRAME BOGIE
D1	40 TON BOGIE WELL WAGON	"	PLATE " "
D1	BOGIE BOLSTER WAGON	"	PLATE " "
SD6	STANDARD GOODS BRAKE VAN	"	
SD6	GOODS BRAKE VAN W.R.	"	
SD6	" " " L.M.R.	"	
	ALL COACHES	"	
SD6	16 TON MINERAL WAGON	"	

Magazine had an article on converting these wagons to the Triang type coupling, but the sheer labour involved in converting this stock was totally uneconomic when no extra charge could be made. I have two wagons which have been professionally adapted with a special white metal cast adaptor plate and the new Triang coupling fitted, but I have never been able to find out who undertook this.

That so much excellence was to end in commercial failure was indeed sad and one small compensation must be the continuance of the name 'Hornby' if not 'Hornby Dublo'. There can be few instances in the history of model railways where after the demise of the original manufacturer, its name went one way and the products remained in production under an entirely different name – Wrenn in this instance.

It is fortunate for the Hornby Dublo production line that they did not suffer the problems of manufacturers in the mid-1970s. Benzine was used far more than petrol due to the reduction in the lead content and polystyrene supplies virtually dried up. For the time being it was panic stations.

4654 Rail Cleaning Wagon from the December 1964 Meccano Magazine.

Extract from the September 1951 Model Railway Constructor.

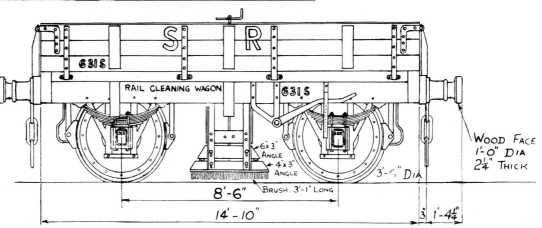

SUPER DETAIL COACHES

You might be under the impression that I have been too high in my praise for the Hornby Dublo model railway locomotives and rolling stock we have covered so far. I make no apologies. Being an ardent enthusiast of the railway locomotive since my earliest childhood, the Hornby Dublo range has always to me been the miniature equivalent of the full-size locomotive. Now, on reflection it fascinates me to inspect the models closely and find how they mirror their full-size prototype in the minutest detail. I stated in the last chapter how I felt that the super detail range of goods rolling stock had never been surpassed.

The same goes for the new range of Hornby Dublo super detail coaches. Nobody has yet produced to my satisfaction a coach of equivalent standards. I know many prefer the plastic moulded sides, but to my mind whatever detail is put on, they all seem far too thick compared with the impression one gets of the real train. The incredible amount of detail incorporated in the super detail Hornby Dublo models with their tinprinted sides, more than counteracts the criticism of 'old fashioned' manufacturing techniques.

The first super detail coaches were advertised in the December 1960 *Meccano Magazine* and were the 4050 Western Region corridor coach, 4051 the brake second, 4052 the British Rail maroon corridor coach and 4053 its matching brake second. The first coaches were the Western Region to go with the 'Red Dragon' train set to be hauled by the newly introduced 'Cardiff Castle' locomotive.

The *Model Railway News* 'Review' of February 1961 stated that 'the model as a whole is very pleasing – but why the corpulent plastic couplings. These over-scale couplings which varied considerably in height and were difficult to bend to the correct horizontal level to me were certainly a retrograde step and I would have far preferred to see the continuation of the old metal coupling.' The *Model Railway News* goes on . . . 'The model possesses a good deal of external and internal detail. It also has just the right amount of weight, heavy enough for smooth running and at the same time sufficiently light to enable a 14-coach train to be hauled at ease behind a Hornby Dublo Ringfield Castle locomotive. We also note that an exceptionally fine effort has been made with the British Railways Crest which adorns each side of the coach.'

The *Model Railway Constructor* 'Review' reported that although underscale in length (57 ft 9 ins against the 64 ft 6 ins) they were nevertheless very smart attractive vehicles . . . 'The new coaches incorporate several departures from normal Hornby practice. The bogies were flexible – this being achieved by pivoting the side frames of the main bogie frame allowing the nylon wheels to follow any slight undulations in trackwork without transmitting them to the bogie. The main bogie pivot is off-centre towards the centre of the coach.'

They go on . . . 'the coach body has tinprinted sides; plastic roof, ends and underframe detail and a metal underframe whose sole bars regrettably have no running boards below the doors. Lack of running boards and the flush tin body sides give a rather flat side appearance.

'End detail is very good. The pullman gangway connection is well produced, steps, lamp brackets, lighting points and communication cord equipment are all there. The water tank filler-cum-hand rail is well represented by thin black wire. The grey plastic

The new Hornby Dublo Western Region coaches – from a Meccano Publicity photograph 6th December 1960.

SUPER-DETAIL COACHES IN HORNBY-DUBLO

The new "super-detail" Corridor Coaches have Polystyrene ends, roofs and underframes, tinprinted sides and die-cast bogie sideframes. The Pullman Cars have moulded bodies and bases.

HORNBY-DUBLO COACHES
(2 or 3 rail)

4021 Suburban Coach, 1st/2nd B.R.		12/-
4025 Suburban Coach, 1st/2nd (S.R.) Green		12/-
★ 4035 Pullman Car, 1st Class		18/6
★ 4036 Pullman Car, 2nd Class		18/6
4037 Pullman Car, Brake/2nd		18/6
4050 Corridor Coach, 1st/2nd (W.R.)		16/-
4051 Corridor Coach, Brake/2nd (W.R.)		16/-
4052 Corridor Coach, 1st/2nd (B.R.)		16/-
4053 Corridor Coach, Brake/2nd (B.R.)		16/-
4075 Passenger Brake Van (B.R.)		14/11
4078 Composite Sleeping Car (B.R.)		16/-

★ With interior fittings.

MADE BY MECCANO LTD.

No. 4037

No. 4036

No. 4035

No. 4052

No. 4053

No. 4078

No. 4050

No. 4051

No. 4075

roof is well detailed although some ventilators are wrongly placed. The accurately modelled interiors are finished in light brown plastic . . . one or two spaces left blank seem to indicate that provision has been made for interior lighting at a later date. The seats have armrests and one compartment in each coach has its double sliding interior doors left open. (BR standard stock has single sliding interior doors.) These are generally very pleasing vehicles which, with some people to give life to the excellent interiors, will make up into a really impressive train.'

The reference to interior lighting detail is once more one of the items which was tried, investigated, but never put into practice. The report admits the fact that on the brake second vehicles there was also representation of the periscopes facing fore and aft provided on some BR vehicles for the guard.

The write up in the *Meccano Magazine* refers to the finely moulded nylon coupling (a classic exaggeration). They also report on the new feature for Hornby Dublo stock incorporating underfloor detail between

Advertisement from the March 1961 Meccano Magazine.

Extract from the September 1961 Meccano Magazine.

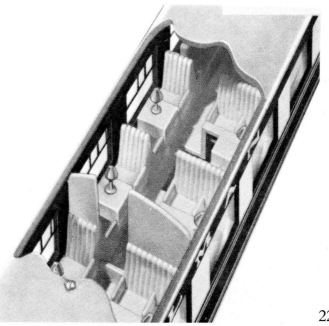

the bogies in the form of a single plastic moulding. This is attached to the base of the coach and represents very effectively the underframe girders, accumulator boxes, brake cylinders and V-hangers, and even the domed end of the lighting dynamo which is quite a prominent feature on many BR standard vehicles.

One of the most pleasing closeup effects to me is when you look inside the first class compartments and see the very effective padded lining of the seats while the second class seats are just plain flat moulding. If only the coach roofs could have been readily removed to allow for seated passengers thus bringing these superb models to full life.

In the March 1961 *Meccano Magazine* five new vehicles were announced – the 4075 full brake, the 4078 sleeping car and the wonderful pullman coaches 4035, 4036 and 4037.

The *Model Railway News* reported that the Meccano Company certainly meant business with their latest 9⅛" long coaches. They stated that the sleeping car was of special interest and afforded another new operation for the timetable in model railway working. The model was fitted out with adequate interior details and represents the standard BR sleeping car containing five first class single berth compartments and six second class two berth compartments. The extra detail in the sleeping car doubtless reflects why its price was 16s. against the super detail coaches introduced to date which were 14s. 11d.

The *Constructor* 'Review' as usual in great detail, goes on to report . . . 'the sleeping car has separate compartments, each fitted with one berth and a dummy wash basin. To be strictly accurate the second class sleeping compartment should also have an upper berth but the absence of such a small detail is not likely to be noticed.' They continue . . . 'although the Hornby Dublo sleeping car has been finished as a composite, the prototypes of which run on the Western Region, the body design is identical to the full first class and full second class cars and hence it will not be difficult to alter the class of this model by painting over the figure one on the door of one end or adding another figure one at the other end. Sleeping cars can either be used singly or in pairs mixed with ordinary stock or with a full brake at each end formed into a complete train such as found on the East coast and West coast mainlines between London and Scotland.'

Publicity photographs of the new pullman coaches issued on 20th January 1961 by the then Meccano agents J. Walter Thompson Co. Ltd.

The exterior and interior views of the real pullman coaches –
from Meccano records.

The full brake coach is thought to have the correct number of ventilators and periscopes and is also virtually near scale length. The prototype is 58 ft against the 75 ft 9 ins scale length we have already mentioned.

However, the highlight of these five new vehicles must be the rake of three pullman cars. There must have been some delay in producing them as it was not until June 1961 that the 'News Special' column of the *Railway Modeller* reported that the first two coaches, the brake second car number 79 and the all second car number 74 were in production. They report . . . 'they are very attractive replicas of the older pattern pullman coach complete with internal detail, seat, tables and lamps. The bogies are a new design which we have noted on some of the latest British Railways stock being similar to the old LNE type without the equalising bar. To enable the coaches to negotiate the 15 inch radius curves there is of necessity greater clearance between the bogie and the underside of the vehicle. One point of criticism is that the characteristic matchboarding of pullman sides is not reproduced and this does detract slightly from an otherwise most satisfactory coach. They are 58 ft 6 ins over buffers and retail at only 18s. 6d.'

The reviewer has made a mistake here, as these particular coaches were never match sided and the *Model Railway Constructor* stated that although originally publicised by Meccano Limited as being for the Southern Region, both models were based on the all-steel cars introduced on the LNER 'Queen of Scots' train in 1928 . . . 'The Hornby cars are shorter than scale, 58 ft against the prototypes 63 ft 10 ins but the discrepancy is not noticeable particularly as the number and details of the prototype doors and windows have been faithfully reproduced. The pullmans are the first coaches from Meccano Limited to have bodies entirely of polystyrene; the mouldings reproduce well the unadorned steel sides of the originals with authentically sparse details such as recessed end doors and handrails and on the brake car, a guard's lookout and (a surprising item still found on the prototype) exterior side lamps a feature which went out of general use about the time the pullmans entered service. Roof detail is however rather simplified, interior detail is good with neat seats, tables and table lamps but some of the realism is sacrificed since tables and seats are formed from one moulding of uniform caramel brown colour.

← *The Super Detail Coaches.*

Extract from letter from the Pullman Car Co. Ltd. to Meccano Ltd. dated 3rd April 1959, listing all Pullman Cars then in service.

We confirm that Pullman Brake Cars are 2nd Class.

Representative names and numbers of cars.

First class cars have names and second class cars have numbers.

Second Class Brakes: Nos. 68, 70, 77, 78, 79, 80.

Second Class Kitchens:" 67, 69, 71, 72, 81, 82, 303* .

Second Class Parlours:" 73, 74, 75, 76, 83, 84.

First Class Kitchens: Belinda, Evadne, Ione, Joan, Loraine, Nilar, Phyllis, Thelma, Aquila,* Aries* Carina* Orion*

First Class Parlours: Agatha, Eunice, Juana, Lucille, Sheila, Ursula, Lena, Cygnus*

Hercules* Perseus* Phoenix*

Colouring of interiors

Usually mahogany panelling; polished brass fittings i.e. parcel racks, sliding lights, table lamps, door handles, electric torch brackets etc., white ceilings, fawn trelis pattern carpets; general upholstery various but often in wine and green patterns.

Colouring of Exterior

Umber and cream (see painting diagram S.2022).

Generally speaking Pullman roofs are now finished in aluminium.

I do not think there will be any objection to finishing in a light shade of grey.

* GOLDEN ARROW CARS.

227

The roof for instance is extended over the doors instead of being recessed as on the other cars; the ends are slightly different in the design of the window. Roof and underframe detail is better than on the previous models. Readers may remember that we commented on the bad lettering of the earlier cars; we are glad to report that it is much clearer on this car (I think they must have been pre-production samples. Ed.). The vehicle rides correctly on Gresley type bogies. With the introduction of this kitchen first, a complete pullman train can now be built up. The price is now 18s. 10d.'

Although I have never seen badly reproduced samples of lettering on the Hornby Dublo coaches, I have found a distinct variation in the shades of the cream colour on the coach sides. One noticeable alteration in the later pullman coaches was that they reverted to the British Railways standard bogie side frame as opposed to the Gresley type fitted earlier.

Extract from the October 1961 Meccano Magazine.

'The pullman brown and cream livery has a matt finish. The specimens we received may have been hand finished pre-production models since the cream is uneven and overlaps the brown in places and the pullman and lining transfers are badly applied.'

They go on . . . 'The coaches are mounted on compensated Gresley type bogies. The prototype so far as we are aware ride on pullman bogies. The now standard plastic coupling is fitted. The removal of three screws underneath the cars allows the interior to be removed so that passengers can be inserted. These pullman cars will certainly make up into a useful train and now that a number of the originals of this type have been transferred to the Southern Region can correctly be used on Southern Region services.'

In the following *Constructor* issue – November 1961 – they reported 'the third Hornby pullman car – a model of the first class kitchen car "Aries" – has now appeared although as yet only in boxed train sets. The prototype car was built in 1952 and is used in the "Golden Arrow" train. Its design is slightly different from that of the Dublo "Queen of Scots" brake second and power second cars reviewed in our June issue.

HORNBY-DUBLO PULLMAN CARS

In your review of the new Hornby-Dublo Pullman cars you express regret that the tongue and groove side panelling characteristic of older Pullmans is not reproduced. May I point out that the Hornby models have been based on genuine prototypes, unlike some other previous proprietary Pullmans? Both parlour second No. 74 (now S.R. allocation) and brake second No. 79 (east coast allocation) are all-steel vehicles built in 1928. In any event most of the timber-panelled cars have now been withdrawn, and those

Extract from readers' letters in the August 196 Railway Modeller.

which remain in service have had, or ar likely to have, their side panels plate over. For any readers who want alterna tive numbers for their Hornby Pullman 73—76, 83 and 84 are suitable for the par lour cars, and 67—72, 77—82 for th brakes. It should be noted that th Southern Region has no allocation o brake cars of the all-steel pattern. Brak seconds Nos. 62, 63 and 65, for use in th "Bournemouth Belle," are of composit construction, although their general ap pearance and layout are similar to the eas coast vehicles.

Unfortunately, no other Pullman i quite like the promised kitchen firs "Aries" (allocated to S.R.). This is a 20 seat car built in 1951. Kitchen first "Aquila," "Carina" and "Orion," whic date from the same year, are all 22-sea vehicles.

To be strictly accurate, both cars 74 an 79 should be mounted on Pullman 10ft. wheelbase bogies. Gresley bogies are, how ever, correct for "Aries."

CHARLES S. E. LONG.

Leatherhead.

Perhaps they had trouble in the tool although I have heard frequent reports that these compensated side frame bogies were somewhat prone to derailing.

Royston Carss, a well-known Hornby collector and past Editor of the *H.R.C.A. Journal* reported that the pre-production 4036 pullman car number 74 in the March 1961 *Meccano Magazine* had the full correct lettering 'Second Class Car No. 74' as per the prototype, but he goes on to say that he has never seen one, and I think this must be a pre-production sample.

Like the earlier coaches, these too had a hole in the centre of the bogie frame and moulded rectangular sections inside the coach which would have been to house the proposed interior lighting.

I have already mentioned the immense detail that the Meccano Company managed to achieve in reproducing their Hornby Dublo models. They were in touch with the main prototype manufacturers and much of their original documentation with the manufacturers is still in existence. I have to thank Colin Parker and his wife Jean for allowing me to pay many calls, at all hours, to inspect these records and of particular interest were the letters from Mr. J. L. Gilbert, Works Manager of the Pullman Car Company.

I was also able to contact Mr. Charles S. E. Long who wrote a correction in the Readers' Letters, *Railway Modeller* August 1961 to the 'Review' of the Hornby Dublo pullman cars about the lack of tongue and grooved side panelling characteristic. He turned out to be none other than the present Editor of *Modern Railways* and in a letter to me on 10th February 1978 reported that he was employed in the Pullman Car Company's offices at Victoria Station in to quote 'what was grandly titled "Traffic Department"' – in fact it was a two man team, concerned with the movement of all pullman vehicles on BR and the make up of Pullman Limited trains.

In September 1961, the French Hornby-Acho appeared on trial to the U.K. market and it was also announced that the 2014 passenger train set the 'Talisman', hauled by the 2-rail 'Golden Fleece' A4 locomotive was now available with the new original super detail coaches 4052 and 4053, the first second maroon corridor coach and the brake second matching corridor coach respectively. In the following month, October, the 'Caledonian' passenger train set, number 2023, was similarly modified. Interestingly

Dear Mr Foster,

Thank you for your letter of 23 January 1978, written to my home address.

Indeed I was the writer of the letter about Hornby-Dublo Pullman cars published in the August 1961 issue of 'Railway Modeller'. At that time, I was employed in the Pullman Car Company's offices at Victoria Station in what was grandly titled the 'Traffic Department' – in fact a two-man section concerned with the movement of all Pullman vehicles on BR and the make-up of Pullman limited trains.

I have no objection at all to your quoting from the letter. After all these years my recollections of it are rather dim, but I seem to remember that I commended Hornby for modelling genuine prototypes (if short of scale length) at the same time remarking on the improbability of ever finding the three particular vehicles chosen in the same formation.

Yours sincerely,

Charles Long

Charles Long
Editor
MODERN RAILWAYS

. . . 'and the writer replies' – 17 years later!

Comparative Dimensions

	BR Standard	Hornby-Dublo	Playcraft	Tri-ang	Trix
Length over body:	64ft 6in	57ft 6in	58ft 6in	64ft 3in	64ft 5in
Length over buffers:	67ft 1in	58ft 3in	59ft 0in	66ft 6in	66ft 0in
Bogie centres:	46ft 6in	41ft 1in	40ft 0in	47ft 6in	47ft 1in
Bogie wheelbase:	8ft 6in	8ft 3in	7ft 6in	8ft 6in	8ft 5in
Wheel diameter:	3ft 6in	3ft 0in	3ft 0in	3ft 3in	3ft 1in
Height to gutter:	10ft 5in	10ft 3in	10ft 6in	10ft 9in	10ft 8in
Height to roof:	12ft 4½in	12ft 0in	12ft 3in	12ft 6in	12ft 0in
Length over headstock:	63ft 5in	55ft 9in	57ft 6in	63ft 3in	63ft 6in
Width over body:	9ft 0in	9ft 0in	9ft 6in	9ft 1in	9ft 5in
Width of door:	2ft 0in	1ft 9in	2ft 0in	2ft 0in	1ft 11in
Width of main windows:	4ft 0in	4ft 0in	3ft 11in	4ft 0in	4ft 0in
Height of windows:	3ft 1½in	3ft 0in	3ft 0in	3ft 7in	3ft 0in
Weight:	—	5¾oz	3oz	3¾oz	4¾oz
Price:		16s 9d	8s 6d	11s 6d	12s 6d

Scale of comparison of proprietary 00 coaches – from the June 1965 Model Railway Constructor.

enough at this period, the September *Meccano Magazine* reported that the new moulded nylon coupling which had arrived with the first super detail coaches was now to be standard on all new items of rolling stock. It must have been quite an exciting period because in the same month the 3-rail 2–6–4 Tank 80059, which we have already covered, arrived and indeed, in October, the West Country 'Barnstaple' locomotive headed the 'Bournemouth Belle' train set. As already mentioned, in November the 'City of Liverpool' arrived as well as the 'Dorchester' locomotive and in December the new super detail open coaches. These were the 4060 open coach first class Western Region, 4061 the open second class coach, Western Region, and 4062 and 4063 the open first class and second class coaches in BR maroon respectively.

The *Constructor* 'Review' in January 1962 reported, although the scale of the vehicles was once more 57 ft against the 64 ft 6 ins, slight compression of all the body side dimensions had enabled the correct number of compartments to be included in each vehicle – eight in the open second and seven in the open first. Although the blue in the latter is somewhat glossy, the overall effect is quite convincing. They continue:

'The most noticeable feature of these new vehicles is the revised bogie designs. Readers may remember that when the new range of super detail coaches was first introduced almost a year ago, new compensated bogies were fitted to all the models. These do not appear to have been entirely satisfactory since these new models are fitted with solid cast metal uncompensated bogie frames. The design of the bogie frame side has been altered and the tie–bar has been omitted. The general appearance of the vehicles which have the usual flat printed tin sides is acceptable but we cannot help thinking of the vast improvement that would have resulted had detailed moulded polystyrene sides been used instead.' (The author is still not convinced.)

Judging by the large stocks of these left over, they do not appear to have been so popular but, as with the super detail rolling stock a summary appears at the end of this chapter of the sale figures for 1964 with the remaining stock details.

The April 1962 *Meccano Magazine* heralded the new super detail suburban coaches, the 4081 and 4082 Southern Region green suburban first/second and suburban brake second coach and the 4083 and 4084 British Rail maroon suburban coaches in a first/ second and brake second format. Just by looking at them one can well understand the reason they are so highly prized and expensive in today's collector's market.

It was not until June that the trade reviewed them and the *Constructor* 'Review' . . . reported . . . 'the first models to reach the shops are the nine compartment composite coaches in lined maroon and a nine compartment second in unlined SR green livery. The composite is a scale length model of 57 ft BR nine compartment composite, examples of which are at work on the London Midland, Scottish and Western Regions. The model has the correct number of compartments at the correct spacing, is tolerably neatly lined and carries a correct coach number. A detailed plastic interior is incorporated and, apart from the lack

HORNBY-DUBLO
Open First and Open Second Coaches
16s 2d

THE latest coaching stock models from Meccano are these Open First and Open Second coaches. Both types of vehicle are available in both Western Region chocolate and cream livery or standard B.R. maroon livery. The fully detailed underframe and end mouldings are the same as those used on the earlier side corridor vehicles. Although the vehicles are only a scale 57ft against the correct 64ft 6in, slight compression of all the bodyside dimensions has enabled the correct number of compartments to be included in each vehicle—eight in the Open Second, and seven in the Open First. Fully detailed interiors are fitted, buff in the second and blue in the first. Although the blue in the latter is somewhat glossy, the overall effect is quite convincing.

The most noticeable feature of these new vehicles is the revised bogie design. Readers may remember that when the new range of super detail coaches was first introduced almost a year ago, new, compensated bogies were fitted to all the models; these do not appear to have been entirely satisfactory, since these new models are fitted with solid cast metal uncompensated bogie frames. The design of the bogie frame side has been altered and the tie-bar has been omitted. The general appearance of the vehicles which have the usual flat, printed tin sides is acceptable, but we cannot help thinking of the vast improvement that would have resulted had detailed moulded polystyrene sides been used instead.

---

of raised door handle detail and the round instead of oval buffers is quite an acceptable model.

'The SR second unfortunately is not quite so accurate. In fact it is not really a second at all as it has exactly the same body shell as the composite reviewed above and carries the coach number of a ten compartment 63 ft 6 ins second. However, as there are no 57 ft seconds or composites allocated to the Southern Region correct numbering would be impossible. In addition to working as an orthodox steam hauled vehicle it is intended that the Southern Region second should be used as an intermediate trailer in the forthcoming Hornby electrical multiple unit.'

Three months later, in September, the *Constructor* 'Review' again goes on to report the recently released suburban brake second coaches but. . . .

'Unfortunately however mistakes have crept in on both models. The lined maroon brake is a scale 57 ft the correct length for an LMR vehicle and carries a correct coach number but the windows in the guard's compartment should be full height like the passenger compartment quarter lights and not only the height of the drop door lights as modelled. The Southern Region brake second also suffers from this discrepancy although all Southern Region BR standard suburban stock is built on the longer 63 ft 5 ins underframes the Hornby model incorporates the same body shell and scale 57 ft underframe as its London Midland contemporary and therefore has one compartment less than its prototype. Apart from the fact that the prefix letter "S" is inadvertently shown as the figure "5" giving the vehicle a six figure no prefix number the remaining five figures are correct for a long underframe Southern Region vehicle. Both vehicles are fitted with standard plastic couplings and wheels with cast metal uncompensated bogies. The realism of the caramel coloured seat units is impaired by the badly modelled compartment partitions which are cut away at each end allowing light to pass from one compartment to the next. The compartment partitions were correctly shaped on the earlier composite and second and we can see no good reason for this retrograde step.

However, despite our criticisms we feel that the models are quite acceptable as proprietary models. . . .'

It is interesting to note this reference to the figure '5' instead of 'S'. I have seen this on one or two sections of the artwork and it stems purely from misreading the lettering on the artwork. This fault was corrected on later models. For some reason also, there are variations in the colour of the interior moulding on the suburban coaches from the carmel cream colour to an almost brilliant white. However, they are still very attractive coaches. Some had green moulded ends, others plain black.

At the same time, April 1962, the new Southern main line standard corridor coaches were announced although they were not advertised until May 1962 in the *Meccano Magazine*. It must have been thrilling for the Southern Railway enthusiast at this period what with the new West Country locomotive and pullman coaches in addition to the Southern green main line corridor coaches although one of the reviewers reported that both vehicles carried the BR coaching

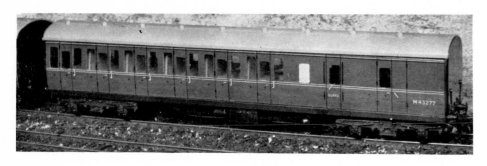

stock crest . . . 'a detail which, strictly speaking, restricts them to use in the "Royal Wessex" formation as the coaches in this train are the only locomotive hauled vehicles on the Southern Region to carry the crest.'

The *Model Railway News* for June 1962 refers to the first/second suburban coaches and the main line Southern corridor coaches bringing a total of 16 vehicles to the Hornby Dublo owner. A choice of vehicles in excess of anything ever offered by a single manufacturer. As with the pullman cars earlier, they reported that a nice touch in the corridor stock is shown in the moulding of the corridor partition, certain sliding compartment doors are shown open – a typical situation rarely depicted in model form.

On the inside front cover of the October 1962 *Meccano Magazine* the suburban electric train set we have referred to earlier is illustrated. With this set was the dummy trailer coach, number 4150 and I could not for the life of me think whether this should be included in this particular chapter or with the powered car itself. I chose the latter, but have mentioned it here just in case you point out to me that I have left it out!

We have now to wait until April 1963, when the most sought after of all super detail coaches, the restaurant cars, were announced. The same month saw the arrival of the new Simplec points as a hurriedly produced item to overcome the complexity of the original 2-rail track for the younger enthusiast. The *Meccano Magazine* for April describes them as identical in construction and detail to the earlier super detail coaches and . . . 'interior furnishings and features are, of course, incorporated these being attractively

represented by plastic moulding that provides the table tops and the seating on either side of the passage through the restaurant section. As in the real vehicles seating is arranged so that there are pairs of seats on one side of the gangway but single seats to the smaller tables on the opposite side. At one end of the car the section representing the kitchen and the pantry is partitioned off where the centre passage becomes a side corridor. Windows are glazed with transparent plastic except those in the kitchen section where obscure glass is the rule as in real practice. The special character of the vehicles as compared with the ordinary corridor coaches is denoted by the roof and underframe details.

There is a representation of the normal torpedo ventilators along the passenger section but at the busy end of the vehicle, where the kitchen and pantry are situated, circular shapes simulate the fans that are so necessary in the actual coach. . . . Lighting is specially important in a restaurant car so the relatively massive character of the battery boxes will not surprise you. Among other underfloor items to intrigue you is the section of moulding just below the central door in the side of the vehicle that represents the refrigerator and the bottle cooler boxes. A restaurant has to be in effect a self-contained hotel on wheels. The new restaurant cars are available as number 4070 in WR brown and

Extract from the September 1962 Model Railway Constructor.

cream livery and as number 4071 in BR maroon. In each case the approximate running numbers appear on the body side, together with the bold wording "Restaurant Car" and the BR emblem. The BR classification of the real vehicles represented is RU which stands for "Restaurant Car Unclassed" – in other words first class or second class passengers can be accommodated. If additional seating is required it is often the practice to run an open coach of either class next to the restaurant car and this practice can be readily followed in Hornby Dublo. . . . The open coaches in Hornby Dublo are therefore very useful vehicles carrying the seating and double accommodation required for such purposes. I can foresee a strong demand for the new restaurant cars on the part of Hornby Dublo owners who want to cater for the needs of their "hungry passengers" on long distance services.'

The drawing for the super detail restaurant car refers to the fact that the interior was in SF-37 blue colour, but changed, on 22nd March 1963, into SF-80 yellow (creamish colour). I have only seen restaurant cars with the yellow interior livery, but it could well be that the original ones had a blue livery. Certainly the models reviewed had a yellow interior.

The *Model Railway News* reported that the maroon 4071 represents one of the Eastern Region's vehicles and was one of a batch of 19 turned out by the Birmingham Railway Carriage & Wagon Company. There were 92 in the class which were allocated to the Western, Eastern and Scottish Regions only. They also have an interesting report that it should not be confused with Triang's model at this period which is the miniature buffet RMB. A discrepancy occurs here,

Photograph from the May 1962 Meccano Magazine.

because the *Constructor* talks about 91 actual cars being employed and that the model in maroon was E1939 (or in the obsolescent WR chocolate and cream livery, W1910). They also state that it was a pity, despite it being an excellent model, that Hornby chose the RU in preference to the BR standard restaurant buffet (RB) examples of which are found on *all* Regions. A vehicle in Southern Region green livery could then

The Southern Region main line coaches from original artwork.

have been produced. Little did they know that a Southern buffet car had already been drawn up, although never to be produced – but more of this in a later chapter.

In October 1963 came the final coach to be issued in the super detail range, Number 4076, the six wheel passenger brake van. There was an interesting report on these original new vehicles in the January issue of the 1934 *Meccano Magazine* referring to the original six vans which had been constructed at the Wolverton Works for the requirements of Mr. W. A. Stanier, the Chief Mechanical Engineer. The underframe of each was constructed entirely of steel and fitted with shock absorbing buffers and steel disc wheels. The body was soundly constructed of hard wood framing members, having holes bored at intervals to allow free circulation of air in the sides. The outer panels were of steel, with the windows particularly flush with the outer surface of the body to facilitate cleaning. Steel sheet projections, or guards' lookouts, were situated on each side of the vehicle and were provided with standard electric side lamps. Gangways were provided at each end of the vehicle and the vans can, therefore, be connected to all types of vestibuled passenger stock. The floors were fireproof and were provided with drain holes for washing out.

The *Meccano Magazine* reports that the windows of the model were glazed with transparent plastic and opposite certain of the window openings were representations of the bars fitted across inside the window glass on the rear vehicles in order to prevent any damage that might be caused by the handling of luggage etc., inside the van. They go on to state . . . 'it is ideal for use in conjunction with other vans particularly the bogie number 4075 passenger brake van in the formation of trains for mails, parcels, milk and so on. In addition it would be quite in order for you to use the new six-wheeler at the tail of your most important express freight trains.'

The *Constructor* 'Review' was really very complimentary and stated that Hornby were to be congratulated on production of a passenger vehicle, for very few vehicles of this type were available on the proprietary market. They go on . . . 'the choice of a long wheelbase six wheel prototype however was a little ambitious as design problems would inevitably have to be faced to enable the vehicle to traverse

HORNBY-DUBLO OO
B.R. Standard Unclassed
Restaurant Car 16s 9d

THE most recent addition to the range of Hornby "Super-Detail" coaches is the B.R. Standard Unclassed Restaurant (RU). In general the model conforms with its immediate predecessors in the series, with printed tin sides, plastic roof and ends, rigid cast metal bogies and a slightly compressed appearance due to the sub-scale length of the vehicle.

The correct number of windows and doors are, however, included and the legend "Restaurant Car" is carried on each side. A somewhat bright yellow interior unit is fitted to the passenger section, while the doors and windows of the kitchen section are correctly painted and frosted over. The 91 prototype cars are employed on the Eastern, Western and Scottish Regions; the Hornby model is available either in maroon as E1939 or in the now obsolescent W.R. chocolate and cream livery as W1910. While this is an excellent model, it is a pity that Hornby chose the RU in preference to the B.R. Standard Restaurant-Buffet (RB), examples of which are to be found on all Regions. A vehicle in Southern Region green livery could then have been produced.

Extract from the September 1963 Model Railway Constructor.

Meccano publicity photograph of the WR restaurant car.

proprietary curves and point work. The centre axle is not carried in the normal way but is held in a bracket giving a considerable amount of lateral and vertical movement, also a small degree of turning movement. Performance of the van suggests that freedom of movement in one or other of the former cases – perhaps both – is too excessive for the centre pair of wheels tend to become derailed very easily even on Hornby Dublo track.'

The new thinner style of moulded coupling was fitted and sprung by a length of thin black rubber tubing fixed at one end to the coupler and held between two moulded pegs at the other. For some

reason there seems to have been objection to the original light colour of this plastic tube as it was recorded at a production meeting in the Company that it would be changed to black – although less flexible. An interesting point is that the LMS style of lining was adopted. Present BR lining has the same yellow–black–yellow lining at waist level, but a yellow and black line instead of two yellow lines at cantrail height.

I am surprised that they did not overcome the problem of the centre axle-derailing as if they had only read the article by 'Great Northern' in the *Model Railway Constructor* in September 1957, on page 234, they would have seen an excellent review on such vehicles using sharp radius curves which even showed a photograph of such a vehicle on the 15 inch radius Hornby Dublo trackwork. The author's suggestion is to have the centre axle fixed securely in the correct position, but to file the flanges flat at the bottom so that although the vehicle has to all intents and purposes a fully flanged wheel no flanges actually proceed beneath rail level and so the rolling characteristics of the vehicle would be the same as for any four wheel vehicle. It would have solved the problem entirely. In earlier days the Clemenson arrangement solved the problem in both reality and tinplate.

All the Hornby Dublo super detail coaches are very popular with collectors these days, especially the suburban coaches and the restaurant cars. Some of the main line corridor stock, particularly the brake second of the Western Region are becoming extremely desirable. The pullman cars were climbing very fast in price until an identical model was put onto the market by the G & R Wrenn Company Limited.

Extract from the January 1934 Meccano Magazine.

The 6-wheel brake – from Meccano publicity photograph.

Lineside Buildings & Structures

PRE-WAR WOODEN BUILDINGS

The introduction of the Hornby Dublo system brought with it a complete range of building accessories. Included in the very first catalogue, reference 7/938/185, there was the main line station measuring 24 inches in length, the island platform, the goods depot, the signal box and the D1 (short) tunnel and the D2 (long) tunnel. These were all made of wood with well printed detail of doors, windows, timetables, luggage, milk churns, and even a letter box. The length of 24 inches was set by the fact that it was planned to accommodate three coaches.

The main line station was drawn on 1st April 1938 with the island platform three days later, on the 4th. I feel almost certain that they were subcontracted outside Binns Road and I have heard rumours that they were manufactured by the company which made all

the wooden cabinets, etc., for them. The box code on these initial sets all refer to 838 i.e. August 1938 and the initial production was 3,250 per unit.

The D407 main line station had Robertson's 'Golden Shred' advertisements on the left hand side of the platform wall looking at the entrance of the station, while on the right hand side, there was the 'Oxo' advertisement. On the platform side of the wall there was a small advertisement for 'Swan Pens' and 'Nestle's Milk'. On 24th May, printed station name panels on triple gummed paper were drawn up. There were the large name panels measuring $1\frac{1}{4}$ inches length for Penrith (for the LMS) Berwick (for the LNER) Truro (for the GWR) and Ashford (for the Southern Re-

gion). At the same time smaller name panels, measuring only $\frac{7}{8}$ inch long, were produced specifically for the signal boxes. The top of the platform wall, or fence as it is called on the drawing, was altered to accommodate the name panels on 8th July 1938, but I must admit that I have never seen a red-roofed version so altered. A year and a week later, on 14th July 1939, the final modification was made when both the station and the island platform, as well as the signal box and goods yard building, were produced with a matt green roof instead of the matt red roof of the 1938 series buildings.

A further modification in the 1939 series main line building – the examples I have still bear the identical shaped platform fence as the 1938 model – now delete

Extract from the November 1938 Meccano Magazine.

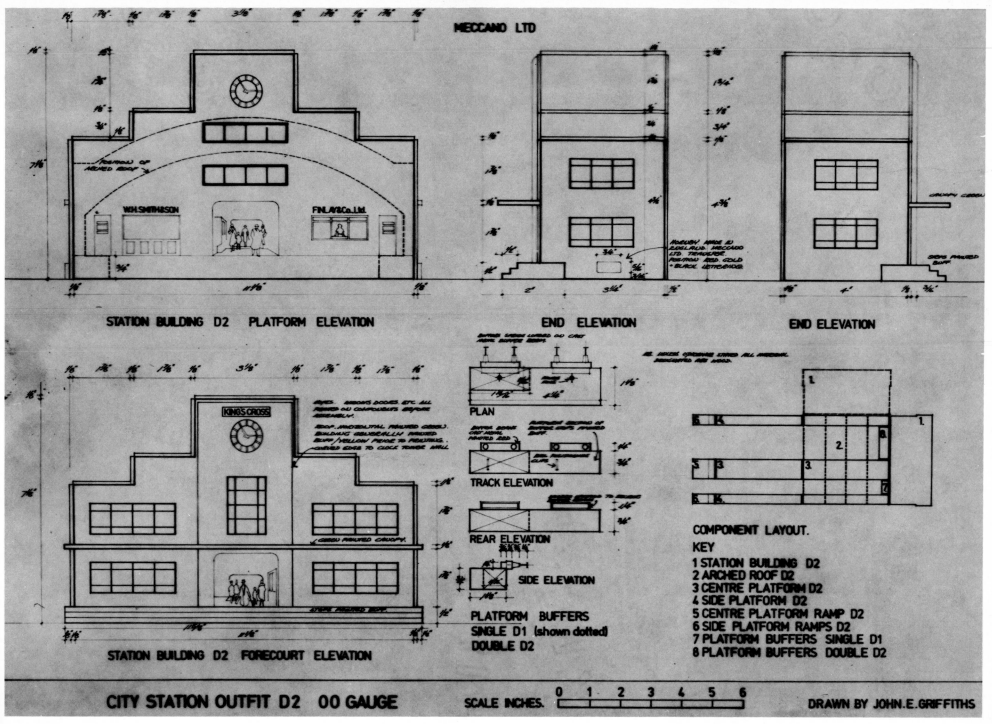

MECCANO LTD

STATION BUILDING D2 PLATFORM ELEVATION

END ELEVATION

END ELEVATION

STATION BUILDING D2 FORECOURT ELEVATION

KINGS CROSS

W.H. SMITH & SON

FINLAY & Co. Ltd.

PLAN

TRACK ELEVATION

REAR ELEVATION

SIDE ELEVATION

PLATFORM BUFFERS
SINGLE D1 (shown dotted)
DOUBLE D2

COMPONENT LAYOUT.
KEY
1 STATION BUILDING D2
2 ARCHED ROOF D2
3 CENTRE PLATFORM D2
4 SIDE PLATFORM D2
5 CENTRE PLATFORM RAMP D2
6 SIDE PLATFORM RAMPS D2
7 PLATFORM BUFFERS SINGLE D1
8 PLATFORM BUFFERS DOUBLE D2

CITY STATION OUTFIT D2 OO GAUGE

SCALE INCHES.   0 1 2 3 4 5 6

DRAWN BY JOHN.E.GRIFFITHS

← *A pre-war scene.*

The John Griffiths' drawings of wooden buildings.

239

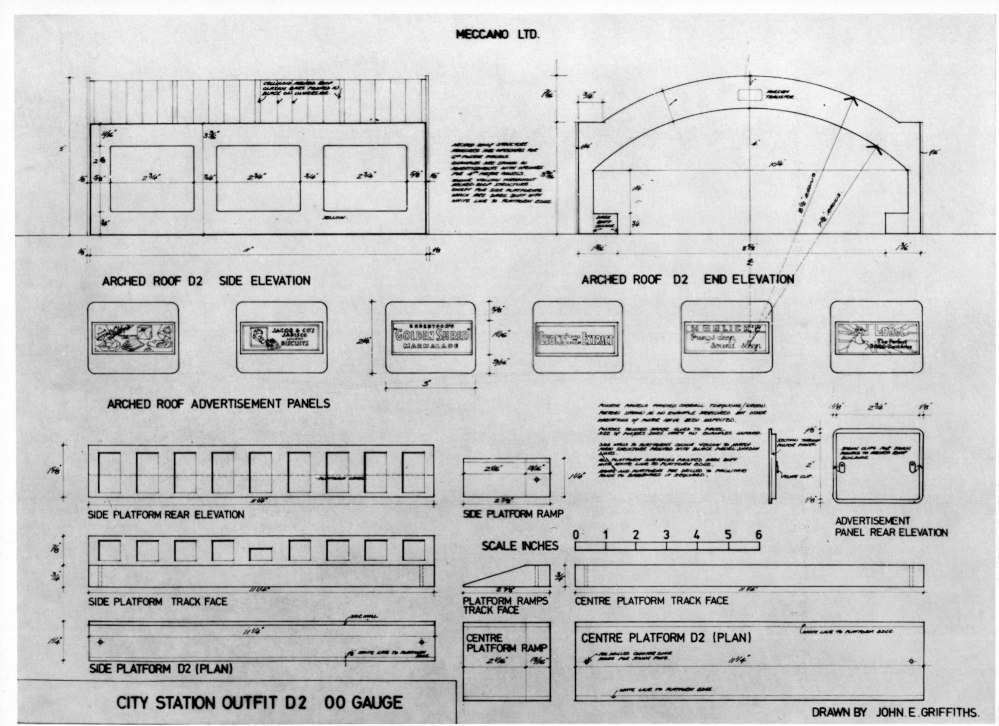

MECCANO LTD.

ARCHED ROOF D2   SIDE ELEVATION

ARCHED ROOF D2   END ELEVATION

ARCHED ROOF ADVERTISEMENT PANELS

SIDE PLATFORM REAR ELEVATION

SIDE PLATFORM   TRACK FACE

SIDE PLATFORM D2 (PLAN)

SIDE PLATFORM RAMP

PLATFORM RAMPS
TRACK FACE

CENTRE
PLATFORM RAMP

SCALE INCHES   0 1 2 3 4 5 6

CENTRE PLATFORM TRACK FACE

CENTRE PLATFORM D2 (PLAN)

ADVERTISEMENT
PANEL REAR ELEVATION

CITY STATION OUTFIT D2   OO GAUGE

DRAWN BY JOHN. E. GRIFFITHS.

The John Griffiths' drawings of wooden buildings.

all four advertisements panels we mentioned and instead have a series of printed architectural recesses, so commonly found on buildings of this period. I do not think the alterations to the platform fence to accommodate the name ever came into being, but I could well be wrong. All the boxes I have seen for the 1939 series of buildings i.e. with the green roof, whether they be for main line station, city station, island platform, goods yard, or engine shed, show a box coding, indicating 1,000 of each.

The D403 island platform, with its red roof, initially had light blue painted wooden seats in the centre. This appears to be the correct finish according to the catalogues and on the semicircular wall were the 'Bovril' and Wills' 'Goldflake' advertisements. I am aware of an interesting variation where the semicircular wall ends were painted the same blue livery as the seats.

All the stations had thick white safety edges to the platforms and this practice continued with the first metal platforms issued after the war. The green-roofed station, had distinctly darker grey cream colour platforms as opposed to the light cream of the 1938 series and according to the drawing, also had a further modification on 19th April 1939, when the width of the platform was reduced from 2¾ inches to 2½ inches. I have not seen the latter.

The D402 goods depot followed closely the two items we have already discussed with respect to the quantities produced and the colour of the roof etc. The printed detail on the goods depot itself, down to the minutest piece of luggage, really is superb. All the versions I have seen had 'Hartley's Marmalade' and 'Atora Beef Suet' advertisements, one at each end.

The signal box was very simple, measuring 3 inches long by 2 inches wide, with a triangular roof section the colour of which matched both the matt red and matt green of the 1938 and 1939 series buildings. All the buildings we have mentioned so far were available in their light blue boxes although I have never been able to find a single light blue box for the signal cabin. Whether they were supplied (as the early Dinky Toys), in boxes of six or in individual boxes I am simply not sure, and it would be interesting to know the D number.

The tunnels were very weird pieces. The short D1 tunnel, measuring 5½ inches and the longer D2 tunnel measuring 11½ inches, were almost identical copies of

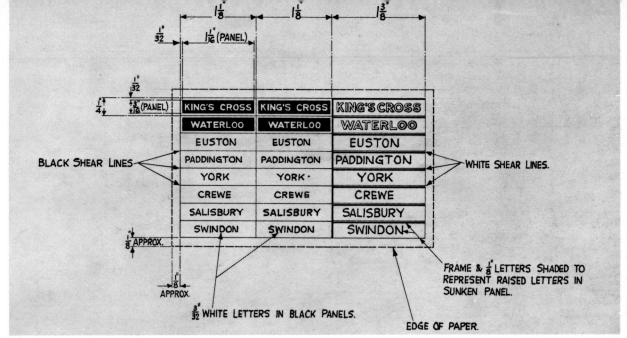

Station and signal cabin nameplates – from original drawings.

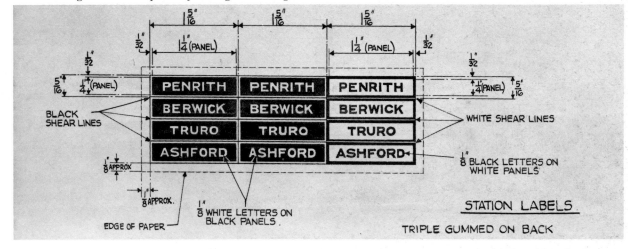

the wooden 0 gauge versions. I know many people have been confused as to whether it was actually produced by the Meccano Company as all the buildings to date have had the little Hornby transfer. . . . However the tunnels merely had a cheap red printed label stuck to the inside with 'Made in England by Meccano Ltd., Liverpool 13', which tends to come off easily thus making identification confusing.

The June 1939 *Meccano Magazine* hinted at the new

buildings later that year and the following issue showed a magnificent layout, including the new city station. Also the wooden footbridge, but more of this later. We had to wait until December 1939 – three months after the declaration of war – for the *Meccano Magazine* to show the new developments which included not only the City Station and Engine Shed, but also the isolating rail and the famous electrically operated points and signals. As well as the *Meccano*

Magazine there was also a folder, on the new developments reference 2/1239/20. The City Station, D419, came out first with the reference BW8530 (the box dated October 1939 and 1,000 produced). I have a mint boxed version, but unfortunately the light blue paper on the cardboard box, which shows the D number, is missing, so as with the signal box, I cannot ascertain the correct D number. It is a magnificent building with a large terminal station and a wooden canopy with a fixed cellophane roof. It spanned three track widths when set out although one could adjust the platforms, which were both wide and narrow to suit. On each side it had six large wooden green-coloured advertisement blocks, which could either be left in position or, by twisting little locking tabs, be removed if one required to back lorries up to the edge of the platform or have them side by side. From the catalogues I am assuming that all the items were available separately, although the whole City Station kit came in one large light blue box. The price of the complete unit was 25s. City Station Components included:

Station building D2 8s. 6d.
Arched roof D2 10s.
Centre platform D2 (Box of two) 1s. 10d.
Side platforms D2 (pair) 3s. 3d.
Centre platform ramps (box of six) 2s.
Side platform ramps (box of six) 1s. 6d.
Platform buffers. Single D1 (box of six) 3s.
Platform buffers. Double D2 (box of three) 3s.

A corner of Mr. Charles Gent's magnificent Hornby Dublo model railway.

The engine shed, number D415, was likewise dated October 1939 and 1,000 were produced and only cost 10s. 6d. It too was made of thick plywood in the design of the period with five windows each side and fixed cellophane roof skylight windows. One could mount these either side by side, or end to end or, as frequent articles in the *Meccano Magazine* stated during the war, one could find alternate uses for them either as a warehouse or shed for Dinky Toy wagons.

Although I have never seen them officially advertised, many of the engine sheds were available after the war when the stocks were unfrozen. It is surprising that the British Industries Fair of 1948 showed the complete set of wooden buildings on the Hornby Dublo stand. The following year the mock-up diecast stations were shown along with the canopy sections of the City station, the wooden signal cabin and the goods yard depot.

The City station was issued with the words 'King's Cross' printed neatly at the top of the building. It had been planned to use similar labels to those supplied earlier for the signal cabin and the following samples were prepared . . .

King's Cross	York
Waterloo	Crewe
Euston	Salisbury
Paddington	Swindon.

DIECAST BUILDINGS AND ACCESSORIES

There were many fascinating accessories which were scheduled for introduction before the commencement of the Second World War but never made it.

WATER CRANE

The water crane was drawn on 14th August 1939, but to my knowledge did not come out before the war. It is impossible to tell its exact introduction date after the war, although from the box code printing, it was April 1949. From the variations we have seen there is a brown painted underside section with no number, the common black painted underside with no number and then the black painted underside with either the number 1 or 2 cast on it. This model was altered to a buff colour for the 1959 modernisation scheme and was in production throughout the post-war years.

THE LOADING GAUGE

This too was planned pre-war, but did not come out until the Autumn of 1949. I put the month as October – as the box code is 10/49 50m (50,000!) – like the water crane it had a diecast post and base unit in this case only 18 mm square (there is no evidence that it was actually available in this form). It must have been considered unstable because very soon, riveted to the

Extracts from the July 1957 Meccano Magazine.

The three variations of the loading gauge.

diecast base was a long flat metal tongue which actually went underneath the rail section. A catalogue 16/450/150 showed this modification. From the advertisements, although one cannot rely totally on their accuracy, it appears that this long metal tongue version was in production right the way through until 1957 when the standard loading gauge with the larger base came in in July that year, this time the base measured 25 mm × 28 mm.

THE FOOTBRIDGE

The story of the footbridge has been an absolute devil to unravel. As far back as June 1939 the footbridge was advertised and indeed there were pictures of a wooden version (although it was probably a mock-up of the metal version). All the 1939 pre-war catalogues showed this particular accessory though only in illustrations of layouts and then with advertisements on the

The unconfirmed Meccano wooden footbridge with the early and final diecast post-war models.

sides; e.g. 13/63a/11,500 together with its price and Alan Ellis even found in a shop in Northumberland, a dealer's copy of his Meccano order dated 5th April 1939 where he had actually ordered one at the price of 3s. 6d.

There was certainly a commercially produced footbridge in wood identical in every detail even to the number of steps as the cast Hornby Dublo model. Its construction and paint finish was practically identical to the pre-war wooden building. The question is who made it? I traced many of the early catalogues and found at least half a dozen manufacturers of wooden building accessories of the period though not one shows a footbridge remotely like this. It is a mystery.

Mr Bob Moy wrote to me on 10th March 1978 stating that precise identification was a problem, but that he thought that one had been made in their woodwork department. He does not recollect that any wooden items were made commercially.

As with the 'Duchess of Atholl' Bob crafted the prototype footbridge in brass.

The original drawing had a thick cast spigot to centralise the ramps onto the footbridge itself and the drawing states that this idea was deleted on 17th Feb-

ruary 1948. The first proof we have of introduction is on page 279 of the June 1950 *Meccano Magazine* where this spigot was replaced by a screw fixing and there were two interlocking lugs at the top of the steps. These lugs were both long and short type and according to the drawing were withdrawn on 28th November 1952, when the triangular reinforcing piece under the stairway was added. The design was based on a standard British Railways pattern which was still being built ten years later as a publicity photograph from British Railways, dated 8th November 1957, shows the new concrete footbridge at Weeley station on the Colchester–Clacton–Walton line, although it was raised to give sufficient clearance to the new overhead electrical equipment.

Proof that the metal footbridge did not come into production before the war is contained in the revised price list for Hornby Dublo items dated 9th October 1939, reference 15/1039/125 where, together with all the 'Duchess of Atholl' items, there is, at the bottom of the list, marked under the heading 'Suspended Indefinitely', the D1 footbridge. I simply do not know what to think.

It would appear that this footbridge was available

Extract from revised price list dated 9th October 1939 reference 16/1039/125.

in late 1948 or early 1949 and numerous colour variations exist plus a number of casting differences, additional to those already mentioned.

THE ALUMINIUM BUILDINGS

Why Hornby Dublo decided to change from its pre-war wooden buildings I do not know. They were certainly attractive in their own right, but probably their experiences pre-war had shown them that they could not hope to meet the anticipated demand using scarce wood. They approached the Birmingham Aluminium Casting Co. Ltd., of Dartmouth Road, Smethwick, Birmingham and proceeded to design the details of a new island platform, main line station and signal box based on modern designs. Each model was made from precision pressure diecast aluminium.

Up to now the *Meccano Magazine* had implored its readers to use boxes or wood or anything they could lay their hands on to simulate platforms as none of their pre-war wooden buildings were available despite them being shown at the British Industries Fair.

Both the main line (through) station and island platform were made the same length as two standard EDB1 straight rails to enable the Hornby Dublo owner to determine what rail space he needed to accommodate them.

Gummed station name strips were available covering Crawford for the Scottish Region in a light blue, Lichfield in the London Midland Region red, Newark Eastern Region in a dark blue, Overton in Southern Region green and finally Westbury in Western Region brown. The initial models were screwed together (supplied in blue boxes with pale blue pictures on the front) latterly however, they were of all riveted construction.

The prototype footbridge, from Meccano records.

One interesting variation in common with the pre-war wooden buildings, is the white line on the platform edge. However, as soon as the new blue with white stripe boxes appeared with a colour picture, the white line was deleted.

I was in correspondence with Mr. J. H. Newman, Works Director for the Birmingham Aluminium Casting Company in November 1972 who kindly enclosed copies of the drawings of these station units and wrote . . . 'You may be interested to know that a tremendous amount of co-operation and liaison went on between Meccano and this Company and we redesigned all of the items to make them suitable for production in aluminium alloy.'

He recalls approximately 86,000 sets, i.e. stations, island platforms and signal boxes were produced.

We had to wait until July 1955 for the island platform extensions to be introduced and, which seems strange today, a further nine months before the platform extensions were available for the through station i.e. the ones with the back wall or fence as it should be called.

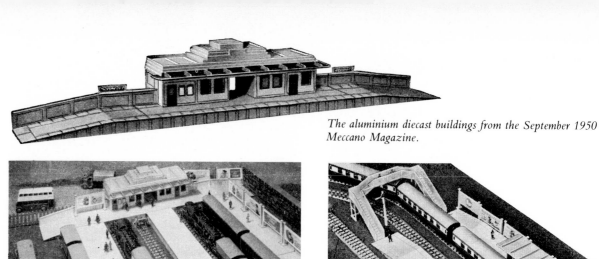

The aluminium diecast buildings from the September 1950 Meccano Magazine.

'The Terminus' – from the July 1956 Meccano Magazine.

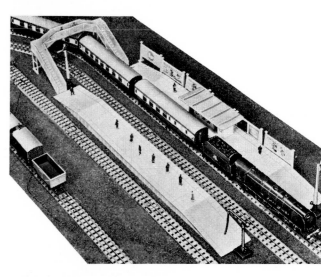

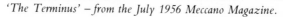

Through station extensions – from the April 1956 Meccano Magazine.

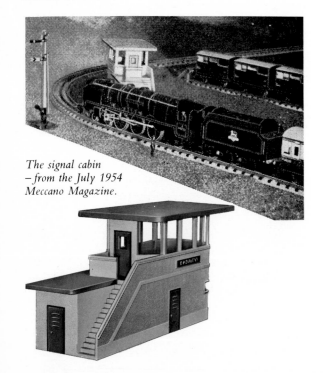

The signal cabin – from the July 1954 Meccano Magazine.

Island platform extensions from the July 1955 Meccano Magazine.

246

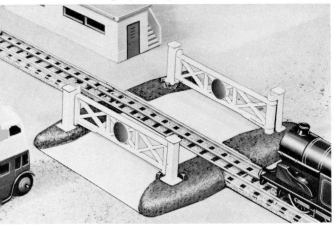

THE LEVEL CROSSING

The D1 level crossing was a very popular introduction arriving in November 1953.

The Meccano Company had been at pains to point out in earlier issues, even pre-war, which Dinky Toys were of the same scale as Hornby Dublo model railways. The model was of similar construction to the station buildings although it must seem surprising that the enthusiast then had to wait almost twelve months, until October 1954 before the road rail was introduced. This was a standard half straight rail with two moulded dummy centre sleeper sections to allow a Dinky Toy to be pushed across the level crossing.

With the advent of the new modernisation programme in 1959, the 3-rail level crossing was recast in polystyrene using the same moulds. It retained the metal cast pillars for the gates, but these were in a cream polystyrene colour.

THE GOODS YARD CRANE

Drawn up and planned at the same time as the aluminium cast station buildings in 1950 was a goods yard unit, complete with swivel crane. It was almost identical to the unit which appeared in the 1959 polystyrene moulding, but such was the shortage of metal at this stage that it was decided to delete the item. Instead an enlarged version of the aluminium cast jib unit and body were produced which, drawn in February 1950, became No. 752 the goods yard crane in the Dinky Super Toys series. There was obviously

immense play value in this model although it was far more suited to gauge 0 operation than Dublo. By March 1960, when an article on this crane appeared in the *Meccano Magazine* the Dinky Toy number had been changed to No. 973.

An almost exact reproduction of this model crane, this time in 00 scale was introduced by B. J. Ward Limited of Westminster Bridge Road, London S.E.1., in their 'Master Model Range' and this was announced as entirely new in the April 1956 *Railway Modeller*.

The depot crane was more suited to 0 gauge operations.

The goods yard crane – from the March 1960 Meccano Magazine.

The girder bridge – from the March 1960 Meccano Magazine.

main line running into Paddington Station (London). I know many enthusiasts have used them as a road bridge and once more a very realistic effect is obtained by putting a double decker bus or Dublo Dinky Toys running across them.

At a Product Committee Meeting on 15th January 1962 it was proposed to make the sides of the bridge in plastic to reduce the cost (at that time there was still a

charge apparently of £1,600 outstanding on the tools). It was decided at the meeting to proceed with this conversion as it would reduce the cost of this item from 19s. 6d. to 11s. 9d.

The girder bridge was drawn on 18th August 1955 and the amendment to the bright SF10 red colour sides in polystyrene is dated 9th March 1962. 3,000 were produced and released from 24th April 1963. I must admit that I had thought that this plastic version of the girder bridge was only produced by the Triang Company and it was only by looking at the records that I found it was indeed produced by the Meccano Company.

THE POLYSTYRENE BUILDINGS

Once more following the massive British Rail modernisation scheme, Hornby Dublo announced its own scheme, in April 1959. The principal item was to be the new 2-rail track, but also shown was the complete range of new buildings, including a suburban through station, island platform, engine shed with extension kit, goods depot, platelayers' hut, gradient post and telegraph poles. All these items were stated to be available later in the year. The first item was the platelayers' hut which appeared in July 1959. It was supplied in boxes of six and was number 5040. The plastic moulding process allowed the inclusion of, to quote the *Meccano Magazine* . . . 'the most convincing details'. The doorway at one end of the hut is represented and although the door is not made to open it is correctly planked and provided with representations of hinges and a door handle while the windows indicate hinged shutters. This item is still made by the G and R Wrenn Company. The first precast concrete platelayers' huts were introduced by the Chief Engineer of the LNER (*Meccano Magazine*, December 1943).

THE SINGLE TRACK TUNNEL

The Hornby Dublo single track tunnel, number 5091, was announced in September 1959. Although highly detailed it was again in polystyrene and I must admit I am surprised, in retrospect, at its inclusion. It was very much a toy item for a table top railway. However, it served its purpose perfectly for the younger enthusiast

THE GIRDER BRIDGE

A D1 viaduct bridge was printed on a Meccano order sheet dated 5th April 1939 with no further information until there was a magnificent full colour advertisement page in the January 1957 *Meccano Magazine* showing all the Hornby Dublo accessories and including item 17 the D1 girder bridge. Its full introductory advertisement came in the following month, February. The sides of the bridge were diecast in metal with a steel base and carried a single line of track. The price was 17s. 11d. each.

The Hornby Dublo engineers had obviously been in some discussion as to whether to have a single or double track bridge but in the end it was planned to have this single track unit as the advertisement continues . . . 'several of these bridge sections can be used together to excellent effect.' How right they were. To me it is still one of the most attractive of all the Hornby Dublo accessories and in its bright orange paint looks exceptionally smart whether singly spanning the main line or as the similar bridge crossing at an angle, the

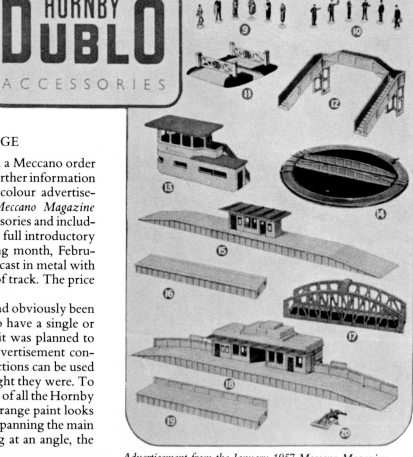

Advertisement from the January 1957 Meccano Magazine.

The terminus in the early 1960s →

working his branch line. In the same month Dinky Toy No. 765 arrived – the advertisement hoarding – and it was a useful scenic accessory for the railway.

THE HORNBY DUBLO ENGINE SHED

If I am inclined to criticise the tunnel I have great praise for the engine shed number 5005. It was fashioned on a standard BR prototype (the LMR main running shed at Chester) and was complete with smoke vents, transparent roof lights and small glazed windows. It was suitable for both 2-rail and 3-rail track and was a standard two road shed unit. Its price was 17s 9d.

THE HORNBY DUBLO ENGINE SHED EXTENSION KIT

However, the extension shed kit number 5006 really made the engine shed because here, by simply providing an extra roof section and centre stanchions, one could double the width from a two road to a four road shed. Not content just with this, one could add more extension shed kits and have a six, eight or ten road shed.

With the possibility of such a large low building all sorts of variations can be used and I have seen many model railway layouts which have included the platform sections running them as a miniature goods depot. To my mind a really superb kit. The *Constructors* 'Review' reports that the engine shed had a superb concrete faced finish to the main walls and some beautifully detailed fall-pipes and guttering. As with all the shortly to be introduced polystyrene buildings the shed was fitted to take the new internal lighting accessory kits.

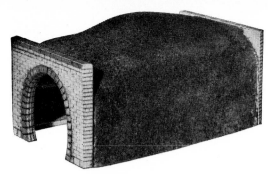

The single track tunnel, from the September 1959 Meccano Magazine.

Advertisement from the April 1959 Meccano Magazine.

From the December 1959 Meccano Magazine.

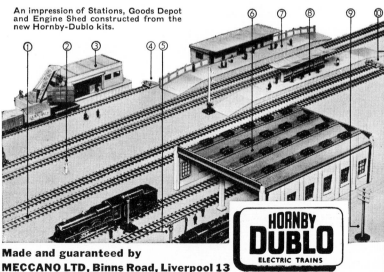
Carnforth Shed in June 1946. BR photograph from Meccano records, almost identical to the Hornby Dublo model which used Chester Shed as its real life counterpart.

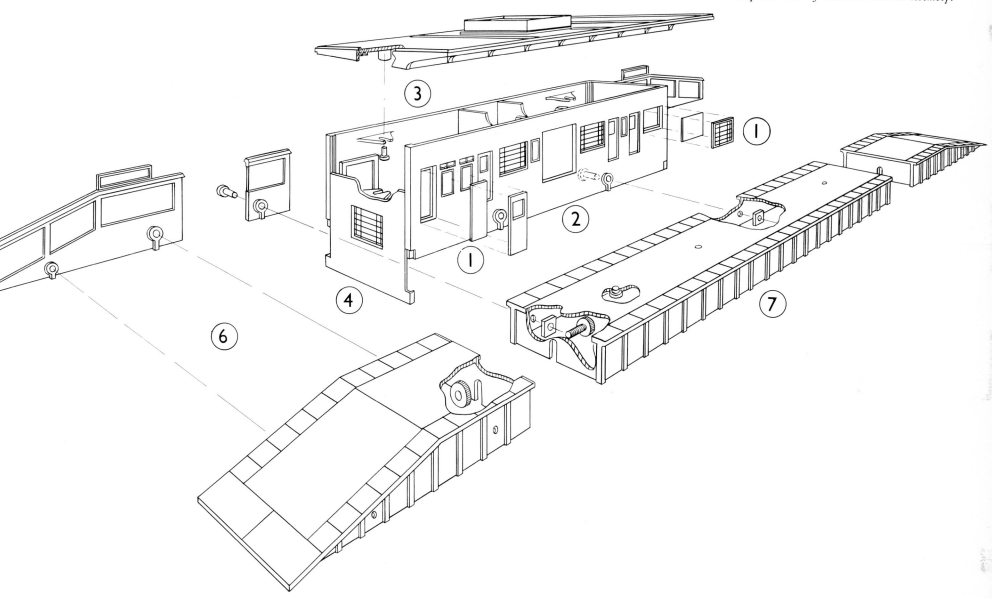

251

The through station.

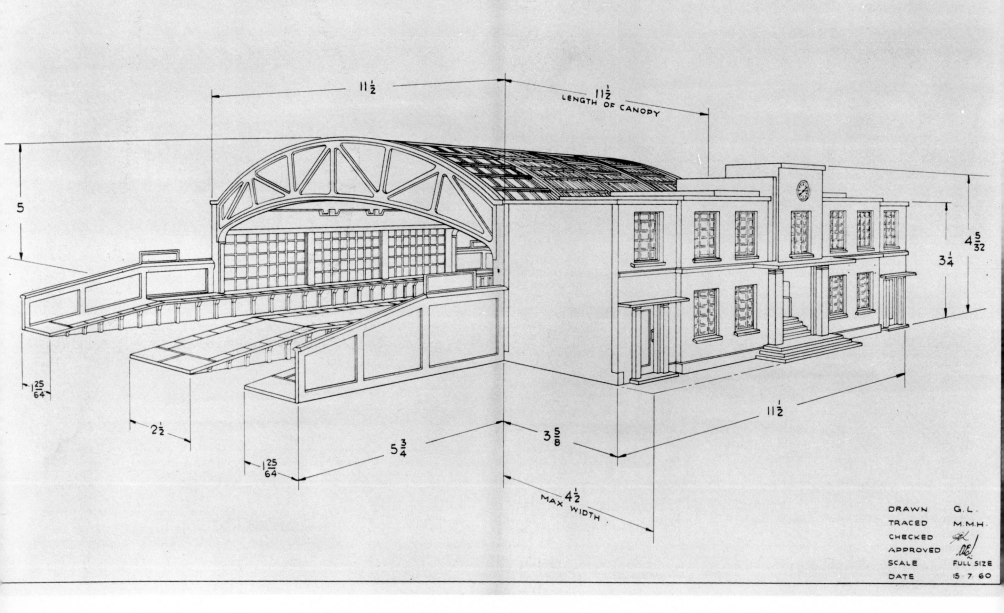

11½

11½
LENGTH OF CANOPY

5

4 5⁄32

3¼

1 25⁄64

2½

1 25⁄64

5¾

3 5⁄8

11½

4½
MAX WIDTH

DRAWN   G.L.
TRACED   M.M.H.
CHECKED
APPROVED
SCALE   FULL SIZE
DATE   15·7·60

252

A nice touch in the February 1960 *Meccano Magazine* was the use of the shed adapted for a diesel motive power depot with the superb feature of using the Dinky Toy pavement sets in between the tracks. A very realistic effect.

THE SUBURBAN STATION

This was announced in January 1960 and sold for 22s. 6d. In keeping with the goods shed detail, it was a two minute (according to the advertisement) accessory kit, with the doors, glazing and windows being pressed or screwed together. Once more a very attractive item and extremely realistic.

I think there must have been customer correspondence on this as in no way could one assemble such a kit inside two minutes and by February they were talking about the five minute kit! This building was arranged to take the working lighting accessory.

THE ISLAND PLATFORM

This was a very simple accessory consisting of a platform unit with a pressed centre wall section with seats and a push on roof canopy. Many of the early box covers show the seats painted in green, but I have never seen these. All the island platforms I have seen had plain stone finish seats, as the walls, with a light grey moulded roof. It is interesting to read that these buildings were specifically designed for 2-rail track and were the scale platform height, although they could be used with 3-rail track, they were a trifle on the low side.

PLATFORM EXTENSIONS AND EXTENSION WALLS

By February 1960 the *Meccano Magazine* had told its readers that the platform extensions were available (number 5086) as well as separate wall sections. The platforms all had holes drilled on their upper face so that the island platform canopy could be fitted anywhere along the platform, even overlapping two platforms and for all the holes not used, there were little moulded caps which one pressed in from the underside to fill in the manhole effect. They were fitted together with knurled brass studs, although later, in an effort to economise, they had moulded rubber lugs.

With these one could build a platform of any suitable length and it was a very good idea to have the suburban station platform and the island platform the same width, unlike the earlier aluminium moulded items. The platform walls, number 5087, were also available separately and they fulfilled many uses on layouts and not just at the back of platforms. Such representations as factory walls or edging to a layout were almost

endless and there still seem to be many of these available.

THE WATER CRANE

There was an article in March 1960 on the water crane, number 5095, and this possibly was to coincide with the appearance of the new water crane in a buff colour. I have been unable to ascertain the exact date of introduction.

Ted Higgs' 5084 canopy extension kit.

253

THE GOODS DEPOT

June 1960 heralded the goods depot number 5020. This, in polystyrene, is an almost exact reproduction of the diecast goods depot planned as far back as 1950, but cancelled due to the shortage of metal. It was similar in construction to the earlier buildings we have just mentioned, with sliding doors and a beautiful little crane unit with a diecast frame, this time, however, with a pressed tin jib unit. The original was to have been diecast. I wonder whether this crane in 00 scale has any link with the pre-war four wheeled crane that Hornby Dublo were planning to bring out.

The goods depot sold for £1. 5s. 0d. and is a relatively rare item to find in good condition today. In this instance when I say it is rare, I do not mean that it is expensive, but that there just do not seem to be many of them about.

Gradient posts and lineside notices.

The handles on the crane were similar to the early Dinky Toy type and there was immense play value from this item provided it was fitted in a suitably accessible place on the layout.

THE DOUBLE TRACK TUNNEL

The March 1961 *Meccano Magazine* introduced the double track tunnel which was added to the system at that time. Identical in construction to the single track with a nicely moulded front brick section, the overall tunnel measured 16¾ inches long – nearly two coach lengths.

As with the single tunnel the portal is, for my liking, too large and too high although one of the reviewers suggested that the portal had to be that height to take a layout system employing overhead pick-up. They said it could easily take three track widths, but it is more likely that the large portal was

254

planned to enable it to take two tracks on the skew – a useful feature for small layouts.

The tunnel portals were available separately and the early models had a 'smoked' effect above the track position. As with the single tunnel, the interior of the tunnel itself was either in green or black moulded plastic with a realistic green powdered velvet effect on the outside. However, through the influence of the *Railway Modeller* and other such magazines, model railways were becoming more and more scale conscious and so the scenery one could expect on the average layout was now receiving far more attention and was more realistic. In fact over the next ten years it seems that the scenic effect received more emphasis than the track and the rolling stock, which to my own mind was a retrograde step.

THE LIGHTING KIT

The June 1961 *Meccano Magazine* made full mention of the frequently advertised lighting kit. It comprised a spring clip fitting that formed a holder for the readily detachable 14 volt bulb which was included. The necessary connecting wire was provided and the complete fixture was made to clip onto suitable projections on the interior surfaces of the roofs of the different buildings. Together with the lighting kit was a small terminal panel to ease the wiring problems and this was mounted inside the building by means of a self-tapping screw included with the building kit. The panel included four terminals, two on one side, designated A, into which the wires from the lighting kit were fitted and the other two, designated B, for connecting the supply from a suitable power source.

'Switch off the lights, will you, please Dad . . .?' Oh magic! It was a great shame that the Meccano Company never introduced a suitable lampost using a small grain wheat bulb or something similar. They did indeed produce very attractive lamposts in their Dinky Toy series (the single arm lampost No. 755, and the double arm No. 756) but unfortunately not a working version.

GRADIENT POSTS

It was in November 1961, together with the 1521 aluminium wire model cable drum that the new set number 5025, gradient and mile posts came. They were very neat accessories, but of course, had to have a fairly large base to give them anything like normal stability.

THE TERMINAL/THROUGH STATION KIT

This extremely attractive model was advertised in the November 1961 *Meccano Magazine*. Kit number 5083, it was the best of all and rightly cost 69s. 6d. An impressive station was a very apt description. The kit fell into three main sections: the imposing station building itself, the overall roof and the various platform pieces. By altering the arrangement of the building either a terminal or through station could be built up.

The *Model Railway Constructor* thought that the arrangement gave unrealistically short platforms stating that – 'arranged as a terminal – the platform can only just house the Dublo "Duchess" locomotive and nothing else'. They did, however, admit that extra extension pieces could be purchased, but as they were only $11\frac{1}{2}$ inches long or just over a coach length, several would have to be purchased to house even a short four or five coach train.

I am not quite sure what they had in mind for the average layout space, but I think Meccano were right in making the kit as they did. The whole secret lies in its flexibility and the ability to extend as necessary. It also has an exceptionally attractive box and was extremely popular in the early 1970s with collectors. Fortunately there were 400 left over at the time of the takeover and indeed the model was brought out by the Triang Company in their own plain red box. However the station building inside the box was the standard Hornby Dublo model, complete with their name engraved on it etc. I have on occasions built layout plans incorporating ten of these moulded canopy units and whether one has twin canopies running over a through station or four canopies side by side spreading a terminus, the effect is really most realistic. It was a pity that the design could not have been so arranged to have a canopy fitting to the front of the station as well, because many main terminal station concourses are covered and it is not necessary always to put platforms and railway tracks underneath the canopy. The Dinky Toy pavement sections and double decker buses and taxis have an equally realistic effect. The *Constructors 'Review'* was not exactly full of its praise and concluded . . . 'Considering the detail achieved on some other makes of plastic building kits sold for no more than a few shillings, the price of this station kit, even allowing for its size, seems a little high.'

CANOPY EXTENSION KIT

There has been a lot of discussion in the Hornby Dublo Collectors Circle on whether there were canopy extension kits for the terminal station. Indeed the redoubtable Ted Higgs once more found a sample so that we were able to finally confirm that it was produced. It was certainly not widely advertised or actively sold to the dealers as on 6th July 1961 Mr. Jack Gahan (fulltime member in Binns Road of the Hornby Railway Company and responsible for setting up many of the scenes etc., which appeared in the *Meccano Magazine*) – received the following memorandum . . .

'Mr. Ernest Lee has given me some very important information this afternoon about the terminal and through stations in kit form which are soon to come on the market as Hornby Dublo accessories.

'Basing the remarks on number 5083 as a Terminal Station Mr. Lee points out that the length of the platforms under the canopy are only such as to accommodate a coach and a half or possibly a locomotive and tender and the barest vestige of a coach. To make this station suitable for holding a complete train there are available, as you will know, Platform Extensions No. 5086 and Fences No. 5087 and these can be used to extend the Terminal Station to a length appropriate to a given train. What has not been made clear in the catalogue is that there will also be available separately if Meccano dealers are approached about this, the canopies for the Station and the Station building itself. In other words the Terminal Station and for that matter the through station can be enlarged ad infinitum, either laterally or longitudinally and likewise any number of Station Buildings (the clocks all guaranteed to be giving the same time!) can be used. A further point is that of course Platform Extensions can be used by the side wall of the Stations which have been left quite plain for that purpose.'

THE 2-RAIL LEVEL CROSSING

With the introduction of the 2-rail track and the different height, it was necessary to redesign the level crossing unit and reintroduce it as a 2-rail version complete with track already in place, as a standard half straight. This was shown in the December 1961 *Meccano Magazine* although, according to the drawing, the original moulding for this and indeed the colour which appeared in many of the catalogues of this period, was in polystyrene SF93 brown, but was changed to SF73 stone i.e. the buff yellow, on 25th October 1961. There has been some conjecture as to whether this brown version ever existed, but I cannot confirm either way at the time of writing. The May 1961 *Hornby Dublo Catalogue* showed it as available later, as well as the new moulded 3460 3-rail level crossing.

There was a lot of talk about making a two track level crossing and, indeed, producing a version with working electric warning lights, but this was never put into production and will be covered in the appropriate chapter under the models that never were. At the same time the Dinky Toy No. 792 arrived – packets of polystyrene packing cases, three per packet.

THE LINESIDE NOTICES

As with the gradient and milepost kit produced earlier, June 1962 introduced the 5037 kit of lineside notices. They were very well produced and indeed well printed, but came in for some criticism from the model railway press in that some were overscale 7 mm (0 gauge scale). These were the two British Rail warning signs. However, in practical terms, if they were in 00 scale they would doubtless be too small to be seen or unstable so one could not really win.

THE TELEGRAPH POLES

Although shown in the introductory modernisation scheme, I am unable to ascertain exactly when the telegraph poles made an appearance. They were supplied in boxes of twelve, numbered 5090, but were remarkably unattractive pieces, totally out of keeping with the rest of the buildings. The original material

256

MODEL RAILWAY NEWS

1'6

MAY 1957

was polythene although in a modification on the drawing, dated 10th February 1961, this was changed to polypropylene SF93 brown. They were just under 4 inches tall with a large circular base stamped 'Hornby Dublo, Meccano Limited' underneath. An ugly item, and to my mind totally out of keeping with the range. Their unpopularity then has contributed to their rarity today.

THE SIGNAL BOX

The signal box, number 5080 was retained in moulded aluminium strangely when the majority of buildings were produced in polystyrene. It retained its bright orange roof sections although later versions were known to have light green roofs.

Why or when they changed the colour I do not know, nor is it recorded anywhere and the green-roofed version is highly sought after.

'Wartime shortages called for improvisation'. This sketch from the September 1941 Meccano Magazine shows a push button switch for the new electrically operated signals.

SIGNALS

The Hornby Dublo signals were fine accessories and to my mind most realistic model signals even by today's standards. They had a diecast base and mast, with brightly printed signal arms operated on the same principle as the large 0 gauge signals, through steel cranks and a wire connecting rod to a counterbalanced lever at the base. All pre-war signals I have seen have an unpainted (i.e. plain metal underside) finish to the base as well as small balance weights. They must have been insufficient in practice because the post-war issue of the signals from 1952 onwards all had enlarged balance weights.

From the very first catalogue there was the upper quadrant single signal arm (D1) in either home or

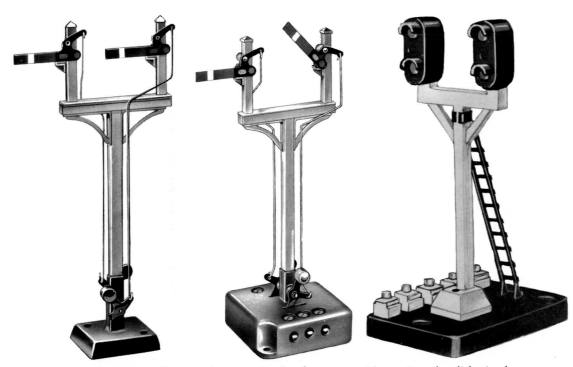

The manual and electrically operated junction signals – from original artwork.

The junction colour light signal – from original artwork.

COLOUR LIGHT SIGNALS
. . . . just like British Railways!

MADE IN ENGLAND BY MECCANO LTD

257

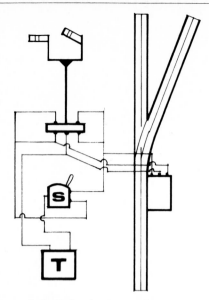

Junction signal. Right hand points set for curve.

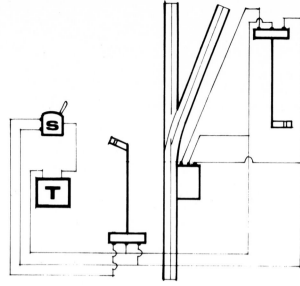

Two home signals and one point controlled from one switch. Set for curve.

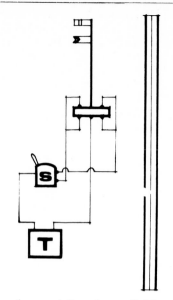

Double arm (home and distant) controlled from one switch.

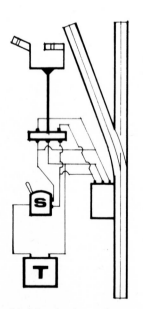

Junction signal left hand point set for curve (signal aspect corresponds with point setting).

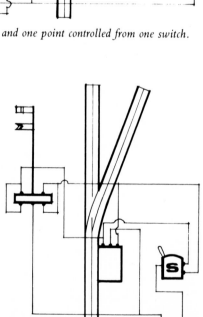

Double arm signal (home and distant) and right hand point controlled from one switch.

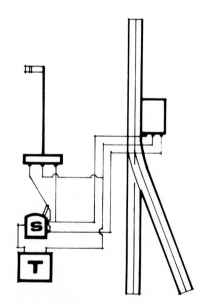

Home signal right hand point. Signal at Danger when points set for curve.

JOHN. E. GRIFFITHS.

Wiring details for signal/point sketches.

distant as well as the upper quadrant double arm (D2) with both home and distant on the same post. Each box contained 6 signals and its coding is 10/38, i.e. October 1938, and they all have the same quantities 1.75M – 1,750 produced.

The next inclusion in the range was the D3 junction signal in home or distant. They were boxed in pairs and had a retail price of 1s. 6d. The trade bulletin is dated February 1939 and it puts the signals as being ready in the Autumn, together with the footbridge and the city station we have already covered, although surprisingly no mention is made of the engine shed. The dealers' catalogue for June 1939 refers to the electrically operated signals. I can find no exact record when the D3 manually operated junction signal came into being, although I would put it at mid-summer. There are photographs in the earlier *Meccano Magazines* as far back as April showing the junction signal.

It was in December 1939 that the electrically operated points and signals first came onto the market – three months after the declaration of war.

The single arm electric signal in both home and distant was box code D418 with a quantity of 5M i.e. 5,000, while the double arm signal, D430, was only 3M i.e. 3,000 and the junction signals, D431, likewise. There was a small sticker on each box to denote whether it contained a home or distant signal. I do not know whether the full quantity was produced immediately, or whether it was snapped up by the scale railway enthusiast. They were, however, in short supply and there were many advertisements in the early war year model railway magazines in the 'Wants' column requesting them.

With the signals came the red D1 switches for the electrically operated points and signals, while the black D2 switch was for the isolating rail. These switches were very soon sold out and there was a fascinating wooden switch which one could make oneself, mentioned in the September 1941 *Meccano Magazine*.

One of the most attractive signal sets, frequently shown in the pre-war *Meccano Magazine* Hornby Dublo illustrations, was the Dinky Toys set No. 15. These were a lot smaller than the Hornby Dublo signals, being only 3 inches tall, against the 4½ inches of the standard semaphore type. They were most realistic in appearance as starter signals in railway station scenes, indeed they were small enough, particularly the junction signals, to be mounted onto the platforms themselves.

After the war, with the resupply situation in Hornby Dublo gaining pace, the manual signals were introduced over a period commencing August 1948 through to 1952. The April 1950 *Meccano Magazine* shows them for the first time. All signals before about 1952 had small counterweights and the bases painted black (underside) or in some cases white. Large counterweights followed around 1952.

In September 1952, the electrically operated points were once more available and two months later, in November, the electrically operated signals.

From the Hornby Railway Company information book at Binns Road, now in the treasured archive category in the care of the 'Hornby Railway Collectors Association', there is a fascinating note marked 'Not for information to the public' stating that the signal solenoid has 700 turns of No. 40 SW gauge wire which must have an approximate resistance of 23 ohms.

For some reason we had to wait until July 1953 for the manually operated junction signal D3 in either home or distant and its electrically operated brother to be available.

In November 1958 there was an article in the *Meccano Magazine* which stated . . . 'Today, colour light signals are replacing semaphore types for controlling the movements of real trains and now Hornby Dublo owners can equip their tracks with this up to the minute colour light signalling system.'

As usual, up to the minute with British Railways practice, the Binns Road factory produced two-aspect

colour light signals in both home and distant. Despite the large, but necessary base they were to quote the January 1959 *Constructors* 'Review' . . . 'well proportioned and look most realistic when in situ.' Indeed they did and were followed in December, by the twin-head colour light junction signal.

To see a night scene on a Hornby Dublo layout, with the buildings illuminated – though not too brightly – and fully operational, with colour light signals, is a wonderful experience. It is a pity that they did not produce working yard lights or platform or road lamps.

Because the signals were in operation the whole time showing either a red/yellow or green aspect, it was not possible to use the existing red D1 switch or black D2 switch. A special switch G3 (green) had to be designed although it was of identical structure to the earlier switches and could be used to form a 'bank'. The signals operated from either an AC or DC current, at 12–15 volts and full instructions for wiring were provided in the box. Four most useful diagrams complete, what is, to quote the *Model Railway Constructor* 'a most acceptable introduction'.

The Hornby Dublo signals, both colour aspect and semaphore type, to my mind copied the Hornby Dublo practice of giving maximum reliability and operational value while retaining very much a scale impression. I say impression deliberately, as they recreate the sight and sound of real life railways far more than the so very fragile-looking, real scale miniature models one sees around today.

On my own layout I always ensure that the voltage to the signals is turned down to about half the recommended voltage as, to my taste, when fully lit the colour aspect signals are too bright and also, with bulbs almost impossible to obtain today this procedure extends their life.

Many signals had the letters in white imprinted into the base '2 T'. This was to signify the second type requiring bulbs of a different diameter.

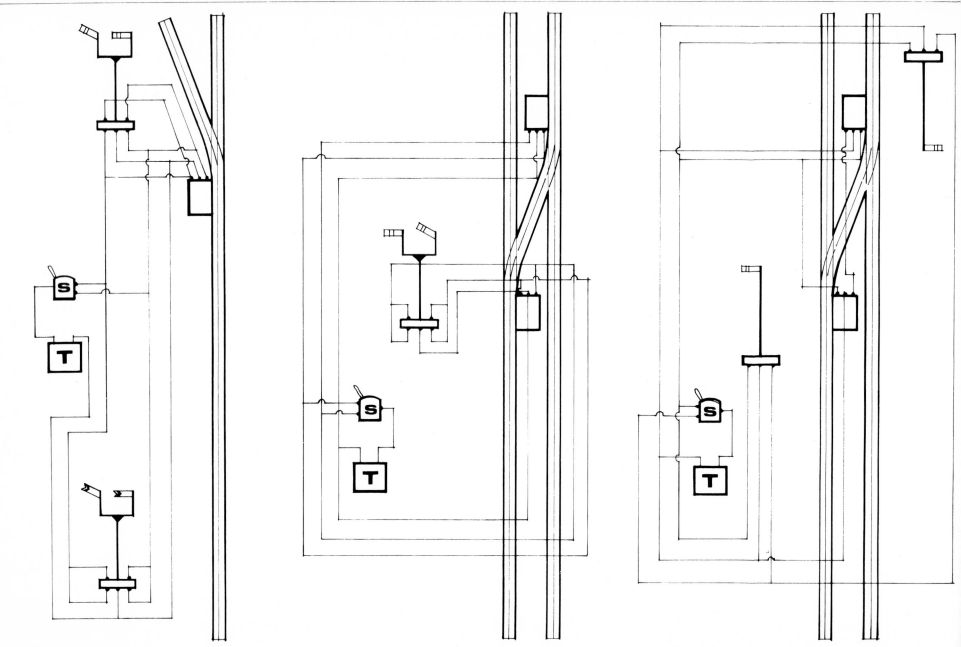

Home and Distant junction signals operated from one switch.

Junction signal home and two points forming crossover operated from one switch (signal aspect corresponds with point setting).

Two home signals and two points forming crossover controlled from one switch (signals when points set for straights).

JOHN. E. GRIFFITHS.

Accessories

Extracts from original Meccano drawings.

1. The station master, job number 11740, complete with greatcoat, reading a piece of official documentation. In this instance there is very little difference between the pre-war and post-war models.

2. The guard, job number 11741. The pre-war guard had four shiny buttons on his double-breasted jacket (little blobs of silver paint) as well as a smart green tie, while the post-war version was all over blue.

3. The ticket collector, job number 11742. Likewise six shiny buttons on the pre-war version only. The pre-war figures always had their faces and hands painted, but with many of the post-war, it was just their faces.

4. The engine driver, job number 11743. The pre-war version was very smart in dark blue with the overall coat commonly used by drivers buttoned at the top only and bright shiny buttons on his inside jacket and a red handkerchief in his top left hand pocket. His post-war counterpart was painted overall in a lighter shade of blue.

5. The porter with bags, job number 11744. Again a very smart porter with bright buttons on the traditional sleeved waistcoat of his trade. He is walking carrying a cream suitcase in his right hand and a red suitcase in his left while his post-war counterpart was painted all over blue with two light brown suitcases.

6. The shunter, job number 11745. He wears his long service mackintosh with the collar turned up and eight shiny buttons and is signalling with his left hand as though giving instructions to the engine driver. The pre-war version had a long piece of wire fitted into the casting to represent what the uneducated call the 'shunter's pole'. I am told the correct terminology should always be the 'coupling stick'. The post-war version, while naturally the same casting, had a cast shunter's pole which finished at the top of his right shoulder.

RAILWAY PERSONNEL AND PLATFORM ACCESSORIES

The famous model shop, Hamblings in London claimed to be the first firm to put scale, hand-painted figures in 00 scale on the market. This was way back in 1935 and they included not only railway station staff and passengers, but also horses, cows, sheep, pigs, etc.

There had been miniature figures shown on the covers of the two Hornby Dublo 1938 catalogues, including the very first one although it was not until the February 1939 *Meccano Magazine* that they were reviewed. They were supplied in little green boxes, about the size of a matchbox and were the D1 railway staff which incorporated a station master, guard, ticket collector, driver, porter with luggage and a shunter. The D2 passenger set incorporated three men and three ladies. It was not surprising, with their small metal content, that they were one of the first models to be introduced after the extreme shortage of metal in the early 1950s. They were advertised in the April 1952 *Meccano Magazine* as the 1001 station staff sets which later became 051 and the 1003 passenger sets which later became 053.

There is considerable difference between the two sets of figures although the same moulds were used. The finish on the pre-war figures was quite exquisite and far superior to their post-war counterparts.

Detail notes on railway personnel:

7. Man carrying a raincoat, job number 11752. The pre-war version was very smart in brown suit, black hat, and a light cream raincoat and grey tie. The post-war version had an overall dark brown suit and again cream raincoat.

8. Man reading newspaper, job number 11753. He looks like a commuter ready for a days work in the city. The pre-war version had a long light blue overcoat and is wearing light grey trousers with a red tie and black bowler hat whereas the post-war version is dressed dark blue throughout.

9. The golfer, job number 11754. The pre-war version is dressed overall in a dark green colour with a green beret and cream golf bag with silver painted golf club heads, dressed very much in the period with 'plus fours'. The post-war version was wearing a light brown set of clothes with a dark brown golf bag only.

10. Woman with rug, job number 11755. The pre-war version is in an overall green colour wearing a green hat and carrying a light brown rug. The post-war version was dressed overall in a light blue colour.

11. Woman walking, job number 11756. I have two variations of the pre-war version: A lady walking briskly dressed in a yellow dress and the other in a light mauve dress. Both carry a black handbag and wear green gloves and hat. On the post-war version the green gloves and hat are retained, but the bag is not painted and she wears a red dress.

12. Woman in fur coat, job number 11757. The pre-war version is dressed overall in a medium grey coat and hat. Just to prove the exception, the post-war figure is dressed overall in a light green, but this time has the collar of the fur coat painted in a light grey.

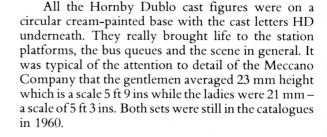

All the Hornby Dublo cast figures were on a circular cream-painted base with the cast letters HD underneath. They really brought life to the station platforms, the bus queues and the scene in general. It was typical of the attention to detail of the Meccano Company that the gentlemen averaged 23 mm height which is a scale 5 ft 9 ins while the ladies were 21 mm – a scale of 5 ft 3 ins. Both sets were still in the catalogues in 1960.

THE PLASTIC MOULDED FIGURES

With the introduction of super detail rolling stock it is not surprising that a super detail range of miniature people was produced. The December 1960 *Meccano Magazine* showed the first photograph of them, although they did state that there would be more information later. In point of fact, it was not until May 1961, that the first railway staff set, number 050, was available. The Meccano announcement recorded . . . 'These excellent figures will populate any 00 gauge railway layout. There is an assorted pack of 12 railway personnel: porter, policeman, guards, driver, maintenance men, etc., masterly sculptured in realistic attitudes and well proportioned. They are hand painted and cost 3s per set of 12.'

The July 1961 *Meccano Magazine* recorded . . . 'It is remarkable how much these attractive little people contribute towards the "life" of the railway. Their attitudes are natural and realistic – which is not surprising as they were modelled on actual railwaymen who entered thoroughly into the spirit of the thing when their individual photographs were taken to form the basis of these fascinating miniatures.

'Thus the engine driver, a well-built man, is making his unhurried way towards his engine, sponge cloth in hand, typically, with his jacket fastened at the top button only. There will always be several of his type coming and going around about your engine shed. The locomotive fitter like several of the other figures is modelled holding something that suggests his calling, quite apart from the fact that he is dressed in a boiler suit and is equipped with fitter's lamp and battery box. His right hand grasps a brake spanner, a tool of formidable proportions needed when brake adjustments on an engine is one of the things to which he has to attend.

← *Personnel – top row pre-war diecast, second row post-war diecast, third and fourth rows the Super Detail Sets.*

'The permanent way ganger is standing in a characteristic attitude with his long handled hammer resting on the ground. Perhaps he is viewing the track or possibly he is simply eyeing a passing train – it all depends where you put him on your layout. His assistant, the length man, has a broad bladed shovel of the kind that he needs when tidying up the track ballast and doing the many other jobs on the line that fall to him. In an engine shed scene he could represent a shed labourer, one of whose tasks will be to keep the engine pits clear of ashes, and so on. The carriage and wagon examiner is shouldering his wheel tapping hammer while he also holds the powerful inspection lamp often needed in his duties. If you look at him through a magnifying glass you will see that he has a short spanner tucked in one of his overall jacket pockets. A lot of unsuspected detail of a similar nature can be discovered if you put your miniature figures "under the glass" in this way.

'Of the uniformed grades, the station master is a dignified figure obviously in charge of things, while the porter is a busy person who is clearly earning his money, being loaded with a suitcase in each hand and a hold-all under his arm. The ticket collector is smart and alert one hand outstretched to take tickets while in the other are the nippers with which to clip them. The passenger guard is in action with his whistle raised to his mouth as he gives the "right away" signal with his green flag held aloft. He is leaning slightly as he does so to make sure that the driver up in the front sees the flag. The corresponding goods guard has no flag but instead he carries a guards lamp.

'Finally we have two policemen, both solid dependable types, one with his hands held behind his back just keeping an eye on things, while the other, with white gloves and arms outstretched, is ideal for road traffic duty outside your station or at any suitable point on the lineside road.'

It is not surprising that these figures are so popular amongst collectors today, and they rank amongst the finest in their class.

I am aware of one or two variations relating to the lamps. The goods guard for instance is usually carrying a black lamp with a red light, although I have seen many model sets with a white light. Likewise the carriage and wheel examiner usually carries a black lamp with a red light, although I have seen many sets with a silver lamp.

With such a popular series, it is not surprising that it should be extended and in December 1961, the 052 railway passenger sets were available, arriving at the same time as the new 2-rail level crossing and Dinky Toy 792 packing cases. The Secretary of the Hornby Railway Company, in March 1962 wrote . . .

'When you see these latest models at close quarters you cannot help noticing how well modelled they are, and if you look at them through a magnifying glass you will find that their features are actually moulded. Their attitudes and clothes look natural too and the flat finish used in colouring them helps to give them a remarkably natural and realistic appearance.

'I have been interested in miniature figures of all kinds for a long time and it is a remarkable fact that of the many varieties that have been produced from time to time for miniature railway owners generally, very few seem to have included any children or young people. Nearly all of them represented a standard range of grown ups, so the opportunity has been taken to introduce some youngsters amongst the figures now featured in the 052 set and the youngest of them forms one of the family trio you can see on the station seat, the seat itself forming an essential part of the set. This small child is modelled as if sitting cosily next to his mother, the two forming a single moulding. This is the first time that seated figures were available in Hornby Dublo.

'The three figures on the seat make a nice group as they wait for their train to arrive, "the train now standing" as the station announcers say at the platform behind them is clearly not the one they want. More interest is being displayed in it by some of the other people in particular the schoolboy near the top of the platform ramp who is admiring the engine "Cardiff Castle". I suspect that he is a keen spotter who has just "copped" 4075. He like his pigtailed sister, the schoolgirl who is standing at a more discreet distance from the engine, opposite the rear driving splasher, is modelled in typical school uniform, blue blazer and cap for him, maroon blazer and beret for her. Both have school bags hung over their shoulders in the usual nonchalant manner.

'Impressed, but not specially interested perhaps, in the locomotive is the young lady, a junior miss, I think, in the light dress who is standing near the tender. Blonde, hatless and with flared skirt she adds variety and colour to the scene. A typical figure whom you can see in real life, at so many stations, is the woman sitting demurely on a large suitcase with other items of luggage alongside. Her baggage suggests that she is going on a fairly long journey, and she is, therefore, appropriately dressed for this. You can see her on the platform almost level with the front of the first coach. She is clearly quite contentedly waiting for the train she wants. Further along the platform, by the first pair of luggage doors is a business man complete with brief case, bowler hat and rolled umbrella. The last mentioned item you cannot see in our picture, as our city gent is turned away from us, and he is holding the umbrella in his right hand. This particular figure, in neat grey suit certainly looks the part.

'In complete contrast is the carefree looking sportsman, with bag containing his gear in front of him. The impression of a casual stance is remarkably

050 railway staff from the May 1961 Meccano Magazine.

052 railway passengers from the January 1962 Meccano Magazine.

264

well conveyed in the figure for he is wearing a double breasted jacket, light trousers and cap.

'Dignity is combined with elegance in the figure of a woman who stands holding a handbag. This matronly person wears an attractive dress and close fitting hat of contrasting colour. To wind up we have a man in a belted raincoat and trilby hat who is carrying a large suitcase. As an example of the mythical Mr. Everyman he would be very hard to beat.'

The *Model Railway Constructor* in their January 1962 'Constructors Review' reported . . . 'The use of subdued matt colours, coupled with the natural attitude of the figures make them all the more credible. The figures stand on unobtrusive, fawn stands but look more realistic if removed from these bases with a sharp knife and cemented into position on the layout.'

For some reason they only put 11 pieces in this set and I feel certain that they could have found something to put in that last empty square.

The original 050 railway staff were supplied in little plastic packets, and I suppose these must have been frequently damaged or broken as they are now packaged in little perspex moulded partitioned boxes.

Following on much quicker, in April 1962, the 054 railway station personnel series arrived. Again in the April 1962 *Meccano Magazine* the Hornby Railway Company Secretary reported . . . 'When the figures and other items in this new set are used in conjunction with the two sets of figures already available, some remarkably realistic effects are to be obtained, particularly if one gives some thought to the placing of the figures and the other pieces. One figure from the new set, a man with his bicycle, is included in the level crossing scene above.' The Secretary goes on . . .

'These new models look good enough by any standards to the naked eye but the faithful character of their modelling is well worth studying with the aid of a magnifying glass. Let us start with the porter, smartly dressed in uniform with his arms extended so that he can be used with the porters barrow which is also included in the set. The barrow is very neatly modelled indeed with its open type of frame and other familiar characteristics. To go with it are several pieces of luggage – a trunk, a case and that familiar item of the present age – the travelling bag. The porter, barrow and luggage can be dispersed about the platform in

any number of ways. It would not be out of place for them to appear outside the station too, as if the porter was dealing with baggage belonging to a passenger arriving or departing by car.

'The porter is suitable for any kind of station, but the next two items to be mentioned a mobile bookstall and a refreshment trolley with their respective attendants are specially suited to stations of the more important type. You would, for instance, have plenty of opportunity for their employment in a large terminal or through station assembled from the components of the 5083 composite station kit. Taking the mobile bookstall first, we find that this is moulded in a pleasing manner to represent a typical vehicle of this kind, having a three tier stand, plentifully supplied with reading material including, no doubt, copies of the MM! In view of the variety suggested by the attractive colourings of the publications represented, I am sure that anything Hornby Dublo passengers may wish to read on their journeys can be provided. The bookstall attendant is a separate figure, smartly attired in a white jacket and clearly keen to please his customers as he pushes his perambulating bookshop along.

'The refreshment trolley represents a popular piece of station furniture, recalling those cups of tea, fruit drinks or eatables which are often in demand before the start of a journey or are eagery sought at an intermediate stop. The trolley is modelled to represent the usual urns, one each end, for the white finished

054 railway station personnel – from the April 1962 Meccano Magazine.

counter at lower level between them. The woman attendant is neatly dressed in a long overall coat attractively coloured in green with a cap to match. I can foresee, on many Hornby Dublo platforms some interesting groupings of the other figures round about the refreshment trolley as it is readily possible to change the grouping of the figures as required. Because of its everyday character the next figure, representing a man with his bicycle is particularly attractive. The cyclist and his machine are separate mouldings and this has made possible some really realistic modelling. The man wears a cap, a grey coat and trousers which are baggy around the ankles as though he was wearing cycle clips. His left hand is thrust into his trousers pocket with the result that his jacket on that side is swept back and sticks out behind him in a delightfully realistic manner. His right hand is extended, to rest on the handle bars of his bike, a splendid piece of simple modelling which includes such details as pedal cranks as well as the saddle, handle bars and more obvious items. Here again is a combination which can be employed very suitably almost anywhere on the layout – on the station platform, along the road, by level crossings and in many other places. I am sure you will be able to think up any number of likely situations.'

*Extract from the June 1962
Model Railway Constructor.*

There is a considerable variety of colours in the luggage items to be found in these sets. They have used a green, light brown and dark brown moulding plastic and the average seems to be green and light brown suitcases, a brown travel bag and a green trunk. However, in the packets I have there are green travel bags, dark brown and light brown trunks and brown suitcases.

In the December 1962 *Meccano Magazine* they reviewed the year's progress of Hornby Dublo and in particular announced that in the original 050 railway passenger set they had made a change. The new sets came out in the new plastic moulded boxes as opposed to the little polythene bags and included a very realistic shunter with a long coupling stick, which replaced one of the two policemen – the one with his hands behind his back.

I could not help feeling that there should be another set, 056, of seated railway passengers or at least figures that could be put inside the super detail coaches. Alas it was not to be and I can find no trace in any records that such a set was ever planned.

Mr. Norman Hatton of Liverpool informed me once that many of the 054 packets of figures he purchased and was selling a few years ago were wrapped in light brown paper with the trade name 'Subbuteo

Company Limited' on them. I wrote to Mr. G. Erik, Director of Development who kindly replied . . . 'I seem to recall being involved with the production of 00 scale railway figures which could have been destined for Hornby years ago – but they might have been for somebody else.' This was in February 1974 and he went on to state that the Subbuteo Sport Games Company Limited had been sold to John Waddingtons in 1969 and unfortunately he could not verify this point.

More Hornby people; since the review above right was written, there seems to have been some redistribution of manpower—the green coated woman has assumed control of the mobile bookstall, while the white coated gentleman now supplies the plastic tea we mentioned last month.

'The Flying Scotsman' — used Head Board No. 1720	THE FLYING SCOTSMAN Coach Board No. 1750	KINGS CROSS — EDINBURGH Destination Board No. 1775
'The White Rose' — used Head Board No. 1721	THE WHITE ROSE Coach Board No. 1751	KINGS CROSS — LEEDS Destination Board No. 1776
'The Fair Maid' — used Head Board No. 1722	THE FAIR MAID Coach Board No. 1752	KINGS CROSS — PERTH Destination Board No. 1777
'Royal Scot' — used Head Board No. 1723	THE ROYAL SCOT Coach Board No. 1753	LONDON — GLASGOW Destination Board No. 1778
'The Red Rose' — used Head Board No. 1724	THE RED ROSE Coach Board No. 1754	LONDON — LIVERPOOL Destination Board No. 1779
'The Mancunian' — used Head Board No. 1725	THE MANCUNIAN Coach Board No. 1755	LONDON — MANCHESTER Destination Board No. 1780
'The Bristolian' — used Head Board No. 1726	THE BRISTOLIAN Coach Board No. 1756	PADDINGTON AND BRISTOL Destination Board No. 1781
'Torbay Express' — used Head Board No. 1727	TORBAY EXPRESS Coach Board No. 1757	Destination Board No. None Made
'Cornish Riviera Express' — used Head Board No. 1728	CORNISH RIVIERA EXPRESS Coach Board No. 1758	Destination Board No. None Made
'The Caledonian' — used Head Board No. 1729	THE CALEDONIAN Coach Board No. 1759	LONDON — GLASGOW Destination Board No. 1782
'The Talisman' — used Head Board No. 1730	THE TALISMAN Coach Board No. 1760	Destination Board No. None Made
'The Red Dragon' — used Head Board No. 1731	THE RED DRAGON Coach Board No. 1761	PADDINGTON NEWPORT CARDIFF AND SWANSEA Destination Board No. 1783
'Bournemouth Belle' — used Head Board No. 1732	BOURNEMOUTH BELLE Coach Board No. 1762	Destination Board No. None Made

The then new 'Royal Scot' headboards – from the August 1950 Model Railway Constructor.

regions put suitable nameboards and destination boards on their principal expresses, although the October 1945 *Meccano Magazine* carried a fascinating advertisement on behalf of the Acton Model Railway Club where they advertised . . . 'Dublo Enthusiasts! Add the latest "Super-Detail" to your coaches. 4 mm true to scale coach nameboards.'

E1 was 'The East Anglian', E2 – 'The Highlandman' and E3 – 'The Aberdonian' while for the Great Western enthusiast they had G1 – 'The Cornish Riviera Ltd.', G2 – 'The Cheltenham Spa Express' and G3 – 'The Bristolian'.

The December 1946 *Meccano Magazine* reported that although not yet a usual practice it had been a pre-war feature of the LNER for the locomotives hauling certain famous expresses to carry headboards bearing the trains' names. They commented that it was pleasing to report that three LNER express headboards had now reappeared in conjunction with improved Winter services as well as the 'Bournemouth Belle' headboard on the Southern Region and the addition to the insignia of the 'Golden Arrow'.

The *Railway Modeller* in its December 1957 issue announced that the Meccano Company had realised the potential of these most attractive new accessories

and had included them in their 'Bristolian' and 'Royal Scot' trains. However, it was not until October 1958, that the first advertisement appeared.

To me they just complete the superb miniature realism of the Hornby Dublo trains and seem even more attractive on the tinplate passenger coaches and 3-rail track than they do on the 2-rail.

You will notice one obvious gap in the 2-rail catalogue number metal headboard 1703 or 3-rail catalogue number 32853. As I mentioned in the chapter on the 'Co-Bo' locomotive this was to be a headboard similar to the A4 locomotive headboard for the Condor freight train – it was projected on British Rail to have a number of special fast named freight trains. In real life they never appeared and as with Hornby Dublo, it was a non-starter. There is an interesting variation too on the destination boards of the London – Glasgow route. The original 'Royal Scot' coaches had the tartan backing for the destination board, whereas the later 'Caledonian' train destination boards had a cream background.

One of the features reported in the October 1961 *Meccano Magazine* was on the elegant new pullman train featuring for the first time number 34005 'Barnstaple' locomotive and the three pullman cars. The

TRAIN NAME HEADBOARDS

The old North British Railway was undoubtedly the first to carry train name headboards. Even before the First World War they had a famous train, the 'Lothian Coast Express' which carried destination boards and a headboard. The *Meccano Magazine* for July 1955 had an excellent article and concluded that the headboard may well have been regarded not only as an advertisement but also as a simple and practical manner of indicating the general destination.

It was in 1928 that the Haymarket (Edinburgh) based Gresley Pacific No. 2580 – 'Shotover' appeared at London King's Cross on the first arrival at that terminus of the non-stop 'Flying Scotsman' train from Waverley carrying a headboard. Gradually the other

Extracts from the October 1958 Meccano Magazine.

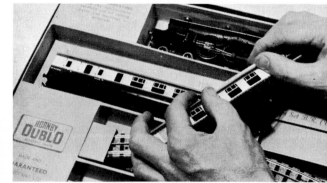

'Putting on the Coachboards' – from the December 1957 Railway Modeller.

Hornby Railway Company Secretary reported that . . . 'There is one small feature of this train set that will, I know, delight all those who buy it. It is the inclusion of a locomotive headboard of correct Southern outline with a self-adhesive label bearing the title "Bournemouth Belle". The lettering and edging of the label have been beautifully executed in aluminium, the background of the nameboard being Southern green. In addition there are attractive "Bournemouth Belle" labels suitable for fitting to the pullman cars.'

Despite the number of headboard and destination board labels the Meccano Company produced for their Hornby Dublo trains, there were as many planned and drawn, but alas never put into production. Perhaps they were going to produce their own special pamphlet on them as there are many drawings showing the correct positions that the destination boards and nameboards should be affixed. The fact is that Hornby Dublo model railways copied in the minutest detail the full size prototypes and through the inclusion of such information, expected their followers would rightly be interested in doing the same.

Among the headboards and destination boards not produced were the 'Merseyside Express', the 'Heart of Midlothian', the 'Elizabethan', the 'Royal Duchy', the 'West Riding', the 'InterCity', the 'Merchant Venturer', the 'Ulster Express', etc. But more of these in a later chapter dealing with models which were planned but never produced.

In fact, so neat were these headboards and in particular the destination labels, that in the January 1959 *Meccano Magazine*, 'Tommy Dodd' the well known author in Hornby train circles, suggested using the destination boards on the 0 gauge coaches as well. Without doubt these accessories are one of my favourites.

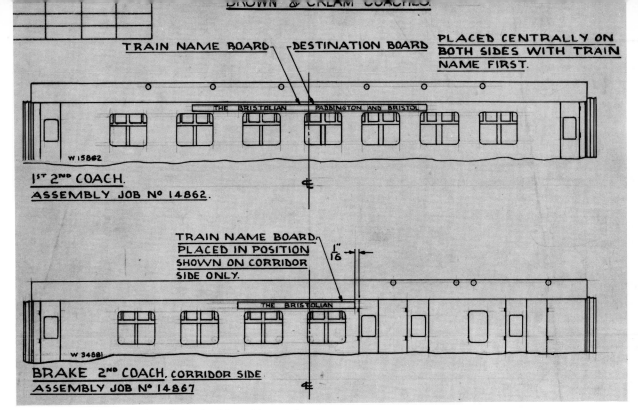

Train name and description board's 'placings' from Meccano drawing.

Headboard and destination boards from Meccano drawing.

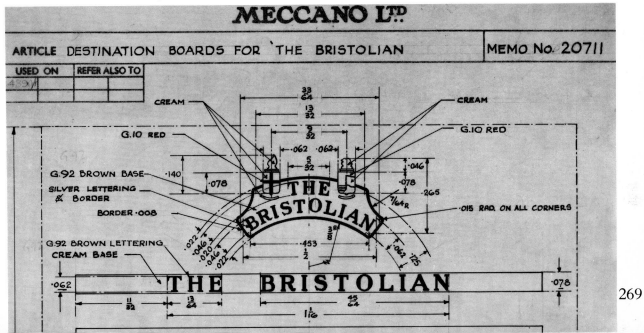

'Sheer nostalgia' from a pre-war Hornby Dublo catalogue reference 12/1039/70.

THE DUBLO DINKY TOYS

Dinky Toys played an essential part of the scene in many of the pre-war and immediate post-war pictures of the Hornby Dublo system. The editor of the *Meccano Magazine* was frequently asked by boys which Dinky Toys he could use with his new Hornby Dublo model railway and he was told . . .

22C Motor Truck	29G Luxury Coach
25R Forward Control lorry	35A Saloon Car
29B Streamline bus	35B Racer
29C Double Decker bus	35C MG Sports car
29E Single Deck bus	35D Austin Seven Car

Of these, only the single deck bus, double decker bus and luxury coach were to the same scale as Hornby Dublo, i.e. 5/32″ although many were passable, in particular the forward control lorry which was 1/16″ scale.

It has always been a bit of a disappointment to me that the incredibly attractive 35R Mechanical Horses and Trailer vans in the four regional liveries could never really be used. Most of the Meccano advertisements showed them with Hornby 0 gauge and there was an article stating that they could be used with Dublo as long as they were not too near to the locomotives.

The Dublo Dinky Toys arrived at the beginning of the period leading up to the peak of Hornby Dublo activity, some two months after the introduction of the 'Bristol Castle' locomotive and two months before the introduction of the super detail goods wagons. The first advertisement went in December 1957 . . . 'Now you can start to build up a model transport system with these new Dublo Dinky Toys made to the scale of 00 gauge railways. They are precision diecast in metal fitted with grey one piece "non-scratch" moulded wheels and tyres and finished in safe Lead Free enamel. Now is the time to start collecting . . .'

I have seen many models with matt black painted tyres – possibly the original finish and deleted as a cost cutting exercise!?

Mr. Warncken, the Sales Director of Meccano (retired 1971) said that the original marketing concept of Dinky Toys was that it should be a collecting hobby, the play value of the individual toy being of secondary importance. In later years this policy seems to have been reversed, but in 1957 it was still very much in force, the object being that these new models would be collected by the railway enthusiasts when issued.

The first models were the 064 Austin lorry, 065 Morris pickup and 066 Bedford flat truck. These

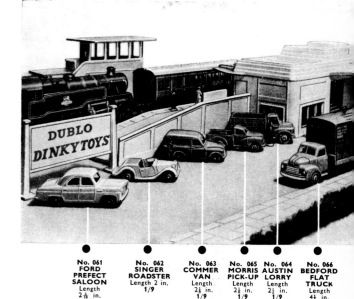
← Rows 1 and 2, Dublo Dinky Toys in order of introduction with other suitable standard Dinky Toys.
(The mechanical horses in row 4 are post-war versions of the very rare pre-war units.)

March 1959 Meccano Magazine.

Number 066, the Bedford flat truck in grey livery had plain grey wheels, treaded grey wheels and the final modification was a hook riveted to the back of the tailboard for towing a trailer. The somewhat elongated appearance of this model was so that it could carry one of the wooden container bodies from the Hornby Dublo series. This had a similar short life to the 065 Morris pickup.

The next model appeared in March 1958. Number 061, Ford Prefect, in a beige colour, had plain grey wheels, and was only in production for one year! It was not ever shown in the 1960 catalogue.

Number 062, the beautiful Singer Roadster, in a yellow and red livery, also had plain grey wheels and that too was deleted by 1961.

September 1959 Meccano Magazine.

Collectors, by the former because they are designed to the same scale as gauge 00 trains and by the latter as fine new Dinky Toys. They are ideal for use with Hornby Dublo Railway layouts and many boys who are interested only in Dinky Toys Collecting are now making a point of starting a separate collection of the latest smaller gauge models.' The same month the very popular Dinky Super Toy, number 943, the Leyland Octopus Esso 8 wheel tanker arrived.

moulded, non-scratch wheels could never have been very popular – whether it was from appearance or competition I do not know – but on 2nd December 1957, the new tyres with 20 treads equally spaced on each wheel were drawn and arrived, with the Dublo Dinky Toy taxi in March 1959. They were not changed to black as the drawing until 29th May 1969, the final modification being on 17th June 1971 when the material was changed from black polystyrene to polyethylene. Although the manufacture of Hornby Dublo model railways was stopped in 1964, some of the Dublo Dinky Toys continued in production right up until 1971.

Number 064, the Austin lorry, was produced in green with plain grey wheels, treaded grey wheels and treaded black wheels. It was in production up to 1962 only.

Number 065, the Morris pickup in a red colour was only produced, I have found, with plain grey wheels. Why this, and others, had such a short life I do not know. It was shown in a June 1960 catalogue but already deleted by the 8th edition Dinky Toy Catalogue.

June 1959 Meccano Magazine.

Number 063, the Commer Van, was finished in a light blue colour, again with plain grey wheels only, deleted by 1961.

The *Meccano Magazine* records . . . 'As we expected, they were enthusiastically welcomed by Hornby Dublo Train owners as well as Dinky Toy

For some reason there was a gap of twelve months before the next most popular of all Dublo Dinky Toys appeared and was ready during March 1959.

The Austin Taxi number 067, in blue and white, first arrived with treaded grey wheels although the later versions had treaded black wheels.

The next model appeared in April 1959, and was the Royal Mail Van. Number 068, Royal Mail Van, only had treaded grey wheels and although the first advertisement appeared without windows, two months later they were advertising this vehicle with

April 1959 Meccano Magazine.

Advertisement from the October 1959 Meccano Magazine.

windows – the first of the series to be so equipped. All future models had this improvement where appropriate. (Deleted by 1965.)

The next model to appear was in June 1959, with the Bedford articulated flat truck. Number 072, the articulated flat truck was in a bright yellow colour with a sharply contrasting bright red trailer, the same length as the 066 Bedford flat truck so that it could carry a container. Strangely enough this model still is common with its smooth grey wheels although the original advertisement showed that it had the treaded type. Obviously both versions were produced. The model was deleted by 1966.

Three months later, in September, the 069 Massey-Harris-Ferguson tractor arrived. This was in an all over blue finish with battleship grey treaded wheels.

This colour version is strange, because a friend working for the Massey-Ferguson Company told me that in 1956 their tractors had a grey bonnet and wings and a gold engine, but were then changed to a red and grey in December 1957. I am not sure, but perhaps this complicated paint structure would not be possible in a toy costing only 1s 6d. I have a note on the drawing of the tractor wheel stating that a new wheel was moulded in polystyrene 45 grey and changed from the original dark grey on 9th July 1959.

The October 1959 Dublo Catalogue showed our tractor (mounted on a low-sided railway wagon No. 4649) which was deleted by 1966. As a footnote one should point out the hole in the seat – was there a figure/driver planned similar to the miniature Dinky army driver . . .?

In October 1959, the Dublo Dinky Toy 070, the AEC tanker, a familiar vehicle of the Shell fleet arrived, finished in correct colours. This too had the treaded grey and treaded black wheel versions and was deleted by 1964.

In February 1960, the Dublo Dinky Toy, number 071, the Volkswagon delivery van appeared. This was a very neat little model in a bright yellow finish with the words 'Hornby-Dublo' in red on the side no doubt delivering Hornby Dublo train sets to the children of the miniature people. This is the only time that the Meccano Company actually advertised Hornby Dublo on a Dinky Toy, they never repeated this on an item of rolling stock. The sole exception was the

mysterious wooden container, mentioned earlier. It is surprising in a way, because they certainly had Meccano and Hornby train private owner wagons in 0 gauge long before the Second World War but they were so concerned with accuracy to prototype that it was never considered (deleted 1968).

We have to wait until June 1960 for the number 076 Lansing Bagnall tractor and trailer set to appear. This was in a rich maroon colour with plain black wheels, the trailers were available separately in boxes of six. These really were a superb platform accessory and very much sought after today. The Lansing Bagnall tractor was deleted by 1966, yet its trailer, No. 078, continued up to 1970 finally being deleted in the 1971 catalogue.

February 1960 Meccano Magazine.

In September 1960, the last Dublo Dinky Toy appeared, the number 073 Landrover with horsetrailer. There appear to be many variations of this such as a bright green Landrover with orange trailer and green flap. Plain grey wheels although the trailer always appears to have treaded grey wheels. There is also a darker green version with a brown flap on the trailer and a final original bright green version with a black flap on the trailer again with treaded black wheels all round. It was provided with a horse from the same moulding as that supplied with the super detail horsebox although it normally appears in brown as opposed to the original light fawn. Funnily

enough this is the only time I have found a trade write up on this little series and this did not appear until the February 1961 *Model Railway Constructor*. They report . . . 'The Dublo Dinky Toys model provides an authentic touch to a country railway scene.' The Editor of the *Meccano Magazine* reported that the Landrover was based on the series 2 model, while the horsetrailer was manufactured by the Smiths Company, model CT86. The trailer, despite being in diecast metal (as all the Dublo Dinky Toy range) still carried a wealth of detail and there was even a groom's door situated on the nearside front giving access to the interior of the body without the necessity of lowering the rear ramp. The movement of horses by rail does form quite an important traffic for British Railways albeit on a limited regional basis. It is fitting that this vehicle should be the last in the series. There was a wonderful picture supplied by Mr. E. C. Griffith in the April 1966 *Model Railway News* where he has a picture of Charlie, the last shunt horse, by coincidence kept at Newmarket where, with his handler, Mr. Lawrence Kelly, is pulling one of the standard British Rail horseboxes.

Shunting horses played a considerable part in railway operations and originally almost all such operations were handled by them which is why the steam locomotive and even the 350 h.p. diesel shunters continue to have the nickname of 'donkey' or 'nag' as already discussed in respective chapters. Railway horses were used for two purposes – cartage and shunting and Mr. Michael Hale wrote a superb article on the story of railway horses at Tipton in the *Black Country Society Magazine*. He records . . . 'Cart horses were more in the public eye and their harnesses often carried decorative brasses which were highly polished, especially for such occasions as May Day Parades. There are many stories told about cart horses who knew their regular round and who could find their own way back to the stables if necessary!'

Mr. Michael Hale continues . . . 'Shunt horses worked in goods yards and station buildings hauling rail wagons along by means of a rope with a hook on the end which was placed in a ring or a hole in the frame of the vehicle. Again some of those horses learned their regular duties. For example they knew which trains had to have parcel vans attached and would wait patiently in a siding until the right moment and then would start to draw the van forward without being told. Charlie the last shunting horse retired in February 1967 spending his last days grazing in the Somerset fields but died in October the following year.'

Meccano never produced any buses in the Dublo Dinky Toy series, but as I mentioned at the beginning of the chapter, the regular Dinky Toy buses, particularly the single deck models were in scale with Hornby Dublo and the beautiful double decker buses were not

Extract from the August 1960 Model Railway News.

Extract from the February 1961 Model Railway Constructor.

Up till now few Dinky Toys could be accurately used with Hornby Dublo Trains, other than the Double and Single decker buses and the Forward Control lorry. The introduction of Dublo Dinky Toys in December 1957 changed all that and allowed very realistic scenes to be recreated.

far out. The world's first regular bus service was itself connected with railways being between Eastbourne station and Meads in East Sussex.

I have often wondered why Meccano never made more of the play factor in trains carrying new cars from the factory. Or indeed in having a special motor vehicle wagon in their range of Hornby Dublo rolling stock. Certainly I could find no trace of one planned. Nor could I find which models were planned to cover numbers 074, 075 and 077 which remained unallocated. Numbers 080 to 099 covered spare tyres, for standard Dinky Toys.

'Runcorn Bridge' – a 1961 display model.

AcHO Trains & Track

HORNBY ACHO TRAINS

No book on Hornby Dublo model trains would be complete without at least a token look at their cousin – Hornby-Acho model railways. As the name implies it was to a slightly different scale – 3.5 mm to 1 ft – hence HO or Acho as it was known.

All the trials, tribulations and experiences of the Meccano Company Limited in Liverpool in developing the Dublo system were put at the disposal of the sister French Company and a completely new train system was introduced at the Nuremberg Toy Fair in January 1960.

I have long been a lover of France and all things French (I even have a French sister-in-law). The French are brilliant engineers as well and I dare not fall into the trap of comparison between the Hornby Dublo system and the new Acho system.

Likewise I would not regard myself as an expert on French railway practice or the variations of their models. Hopefully, a complete book on the subject will be produced in the not too distant future.

The quality of their motors, the sheer sweet running capability and marvellous attention to detail on the bodywork, matches the unique standards set by Hornby Dublo earlier and I would like to express my sincere thanks to Mr. Michel Bucher, the Marketing Manager in the Paris Office, together with Mr. Pierre Delfeld, Works Director of their Calais Factory and his colleagues Mr. Roger Lassere and Mr. Albert Montserrad, and by no means least Mr. Delfeld's secretary Mlle Renee Elleboode.

Mr. Andre Rio, Manager of International Operations kindly wrote to me on 6th October 1972 when I began my investigations, and sent me an article he had written in 1959, putting the design philosophy behind this new system.

← Hornby-Acho motive power.

JUST ARRIVED from Paris

French-type Electric Locomotive and Coaches. Suitable for Hornby-Dublo 2-rail track

No. 638 Locomotive Series BB 16000 (with pantographs) Length 8 in. Price £5.10.0

This attractive model represents the French railways (S.N.C.F.) BB 16000 class express passenger locomotive built for use between Paris and Lille. It is produced by our Paris Works under the trade name of Hornby-Acho, which is HO gauge, but suitable for running on Hornby-Dublo 2-rail track. Dummy pantographs are fitted on the roof.

The passenger coaches are representative of those used in main line service in France. They are of corridor type, with doors at each end.

No. 734 Coach 1st Class
Length 9¼ in. Price 16/6

No. 733 Coach 2nd Class
Length 9¼ in. Price 16/6

HORNBY-DUBLO
ELECTRIC TRAINS
MADE BY MECCANO (FRANCE) LTD.

The first advertisement in England – from the September 1961 Meccano Magazine.

INTERNAL MEMORANDUM: MECCANO FRANCE 1959

A New Product: The Hornby-Acho Train

Some of you, particularly those who belong to the Design Office, the Buying Department or the Electrical Department, must already have heard of a new train which we are preparing to bring out for the Spring of 1960. Why a new train? Do we not have enough with the Express and M mechanical trains and the O or T electric trains? The answer lies in the trade mark which our Company has given this new item. Hornby indicates that it belongs to the range of trains, AcHO is a registered trade mark inspired by the two letters HO which, throughout the world, designate tracks of a distance which is half the 0 gauge (Half-0 in English). The mark is very easy to remember and that is not the least of its advantages both in the minds of our dealer customers and in the mind of the public.

It is therefore a question of a new range of trains, completely different from the Hornby 0 with which it

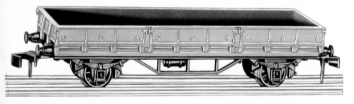

Typical Acho wagons available in England.

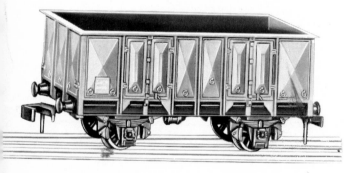

has nothing in common. To make things clear, let's say that a BB locomotive in the 0 range measures 275 millimeters, the same locomotive in H0 will measure 200 millimeters. But, you will say, the difference is not a half. Quite correct, but the AcHO locomotive will be much more in proportion with reality than the 0 locomotive was. In fact, if we had made 0 locomotives and wagons to the required scale, the length of them would have been such that they would have been unable to go round the bends without leaving the rails. Two other figures which it is also helpful to know are those of the rail gauges (taken from their insides): in the 0 track: 32 and in the H0 track: $16\frac{1}{2}$ millimeters.

It is therefore at the birth of an entirely new article that you are going to be present, a very rare event at Meccano since the present products started in 1924 (Meccano and Hornby 0) and in 1934 (Dinky Toys). You would be right in thinking that our Management did not make this decision lightly, a decision which entails considerable investment and the risk which exists with any innovation. There is no doubt that in France there is a market for these small trains which is developing from day to day. The advantage of the H0 is first of all the small space required which allows for having a very interesting network with point changing, engine shed tracks etc. all in a space of one square meter. In addition, the reproductions of locomotives and wagons will be much finer and be much more detailed, particularly due to the use of raw materials such as Zamak (already used to manufacture the Dinky Toys) and plastics. The H0 is indisputably better than 0. This does not mean, of course, that the 0 is going to disappear. We certainly hope, indeed, to be able to manufacture and sell our two trains alongside each other for very many years for the 0 will be aimed in particular at our younger customers (5 to 10 year olds) while the H0 will suit the older ones better.

However, the risk lies in the fact particularly that we already have innumerable competitors, one of whom produces H0 trains at a very low price while another manufactures in a distinctly higher price range. We are, therefore, neither the only ones nor the first in this field. Our trump card will be essentially an article of impeccable quality at the lowest possible price. We shall obtain the quality thanks to careful manufacture and very strict inspection. The price will be our main concern for there is no point in bringing

out a sensational product if it can only be bought by a small number of people with a very high purchasing power. Further, we need to look further than the French market only and we would not be annoyed if we could export our Hornby-AcHO to various countries in Europe.

In a word, with the AcHO train we have a fine card to play. Some departments such as the Design Office have already given of their best in the preparation of all the parts (and how many there are!) which, assembled together, will give locomotives, wagons, points systems, signals etc. Other departments have already, or will have within the next few months, the opportunity of showing that they too are capable of contributing towards producing a new article in the Meccano tradition, in the interest of all.

A.R.

The introductory leaflet in their dealers' catalogue for 1960 talks of 'the H0 trains you have wanted at a price you wished for'.

The orders recorded at both the Nuremberg and Lyon Toy Fairs completely fulfilled their expectations and Meccano France were executing a big publicity campaign which had in fact already begun. It was to have wide media coverage. One of their advertisements stated . . . 'We can tell you that it will cover not only the youngsters by the juvenile press but their parents in the main periodicals, the cinema, catalogue, leaflets etc.' They pleaded with their dealers that if they had not already ordered Hornby-Acho that they must not delay as they would certainly be low in stocks by the end of the year and it would be a pity if

the dealer could not satisfy the demands of his customers. The Meccano France Company made an all out effort to launch their new Hornby-Acho trains and were very proud and happy when the big French women's magazine *Marie Claire* awarded a star to the new Acho system. The star signified that the editors of the magazine had tried their new trains and for their quality and sales price had found them well worthy of bringing them to the attention of their readers.

As they were tooling up from scratch many of the costs involved in altering old tools etc., were avoided unlike the experience at Binns Road, and furthermore they decided to have needle type bearings for their rolling stock. On 22nd March 1963, Mr. Mike Rickett, then running the information service at Meccano, Binns Road, wrote to Mr. Ray Riisnaes, one of the founder members of Hornby Railway Collectors Association, stating that . . . 'Hornby Dublo had not yet produced pinpoint bearings but that the French Hornby-Acho did with the resultant smoothness of

travel, and that Hornby Dublo may well consider improving their rolling stock in similar fashion in the near future.'

I have often been surprised that Hornby Dublo Directors allowed Hornby-Acho into the U.K., when their own products, in the beginning of the 1960s were undergoing such competition and slow turn round in stocks.

In September 1961 the first Acho products appeared in this country – number 638 'Bo-Bo' 16009 locomotive with pantographs and number 733 second class and 734 first class coach. Limited supplies were brought over for a trial run although very soon Mr. Cyril Vincent of Adur Models in Shoreham, Sussex, was supplying the complete range. The *Model Railway Constructor* in reviewing these new products in their

December 1961 issue stated . . . 'The power is provided by a single motor bogie of a design produced in Meccano's Paris factory which does not incorporate the Ringfield motor now standard on new Hornby Dublo models. Nevertheless performance is fully up to the standards of the British models, fitted with the Ringfield motor. The three pole horizontally mounted motor drives the two axles through substantial worm gearing. The locomotive is mechanically almost silent when running, the only noise being a realistic "electric locomotive whine" which disappears as the locomotive reaches full speed.' The *Model Railway News* reported . . . 'Beneath the smooth external lines of the body can be found one of the most silent and smooth running motors we have yet experienced.' By January the new goods wagons were being

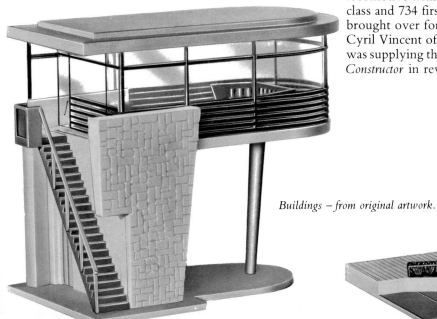

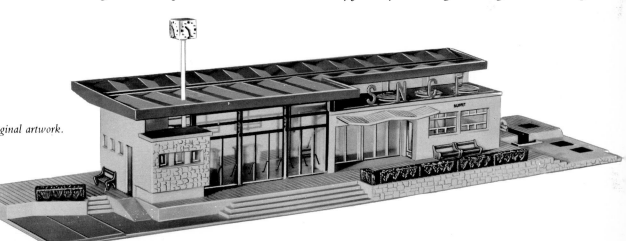

Buildings – from original artwork.

HORNBY-acHO

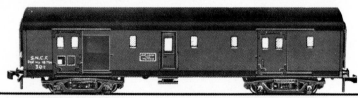

● **7310** - Fourgon de queue à bogies avec éclairage. 4 portes ouvrantes. Long. 200 mm.

● **7370** - Voiture voyageurs inox 1re classe avec glaces et aménagements intérieurs. Long. 280 mm.

la rame Rheingold
Reproduction des voitures du célèbre rapide Amsterdam-Bâle de la Deutsche Bundesbahn, qui suit la magnifique vallée du Rhin, dont il tire son nom ("l'Or du Rhin") ; c'est une exclusivité HOrnby-acHO.

7444 - Wagon salon. Long. 250 mm.

7446 - Wagon restaurant. Long. 250 mm.

7448 - Wagon panoramique. Long. 250 mm.

7450 - Wagon compartiments. Long. 250 mm.

● **7390** - Voiture restaurant avec glaces et aménagements intérieurs. Long. 265 mm.

● **7420** - Voiture postale avec glaces. Long. 256 mm.

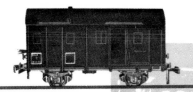

7000 - Fourgon de queue avec porte ouverte et éclairage arrière. Long. 110 mm.

● **7030** - Wagon transport de ciment. L. 110 mm.

7060 - Wagon transport de céréales C.T.C. Long. 110 mm.

● **7082** - Wagon tombereau avec charge de charbon. Long. 110 mm.

7010 - Wagon-tombereau à claires-voies. Long. 128 mm.

● **7040** - Wagon couvert à portes coulissantes. Long. 128 mm.

● **7070** - Wagon transport de produits chimiques. Long. 110 mm.

● **7090** - Wagon transport de minerai "Simotra". Long. 128 mm.

7020 - Wagon-citerne "Primagaz". Long. 110 mm.

7050 - Wagon frigorifique STEF. Long. 128 mm.

7080 - Wagon tombereau. Long. 110 mm.

7100 - Wagon-citerne "ESSO". Long. 110 mm

7120 - Wagon isotherme à lait. Long. 128 mm.

7170 - Wagon plateau à ranchers. Long. 128 mm.

7250 - Wagon-citerne "BP" à bogies
Long. 138 mm.

7270 - Wagon à ridelles à bogies. Long.
146 mm.

7130 - Wagon couvert "Evian". Long.
128 mm.

7172 - Wagon plateau avec charge de bois.
Long. 128 mm. La charge de bois est amovible.

7260 - Wagon "Arbel" à bogies. Long.
137 mm.

7280 - Wagon tombereau à bogies. Long.
146 mm.

7160 - Wagon porte-essieux (essieux amo-
vibles). Long. 128 mm.

7180 - Wagon à ridelles basses. Long. 128 mm.

7262 - Wagon "Arbel" à bogies avec charge
de minerai. Long. 137 mm.

7282 - Wagon tombereau à bogies avec charge
de sable. Long. 146 mm.

7240 - Wagon couvert à bogies. 2 portes ouvrantes. Long. 146 mm.

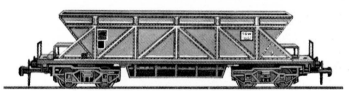

7290 - Wagon houiller à bogies. Long. 187 mm.

282

reviewed. The *Model Railway Constructor* called them 'very steady free running vehicles and although based on French prototypes all three could be used on British 00 layouts for they are quite acceptable as train ferry vehicles'.

In April 1962 the railway station buildings in Acho were reviewed and rather than do a blow-by-blow account of the models which in any event are covered in tabular form at the back of this book I thought the reproduction of a typical catalogue would show the main items which were produced.

One beautiful item was the heurtoir, or rail made buffer No. 6610, as well as the 6650 gantry colour aspect signal and 6950 – passage de voires – the platform sets.

By November and December 1962 the Meccano France Company was taking direct full page advertisements in the *Railway Modeller* and *Model Railway Constructor*. The *Model Railway Constructor* in February 1963 concentrated two whole pages on the new Acho models, including the 'Co-Co' locomotive, type CC65, the colour light signals and new items of rolling stock.

One fascinating piece was the speed reducer device which in the U.K. cost 22s. In operation the resistance did not bring the speed of the locomotive to a particular level, but roughly halved the train's speed from that given by the controller at the time. It was supplied with two one-third length track sections with insulation gaps and a coil of wire so one could adjust the restricted zone as necessary, there was also an override button.

The April 1963 *Meccano Magazine* had three pages covering the latest products from France reproduced here.

They produced twelve locomotives, six with pantographs, three diesels, ranging from a 'Co-Co' to a 0–6–0 shunter, a two coach railcar set, and three steam locomotives – the famous 2–6–2 or, as it is called on the Continent, 1–3–1 Tank locomotive and perhaps the most desirable of all by U.K. requirements, the 0–6–0 American dock saddle tank which came over during the Second World War in real life. There was both the standard SNCF green loco and a simplified all-black version of this without the valve gear.

An early publicity photograph.

Early publicity photographs of Hornby-Acho.

These locomotives, 'switchers', to give them their correct title, were brought over to Europe to work on the devastated railways of the Continent and a few remained behind in Britain on the Southern Region. One of them has fortunately been restored and is now on the Keighley and Worth Valley Railway. The reviewers were full of praise for this new model which did not appear until the Summer of 1969. The drivers were all fully flanged and ran dead true and there was no tendency for the model to waddle along the track as can sometimes happen with short wheel base locomotives. It was complete with working lights and was still available in this country up to 1973. It was the last locomotive brought out by the Hornby-Acho Com-

pany who continued in full production until 1973 although by the time of their last catalogue many items had been deleted.

The system was in no way affected by the collapse of the English Meccano Company and the suspension of manufacturing of the Hornby Dublo system. Indeed, many of the immediate post take-over catalogues, 1964, 1965 and 1966 for Hornby-Acho showed not only their own product range, but also some of the Hornby Dublo locomotives and items of rolling stock as well as some of the Triang models!

The reason for the collapse of the Acho system was referred to even in the very first letter of introduction by Mr. Rio when he stated . . . 'We already have

innumerable competitors, one of whom produces H0 trains at a very low price while another manufacturers in a distinctly higher price range.'

When I visisted the factory in Calais with Royston Carss in 1974, the collapse was put down to the lack of standardisation such as chassis, etc. Each one had been separately designed for its particular locomotive and as inflation and costs increased, particularly in the early 1970s, the system was no longer competitive on the continental market.

Mr. Delfeld, the Works Director, asked Mr. Roger Lasserre, an engineer who had been with the Meccano factory in Calais for some considerable time to show us round and it was a wonderful experience. The stores contained the last remnants of the Hornby-Acho system – half a dozen bakers' trays with just a few odd coaches and models of the CC7121 locomotive which had held the world speed record of 340 kilometres per hour. Mr. Lasserre took me back to his office where he showed me his personal collection of Acho models with the original cut away bodies he had made for the exhibitions and, in keeping with the superb generosity and hospitality of the French people, kindly presented me with the special 'Bo-Bo' locomotive number 8144, not in the usual SNCF green colour, but in a dark matt blue made, I believe, as a trial run for the Netherlands market.

Some of the items which were inaugurated at Binns Road, found their way onto the French market while others were jointly developed or conversely developed in France and marketed in the U.K. I am thinking of such items as the elevated track section which was sold briefly in this country and the barrier railway crossing which was available either in automatic form or for manual operation. Correspondence between the two companies also referred to imitation diesel horns and diesel fueling depots.

I am still looking for some French Acho models which I could never find in this country and in particular would love to have a rake of the wagon Houiller à bogies number 7290 (187 mm long).

So by the end of 1973 the French Hornby-Acho production ceased and I feel certain it will be collected as much as the old Hornby 0 gauge and other tinplate toys.

HORNBY DUBLO TRACK

In the 1920s there was a classic book published by Mr. Ellis Parker Butler entitled *Pigs is Pigs*. It dealt with the unhappy predicament of a railway station clerk who could not ascertain under which tariff to charge guinea pigs and while he kept the two pigs in his office wrote off to his Chief Clerk for a ruling. The subsequent bureaucracy and delay did not allow for the rapid increase in the guinea pig family.

Well – 'pigs is pigs' and to me 'track is track'. The many variations that have been found to date are listed in Alan Ellis's compendium, and so I am going to aim my chapter at the more general aspects by reproducing articles from the *Meccano Magazine* and Hornby Dublo booklets, trying to ensure that you, my reader, have all the basic information to operate and obtain the best from your Hornby Dublo model railway.

The Hornby Railway Company information book recorded:

'Hornby-Dublo track conforms to the usual 16.5 mm gauge for standard 4 mm scale. On Hornby Dublo points the wing rails at the frog allow a flangeway of 1/16th in. The same dimension applies to the check rail on the straight length of points; on the curved length the check rail spacing is 5/64th in. These dimensions ensure satisfactory running of our wheels over our points.'

The initial track had brass running rails, fishplates and centre tags, but the electric version had a steel centre rail. The later type 2 version had plated brass running rails, on a rigid steel tinprinted base.

From its very inception the Meccano Company ran two distinct systems – the clockwork track and the electric track which were basically identical – the former without the centre running rail. The clockwork track looked very realistic indeed because it had a '2-rail' appearance. The whole object of the system was that it should be capable and sturdy enough to be used for a short period and hastily put away when dad came home for his tea. Permanent layouts on base boards were a rarity in those days.

The points were particularly interesting in that all the pre-war issues had a printed sleeper base identical to the track section. Also on the straight section there were large letters 'LH' printed for lefthand or 'RH' for righthand points.

They did have one design failure in that the pre-war points had a very weak cast rail section to the frog which, considering the rails were normally forced and twisted together, broke all too soon. This frog was in a 'Y' configuration, whereas the post-war frogs were a fully webbed diecast unit and much stronger (although there were pre-war modifications to the frog).

On all the post-war points I have examined, the point lever was painted red on the side indicating the turn-off. Reverse the lever 180° and it was just the standard diecast metal colour for the straight rail. However, we go too fast.

The initial curved track was all set to a 15 inch radius and it was not until twelve months after the introduction of the Hornby Dublo, system that the new large radius curves to 17½ inches were introduced. They were all shown in the famous 'New Developments' catalogue, reference 2/1239/20, and it was stated that the use of the new large radius curves, in conjunction with the standard Hornby Dublo 15 inch radius curves, would provide a perfectly symmetrical double track – 'no miniature railway is complete without double track'.

One point from the reference book of the Hornby Railway Company was the fact that to copy the standard 6 ft way between the two tracks in mainline railway practice, one must allow 1¼ inches (32 mm)

Hornby Dublo track data, from original drawing.

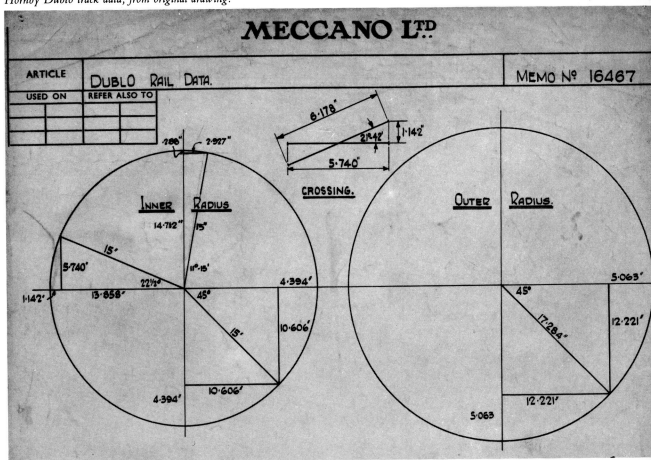

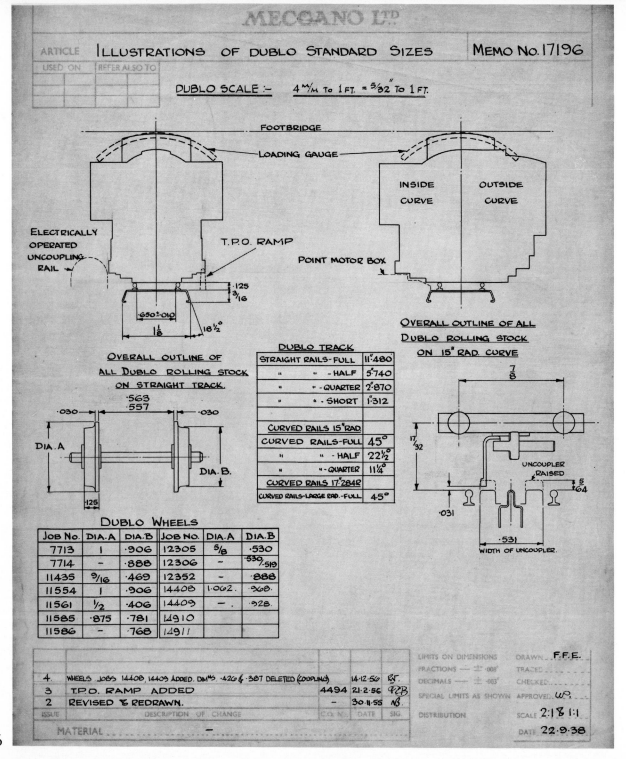

Hornby Dublo standard sizes, from original drawing.

between the bases of the Hornby Dublo track, to be really accurate.

At the same time as the introduction of the large radius track, the electrically operated points, signals and isolating rail appeared.

I and my fellow Hornby Dublo colleagues have never seen any pre-war electrically operated points with tin printed sleepers on the base. They all had the light grey finish of the post-war points and came boxed in pairs. It is interesting to note the box printing codes. The pre-war reference was BW9053–5M (five thousand) dated 11–39, i.e. November 1939, while the first post-war reference I have found is from box code BW7233–49 i.e. March 1949 where the quantity was 80M (eighty thousand). No wonder the pre-war electric points were so rare and there were so many advertisements in the war time *Meccano Magazines* for them. Perhaps the most interesting piece though was the isolating rail.

The write-up in the 'New Developments' catalogue reads . . . 'This is a real triumph in Hornby Dublo railway practice. You can now divide your layout into separate sections that can be made "alive" or "dead" as required. This means that endless fun can be had by controlling two or more trains independently at the same time. All kinds of fascinating shunting operations can be carried out, every movement being made as on real railways.'

After the Second World War, in December 1947 the Hornby Dublo system was reinstated but only complete train sets were available. The 0–6–2 Tank sets were available first and as already mentioned, it was not until the latter part of the next year that the Pacific locomotives came onto the market. Twelve months after the recommencement the December 1948 *Meccano Magazine* reported that individual rails were still not available separately!

It was not until twelve months later, in December 1949, that, to quote: . . . 'One of the most important post-war developments in the Hornby Dublo system has been the introduction of new and greatly improved automatic couplings (by Mr. Pritchard). . . . The special advantage of the new couplings, however, is that they are designed in conjunction with the Hornby Dublo uncoupling rail.' The fun of such operation, even when manually controlled was immense,

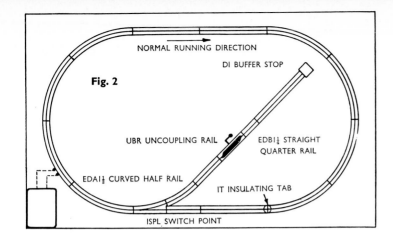

Fig. 2

NORMAL RUNNING DIRECTION

DI BUFFER STOP

UBR UNCOUPLING RAIL

EDBI¼ STRAIGHT QUARTER RAIL

EDAI¼ CURVED HALF RAIL

IT INSULATING TAB

ISPL SWITCH POINT

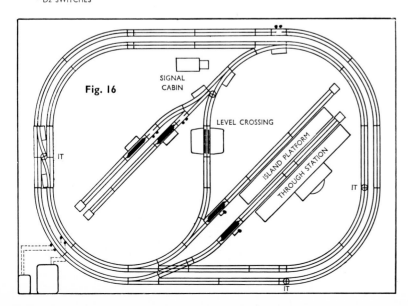

Fig. 15

IT

LOADING GAUGE

IT

THROUGH STATION

ISLAND PLATFORM

WATER CRANE

IT

PUSH BUTTON FOR EUBR

DI SWITCHES

D2 SWITCHES

Fig. 16

SIGNAL CABIN

LEVEL CROSSING

ISLAND PLATFORM

THROUGH STATION

IT

IT

IT

Suggested 3-rail layout from Meccano Layouts Book reference 16/159/50M.

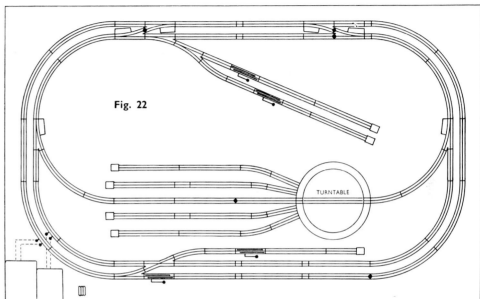

Fig. 22

TURNTABLE

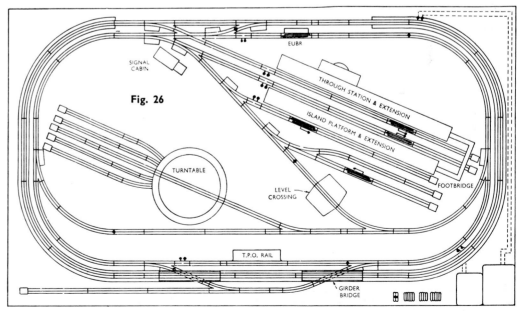

Fig. 26

EUBR

SIGNAL CABIN

THROUGH STATION & EXTENSION

ISLAND PLATFORM & EXTENSION

FOOTBRIDGE

TURNTABLE

LEVEL CROSSING

T.P.O. RAIL

GIRDER BRIDGE

287

but really it needed the rails screwed to a base board. Later reports talk about number 3 roundhead screws by ½ inch long as being the most suitable.

It was not until October 1954 that the electrically operated uncoupling rail was introduced.

The supply situation greatly eased in 1950 and there was the new rail layout suggestion booklet together with the introduction and reintroduction of such items as the water crane, the buffer stops, signals, the footbridge, in September the new mainline aluminium diecast station and island platform etc.

One item which had a lot of attention and which was discussed in the first chapter, was the radio suppression in Hornby Dublo trains and the new EDBT1 rail was introduced with a suppressor in March 1950, although the suppressor itself had been deleted by 1952, EDBT1 still continued in production until mid-1955.

There was no addition in 1951, just advice on layouts and various running schemes terminating with an advertisement on the back page of the December 1951 *Meccano Magazine* stating replace-ments and spares were not easily available and all materials would be needed for making *new* sets for other boys! There was, however, a write-up on the buffer stop which had most definitely been in production pre-war and had been drawn on 10th January 1938. They fitted very neatly to the straight track and had two hook wires which fitted into slots provided at one end of the EDB1 straight rail and EDB1 half straight half rail. It was emphasised that buffers should always be put onto the straight rails as if they were put onto curved rails the buffers of the vehicles running on them would not meet the buffer stop squarely and a derailment might result. For this reason Hornby Dublo curved rails have no slots for the attachment of the spring wires of the buffer stop.

The February 1952 *Meccano Magazine* had a fascinating article on one of my favourite items, the little insulating tabs. The isolating rail was a very useful introduction but what happens if we want to join the two main tracks by means of points forming a crossover? The use of the isolating rail would set the two

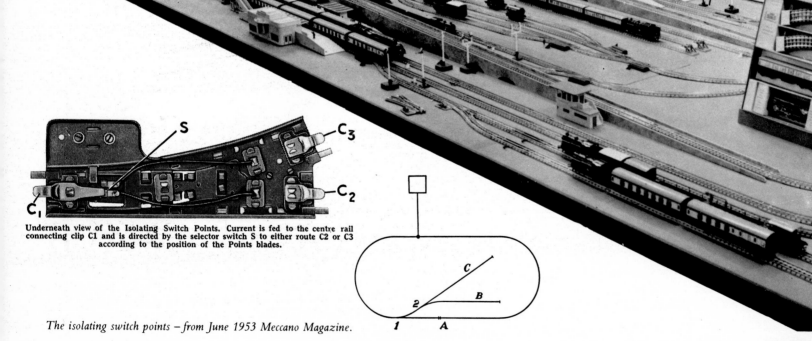

Underneath view of the Isolating Switch Points. Current is fed to the centre rail connecting clip C1 and is directed by the selector switch S to either route C2 or C3 according to the position of the Points blades.

The isolating switch points – from June 1953 Meccano Magazine.

1953 British Industries Fair Exhibition layout.

tracks further apart than the standard Hornby Dublo double track distance and this was the reason for the introduction of the insulating tab. It just slipped in between the centre rail clips and so made the necessary electrical break.

By September 1952, the electrically operated points reappeared and the following month, October, the railer – a very easy method for ensuring the locomotive and rolling stock, particularly the multi-wheeled variety, could be fed onto the track. For some reason it was soon deleted, as I have a dealers' announcement leaflet dated 25th October 1955 mentioning its reintroduction! A shortage of metal perhaps? – I have no idea. The following month, in November the electrically operated signals returned and in the January 1953 *Meccano Magazine*, there was an excellent article on combined operations.

In June 1953 the isolating switch points arrived and made Hornby Dublo railway working simple, for when the points lever was moved to set the road for the train it also directed the current to the route on which the train was to go.

It was not until October 1953 that the reintroduction of the EDA2 large radius curves appeared, to be followed in the next month by the level crossing we have already mentioned.

In May 1954 the diamond crossings, left and right hand appeared. They had been shown earlier in a catalogue marked as 'available later', but only at this time were supplies coming onto the market. Articles on crossings, sidings and loops followed and in October came the advertisement (marked as new) for them together with the electrically operated uncoupling rail and switch we have already mentioned and indeed the EDBX half straight rail with roadway to go with the level crossing unit which had been introduced twelve months earlier.

The 3-rail track programme was basically complete and in 1955 and 1956 there were many excellent articles on the correct operation of the various rail accessories.

It was in 1957 that the last two items of new railway track accessories appeared. The first, in January was the wonderful turntable accessory. The need

Mr. Roland Hornby (right) at the opening of the 1953 British Industries Fair.

for a turntable, or at least a method of turning round the locomotives on the track (picking them up by hand I think is cheating!) had long been recognised and even back in 1947 there was an article on a triangular Hornby Dublo track formation, although this was simplified in a November 1949 *Meccano Magazine* article.

In the *Meccano Magazine* for January 1955, there was an article about Mr. M. A. Houghton and his son Peter of Edgware, Middlesex, who had made their own turntable unit to their base board system with a small electric motor fitted beneath it, the gear train used for transmission being salvaged from an old clock. The article is headed 'Why not a Turntable?' – why not indeed, and some eight months later, on 11th August 1955, the drawing was commenced at Binns Road. The D1 turntable was always manually operated and had four tracks coming off it which necessitated the inclusion of a curved quarter rail EDA1 ¼. These little rails are very hard to find today. No switches or other devices were needed with the turntable and each of the outlet tracks was electrified when the turntable was correctly aligned with it, the other track outlets then being dead. To ensure a correct track alignment, there was a little spring-mounted locking tab which fitted into slots cut into the circular base of the turntable itself. Despite taking up a lot of space it was truly a first class accessory and it was a pity there were not cast aluminium engine sheds in the building accessories to go with it, although we only had to wait a couple of years until the polystyrene engine sheds appeared.

There had been a lot of discussion at Binns Road with the New Products Committee on whether they should bring out an electrically operated turntable, or indeed, a 2-rail turntable and design projects were undertaken, but never came to fruition.

The rival Marklin system has long had an electrically operated turntable and there is a photograph of this in the September 1956 *Meccano Magazine*. The reason the Meccano Company did not emulate this item was due to the high production costs and this has been borne out by the Marklin accessory part number 7186 which, although still available today, costs some £57. Did you know that Hornby Dublo track will mate with the Marklin track? It is a perfect fit although the Marklin track is higher and one does need small

timber packing ramps or the equivalent initially to bring the rail up to the level or alternatively sink the turntable about 7 mm lower.

Another coincidence is that the original small electrical contact spades on the centre rail were of the wider square pattern on both the turntable and mail operating set and were once more identical to that of the Marklin turntable. This was obviously to improve the electrical contact.

If you have a turntable on your model railway which is copying various points of the famous Settle and Carlisle line, you should ensure that you build a palisade around it because there is a wonderful story in

Remote control – linking electrically operated points and signals from the October 1955 Meccano Magazine.

Extract from the January 1955 Meccano Magazine.

The Hornby-Dublo "Duchess of Atholl" being worked round the triangular junction described on this page. Its Coaches are standing clear of the main line Points.

'Picking up your locomotive to turn it is cheating!' extract from the November 1949 Meccano Magazine.

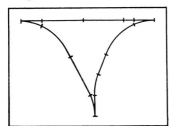

Rails required: 2 EDA1 Curved Rails, 1 EDA1½ Curved Half Rail, 3 EDB1 Straight Rails, 1 EDB1½ Straight Half Rail, 1 EDB1¼ Straight Quarter Rail, 1 EDPR Points (R.H.), 2 EDPL Points (L.H.).

"Duchess of Montrose" on the Turntable. The spring loaded locking device on the edge of the Turntable base is prominent in the foreground.

'The Turntable' – from the January 1957 Meccano Magazine.

the March 1946 *Meccano Magazine* referring to an occasion, even then many years earlier, when an engine was being turned at Garsdale Station. In a bleak and lonely spot such as this it was not surprising that during a gale the wind reaches a very high velocity and it blew so much that the engine acted as a sail and the turntable went round and round and round, much to the consternation of the railway staff. It was to prevent a recurrence of this that the palisade was built.

It was in March 1957 that the new TPO mail train set was announced, which was the same length as a full straight rail with its base for the little hut and mail bag apparatus. If you had a spare or damaged rail unit it was a simple matter to remove the accessories and just bolt into place the body of a D13 suburban coach and you had a little rest room for your railway staff!

The Meccano Company had massive stocks of 3-rail track, but with the introduction of 2-rail the market waned. In November 1964, Beatties were announcing wonderful reductions of factory-fresh new stock which they were selling at lower than the average secondhand price. Their October 1965 advertisement stated that they had purchased over 15,000 straight rails and 100,000 other pieces of 3-rail track to get a keen price and were passing on their 'good buy' to their customers, although much still remained.

From original artwork.

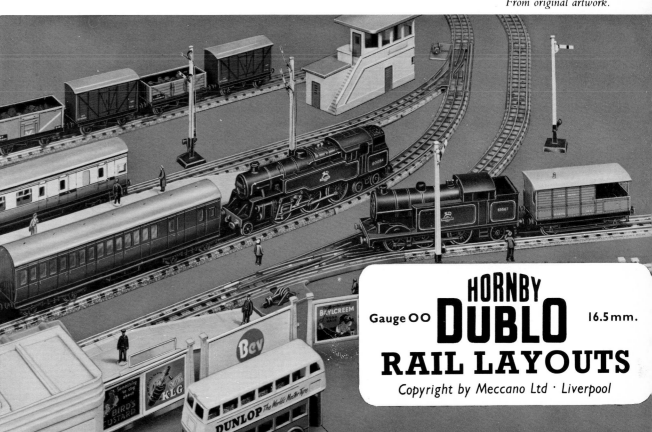

HORNBY DUBLO RAIL LAYOUTS

Gauge OO   16.5mm.

Copyright by Meccano Ltd · Liverpool

291

3-rail track to many has a particular appeal and is still collected today with more than a little nostalgia as boys of the 1940s and 1950s now have sons of a train age and up they go into their loft to retrieve their old train set and seeing secondhand track in model train shops or secondhand shops, start adding one or two pieces to it thus starting the model railway cycle again.

I have purposely excluded any real reference to the Hornby Dublo power controllers and transformers. At their introduction they were capable of doing the task assigned to them and by the middle 1950s (the A2 controller appeared in October 1956), were supreme in the model railway world. I do however warn any of my readers who continue to use the early black and pre-war blue transformers and controllers that there is a high risk involved, the reason for this being that the quality of rubber etc., used in the insulation of wires on all the ones I have seen, has fatigued to such a dangerous extent that I would think that they are now totally unsafe for operation.

LIST OF COMPONENTS.

DESIGN N°	SYMBOL	DESCRIPTION	N° OFF	DESIGN N°	SYMBOL	DESCRIPTION	N° OFF
EDB1		STRAIGHT RAILS - FULL	18	D1		THROUGH STATION	1
EDB1½		" - HALF	19	D1		" " EXTENSION	1
EDB1¼		" - QUARTER	12	D1		ISLAND PLATFORM	1
EDBS		" - SHORT	13	D1		" " EXTENSION	2
EDBX½		" - HALF (for LEVEL CROSSING)	1	D1		" " RAMPS (for EXTENSION)	2
EDA		CURVED RAILS - FULL	8	D1		SIGNAL CABIN	1
EDA1½		" - HALF	4	D1		FOOTBRIDGE	1
EDA1¼		" - QUARTER	3	D1		TURNTABLE	1
EDAT1		" - TERMINAL	1	D1		TPO RAIL	1
EDA2		" - LARGE RADIUS	7	D1		GIRDER BRIDGE	2
EDAT2		" " TERMINAL	1	D1		LEVEL CROSSING	1
EUBR		UNCOUPLING RAIL - ELECTRICALLY OPER?	7	D1	B	SIGNALS - S/A MANUALLY OPERATED	2
UBR		" - MANUALLY OPERATED	3	D2	F	" - D/A "	1
IBR		" ATING "	3	ED1	B	" - S/A ELECT? "	1
ISPR		" ATING SWITCH POINTS - R.H	4	ED2	C	" - D/A ELECT? "	1
ISPL		" " " - L.H	2	ED3	D	" - JUNCTION. ELECT? "	2
EODPL		ELECTRICALLY OPERATED POINTS - L.H	5	D1	A	BUFFER STOPS	9
EODCR		DIAMOND CROSSING - R.H	1	D1	G	LOADING GAUGE	2
IT	•	INSULATING TABS	7	D1	H	WATER CRANE	1
				A3		POWER CONTROL UNIT	1
				A2		" " "	1
				D1		POINTS & SIGNAL SWITCHES	4
				D2		ISOLATING SWITCHES	3
						PUSH BUTTON for T.P.O.	1
						" " for EUBR	1
					O	COLOURED BUTTONS	40

Suggested 3-rail layout from Meccano Layouts book 16/159/50 m.

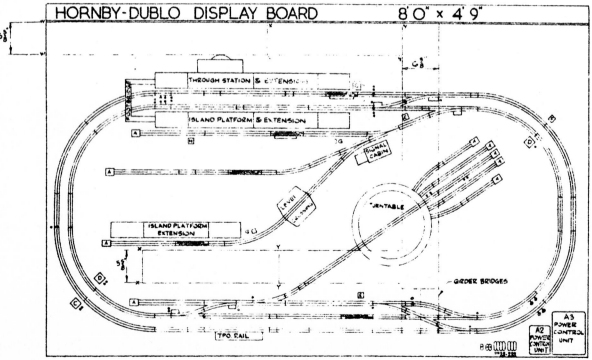

HORNBY-DUBLO DISPLAY BOARD   8 0" × 4 9"

THROUGH STATION & EXTENSION

ISLAND PLATFORM & EXTENSION

SIGNAL CABIN

LEVEL CROSSING

ISLAND PLATFORM EXTENSION

TURNTABLE

GIRDER BRIDGES

TPO RAIL

A2 POWER CONTROL UNIT

A3 POWER CONTROL UNIT

DIMENSIONS TO UNDERSIDE ROADWAY (FROM BASEBOARD)
ROADWAY RISING FROM 0" TO 2⅝" BETWEEN POINTS XX & YY
" HORIZONTAL AT 0" " " WW & XX
" " " 2⅝" FOR REMAINDER.

NEW
- 2-RAIL TRACK
- TRAIN SETS
- LOCOMOTIVES
- ACCESSORIES

Set 2006
Set 2007
Set 2019
Set 2030
Set 2015
Set 2025
Set 2020
Set 2022

*A separate folder is available giving particulars of the range of Hornby-Dublo 3-rail Train Sets and Accessories. Ask your dealer for a copy.

THE 2-RAIL TRACK

The Hornby Dublo designers decided that they must go to 2-rail operation. Their aim was quite simple – to have the best in the business – and they did! Even in retrospect in February 1965 when the *Model Railway Constructor* undertook a survey of all the proprietary track on the market at that time, reviewing ten different products, they stated that the Hornby Track was . . . 'the most realistic of the "big three" proprietary tracks, it was sturdy and reliable in operation and will accept most wheel standards – although the flanges of the coarser Tri-ang wheels tended to run on the chairs!'

The 2-rail track was introduced with the 1959 Hornby Dublo modernisation scheme and incorporated solid drawn nickel silver rails and individual moulded sleepers and, to quote their September advertisement, was . . . 'already accepted as the finest model railway track ever produced.'

The 2-rail hand-operated isolating switch point and double isolating rail appeared in December 1959 and the *Model Railway News* stated that the three terminals at the toe end of the point were to be used for wiring colour light signals for switching, in conjunction with the point and also for reverse loop operation. The *Constructors* 'Review' reported . . . 'The cast metal frog unit changes polarity through the switching of the point blades which are again a single electrical unit. Thus current *must* always be fed from the toe of the point and prevent it from reaching a point from its heel. For this purpose double isolating rails are used. Readers unfamiliar with this type of 2-rail wiring should read the instruction sheet packed with the points very carefully. . . . We think this is a pity as it means, in many cases, that compensating fractional track units have to be brought to "balance" the points in layouts. We also think the term "isolating point" under which they are marketed could perhaps be misleading. As we have explained these points are not self-isolating and isolating rails must be used to stop current reaching the point from the heel.'

The points worked well and locomotives and rolling stock ran through them very smoothly, but herein

From Meccano leaflet 13/1059/25.

293

lay the crux of the matter. The very complicated system that had been introduced meant the Meccano Company and its dealers were inundated with letters asking how the system worked. However one useful feature was that the switch apparatus was now put on the straight rail side of the point as opposed to 3-rail point units which always had the switch housing, particularly on the electric points, on the curved i.e. inside edge. This prevented points from being grouped together one after another to realistically recreate sidings in goods yards and Mr. Jack Wheeler who we mentioned in the first chapter, strongly suggested to Meccano that they be transferred, as they are now, to the straight side. The housing of the switch unit had also been set very low but even so it caused trouble with the travelling post office coach operating contact lever which just missed – by $\frac{1}{64}$th inch – the housing of the 3-rail electric points motors.

By May 1960, the *Meccano Magazine* reported that 2-rail track was now fully available and in the July issue an editorial assured readers that 3-rail track would continue to be supplied as long as demand lasts. The manual uncoupling rail, 2745, was available from the outset, and by May 1960 the electrical uncoupling rail No. 2746 was also ready. There seemed to be a moulding fault because many would not work. However with the use of a file and screwdriver they could be repaired though this did make for bad customer relations.

The buffer stop was immediately available in 2-rail No. 2450 and had an illuminated brother (No. 2451) though only in the 2-rail version.

The February 1961 *Model Railway Constructor* highlighted the electrically operated points which had just become available, and were similar to the hand operated models, once more requiring the isolating rails.

In September the 2-rail polystyrene railer, number 2900, appeared . . .

The following month, in October 1961, a new series of articles appeared in the *Meccano Magazine* by Linesman, in point of fact our friend Mr. Jack Gahan. In an effort to try and overcome the immense difficulty their enthusiasts were having with the operation of the new 2-rail system and these appeared almost monthy right up until the end of 1964.

Advertisement from the September 1959 Meccano Magazine.

Jack wrote to me on 16th October 1972 . . . 'All the illustrations that accompanied the monthly Hornby and Hornby Dublo articles in the *Meccano Magazine* were of layouts and scenes I myself laid out, while Mr. L. Norman usually wrote the text. We had a good job! It is a pity it all came to an end – going to work at Meccano was no hardship and I wish I could live it once again.'

However, much discussion was going on in the Hornby Dublo Development Room and at a meeting on 28th September, ways of reducing the cost of the 2-rail track by using roll formed brass rail (tinned) as well as plans to investigate the track of their competitors were on the agenda. The following month the minutes of the New Products Committee, on 26th October stated . . . 'It was suggested that perhaps the existing 2-rail point might be modified only to the extent of altering the switching arrangement, which is the subject of patent infringement, and it was agreed to investigate this possibility.'

Therein perhaps lies a tale. In December the 2-rail 2460 single track level crossing appeared and as we have already mentioned, many advertisements showing it in a dark brown base moulding. Despite exhaustive enquiries I have still not been able to confirm whether, in fact, this was ever issued though, I, in my mind, still feel convinced I have seen one.

The January 1962 *Meccano Magazine* announced the 2734 right hand 2-rail diamond crossing and the 2735 left hand item. The *Model Railway Constructor* reported in their April issue . . . 'The crossing is mounted on a plastic base in which sleepers and ballast are formed from a solid moulding. Solid drawn nickel silver rails are isolated by short pieces of plastic "rail" at the intersections of the two tracks. The rails in the diamond of the crossing are plated diecastings which,

From original artwork.

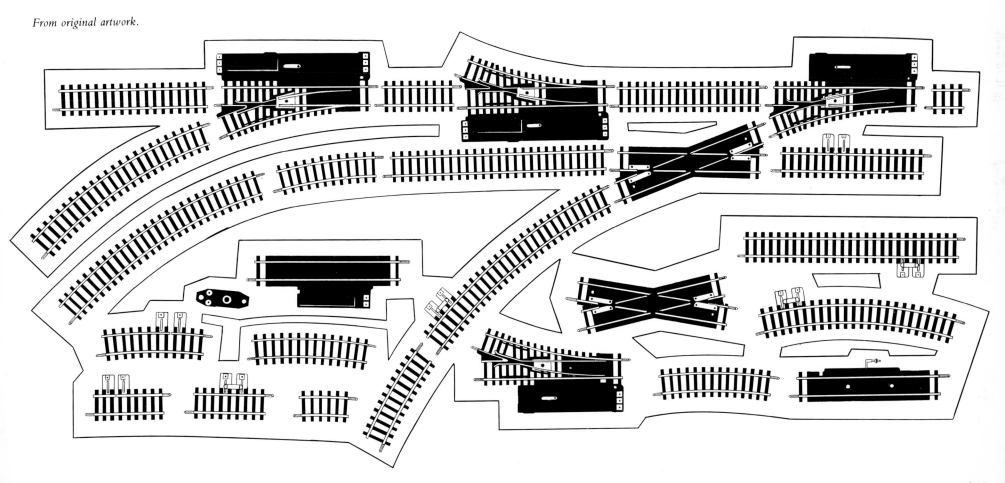

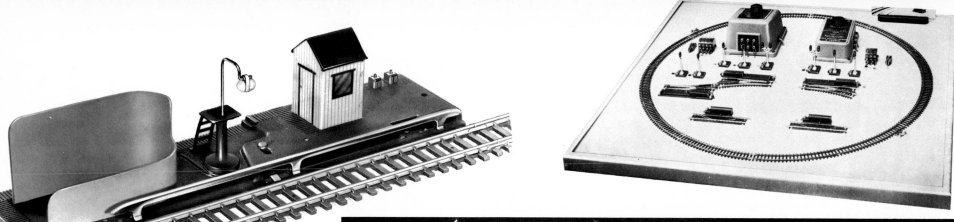

The 2-rail TPO set. From original artwork.

Trade display of the new track packs January 1964.

to avoid 2-rail isolation problems, are not extended alongside the frog nose to form wing rails. The first samples we received suffered because the nickel silver, plastic and diecast rails were not in true vertical alignment giving a bumpy ride with occasional derailments but we understand from Meccano Limited that the manufacturing fault which caused this has been corrected. There was no trace of the trouble in a later sample submitted which we subjected to intensive tests and found to be quite satisfactory.'

In April 1963 the new starter set was announced with the 0–4–0 locomotive and in their design concept for this, the Hornby Dublo engineers felt that the existing 2-rail track was not strong enough as this set was planned for the younger and more heavy-handed enthusiast. They brought out a new track, number 2709, curved rails only, which employed the same sleeper spacer and integral rail fastenings as the existing 2-rail track, but the intermediate web was much thicker detracting somewhat from the overall appearance. The rail section was identical to the earlier type but was drawn from treated steel and not the more expensive nickel-silver. It was only ever intended for this starter set.

Dealer display layouts, from Meccano Catalogue reference 8/162/8.

The double junction from the December 1964 Meccano Magazine.

Extract from the August 1963 Model Railway Constructor.

The Hornby Railway Company Secretary reports in the same issue that they were introducing a new design point to simplify the system and ease the wiring difficulties. These were to be known as 'Simplec' points and their principal characteristic was the inclusion of an insulated frog – that is the 'V' shaped section where the two rails intersect. The trade bulletin to Meccano dealers covering April, May and June 1963, stated these new points were ideal for the boy who wants to increase his layout by adding a siding . . . 'These new points – as their name implies are simplicity itself. They are self isolating, so there is no need for any added complications such as double isolating rails etc., when you wish to include them on your layout. Simple to include, simple to operate – the Simplec point has arrived!'

They did, however, go on to state that . . . 'For the advanced model enthusiast, the current Hornby Dublo points will have great appeal of course, having perhaps a more technical flavour than the new, easily understood Simplec points.' . . . I wonder?

The same bulletin also mentioned the Hornby Dublo track packs and the Hornby Dublo elevated track, but more of these in a moment.

By August, the electrically operated Simplec points appeared. Yet again I would refer the reader to an excellent article in the *Model Railway Constructor* magazine. So excellent in fact, that it was reproduced in the October 1963 *Meccano Magazine* by courtesy of the editor of the *Model Railway Constructor*.

Another item to make Hornby Dublo 'Easier and easier', was the introduction of the Hornby Dublo terminal connector with suppressor. The purchase of

HORNBY-DUBLO   **OO**
Hand-operated "Simplec"
Points   **7s 9d**

ONE of the snags in two-rail electrification occurs at points and crossings when current at one polarity in one rail must be led across current of the opposing polarity in the other rail, without causing a short circuit. The two most common methods of overcoming this difficulty are either by having a "dead" frog or by bonding the point blade-wing rail-frog assembly together as one electrical unit. Both methods have their advantages and disadvantages. The "dead" frog arrangement is simpler but the conducting rail surface from which the wheels pick up current is not continuous, and adjoining rails must be perfectly clean to ensure adequate current collection, otherwise the locomotive may be jerky or even stop on the point. In the "dead" frog method the two point blades are electrically isolated from each other, and are permanently connected to the continuation rail beyond the frog. With a "live" frog, both point blades are electrically connected to each other, but not to the wing rails so that the polarity of the blades-stock rail-frog assembly depends on which way the point blades are set and, in consequence, which of the stock rails they are touching However, this method needs an insulated rail joint beyond the frog on a continuous track to prevent a short circuit when the points are reversed towards a track deviating from the main line. It is the second method that has been used by Meccano Limited since they introduced the two-rail system to the Hornby-Dublo range. To obtain the necessary insulation near point frogs special isolating rail-sections have been needed, and in some cases double isolating rails as well. To overcome the complications of this method, Meccano Limited have now introduced points working on the "dead" frog principle, which do not normally need additional isolating rails, although the latter can be used to provide automatic stop sections if points are not set correctly. The new Hornby points, which are of the usual 15in radius, are mounted on a plastic sleeper base which incorporates frog and check rail mouldings. The back-to-back measurements of the check to wing rails is 12.5mm and the check rail to frog nose nominally 15mm. We found that scale wheels passed through the points with but a slight bump. The point blades themselves are cast to a modified rail section. An improvement over the earlier types of Hornby-Dublo points is the compact operating mechanism.

We welcome these points, for they simplify some of the complications of two-rail electrification, and with the model railway hobby daily becoming more complicated, any move towards simplification is desirable.

Trade display at the Grosvenor Hotel, January 1961.

this handy item enabled the owner to change an ordinary rail into a terminal rail so that he could connect the power supply to any convenient part of the track. It was fitted with a suppressor to counter any interference to radio and television sets.

To promote their new Simplec points, the Hornby Dublo Company also introduced a set of track packs which contained extra rails and points and provided an easy way to track extensions and more interesting layouts. They were warmly received by the trade and model railway owner alike. However it was regrettably too late. The damage the complicated 2-rail system had done to the Hornby Dublo name was a further nail in their coffin, forcing many customers to either return their 2-rail sets, or having heard of the difficulties their friends were having, choosing a simpler system such as the one made by Triang.

ELEVATED TRACK

On 25th June 1962, Mr. Norman received a memo to the effect that the Meccano Company had been sent drawings from Meccano France of proposed ramps for elevating their Dublo track and that Binns Road had examined the possibility of using them for their 2-rail and 3-rail systems. The report reads . . . 'The basic elements consist of straight and curved ramps which match the 2-rail system, both in the straight track length and the curvature and angles of the curved rails, both inner and outer radii. There is a straight access ramp followed by a series of straight and curved ramps raised on piers. The piers are raised in successive increments of 9 mm (23/64 inches). The piers are in three sizes of one (23/64 inches), three (in $1\frac{1}{16}$th inches) and five (in $2\frac{7}{8}$ inches) increments of height and they will all stand upon a base which may be screwed down. The sides of the ramps are made from a pliable extruded plastic which may be slid on and off the edge of the ramps to allow for modifications in the layout. There is another pliable plastic extrusion which joins two ramps together down the centre to make a double rail ramp.

'Both these extruded sections will be made in long lengths and cut to the necessary size, and their pliability makes them adaptable to curved sections.' Mr.

Bonneau reported that a plastic part representing a metallic bridge was under consideration and this would be designed to replace the straight ramp sides and could be assembled by the customer at any time and in any quantity. This would probably be cheaper than the existing girder bridge.

'The length of the ramp and the height of the piers ensures a rise of 1:25 and by adding parts, an indefinite height or length may be achieved according to the space available. Also the length may be continued at any desired height by using a series of equal piers. This also ensures that the ramps will clear any present or future catenary system and a scheme has been devised for adding catenary posts to the ramps at a later date. Tests made by the performance of 2-rail locomotives hauling corridor coaches up a ramp of 1 in 25 on large radius rails produced the following result:

0–6–0 Tank	2 coaches
0–6–2 Tank	
2–6–4 Tank	
Diesel Shunter	3 coaches
Castle Locomotive	
West Country Class	
Bo-Bo Diesel	4 coaches
2–8–0 Freight	
City Class locomotive	5 coaches
Deltic & Co-Bo	12 coaches.

'The Deltic and Co-Bo locomotives could have hauled more coaches if the track had been longer. Wooden models of the ramps were made and erected on a layout similar to the one illustrated on the back page of the 3-rail layout booklet. This layout tests the effect of overhang on locomotives and rolling stock when passing the ramps on the inner rail (which is not a ramp). Under these conditions it was found that the "City" Class locomotive touched the ramp as it passed, and that the handle of the Breakdown Crane interfered with its passage. Neither of these interferences occurred on double track ramps. It was also found that the operating contact projecting from the side of the T.P.O. coach interfered with the inside wall of the ramp.

'The piers and ramps are connected by push fit, and the rails lie in a trough moulded in the ramps. For normal use this is sufficient, but for transportation of a layout on a board, or if the board stands on one edge when not in use, then the parts would need to be secured together with plastic cement, and the sleepers secured to the ramps in the same way.

'The ramp system will accommodate 3-rail layouts. Two rail curves are 12 to a circle, and 3-rail are 8 to a circle. Consequently, with 3-rail curves the rail joints do not correspond to the ramp joints, but this is not essential. If the user requires the ramps to follow a serpentine path then he may find some limitations because the ramp and rail joints correspond only at intervals of 90°. The 3-rail full straight rail is too long for the straight and access ramps, but a straight half rail plus a straight quarter rail would be the correct length. Three rail bases will fit into the trough in the ramps, but there is no provision for securing the rail. This could be done by the user drilling the ramps and using screws.

'The general conclusion drawn from this investigation is that the ramps are suitable for use with our 2 and 3-rail systems, with slight reservations regarding the "City" Class locomotive, the Breakdown Crane and the T.P.O. Van.'

I have found many of these items sufficient to build a flyover unit but they did not seem to fit together very easily and although definitely marketed, could not have been a very popular item in this country. (All the parts were available separately.) Considerable fears had been expressed at the time of its proposed introduction into the U.K. because the famous Kibri Company were selling a similar system at a cost of £2 and Triang at £3. 3s. 10d. whereas the Meccano France item was approximately £5.

And so concluded the 2-rail system and although today the purest collector insists that Hornby Dublo Model Railways should always run on Hornby Dublo track, the shortly to be introduced Tri-ang super six track and the other proprietary model railway tracks particularly the flexible tracks, were much sought after, and quickly overtook the Dublo 2-rail sales which virtually went into oblivion. There is still an exceptionally healthy demand for secondhand Dublo 3-rail track but rarely is Dublo 2-rail track sought.

Meccano France exhibition display.

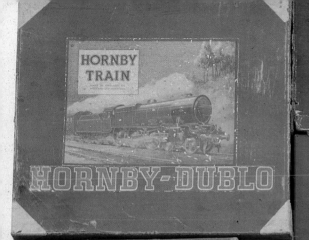

HORNBY TRAIN

HORNBY-DUBLO

HORNBY-DUBLO TRAIN

THE PERFECT MINIATURE RAILWAY

HORNBY DUBLO ELECTRIC TRAIN

MADE AND GUARANTEED BY MECCANO LTD.

HORNBY DUBLO ELECTRIC TRAIN

Made in England by MECCANO LIMITED

HORNBY DUBLO ELECTRIC TRAIN

Made and Guaranteed by Meccano Ltd

The Luxury Set of the Year

Hornby

DUBLO
2 RAIL ELECTRIC TRAIN

REALISTIC
RELIABLE
GUARANTEED

MADE IN ENGLAND BY MECCANO LTD

Set 2035 'Bournemouth Belle' Pullman Train S.R.

HORNBY MOTORS for POWER

Hornby Dublo Train Sets

It is little wonder that the pre-war boxed Hornby Dublo sets command so much in the collector's market. To my mind any boxed set is a gem and one can well imagine, indeed many of us well remember, the thrill on a birthday or at Christmas as unpacking one of the attractive boxes containing a Hornby Dublo train set.

The sets were complete and ready to run, with sufficient track, controller and full instructions right the way down to the little spanner and oil bottle.

If one had been given a catalogue to go with the set, it was indeed unfortunate for the parents, grandparents, uncles, etc., as the young enthusiast pored over it looking for items to add to the collection with a . . . 'Please Dad, can I have one of those next?'

Before the Second World War both electric and clockwork train sets were available.

The EDP1 Hornby Dublo Electric Passenger Train included the LNER EDL1 Streamlined six coupled locomotive 'Sir Nigel Gresley' with automatic reversing, a D1 tender and D2 two coach articulated unit, a Dublo controller No. 1, seven EDA curved rails, one EDAT curved terminal rail, and two EDB straight rails.

The initial catalogue 7/938/185 put the price at 70s. – a princely sum in those days.

The clockwork DP1 train set naturally had the clockwork DL1 locomotive, the articulated coach unit, 8 DA curved rails and two DB straight rails and a key. It sold for 39s. 6d.

There was an alternative electric train set, EDPA1, which had the No. 1A controller for use with the 12 volt accumulators. This price was considerably cheaper at 61s. 6d.

The faithful 0–6–2 Tank locomotive was available in four liveries LMS, LNER, GWR and SR as in the electric version set, EDG7. It contained the EDL7 six coupled Tank locomotive, with automatic reversing, the open goods wagon D1, the goods van D1, the goods brake van D1, the Dublo controller No. 1, seven EDA curved rails, one EDAT curved terminal rail and two EDB straight rails. Its original sales price was 55s. Alternatively, the EDGA set with the number 1A controller for use with accumulators only, cost 46s. 6d.

The DG7 clockwork Tank Goods set was once more basically identical, but with the clockwork locomotive, eight DA curved rails and 2 DB straight rails and a key. Its price was 27s. 6d.

The 'Duchess of Atholl' locomotive did not appear before the war, but was frequently advertised in both trade bulletins and sales catalogues in the latter half of 1939, as available in Autumn.

EDP2 was to be the full LMS train set with No. 1 controller at 92s. 6d. while EDPA2 with the number 1A controller would cost 84s. The EDLT2 (it gets a little complicated doesn't it?) was to be the 'Duchess of Atholl' locomotive packed together with its tender and its original retail price was to be 45s., while the EDL2 locomotive on its own was 39s. The LMS D3 coaches were originally planned to be 6s. 9d. each as opposed to a standard LNER coach which was only 3s. 6d. and was even more expensive than the beautiful articulated coach set which was selling at this time for 6s. 6d.

The pre-war sets were shown to superb effect in the last pre-war *Hornby Book of Trains* 1939–1940 code 7/739/100 (see Volume 1 *Hornby Companion Series*). They were also shown on the front cover of the last individual pre-war Hornby Dublo catalogue, code 12/1039/70 where a 'Duchess of Atholl' is seen accelerating away out of the terminus station and a further locomotive is depicted, its smoke box just protruding from the engine shed. My catalogue has a little slip printed, attached to the front which states . . .

'All prices in this catalogue are now obsolete. Current prices will be found in the accompanying list issued on 21st October 1940. All prices are subject to alteration without notice.'

Despite this catalogue showing the 'Duchess of Atholl' locomotive on its front cover, on opening it up there is no reference to it whatsoever.

Interestingly enough a dealers' copy of an order sheet, lists a clockwork DP2 ('Duchess') passenger train set in addition to set DP1. This is the only reference that they were going to produce a clockwork 'Duchess' with the engine being coded DL2.

Price lists continued to be put out during the initial war years in January 1940, in August 1940, and a special on 21st October 1940 on which date purchase tax came into operation.

The EDP1 LNER train set previously 57s. 6d. cost, with tax, 94s., there were similar increases on the other sets.

The final price list I have is dated 1st November 1941 showing the EDP1 train set at 115s. and, with tax added 140s. In none of these price lists was the 'Duchess of Atholl' locomotive shown or the elusive footbridge.

POST-WAR, PRENATIONALISATION SETS

As we have read, the first advertisement announcing that Hornby Dublo trains were again available after the war was in December 1947.

However these were only the EDG7 Tank goods train sets, in the four liveries, and the price, including the increased purchase tax from that date, was 148s. 9d. Very few must have been available before Christmas and although advertisements claimed that the streamlined 'Sir Nigel Gresley' locomotive and 'The Duchess of Atholl' train sets were to be available in the new year, it was not in fact well into that year, that these sets became available. Indeed, the 'Duchess of Atholl' was not available until the latter part of the year, around October/November, when sets began trickling through onto the English market. The Meccano products catalogue dated 1st February 1950 shows the EDG7 0-6-2 Tank goods set costing 142s. 6d. while the EDP1 'Sir Nigel Gresley' passenger train set was 162s. 6d. and EDP2 'Duchess of Atholl' passenger train set was 175s.

By October that year EDG7 was 152s. 6d. the EDP1 was 172s. 6d. and the EDP2 was 185s. In the March 1951 price list these had increased to 162s. 2d. for the EDG7, EDP1 was 181s. and the EDP2 set was 195s. 4d. but they did remain the same in the October 1951 price sheet.

From old notes of the Hornby Railway Company it appears sets number 1–6 were reserved for passenger trains and the goods sets started at number 7. However, in an announcement to the trade in a bulletin dated 25th February 1953 – an almost identical bulletin being released to the general public on April 1953, the numbers were increased by 10 and it was stated that the 0–6–2 Tank set was to become EDG17 in its gloss BR livery and was to have a D1 ventilated van, the Royal Daylight tank wagon with the Esso badge above it, the standard five plank BR goods wagon and the Eastern region brake van. It was stated that it was hoped that this set would be ready for May. There was a dramatic reduction to the prices as these sets, without a controller, were retailing for 107s. 6d.

The EDP1 train set became the EDP11 with the streamlined 'Silver King' locomotive and the Eastern Region D11 coaches in plum and spilt milk livery. This set was to be ready during April 1953 at a cost, excluding controller of 127s. 6d.

Finally we had the new EDP12 train set which included the EDL12 'Duchess of Montrose' locomotive and the D12 BR mainline corridor coaches, again in plum and spilt milk livery. This set, without controller, cost 140s. (including purchase tax).

A further dealers' leaflet dated 29th May 1953 and received by one particular shop on 9th June, 1953 stated that the EDG17 Tank goods train set was ready.

In the first colour catalogue released after the Second World War dated 1953/54 code 7/1053/250, there was a further massive reduction in train set prices. The EDG17 was now 98s. 6d. while the EDP11 was 122s. and the EDP12 was 133s. 9d.

The introduction of the 2–6–4 Tank locomotive brought two new sets into production from the following year's colour catalogue, reference 7/754/200. The first of these was the EDP13 train set which had two brake third suburban coaches, and one first third suburban coach. These were with the tinprinted windows, type D13. Its sales price was 127s. 6d. while there was also the EDG18 set with the 2–6–4 Tank locomotive, the bogie brick wagon, the bogie bolster wagon and the Eastern Region brake van, this sold for 122s. 6d.

The September 1955 issue of the *Railway Modeller* had a full page advertisement on the Hornby Dublo train sets and bar marginal increase in prices – for instance the EDP11 'Silver King' Passenger set had increased from £6. 10s. to £6. 15s. – there was only one physical change. This was in the EDG17 0–6–2 Tank Goods set, where the Royal Daylight tanker had been exchanged for the recently introduced Vacuum tanker. This was shown to good effect in the 1955/56 colour catalogue reference 7/755/550 (over half a million printed).

The bulletin to Meccano dealers, dated 17th February 1956, asks them to visit the British Industries Fair at Earls Court, London to be held between the 22nd February and 2nd March. They wrote . . . 'The make up and presentation of several Hornby Dublo train sets have been altered and an 0–6–2 Tank passenger set is being added to the range.'

The first to be announced was again in a Meccano dealers' bulletin dated 23rd March 1956, reference 18/356/4.75 where a new passenger train set the EDP15 was now available for ordering. This was our old friend the EDL11 'Silver King' locomotive, but with the D12 first third and brake third coaches.

On 27th August, in a further bulletin to Meccano dealers, the 0–6–2 Tank passenger train set, including one of the new D14 suburban first/second and brake/second coaches with the transparent windows appeared. This was to be set EDP10 and had a retail price of £5. 7s. 6d. The trade price was exactly £3.

At the same time the EDP13 train set was brought up to date with the new D14 suburban coaches and was called the EDP14 2–6–4 Tank passenger train set with a retail price of £6. 13s. 6d.

Other changes included the exchange in the EDG18 2–6–4 Goods set which had the grey LMR brake van against the earlier Eastern Region van and in the 0–6–2 Tank Goods set, EDG17, the ventilated van was exchanged for a white refrigerated van and the Vacuum tanker exchanged for the Mobil tanker – still with the two Mobilgas crests either side of the logo. These were shown to good effect in a beautiful photograph in the 1956/57 colour catalogue reference 7/556/500.

In 1957 further changes in the composition of the sets took place and the dealers' bulletin for 27th May that year brought their attention to the new 2–6–4 Goods set, EDG19, which included the LMR goods brake van, the D1 20-ton tube wagon, the D2 double bolster wagon, the D1 tank wagon, Mobil, with the single logo and the long wheel base D1 ventilated van. The retail price was 137s. 6d.

A further change in a dealers' bulletin dated 27th June, referred to the new EDP22 'Royal Scot' set. This was our old friend 'The Duchess of Montrose' locomotive, but this time hauling two of the new, all maroon, D22 corridor coaches. The retail price was 147s. 6d.

A lot of dealers were having problems with displaying sets within the reach of their younger customers and to overcome this the Meccano Company had

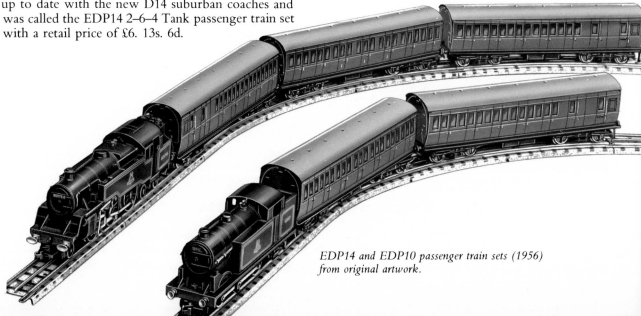

EDP14 and EDP10 passenger train sets (1956) from original artwork.

EDP15 train set (1956) from original artwork.

special glass topped lids made for their various train sets. The large lid covered the EDP12, 15, 19, 20 and 22 sets while the medium size covered the EDP14 and the small size, the EDG16. This last set was shown in the 1957 colour catalogue reference, 7/857/500, and incorporated the 0–6–2 Tank Goods set with two D1 five plank BR open wagons and an Eastern Region brake van. The whole set sold for 97s. 6d. It was mentioned in this catalogue that the EDP12 'The Duchess of Montrose' set was still available with the standard D12 plum and spilt milk coaches.

Obviously though the highlight of the catalogue was the new EDP20 which showed the new EDLT20 'Bristol Castle' locomotive and tender and the new Western Region D21 brake second and first/second coaches. Prices were shown as . . . 'available later'. It has always surprised me that they never introduced the 'Cornish Riviera' set (in 1904 this was the first train to run regularly for more than 200 miles non stop).

Another leaflet never released in the United Kingdom to my knowledge, was issued by the Meccano Company in Canada from their 675 King Street West, Toronto office. This coding was 16/957/30 and showed their EDL2 'Canadian Pacific' locomotive in

EDP20
– the incomparable
'Bristol Castle' train set (1957)
from original artwork.

the EDP2 passenger train set, with the two D12 coaches although all the sets I have seen have had the later D3 coaches. The Goods set was the EDG3 which strangely had the bogie brick wagon instead of the far more applicable bogie bolster wagon and the special CPR caboose. Both train sets cost $24.95 while the D1 caboose cost $1.55 and the locomotive $11.50 and the tender an extra $1.95. A slight mystery surrounds the extended lead time of this locomotive between its original drawing in 1952/53 and its eventual release some five years later.

By 1958 many of the sets had again altered in their content. The dealers were advised on 27th May that there would be two new goods train sets incorporating the new super detail wagon range which had

recently been released. The first was the G16 set which was our old friend the 0–6–2 Tank Goods set, but it was to have two super detail steel type wagons and a grey Western Region super detail brake van.

The G19 set incorporated the 2–6–4 Tank Goods locomotive with the super detail cattle wagon, the D2 double bolster wagon, the Mobil tank wagon, the super detail steel type goods wagon and again the Western Region super detail brake van. The remaining sets dropped their ED letters and looking at the list in the colour catalogue reference 7/858/500 there was the P14 Tank Set – the 2–6–4 Tank locomotive and three D14 suburban coaches; the P15 'Flying Scotsman' passenger train set showing the 'Mallard' locomotive, complete with headboard and the D12 coaches; the P20 Bristolian train set with the 'Bristol Castle' locomotive and headboard and the D21 coaches; the P22 'Royal Scot' passenger train set with the 'Duchess of Montrose' locomotive and headboard and D22 coaches. (What a beautiful set!) And finally, heralded as new, the G25 Goods set which included the new 48158 8F freight locomotive which had the super detail refrigerated van, the bogie well wagon,

EDG17 Tank Goods set from original artwork.

303

the Shell lubricating oil tanker, the steel type standard goods wagon and surprisingly, according to the catalogue, the tinplate LMR brake van although the LMR super detail brake van was already on the market. The Meccano 'Toys of Quality' catalogue, reference 13/758/450, also stated that the P10 0–6–2 Tank passenger set was still available.

The 1958 catalogue 7/858/500 had a very attractive inside layout showing all the sets, so attractive that it was specially printed as an advertisement picture for shops.

TWO-RAIL SETS

In the latter part of 1959 the new 2-rail sets became available. There was the Hornby Dublo catalogue

marked 'first edition' some copies indicating a printing code 13/1059/25. Two months later, in December, the superb *Hornby Dublo Book of Trains* arrived.

The 1959 catalogue showed eight new 2-rail sets. Set number 2006 was the new green 0–6–0 R1 Southern Tank locomotive with the super detail United Glass wagon and steel type open goods wagon with the Western Region brake van, while its partner, set 2007, was the same locomotive with the D14 type suburban coaches now in Southern green and numbered 4025 and 4026.

Set 2019 was the 2–6–4 Tank locomotive 80033 with the low-sided wagon and the Dublo Dinky Toy tractor, low-sided wagon with the insulated meat container and the double bolster wagon, with timber load under the care of an Eastern Region super detail bauxite brown brake van.

Set 2030 was the ill-fated, 2-rail 'Bo-Bo' locomotive, number D8017, with a rake of super detail wagons including the 16 ton mineral wagon, the refrigerated wagon, the bulk grain wagon and the standard 12 ton covered wagon with the grey LMR super detail brake van.

Set 2015 showed the new 'Golden Fleece' A4 Class locomotive hauling the 'Talisman' train with somewhat surprisingly, the adapted 2-rail D12 tinplate plum and spilt milk coaches.

Set 2025 showed the new 2-rail 8F locomotive, number 48109, hauling the refrigerated van, the bogie weltrol wagon, the Shell Lubricating Oil tanker, the five plank standard goods wagon and the grey LMR brake van.

Set 2020 had the new 'Castle' Class locomotive, number 7032 'Denbigh Castle' hauling the 'Torbay Express' with the D21 coaches.

Finally, set 2022 showed the revised and rebuilt 'City of London' Class locomotive hauling the 'Caledonian' train with the D22 new BR standard all maroon coaches.

No. 2019 2–6–4 Tank Goods train set from original artwork.

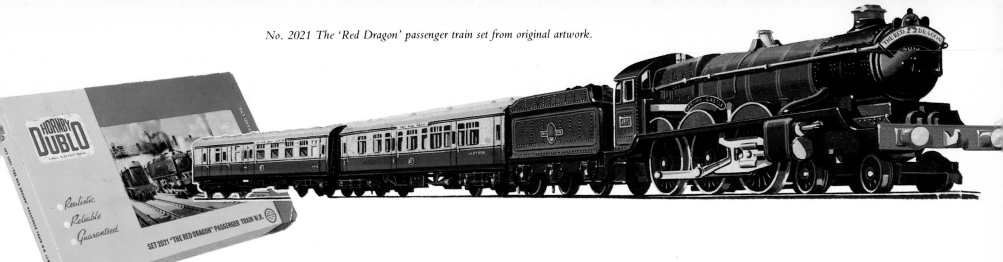

No. 2021 The 'Red Dragon' passenger train set from original artwork.

The catalogue also informed its reader that a separate folder giving particulars of the 3-rail train sets and accessories was also available. The *Hornby Dublo Book of Trains* showed set 2007 with the black 0–6–0 R1 Class locomotive hauling the Southern suburban coaches, although a single page leaflet on the 2-rail electric trains a year later (reference 8/760/250) listed two other sets – number 2008 which was the 0–6–0 Tank Goods set identical to 2006, but with a black

2030 'Bo-Bo' goods train from a publicity photograph.

No. 2016 0–6–2 Tank Goods set from original artwork.

locomotive, while 2009 was the 0–6–0 black locomotive, but this time with maroon D14 coaches suitably adapted to 2-rail by fitting the nylon wheels.

Other sets shown in this catalogue for the first time were set 2016 which was the recently introduced 0–6–0 N2 Tank locomotive, the last of all to be converted to 2-rail, number 69550, hauling the super detail Saxa Salt wagon, the Mobil tanker, the low-sided cable drum wagon and the LMR super detail brake van.

A further interesting feature of this very scarce piece of literature which eluded me for a long time, was that it showed the new 8F locomotive and 'Castle' Class locomotive fitted with the newly introduced Ringfield motor. The 8F goods freight set was number 2024 hauled by Ringfield locomotive number 48073. The new Western Region express train was set number 2021 hauled by 'Cardiff Castle' locomotive and retitled the 'Red Dragon' passenger train but at that time showing tinplate D21 coaches in the artwork.

There was a very attractive export catalogue for Meccano dealers, reference 9/560/2.5 which showed the 0–6–0 Tank set number 2016 that we have already discussed and also the new 'Red Dragon' train set with a small paragraph stating . . . 'This set has new coaches and the locomotive is fitted with the new highly efficient Ringfield motor. (Available 1961.)' It also listed the first nine super detail coaches – the Western Region corridor coaches number 4050 and 4051 with the British Rail 4052 and 53. The 4078 composite sleeping car, the 4075 full brake van and the three pullman cars although these were not released until the end of the year. The December 1960 *Meccano Magazine* had an advertisement for the first four coaches.

The 3-rail catalogue 16/959/100 listed all the 3-rail sets that have already been dealt with in detail.

3010 Hornby Dublo 0–6–0 Tank Passenger Train Set (P10)
3014 Hornby Dublo 2–6–4 Tank Passenger Train Set (P14)
3015 Hornby Dublo Flying Scotsman Passenger Train Set (P15)
3016 Hornby Dublo 0–6–2 Tank Goods Set (G16)
3019 Hornby Dublo 2–6–4 Tank Goods Set (G19)
3020 Hornby Dublo Bristolian Passenger Train Set (P20)
3022 Hornby Dublo Royal Scot Passenger Train Set (P22)
3025 Hornby Dublo LMR 2–8–0 Freight Train Set (G25)

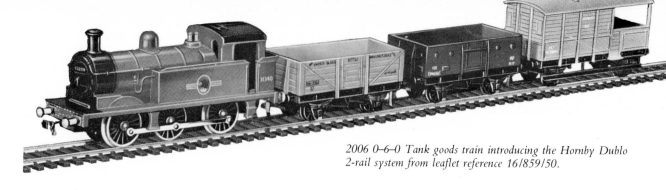

2006 0–6–0 Tank goods train introducing the Hornby Dublo 2-rail system from leaflet reference 16/859/50.

It is interesting to see the 'Duchess of Montrose' locomotive was still the mainstay of set 3022 and the later versions having nickel wheels and plastic bogies which were standard on the 2-rail sets. It was not until November 1961 that she was finally replaced by the 'City of Liverpool'.

The new Hornby Dublo catalogue announced in October 1960 showing the blue prototype Deltic locomotive being admired by a group of trainspotters, again refers to the 2021 'Red Dragon' passenger train set, but states that this was supplied with super detail coaches 4050 and 4051.

In September 1961, the new year's Hornby Dublo catalogue showing the 34005 'Barnstaple' locomotive was announced and stated that set 2014 the 'Talisman' passenger train set was equipped with the new 4052 and 4053 super detail locomotives. While the Eastern Region train set dropped a number from 2015 to 2014 the LMR principal passenger train the 'Caledonian' increased from 2022 to set number 2023 with the inclusion a month later of the super detail coaches.

The September catalogue also showed as new the pullman train set incorporating three cars and the arrival of the 'Barnstaple' West Country locomotive. However, it was not advertised until the November 1961 *Meccano Magazine* and was heralded as 'The luxury train set of the year' and catalogued at £9. 18s. 1d.

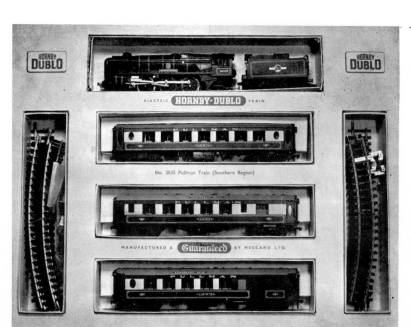

"Bournemouth Belle" set   **£9 18s 1d**

CONCURRENT with the introduction of the Pullman car *Aries* and the rebuilt "West Country" class locomotive, both reviewed above, comes this new Pullman Train Set, No. 2035. Like the other Hornby sets, it is complete except for a power unit. The set consists of a rebuilt "West Country" locomotive, one each of the three Pullman cars, a brake second, a parlour second and a kitchen first, a circle of two-rail track, and a headboard and six roofboards for the "Bournemouth Belle." Technically, the formation is not entirely accurate, since the very short rake includes a "Golden Arrow" car. However, for the junior, for whom the sets are obviously intended, it is a very good representation of the Southern's last steam-hauled Pullman train.

'Luxury Train Set of the Year' – the 2035 'Bournemouth Belle' set. Extract from the November 1961 Model Railway Constructor.

It was by far the most expensive set in the range at that time. The 2041 'Talisman' train set was retailing at £6. 12s. 6d. while the 'Red Dragon' passenger train set was £6. 17s. 6d. and the 'Caledonian' £7. 2s. 6d.

The set was introduced concurrent with the introduction of the last of the three pullman cars 'Aries' and was complete with a circle of 2-rail track, a headboard and six roof boards for the 'Bournemouth Belle'. The *Model Railway Constructor* 'Review' reported that technically the formation was not entirely accurate since the very short rake includes a 'Golden Arrow' car but to quote: . . . 'However for the junior for whom the sets are obviously intended, it is a very good representation of Southern's last steam hauled pullman train.'

This famous September 1961 catalogue also showed for the first time the new 3-rail locomotives, or at least the 3-rail equivalent of these new 2-rail models, although many of them had been shown a couple of months earlier in the special 3-rail system catalogue, reference 13/761/150. The locomotives illustrated were the 3235 'Dorchester' West Country locomotive, the 3226 4–6–2 LMR 'City of Liverpool' locomotive, 3221 The 'Castle' Class locomotive 'Ludlow Castle' as well as the 3-rail diesel locomotives. The 3211 'Mallard' locomotive was obviously retained. They were not in fact available until December 1961.

It seems the production runs of these 3-rail locomotives were very small and I regret that it is impossible to record the actual figures. I know 2–8–0 '8F' freight locomotive, number 48094, together with the 'Ludlow Castle' and 'City of Liverpool' are particularly sought-after models by the collector fetching really quite high prices now in relationship to their 2-rail sisters. Strangely enough, this 3-rail catalogue together with the later ones never once showed 3-rail train sets and, to my surprise, as I write this I can only conclude that no 3-rail sets of these later trains were issued – just the locomotives as individual items.

In April 1962, a fascinating little set was announced, number 2049 the breakdown crane and to quote the introduction in the *Meccano Magazine* . . . 'This train, introduced as an addition to an existing railway is available without rails, and provides scope for all kinds of fascinating breakdown jobs on the "00" line. Headed by the 0–6–2 Hornby Dublo Tank

2033 Co-Bo freight set which introduced the bauxite LMR brake van 1962 from original artwork.

locomotive, it consists of the breakdown crane, with relieving bogies and match truck, a packing van a new vehicle in the range and a brake second suburban coach for the breakdown crew.'

Its U.K. price was £4. 19s. 11d. although surprisingly the identical advertisement in the November 1962 *Meccano Magazine* shows it as only £4. 18s. 6d. This is a very rare set to find today.

In May 1962 the new superb Hornby Dublo catalogue with the Deltic locomotive on the cover arrived and for the first time showed the more popular 2008 0–6–0 Tank Goods set with the black locomotive and at the same time the 2009 passenger train again with the black locomotive and still with the old D14 coaches now numbered 4022 and 4021.

Three new train sets were also shown. The first was a very rare mistake in the marketing department of the Hornby Dublo offices. It showed the Deltic locomotive, number 2234 Crepello, hauling the famous 'Royal Scot' train with the two super detail maroon coaches. As was immediately pointed out by the model railway press, the Deltic locomotives were primarily running on the Eastern Region mainline. In fairness to Binns Road, it was possible that BR were planning for the Deltics to have a far wider area of operation than that that finally appeared. This set was number 2034. Appearing with this set in the catalogue, although not advertised until the June 1962 *Meccano Magazine*, was the 2033 Goods Diesel electric train set. This was an effort to try and move the very unpopular (in both real life and model form) 'Co-Bo' diesel locomotive. It was planned to copy the famous 'Condor' overnight freight train and include four super detail goods vehicles – the refrigerated van, the bulk grain wagon, the 12-ton covered van and the bauxite brown LMR brake van, as the advertisement said . . .

'For fast train working!' There must have been some scarcity of the inside wall sections of this van as many I have seen have the grey LMR partition.

It was not until October that the final set appeared: the 2050 suburban electric train set and the first advertisements showed them without their yellow visual warning panels. The catalogue photograph shows the three coach unit which was originally planned incorporating the motor coach, the dummy trailer coach and a suburban super detail Southern Region car acting as the centre coach. However, as discussed in its relevant chapter, it was decided that this would be too expensive and so it was only marketed as a two coach set. As with all these later items, it is very rare to find today.

The next train set to be announced was in the strange, almost postcard size, eight page colour catalogue, reference 10/363/400 again with a Deltic locomotive on the cover. This was the new 'ready-to-run' 0–4–0 Tank Goods set, number 2001 which received a full page advertisement in the April 1963 *Meccano Magazine* and was complete with a circle of what may be described as heavy duty 2-rail track and a new Hornby No. 1 power control unit. It was a last attempt to try and gather the lost younger enthusiast who had defected to the considerably cheaper train sets marketed by competitors. The set retailed in the U.K. for 89s. 6d., and was followed, almost twelve months later, in December 1964, by the 0–4–0 Diesel Shunter outline. This item was heavily advertised and by all accounts sold well. The sets were not put under the critical eye of the *Constructors* 'Review' until the August 1963 issue when there was a full page article which concluded . . . 'An excellent and robust first set for the junior enthusiast which should provide hours of safe and trouble free running.'

No. 2049 The breakdown crane train set from original artwork.

No. 2034 The 'Royal Scot' passenger train set. Though, to my knowledge, no Deltic locomotive ever hauled this train in real life.

No. 2050 Suburban electric train set of the Southern Region.

No. 2001 0–4–0 Tank goods train set of the 'ready to run' series.

No. 2245 Passenger train set incorporating the E3002 locomotive and three Super-Detail coaches advertised in the 1964 catalogue 13/464/100. To my knowledge this set never came into production.

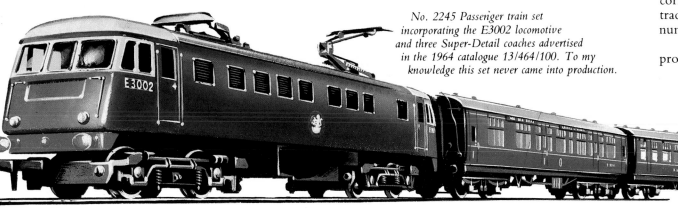

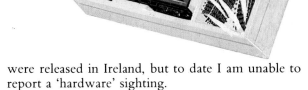

were going to be? – perhaps they would have included the little 'bug box' four wheel coaches similar to those brought out by the Hornby Company ten years later.

The last advertised train set of all never to my knowledge appeared. This was the 'Red Rose' set which had the new 3,300 h.p. electric locomotive, number E3002, with the 4052 and 4053 corridor first second and brake second coaches and the 4071 BR restaurant car. It was shown at the Grosvenor Fair in January 1964 to the trade and to my knowledge was never issued. The artwork shows it in a pressed foam carton with the electric locomotive in the top lefthand corner and the three coaches underneath, with the track sections on the righthand side. It was to be set number 2245.

I have heard one or two rumours that this set was produced in a very limited number and that some

In July 1963 *Railway Modeller* reported on a sample of one of Triang's own 'starter' electric sets which sold for the remarkably low price of 39s. 11d., although without a power controller and this was contrasted with the Hornby starter set offering. To quote the write-up . . . 'For this one gets the basic necessities – a circle of super 4 track, a power clip, a bottle of oil, a short bogie coach – one of the earlier pattern mainline coaches now superceded by the scale length types and last, but most important of all, the locomotive. This was our old friend "Nellie" 0–4–0 in black plastic with a set of the latest BR transfers to relieve the tank sides. This set brings electric trains within reach of anyone and since everything included is basically a standard Triang product there will be no difficulty in expanding this starter set.

'These little Triang 0–4–0 locomotives I find very sweet and eminently collectable. As they were naturally designed for the younger enthusiast they are very

hard to find in good original condition and there are at least ten distinct colour variations as well as two all black models showing the original BR crest and the later BR crest respectively. But I digress. . . .'

The May 1962 Hornby Dublo colour catalogue, with the Deltic cover, surprisingly does not show the 2023 'Caledonian' passenger set with the 'City of London' locomotive although it was printed on the April 1962 price list. Neither was it shown on the next 2-rail electric trains catalogue, reference 11/662/200 although it was still listed in the price list in the little postcard size catalogues already mentioned. Surprisingly it was never to appear again in any of the last catalogues so I can only assume that the artwork was damaged or mislaid.

The very last catalogue, with the red cover, reference 13/464/100, showed two new train sets; the first being number 2004 which was the extension of the ready-to-run series and included the 0–4–0 diesel shunter locomotive. I wonder what sets 2002 and 2003

were released in Ireland, but to date I am unable to report a 'hardware' sighting.

No more sets were issued by the Company, although a rare amalgamation catalogue of Triang Railways and Hornby Dublo, dated May 1965, listed many of the building accessories and six locomotives number R2235 the 'Barnstaple' West Country locomotive, number R2233 the 'Co-Bo' diesel electric locomotive, number R2217 the 0–6–2 Tank locomotive, the R2207 0–6–0 green Tank locomotive and R2231 the 0–6–0 diesel shunting locomotive as well as number 2250 the electric motor coach and 4150 non-powered trailer coach and the final locomotive of all – number 2245 the E3002 electric locomotive.

Models that might have been

I am hard put to give any precise chronology to the models which were either definitely planned (or from the photographs that remained in the Meccano Company and from the memories of past and present employees were at least being considered). In many ways it would be a hotchpotch so I list them in approximate date order, only.

PRE-WAR

Such is the nature of man that you might well ask which war? I mean the Second World War, and there is an interesting Meccano trade bulletin marked 1/239/4.5 i.e. February 1939 which showed the wooden terminus station, the electrically operated points and signals as well as the large radius curves and footbridge (metal) and included a final paragraph which reads. . . .

FURTHER HORNBY DUBLO DEVELOPMENTS

'In addition to the new Hornby Dublo items mentioned above many more attractive models of rolling stock and accessories are in course of preparation. They include a Breakdown Crane, Flat Truck, Goods Container, Engine Shed, Telegraph Poles, Signals, Lighting accessories, Water Crane and others. Details of these will be given in our next trade bulletin.'

Well the tragic circumstances of 1939 to 1945 stopped or postponed many of them.

A copy of the order from Mr. J. Lynch of 19, The High Street, Hawick, records other fascinating items such as tarpaulins for the standard wagons in the four main liveries closely following the Hornby 0 gauge pattern. The drawing was dated 8th February 1939 and was curiously enough overstamped 'production, 15th March 1946!'

There were also D1 lamp standards, D1 platelayers' huts, D1 telegraph poles, and finally D1 viaduct bridges! There was a Dublo drawing of water

Tarpaulin sheets, drawn 8.2.39 and marked 'for production 15.3.46'. Shortage of materials perhaps?

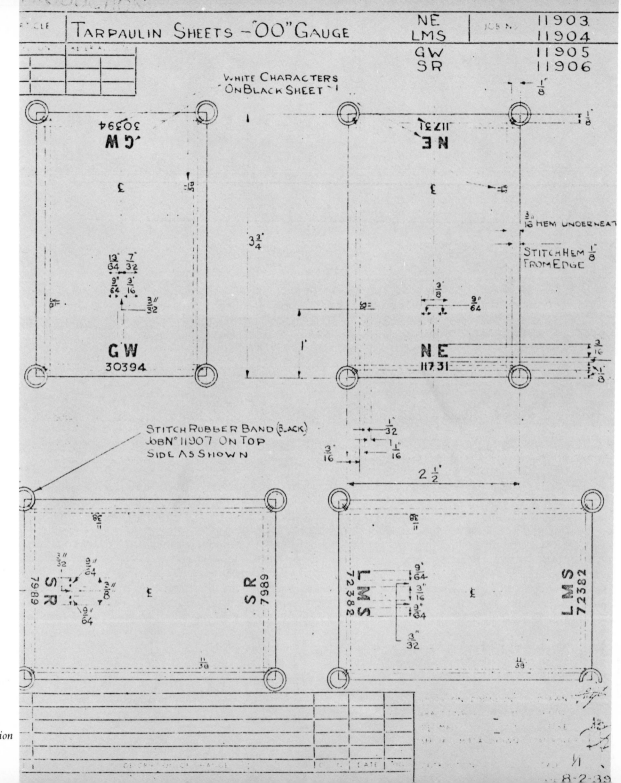

MECCANO LTD.

CONTINUATION of ORDER No. **T**

DEALER'S COPY

PLEASE RETAIN THIS COPY FOR REFERENCE

ORDER.
HORNBY-DUBLO

DATE 1939

FROM ....
PER ....
DELIVERY .... INVOICE .... DUE LESS 2½% 15TH
SIGNATURE .... DUE NETT

THIS ORDER MUST BE SIGNED BY THE PURCHASER OR WRITTEN CONFIRMATION GIVEN.
THE QUANTITY FILLED IN WILL ALWAYS BE TAKEN TO REFER TO THE PACKED UNIT (SET OR BOX); BROKEN QUANTITIES CANNOT BE SUPPLIED

Train Sets and Rolling Stock

		Price	LMS	LNE	GW	S
SETS (Clockwork)						
DP1	PASSENGER (Streamlined)	39/6	—			—
DP2	PASSENGER (Duchess)	—	—			—
DG7	TANK GOODS	27/6				—
SETS (Electric)						
EDP1	PASSENGER (Streamlined)	70/-	—			—
EDP2	PASSENGER (Duchess)	55/-				—
EDG7	TANK GOODS					—
	SETS PACKED WITH No. 1A CONTROLLER					
EDPA1	PASSENGER (Streamlined)	61/6				—
EDPA2	PASSENGER (Duchess)					—
EDGA7	TANK GOODS	46/6				—
LOCOS. (Clockwork)						
DL1	PASSENGER (Streamlined)	18/6	—			—
DL2	PASSENGER (Duchess)					—
DL7	TANK	12/6				—
LOCOS. (Electric)						
EDL1	PASSENGER (Streamlined)	25/-	—			—
EDL2	PASSENGER (Duchess)					—
EDL7	TANK	17/6	—			—
ROLLING STOCK						
D1	TENDERS (Streamlined)	4/6	—			—
D2	TENDERS	3/6				—
D1	CORRIDOR COACHES	6/6			—	—
D2	ARTICULATED COACHES			—		—
D3	COACHES	2/6		—		—
D1	BRAKE VANS	1/7		—		—
D1	COAL WAGONS	1/9		—		
D2	HIGH SIDED	1/6				
D2	CATTLE TRUCKS	3/6		—		
D1	HIGH CAPACITY WAGONS	1/6				
D2	HIGH-SIDED WAGONS	1/6		—		
D1	HORSE BOXES	1/6		—		
D1	FISH VANS	1/6				
D1	GOODS VANS	1/4		—		
D1	OPEN GOODS WAGONS	1/6				
D1	MEAT VANS	1/6		—		
D1	TANK WAGONS, "ESSO"	2/6		—		
D1	TANK WAGONS, "POWER"	2/6				
D1	TANK WAGONS, "ROYAL DAYLIGHT"	2/6		—		
D1	TARPAULINS (for Wagons)					

ACCESSORIES

		Bxd in	Each
D1	BUFFER STOPS	6	-/9
D1	DEPOT, Goods	1	4/-
D1	ENGINE SHEDS	1	
D1	FOOTBRIDGES	1	3/6
D1	LAMP STANDARDS		
D1	PLATELAYERS' HUT		
D1	PLATFORMS, Island	1	4/-
D1	SIGNALS, Single-arm	6	1/-
ED1	SIGNALS, Single-arm (electrically operated)		
D2	SIGNALS, Double-arm	6	1/3
D3	SIGNALS, Junction	2	1/6
D1	SIGNAL CABINS	6	-/11
D1	STATIONS, Main	1	6/9
D2	STATIONS, Terminus	1	
D1	TELEGRAPH POLES	1	
D1	TUNNELS (Short)	6	1/3
D2	TUNNELS (Long)	6	1/8
D1	VIADUCT BRIDGES	1	
D1	MINIATURES (Station Staff)	—	1/-
D2	MINIATURES (Passengers)	—	1/-
D1	OIL (Clockwork)	1	-/2
D2	OIL (Electric)	1	-/2

TRANSFORMERS & CONTROLLERS

		Bxd in	Each
	No. 1 CONTROLLER	1	21/-
	No. 1A CONTROLLER (for Accumulator)	1	12/6
No. 1	TRANSFORMER for 1 Train	1	9/6
No. 2	TRANSFORMER for 2 Trains	1	12/6
	SWITCH for electrically operated points & signals		
	SWITCH for isolating rails		

TRACK

		Bxd in	Doz.	Boxes
CLOCKWORK				
DB1	STRAIGHT RAILS	6	12/-	
DB1¼	STRAIGHT HALF RAILS	6	9/-	
DA1	CURVED RAILS	8	12/-	
DA1¼	CURVED HALF RAILS	6	9/-	
DBS	SHORT RAILS	6	6/-	
DPR	POINTS, R.H. } pair	Pr.	Pr.	
DPL	POINTS, L.H. } pair		6/6	
ELECTRIC				
EDB1	STRAIGHT RAILS	6	15/-	
EDBT1	STRAIGHT TERMINAL RAILS	3	21/-	
EDB1¼	STRAIGHT HALF RAILS	6	12/-	
EDA1	CURVED	8	15/-	
EDA1¼	CURVED HALF RAILS	6	12/-	
EDAT1	CURVED TERMINAL RAILS	3	21/-	
EDA2	CURVED LARGE RAILS	8	18/-	
EDAT2	CURVED LARGE TERMINAL RAILS	3	27/-	
EDBS	SHORT RAILS	6	9/-	
EDPR	R.H. POINTS } pair	Pr.	Pr.	
EDPL	L.H. POINTS } pair	Pr.	9/6	
EODPR	R.H. POINTS } pair			
EODPL	L.H. POINTS } pair (electrically operated)			
IBR	ISOLATING RAIL			

A printed Meccano order sheet, completed 5th April 1939. Note a footbridge was ordered for 3s. 6d. (17½p) and also due a clockwork 'Duchess' loco, lamp standards, platelayers' hut, telegraph pole and viaduct bridges!

311

cranes with a header tank above them as issued by the general Drawing Office of the LMS in 1932.

On the locomotive side a fascinating model has been found by collector Mr. Gordon Monks. I visited him and he kindly had some photographs taken ready for me which showed the only pre-war issue of the LMS Hornby Dublo tender, albeit a pre-production mock-up. It showed the pre-war flat spring coupling riveted to a central spigot by the rear tender wheels, but, perhaps the most interesting of all was its wooden body in the shape of an LMS streamlined 'Coronation' which fitted neatly onto the streamlined A4 – 'Sir

Mr. Gordon Monks' factory mock-up streamlined LMS 'Coronation' Class locomotive using a pre-war A4 chassis and the pre-war LMS 'Duchess' tender – note metal fatigue on tender chassis.

The following details on the 'Duchess of Atholl' were supplied in a letter from J. D. McHard.

1. The model of the Duchess of Atholl to which you refer was hand built in nickel and brass by Mr. Bob Moy in either 1938 or 1939.
2. The coaches are hand painted but the metal appears to have been die-stamped and it is, therefore, a reasonable supposition that the press tools for the coaches were made before the war but that none of the litho printing plates were available.
3. In its original form as Mr. Moy made it, the locomotive had a single chimney and examination of the inside of the smokebox clearly shows its original location. The paintwork on top of the smokebox around the double chimney base also reveals evidence of later alteration as does that around the dome.
4. The model was used for all the pre-war photographs of the Duchess of Atholl both in Meccano Magazine and in other promotional sales literature.
5. At some stage, either during the war or immediately after it, Mr. Moy updated his model to incorporate the twin chimney, and in this form the model was again used for promotional and photographic purposes. More significantly it was also used for running demonstrations at the first B.I.F. Show in which Meccano Limited participated following the cessation of hostilities.
6. It seems most unlikely that this hand made model would have been altered in this way had castings at that time been available and to my mind, this is a significant fact in connection with the dispute over whether or not Atholls were cast before the war.
7. Like the rest of the locomotive, the linkage was hand made but the wheels appear to have been taken from a Dublo Sir Nigel Gresley. They were cast in impure mazak and have since disintegrated to a very large extent.

I do hope that the foregoing information which was largely built up as a result of talking to both Mr. Moy and some of his contemporaries during my association with Meccano Limited from 1967 - 1977, adequately answers your queries.

J.D. McHard

The original factory sample – in brass – note drilling for single chimney

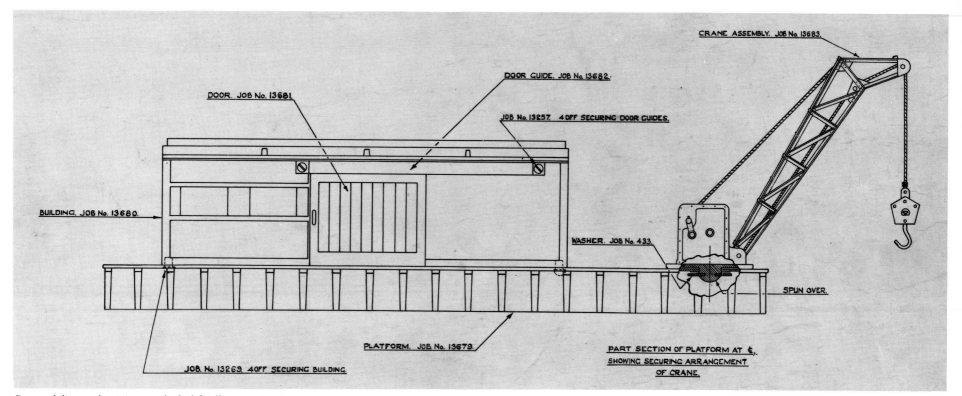

CRANE ASSEMBLY. JOB No. 13683

DOOR GUIDE. JOB No. 13682.

DOOR. JOB No. 13681.

JOB No. 13257. 4 OFF SECURING DOOR GUIDES.

BUILDING. JOB No. 13680.

WASHER. JOB No. 433.

SPUN OVER.

PLATFORM. JOB No. 13679.

PART SECTION OF PLATFORM AT ℄.
SHOWING SECURING ARRANGEMENT
OF CRANE.

JOB No. 13269. 4 OFF SECURING BUILDING.

Proposed diecast aluminium goods shed finally appearing in 'plastic' nine years later.

Nigel Gresley' chassis. This probably accounts for the fact that all the details of this chassis were headed streamline type and could have been used for both locomotives. Whether it was planned before or after the introduction of the Trix model, I do not know. June 1938 *Meccano Magazine* announced that ten new LMS Pacific Duchess type locomotives were being built, the first five being similar to the blue and silver 'Coronation' engines but in LMS red whilst numbers 6230 to 6234 would be non-streamline. The original 'Duchess' firm sample, with a drilling for the single chimney is illustrated and strictly speaking the single chimney version must be considered as a model that might have been.

POST-WAR
GOODS STATION ASSEMBLY

On 4th July 1950, a Goods Station Assembly was drawn, but Meccano did not produce it as they did not

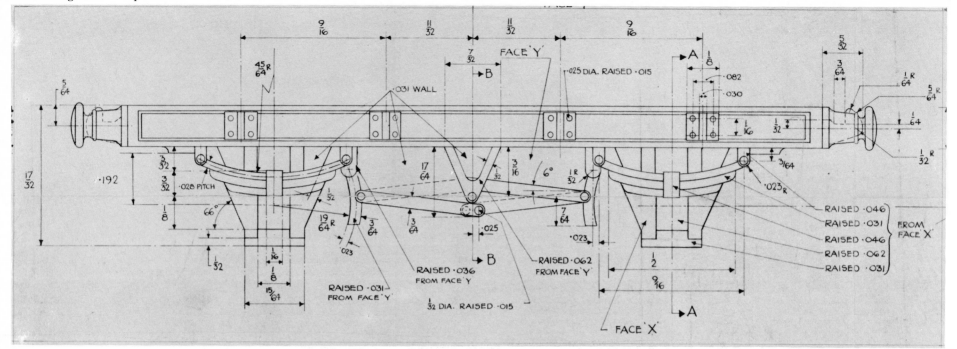

have the equipment to make aluminium castings. The project was put out to a contractor – the Birmingham Cast Aluminium Company mentioned earlier but, owing to a shortage of metal and the fact that it was too expensive it was shelved as a commercial proposition. It was to all intents and purposes identical in design to the polystyrene model, which came out ten years later. The crane unit was fascinating because it was scaled up and became the Dublo Dinky Supertoys Goods Yard Crane.

A HOPPER COAL STAGE

It has always been a surprise to me that no model company has ever produced a commercial hopper coaling stage in 00 scale. The Meccano Company certainly discussed it, but doubtless rejected it on the same grounds as the goods yard in 1950. The Trix Company had a fascinating ore loading set, but I am talking about the large reinforced concrete coaling stage, similar to those on LNER practice, which would take a four wheel coal wagon up the side and tip it over into the hopper. With today's affluent society I

am sure it would be well within the bounds of one commercial company to produce such an item. It would have immense play value and could use imitation coal such as the Dinky Toys model number 791 which was available in the early 1960s in little plastic bags.

HEADLIGHTS

One must remember that Hornby Dublo railways were distinctly designed for the toy market as opposed to the scale enthusiast and such items as headlamps, although considered, were rejected as they could not find ways to secure them and incorporate the interchangeability to copy correct locomotive practice. They were however, certainly considered. It was not until the end of their era that they tried putting very crude dummy headlamps into the 'Co-Bo' and the 'Co-Co' locomotives. It was a clumsy modification as shown and not a patch on the superb little headlamps which appeared on the Acho Models. Continental manufacturers were well ahead of us at the time in their attention to this sort of detail.

PLASTIC WAGON BASE

As far back as 21st November 1951, with the scarcity of metals, it was planned (indeed drawings were made) to have a plastic wagon base for the four wheel items of rolling stock. The metal supply position improved and so the project was never finalised.

They did, however, have plastic moulded bodies on the later items of their super detail rolling stock and with the cheap wagons in the starter set series had planned to introduce the moulded base used here throughout the range, but as we have already mentioned, it was considered a retrograde step due to the increased competition.

OTHER LOCOMOTIVE MODELS
(1950s)

HRCA member, Mr. Bernard Simpson wrote in the Journal some years back that he had been informed by Mr. L. A. Norman of the Information Department in Binns Road that all drawings and some preliminary toolings had been completed on a Great Western

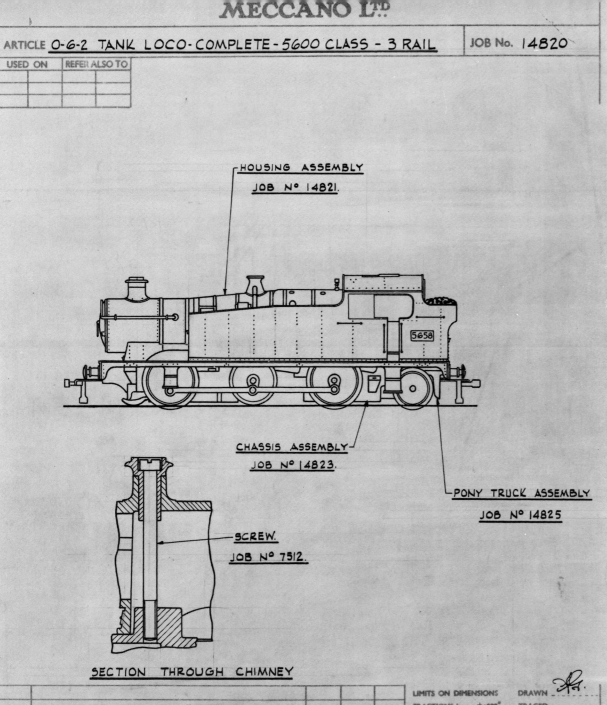

ARTICLE	0-6-2 TANK LOCO-COMPLETE-5600 CLASS - 3 RAIL			JOB No.	14820
USED ON	REFER ALSO TO				

HOUSING ASSEMBLY
JOB Nº 14821.

5658

CHASSIS ASSEMBLY
JOB Nº 14823.

PONY TRUCK ASSEMBLY
JOB Nº 14825

SCREW.
JOB Nº 7512.

SECTION THROUGH CHIMNEY

ISSUE	DESCRIPTION OF CHANGE				C.O. No.	DATE	SIG.
MATERIAL	SEE JOB LIST Nº 436						

LIMITS ON DIMENSIONS   DRAWN
FRACTIONS :— ± ·005″   TRACED
DECIMALS :— ± ·003″   CHECKED
SPECIAL LIMITS AS SHOWN   APPROVED
DISTRIBUTION   SCALE 1:1 & 2:1
                                         DATE 2-1-58

'Castle' Class locomotive prior to 1939 and that in 1939 drawings had been completed for a Southern Region 'Lord Nelson'. Sadly no trace of them has been found. These were dropped after the Second World War in favour of the West Country locomotive. In a letter to Mr. McTaggart of Australia, Mr. Roland Hornby stated that it was planned to produce a famous locomotive from each of the four main companies, but he did state that Number 4472 'Flying Scotsman' was not to be produced. He went on to say that producing Hornby Dublo in Australian colours was not viable unless large quantities could be guaranteed – 10,000 minimum. However collector John Ridley brought many boxed CPR tenders back from Canada, one had a code BW 468–600–8/52 and a further box BW8011–550–9/53 which would indicate a run of some 600 in August 1952.

However, what was fully drawn on 2nd January 1958, was a superb little 0–6–2 Tank locomotive based on the Great Western 5600 Class, Number 5658. It was planned to produce this both in 2-rail and 3-rail, but in October 1959, the Trix Company had introduced their own 0–6–2 Great Western Tank in the form of the 66XX Class.

The only other locomotive I could find that was definitely planned, perhaps would have been the most attractive of all, the 2–6–2 Class 'Green Arrow' locomotive of the LNER. This was definitely drawn in great detail and, from a scale drawing I have, would have fitted the wheel arrangement of the 2–6–4 Tank locomotive exactly. One could have used the front pony from the '8F' locomotive and the rear bogie from the 4–6–2 'Duchess' locomotive. Collector Chris Willis tells me that from his own researches the number for this locomotive would have been 2240 in 2-rail and 3240 in 3-rail. I cannot find any trace of even a mock-up locomotive being prepared, but I feel certain that it was.

In my earlier researches at the Meccano factory I came across all the drawings for the body and tender of this locomotive and was given a copy of the two main body drawings. I mentioned this model on a visit shortly afterwards to Mr. George Wrenn and naturally he too was more than enthusiastic and contacted the Meccano Company to see if they were obtainable

Class 56XX 0–6–2 Tank locomotive, drawn 2nd January 1958. Not to be confused with the Trix 66XX Class loco which was available from October 1959.

315

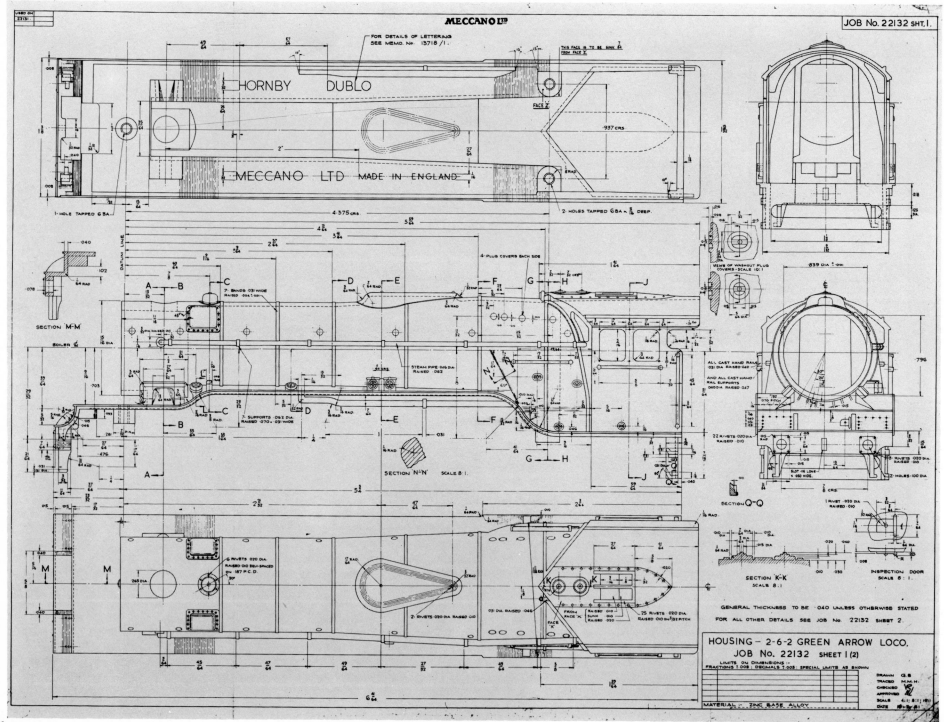

316 *The 'Green Arrow'. The LNER's famous 2–6–2 design. What a pity it was never produced. Drawings dated 18.7.61.*

so that he could reproduce the model. The drawings were dutifully taken out of the drawer and put together, but terms could not be agreed and the negotiations failed. Sadly, since then, this roll of drawings has been lost.

Mr. L. C. Norman of the Hornby Railway company in Binns Road wrote to Mr. Ray Rissnaes – co-founder of the HRCA on 6th October 1960 . . .

'It is unlikely that a further Doncaster 4–6–2 will be introduced, but we might possibly be able to introduce a tender loco of typical Gresley character.'

The drawings were dated 18th July 1961, but owing to the poor sales in the early 1960s and high stocks of existing models it was not possible to introduce a new model.

HALF LENGTH PLATFORM EXTENSIONS

On 2nd May 1949, half length ($5\frac{1}{2}$ inches) platform extensions were drawn, but never brought into practice.

ADDITIONAL NAMES AND NUMBERS FOR MAINLINE LOCOMOTIVES

Between January and March 1958, a whole range of engine nameplates and number plates for the 'Duchess', 'A4' and 'Castle' Class locomotives were drawn up but in fact never issued.

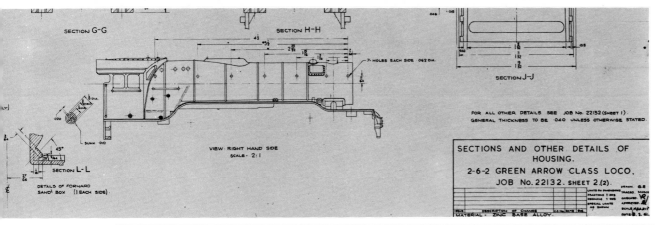

SECTION G-G
SECTION H-H
SECTION J-J
VIEW RIGHT HAND SIDE
SCALE · 2:1
SECTION L-L
DETAILS OF FORWARD SAND BOX (1 EACH SIDE)

FOR ALL OTHER DETAILS SEE JOB No. 22132 (SHEET 1)
GENERAL THICKNESS TO BE ·040 UNLESS OTHERWISE STATED.

SECTIONS AND OTHER DETAILS OF HOUSING.
2-6-2 GREEN ARROW CLASS LOCO.
JOB No. 22132. SHEET 2 (2).

MATERIAL · ZINC BASE ALLOY

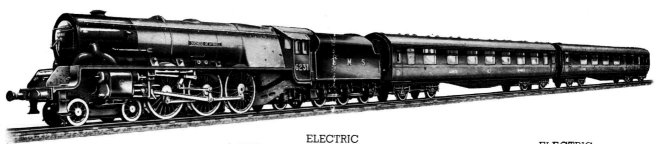

New Hornby-Dublo L.M.S. Express Passenger Train Set

The fine new Hornby-Dublo Train Set illustrated below comprises a perfect representation of the L.M.S. "Duchess of Atholl" one of the magnificent "Duchess" class express locomotives recently introduced, with tender, first-third and brake-third corridor coaches of standard L.M.S. types. For Autumn delivery.

CLOCKWORK

DP2 Hornby-Dublo Clockwork Passenger Train Set, L.M.S. contains DL2 Locomotive "Duchess of Atholl" (reversing). Tender D2, first-third Corridor Coach D3, brake-third Corridor Coach D3, eight DA Curved Rails and two DB Straight Rails.

ELECTRIC

EDP2 Hornby-Dublo Electric Passenger Train Set, L.M.S. (for use with Dublo Controller No. 1) contains EDL2 Locomotive "Duchess of Atholl" (automatic reversing) Tender D2, first-third Corridor Coach D3, brake-third Corridor Coach D3, Dublo Controller No. 1, seven EDA Curved Rails, one EDAT Curved Terminal Rail and two EDB Straight Rails. (Transformer not included).

ELECTRIC

EDPA2 Hornby-Dublo Electric Passenger Train Set L.M.S. (with Dublo Controller No. 1a for use with 12-volt accumulators). For districts where the electric mains supply is Direct Current, or where there is no electric supply.

PRICES OF THESE NEW TRAIN SETS WILL BE ANNOUNCED LATER

317

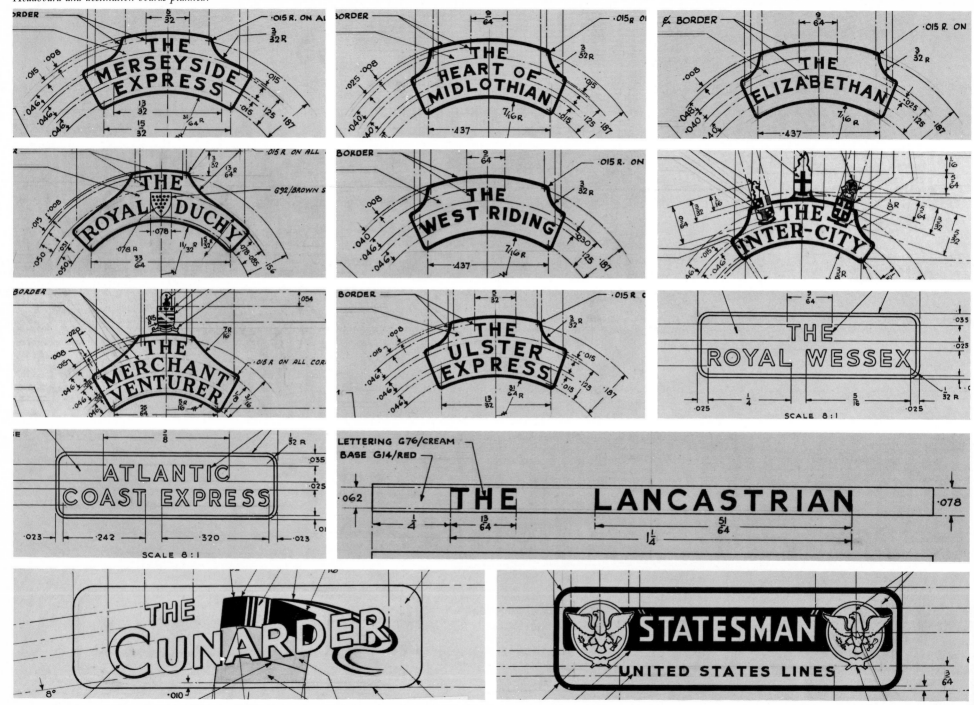

ALTERNATIVE HEADBOARDS AND DESTINATION BOARDS

During the same period a considerably larger range than those produced were planned as follows:

The Merseyside Express
The Heart of Midlothian
The Elizabethan
The Royal Duchy
The West Riding
The InterCity
The Merchant Venturer
The Ulster Express
The Cunarder
The Statesman (United States Lines)
The Lancastrian
The Royal Wessex
The Atlantic Coast Express.

The Cunarder and Statesman trains would have been of particular fascination, as this was the heyday of the great transatlantic liners with the 'Queen Mary', 'Queen Elizabeth', 'United States' and the 'America' all arriving at Southampton Dock to be met by pullman trains. The Cunarder and Statesman trains, however, had already been cancelled before the end of steam, due to the high operating costs. Adverse weather etc., frequently delayed ships' arrivals and British Railways could have had these special trains extravagantly standing with crew and staff idle for hours.

Mr. Ronald Wyborn (right) with Chief Draughtsman Mr. Ernest Lee, discussing a technical point on a 'Castle' Class 3-rail prototype having tender pick-up and remote operated 'whistle'.

1961

There were many fascinating accessories being considered in 1961 and Mr. Ronald Wyborn, highlighted them to me in his usual exceptional detail. He wrote . . . 'Over the years many projects in connection with Dublo were undertaken and mostly brought to successful conclusion without ever reaching production. To mention just a few at random there was a fully developed overhead pick-up system complete with associated pantographs for attachment to the locomotives. Remote operation of horns for the diesels with sound of authentic pitch. A high frequency supply unit to provide a superimposed track supply for coach lighting etc. Most were considered too costly to command a sufficiently high market. Certainly early super detail coaches had moulded spaces for an interior lighting system.'

A STEAM REMOTE OPERATED WHISTLE

There is a fascinating photograph of Mr. Wyborn and his Chief Draughtsman Mr. Ernest Lee, discussing a technical point on a 'Castle' Class 3-rail prototype having a tender pick-up and a remote control whistle.

The 'Bo-Bo' passenger train set from original artwork.

A 2-RAIL TURNTABLE

This was discussed at length and there was a plan to modify the 3-rail turntable reported to the New Products Committee Meeting on 5th October 1961 but the project was finally abandoned on 2nd February 1962.

DIESEL RAIL CAR

There was also a diesel rail car discussed, but delayed because of the problems with the 'Bo-Bo' 2-rail chassis unit and although it was drawn on 10th November 1961, two weeks later by 24th, it was withdrawn due to the similarity with the Southern Electric set. No trace of this drawing has been found.

LEVEL CROSSING

At the same meeting, on 24th November 1961, a double track level crossing was planned to be available for marketing in 1963. It was initially planned to be automatic and details were to be sent by Meccano France, but by 1st March 1962 it was changed to mechanical operation and eventually abandoned.

A LINESIDE WHISTLE

A Lineside whistle, not unlike the Trix item, was planned to simulate a diesel horn and apparently was exceptionally realistic. It was planned on 29th

December 1961 and would be on a moving drum or tape system to be marketed in 1964. By 2nd January 1963, a sample had been produced and was shown to the meeting and it was decided to continue with its development, but by 28th February that year on conclusion of the experimental stage it was decided to cease further work.

A SOUTHERN REGION SUPER DETAIL GOODS BRAKE VAN

Mr. Lee had drawings and photographs forwarded to him of a Southern Region brake van. The memo reported that the sand boxes and side doors were not

The SR buffet restaurant car assembly No. 4072.

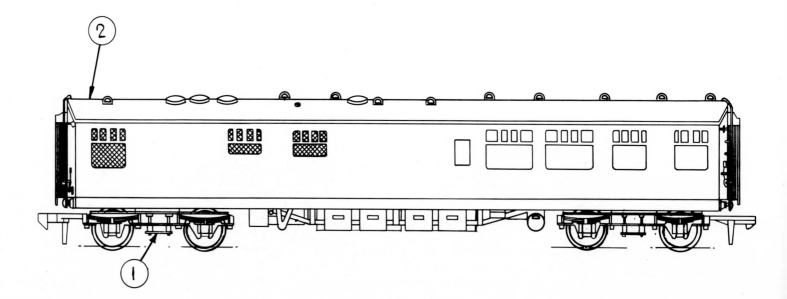

MECCANO L™.

TITLE. BUFFET RESTAURANT CAR ASSEMBLY S.R. GREEN.

ITEM No.	DESCRIPTION	JOB No.	No. OFF
1	BASE ASSEMBLY	21245	1
2	BODY ASSEMBLY	21177	1
3	INTERIOR	21259	1

fitted and so these items should be disregarded. The British Rail standard finish of the vaccuum fitted van is bauxite brown for the bodywork with a grey roof and black base and suitable present day markings (the memo was dated 18th August 1961) for the Southern Region would be S55980 placed where 56365 appears in the photograph. Also the 25–6 should be placed where 23–12 appeared in the photograph.

Trix Western Class in HO.

WESTERN AND WARSHIP LOCOMOTIVES

Both the famous Western Class and the Warship Class were planned to be produced, but the idea was dropped when Trix produced their models. (The Ringfield motor was to have powered the Western.)

SOUTHERN REGION BUFFET CAR

The model railway trade criticised the Meccano Company for introducing their super detail restaurant cars for all regions *except* the Southern. Naturally they did not know that on 9th December 1960 a Southern Region buffet car was drawn which was included on the four pages of Dublo dimensions drawn on 1st June 1961 and was to have been 4072 buffet restaurant car in Southern Region green.

PASSENGER BRAKE VAN IN WESTERN REGION BROWN AND CREAM LIVERY

A super detail Western Region full brake van was drawn and indeed was once more included on this list of Dublo dimensions and would have been number

'Diesel Fueling Bay' BR photograph in Meccano records.

4074. It was never issued as its real life prototype never existed in British Railways practice.

There are many gaps in the super detail list of coaches, in particular numbers 4046–4059, 4064–4073 and 4077 as well as 4079 and 4080. I have been unable to find any reference to how these numbers were likely to have been applied.

SUPER DETAIL TRAVELLING POST OFFICE SET

From the drawings in the archives there is brief mention of parts for a super detail travelling post office coach to replace the earlier tin-sided model. At the time of writing I have no further details.

The March 1965 *Model Railway Constructor* reported . . . 'Hornby have, as yet, released no detail plans for 1965, but we understand re-designed coaches are a possibility for the near future!'

A DIESEL REFUELLING PLANT

With the modernisation scheme in full force and rolling stock being pulled by mainline diesel locomotives, there was an engine shed which could easily be used as a diesel depot, so it was decided that a diesel refuelling plant would be a useful accessory, and one

was drawn up. However, at a New Products Committee Meeting on 10th July 1962 it was decided, in view of other commitments, to ask Mr. Bonneau of Meccano France if he would be interested in the project himself. Mr. Bonneau and his colleagues were not and sadly I have not been able to find any trace of this drawing. The nearest equivalent is doubtless the one produced by the Triang Company in their TT range. With the Dinky Toy pavement sections between the tracks it would have made a most attractive accessory.

THE BOGIE TIMBER WAGON

This was drawn on 7th December 1962 using a standard super detail coach chassis unit and the transfer markings of a bogie weltrol wagon. There was a trade bulletin for Meccano printed 8/1163/10 which showed its number was to be 4612. A sample was made up and shown at the Toy Fair, but obviously the dealers' reaction was negative.

THE CONFLAT CONTAINER WAGON

On 18th June 1963 it was proposed, following Dr. Beeching's freight extension policy, that a new container wagon would be produced and the drawing of a

4612 bogie wagon with timber load from Trade Catalogue reference 8/1162/104 U.K.

this time with two Gresley type bogies. The conflat 'P' was to be number 4638 in the Hornby Dublo listing.

THE OPEN SOUTHERN REGION FERRY WAGON

This too was to be introduced and was drawn on 10th March 1961. It was to be Hornby Dublo number 4639 and was another wagon in what I call the Channel Tunnel period when they were hoping to link the Hornby Dublo and the Hornby-Acho systems. If only that project had gone ahead.

four wheel wagon was made. They also drew up a type A container in high impact polystyrene, colour to be used with the conflat SF/14 red-bauxite brown 'P' as well as a type BD container.

There was a superb photograph in the February 1965 *Railway Modeller* showing a bogie conflat wagon using the plate bogies carrying three of the BD type containers as used on the famous LMR Condor overnight express freight train from Hendon, London to Gushet Faulds, Glasgow. Do you remember the comments we made on the chapter dealing with the 'Co-Bo' locomotive and the headboard that never was number 1703? There was an excellent British Railways photograph showing an experimental conflat wagon loaded with three such containers which appears to be mounted onto a full size coach chassis

The range of Conflat wagons and containers.

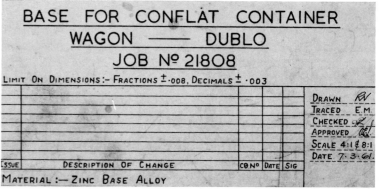

BASE FOR CONFLAT CONTAINER
WAGON ———— DUBLO
JOB № 21808

'B D' TYPE CONTAINER.
JOB № 21809.
FOR USE WITH CONFLAT 'P' WAGON.

'A' TYPE CONTAINER
JOB № 21813.
FOR USE WITH CONFLAT 'P' WAGON

322

THE 12 TON SHOCK ABSORBING WAGON

This was drawn between 17th April 1961 and finalised 16th June. Shock absorbing wagons had been in operation a long time and were designed for carrying fragile loads such as glass and other sensitive-to-impact items including delicate machinery etc. To my knowledge nobody has yet made a commercial model in 00 scale of this vehicle. The notes I have refer to the introduction of such a wagon by the LMS in October 1937 with a capacity of 12 tons. The shock absorbing wagon was to be Hornby Dublo number 4667.

4653 SUPER DETAIL HIGH SIDED COAL WAGON

There was much correspondence about this in collectors circles some five years ago, but unfortunately I

The SR open ferry wagon.

have been unable to add to this. However, I mention this merely as a signpost for more energetic Dublo historians.

A REAL 00 SCALE STEAM LOCOMOTIVE

The New Products Committee minutes of 23rd August 1963 considered an 00 scale, real model steam locomotive to stimulate 00 sales. The meeting records

later that unfortunately the technical problems involved were too great to justify further consideration. I have recently seen models of a live steam 00 scale 'Rocket' locomotive made on the continent.

A SIMPLE CRANE TRUCK

In the minutes for 24th September 1963 it was decided to investigate the possibility of a simple four wheel crane truck. This was drawn up although drawings have not survived nor a sample made, and the idea was abandoned at a meeting on 22nd November. Both Marklin and Trix had small crane trucks based on the 6-wheel chassis although the centre wheel on the Trix model was a dummy. Perhaps it was to be used in conjunction with the double bolster wagon similar to the Taylor Hubbard 5 ton steam crane number DS525 and I am indebted to Mr. E. B. Trotter who wrote an article on such a crane in the *Model Railway Constructor* in June 1957.

Alternatively, it could have been similar to the Triang model R127 crane truck which was announced

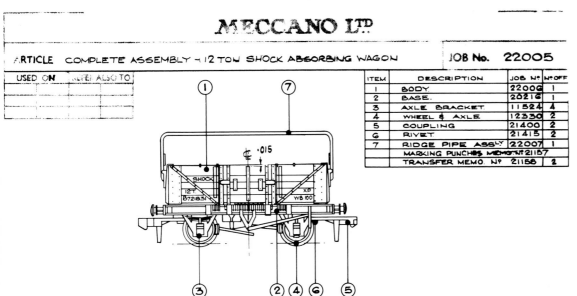

The 12 ton shock absorbing wagon.

in their 8th Edition Catalogue for 1962. This four wheel crane truck had a heavy diecast base and there was also number R17 a four wheel bolster wagon and matching truck for the crane. It could just be that because of the introduction by Triang of this four wheel crane unit that the proposed Hornby Dublo model was itself cancelled.

CAR TRANSPORTER

As I have mentioned before in the chapter on Dublo Dinky Toys I have been very surprised that far more use was not made of hauling motor vehicles by railway wagons. The practice goes back for as long as there have been motor cars and even before the initial grouping of the main railways into the big four companies in 1923. The London North Western Railway Company had special wagons for motor car vehicles and indeed models appeared in 0 gauge and larger principally through Bassett-Lowke. Even the English Brimtoy Company had a fascinating little four wheel van marked 'for motor traffic only'.

The new car transporters were, according to the *Meccano Magazine*, shown at King's Cross Station in July 1961 and were expected to be ready for the 'Car Sleeper Limited' which was an overnight express between King's Cross and Perth, for the convenience of motorists touring the Highlands. These transporter cars could carry up to six cars, four in the upper deck and two in the lower and loading was by a ramp to the top deck and by connecting bridges between adjacent similar vans in the same train. The cars to travel on the lower deck were put down by an electric hoist and they conclude that the formation of this express was likely to be six of these new type of car transporters, one van for large motor cars, six sleeping cars and a passenger brake coach.

In a pile of old photographs kindly loaned by Colin Parker I found a photograph of this vehicle, complete with plate bogies and although no mention has been made in the Hornby Dublo literature I feel certain a lot of work had been done, as by coincidence, it was announced in the 11th edition of the 1965 Triang catalogue as part of the 'Car-a-Belle' train set and was shown as a separate item available the following year as number R342.

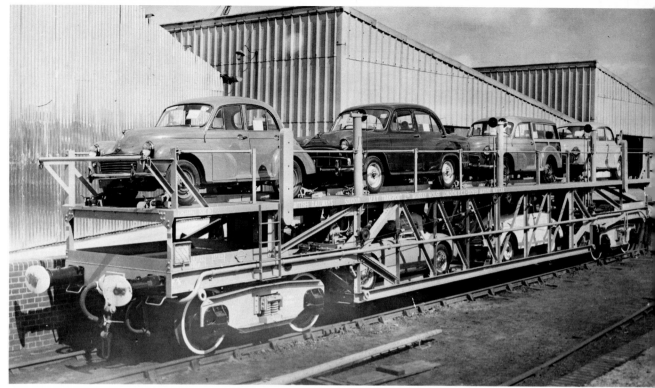

The car transporter.

2–10–0 9F LOCOMOTIVE

It was in edition 17 – 1971 that the Triang Hornby Company announced their 2–10–0 locomotive 'Evening Star' complete with tender drive Ringfield motor. However, Mr. Ronald Wyborn responded in a letter dated 8th March 1973 to my many queries as follows . . .

'We first began thinking in terms of tender drives some ten years ago (1963) and several sketches of various arrangements were made. With the advent of the Ringfield motor interest was revived and just when I left the Company in 1964 an initial design of a 2–10–0 locomotive was on the board. I don't know what became of it subsequently.

'I remember a model of the Green Arrow being started but for some reason or other I don't think it was ever finished. I am fairly sure it would have been on a new chassis.

'I know nothing about a Black 5 locomotive.'

I have heard one or two rumours that the 9F 2–10–0 locomotive was definitely drawn at Meccano and that all the drawings went down to Margate with the Triang Hornby Company on the takeover and that the model was subsequently released by them in 1971. I would love to see a copy of this original drawing as I feel certain that it must still exist although in fairness to the Triang Company I have been assured that together with many other Hornby Dublo drawings it was destroyed in order to make more space available.

FISONS NITROGEN LIQUOR TANKER

From Colin Parker's excellent photographs there was shown a four wheel Nitrogen Liquor tanker very similar to the traffic services vehicle. It could well have been that such a modification was being prepared.

SINGLE TRACK LEVEL CROSSING WITH LIGHTS!

I have already discussed the single track level crossing which was produced in SF73 HI polystyrene stone colour. The interesting point is that listed as the third modification, dated 25th October 1961, was the fact that it was made in an earlier colour – SF93 brown – the rich dark brown which was featured in many of the catalogues. Examining the drawing there is a heading (crossed out) showing that this was a single track level crossing with lighting! Did this mean that it was to have red warning lights rather like the colour aspect signal bulbs on the gates?

THE 'ROYAL SCOT' LOCOMOTIVE

A lot of interest was created in the late 1978 HRCA Journals by collector Frank Sheeran who reported that a well known and reputable Australian dealer who imports directly from the U.K. had examined the prototype model that the Wrenn Company had recently put out on their new 'Royal Scot' locomotive with the parallel boiler and found the Binns Road Trade Mark underneath! He pleaded that members of 'initiative' should corner Mr. George Wrenn in his den and asked him what light he could throw on this. Well, I did and in discussing this matter with both Mr. George Wrenn and his Works Manager, Mr. George Porter they confirmed that this model was wholly the idea of the Wrenn Company and was not planned by Hornby Dublo. The body used a Wills kit and the tender was an old Hornby Dublo '8F' tender quite literally taken off the windowsill. The model was first painted in LMS red and then, for their latest number 4 issue catalogue, stripped and repainted in both British Railways green and the post-war LMS black livery. Photographs at each stage were taken for inclusion in the catalogue.

This leads us nicely on to . . .

CAST WHITE METAL KITS

To help promote the sales of Hornby Dublo 'linesman' in September 1964, the *Meccano Magazine* commenced a series of three articles wherein they stated that they wanted to describe the wonderful range of locomotive kits available to the enthusiast and to demonstrate how a Hornby Dublo locomotive chassis could be used in conjunction with them:

'Many enthusiasts will prefer to use a Hornby Dublo chassis with a cast locomotive since it combines the reliability of a Hornby Dublo chassis with the individuality of a kit. The prices for the complete 2-rail chassis assemblies were:

2–8–0 Chassis £3. 4s. 0d. (£3. 20p)
0–6–2 Chassis £2. 3s. 6d. (£2. 17p)
Castle Chassis £2. 18s. 3d. (£2. 91p)
2–6–4 Chassis £2. 18s. 3d. (£2. 91p)
0–6–0 Chassis £1. 13s. 9d. (£1. 68p)
Golden Fleece Chassis £2. 12s. 3d. (£2. 61p)
West Country Chassis £3. 12s. 9d. (£3. 63p)
The City Chassis £2. 19s. 3d. (£2. 96p)

All these units were available from Service Agents or direct from their local dealer.

The firms producing the vast range of kits were Messrs. K's, Wills, Bec and Gem but only Bob Wills replied to my request some years ago for photographs of their models using the Hornby Dublo chassis. His name is interwoven with our subject. What with his original Track Cleaning Wagon and the fact that on

The Fisons Nitrogen Liquor tanker.

SR E.6 Tank by Wills Finecast Ltd.

more than one occasion one or two of the main proprietary model railway manufacturers had used his kits to display one of their new planned prototypes. Many thanks indeed Bob for all your help. I think the finest kit of all for me was reviewed in the September 1962 *Railway Modeller* under the heading 'A Magnificent Replica' this being the model of the three cylinder Stannier 4P4F Tank locomotive. It records that the then editor of the *Railway Modeller*, Mr. Cyril Freezer had contacted Bob at the Model Railway Exhibition and suggested that a model 2–6–4 Tank locomotive fitted with a Hornby Dublo Chassis was badly needed.

The entire 37 locomotives of this Class spent almost their whole career on the LTSR mainline, hauling packed trains from Fenchurch Street to Southend and Shoeburyness on a tight schedule, and although rated as Class 4 performed duties that would have fallen to Class 5 locomotives elsewhere. Plaistow Shed kept them all in perfect mechanical condition and one was scheduled for preservation.

I was sad to read in the *Railway Modeller* for June 1969 an obituary to one of the greatest pioneers of the model railway hobby Mr. Stewart Reidpath. More than anyone else he had laid the foundations for modern small scale modelling. In the first issue of the *Model Railway News* in January 1925 he contributed an article on a superb H0 dining car which would stand comparison with anything produced today, over half a century later. He was one of the first to move clearly from the super toy into the scale field and during the 1930s there can have been few H0 and 00 gauge layouts which did not rely heavily on Reidpath components. He produced one of the first reliable 00 gauge mechanisms and was the pioneer of the cast white metal locomotive body.

LMS Stanier Class 4 Tank also by Bob Wills.

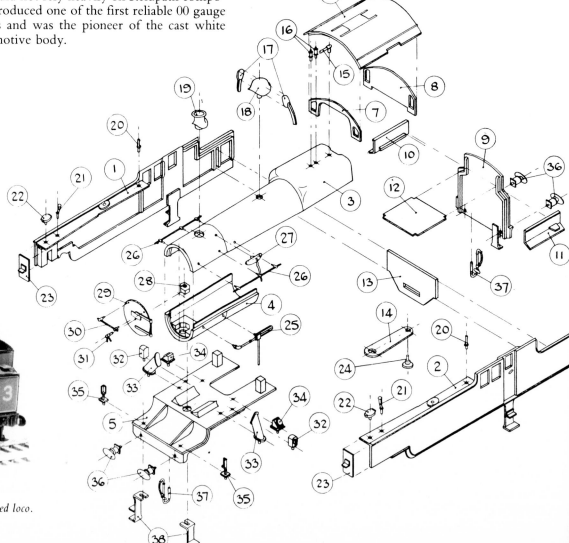

The very attractive finished loco.

The Compendium
by Alan F. Ellis

A COMPILATION OF HORNBY-DUBLO ITEMS

As Manufactured, or Noted by Meccano Limited, Liverpool.

The following pages have been compiled by enthusiasts for enthusiasts. Information has been obtained from the Hornby-Dublo Circle and almost two hundred catalogues, price lists and folders issued by Meccano Limited, Rovex Limited and G. & R. Wrenn Limited, plus the Meccano Magazine. Variations are noted from the above literature and from hours of analysis by ardent collectors, to whom we are very grateful. Without their help and cooperation we would not have been able to create this list.

My thanks and appreciation go to those whom I am always pleased to meet to discuss our common interest, especially Messrs. J. Callow, A. Bianco, J. Marr and M. Foster, plus many others far too numerous to mention.

Alan F. Ellis

The list is not meant to be a history — that has already been amply covered by our fellow collector Mr. Michael Foster — but a list of all known items and their variations derived from the available information and innumerable collections.

This does not mean that all variations are necessarily known and listed here, but only those that are known to this point in time. We are certain that others will turn up as a result of this list — in fact we expect it — but hope that they will be few in number.

We have tried to ensure that all variations listed are genuine, by studying the available literature and the items in question. There may be some that don't appear to be the genuine article, but we can assure you that they have been confirmed to be genuine.

The occasional item that has yet to be confirmed is noted as such. This does not mean that the item is a fake, but that proof of originality has yet to be established.

Freak items are well known as having been made at Binns Road, and these are also noted accordingly. Others are shown in catalogues and folders but were never actually sold.

Minute colour variations are not noted, as they are often a result of sunlight and fading with the years. Both boxes and wagons etc are susceptible to this problem. Major colour differences are noted, as items with odd colours are often rare and therefore are keenly sought after.

Finally, this section is dedicated to the wives and sweethearts, especially to my own good wife, who have all had to put up with men talking of toy trains.

GLOSSARY OF TERMS AND ABBREVIATIONS

In order to keep the information in a short format and to a practical length, abbreviations are essential to simplify the list. Common model railway terms are utilized and should present no problems.

ABBREVIATIONS.

WHEELS

PWW Prewar wheels. These are identified by their 'square' section and are of soft zinc alloy material, which when impure deteriorates with age. All too often prewar wheels have, or are in the process of, breaking up.

EPW Early postwar wheel. These have the same 'square' section as prewar, but do not break up. The reason being that the zinc alloy no longer has the impurities of the prewar metal.

FPW Final postwar type (metal). These were used until the change over to plastic wheels in the late 1950's. These are made of sintered iron and have no 'square' sections, but have rounded profiles both in front of and behind the flange.

SO Solid plastic (disc) wheels. Plastic material is polypropylene. The two wheels and axle are one moulded piece.

SP Spoked plastic wheels.

COUPLINGS

PW Prewar. These are of spring steel, basically flat with an oval end having a tongue which engages with the coupling of the next vehicle. They are not suitable for automatic uncoupling.

EMC Early metal 'hook' type coupling. Can be used for both automatic coupling and uncoupling. Uncoupling is accomplished by a vertical drop piece (striker) which engages the uncoupling ramps. This type is distinguished by a small vertical portion at the end of the hook piece and no patent number around the pivot hole. A registered design (RD) number exists along the shank.

LMC Basically identical to the EMC type above, but have patent numbers around the pivot hole and still the same length of vertical portion at the end of the 'hook' piece.

FMC Final type of metal coupling. These have patent numbers plus a much longer vertical portion at the end of the 'hook' piece.

EPC Early type plastic coupling. About 6/60. Made of nylon with the same basic shape as the metal couplings above, but much thicker.

NPC New plastic coupling. About 3/63. This was the last type of coupling to be made by Meccano Limited. This coupling was made of black delrin, and is much finer than the EPC type.

Many of these were screwed into place, as were a few of the above, rather than rivetted. The later items of rolling stock had special plastic clip-in plugs to secure the couplings to the chassis.

In addition to the basic styles of couplings noted above, each coupling was also made in varying types to allow for the differences in rolling stock or locomotive height above track level. In some cases the coupling was extended in length, between the pivot hole and the 'hook', in order to protrude and clear buffers etc. In addition to the basic type, there are two others. a) With the stops to prevent excessive swinging located on each side, rather than a single stop at the rear behind the pivot hole, and b) With an extended arm and curvature. Metal couplings can also be found to have a coat of black paint, 'blued' or nickel plated.

BOGIE FRAMES

SGa Standard Gresley type frames. Prewar.

SGb As SGa, but postwar. Only the type of metal varies between the two types.

CG Compensated Gresley type. Used on early Pullman coaches. Bogie frame has pivots to allow vertical play.

DBa Diamond bogies. Named after their shape. Prewar. Used on High Capacity Wagon prewar.

DBb Diamond bogies. Common to all postwar bogied freight wagons until replaced with the later Plate Bogie. The metal is the only variation from the prewar type.

PB Plate Bogie. Appeared in the late 1950's although the Diamond type did not disappear altogether.

LMS Bogie frame type to be found on LMS coaches and early red and cream coaches of B.R. livery. Readily noticed by two small stars on the side frame near the centre of each bogie.

SB Standard B.R. type bogie. Recognised by two small springs below the centre of the side of frame and no stars, but rods where the stars were located on the LMS type.

CSB Compensated standard bogie type. As the SB above, but has pivot to allow vertical movement, like the compensated Gresley type.

BASES

Meccano Limited have already provided numbers on the underside of three bases. These are numbers 5, 6 and 7 and they appear on the three latest type of wagons having open brake gear. To prevent any confusion, these numbers have been retained.

As there are four basic base types prior to the three noted above with open brake gear, it is easy to number them 1 through 4, but with suffixes where necessary to distinguish variations within the types. Other bases are

...numbered after 7. Many of the later bases were only used for one model, but are numbered in order to correspond with the base illustrations.

Type 1a	Prewar standard bases, with the word 'Hornby' and moulded for use with the prewar spring steel couplings. They have a raised centre circular piece.
Type 1b	Identical to the above, but moulded for postwar couplings. The metal also varies from that of the prewar as noted under bogie frames previously. These were used for all pre-nationalised stock and early B.R. stock. The change occurred about 1955/6.
Type 1c	As type 1a, but with longer wheel base as used on the Goods Brake Vans prewar.
Type 1d	As type 1c, but postwar metal, for Goods Brake Vans.
Type 2a	Much later chronologically, identical to type 1b, but with no raised centre circular piece.
Type 2b	As type 2a, but with hole for fastening bodies of vans to the base with a screw.
Type 2c	As type 2a, but for longer wheel base vehicles, such as the Goods Brake Vans.
Type 3a	These have the words 'HORNBY DUBLO' on the underside and were used on nearly all tin plate wagons and on the early superdetailed stock. These are by far the most common base type to be found. They also have a raised centre circular piece, except for the Goods Brake Vans, see note below.
Type 3b	As type 3a but used on Goods Brake Vans. Base plate is of tin and is separate from the main casting.
Type 3c	Identical to type 3b above except that the casting now has long running boards.
Type 3d	Base plate cast as part of the whole chassis frame. Continues to have long running boards.
Type 3e	Same basic style as type 3a, but is elongated for use on the Low Sided Wagons.
Type 3f	As type 3e, but with raised stops on the upper side for use with the Cable Drums.
Type 4a	Same as type 3a, but no longer has a raised centre circular piece.
Type 4b	As type 4a, but with hole for securing van bodies to the base.
Type 5	These have the number cast into the underside of the base. Used mostly on Tank Wagons. Base has open brake gear.
Type 6	Number 6 is cast into underside of base. Used mostly on Vans. Has open brake gear and is vacuum fitted.
Type 7	Number 7 cast into underside of base. Used mostly on open wagons. Has open brake gear.
Type 8	Long Wheel base vehicles. These have a square raised area adjacent to the vacuum pot, through which a hole is drilled.
Type 9	Basically as type 8, but with no square raised area. The words 'Meccano Ltd' etc are in a different location to those on the type 8 base.
Type 10	Bases as used on the Bulk Grain and Cattle Wagons, superdetailed. Has the words 'Hornby Dublo' plus semi open brake gear.
Type 11a	Used on High Capacity Wagons, prewar. Flat base with raised centre circular piece.
Type 11b	Postwar variation of type 11a. Metal is only difference.
Type 11c	As type 11b, but wording is now in a depressed area from the rest of the base. Still retains the centre circular raised piece.
Type 11d	As type 11c, with depressed area, but no longer has a centre circular raised piece.
Type 12	Bulk Cement and Bulk Salt Wagons. Similar to type 4, but slight change in location of the lettering, and shorter in length. Has open brake gear.
Type 13	Double Bolster Wagon.
Type 14	Bogie Bolster Wagon.
Type 15	Bogie Well Wagon.
Type 16	Traffic Services Tank Wagon.
Type 17	ICI Chlorine Tank Wagon.
Type 18	United Dairies Tank Wagon.
Type 19	Utility Van.
Type 20	Hopper Wagon.
Type 21	Rail Cleaning Wagon.
Type 22	6-wheel Passenger Brake Van.
Type 23	Lowmac Machine Wagon.
Type 24	Blue Spot Fish Van.
Type 25	ICI Caustic Liquor Bogie Tank Wagon.

Types 13 through 25 are special to specific types of wagons and vans only, and do not appear on more than one type.

BOXES — WAGONS & COACHES

Type	Description	Date
Type 1a & 4a	Standard wagon, van and tender boxes. Pale blue with dark blue printing. Code on side includes production run with month and year. End flaps locate contents. End flaps identically printed including D (Dublo) or DRxxx (R-Rolling Stock) reference numbers. Colour stickers identify railway company where necessary. NOTE Some early postwar items issued in this type box.	1938-40
Type 1b & 4b	As 1a, but D/DRxxx deleted. Still pale blue.	1948
	Slight variation to above, darker in colour but with distinctly smooth 'varnish' finish.	1948
	Blue is now more turquoise and slightly speckled, still with dark blue printing. D/DR numbers back in use and multilingual descriptions.	1949
Type 1c & 4c	Blue much darker, or 'Mid' blue, dark blue printing on early ones and white on later, D/DR numbers and multilingual.	1950
Type 1d & 4d	As (c) but D/DR numbers replaced with 32xxx reference at bottom left hand corner, and later at top centre. Railway companies identified by sticker where applicable.	1951-2
Type 1e & 4e	As (d) but dark blue. 'BR' sticker used in late 1952.	1952

Type	Date	Description
Type 1f	1953-4	As (c) but date code on side deleted. 'BR' now printed as part of description. A hand stamped date code can often be found on one inside flap.
Type 2a & 4a	1955 onward	Box has blue and white stripes. 32xxx number and is multilingual on one end flap. A hand stamped date code is often to be found inside one end flap. Early boxes had light blue internal colour, later boxes are grey-brown inside.
Type 2b		As type 2a, but for SD 6 (Super-Detailed) series. These have a white instruction panel on one side, a 32xxx number and a hand printed code within the box on one end flap. An illustration of the wagon inside is depicted on the side of the box.
Type 2c & 5c		As type 2a, but a red sticker can be found on at least one end flap, indicating that the item is suitable for both 2 and 3-rail running.
Type 2d		As type 2b, but no longer has a 32xxx number. A 4xxx number is used instead.
Type 3a & 6a		Box is now red and white stripes, a 4xxx code is shown in white lettering in a large red oval. Some have an illustration of the article on the outside.
Type 3b & 6b		Basically as type 3a, but with an additional 36xxx or 37xxx box code. The 4xxx code is now in a small red oval.
Type 3c & 6c		Similar to type 3b, but with new Hornby insignia. The 4xxx number is now in red printing in a small white oval having a red outline.

Types 4a through 6c noted above are for coaches. Except for length, these are all identical to the wagon boxes. Where no 4, 5 or 6 code appears there is no corresponding coach box type. Additional coach boxes, which have no corresponding wagon type boxes are as follows:—

Type	Date	Description
Type 4g		Plain unprinted mid-blue box with labels on the ends only. Labels show a 32xxx code.
Type 4h		Plain brown cardboard box. (These vary from those used as repair boxes, in that they have end flaps, and repair boxes have two sections, a lid and a bottom).

BOXES — LOCOMOTIVES

Type	Date	Description
Type 7a		Prewar locos. clockwork. Pale blue in colour, and much larger than postwar boxes. Printing is also blue. The D series numbering and date code appear on side of box. Two piece box. Locos packed in corrugated cardboard.
Type 7b		Prewar electric locos. Pale blue box with mauve print. Larger than postwar type. Two piece box. Cardboard packing.
Type 7c		Early postwar box, pale blue in colour but only large enough to contain loco. Cardboard no longer used for packing. Printing is blue. Date and code on side of box. Two piece box.
Type 7d		Plain mid-blue box and no printing. Information on end labels, with dark blue printing on a light blue label. Two piece box. No date code or 31xxx number.
Type 7e	1955 onward	As type 7d, but label includes a 31xxx code number. Box large enough for loco only. i.e. Tender locos came without tender, which was available separately.
Type 7f		As type 7e, but box now large enough to contain loco and tender.
Type 7g		As 7e for tank engines and as 7f for tender locos. End label now shows 32xxx number. Some labels include a 34xxx number. Labels vary from turquoise to a pale blue with dark blue lettering. This type is much later chronologically than the type 8 series, and was used for the last 3-rail locomotives.
Type 8a		Lid of box is finished with blue and white stripes. Yellow oval end panels contain loco information and an EDL xx number code or LT xx number code. Boxes large enough to contain loco only where applicable. A picture of the loco is illustrated on top of the box. The box bottom is plain mid-blue.
Type 8b		As type 8a, but box now large enough to contain loco and tender where applicable.
Type 8c		As type 8b, but end panel is now rectangular having rounded corners and a 32xxx loco code number and a 34xxx box code number.
Type 8d		Similar to 8c, but end labels have square corners and top of box is yellow with illustration and no blue and white stripes.
Type 9a		Plain red boxes for early two rail locos. These have square white end labels with red printing and a 22xx loco code in a red oval. No box codes. Some have a linen finish to the box, which was mostly used on export items. Export boxes are not listed as a variation.
Type 9b		Red and white stripe one piece box, as type 3b, for locos 2206 and 2207 only. The only one piece box used for locos. The 22xx code is printed in white in a red oval. A 31xxx box code is also printed on box.
Type 9c		Similar to type 8c, but with red and white stripes and 22xx loco code number plus a 31xxx box code. A picture of the loco is illustrated on top of box. The end panels have rounded off corners.
Type 9d		As type 8d, but with red and white stripes on sides.
Type 9e		As type 9d, but with new 'Hornby' insignia.

BOXES — SETS

Type	Date	Description
Type 10a		Prewar type. Essentially dark blue with illustration of passenger and goods train on top. Narrow, deep and long box. Includes a controller.
Type 10b		Early postwar. Almost square as compared to the prewar set boxes. Has picture of

Type 10c	LMS loco in red on top label, which originates from prewar 'O' gauge sets. Includes a controller.
Type 10d	As 10b type, but has small rectangular label showing prewar items on top of lid.
Type 10e	As 10c type, but with label showing boy and postwar items. Blue end labels, some having a 30xxx box number. No longer contains a controller.
Type 10f	End labels are yellow and the top picture is much larger. Otherwise as above.
Type 11	Long narrow box, similar to prewar but not so deep. Label as above but elongated to cover top of box. Yellow end labels. Used for certain 0-6-2T and 2-6-4T sets in the mid-1950's.
Type 12	Early 2-rail sets. Box similar to type 10b, but top has a multi-colour illustration and is a light blue with yellow background to picture.
Type 13a	Later 2-rail sets. White and light blue with light and dark brown panels.
Type 13b	Ready to run sets. Have a mottled brown finish with the new 'Hornby' insignia in blue. Lid folds over bottom and is all one piece. Sets contain a No. 1 Transformer-Controller.
Type 13c	Ready to run sets. Foamed polystyrene base with a clear celluloid lid. Contain a No 1 Transformer-Controller. Polystyrene base and celluloid lid, similar to above but as illustrated in the 1964 folder. There is no confirmation that this type of box ever existed for sets other than the ready to run sets as noted above.

BOXES — ACCESSORIES AND TRACK — 3-RAIL

Type 14a	Prewar. Pale blue with blue printing. D and DA numbers plus code in most cases.
Type 14b	As type 14a except for date code. No D or DA (Dublo Accessories) numbers in many cases. No D numbers for track boxes.
Type 14c	Boxes are now a mid-blue colour. DA numbers continue except for track boxes, which are slightly lighter in colour. Many boxes have a linen finish.
Type 14d	As type 14c, but no longer have DA numbers. Track boxes are now identical in colour.
Type 14e	Dark blue in colour. Some have date code on side, and 32xxx numbers have been added to most.
Type 14f	Box now has blue and white stripes. Continues with 32xxx number. Later ones have a 37xxx code. Most have colour illustration on box top, except for track. Gloss finish.
Type 14g	As above, but matt finish. Codes are now 3xxx and 35xxx for the box. No longer illustrated on top.
Type 14h	As 14e type, but white box and blue lettering for D2 switch.
Type 14j	As type 14e, but green with blue lettering, for G3 switch.
Type 14k	Very early postwar box. Plain brown cardboard with blue printing. Includes a date code. Used for track. This item out of basic chronological sequence due to its recent discovery.
Type 14l	Identical to type 14f, except no picture and used only for track. Blue is glossy like 14g.

BOXES — ACCESSORIES AND TRACK — 2-RAIL

Type 15a	Red and white stripes plus illustration of item on top. 2xxx and 5xxx code numbers plus 32xxx and 37xxx box code numbers respectively.
Type 15b	Identical to above but with no illustration.
Type 15c	White box with red printing, as used for straight short rail.
Type 15d	As type 15b but with new 'Hornby' insignia.
Type 15e	Mottled brown boxes plus label. As used on the Track Packs.
Type 16	Plain red boxes with white number in red oval. As used for plastic building kits and early Breakdown Cranes. Also electrically operated signals, but with different labels.
Type 17	Red and white striped boxes, with plain red bottom. Has yellow end labels and illustration of item on top with yellow back ground.
Type 18	Light blue box with multi-coloured illustration, as used for the Terminal Station Kit.
Type 19	Polyethylene packets or bags. May have red or blue or no printing.
Type 20	Plastic bubble pack with cardboard back plate.
Type 21	Small white box with red printing. Mainly for parts.
Type 22a	Yellow box with blue band having blue printing.
Type 22b	White box with blue band and blue lettering.
Type 22c	Yellow box with white band and red printing.
Type 23a	Paper envelopes with either blue or mauve printing.
Type 23b	Cellophane envelopes with blue printing.
Type 24	Grey-brown box with red printing. Used for tunnels.
Type 25a	Tin box with green wrapper and printing. White cardboard box with yellow label.
Type 25b	This and 25a above are used for the spare colour light bulbs.

Track boxes are included with accessories as the box types and colours are basically identical. Minor variations are noted in the above list.

To enlarge upon the various sizes of boxes, in addition to major items noted, would be a gigantic task, as sizes varied from item to item. Similarly, to list all the variations in dimensions in the following pages would not serve any real purpose. Certain dimensions of many of the items are to be found in the numerous catalogues and folders, as issued by Meccano Limited.

BASIS OF BOOK LAYOUT

Obviously the layout of this list has to be based upon some logical method. The problem is which method should work best and make the list easy to follow.

The first few pages are used for prewar items. This should present no trouble. The order chosen for the prewar arrangement is not based upon any order of Meccano Limited, but is simply an extension of my original inventory sheets, from which the idea of publishing a complete list originated.

The postwar list is an entirely different situation. Again, the list evolved from my own inventory sheets. This has a foundation based upon Meccano Limited's own numbering system used from 1959 onwards.

In the 1959 Hornby Book of Trains, the following basic numbering system was used for the first time:—

0 – 1999	Sundries, Parts and Electrical Control Equipment.
2000 – 2100	2-rail Locomotives.
2200 – 2300	2-rail Sets.
2400 – 2999	2-rail Track and associated items such as Buffer Stops.
3000 – 3199	3-rail Sets.
3200 – 3399	3-rail Locomotives.
3400 – 3999	3-rail Track etc.
4000 – 4299	Coach Stock.
4300 – 4699	Rolling Stock excluding Coaches.
5000 – 5099	Accessories.
6000 – 6999	Hornby-Acho Items available in Britain and elsewhere, but excluding France.

There were many gaps in the numbering system, but I have tried to utilise it in the following pages. However, there are a couple of exceptions. These have been made to put groups together, such as the 2 and 3-rail track, sets and locomotives.

Due to using the above series of numbers the lists are laid out with this last number series being noted first. Immediately before the above number series, all items had a 32xxx code and these are listed second. Prior to the 32xxx code, all items were noted by a D1 or D2 etc and therefore the D series is shown last. Chronologically these appeared first.

The D numbers appeared in 1938 and were an extension of the 'O' gauge numbering, the D being a prefix to show that the item was a Dublo one. The 32xxx numbers was first used as a box reference code and originated about 1950. The 32xxx code was first used for catalogue numbers in early 1956.

One exception exists in the reverse chronological order, and that is in the 3-rail sets, where the 'EDP and EDG' sets are listed first, as the 3xxx series, although listed in a few catalogues and price lists, was never known to have been used on the set boxes and therefore full information is not available.

Numbers in brackets in the 'BOX NO.' column signify no confirmation of the numbers in the case of the prewar items, and that the noted box numbers do not appear on the specific boxes in the case of the postwar items, but are referred to in dealers lists.

Although originally presumed to be box code numbers for postwar stock, it has recently been confirmed that the numbers on the boxes are a Data Processing code used by Binns Road for order purposes and presumably stock purposes also, as all Meccano Ltd. products have a five figure number according to dealer's delivery and invoice sheets.

Dates and prices of items are either as listed in the Meccano Magazine, or other literature, in the event that the item did not appear originally in the Meccano Magazine. The last date and price is as noted in retail catalogues or price lists. Over the years, as previously noted, each item may have been listed under a Dx, 32xxx or the latest four figure number, and therefore the prices and dates between the first and last reference to a particular item and variation are noted if other references and/or variations of the item are illustrated or noted in the literature, i.e. An item was originally shown with early metal couplings (EPW) and listed under a D1 number. It would next be listed under a 32xxx number, and so there is a reference change. Next the item might appear with the final postwar couplings (FPW), or plastic couplings or open brake gear chassis etc., and therefore the reference and date/price changes each time, so that an idea of when a variation occurred may be determined.

Box code dates are shown either as 12.52 or 4/53. The first signifies the code printed on the box side, the latter indicates a code hand stamped on the inside of one of the end flaps, underside of the lid or box bottom, depending upon the type of box.

In general, no box can be said to contain any particular variation of an item, due to extensive overlapping which occurred. The list shows approximately when variations and types of boxes coincided.

Brackets along side various references indicate that there is no change or variation in the item, but only in the reference or box type. Similarly, brackets alongside the boxes indicate that the box type remains static, although the item or reference might change.

This all sounds very confusing, but once one becomes familiar with the variations and codes, the list is not too difficult to follow.

KEY:
- C — Catalogue
- F — Folder
- PL — Price List
- DPL — Dealer's Price List
- B — Book
- P — Pamphlet
- IPL — Illustrated Price List
- S — Single Sheet
- Su — Supplement
- DL — Dealer's List

CATALOGUES, FOLDERS AND PRICE LISTS ETC.

N.B. Unless noted otherwise, the items are UK.

NO.	REFERENCE NO.	OTHER REF.	DATE	TYPE	COLOUR	COMMENTS
1	13/638/1150	—	1938/9	C	Black & White	Meccano Products.
2	17/738/30	—	1938/9	C	Black & White	Meccano Products. Canada. Unpriced.
3	7/938/4	—	1938/9	F	Full Colour	Dublo Only. New Zealand.
4	7/938/185	—	1938/9	F	Full Colour	Dublo Only.
5	2/1238/50	—	—	F	Black, White & Blue	Dublo Only.
6	2/1238/50	—	—	F	Black, White & Blue	As above, Black 'Hornby-Dublo'.
7	1/239/4.5	—	1939	DL	Brown on Cream	Dublo, O and Dinky Toys.
8	1/239/10	—	1939	P	Black on Grey-Blue	'Perfect Train Control'.
9	5-4-39	—	—	DL	Black & White	Dealer's Order Form.
10	—	—	1939	DL	Black on Pink	Dealer's Stock List.
11	1/539/5	—	June 1939	P	Ochre on Cream	'Part Exchange Scheme'.
12	13/639/1,1500	—	1939/40	C	Black & White	Meccano Products.
13	7/739/3/N.P.	—	1939/40	C	Colour	Hornby Book of Trains. Canada.
14	—	—	8 Nov. 1939	PL	Black on Blue	Revised Prices, H-D & D.T. Canada.
15	7/739/100	—	1939/40	C	Colour	Hornby Book of Trains.
16	1/939/27	—	1939	P	Black on Green	'Perfect Train Control'.
17	12/1039/70	—	1939	F	Orange, Black on Wh.	Dublo Only.
18	16/1039/125	—	9 Oct. 1939	PL	Black & White	Dublo Only. Revised Prices.
19	2/1139/70	—	1939/40	F	Brown on Cream	New Features.
20	2/1239/20 (2nd P.)	—	1939/40	F	Brown on Cream	New Features.
21	1/140/50	—	1 Jan. 1940	PL	Brown on P. Yellow	Meccano Products. Revised Prices.
22	13/840/15	—	Aug. 1940	C	Brown on Buff	Meccano Products. Australia.
23	16/840/50	—	Aug. 1940	PL	Blue on White	Meccano Products.
24	16/1040/100	—	21 Oct. 1940	PL	L. Green on White	Meccano Products.
25	16/641/25	—	May 1941	PL	Blue on Buff	Meccano Products. Australia.
26	—	—	Sept. 1941	C	Brown on Buff	Meccano Products. Canada.
27	13/741/20	—	—	PL	Black on L. Green	Meccano Products.
28	16/1141/20	—	1 Nov. 1941	PL	Brown on White	Meccano Products.
29	1947	—	—	IPL	Blue on White	Meccano Products. First Post-War List
30	16/248/10	—	—	IPL	Black, Orange & White	Meccano Products. South Africa.
31	13/248/20	—	—	IPL	Black, Orange & White	Meccano Products. New Zealand.
32	13/448/15	—	—	IPL	P. Green on Off White	Meccano Products. Australia.
33	16/448/30	—	1 May 1948	IPL	Black, Orange & White	Meccano Products.
34	13/648/5	—	—	IPL	Violet on Off White	Meccano Products. Prewar Cplgs.
35	16/948/200	—	Oct. 1948	IPL	Black & White	Meccano Products.
36	—	—	Approx. 1948	C	L. Brown on Off Wh.	Dublo & O Gauge. USA.
37	16/449/100	—	—	IPL	L. Brown on Off Wh.	Meccano Products.
38	16/549/10	—	May 1949	IPL	Blue on Buff	Meccano Products. New Zealand.
39	—	—	July 1949	PL	Violet on Off White	Meccano Products. Australia.
40	16/1049/100	—	—	IPL	Black on Buff & Wh.	Meccano Products.
41	13/1049/150	—	—	C	Brown on White	Meccano Products.
42	16/250/100	C2091	1 Feb. 1950	IPL	Black, P. Blue & Wh.	Meccano Products.
43	16/450/150	C2495	June 1950	IPL	Black, P. Blue & Wh.	Meccano Products. Canada.
44	16/550/50	C2685	June 1950	IPL	Black, Buff & White	Meccano Products. Australia.
45	16/550/68	C3103	May 1950	IPL	Black, Blue & White	Meccano Products. New Zealand.
46	—	—	—	IPL	Blue on White	Meccano Products.
47	16/750/20	—	—	IPL	Black, Blue on White	Meccano Products. New Zealand.
48	16/1050/160	C3476	Oct. 1950	IPL	Blue on White	Meccano Products.
49	16/151/23.5	C4246	1951	IPL	Black, Blue on White	Meccano Products. New Zealand.
50	16/251/33	C4445	March 1951	IPL	Brown on Cream	Meccano Products.
51	5/451/75	C5198	Jan. 1951	IPL	Brown on Off White	Meccano Products. Australia.
52	16/651/75	C5658	March 1951	IPL	Blue on White	Meccano Products. Italy.
53	5/951/10	—	Aug. 1951	IPL	Brown on Off White	Meccano Products. South Africa.
54	16/951/10	—	Aug. 1951	IPL	Brown on Off White	Meccano Products.
55	16/1051/25	C5745	Oct. 1951	IPL	Mauve on White	Meccano Products.

NO.	REFERENCE NO.	OTHER REF.	DATE	TYPE	COLOUR	COMMENTS
56	16/152/5	C6319	March 1952	IPL	Blue on White	Meccano Products. New Zealand.
57	16/152/50	C6321	Feb. 1952	C	Brown on White	Meccano Products.
58	16/452/50	C6755	April 1952	C	Blue on White	Meccano Products. New Zealand.
59	16/552/50	C6921	March 1952	C	Blue on Blue	Meccano Products. South Africa.
60	5/752/10	—	—	C	Black & White	Meccano Products. Canada.
61	16/752/90	—	1952	C	Blue on White	Meccano Products. Canada.
62	16/852/500	C7401	Sept. 1952	C	L. Brown on Off Wh.	Dublo & O Gauge. USA.
63	—	C8054	Oct. 1952	IPL	Black & White	Meccano Products.
64	16/153/50	—	1 Feb. 1953	C	Blue on White	Meccano Products. Australia.
65	—	—	1 Mar. 1953	PL	Blue on Buff	Meccano Products. New Zealand.
66	17/253/5	—	April 1953	IPL	Blue, Buff on White	Announcement of B.R. Liveries. N.Z.
67	8/253/5	—	25 Feb. 1953	DL		Announcement of B.R. Liveries. N.Z.
68	8/353/10	C8483	April 1953	DL		Meccano Products.
69	16/453/50	—	15 Apr. 1953	C	Mauve on White	Meccano Products.
70	8/553/5	—	29 May 1953	DL		Dublo & Meccano Only.
71	13/653/5	—	1 Oct. 1953	C	Black & White	Meccano Products.
72	13/953/17	—	1953	C	Black & White	Meccano Products. Italy.
73	13/953/25	—	1 Oct. 1953	C	Black & White	Meccano Products. Australia.
74	13/953/50	—	1 Oct. 1953	C	Black & White	Meccano Products. New Zealand.
75	13/953/678	—	1 Oct. 1953	C	Black & White	Meccano Products.
76	13/1053/10	—	1 Oct. 1953	C	Black & White	Meccano Products. South Africa.
77	13/1053/90	—	1953	C	Black & White	Meccano Products.Canada.Shows CPR
78	7/1053/250	—	1953/54	F	Colour	Dublo Only. Priced.
79	7/1053/250	—	1953/54	F	Colour	Dublo Only. Unpriced.
80	16/1053/150	—	1 Oct. 1953	PL	L. Green on White	Meccano Products.
81	13/1053/350 (2nd P)	—	1 Oct. 1953	C	Black & White	Meccano Products. Italy.
82	13/1053/350 (2nd P)	—	1 Oct. 1953	C	Black & White	Meccano Prod.'Rev. Prices, 1 Apr.1954'
83	16/154/5	—	1 Apr. 1954	PL	Blue on White	Meccano Products. South Africa.
84	16/154/10	—	1 Apr. 1954	PL	Blue on White	Meccano Products. New Zealand.
85	16/354/50	—	1 Apr. 1954	PL	Brown on Yellow	Meccano Products.
86	—	—	1 Apr. 1954	PL	Blue on Apricot	Meccano Products. Australia.
87	16/454/50	—	1 May 1954	PL	Brown on Yellow	Meccano Products. New Zealand.
88	13/654/50	—	1954/55	C	Black & White	Meccano Products. Australia.
89	13/654/50	—	1954/55	C	Black & White	Meccano Products.
90	13/654/995	—	1954/55	C	Black & White	Meccano Products.
91	7/754/28	—	1954/55	F	Colour	Dublo Only. Unpriced.
92	7/754/200	—	1954/55	F	Colour	Dublo Only. Priced.
93	7/754/200	—	1954/55	F	Colour	Dublo. 'Revised Prices, 1 Feb. 1955'.
94	16/754/20	—	—	PL	Brown on Off White	Meccano Products.
95	7/854/12	—	1954/55	F	Colour	Dublo Only. Australia.
96	7/954/20	—	1954/55	F	Colour	Dublo Only. Priced. Canada.
97	16/954/50	—	—	PL	Blue on White	Meccano Products.
98	7/1054/7	—	1954/55	F	Colour	Dublo Only. Priced. New Zealand.
99	16/1054/3	—	1 Sept. 1954	F	Colour	Meccano Products. Italy.
100	7/1154/4	—	1954/55	F	Black, Blue on White	Dublo Only. Eire.
101	7/1154/40	—	1954/55	F	Colour	Dublo Only. Unpriced.
102	16/1154/250	HD/PL/1	—	P	Blue on White	'Dublo can be yours etc.'
103	16/155/10	—	March 1955	PL	Black & White	Meccano Products. New Zealand.
104	16/155/15	—	March 1955	PL	Brown on Yellow	Meccano Products. New Zealand.
105	16/155/100	—	Feb. 1955	PL	Brown on Yellow	Meccano Products. New Zealand.
106	16/255/100	—	Feb. 1955	PL	Brown on Buff	Meccano Products.
107	16/355/50	HD/PL/1	1 Feb. 1955	PL	Black on Green	Dublo Only.
108	16/355/50	MP/PL/1	March 1955	PL	Brown on Yellow	Meccano Products.
109	16/355/100	MP/PL/1	March 1955	PL	Brown on Yellow	Meccano Products.
110	16/555/100	MP/PL/1	May 1955	PL	Brown on Yellow	Meccano Products.

NO.	REFERENCE NO.	OTHER REF.	DATE	TYPE	COLOUR	COMMENTS
111	13/655/50	MP/B/1	1955/56	C	Black & White	Meccano Products. New Zealand.
112	13/655/50	MP/B/1	1955/56	C	Black & White	Meccano Products. Australia.
113	13/655/797	MP/B/1	1955/56	C	Black & White	Meccano Products.
114	7/755/20	HD/CF/1	1955/56	F	Colour	Dublo Only. New Zealand.
115	7/755/20	HD/CF/1	1955/56	F	Colour	Dublo Only. Australia.
116						
117	7/755/70	HD/CF/1	1955/56	F	Colour	Dublo Only. Unpriced.
118	7/755/550	HD/CF/1	1955/56	F	Colour	Dublo Only. Priced.
119	7/755/550	HD/CF/1	1955/56	F	Colour	Dublo Only. Overprinted 'Rev. Prices'
120	7/855/10	HD/CF/1	1955/56	F	Colour	Dublo Only. Canada.
121	7/855/2	HD/CF/1	1955/56	F	Colour	Dublo Only. Italy.
122	16/1055/500	MP/PL/2	27 Oct. 1955	PL	Black on Green	Meccano Products.
123	16/156/100M 1st P	MP/PL/3	1 Feb. 1956	PL	Brown on Pink	Meccano Products.
124	16/256/7.5 1st P	MP/PL/3	Feb. 1956	PL	Brown on Apricot	Meccano Products. New Zealand.
125	7/256/400					
126	16/456/20	MP/PL/3	Feb. 1956	PL	Brown on Apricot	Meccano Products. Australia.
127	16/456/100M 2nd P	MP/PL/4	April 1956	PL	Brown on Pink	Meccano Products.
128	7/556/20	HD/CF/2	1956/57	F	Colour	Dublo Only. New Zealand.
129	7/556/20	HD/CF/2	1956/57	F	Colour	Dublo Only. Australia.
130	7/556/500	HD/CF/2	1956/57	F	Colour	Dublo Only. Priced.
131	10/656/32.5	MP/PL/4	July 1956	PL	Blue On Blue	Dublo Only. New Zealand
132	13/656/525	MP/PL/4	July 1956	PL	Black on Yellow	Meccano Products.
133	13/756/50	—	—	C	Colour	Meccano Products. New Zealand.
134	13/756/50	—	—	C	Colour	Meccano Products. Australia.
135	13/756/100	—	—	C	Colour	Meccano Products. Canada.
136	13/756/525	—	—	C	Colour	Meccano Products.
137	7/856/10	HD/CF/2	1956/57	F	Colour	Dublo Only. Priced. Canada.
138	7/856/15	HD/CF/2	1956/57	F	Colour	Dublo Only. Priced. South Africa.
139	7/956/25	HD/CF/2	1956/57	F	Colour	Dublo Only. Unpriced.
140	9/956/25	HD/CF/2	1956/57	F	Colour	Dublo Only. Unpriced. Canada.
141	—	—	—	S	Black & White	Sheet showing CPR Sets.
142	16/956/200	MP/PL/5	Sept. 1956	PL	Black on L. Green	Meccano Products.
143	8/1256/50	2407/56	Dec. 1956	IPL	Brown on Buff	Dublo Sets & Accessories Only.
144	16/157/100M	MP/PL/6	1 Feb. 1967	PL	Brown on Pink	Meccano Products.
145	—	MP/PL/5	1957	PL	Black on White	Dublo Only. U.S.A.
146	16/257/17.5 1st P	—	1957	PL	Black on Apricot	Meccano Products. New Zealand.
147	7/457/150	—	1957	F	Colour	Meccano Products. New Zealand.
148	7/457/150	—	1957	F	Colour	Meccano Prod. Rev. Prices 1 Feb 1958
149	—/457/50	—	—	S	Colour	Girder Bridge, Turntable & TPO.
150	16/457/100M 2nd P	MP/PL/7	April 1957	PL	Black on Pink	Meccano Products.
151	16/557/25 2nd P	MP/PL/6	1 May 1957	PL	Black on Apricot	Meccano Products. New Zealand
152	20M/6/57	—	1 June 1957	PL	Rust on Yellow	Meccano Products. New Zealand.
153	7/757/20	HD/CF/4	1957	F	Colour	Dublo Only. New Zealand.
154	13/757/15	—	1957	C	Colour	Meccano Products. Eire.
155	13/757/80	—	1957	C	Colour	Meccano Products. Canada.
156	13/757/500	—	1957	C	Colour	Meccano Products.
157	13/757/500	—	1957	C	Colour	Meccano Prod. Rev. Prices 1 Feb 1958
158	16/757/100 3rd P	MP/PL/8	Aug.1957	PL	Blue on L. Blue	Meccano Products.
159	7/857/20	HD/CF/4	1957	F	Colour	Dublo Only. Priced. Canada.
160	7/857/26	HD/CF/4	1957	F	Colour	Dublo Only. Unpriced
161	7/857/500	HD/CF/3	1957	F	Colour	Dublo Only. Priced.
162	7/857/500	HD/CF/3	1957	F	Colour	Dublo Only. Rev. Prices 1 Feb 1958.
163	16/857/500	MP/PL/9	Sept. 1957	PL	Black on Yellow	Meccano Products.
164	16/857/500	MP/PL/9	Sept.1957	PL	Rust on L. Yellow	Meccano Products. Identical to above
165	7/957/15	HD/CF/4	1957	F	Colour	Dublo Only. Priced. South Africa.

NO.	REFERENCE NO.	OTHER REF.	DATE	TYPE	COLOUR	COMMENTS
166	16/957/30	—	1957	S	Brown on Cream	Sheet showing CPR Sets.
167	16/1057/100 4th P	MP/PL/8	Oct. 1957	PL	Black on Green	Meccano Products.
168	16/1057/100M	—	—	P	Brown on Cream	Single sheet on Bristol Castle.
169	16/1157/6	DT/CL/20	—	S	Colour	Single sheet on Dublo Dinkys. Aust.
170	16/1157/100	DT/CL/20	—	S	Colour	Single sheet on Dublo Dinkys. Aust.
171	16/158/100 1st P	MP/PL/9	1 Feb. 1958	PL	Black on Orange	Meccano Products.
172	16/258/27.5 1st P	MP/PL/6	March 1958	PL	Black on Orange	Meccano Products. Canada.
173	8/558/5	DA 658	27 May 1958	DL	Brown on Buff	Dublo Only.
174	16/558/50 2nd P	MP/PL/10	1 May 1958	PL	Black on Orange	Meccano Products.
175	16/558/5	MP/PL/6	May 1958	PL	Black on Pink	Meccano Products. Cyprus.
176	16/658/27.5 2nd P	MP/PL/7	July 1958	PL	Black on Blue	Meccano Products. Canada.
177	16/658/30 3rd P	MP/PL/11	1 July 1958	PL	Black on Yellow	Meccano Products.
178	16/658/70 3rd P	MP/PL/11	1 July 1958	PL	Black on Blue	Meccano Products
179	8/6/58/5000	DA 758	1958	DL	Brown on Cream	Dublo, Dinkys & Meccano.
180	13/758/450	MP/CB/3	1958	C	Colour	Meccano Products.
181	10/758/450	MP/PL/12	1958	PL	Black on Orange	Meccano Products.
182	7/858/50	HD/CF/5	1958	F	Colour	Dublo Only. Unpriced.
183	7/858/500	HD/CF/5	1958	F	Colour	Dublo Only. Priced.
184	7/858/500	HD/CF/5	1958	F	Colour	Dublo. Revised Prices May 1959.
185	16/858/58 4th P	MP/PL/12	1 Aug. 1958	PL	Black on Blue	Meccano Products.
186	16/958/50 5th P	MP/PL/12	1 Nov. 1958	PL	Black on L. Blue	Meccano Products.
187	7/1058/15	HD/CF/5	1958	F	Colour	Dublo Only. Canada.
188	16/1258/70 6th P	MP/PL/13	—	PL	Black on L. Blue	Meccano Products.
189	—	—	Dec. 1958	DL	Blue on White	Dealer's Copy Order Form.
190	18/259/300	(92017)	1959	C	Colour	Hornby Book of Trains.
191	16/359/5 1st P	MP/PL/7	June 1959	PL	Black on Pink	Meccano Products. New Zealand
192	16/459/100 1st P	—	1 May 1959	PL	Black on Green	Dublo & O Gauge Only.
193	16/759/5 2nd P	—	1959	PL	Black on Green	Dublo & O Gauge Only. New Zealand.
194	16/859/50	—	1959	P	Colour	2006/7 Sets Only.
195	16/959/100 2nd P	—	1 Sept. 1959	PL	Black on Pink	Dublo & O Gauge Only.
196	16/959/100	HD/CF/7	7th Ed. 1959	F	Black, Yellow on Wh.	Dublo Only.
197	—	—	23/10/59	DL	Blue on L. Blue	Dealer's Copy Order List.
198	—	—	—	DL	Blue on Off White	Dealer's Copy Advice Note.
199	—	HD/CF/1	1st Ed. 1959	F	Colour	Dublo Only. Priced.
200	13/1059/25	HD/CF/1	1st Ed. 1959	F	Colour	Dublo Only. Unpriced.
201	16/1049/145 3rd P	—	1 Oct. 1959	PL	Black on Green	Dublo & O Gauge Only.
202	16/1259/7.5 1st P	MP/PL/10	1960	PL	Black on Green	Meccano Products. Canada English.
203	16/1259/145 4th P	—	Dec. 1959	PL	Black on Pink	Dublo & O Gauge Only.
204	8/160/5 1st P	—	1960	PL	Black on Green	Dublo & O Gauge Only. New Zealand
205	13/160/40	HD/CF/1	1st Ed. 1959	F	Colour	Dublo Only. Australia.
206	—/260/15	MP/TF/7	1960	DPL	Black on Buff	Dublo, O & Meccano.
207	13/260/4	HD/CF/1	1st Ed. 1959	F	Colour	Dublo Only. Malay & Singapore
208	13/360/15	HD/CF/1	1st Ed. 1959	F	Colour	Dublo Only. New Zealand.
209	9/560/2.5	—	1960	DC	Colour	Dublo & O. Etc.
210	9/560/2.5	—	1960	DC	Colour	Dublo & O, Etc. Export.
211	8/660/30	—	—	P	Colour	2-rail Sets Only. Canada English.
212	8/660/400	—	—	P	Colour	2-rail Sets Only. Canada English.
213	8/760/250	—	—	P	Colour	2-rail Sets Only. Canada English.
214	8/760/12.5 2nd P	MP/PL/11	1960	PL	Black on Off Yellow	Meccano Products. Canada English.
215	8/760/5 2nd P	MP/PL/10	1960	PL	Black on Buff	Meccano Products. New Zealand.
216	8/760/125 1st P	—	Aug. 1960	PL	Black on Green	Dublo & O Gauge.
217	16/1060/100 2nd P	—	Aug. 1960	PL	Black on Yellow	Dublo & O Gauge.
218	1885/10/60/5000	DA1160	31 Oct. 1960	DL	Colour	Dublo Dinkys & Dinky Toys.
219	(Oct. 1960)	(92016)	2nd Ed. 1960	C	Colour	Dublo Only. 'Erratum p. 3'.
220	(Oct. 1960)	(92016)	2nd Ed. 1960	C	Colour	Dublo Only. 'Erratum p. 3'.

NO.	REFERENCE NO.	OTHER REF.	DATE	TYPE	COLOUR	COMMENTS
221	(Oct. 1960)	(92016)	2nd Ed. 1960	C	Colour	Dublo Only. Revised Prices 1 Feb. '61.
222	(Oct. 1960)	(92016)	2nd Ed. 1960	C	Colour	Dublo Only. Export.
223	16/261/2.5	72823/04	1 Feb. 1961	PL	Black on Yellow	Dublo & O Gauge. Eire.
224	16/261/5	72823/19	—	PL	Black on Green	Meccano Products. New Zealand.
225	16/261/100 1st P	72823/02	1 Feb. 1961	PL	Black on Yellow	Meccano Products.
226	16/561/50 2nd P	72823/02		PL		
227	18/561/500	72236/02	3rd Ed. 1961	C	Colour	Dublo Only. Priced.
228	18/561/500	72236/02	3rd Ed. 1961	C	Colour	Dublo Red. Revised Prices 26 July '61
229	18/561/500	72236/02	3rd Ed. 1961	C	Colour	Dublo Black. Rev. Prices 26 July 1961
230	13/761/150	72240/02	8th Ed. 1961	F	Colour	Dublo Only.
231	16/861/12	72825/42	1961	PL	Black on Green	Meccano Products. Canada English.
232	16/861/60	72825/02	1961	PL	Black on Green	Meccano Products.
233	16/861/100 3rd P	72823/02	1 Sept. 1961	PL	Black on Pink	Dublo & O Gauge.
234	—	—	1961	F	Colour	French Meccano Products.
235	—	—	Sept. 1961	PL	Black & White	French Meccano Products.
236	—	—	Oct. 1961	DL	Black & White	Dealer's Order List.
237	16/1161/100 4th P	72823/02	1 Nov. 1961	PL	Black on Blue	Dublo & Acho.
238	16/1261/100 1st P	72847/02	Feb. 1962	PL	Black & White	Dublo & Acho.
239	—		1961/62	C	Black & White	Dublo & Acho. English.
240	—		Feb. 1962	PL	Black & White	Dublo & Acho. English.
241	—		Jan. 1962	DL	Black & White	Dealer's Order List.
242	—		1 Feb. 1962	PL	Blue on White	Meccano Products. Canada Typed.
243	13/162/500	92021	4th Ed. 1962	C	Colour	Dublo Only.
244	16/262/3	72841/43	1962	PL	Black on Pink	Meccano Products. Canada French.
245	16/262/10M	72847/04	Feb. 1962	PL	Black on Buff	Dublo & O Gauge. Eire.
246	8/262/50 1st P	72252/02	Feb. 1962	PL	Black on Buff	Dublo & O Gauge. Eire.
247	8/462/250 2nd P	72254/02	April 1962	PL	L. Green on White	Dublo & O Gauge. Eire.
248	16/462/170M 3rd P	72877/02	April 1962	PL	Black on Orange	Dublo & Acho.
249	—	—	May/June '62	DL	Black & White	Dealer's Order List.
250	16/662/100M 4th P	72877/02	June 1962	PL	Black on Buff	Dublo, Acho & O Gauge.
251	—	72250/02	9th Ed. 1962	F	Colour	Dublo, 3-rail.
252	11/662/35	72245/07	2nd Ed. 1962	F	Colour	Dublo, 2-rail.
253	11/662/200	72245/02	2nd Ed. 1962	F	Colour	Dublo, 2-rail.
254	11/762/5	72245/42	2nd Ed. 1962	F	Colour	Dublo, 2-rail. Canada.
255	11/762/5	72245/40	2nd Ed. 1962	F	Colour	Dublo, 2-rail. New Zealand.
256	16/962/150M 5th P	72877/02	Sept. 1962	PL	Black on Green	Dublo & Acho.
257	(13/962/5 ?)	72881/02	—	C	Colour	Dublo & Acho. English.
258	8/962/100 3rd P	72254/02	Sept. 1962	PL	Green on White	Dublo Only.
259	—	—	Jan. 1963	DL	Black on White	Dealer's Order List.
260	16/163/50M 1st P	72886/02	Jan. 1963	PL	Black on Buff	Dublo & Acho.
261	—	—	March 1963	DL	Black & White	Dealer's Order List.
262	13/363/10	72885/19	1963	PL	Black on Yellow	Meccano Products. New Zealand.
263	7/363/5	72256/19	—	C	Colour	Dublo Sets Only. New Zealand.
264	7/363/5	72256/19	—	PL	Black on Green	Price List inside above. New Zealand.
265	7/363/5	72256/42	—	C	Colour	Dublo Sets Only. Canada.
266	7/463/5	72256/42	—	PL	Black on Green	Price List inside above. Canada.
267	7/363/400	72257/02	—	C	Colour	Dublo Excl. Sets.
268	7/463/400	72257/02	—	PL	Black on Buff	Price List inside above.
269	—	72256/400	—	C	Colour	Dublo Sets Only.
270	10/363/400	72256/02	—	PL	Black on Buff	Price List inside above.
271	7/563/35	72257/07	—	C	Colour	Dublo Excl. Sets. Australia.
272	7/563/35	72257/07	—	PL	Black on D. Green	Price List inside above. Australia.
273	7/663/5	72257/19	—	C	Colour	Dublo Excl. Sets. New Zealand.
274	7/663/5	72257/19	—	PL		Price List inside above. New Zealand.
275	7/663/5	72257/42	—	C	Colour	Dublo Excl. Sets. Canada English.

NO.	REFERENCE NO.	OTHER REF.	DATE	TYPE	COLOUR	COMMENTS
276	7/663/5	—	—	PL	Black on Green	Price List inside above. Canada Eng.
277	16/563/60	72257/42	1963	PL	Black on Buff	Meccano Products.
278	E.P.C. 25404	72900/02	April 1963	DL	Black & White	Dealer's Order List.
279	512/4/63/15,000	—	May 1963	DL	Black & White	Dealer's Order List.
280	E.P.P. 2564/4/63/14M	—	—	DL	Black & White	Dealer's Order List.
281	764/6/63/14,000	—	July 1963	DL	Black & White	Dealer's Order List.
282	Main Season Order 1963	—	1963	DL	Black & White	Dealer's Order List.
283	—	—	—	DL	Black & White	Elevated Track Order Form.
284	Main Season Order 1963	—	1963	DL	Black & White	New Goods Order Form. 2245 & 32451
285	16/963/125/ 2nd P	72886/02	Sept. 1963	PL	Black on P. Green	Dublo & Acho.
286	8/1163/10	72038/02	1963	DL	Black, Orange on Wh.	New Items for 1963.
287	—	Apr. May, June	1963	DL	Black, Orange on Wh.	Dealer's Announcement. Shows 4071.
288	—	Jul. Aug. Sept.	1963	DL	Black, Blue on White	Dealer's Announ. Shows 4644 & 4076.
289	—	—	1964	C	Colour	Acho, Meccano & Triang.
290	16/164/100	72904/02	1964	PL	Black on Buff	Meccano Products.
291	16/164/10	72904/19	1964	DL	Black, Yellow on Wh.	Meccano Products. New Zealand.
292	13/464/100	72265/02	1964	F	Colour	Dublo. Priced.
293	13/564/1	72265/42	1964	F	Colour	Dublo. Priced. Canada
294	13/564/20	72265/06	1964	F	Colour	Dublo. Unpriced.
295	13/564/5	72265/04	1964	F	Colour	Dublo. Priced. Eire.
296	13/564/70	72265/07	1964	F	Colour	Dublo. Priced. Australia.
297	13/664/5	72265/19	1964	F	Colour	Dublo. Priced. New Zealand.
298	16/964/60	72904/02	1964	PL	Black on Blue	Meccano Products.
299	16/1264/150 1st P	92918/02	1965	PL	Black on P. Green	Meccano Products.
300	—	—	1965	DL	Black & White	2-rail sets plus others.
301	—	—	(11/4/61)	F	Black, Orange on White	Mecc. Prods. for sale in Russia.
302	—	—	22 June 1964	PL	Blue on White	Dublo Only. Typed. Canada.
303	—	—	1965	PL	Blue on L. Blue	Dublo Only. Typed. Canada.
304	—	—	1965	PL	Black on Blue	Meccano Products. Australia.
305	—	—	Sept. 1966	PL	Blue on White	Dublo Only. Typed. Canada.

LITERATURE OF TRIANG AND WRENN NOTING HORNBY-DUBLO

NO.	REFERENCE NO.	OTHER REF.	DATE	TYPE	COLOUR	COMMENTS
306	Triang 11th Ed.	R280S	May 1965	Su	Colour	Amalgamation Announcement.
307	Triang 11th Ed.	—	1 May 1965	PL	Black & White	Dublo included.
308	Rovex	—	1 June 1965	PL	Black on Green	Dublo Only.
309	Triang	—	1 Aug. 1965	PL	Black & White	Dublo included.
310	Triang	—	1 Sept.1965	PL	Black & White	Dublo included.
311	Triang 12th Ed.	R280	1966	C	Colour	Dublo included.
312	Triang 12th Ed.	—	24 Jan. 1966	PL	Black & White	Dublo included.
313	Rovex	R280	24 Jan. 1966	PL	Black on Green	Dublo Only.
314	Triang 13th Ed.	—	1967	C	Colour	Dublo included.
315	Triang 13th Ed.	—	23 Jan. 1967	PL	Black & White	Dublo included.
316	Triang 13th Ed.	—	12 April 1967	PL	Black & White	Dublo included.
317	Triang 13th Ed.	—	12 April 1967	DPL	Black on Green	Dublo included.
318	Rovex	—	12 Apr. 1967	PL	Black on Green	Dublo Only.
319	Triang	—	22 June 1967	PL	Black & White	Dublo included.
320	Triang	—	15 Sept. 1967	PL	Black & White	Dublo included.
321	Triang 14th Ed.	RM280	1968	C	Colour	Dublo included.
322	Triang	—	1 Jan. 1968	PL	Black & White	Dublo included.
323	Triang	—	1 Jan. 1968	DPL	Black on Green	Dublo included.
324	Triang	—	5 April 1968	PL	Black & White	Dublo included.
325	Wrenn	R2/5/68		F	Black & White	Dublo included.
326	Wrenn	—	1 May 1968	DPL	Black on Grey	Dublo included.
327	Triang	—	1 Sept. 1968	PL	Black & White	Dublo included.
328	Triang 15th Ed.	RM280	1969	C	Colour	Dublo included.
329	Triang 15th Ed.	—	1 Jan. 1969	PL	Black & White	Dublo included.

NO.	REFERENCE NO.	OTHER REF.	DATE	TYPE	COLOUR	COMMENTS
330	Triang	—	1 May 1969	PL	Black & White	Dublo included.
331	Triang	—	1 May 1969	DPL	Black on Green	Dublo included.
332	Triang	—	1 Aug. 1969	PL	Black & White	Dublo included.
333	Triang	—	1 Oct. 1969	PL	Black & White	Dublo included.
334	Triang 'Hornby Book of Trains'	—	1969	B	Colour	Terminal Station & Engine Shed.
335	Triang 16th Ed.	RM280	1970	C	Colour	Dublo included.
336	Triang 16th Ed.	—	1 Jan. 1970	PL	Black & White	Dublo included.
337	Triang 16th Ed.	—	1 Feb. 1970	PL	Black & White	Dublo included.
338	Triang 16th Ed.	—	1 June 1970	PL	Black & White	Dublo included.
339	Triang 17th Ed.	R280	1971	C	Colour	Dublo included.
340	Triang 17th Ed.	—	1 Jan. 1971	PL	Black & White	Dublo included.
341	Triang 17th Ed.	—	1 Jan. 1971	PL	Black & White	Dublo. Typed.
342	Triang 17th Ed.	—	22 Jul. 1971	DPL	Black on Blue	R5083 still shown.
343	Triang 17th Ed.	—	27 Sept. 1971	DPL	Black on Green	R5083 shown as withdrawn.
344	Triang 17th Ed.	—	1 Oct. 1971	PL	Black & White	Still lists R5083 Term. Stat.

LOCOMOTIVE OPERATING AND MAINTENANCE INSTRUCTIONS.

NO.	REFERENCE NO.	OTHER REF.	TYPE	COLOUR	LOCOMOTIVE	COMMENTS
1	2/938/25	—	F	Blk/Pk/Wh.	A4 & 0-6-2T	Clockwork locos, prewar.
2	2/938/25	—	F	Ble/Blk/Wh.	A4 & 0-6-2T	Electric locos, prewar.
3	1/1038/35	—	S	Blk/Pink	A4 & 0-6-2T	Sticker attached to item no. 1 above.
4	1/1038/45	—	S	Blk/Blue	A4 & 0-6-2T	Sticker attached to item no. 2 above.
4a	2/739/5	—	F	Blk/Lt. Ble/Wh.	A4 & 0-6-2T	Reprint item 2, incorp. 4
5	12/947/25	—	F	Blk/Blue	0-6-2T	Post war electric – horseshoe magnet, prewar 0-6-2T GWR illustrated, and shows prewar wood buildings.
6	12/548/30	—	F	Blk/Blue	A4	No longer shows 0-6-2T
7	6/549/10	—	F	Blk/Blue	A4	No longer shows 0-6-2T
8	16/649/10	2nd EM	F	Blk/Blue	A4	No longer shows 0-6-2T, & now shows capacitor.
9	16/849/25	—	F	Blk/Blue	Atholl & 0-6-2T	Shows new magnet, prewar buildings.
10	16/150/20	C1966	F	Blk/Blue	Atholl	New magnet, capacitor and wood buildings.
11	16/450/20	C2366	F	Blk/L. Green	Atholl	New magnet, capacitor and metal buildings.
12	16/1150/20	C3912 (2P)	F	Blk/L. Green	Atholl	New magnet, capacitor and metal buildings.
13	5/151/2	—	F	Blk/L. Green	Atholl	As above, but in German.
14	16/2/51/50M	C3944	F	Blk/L. Green	Atholl	New magnet, capacitor and metal buildings.
15	16/7/51/25M	C5442	F	Blk/L. Green	Atholl	New magnet, capacitor and metal buildings.
16	7/151/2501	—	S	Red/Yellow	Atholl	Note 'Oil this train before running'.
17	16/1251/10M	C6096	F	Blk/L. Green	Atholl & 0-6-2T	New magnet, capacitor and metal buildings.
18	16/752/20	C7106	F	Blk/L. Green	Atholl	Shows new flat capacitor.
18a	6/1252/25	C7990	F	Blk/L. Green	Atholl	Shows new flat capacitor.
19	16/253/25	C8236	B	Blk/Blue	Atholl	Booklet form, rerailer on back page.
20	16/753/25	C9117	B	Blk/Blue	Atholl	Booklet form, rerailer on back page.
21	16/1053/20	C9536	B	Blk/Blue	Atholl	Booklet form, rerailer on back page.
22	16/1253/15	C9888	B	Blk/Blue	Atholl	Booklet form, rerailer on back page.
23	16/254/60 (1st P)	D169	B	Blk/Blue	Atholl	Booklet form. Electrical inform. on back page.
24	16/654/65 (2nd P)	D169	B	Blk/Blue	Atholl	Booklet (Larger than 19 etc.).
25	16/954/100 (1st P)	D1477	B	Blk/Blue	Atholl	Booklet Now includes 2-6-4T.
26	16/954/100 (1st P)	D1477	B	Blk/Blue	Atholl & 2-6-4T	Special note attached re 2-6-4T cplgs.
27	16/355/75 (2nd P)	D2864	B	Blk/Blue	Atholl & 2-6-4T	As no. 25, with revised note back page.
28	16/156/90	D3995	B	Blk/Blue	Atholl & 2-6-4T	Now shows inductor-capacitor combination.
29	16/1056/50	D6117	B	Blk/Blue	Atholl & 2-6-4T	Now shows inductor-capacitor combination.
30	16/357/40	D7200	B	Blk/Blue	Atholl & 2-6-4T	Now shows inductor-capacitor combination.
31	16/857/30	D7676	B	Blk/Yellow	EDLT20-Castle	½-in. motor. P.8 has correction on paper.
32	16/11/57/30 57045	D8540	B	Blk/Yellow	EDLT20-Castle	Correction now printed bottom of page.
33	16/258/50	D9185	B	Blk/Green	4-6-2, 0-6-2T & 2-6-4T	As no. 28 etc.
34	16/258/50	D9815	B	Blk/Green	4-6-2, 0-6-2T & 2-6-4T	As no. 28 etc.
35	16/758/50 57042	E410	B	Blk/Yellow	LT20-Castle & LT25 - 2-8-0	As 32, but rewritten & no footnote.
36	16/1058/25 57042	E1451	B	L. Green	L30 Bo-Bo	Includes 2-8-0 loco.

NO.	REFERENCE	OTHER REF.	TYPE	COLOUR	LOCOMOTIVE	COMMENTS
37	—	57044/1	S	Red	L30 Bo-Bo	Bogie replacement slip with no. 36.
38	16/1158/12.5 (2P)	E1451, 57044	B	Pale Gr./Blk.	L30 Bo-Bo	As no. 36, but rewritten.
39	16/259/25 57050	E2203	B	Blk/Blue	4-6-2, 0-6-2T & 2-6-4T	As no. 33.
39a	16/559/50	E2921	B	Blue/White	2206/7	Locos 2206 and 7. No white parts to pages.
40	16/659/40(2nd P)57046	E2921	B	Blk/Blue-Grn.	0-6-0T(2-rail)	
41	8/859/40	57048	B	Brown/Cream	Denbigh Castle & 2-8-0(2-rail)	As no. 42, but without the 57xxx no.
42	8/859/40	—	B	Brown/Cream	Denbigh Castle & 2-8-0(2-rail)	
43	16/959/10(3P)57046	E3844	B	Blue/Blue-Grn.	0-6-0T (2-rail)	As no. 40, but reprinted.
44	16/1059/60	57047	B	Blue/Blue	2-6-4T, 4-6-2's (2-rail)	For 'Golden Fleece & City of London'.
45	16/1059/7.5 57044	E3967	B	Pale Grn.,Blk.	L30 Bo-Bo	As no 38, but reference to accumulator deleted.
46	October 1959	—	S	Typewritten	L30 Bo-Bo	Insert for use with no. 45 for 2-rail.
47	16/1159/7.5 57044	E4317	B	Pale Grn./Blk.	L30 Bo-Bo	As no. 45.
48	8/1159/30	57049	B	Brown/Orange	2230 Bo-Bo (2-rail)	
49	16/1159/50(4P)57046	E4166	B	Blue/Blue	0-6-0T (2-rail)	As no. 43, but rewritten.
50	16/460/25	57047	B	Blue/Blue	2-6-4T, 4-6-2's (2-rail)	As no. 44, but rewritten.
51	16/760/40	57231	B	Blk/Pale Orange	0-6-2T(2-rail)	
52	5/760/35	57236	B	Blk/Pale Yellow	2232 Co-Co (2-rail)	Co-Co Diesel.
53	8/760/30	57235	B	Blk/Pale Pink	0-6-0DS(2-rail)	Diesel Shunter.
54	13/860/15	57240	B	Black/Green	3232 (3-rail)	Ringfield motor.
55	13/860/40	57237	B	Blk/Pale Pink	Cardiff & 2-8-0 (2-rail)	
56	13/860/15	57238	B	Blk/Mauve	0-6-0DS (3-rail)	Diesel Shunter.
57	—	57317	S	Red/White	0-6-0DS (2, 3-rail)	Amended Instructions for 'oiling top motor bearing'.
58	16/960/25	57047	B	Blue/Blue	2-6-4T, 4-6-2's (2-rail)	As no. 50, amendments to electrical information.
59	16/960/50	57046	B	Blk/Pale Grn.	0-6-0T (2-rail)	As no. 49, but rewritten.
60	16/1260/5 57044	E7208	B	Black/White	L30 Bo-Bo(3-rail)	As no. 47, but rewritten.
61	16/1260/30	57046	B	Blk/Pale Grn.	0-6-0T (2-rail)	As no. 59, slight change to page 20.
62	16/1260/25	57047	B	Blue/Blue	2-6-4T, 4-6-2's (2-rail)	As no. 58, minor rearrangements.
63	16/1260/30	57231	B	Blk/Pale Orange	0-6-2T (2-rail)	As no. 51, minor change to page 11.
64	13/261/7.5	57246	B	Black/Yellow	Ludlow Castle & 2-8-0(3-rail)	Ringfield Motor.
65	13/261/40	57237	B	Blk/Pale Pink	Cardiff & 2-8-0	As no. 55.
66	8/361/40	57232	B	Black/Yellow	Barnstaple 4-6-2	
67	13/361/10	57248	B	Black/Pink	Co-Co, Co-Bo (3-rail)	
68	5/361/35	57247	B	Blue/Pale Blue	Co-Co, Co-Bo (2-rail)	
69	16/361/10	57239	B	Blk/Blue	Dorchester 4-6-2 (3-rail)	
70	16/461/40 Apr. '61	57319	S	Red/White	0-6-2T (2-rail)	Note to amend 'oiling points'.
71	16/461/125 Apr. '61	57326	S	Red/White	?	Note to amend 'oiling points'.
72	16/661/100 June '61	57343	S	Red/White	Castle, 2-8-0 & W.C.'s (2&3-rail)	Note to amend 'oiling rear bearing'.
73	13/462/12.5	57249	B	Blue/White	EMU (3-rail)	Suburban Electric Motor Coach.
74	5/462/25	57223	B	Blue/Blue	EMU (2-rail)	Suburban Electric Motor Coach.
75	16/163/50	57043	S	Blk/White	0-4-0T (2-rail)	Ready to Run locos.
76	16/963/10m	57072	S	Blue/Blue	2245 & 3245	Instructions for operating locos with pantograph
77	—	57073	F	Blue/Blue	2232, 3232, 2233, 3250, 2245 and 3245. (2 & 3-rail)	
78	—	57249	S	Black/Blue	BB16.009 No 638 Hornby-Acho.	

ACCESSORY OPERATING INSTRUCTIONS.

NO.	REFERENCE NO.	OTHER REF.	TYPE	COLOUR	ITEM	COMMENTS
1	17/650/25	—	S	Black/Blue	Footbridge	Various Languages.
2	17/1250/30	—	S	Black/Blue	Footbridge	Various Languages.
2a	17/153/25	—	S	Black/Blue	Footbridge	Various Languages.
3	17/1255/20		S	Blue/Blue	Footbridge	
4	16/1056/30	57085	S	Black/Grey	Turntable	
5	16/157/50	57084	F	Black/Grey	T.P.O. Mail Van Set	Identical to above.
6	16/657/30	57084	F	Violet/Blue	T.P.O. Mail Van Set	
7	17/1157/25	57051	S	Blue/Blue	Footbridge	
8	16/1157/10	57085	S	Blue/White	Turntable	Identical to no. 4.
9	16/1157/30 D8540	57045	F	Violet/Blue	T.P.O. Mail Van Set	
10	16/359/10	57084	F	Violet/Blue	T.P.O. Mail Van Set	Identical to no. 5.
11	15/759/	57071	S	Red/White	Breakdown Crane	Printed one side only.
12	16/1059/30	57233	S	Red/White	Suburban Station Assembly, No. 5085.	
12a	17/259/20	57051	S	Black/Blue	Footbridge	
13	260/15	57071	S	Red/White	Breakdown Crane	Identical to no. 11.
14	16/360/30	57241	F	Blue/Pale Buff	T.P.O. Mail Van Set	
15	16/1060/30	57233	S	Red/White	Suburban Station Assembly no. 5085; as no 12.	
16	17/1260/10	57051	S	Blue/Pale Buff	Footbridge	Now no. 5010.
17	16/1260/30	57241	F	Blue/Pale Buff	T.P.O. Mail Van Set	
18	261/10	57071	S	Red/White.	Breakdown Crane	Identical to no. 11.
19	—	57234	S	Red/White	Goods Station Assembly no. 5020.	

CONTROLLER AND TRANSFORMER OPERATING INSTRUCTIONS

NO.	REFERENCE NO.	OTHER REF.	TYPE	COLOUR	POWER UNIT	COMMENTS
1	2/938/20	—	S	Black/Blue	Trans. No. 1	For Use with Controller No. 1.
2	2/938/8	—	S	Black/Blue	Trans. No. 2	As above. One pair of terminals.
3	—	—	S	Black/Green	Trans. No. 2	Has two pairs of output terminals
4	2/739/10	—	S	Black/White	Controller No. 1	
5	1/739/.5	—	S	Orange/Black	Controller No. 1A	
6	—	—	S	Lt./Grn/White	—	'Why Transfo. Fuses Blow'.
7	16/149/50	—	S	Violet/White	Trans. No. 1	
8	16/849/10	—	S		Controller No. 1	
9	5/250/50	—	S		Trans. No. 1	
10	16/550/10	—	S		Controller No. 1	
11	16/1250/15	—	S	Black/Pink	Controller No. 1	
12	16/1250/75	—	S	Violet/White	Transformer No. 1	
13	16/652/10	—	Card	Red/White	Controller No. 1	'When the Red Button Rises'.
14	16/353/25	—	S	Black/Pink	Controller No. 1	
15	16/753/10	—	Card	Red/White	Controller No. 1	'When the Red Button Rises'.
16	16/1053/55	—	S	Black/Blue	Power Control No. A3	
17	16/154/15	—	S	Black/Pink	Controller No. 1	
18	16/154/15	—	Card	Red/White	Controller No. 1	'When the Red Button Rises'.
19	—	—	S	Blue/Green	Power Control No. A3	No code. Attached to 7/754/200
20	16/254/1	—	S	Blue/Blue	Power Control No. A3	Canada.
21	16/254/4	—	S	Blue/Blue	Power Control No. A3	England/Export.
22	16/754/25	—	S	Black/Blue	Power Control No. A3	
23	16/1054/12.5	—	S	Black/Blue	Power Control No. A3	
24	16/1154/5	—	S	Black/Pink	Controller No. 1	
25	16/1254/50	—	S	Black/Blue	Power Control No. A3	
26	13/755/1,300	—	S	Black/Cream	Power Control No. A3	
27	—	—	S	Black/Lt.Grn.	Power Control No. A3	
28	17/955/20	—	B	Blue/Blue	Controller C3	
29	10/655/100	72259/02	S	Yellow/Black	Hornby Mains Units	
30	16/1255/30	—	S	Black/Blue	Power Control No. A3	
31	10/556/5	57095	S		Battery Control Unit	
32	16/656/12.5	57101	B	Blue/Blue	Power Control No. A3	
33	16/856/50	57222	S	Blue/Blue	Power Control No. A2	
34	10/956/100	—	S	Brown/Wh.	Power Control Units	
35	13/1056/500	—	S	Brown/Crm.	Power Controls Nos. As & A3	
36	16/1156/50	57222	S	Blue/Blue	Power Control No. A2	
37	13/557/500	—	S	Blue/Grey	A2, A3 and T15	Trans.

NO.	REFERENCE NO.	OTHER REF.	TYPE	COLOUR	POWER UNIT	COMMENTS
38	16/358/25	57222	S	Blue/Blue	Power Control No. A2	
39	16/558/25	—	S	Blue/Blue	T15 Transformer.	
40	13/557/500	—	S	Blue/Pale Blue	A2, A3 and M20 Trans.	
41	5/958/500	—	S	Blue/Cream	A2, A3, T15, C3 and Battery Control.	
42	16/1059/250 UK	—	S	Blk/Wh/Yellow	Marshall 11 and 111	
43	17/959/100	57224	S	Blue/Blue	Marshall 11	
44	16/160/50	57230	S	Blue/Blue	Marshall 111	
45	17/260/60	57224	S	Blue/Blue	Marshall 11	
46	16/560/25	57230	S	Blue/Blue	Marshall 111	
47	17/760/5	57220	S	Blue/Blue	Marshall 11	
48	8/960/50	57221	S	Blue/Blue	Marshall Controller for use with Marshall 111.	
49	13/1160/100 UK	—	S	Orange/Blk.	Marshall Power Units.	
50	16/1260/25	57230	S	Blue/Blue	Hornby 111	
51	17/1260/65	57224	S	Blue/Blue	Hornby 11	
52	5/861/15	72242/02	S	Blue/White	Hornby (Marshall) 111	
53	8/861/1	57111	S	Blue/Blue	Hornby 111	Canada.
54	16/163/30	57101	S	Black/Blue	Hornby 1	
55	16/563	57102	S		GP 15 Trans.	
56	10/563/100	72259/02	S	Blk/Cream	Mains Units and Controllers	
57	—	72253/02	S	Black/Buff	Mains Units and Controllers	
58	—	72241/02	S	Blk/Crm/Brn.	Mains Units and Controllers	

TRACK AND SIGNALLING OPERATING AND WIRING INSTRUCTIONS

NO.	REFERENCE NO.	OTHER REF.	TYPE	COLOUR	ITEM	COMMENTS
1	1/1139/15		S		Isolating Rail	
2	1/1139/20		S		Points and Signals – Electric	
3	16/1247/10		S	Blue/Blue	Isolating Rail	
3a	16/148/25		S	Blue/Blue	Uncoupling Rail	
4	16/449/30		S	Blue/Blue	Isolating Rail	
5	16/449/30		S	Blue/Blue	Uncoupling Rail – UBR	
6	16/550/50		S	Blue/Blue	Uncoupling Rail – UBR	
7	16/650/30		S		Isolating Rail	
8	17/1250/50		S	Black/Blue	Uncoupling Rail – UBR	
9	17/1250/35		S	Black/Blue	Isolating Rail	
10	16/251/35		S	Black/Blue	Points and Signals – Electric	
11	12/1251/16		S	Blue/Blue	Uncoupling Rail – UBR	
12	17/1251/10		S	Blue/Blue	Uncoupling Rail – UBR	
13	16/652/40		S	Black/Blue	Points and Signals – Electric	
14	16/852/25		S	Black/Blue	Points and Signals – Electric	
15	16/1152/25		S	Black/Blue	Points and Signals – Electric	
16	17/1152/15		S	Black/Blue	Isolating Rail	
17	17/153/40		S	Black/Blue	Isolating Rail	
18	16/253/80		S	Black/Blue	Points and Signals – Electric	
19	16/453/50		S	Black/Blue	Isolating Switch Points – Manual	
20	16/154/80		S	Black/Blue	Isolating Switch Points – Manual	
21	16/354/80		S	Black/Blue	Points and Signals – Electric	
22	17/554/25		S	Black/Blue	Isolating Rail	
23	17/554/25		S	Blue/Blue	Uncoupling Rail – UBR	
24	8/754/50		S	Blue/Blue	Uncoupling Rail – EUBR	
25	16/754/50		S	Black/Blue	Isolating Switch Points – Manual	
26	8/1154/32		S	Blue/Blue	Uncoupling Rail – EUBR	
27	8/1154/32		S	Blue/Blue	Uncoupling Rail – EUBR	
28	17/1154/30		S	Black/Blue	Uncoupling Rail – UBR	
29	16/1254/100		S	Black/Blue	Isolating Switch Points – Manual	
30	17/1254/45		S	Blue/Blue	Isolating Rail	
31	16/355/80		S	Black/Blue	Points and Signals – Electric	
32	17/955/45		S	Blue/Blue	Isolating Rail	
33	16/955/100		S	Black/Blue	Isolating Switch Points – Manual	
34	16/1155/50		S	Blue/Blue	Points and Signals – Electric	
35	16/1155/75		S	Blue/Blue	Points and Signals – Electric	
36	10/856/25	57068	S	Blue/Blue	Points and Signals – Electric	

NO.	REFERENCE NO.	OTHER REF.	TYPE	COLOUR	ITEM	COMMENTS
37	10/856/25	57052	S	Blue/Blue	Isolating Rail	
38	16/1056/150	—	S	Blue/Blue	Isolating Switch Points – Manual	
39	17/157/35	57059	S	Blue/Blue	Uncoupling Rail – UBR	
40	10/157/50	57068	S	Blue/Blue	Points and Signals – Electric	
41	10/1157/30	57052	S	Blue/Blue	Isolating Rail	
42	16/1157/100	57067	S	Blue/Blue	Isolating Switch Points – Manual	
43	10/1157/50	57068	S	Blue/Blue	Points and Signals – Electric	
44	17/1157/25	57059	S	Blue/Blue	Uncoupling Rail – UBR	
45	16/1058/75	57067	S	Blue/Blue	Isolating Switch Points – Manual	
46	16/1058/75	57070	S	Blue/Blue	Colour Light Signals	
47	16/1058/55 (2nd P)	57070	S	Blue/Blue	Colour Light Signals	
48	17/159/25	57059	S	Blue/Blue	Uncoupling Rail – UBR	
49	10/259/50	57068	S	Blue/Blue	Points and Signals – Electric	
50	10/259/75	57228	S	Blue/Blue	Uncoupling Rail 2745 (2-rail)	
51	16/359/80	57067	S	Blue/Blue	Isolating Switch Points – Manual	
53	16/359/50	57067	S	Blue/Blue	Isolating Switch Points – Manual	
54	16/359/50	57070	S	Blue/Blue	Colour Light Signals	
55	10/459/20	57052	S	Blue/Blue	Isolating Rail	
56	8/1159/300	57225	F	Blue/Blue	Hand & Electrically Operated Points – (2-rail)	
57	8/1159/100	57226	S	Blue/Blue	Isolating Rail 2738 (2-rail)	
58	8/1159/75	57229	S	Blue/Blue	Illuminated Buffer Stop 2451 (2-rail)	
59	10/1259/75	57228	S	Blue/Blue	Uncoupling Rail 2745 (2-rail)	
60	8/260/100	57226	S	Blue/Blue	Isolating Rail 2738 (2-rail)	
61	16/260/40	57067	S	Blue/Blue	Isolating Switch Points – Manual	
62	16/260/25	57070	S	Blue/Blue	Colour Light Signals	
63	10/560/25	57227	S	Blue/Blue	Isolating Switch Points – Manual	
64	8/960/50	57225	F	Blue/Blue	Hand & Electrically Operated Points – (2-rail)	
65	8/960/90	57243	S	Blue/Blue	Curved Isolating Rail 2741 (2-rail)	
66	8/960/90	57244	S	Blue/Blue	Straight Isolating Rail 2742 (2-rail)	
67	8/1060/150	57242	F	Blue/Blue	Electrically Operated Points, 2-rail	
68	8/1060/250	57245	S	Blue/Blue	Manually Operated Points, 2-rail	
69	16/1260/35	57070	S	Blue/Blue	Colour Light Signals	
70	16/1260/75	57067	S	Blue/Blue	Isolating Switch Points – Manual	
71	10/161/30	57068	S	Blue/Blue	Points and Signals – Electric	
72	8/161/10	57066	S	Blue/Blue	Uncoupling Rail – EUBR	
73	10/261/50	57228	S	Blue/Blue	Uncoupling 2745 – Manual 2-rail	
74	10/261/25	57227	S	Blue/Blue	Uncoupling Rail 2746 – Electric 2-rail	
75	16/861/100	57074	S	Red/White	Nylon Fish-plate	Amended Instructions.
76	16/362/75m	57074	S	Red/White	Nylon Fish-plate	Amended Instructions.
77	5/163/15	57122	S	Black/Blue	Switch Coupling Handle 1612	
78	16/163/100	57120	S	Black/Blue	Simplec Hand Operated Points, 2-rail	
79	5/163/50	57121	S	Black/Blue	Simplec Electrically Operated Points, 2-rail	
80	10/263/50	57123	S	Black/Blue	Terminal Connector 2725, with Suppressor, 2-rail	
81	5/163/2.5	57075	S	Black/White	Track Pack No. 1, 2-rail track arrangement	
82	5/163/2.5	57076	S	Black/White	Track Pack No. 2, 2-rail track arrangement	
83	5/163/2.5	57077	S	Black/White	Track Pack No. 3, 2-rail track arrangement	
84	5/663/2.5	57076	S	Black/White	Track Pack No. 2, 2-rail track arrangement	
85	5/1063/2.5	57075	S	Black/White	Track Pack No. 1, 2-rail track arrangement	
86	16/1164/25	57120	S	Blue/Blue	Simplec Hand Operated Points, 2-rail	

RAIL LAYOUT LITERATURE

NO.	REFERENCE NO.	OTHER REF.	TYPE	COLOUR	PAGES	2 or 3-rail	COMMENTS
1	1/1138/25	—	F	Black/Green	6	3	Electric & Clockwork.
2	1/839/14	—	F	Black/Green	6	3	Electric
3	16/1139/.25	—	S	Black/White	2	3	Electric Layout no. 2A
4	1/440/3	—	F	Black/Green	6	3	Clockwork.
5	16/1249/50	—	B	Blue/Blue	16	3	Shows prewar track.
6	16/1050/20	—	B	Black/Blue	16	3	
7	16/451/25	—	B	Black/Blue	16	3	As no. 5.
8	16/751/25	—	B	Black/Blue	16	3	Shows postwar track.
9	16/1051/25	—	B	Black/Blue	16	3	As no. 8.
10	16/1052/25	—	B	Blue/Blue	16	3	As no. 8.

REF. NO.	CODE NO.	EDITION	REF. NO.	B/F/S	COLOUR	QTY	PRICE	COMMENTS
11	16/653/25	—		B	Blue/Blue	16	3	Reference to EODPR/L in red.
12	16/1053/15	—		B	Blue/Blue	16	3	Shows BR locos on front, and
12a	16/1053/15	—		B	Blue/Blue	4 only	3 Misprint	prewar track within.
13	16/1053/30	—		F	Blue/Blue	4	3	Use of ISPR/L.
14	16/1253/5	—		B	Blue/Blue	16	3	As no. 12.
15	16/3/5	—		F	Blue/Blue	4	3	As no. 13.
16	16/1253/20	—		B	Blue/Blue	16	3	As no. 12.
17	16/354/15	—		B	Blue/Blue	16	3	Shows BR locos on front, & prewar
18	16/554/25	—		B	Blue/Blue	16	3	track within.
19	16/1054/125			B	Blue/Blue/Wh.	12	3 Price 3d	0-6-2T on front. Long format.
20	16/355/100			B	Blue/Blue/Wh.	12	3 Price 3d	0-6-2T on front. Long format.
21	16/156/30			B	Blue/Blue/Wh.	12	3 Price 3d	0-6-2T on front. Long format.
22	16/356/30			B	Blue/Blue/Wh.	12	3 Price 3d	0-6-2T on front. Long format.
23	16/856/100M			B	Blue/Blue/Wh.	16	3 Price 3d	0-6-2T & 2-6-4T on cover. Long format.
24	16/357/35M			B	Blue/Blue/Wh.	16	3 Price 3d	0-6-2T & 2-6-4T on cover. Long format.
25	16/1057/15M			B	Blue/Blue/Wh.	16	3 Price 3d	0-6-2T & 2-6-4T on cover. Long format.
26	16/1157/30M			B	Blue/Blue/Wh.	16	3 Price 3d	0-6-2T & 2-6-4T on cover. Long format.
27	16/358/20M			B	Blue/Blue/Wh.	16	3 Price 3d	0-6-2T & 2-6-4T on cover. Long format.
28	16/458/50M			B	Brown/White	24	3 Price 6d	0-6-2T. As no. 23 etc. but more layouts.
29	16/858/35M			B	Brown/White	24	3 Price 6d	0-6-2T. As no. 23 etc. but more layouts.
30	16/159/50M			B	Brown/White	24	3 Price 6d	0-6-2T. As no. 23 etc. but more layouts.
31	8/660/100	1st Edition		B	Blk/Or/White	24	2 Price 6d	0-6-0T & 2-8-0 on front.
32	8/660/50	2nd Edition		B	Blk/Or/White	24	2 Price 6d	0-6-0T & 2-8-0 on front.
33	8/660/100	3rd Edition		B	Blk/Or/White	24	2 Price 6d	0-6-0T & 2-8-0 on front.
34		April 1961	72237/03	S	Red/White	1	2	Corrections for above books.
35	8/1161/50	4th Ed.	72244/02	B	Blk/Rd/Wh.	24	2 Price 6d	As nos. 31–33.
36	16/462/10		72207/03	B	Brown/White	24	3 Price 6d	As nos. 28–30.
37	8/1062/50	5th Ed.	72244/02	B	Blk/Or/White	24	2 Price 6d	As no 35.
38	8/12/62/50		72258/02	B	Blk/Or/White	32	2 Price 6d	Simplec Track Layouts.
39	8/1/64/50		72258/02	B	Blk/Or/White	32	2 Price 6d	Simplec Track Layouts.
40	8/163/10		72255/02	S	Blk/Or/White	2	2	2-rail track formations X-1 to X-4.

LOCOMOTIVE SERVICING LEAFLETS

REF. NO.	CODE NO.	REF. DATE	COLOUR	ITEM	COMMENTS
1	72851/02	Dec. 1962	Black/Yellow/White	½-in motor 2 and 3-rail	
2	72852/02	Dec. 1962	Black/Yellow/White	5/8-in motor 2 and 3-rail. Ringfield, old and new.	
3	72853/02	Dec. 1961/Dec. 1962	Black/Yellow/White	0-6-0T loco 2-rail.	
4	72854/02	Dec. 1961/Dec. 1962	Black/Yellow/White	4-6-2 streamlined loco (A4) 2 and 3-rail.	
5	72855/02	Dec. 1961/Dec. 1962	Black/Yellow/White	4-6-2 Duchess of Montrose 3-rail.	
6	72856/02	Dec. 1961/Dec. 1962	Black/Yellow/White	0-6-2T, 2 and 3-rail.	
7	72857/02	Dec. 1961/Dec. 1962	Black/Yellow/White	2-6-4T, 2 and 3-rail.	
8	72858/02	Dec. 1961/Dec. 1962	Black/Yellow/White	4-6-0 Castle. 3-rail.	
9	72859/02	Dec. 1961/Dec. 1962	Black/Yellow/White	4-6-0 Castle. 2-rail.	
10	72860/02	Dec. 1961/Dec. 1962	Black/Yellow/White	2-8-0 freight loco. 2-rail.	
11	72861/02	Dec. 1961/Dec. 1962	Black/Yellow/White	2-8-0 freight loco. and tender, 3-rail.	
12	72862/02	Dec. 1961/Dec. 1962	Black/Yellow/White	4-6-2 City class loco. 2 and 3-rail.	
13	72863/02	Dec. 1961/Dec. 1962	Black/Yellow/White	Bo-Bo Diesel. 2 and 3-rail.	
14	72864/02	Dec. 1961/Dec. 1962	Black/Yellow/White	0-6-0 Diesel Shunter. 2 and 3-rail.	
15	72865/02	Dec. 1961/Dec. 1962	Black/Yellow/White	Co-Co Diesel. 2 and 3-rail.	
16	72866/02	Dec. 1961/Dec. 1962	Black/Yellow/White	Co-Bo Diesel. 2 and 3-rail.	
17	72867/02	Dec. 1961/Dec. 1962	Black/Yellow/White	West Country loco. 2 and 3-rail.	
18	72868/02	Dec. 1961/Dec. 1962	Black/Yellow/White	No. 20 Clockwork. (O gauge)	
19	72869/02	Dec. 1961/Dec. 1962	Black/Yellow/White	No. 30 Clockwork. (O gauge)	
20	72870/02	Dec. 1961/Dec. 1962	Black/Yellow/White	No. 40 Clockwork. (O gauge)	
21	72871/02	Dec. 1961/Dec. 1962	Black/Yellow/White	No. 50 Clockwork. (O gauge)	
22	72872/02	Dec. 1962	Black/Yellow/White	Electric Motor Coach. 2 and 3-rail.	
23	Does not exist . . . possibly reserved for AL6 electric loco. no. 2245, although drive bogie same as no. 22 above.				
24	72874/02	May 1962	Black/Yellow/White	Meccano Magic Clockwork Motor.	
25	72875/02	May 1962	Black/Yellow/White	Meccano no. 1 Clockwork Motor.	
26	72878/02	May 1962	Black/Yellow/White	Meccano 'Emebo' Motor.	
—	—	1963/4	Typed	Parts List, price list and associated information.	

CAT. NO.	DESCRIPTION	CODE	LENGTH	VARIATION	BOX TYPE NO.	BOX NO.	BOX CODE	MECC. MAG.	MECC. PRICE	MECC. LAST CAT.	LAST PRICE
CLOCKWORK											
—	Straight Rail	DB	11½"	Type 1	14a	D501	5M 8.38	10/38	1/-	11/41	2/3
—	Straight Rail	DB1	11½"	Type 2	14a	D501	5M 8.38	10/38	1/-	11/41	2/3
—	Straight Half Rail	DB½	5¾"	Type 1	14a	D502	2.5M 8.38	10/38	-/9	11/41	1/9
—	Straight Half Rail	DB1½	5¾"	Type 2	14a	D502	2.5M 8.38	10/38	-/9	11/41	1/9
—	Straight Half Rail	DB1½	5¾"	Type 3 - Label on side	14a	D502	2.5M 8.38	10/38	-/9	11/41	1/9
—	Straight Short Rail	DBS	1 5/16"	Type 1 - No label	14a	D512	0.75M10.39	10/38	-/6	11/41	1/2
—	Straight Short Rail	DBS	1 5/16"	Type 2 - No label	14a	D512	0.75M10.39	10/38	-/6	11/41	1/2
—	Curved Rail	DA	15" rad.	Type 1 - 8 to circle	14a	D503	6M 9.38	10/38	1/-	11/41	2/3
—	Curved Rail	DA1	15" rad.	Type 2 - 8 to circle	14a	D503	6M 9.38	10/38	1/-	11/41	2/3
—	Curved Half Rail	DA½	15" rad.	Type 1 - 16 to circle	14a	D504	1.5M10.38	10/38	-/9	11/41	1/9
—	Curved Half Rail	DA1½	15" rad.	Type 2 - 16 to circle	14a	D504	0.85M4.40	10/38	-/9	11/41	1/9
—	Curved Half Rail	DA1½	15" rad	Type 3 - 16 to circle	14a	D504	0.85M4.40	10/38	-/9	11/41	1/9
—	Switch Point - Right Hand	DPR	5¾"	Type 1	14a	(D505)	0.85M4.40	10/38	6/6	11/41	16/-
—	Switch Point - Left Hand	DPL	5¾"	Type 1							

Points came in pairs in one box. Price is per pair.
(One pair is one left & one right hand).

CAT. NO.	DESCRIPTION	CODE	LENGTH	VARIATION	BOX TYPE NO.	BOX NO.					
—	Switch Point - Right Hand	DPR	5¾"	Type 1	14a	(D505)					
—	Switch Point - Left Hand	DPL	5¾"	Type 1							
—	Switch Point - Left/Right Hand		5¾"	Type 2 - This type not known to exist.							

As above but with 'Y' shaped frogs.

CAT. NO.	DESCRIPTION	CODE	LENGTH	VARIATION	BOX TYPE NO.	BOX NO.	BOX CODE	MECC. MAG.	MECC. PRICE	MECC. LAST CAT.	LAST PRICE
ELECTRIC											
—	Straight Rail	EDB	11½"	Type 1	14a	D506	5M 8.38	10/38	1/3	11/41	3/-
—	Straight Rail	EDB1	11½"	Type 2	14a	D506	8.5M 4.40	10/38	1/3	11/41	3/-
—	Straight Rail	EDB1	11½"	Type 2 Matted Insulators	14a	D506	8.5M 4.40	10/38	1/3	11/41	3/-
—	Straight Half Rail	EDB½	5¾"	Type 1	14a	D507	.75M 7.39	10/38	1/-	11/41	2/6
—	Straight Half Rail	EDB1½	5¾"	Type 2	14a	D507		10/38	1/-	11/41	2/6
—	Straight Half Rail	EDB1½	5¾"	Type 2 Matted Insulators	14a	D507		10/38	1/-	11/41	2/6
—	Straight Quarter Rail	EDB1¼	2 7/8"	Type 3 - Label on side	14a	D519	3.5M11.39	(5.39	-/10)	11/41	2/3
—	Straight Short Rail	EDBS	1 5/16"	Type 1	14a	D513	0.275M8.39	10/38	-/9	11/41	1/9
—	Straight Short Rail	EDBS	1 5/16"	Type 2 - No label	14a	D513	0.275M8.39	10/38	-/9	11/41	1/9
—	Straight Terminal Rail	EDBT1	11½"	Type 2	14a	(D516)		(6.39	1/9)	11/41	3/9
—	Curved Rail	EDA	15" rad	Type 1 - 8 to circle	14a	D508	7.5M 9.38	10/38	1/3	11/41	3/-
—	Curved Rail	EDA1	15" rad	Type 2 - 8 to circle	14a	D508		10/38	1/3	11/41	3/-
—	Curved Half Rail	EDA½	15" rad	Type 1 - 16 to circle	14a	(D509)		10/38	1/-	11/41	2/6
—	Curved Half Rail	EDA1½	15" rad	Type 2 - 16 to circle	14a	(D509)		10/38	1/-	11/41	2/6
—	Curved Half Rail	EDA1½	15" rad	Type 3 - Label on side	14a	(D509)		10/38	1/-	11/41	2/6
—	Curved Terminal Rail	EDAT	15" rad	Type 1 - 8 to circle	14a	(D510)		10/38	1/9	11/41	3/9
—	Curved Terminal Rail	EDAT1	15" rad	Type 2 - 8 to circle	14a	(D510)		10/38	1/9	11/41	3/9
—	Curved Rail - Large Radius	EDA2	17¼" rad	Type 3 - 8 to circle / Label on side	14a	D514	3.5M10.39	12/39	1/9	11/41	3/9
—	Curved Terminal Rail - L.R.	EDAT2	17¼" rad	Type 3 - 8 to circle / Label on side	14a	(D515)		2/40	2/6	11/41	4/6
—	Isolating Rail with switch	IBR	2 7/8"	Type 3 - Label on side	14a	D518	3.5M11.39	12/39	1/9	11/41	3/6
—	Switch Point - Right Hand	EDPR	5¾"	Type 1 - With Sleepers	14a	D511	12.5M10.38	10/38	9/6	6/41	19/-

Points came in pairs in one box. Price is per pair.

—	Switch Point - Left Hand	EDPL	5¾"	Type 1 - With Sleepers	14a	D511	12.5M10.38	10/38	9/6	6/41	19/-
—	Switch Point - Right Hand	EDPR	5¾"	Type 2 - With Sleepers	14a	D511	12.5M10.38	10/38	9/6	6/41	19/-

Points came in pairs in one box. Price is per pair.

—	Switch Point - Left Hand	EDPL	5¾"	Type 2 - With Sleepers	14a	D511	7500 4.40	10/38	9/6	6/41	19/-
—	Switch Point - Right Hand	EDPR	5¾"	Type 3 - No Sleepers	14a	D511	7500 4.40	10/38	9/6	6/41	19/-
—	Switch Point - Left Hand	EDPL	5¾"	Type 3 - No Sleepers	14a	D511	7500 4.40	10/38	9/6	6/41	19/-
—	Switch Point - Right H. Elec.	EODPR	5¼"	Type 1 - With Sleepers	14a	D511	7500 4.40	10/38	9/6	6/41	19/-

Electrically operated points not known to exist with sleepers on base.

—	Switch Point - Left H. Elec.	EODPL	5¾"	Type 1 - With Sleepers							
—	Switch Point - Right H. Elec.	EODPR	5¾"	Type 2 - No Sleepers.	14a	D517	5M 11.39	12/39	17/-	11/41	37/6
—	Switch Point - Left H. Elec.	EODPL	5¾"	Type 2 - No Sleepers.							

*Points came in pairs in one box. Price is per pair.

—Box Nos. in Brackets are presumed & unconfirmed

* Although points normally in pairs, a single switch point is known to exist in a plain blue box with 1,250 4/40 date code and no 'D' number.   Dates and Prices in Brackets refer to earliest references, where item not in Meccano Magazine.

Type 1: Early prewar. Have brass running rails and steel centre rail, with brass tongue. (Centre rail electric only.) Label in centre of rail. Points have rails as above and with sleepers on base. Label is yellow and black. Frogs are in form of open 'Y'. Insulators are plain.

Type 2: Plated running rails, continued steel centre rails on electric track. Label still in centre. Points as above except that frog although still open 'Y' has distinct curve to inside of curve piece. Some matted insulators in use. Plated tongues. Some also have filled in frog.

Type 3: Generally applicable to unusual rails having label on side. Printing is smaller than postwar. Points no longer have sleepers and the frogs are one solid piece, and no longer in shape of open 'Y'. Now have gold label on points.

All prewar points have single travel pieces, unlike postwar which have one stationary piece and one shorter travel piece.

Minor variations exist in regard to cut-outs for curves and indentations for many rails.

PREWAR TRACK LAYOUTS

CAT. NO.	DESCRIPTION	TYPE OF TRACK	BOARD SIZE	PRICE	BOARD ACCESSORIES	PRICE	1/1138 /25	2/1238 /50	1/440 /3	1/539 /5	1/839 /14
No. 1	Track Layout with:	Electric Track	6' x 3'	10/1		15/-	43/1	43/1	—	—	—
No. 1	Track Layout with:	Clockwork Track	6' x 3'	10/1		15/-	32/4	32/4	36/11	—	—
No. 2	Track Layout with:	Electric Track	6' x 3'	19/4		15/-	39/10	—	—	—	—
No. 2	Track Layout with:	Clockwork Track	6' x 3'	19/4		15/-	29/10	—	34/9	—	—
No. 3	Track Layout with:	Electric Track	6' x 3'	19/4		15/-	31/-	31/-	—	—	—
No. 3	Track Layout with:	Clockwork Track	6' x 3'	19/4		15/-	23/-	23/-	25/2	—	—
No. 4	Track Layout with:	Electric Track	6' x 4'	19/9		20/-	56/1	56/1	—	—	—
No. 4	Track Layout with:	Clockwork Track	6' x 4'	19/9		20/-	42/10	42/10	49/1	—	—
No. 5	Track Layout with:	Electric Track	6' x 4'	19/9		20/-	79/7	79/7	—	—	—
No. 5	Track Layout with:	Clockwork Track	6' x 4'	19/9		20/-	59/1	59/1	67/2	—	—
No. 6	Track Layout with:	Electric Track	8' x 4'	19/9		27/-	74/8	—	—	—	—
No. 6	Track Layout with:	Clockwork Track	8' x 4'	19/9		27/-	57/2	—	65/6	—	—
No. 1a	Display Board - Dealer		6' x 3'	—	Includes track &	—	—	—	—	2/10/-	—
No. 2a	Display Board - Dealer		8' x 4'	—	accessories.	—	—	—	—	6/17/6	—
A	Track Layout with:	Electric Track	6' x 3'	32/3	Electric Operated Points	15/-	—	—	—	—	87/3
A	Track Layout with:	Electric Track	6' x 3'	32/3	Manually Operated Points	15/-	—	—	—	—	68/3
B	Track Layout with:	Electric Track	6' x 3'	26/7	Electric Operated Points	15/-	—	—	—	—	87/2
B	Track Layout with:	Electric Track	6' x 3'	26/7	Manually Operated Points	15/-	—	—	—	—	68/2
C	Track Layout with:	Electric Track	6' x 3'	25/9	Electric Operated Points	15/-	—	—	—	—	75/4
C	Track Layout with:	Electric Track	6' x 3'	25/9	Manually Operated Points	15/-	—	—	—	—	56/4
D	Track Layout with:	Electric Track	6' x 4'	26/7	Electric Operated Points	20/-	—	—	—	—	107/3
D	Track Layout with:	Electric Track	6' x 4'	26/7	Manually Operated Points	20/-	—	—	—	—	85/6
E	Track Layout with:	Electric Track	6' x 4'	28/9	Electric Operated Points	20/-	—	—	—	—	135/10
E	Track Layout with:	Electric Track	6' x 4'	28/9	Manually Operated Points	20/-	—	—	—	—	102/7
F	Track Layout with:	Electric Track	8' x 4'	41/1	Electric Operated Points	27/-	—	—	—	—	185/3
F	Track Layout with:	Electric Track	8' x 4'	41/1	Manually Operated Points	27/-	—	—	—	—	149/3

PREWAR ACCESSORIES

CAT. NO.	DESCRIPTION	VARIATIONS	BOX TYPE	BOX NO.	BOX CODE	MECC. MAG	MECC. PRICE	LAST MECC.	LAST CAT. PRICE
D1	Switch Red	For electrically operated points & signals	14a	D605	7.5M11.39	12/39	2/4	11/41	4/3
D2	Switch Black	For isolating rails. Box has illustrations.	14a	D606	7.5M12.39	12/39	2/-	11/41	3/9
D2	Switch Black	For isolating rails. No illustrations.	14a	D606	11.39	12/39	2/-	11/41	3/9
D1	Lubrication Oil	Blue Seal for Clockwork motors	—	—	—	(6/39)	-/2	11/41	-/4
D2	Lubrication Oil	Red Seal for Electric motors	—	—	—	(6/39)	-/2	11/41	-/4
D1	Spanner	(Normally came with loco)	—	—	—	(6/39)	-/1	11/41	-/2½
D1	Key	(Normally came with loco in envelope marked 'Key')	—	—	—	(6/39)	-/3	11/41	-/3½
—	Switch Grouping Rods Long		—	—	—	(6/39)	-/3	11/41	-/6
—	Switch Grouping Rods Short		—	—	—	(6/39)	-/2	11/41	-/4½
—	Herculacker Wire		—	—	—	(1/40)	-/6	11/41	-/11
D1	Buffer Stop	6 per box	14a	D401	3.5M10.38	10/38	-/10	11/41	1/6
D1	Engine Shed	Wooden 12"x 6" approx. Green Roof	14a	D415	1M 10.39	12/39	11/6	11/41	21/-
D1	Footbridge	Wooden (Illustrated Only - but exists)	—	—	—	—	—	—	—
D1	Footbridge	Metal. (Illustrated & Priced - not available prewar)	—	—	—	(6/39)	3/6	9/39	3/6
D1	Goods Depot	Wooden 12"x 3½". Red Roof	14a	D402	3,2508.38	10/38	4/11	12/38	4/11

CAT. NO.	DESCRIPTION	VARIATIONS	BOX TYPE	BOX NO.	BOX CODE	MECC. MAG.	MECC. PRICE	LAST CAT.	LAST PRICE
D1	Goods Depot	Wooden 12"x 3½". Green Roof	14a	D402	650 8.39	(6/39	4/-)	11/41	8/3
D1	Island Platform	Wooden 24"x 2½". Red Roof	14a	D403	3,250 8.38	10/38	4/9	12/38	4/9
D1	Island Platform	Wooden 24"x 2½". Green Roof	14a	D403	350 8.39	(6/39	4/-)	11/41	8/3
D1	Home Signal	Manual. Box of 6. Unpainted underside	14a	D404	1.75M 10.38	10/38	1/-	11/41	1/10
D1	Distant Signal	Manual. Box of 6. Unpainted underside	14a	D404	1.75M 10.38	10/38	1/-	11/41	1/10
D2	Double Arm Signal	Manual. Box of 6. Unpainted underside	14a	D405	1.75M 10.38	10/38	1/4	11/41	2/6
D3	Home Junction Signal	Manual. Box of 2. Unpainted underside	14a	(D406)		(6/39	1/6)	11/41	3/-
D3	Distant Junction Signal	Manual. Box of 2. Unpainted underside	14a	(D406)		(6/39	1/6)	11/41	3/-
ED1	Home Signal	Electric. 1 in box. Unpainted underside	*14a	D418	5M 12.39	3/40	3/6	11/41	4/11
ED1	Distant Signal	Electric. 1 in box. Unpainted underside	*14a	D418	5M 12.39	3/40	3/6	11/41	4/11
ED2	Double Arm Signal	Electric. 1 in box. Unpainted underside	14a	D430	3M 12.39	12/39	6/-	11/41	8/6
ED3	Home Junction Signal	Electric. 1 in box. Unpainted underside	*14a	D431	3M 11.39	12/39	7/3	11/41	15/9
ED3	Distant Junction Signal	Electric. 1 in box. Unpainted underside	*14a	D431	3M 11.39	12/39	7/3	11/41	15/9

*Signifies box comes with either Home or Distant sticker.

CAT. NO.	DESCRIPTION	VARIATIONS	BOX TYPE	BOX NO.	BOX CODE	MECC. MAG.	MECC. PRICE	LAST CAT.	LAST PRICE
D1	Signal Cabin	Wooden 1¾"x 2⅞". Red Roof	14a	?	?	10/38	-/11	12/38	-/11
D1	Signal Cabin	Wooden 1¾"x 2⅞". Green Roof	14a	?	?	(6/39	-/11)	11/41	1/10
D2	City Station Outfit	Wooden. Green Roof	14a		1M 10.39	12/39	28/6	11/41	52/6
D2	Centre Platform	Part of City Station.	—			(5/39	-/11)	10/40	1/2½
D2	Station Building	Part of City Station. Green Roof	—			(5/39	8/6)	8/40	9/6
D2	Arched Roof	Part of City Station. Celluloid Covering	—			(5/39	10/-)	10/40	13/6
D2	Side Platform	Part of City Station.	—			(5/39	1/7½)	10/40	2/1½
D2	Centre Platform Ramps	Part of City Station.	—			(5/39	-/4)	8/40	-/5
D2	Side Platform Ramps	Part of City Station.	—			(5/39	-/3)	8/40	-/4
D2	Platform Buffers – Single	Part of City Station.	—			(5/39	-/6)	10/40	-/8½
D2	Platform Buffers – Double	Part of City Station.	—			(5/39	1/-)	10/40	1/4
D1	Main Line Station	Wooden 24"x 4⅛". Red Roof	14a	D407	3,250 8.38	6/38	7/6	12/38	7/6
D1	Main Line Station	Wooden 24"x 4⅛". Green Roof	14a	D407	1,500 1.39	(6/99	6/9)	11/41	14/-
D1	Tunnel – Short	Wooden. 5½" long. Green cardboard	?			10/38	1/3	11/41	2/6
D2	Tunnel – Long	Wooden. 11½" long. Green cardboard	?			10/38	1/8	11/41	3/6
D1	Miniature Station Staff Metal(6)	Light Colours. Green box with green printing.				10/38	1/-	11/41	2/2
D1	Miniature Passengers Metal (6)	Light Colours. Yellow printing on bright red box.				10/38	1/-	11/41	2/2

— Boxes list contents but have no codes.

CAT. NO.	DESCRIPTION	VARIATIONS	BOX TYPE	BOX NO.	BOX CODE	MECC. MAG.	MECC. PRICE	LAST CAT.	LAST PRICE
No.1	Transformer – Dublo (001)	Light Blue. Two Terminals	14a	D601	20M 10.38	10/38	10/6	11/41	20/-
No.2	Transformer – Dublo	Light Blue. Four Terminals	14a	D604	7.5M 10.38	10/38	12/6	11/41	26/-
No.1	Controller	Light Blue.	14a	D602	2M 6.39	10/38	21/-	11/41	42/-
No.1a	Controller	For Accumulator	14a	D603	2M 6.39	10/38	12/6	10/40	16/9
—	D.C. Converter	For Special Winding	?			12/39	(39/-)	1/40	45/-
—	D.C. Converter	*White on Black background	?			(10/39	55/-)	1/40	55/-
—	Station Names	Plain transparent envelope.	23B						

*— Came with Main Line Station Building & Signal Cabin. Never Listed or illustrated.

CAT. NO.	DESCRIPTION	VARIATIONS/COMMENTS							
D1	Tarpaulins (for wagons)	Certain of these items						Dealers 1939. Order List Only.	
D1	Lamp Standards	are rumoured, but this						Dealers 1939. Order List Only.	
D1	Platelayer's Hut	is the only known						Dealers 1939. Order List Only.	
D1	Telegraph Poles	dealer's reference to						Dealers 1939. Order List Only.	
D1	Viaduct Bridges	them. There is no known						Dealers 1939. Order List Only.	
		retail informations about these items.							

Breakdown Crane, Flat Truck, Goods Container, Water Crane and Lighting Accessories were other items noted in a prewar Dealer's Announcement bulletin dated February 1939, but again were never listed on retail lists or available for sale.

DINKY TOYS — DUBLO SIZED

CAT. NO.	DESCRIPTION	VARIATIONS/COMMENTS	BOX TYPE	BOX NO.	BOX CODE	FIRST DATE	FIRST PRICE	LAST DATE	LAST PRICE
No.15	Railway Signals	Set of six in box	Yellow with Mauve Inside	A2172	—	6/38	1/6	11/41	3/9
15a	Home Signal	Manual. Not Available Separately				6/38	-/2	6/41	-/4
15a	Distant Signal	Manual. Not Available Separately				6/38	-/2	6/41	-/4
15b	Double Arm Signal	Manual. Not Available Separately				6/38	-/3	11/41	-/7½
15c	Home Junction Signal	Manual. Not Available Separately				6/38	-/4	11/41	-/10
15c	Distant Junction Signal	Manual. Not Available Separately				6/38	-/4	11/41	-/10

PREWAR CARS

CAT. NO.	DESCRIPTION/NAME					MECC. MAG.	MECC. MAG. PRICE	LAST DATE	LAST PRICE
No.35	'Small Cars'	Set of 3 in box		—		6/38	-/9	11/41	2/6
35a	Saloon Car		Not Available Separately	—		6/38	-/3	11/41	-/10
35b	Racer		Not Available Separately			6/38	-/3	11/41	-/10
35c	M.G. Sports Car		Not Available Separately			6/38	-/3	11/41	-/10
35d	Austin Seven		?			6/38	-/4	11/41	-/10

PREWAR LOCOMOTIVES

CAT. NO.	DESCRIPTION/NAME	LOCO. NO.	WHEEL ARR.	COLOUR	MOTOR	LABEL COLOUR	VARIATIONS	BOX TYPE NO.	BOX NO.	BOX CODE	MECC. MAG.	MECC. MAG. PRICE	LAST DATE	LAST PRICE
CLOCKWORK														
DL7	S.R.	2594	0-6-2T	Ol.Green	C/W	Gold		7a	D152	7,500 9.38	10/38	12/6	8/40	14/-
DL7	L.M.S.	6917	0-6-2T	Black	C/W	Gold		7a	Locos used same		10/38	12/6	8/40	14/-
DL7	L.N.E.R.	2690	0-6-2T	Black	C/W	Gold		7a	boxes. Small		10/38	12/6	8/40	14/-
DL7	G.W.R.	6699	0-6-2T	Green	C/W	Gold		7a	stickers on end indicated region.		10/38	12/6	8/40	14/-
DL1	'Sir Nigel Gresley'	4498	4-6-2	Blue	C/W	Silver	—	7a	D171	4,250 9.38	10/38	18/6	11/41	37/6
D1	Tender L.N.E.R.	—	—	*Blue		Silver	—	1a	?		10/38	4/6	10/40	6/-

*— Bogie frames are unpainted and base plate is black.

CAT. NO.	DESCRIPTION/NAME	LOCO. NO.	WHEEL ARR.	COLOUR	MOTOR	LABEL COLOUR	VARIATIONS	BOX TYPE NO.	BOX NO.	BOX CODE	MECC. MAG.	MECC. MAG. PRICE	LAST DATE	LAST PRICE
ELECTRIC														
DLT 1	'Sir Nigel Gresley'	4498	Locomotive and Tender					7a	D171	4,250 9.38	(6/38) 10/38	23/-	11/41	45/-
EDL 7	S.R.	2594	0-6-2T	Ol. Green	H/S	Gold		7b	D154	5M 9.38	10/38	17/6	11/41	37/6
EDL 7	L.M.S.	6917	0-6-2T	Black	H/S	Gold		7b	Locos in same type		10/38	17/6	11/41	37/6
EDL 7	L.N.E.R.	2690	0-6-2T	Black	H/S	Gold		7b	of boxes as above. Stickers on end indicated region.		10/38	17/6	11/41	37/6
EDL 7	G.W.R.	6699	0-6-2T	Green	H/S	Gold		7b			10/38	17/6	11/41	37/6
EDL 1	'Sir Nigel Gresley'	4498	4-6-2	Blue	H/S	Silver	(1)	7b	D173	3M 9.38	10/38	25/-	8/40	27/6
EDL 1	'Sir Nigel Gresley'	4498	4-6-2	Blue	H/S	Silver	(2)	7b	D173	3M 9.38	10/38	25/-	8/40	27/6
EDLT 1	'Sir Nigel Gresley'	4498	Locomotive and Tender					7b	D173	3M 9.38	(6/38)	29/6	11/41	60/-
EDL 2	'Duchess of Atholl'	6231	4-6-2	Maroon	H/S	—					(5/39)	39/-	7/39	39/-
	(Single chimney)													
D2	Tender L.M.S.	—	—	Maroon		—		Loco and tender not sold before the war.			(5/39)	6/-	7/39	6/-
EDLT 2	'Duchess of Atholl'	6231	Locomotive and Tender					(Not sold before the war)			(5/39)	45/-	7/39	45/-

One prewar tender is known to exist with prewar couplings. It appears to be a pre-production item as it has no L.M.S. lettering and came with a mock wooden loco.

(1) Early locos have approximately 1/8" deep slot for drawbar.

(2) Later locos have approximately ¼" deep slot for drawbar.

PREWAR SETS

CAT. NO.	DESCRIPTION	ITEMS IN SETS	BOX TYPE	BOX NO.	BOX CODE	MECC. MAG.	MECC. MAG. PRICE	LAST DATE	LAST PRICE
DG 7	S.R. Goods Set	S.R. Open Wagon, Goods Van & Guards Van	10a	(D102)	- No codes	9/38	27/6	11/41	55/-
DG 7	L.M.S. Goods Set	L.M.S. Open Wagon, Goods Van & Guards Van	10a	(D102)	- or dates	9/38	27/6	11/41	55/-
DG 7	L.N.E.R. Goods Set	L.N.E.R. Open Wagon, Goods Van & Guards Van	10a	(D102)	- on boxes	9/38	27/6	11/41	55/-
DG 7	G.W.R. Goods Set	G.W.R. Open Wagon, Goods Van & Guards Van	10a	(D102)	- Region	9/38	27/6	11/41	55/-
					Stickers only.				
DP 1	L.N.E.R. Passenger Set	Articulated Coaches	10a	D101		9/38	39/6	11/41	80/-

— Above sets contain clockwork locos and track. Track consists of 8 curves and two straight rails.

CAT. NO.	DESCRIPTION	ITEMS IN SETS	BOX TYPE	BOX NO.	BOX CODE	MECC. MAG.	MECC. MAG. PRICE	LAST DATE	LAST PRICE
EDG 7	S.R. Goods Set	S.R. Open Wagon, Goods Van & Guards Van	10a	D104	- No codes	9/38	55/-	11/41	115/-
EDG 7	L.M.S. Goods Set	L.M.S. Open Wagon, Goods Van & Guards Van	10a	D104	- or dates	9/38	55/-	11/41	115/-
EDG 7	L.N.E.R. Goods Set	L.N.E.R. Open Wagon, Goods Van & Guards Van	10a	D104	- on boxes	9/38	55/-	11/41	115/-
EDG 7	G.W.R. Goods Set	G.W.R. Open Wagon, Goods Van & Guards Van	10a	D104	- Region	9/38	55/-	11/41	115/-
					Stickers only.				
EDP 1	L.N.E.R. Passenger Set	Articulated Coaches	10a	D103	- As above	9/38	70/-	11/41	140/-
EDGA 7	S.R. Goods Set	S.R. Open Wagon, Goods Van & Guards Van	?	?		9/38	46/6	10/40	64/-
EDGA 7	L.M.S. Goods Set	L.M.S. Open Wagon, Goods Van & Guards Van	?	?		9/38	46/6	10/40	64/-
EDGA 7	L.N.E.R. Goods Set	L.N.E.R. Open Wagon, Goods Van & Guards Van	?	?		9/38	46/6	10/40	64/-
EDGA 7	G.W.R. Goods Set	G.W.R. Open Wagon, Goods Van & Guards Van	?	?		9/38	46/6	10/40	64/-
EDPA 1	L.N.E.R. Passenger Set	Articulated Coaches	?	?		9/38	61/6	10/40	82/-

— Above sets contain electric locos and track. Track consists of seven curves, one curved terminal rail and two straight rails. EDG & EDP Sets contained a No. 1 Controller. EDGA & EDPA Sets contained a No. 1a Controller suitable for an accumulator.

CAT. NO.	DESCRIPTION	ITEMS IN SETS	COMPANY	COACH OR WAGON NO.	COLOUR	ROOF	BASE	BOX TYPE NO.	BOX CODE	MECC. MAG.	MECC. PRICE DATE	MECC. LAST DATE	LAST PRICE
EDP 2	L.M.S. Passenger Set	Br/3rd and 1st/3rd L.M.S. Coaches			Not sold before the war					(5/39)	92/6	9/39	92/6
EDPA 2	L.M.S. Passenger Set	Br/3rd and 1st/3rd L.M.S. Coaches			Not sold before the war					(5/39)	84/-	9/39	84/-

— Above two sets would have presumably have contained same track as in electric sets noted above.

PREWAR ROLLING STOCK

CAT. DESCRIPTION		COMPANY	COACH OR WAGON NO.	COLOUR	ROOF	BASE	BOX TYPE NO.	BOX CODE	MECC. MAG.	MECC. PRICE DATE	MECC. LAST DATE	LAST PRICE
D1 1st/3rd Corridor Coach	L.N.E.R.		L.N.E.R.42759	Teak	White	SGa	4a	D251	2.5M11.38	10/38	3/6	11/41	6/9
D2 All 3rd & Br/3rd Articulated Set	L.N.E.R.		LNER45401 & LNER45402	Teak	White	SGa	4a	D252	2.5M8.38	10/38	6/6	6/41	10/6
D3 1st/3rd Corridor Coach	L.M.S.		LMS4183	Maroon	Silver	—	Never sold prewar.			(5/39)	6/9	9/39	6/9
D3 Br/3rd Corridor Cch.	L.M.S.		LMS26133	Maroon	Silver	—	Never sold prewar.			(5/39)	6/9	9/39	6/9

There are strong indications that a few may have been sold before the war, but there is no confirmation of this available at the present time.

D1 Goods Brake Van	S.R.		SR55975	Brown	White	1c	1a	D301	3M8.38	10/38	2/6	11/41	5/3
D1 Goods Brake Van	G.W.R.		GW68796	Grey	White	1c	1a	D301	Same boxes	10/38	2/6	11/41	5/3
D1 Goods Brake Van	L.N.E.R.		NE20T178717	Brown	White	1c	1a	D301	but with	10/38	2/6	11/41	5/3
D1 Goods Brake Van	L.M.S.		LMS730026	Brown	Silver	1c	1a	D301	region stickers.	10/38	2/6	11/41	5/3
D1 Open Wagon	S.R.		SR12T19260	Brown	—	1a	1a	D303	15M8.38	10/38	1/4	11/41	3/-
D1 Open Wagon	G.W.R.		GW12T109458	Grey	—	1a	1a	D303	Same boxes	10/38	1/4	11/41	3/-
D1 Open Wagon	L.N.E.R.		NE12T404844	Grey	—	1a	1a	D303	but with	10/38	1/4	11/41	3/-
D1 Open Wagon	L.M.S.		LMS12T210112	Brown	—	1a	1a	D303	region stickers.	10/38	1/4	11/41	3/-
D1 Coal Wagon	S.R.		SR12T19260	Brown	—	1a	1a	D305	10M3.39	3/39	1/7	11/41	3/6
D1 Coal Wagon	G.W.R.		GW12T109458	Grey	—	1a	1a	D305	Same boxes	3/39	1/7	11/41	3/6
D1 Coal Wagon	L.N.E.R.		NE12T404844	Grey	—	1a	1a	D305	but with	3/39	1/7	11/41	3/6
D1 Coal Wagon	L.M.S.		LMS12T210112	Brown	—	1a	1a	D305	region stickers.	3/39	1/7	11/41	3/6
D2 High Sided Wagon	L.N.E.R.		NE12T91508	Grey	—	1a	1a	D311	7.5M8.39	9/39	1/6	11/41	3/6
D2 High Sided Wagon	L.M.S.		LMS12T608344	Brown	—	1a	1a	D311	5M1.40	9/39	1/6	11/41	3/6

— Above two boxes are same except for region stickers.

D2 High Sided Coal Wagon	L.N.E.R.		NE12T91508	Grey	—	1a	1a	D312	8M12.39	9/39	1/9	11/41	3/9
D2 High Sided Coal Wagon	L.M.S.		LMS12T608344	Brown	—	1a	1a	D312	8M12.39	9/39	1/9	11/41	3/9

— Above two boxes also same except for region stickers.
— All above wagons have prewar type wheels (PWW) and couplings (PW).

D1 Goods Van	S.R.		SR12T48277	Brown	White	1a	1a	D302	5M7.38	10/38	1/6	11/41	3/6
D1 Goods Van	G.W.R.		GW12T112699	Grey	White	1a	1a	D302	Same boxes	10/38	1/6	11/41	3/6
D1 Goods Van	L.N.E.R.		NE12TN182153	Grey	White	1a	1a	D307	but with	10/38	1/6	11/41	3/6
D1 Goods Van	L.M.S.		LMS12T508194	Brown	Silver	1a	1a	D302	region stickers.	10/38	1/6	11/41	3/6
D1 Meat Van	S.R.		SR10T51298	Buff	Silver	1a	1a	D308	7.5M4.39	4/39	1/6	11/41	3/6
D1 Meat Van	L.M.S.		LMS6TN19631	Brown	Silver	1a	1a	D308	7.5M4.39	4/39	1/6	11/41	3/6
D1 Fish Van	L.N.E.R.		NE10T168975	Lt. Brown	White	1a	1a	D307	7.5M4.39	4/39	1/6	11/41	3/6
D1 Cattle Truck	G.W.R.		GW8T106324	Grey	White	1a	1a	D306	7.5M4.39	4/39	1/6	11/41	3/6
D1 Cattle Truck	L.M.S.		LMS710018	Brown	Silver	1a	1a	D306	7.5M4.39	4/39	1/6	11/41	3/6
D1 Horse Box	L.N.E.R.		NE2337	Teak	White	1a	1a	D309	7.5M4.39	4/39	1/6	11/41	3/6
D1 High Capacity Wagon	L.N.E.R.		NE50TN163535	Brown	—	11a	1a	D310	5M12.39	9/39	3/6	11/41	6/9

Brown Base, DBa type bogies.

D1 High Capacity Wagon	L.N.E.R.		NE50TN163535	Brown	—	11a	1a	D310	5M12.39	9/39	3/6	11/41	6/9

Black Base, DBa type bogies.

D1 Tank Wagon 'Esso'	(Petrol)			Buff	—	1a	1a	D304	1OM3.39	3/39	2/6	11/41	5/3
D1 Tank Wagon 'Power'	(Petrol)			Green	—	1a	1a	D304	1OM3.39	3/39	2/6	11/41	5/3
D1 Tank Wagon 'Royal Daylight' (Oil)				Red	—	1a	1a	D304	1OM3.39	3/39	2/6	11/41	5/3

— All above wagons have prewar type wheels (PWW) and couplings (PW).
— Region stickers can be found on the ends of relative boxes for Meat Vans and Cattle Trucks.

DUBLO-DINKYS AND OTHER ACCESSORIES

CAT. NO.	DESCRIPTION	NO./COLOUR	COMMENTS	BOX TYPE	BOX NO.	BOX CODE	MECC. MAG.	MECC. PRICE	MECC. LAST DATE	LAST PRICE
050	Railway Staff	(12)	Plastic. Set contains policeman with hands behind his back.	19	50050	—	12/60	2/11	12/64	2/11
050	Railway Staff	(12)	Plastic. Set contains shunter with pole in place of above.	20	—	—	—	—	—	—
051	Station Staff	(6)	Metal. Formerly Dinky Toys No. 1001 and 50 051	Green	051 (1001 50250)	—	4/52	3/3	9/59	2/11
052	Railway Passengers	(11)	Plastic	20	—	—	12/61	4/3	12/64	3/11
053	Passengers	(6)	Metal. Formerly Dinky Toys No. 1003 and 50 053	Red	053 (1003 50251)	—	4/52	3/3	9/59	2/11
054	Station Personnel	(12)	Plastic	20	—	—	4/62	4/3	12/64	3/11
061	Ford Prefect	Beige	Plain Grey Wheels.	Yellow/Orange	061	in Black	3/58	1/9	9/59	1/6
062	Singer Roadster	Yellow/Red	Plain Grey Wheels.	Yellow/Orange	062	in Black	3/58	1/9	10/60	1/6
063	Commer Van	Blue	Plain Grey Wheels.	Yellow/Orange	063	in Black	3/58	1/9	10/60	1/6
064	Austin Lorry	Green	Plain Grey Wheels.	Yellow/Orange	064	in Black	12/57	1/9	4/62	1/6
064	Austin Lorry	Green	Treaded Grey Wheels.	Yellow	064	in Black	12/57	1/9	4/62	1/6
064	Austin Lorry	Green	Treaded Black Wheels.	Yellow/Red	064 in Red (no pict)		12/57	1/9	4/62	1/6
065	Morris Pickup	Red	Plain Grey Wheels.	Yellow/Orange	065	in Black	12/57	1/9	9/59	1/6
066	Bedford Flat Truck	Grey	Plain Grey Wheels. No Hook	Yellow/Orange	066	in Black	12/57	2/-	10/60	1/9
066	Bedford Flat Truck	Grey	Treaded Grey Wheels. No Hook	Yellow/Orange	066	in Black	12/57	2/-	10/60	1/9
066	Bedford Flat Truck	Grey	Treaded Grey Wheels & Hook	Yellow/Orange	066	in Black	12/57	2/-	10/60	1/9
067	Austin Taxi	Blue/White	Treaded Grey Wheels.	Yellow/Black	067	in Black	3/59	2/6	12/64	2/6
067	Austin Taxi	Blue/White	Treaded Black Wheels.	Yellow/Black	067	in Black	3/59	2/6	12/64	2/6
068	Royal Mail Van	Red	Treaded Grey Wheels.	Yellow/Orange	068	in Black	4/59	2/3	4/64	2/3
069	Massey-Ferguson Tractor	Blue	Treaded Grey Wheels.	Yellow/Orange	069 in Red (no pict.)		9/59	1/6	12/64	1/6
070	AEC Mercury Tanker	Red/Green	Treaded Grey Wheels.	Yellow & Red	070 in Red (no pict.)		10/59	2/6	4/62	2/6
070	AEC Mercury Tanker	Red/Green	Treaded Black Wheels.	Yellow & Red	070 in Red (no pict.)		10/59	2/6	4/62	2/6
071	Volkswagen Delivery Van	Yellow	Treaded Grey Wheels.	Yellow & Red	071 in Red (no pict.)		3/60	2/-	12/64	2/-
071	Volkswagen Delivery Van	Yellow	Treaded Black Wheels.	Yellow & Red	071 in Red (no pict.)		3/60	2/-	12/64	2/-
072	Bedford Articulated Flat Truck	Orange/Red	Has no. 1 cast into cab & Grey Plain Wheels.	Yellow/Orange	072	in Black	6/59	2/6	12/64	2/6
072	Bedford Articulated Flat Truck	Orange/Red	Has no. 1 cast into cab & Grey Treaded Wheels.	Yellow	072	in Black	6/59	2/6	12/64	2/6
072	Bedford Articulated Flat Truck	Orange/Red	Cab has no. 3 cast into it. Treaded Black Wheels.	Yellow/Orange	072 in Red (no pict.)		6/59	2/6	12/64	2/6
073	Land Rover & Horse Trailer	Br. Green	Green Flap on Trailer & Plain Grey Wheels.	Yellow/Orange	073	in Black	9/60	4/3	12/64	3/11
073	Land Rover & Horse Trailer	Green	Brown Flap on Trailer & Treaded Grey Wheels.	Yellow/Orange	073	in Black	9/60	4/3	12/64	3/11
073	Land Rover & Horse Trailer	Bt. Green	Black Flap on Trailer & Treaded Black Wheels.	Yellow	073 in Black (50073)		9/60	4/3	12/64	3/11
076	Lansing Bagnall Tractor & Trailer	Maroon	Plain Black Wheels.	Yellow	076 in Black		6/60	2/9	12/64	2/11
078	Trailer Only.	Maroon	Plain Black Wheels. (6 per box)	Yellow/Orange	078 in Black		(5/61)	1/6	12/64	1/6
790	Granite Chippings	—	—	19	50790	—	(10/59)	(-/9)	9/62	-/9
791	Imitation Coal	—	—	19	50791	—	12/61	1/6	9/62	-/9
792	Packing Cases & Lids (3)	—	Listed only as Dinky Toy Item & number.	19	—	—	12/61	1/6	12/64	1/6
846	Oil Drums	(6)	— Hornby-Acho Products.	19	—	—	5/61	1/3	—	—
849	Packing Cases	(6)	— Hornby-Acho Products.	19	—	—	5/61	1/3	—	—
850	Crates of Bottles	(6)	— Hornby-Acho Products.	19	—	—	5/61	1/3	—	—
851	Two of each of above	—	— Hornby-Acho Products.	19	—	—	5/61	1/9	—	—

CONTROLLERS AND TRANSFORMERS

CAT. NO.	DESCRIPTION	TYPE	COLOUR	BOX TYPE NO.	BOX CODE	MECC. MAG.	MECC. PRICE	MECC. LAST DATE	LAST PRICE
D1	Controller	12v DC Input. 2 part box.	Black	14e 32300	—	(4/49	37/6	5/55	47/6
D1	Controller	12v DC Input. 2 part box.	Black	14b	—	(4/49	37/6	5/55	47/6
No. 1	Transformer	AC Mains Input. 2 part box.	Black	14e	16/250/50	1947	19/6	5/55	47/6
—	Transformer	AC Mains Input. 2 part box.	Black	14b	—	1947	19/6	5/55	47/6

351

CAT. NO.	DESCRIPTION	TYPE	COLOUR	BOX TYPE NO.	BOX CODE	MECC. MAG.	MECC. PRICE	MECC. LAST DATE	LAST PRICE
A2	Power Controller	Trans. & Contr. 2 part box	Grey	14f	—	10/56	2/12/6	5/57	2/12/6
A3	Power Controller	Trans. & Contr. 2 part box.	Grey	14f	—	12/54	4/17/6	5/57	5/5/-
1040	Controller	16v AC Input. 1 piece box.	Grey	Plain Cardboard & Label		(4/59	3/10/6)	4/59	3/10/6
32304	Controller	16v AC Input. 2 part box.	Grey	14f	32304	(5/56	3/12/6)	12/58	3/12/6
C3	Controller	16v AC Input. 2 part box.	Grey	14f	32304	12/55	72/-	4/57	3/12/6
1080	Battery Controller	Battery/Accum. 1 piece box	Grey	15b	38080 12/59	(10/59	5/-)	5/64	5/-
1849	Battery Controller	Battery/Accum. 1 piece box	Grey	Plain Cardboard & Label		(4/59	9/9	4/59	9/9
32849	Battery Controller	Battery/Accum. 2 part box	Grey	14f	32849 11/54	12/54	(30/-)	9/58	1/11/6
—	Battery Controller	Battery/Accum. 2 part box.	Grey	14f	32849 11/54	12/54	(30/-)	9/58	1/11/6
1041	Controller for Marshall 2 & 3	16v AC Input. 1 piece box	Grey	Plain Cardboard & Label 38041		(1961	35/-)	5/64	23/11
1050	Accessory Transformer	AC Mains Input. 1 piece box	Grey	Plain Cardboard & Label		(4/63	—)	5/64	—
GP15	Accessory Transformer	AC Mains Input. 1 piece box	Grey	Plain Cardboard & Label		(4/63	—)	5/64	—
1060	Safety Transformer	AC Mains Input. 2 part box.	Grey	Plain Cardboard & Label		10/58	1/19/9	5/64	35/11
T15	Safety Transformer	AC Mains Input. 2 part box.	Grey	14f		10/58	1/19/9	5/64	35/11
1090	Hornby No.1 Control Unit	AC Mains Input. 1 piece box	Grey	Plain Cardboard & Label		4/63	35/-	5/64	35/-
1100	Hornby No.2 Power Control Unit	AC Mains Input. 1 piece box	Grey	Plain Cdbrd. & label. (38100)		(10/59	49/6)	5/64	45/-
1103	Marshall 2 Control Unit	AC Mains Input. 1 piece box	Grey	Plain Cardboard & Label		11/59	46/-	5/64	—
1120	Hornby 3 Control Unit	AC Mains Input. 2 part box.	Grey	Plain Cdbrd. & label. (38120)		(10/59	75/-)	5/64	69/11
1123	Marshall 3 Control Unit	AC Mains Input. 1 piece box	Grey	Plain Cardboard & Label		1/60	75/-	—	—
M20	Transformer	AC Mains Input. 2 part box. & 20v AC Output. (Meccano – Not Hornby Dublo).	Grey	14f		(5/57	1/19/9)	5/57	1/19/9

POSTWAR SUNDRIES

CAT. NO.	DESCRIPTION	TYPE	PART NO.	BOX TYPE	BOX NO.	BOX CODE	FIRST DATE	FIRST PRICE	LAST DATE	PRICE
1505	Brushes	½-in. motor. Integral type.	11543	—	—	—	4/59	-/5	12/64	-/5
32652	Brushes	½-in. motor. Integral type.	R300	22a	—	—	5/56	2/3 (for 6)	12/58	-/5
—	Brushes	½-in. motor. Integral type.	R300	22a	—	—	4/53	-/4½	4/56	2/3 (for 6)
1506	Brush Springs	½-in. motor. Integral type.	11544A	—	—	—	4/59	-/1	12/64	-/1
32653	Brush Springs	½-in. motor. Integral type.	R307	22a	35307	—	5/56	-/6	12/58	-/1
—	Brush Springs	½-in. motor. Integral type.	R307 (11544)	22a	—	—	4/53	-/1 (for 6)	4/56	-/6 (for 6)
1507	Brushes	Ringfield Motor.	21461	22	—	—	10/60	-/6	12/64	-/6
1508	Brush Springs	Ringfield Motor. Left & Right.	21464/5	22a & 22b	35508	—	5/61	-/4	12/64	-/4
1510	Brush Arms	2207/8, 3220/5 locos.	14467	22a	14467	(39510)	4/59	-/7	12/64	-/8
32661	Brush Arms	2207/8, 3220/5 locos.	R190	22a	14467/C707		1/58	-/7	12/58	-/7
1511	Brush Arms	2230/3230 locos.	20237	22a & 22b	20237	—	4/59	-/9	12/64	-/9
1511	Brush Arms	2230/3230 locos.	20237	19	—	—	4/59	-/9	12/64	-/9
32668	Brush Arms	2230/3230 locos.	R240	22a	—	—	12/58	-/9	12/58	-/9
1520	Cable Drum	'Liverpool'. Wood.	—	No box with this number.			4/59	-/9	11/61	-/9
32947	Cable Drum	'Liverpool'. Wood.	—	2a	32947	2/58	5/56	-/9	12/58	-/9
D1	Cable Drum	'Liverpool'. Wood.	—	2a	32947	2/58	1/56	-/9	1/56	-/9
1521	Cable Drum	'Aluminium Wire and Cable'.	Plastic	3a	39521	10/62	11/61	-/9	12/64	-/9
1525	Meat Container	British Railways - Insul-Meat.	White	3a	—	—	4/59	1/6	12/64	1/9
32945	Meat Container	British Railways - Insul-Meat.	White	2a	32945	10/56	5/56	1/6	12/58	1/6
D1	Meat Container	British Railways - Insul-Meat.	White	2a	32945	10/56	1/56	1/6	1/56	1/6
1526	Furniture Container	British Railways - Furniture.	Maroon	3a	—	—	4/59	1/6	12/64	1/9
32946	Furniture Container	British Railways - Furniture.	Maroon	2a	32946	2/57	5/56	1/6	12/58	1/6
D1	Furniture Container	British Railways - Furniture.	Maroon	2a	32946	2/57	1/56	1/6	1/56	1/6
1530	Wire 5-yards	Coils of Red, Green or Black.	—	—	—	—	4/59	1/6	12/64	1/9
32657	Wire 5-yards	Coils of Red, Green or Black.	—	—	—	—	5/56	1/6	12/58	1/6
—	Wire 5-yards	Coils of Red, Green or Black.	—	—	—	—	1/53	1/-	4/56	1/6
1531	Wire 50-yards	Coils of Red, Green or Black on cardboard or wood formers.	—	—	—	—	4/59	13/6	12/64	15/-
32659	Wire 50-yards	Coils of Red, Green or Black on cardboard or wood formers.	—	—	—	—	5/56	13/6	12/58	13/6
—	Wire 50-yards	Coils of Red, Green or Black on cardboard or wood formers.	—	—	—	—	10/55	13/6	4/56	13/6

CAT. NO.	DESCRIPTION		PART NO.	BOX TYPE	BOX NO.	BOX CODE	FIRST DATE	FIRST PRICE	LAST DATE	LAST PRICE
1535	Fishplates	3-rail					4/62	-/2	9/63	-/2
1545	Fuses	1½-amps. (6)	—	22a	32660	—	5/61	1/-	12/64	1/-
32660	Fuses	1½-amps. (6)	—	—	—	—	6/56	-/9	12/58	-/9
—	Fuses	1½-amps. (6)	—	22a	—	—	10/50	-/9	4/56	-/9
1550	Lamp	Marshall 3 Control Unit.	—		—	—	Never listed for retail sale.			
1560	Lamp-15v	For Signals. (6)	—	25a	39560	—	4/59	2/2	10/60	2/2
1561	Lamp-15v	Type 2T for Signals. (6)	—	25b	39561	—	10/59	2/2	12/64	2/4
1565	Lamp-10v	For A3 Power Control Unit. (6)	13377	16	39565	—	Never listed for retail sale.			
1565	Lamp-10v	For A3 Power Control Unit. (6)	13377	14e	39565	—	Never listed for retail sale.			
—	Lamp-10v	For A3 Power Control Unit. (6)	R502	14e	—	—	Never listed for retail sale.			
1566	Lamp-2.5v	For A2 Power Control Unit. (6)	7828	16	—	—	Never listed for retail sale.			
1566	Lamp-2.5v	For A2 Power Control Unit. (6)	7828	14e	—	—	Never listed for retail sale.			
—	Lamp-2.5v	For A2 Power Control Unit. (6)	R551	14e	—	—	Never listed for retail sale.			
1575	Lighting Kit.	For Buildings. Dinky No. 787	—	21	39575	—	12/59	3/3	4/64	3/3
1576	Terminal Panel	For 1575 above.	—	19	57314	—	12/59	2/-	12/64	2/-
1577	Lamp-14v	For 1575 above.	20918	16	—	—	Never listed for retail sale.			
1585	Lubricating Oil	Tube.	—	Tube	—	(39585)	4/59	-/6	12/64	-/6
32655	Lubricating Oil	Tube	—	Tube	—	—	5/56	-/6	12/58	-/6
—	Lubricating Oil	Tube	—	Tube	—	—	4/53	-/7½	4/56	-/6
—	Lubricating Oil	Vial	—	Glass Vial	—	—	4/53	-/7½	4/56	-/6
1590	Nut	For 3-rail Terminal Rails etc.	—	19	—	—	Never listed for retail sale.			
1591	Knurled Nuts	For Plastic Kits. (12)	—	19	—	—	Never listed for retail sale.			
1595	Plug & Nut Assembly	For A3 Power Control Unit.	13316/C1141	22a & 22b	—	—	Never listed for retail sale.			
1600	Screw	For Plastic Kits. (6)	—	19	—	—	Never listed for retail sale.			
1601	Knurled Screws	For Plastic Kits. (12)	—	19	—	—	Never listed for retail sale.			
1605	Spanner	For locos. – Chrome Plated.	—	Packaging Unknown.			4/59	-/2	12/64	-/3
32654	Spanner	For locos. 'Blacked'.	—	Packaging Unknown.		—	5/56	-/1½	12/58	-/2
—	Spanner	For locos.	—	Packaging Unknown.		—	1/52	-/1½	4/56	-/1½
1610	Station Names	For Buildings.	—	No Packet with this number			4/59	-/3	12/64	-/4
32171	Station Names	For Buildings.	—	23b	32171	—	5/56	-/3	12/58	-/3
32171	Station Names	For Buildings.	—	23a	32171	—	5/56	-/3	12/58	-/3
D1	Station Names	For Buildings.	—	23a	—	(No.D1)	10/53	-/2½	4/56	-/3
—	Station Names	For Buildings.	—	23a	(DA460)	—	10/50	-/2½	10/53	-/2½
1612	Switch Handle	For coupling two switches together		19	57122	—	4/63	-/9	12/64	-/9
1613	Switch	Maroon for points and signals.	—	15a	39613	6/62	4/62	4/11	12/64	4/11
1614	Switch	Maroon for points and signals.	—	15a	39164	10/61	10/60	4/4	9/62	4/9
1615	Switch	Red, for points and signals.	—	14k	39615	—	4/59	4/4	10/60	4/4
				(Also type 14e, red in colour, no. 1615, but date code 1/64).						
32302	Switch	Red, for points and signals.	—	14e	32302	4/56	5/56	4/2	8/58	4/6
D1	Switch	Red, for points and signals.	—	14e	32302	4/56	8/52	4/-	4/56	4/2
1616	Switch	Black, for Isolating Rails.	—	14e	39616	4/61	4/59	4/-	12/64	4/4
32303	Switch	Black, for Isolating Rails.	—	14h	32303	2/58	5/56	3/11	8/58	4/3
32303	Switch	Black, for Isolating Rails.	—	14e	32303	11/56	5/56	3/11	8/58	4/3
D2	Switch	Black, for Isolating Rails.	—	14e	32303	10/54	6/54	3/6	4/56	3/11
D2	Switch	Black, for Isolating Rails.	—	14h	32303	9/58	6/54	3/6	4/56	3/11
1620	Switch	Green, for Colour Light Signals.	—	14j	39620	5/59	4/59	4/4	12/64	4/9
32305	Switch	Green, for Colour Light Signals.	—	14j	32305	10/58	9/58	4/6	9/58	4/6
G3	Switch	Green, for Colour Light Signals.	—	14j	32305	5/59	9/58	4/6	9/58	4/6
1625	Switch Group Rods	Pair of Long type for 6 switches.	—	19	1625	—	4/59	-/2	12/64	-/2
32148	Switch Group Rods	Pair of Long type for 6 switches.	—	23a	32148	—	5/56	-/2	12/58	-/2
—	Switch Group Rods	Pair of Long type for 6 switches.	—	23a	32148	—	1/52	-/4	4/56	-/2
1626	Switch Group Rods	Pair of Short type for 4 switches.	—	19	1626	—	4/59	-/2	12/64	-/2
32149	Switch Group Rods	Pair of Short type for 4 switches.	—	23a	32149	—	5/56	-/2	12/58	-/2
—	Switch Grcup Rods	Pair of Short type for 4 switches.	—	23a	32149	—	1/52	-/4	4/56	-/2
1628	Terminal Nuts	For Transformer/Controller 1100/20			—	—	Never listed for retail sale.			
1630	TPO Mail Bags (12)	For TPO Mail Train.	—	No box known with this number			4/59	-/2	12/64	-/2
32948	TPO Mail Bags (12)	For TPO Mail Train.	—	22a	32948	—	4/57	-/2	12/58	-/2
D1	TPO Mail Bags (12)	For TPO Mail Train.	—	22a	32498	—	4/57	-/2	12/58	-/2
1631	Locomotive tyres (12)	For locos. 2230/32/33/34/45 & 2250.	20252	22a	20252	—	5/61	-/5 (per pair)	12/64	-/2½

CAT. NO.	DESCRIPTION		PART NO.	BOX TYPE	BOX NO.	BOX CODE	FIRST DATE	FIRST PRICE	LAST DATE	LAST PRICE
1631	Locomotive tyres (12)	For locos. 2230/32/33/34/45 plus corresponding 3-rail.	20252	22a	35244	—	5/61	/5	12/64	-/2½
1631	Locomotive tyres (12)	plus corresponding 3-rail.	R244	22b	20252	—	5/61	-/5-	12/64	-/2½
1631	Locomotive tyres (12)	plus corresponding 3-rail.	—	19	—	—	5/61	-/5	12/64	-/2½
1635	Wheels 2-rail	Spoked – Twelve Pairs.	—	22a	39635	—	4/59	-/3	12/64	-/6
32912	Wheels 2-rail	Spoked – Twelve Pairs.	—		Black Printing.		12/58	-/3	12/58	-/3
1636	Wheels 2-rail	Solid Disc – Twelve Pairs.	—	22a	39636	—	4/59	-/3	12/64	-/6
32913	Wheels 3-rail	Solid Disc – Twelve Pairs.	—		Red Printing.		12/58	-/3	12/58	-/3
32911	Wheels 3-rail	Solid – Six Pairs.	—	22a	32911	—	5/56	-/6	12/58	-/6
32911	Wheels 3-rail	Solid – Six Pairs.	—	22b	32911	—	5/56	-/6	12/58	-/6
	Wheels 2-rail	Solid – Six Pairs	—		—		4/54	-/6	4/56	-/6
48125	Graphite Grease	Tube	—		—		1/63	1/6	12/64	1/6
60125	Graphite Grease	Tube	—		Yellow/Black 60125		12/61	1/6	9/62	1/6
—	Front Bogie Assembly	A4 – L11 locos.	R110	22a	—		Never listed for retail sale.			
—	Front Bogie Assembly	A4 – L11 locos.	11557/C1087	22a	—		Never listed for retail sale.			
—	Pony Truck Assembly	A4 – L11 locos.	R111	22a	—		Never listed for retail sale.			
—	Pony Truck Assembly	A4 – L11 locos.	11518/C1067	22a	—		Never listed for retail sale.			
—	Pony Truck Assembly	L12 locos.	R125	22a	—		Never listed for retail sale.			
—	Pony Truck Assembly	L12 locos.	12373/C1179	22a	—		Never listed for retail sale.			
—	Pony Truck Assembly	L12 locos.	R120	22a	—		Never listed for retail sale.			
—	Front Bogie Assembly	L12 locos.	12377	22a	—		Never listed for retail sale.			
—	Pony Truck Assembly	0-6-2T locos.	R172		—		Never listed for retail sale.			
—	Pony Truck Assembly	0-6-2T locos.	11587		—		Never listed for retail sale.			
—	Rear Bogie Assembly	2-6-4T locos.	R180		—		Never listed for retail sale.			
—	Rear Bogie Assembly	2-6-4T locos.	7734		—		Never listed for retail sale.			
—	Pony Truck Assembly	2-6-4T locos.	R181		—		Never listed for retail sale.			
—	Pony Truck Assembly	2-6-4T locos.	7732		—		Never listed for retail sale.			
—	Pony Truck Assembly	2-8-0 locos.	R220		—		Never listed for retail sale.			
—	Pony Truck Assembly	2-8-0 locos.	7732		—		Never listed for retail sale.			
—	Front Bogie Assembly	Castle locos.	(R125)		—		Never listed for retail sale.			
—	Front Bogie Assembly	Castle locos.	12373/C1179		—		Never listed for retail sale.			

N.B. The above Pony Truck & Bogie Assemblies are for three rail locos.

LOCOMOTIVE HEADBOARDS AND TRAIN NAME LABELS.

CAT. NO.	DESCRIPTION	TRAIN NAME:	FOR:	COLOUR	PACKET TYPE	PACKET NO.	FIRST DATE	FIRST PRICE	LAST DATE	LAST PRICE
1700	Headboards (12)	—	Mallard/Fleece Headboard	—	19	—	1/62	—	1/62	—
32850	Headboards (12)	—	L11 loco. Mallard.	—	19	32850	8/58	-/2	8/58	-/2
1701	Headboards (12)	—	Duchess/City locos.	—	—	—	1/62	—	1/62	—
32851	Headboards (12)	—	L12 Duchess	—	19	32851	8/58	-/2	8/58	-/2
1702	Headboards (12)	—	Castle locos.	—	—	—	1/62	—	1/62	—
32852	Headboards (12)	—	LT20 loco.	—	19	32852	8/58	-/2	8/58	-/2
1704	Headboards (12)	—	2235/3235 West Country	—	19	—	1/62	—	1/62	—
1705	Headboards (12)	—	Deltic locos.	—	19	—	1/62	—	1/62	—
1720	Headboard Label (12)	Flying Scotsman	1700/32850 headboards	Silver/Black	19	—	1/62	—	1/62	—
32860	Headboard Label (12)	Flying Scotsman	1700/32850 headboards	Silver/Black	19	32860	8/58	-/1	8/58	-/1
1721	Headboard Label (12)	White Rose	1700/32850 headboards	Silver/Black	—	—	1/62	—	1/62	—
32861	Headboard Label (12)	White Rose	1700/32850 headboards	Silver/Black	19	32861	8/58	-/1	8/58	-/1
1722	Headboard Label (12)	Fair Maid	1700/32850 headboards	Silver/Black	19	—	1/62	—	1/62	—
32862	Headboard Label (12)	Fair Maid	1700/32850 headboards	Silver/Black	19	32862	8/58	-/1	8/58	-/1
1723	Headboard Label (12)	Royal Scot	1701/32851 headboards	White/Tartan	19	32863	1/62	—	1/62	—
32863	Headboard Label (12)	Royal Scot	1701/32851 headboards	White/Tartan	19	32863	8/58	-/1	8/58	—
1724	Headboard Label (12)	Red Rose	1701/32851 headboards	Silver/Red	19	—	1/62	—	1/62	—
32864	Headboard Label (12)	Red Rose	1701/32851 headboards	Silver/Red	19	32864	8/58	-/1	8/58	-/1
1725	Headboard Label (12)	Mancunian	1701/32851 headboards	Silver/Red	19	—	1/62	—	1/62	—
32865	Headboard Label (12)	Mancunian	1701/32851 headboards	Silver/Red	19	32865	8/58	-/1	8/58	-/1

CAT. NO.	DESCRIPTION	TRAIN NAME	FOR:	COLOUR	PACKET TYPE	PACKET NO.	FIRST DATE	FIRST PRICE	LAST DATE	LAST PRICE
1726	Headboard Label (12)	Bristolian	1702/32852 headboards	Silver/Brown	—	—	1/62	—	1/62	—
32866	Headboard Label (12)	Bristolian	1702/32852 headboards	Silver/Brown	19	32866	8/58	-/1	8/58	-/1
1727	Headboard Label (12)	Torbay Express	1702/32852 headboards	Brown/Cream	—	—	1/62	—	1/62	—
32867	Headboard Label (12)	Torbay Express	1702/32852 headboards	Brown/Cream	19	32867	8/58	-/1	8/58	-/1
1728	Headboard Label (12)	Cornish Riviera	1702/32852 headboards	Brown/Cream	—	—	1/62	—	1/62	—
32868	Headboard Label (12)	Cornish Riviera	1702/32852 headboards	Brown/Cream	19	32868	8/58	-/1	8/58	-/1
1729	Headboard Label (12)	Caledonian	1701/32851 headboards	White/Red/Blue	19	39729	1/62	—	1/62	—
1730	Headboard Label (12)	Talisman	1700/32850 headboards	Silver/Black	19	39730	1/62	—	1/62	—
1731	Headboard Label (12)	Red Dragon	1702/32852 headboards	Brown/Cream	19	32871	1/62	—	1/62	—
32871	Headboard Label (12)	Red Dragon	1702/32852 headboards	Brown/Cream	—	—	Not listed with this number.			
1732	Headboard Label (12)	Bournemouth Belle	1704 headboards	Silver/Green	19	32872	1/62	—	1/62	—
32872	Headboard Label (12)	Bournemouth Belle	1704 headboards	Silver/Green	—	—	Not listed with this number.			
1750	Coach Train Label	Flying Scotsman	D12 Coaches	White/Maroon	—	—	—	—	—	—
32880	Coach Train Label	Flying Scotsman	D12 Coaches	White/Maroon	19	32880	—	—	—	—
1751	Coach Train Label	White Rose	D12 Coaches	White/Maroon	—	—	—	—	—	—
32881	Coach Train Label	White Rose	D12 Coaches	White/Maroon	19	32881	—	—	—	—
1752	Coach Train Label	Fair Maid	D12 Coaches	White/Maroon	—	—	—	—	—	—
32882	Coach Train Label	Fair Maid	D12 Coaches	White/Maroon	19	32882	—	—	—	—
1753	Coach Train Label	Royal Scot	D22 Coaches	White/Tartan	—	—	—	—	—	—
32883	Coach Train Label	Royal Scot	D22 Coaches	White/Tartan	19	32883	—	—	—	—
1754	Coach Train Label	Red Rose	D22 Coaches	White/Maroon	—	—	—	—	—	—
32884	Coach Train Label	Red Rose	D22 Coaches	White/Maroon	19	32884	—	—	—	—
1755	Coach Train Label	Mancunian	D22 Coaches	Red/Blue	—	—	—	—	—	—
32885	Coach Train Label	Mancunian	D22 Coaches	Red/Blue	19	32885	—	—	—	—
1756	Coach Train Label	Bristolian	D21 Coaches	Brown/Cream	—	—	—	—	—	—
32886	Coach Train Label	Bristolian	D21 Coaches	Brown/Cream	19	32886	—	—	—	—
1757	Coach Train Label	Torbay Express	D21 Coaches	Brown/Cream	—	—	—	—	—	—
32887	Coach Train Label	Torbay Express	D21 Coaches	Brown/Cream	19	32887	—	—	—	—
1758	Coach Train Label	Cornish Riviera	D21 Coaches	Cream/Brown	—	—	—	—	—	—
32888	Coach Train Label	Cornish Riviera	D21 Coaches	Cream/Brown	19	32888	—	—	—	—
1759	Coach Train Label	Caledonian	Maroon S-D Coaches	Brown/Cream	19	39759	—	—	—	—
1760	Coach Train Label	Talisman	Maroon S-D Coaches	White/Maroon	19	39760	—	—	—	—
1761	Coach Train Label	Red Dragon	Chocolate/Cream S-D	Brown/Cream	19	32891	—	—	—	—
32891	Coach Train Label	Red Dragon	Chocolate/Cream S-D	Brown/Cream	—	—	—	—	—	—
1762	Coach Train Label	Bournemouth Belle	Pullman Coaches	White/Maroon	—	—	Not listed with this number.			
32892	Coach Train Label	Bournemouth Belle	Pullman Coaches	White/Maroon	—	—	Not listed with this number.			

The White on most is more Off-White or Cream, except for the Tartan Labels.

N.B. The Brown used for W.R. Labels is sometimes referred to as Umber.

CAT. NO.	DESCRIPTION	TRAIN NAME	FOR:	COLOUR	PACKET TYPE	PACKET NO.	FIRST DATE	FIRST PRICE	LAST DATE	LAST PRICE
—	Headboard, Label & 6 Train Nameboards.	Bournemouth Belle	2035 Set.	White/Maroon	19	—	—	—	—	—
1775	Coach Destination Label	Kings Cross-Edinburgh	1750/60 Trains	White/Maroon	—	—	—	—	—	—
32893	Coach Destination Label	Kings Cross-Edinburgh	1750/60 Trains	White/Maroon	19	32893	7/58	—	8/58	1/- per doz.
1776	Coach Destination Label	Kings Cross-Leeds	1751 Trains	White/Maroon	—	—	—	—	—	—
32894	Coach Destination Label	Kings Cross-Leeds	1751 Trains	White/Maroon	19	32894	7/58	—	8/58	1/-
1777	Coach Destination Label	Kings Cross-Perth	1752 Trains	White/Maroon	—	—	—	—	—	—
32895	Coach Destination Label	Kings Cross-Perth	1752 Trains	White/Maroon	19	32895	7/58	—	8/58	1/-
1778	Coach Destination Label	London-Glasgow	1753 Trains	White/Tartan	—	—	—	—	—	—
32896	Coach Destination Label	London-Glasgow	1753 Trains	White/Tartan	19	32896	7/58	—	8/58	1/-
1779	Coach Destination Label	London-Liverpool	1754 Trains	White/Maroon	—	—	—	—	—	—
32897	Coach Destination Label	London-Liverpool	1754 Trains	White/Maroon	19	32897	7/58	—	8/58	1/-
1780	Coach Destination Label	London-Manchester	1755 Trains	White/Maroon	—	—	—	—	—	—
32898	Coach Destination Label	London-Manchester	1755 Trains	Red/Blue	19	32898	7/58	—	8/58	1/-
1781	Coach Destination Label	Paddington-Bristol	1756 Trains	Red/Blue	—	—	—	—	—	—
32899	Coach Destination Label	Paddington-Bristol	1756 Trains	Brown/Cream	19	32899	7/58	—	8/58	1/-
1782	Coach Destination Label	London-Glasgow	1759 Trains	Brown/Cream	19	39782	—	—	—	—
1783	Coach Destination Label	Paddington-Newport	1761 Trains	Brown/Cream	19	32901	—	—	—	—
32901	Coach Destination Label	Cardiff-Swansea	Cardiff-Swansea	Brown/Cream	—	—	Not listed with this number.			

355

See page 357 for details of TRACK CODE letters.

CAT. NO.	DESCRIPTION	TRAIN NAME FOR:	COLOUR	PACKET TYPE	PACKET NO.	FIRST DATE	FIRST PRICE	LAST DATE	LAST PRICE
—	Headboard for Locomotive (1)	—	—	19	57520	7/58	-/2	12/64	-/2
—	Headboard Name Labels for Locomotive Headboards (12)	—	—	—	—	7/58	-/1	12/64	-/1
—	Coach Train Name Labels (12)	—	—	—	—	7/58	1/-	12/64	1/- per dozen.
—	Coach Destination Labels (12)	—	—	—	—	7/58	1/-		1/- per dozen.

POSTWAR PRENATIONALIZATION SETS

NO.	DESCRIPTION	LOCO	WAGONS/COACHES IN SET	TRACK CODE	BOX TYPE	BOX NO.	BOX CODE	MECC. MAG. DATE	MECC. MAG. PRICE	MECC. LAST DATE	LAST PRICE
EDP1	Passenger Train	*7	Br/3rd & 1st Teak	A	10c	—	—	12/47	157/6	4/53	175/-
EDP2	Passenger Train	*6231	Br/3rd & 1st/3rd LMS Mar'n.	A	10c	—	—	12/47	177/6	4/53	185/-
EDP2	Passenger (Canadian Pacific)	1215	Br/3rd & 1st/3rd LMS Mar'n.	A	10c	30004	—	(1956)	$24.50	2/58	$24.95
EDP2	Passenger (Canadian Pacific)	1215	Br/3rd & 1st/3rd B.R.	B	10c	30004	—	(1956)	$24.50	2/58	$24.95
EDG3	Freight Train (C.P.R.)	1215	Hi. Cap., Bog. Bol. & Caboose.	A	10c	30008	—	(1956)	$23.95	2/58	$24.95
EDG3	Freight Train (C.P.R.)	1215	Hi. Cap., Weltrol & Caboose.	A	10c	30008	—	(1956)	$23.95	2/58	$24.95
EDG7	Tank Goods Train 'Southern'	2594	Open Wag., Goods & Guards Van (Dark Olive Green)	A	10b	—	—				
EDG7	Tank Goods Train 'Southern'	2594	Open Wag., Goods & Guards Van (Malachite Green - Gold Label)	A	10c	—	—	12/47	135/-	4/53	152/6
EDG7	Tank Goods Train 'Southern'	2594	Open Wag., Goods & Guards Van (Malachite Green - Silver Label)	A	10c	—	—	12/47	135/-	4/53	152/6
EDG7	Tank Goods Train 'L.M.S.'	6917	Open Wag., Goods & Guards Van (As prewar - Serif lettering)	B	10b	—	—				
EDG7	Tank Goods Train 'L.M.S.'	6917	Open Wag., Goods & Guards Van (Postwar - Gold Label)	A	10c	—	—	12/47	135/-	4/53	152/6
EDG7	Tank Goods Train 'L.M.S.'	6917	Open Wag., Goods & Guards Van (Postwar - Silver Label)	A	10c	—	—	12/47	135/-	4/53	152/6
EDG7	Tank Goods Train 'L.N.E.R.'	2690	Open Wag., Goods & Guards Van (As prewar)	A	10b	—	—				
EDG7	Tank Goods Train 'L.N.E.R.'	9596	Open Wag., Goods & Guards Van (Black Loco)	A	10b	—	—	12/47	135/-	4/53	152/6
EDG7	Tank Goods Train 'L.N.E.R.'	9596	Open Wag., Goods & Guards Van (Green Loco - Gold Label)	A	10c	—	—	12/47	135/-	4/53	152/6
EDG7	Tank Goods Train 'L.N.E.R.'	9596	Open Wag., Goods & Guards Van (Green Loco - Silver Label)	A	10c	—	—	12/47	135/-	4/53	152/6
EDG7	Tank Goods Train	6699	Open Wag., Goods & Guards (as prewar)	A	10b	—	—	— This loco and set is unconfirmed, see note re. loco on page 31.			
EDG7	Tank Goods Train	6699	Open Wag., Goods & Guards (Postwar - Gold Label)	A	10c	—	—	12/47	135/-	4/53	152/6
EDG7	Tank Goods Train	6699	Open Wag., Goods & Guards (Postwar - Silver Label)	A	10c	—	—	12/47	135/-	4/53	152/6
EDG7	Tank Goods Train	6231	Open Wag., Goods & Guards	A	10c	—	—				

— This loco has freak number, see loco note on page 362   * See page 357 for details of TRACK CODE letters.

* Loco nos. 7 and 6231 (Duchess of Atholl) come in several variations. See Locomotive pages for details.

BRITISH RAIL SETS — 3-RAIL

NO.	DESCRIPTION	LOCO	WAGONS/COACHES IN SET	TRACK CODE	BOX TYPE	BOX NO.	BOX CODE	MECC. MAG. DATE	MECC. MAG. PRICE	MECC. LAST DATE	LAST PRICE
EDP10	Passenger Train	69567	D14 Sub. 1st/3rd & Br/3rd	B	10f	30010	—	9/56	5/7/6	5/58	5/7/6
P10	Passenger Train	69567	D14 Sub. 1st/3rd & Br/3rd	C	—	30010	—	(6/58)	5/7/6)	12/58	5/7/6
3010	Passenger Train	69567	D14 Sub. 1st/3rd & Br/3rd	—	No box with this number			(4/59)	5/5/-)	12/59	5/5/-
EDP11	Passenger Train	60016	D11 Corr. 1st/3rd & Br/3rd (Gloss Loco)	A	10d	30011	—	4/53	122/-	4/54	122/-
EDP11	Passenger Train	60016	D11 Corr. 1st/3rd & Br/3rd (Matt Loco)	B	10d	30011	—	(6/54)	122/-)	4/56	6/8/6
EDP12	Passenger Train	46232	D12 Corr. 1st/3rd & Br/3rd (Gloss Loco)	A	10d	30012	—	4/53	—	4/54	133/9
EDP12	Passenger Train	46232	D12 Corr. 1st/3rd & Br/3rd (Matt Loco)	B	10d	30012	—	(6/54)	133/9)	1/58	7/7/6

NO.	DESCRIPTION	LOCO	WAGONS/COACHES IN SET	TRACK CODE	BOX TYPE	BOX NO.	BOX CODE	MECC. MAG.	MECC. PRICE	LAST DATE	LAST PRICE
EDP13	Passenger Train	80054	D13 Sub. 2xBr/3rd & 1x1st/3rd	B	10d	30013	—	11/54	—	4/56	6/13/6
EDP14	Passenger Train	80054	D14 Sub. As Above.	B			—	9/56	6/13/6	5/58	6/17/6
P14	Passenger Train	80054	D14 Sub. As Above.	B		(30014)	—	(6/58)	6/17/6	12/58	6/17/6
3014	Passenger Train	80054	D14 Sub. As Above.	—	No box with this number			(4/59)	6/13/6	12/59	6/13/6
EDP15	Passenger Train	60016	D12 Corr. 1st/3rd & Br/3rd	B			—	8/56	—	5/58	6/19/6
P15	Passenger Train	60022	D12 Corr. 1st/3rd & Br/3rd	B		(30015)	—	(6/58)	6/19/6	12/58	6/19/6
3015	Passenger Train	60022	D12 Corr. 1st/3rd & Br/3rd	B	No box with this number			(4/59)	6/16/-	12/59	6/16/-
EDG16	Tank Goods Train	69567	2xD1 Open Wags., E.R.Grds. Van	C			—	(4/57)	4/17/6	5/58	4/18/6
G16	Tank Goods Train	69567	2xSD6 Steel Wags., W.R. Grds. Van	C		(30016)	—	6/58	4/18/6	12/58	4/18/6
3016	Tank Goods Train	69567	2xSD6 SteelWags., W.R. Grds. Van	—	No box with this number			(4/59)	4/16/-	12/59	4/16/-
EDG17	Tank Goods Train	69567 (Gloss)	D1 Open Wag., Goods Van, Royal Daylight Tank & E.R. Guards Van.	A	10c	30017	—	4/53	—	4/54	98/6
EDG17	Tank Goods Train	69567 (Matt)	D1 Open Wag., Goods Van, Royal Daylight Tank & E.R. Guards Van.	B	10c		—	(6/54)	98/6	6/55	99/6
EDG17	Tank Goods Train	69567	D1 Open Wag., Goods Van Vacuum Tank replaces Royal Daylight	B	10c	30017	—	(7/55)	4/19/6	4/56	5/7/6
EDG17	Tank Goods Train	69567	Meat Van replaces Goods Van & Mobil Oil Co. replaces Vacuum.	B	10f	30017	—	(5/56)	5/7/6	5/58	5/7/6
G17	Tank Goods Train	69567	Mobil replaces Mobil Oil	C	10f	30017	—	(6/58)	5/7/6	8/58	5/7/6
G17	Tank Goods Train	69567	Esso replaces Mobil Tank.	C	10f	30017	—	(9/58)	5/7/6	12/58	5/7/6
EDG18	Tank Goods Train	80054	Hi. Cap. Wag., Bog. Bolster & E.R. Guards Van.	B	10d	30018	—	11/54	—	4/56	6/8/6
EDG18	Tank Goods Train	80054	Hi. Cap. Wag., Weltrol & L.M.R. Guards Van.	B	10d		—	(5/56)	6/8/6	5/58	6/8/6
G18	Tank Goods Train	80054	Hi. Cap. Wag., Weltrol & L.M.R. Guards Van.	B	10d	30018	—	(6/58)	6/8/6	12/58	6/8/6
EDG19	Tank Goods Train	80054	Long Wheel Base Vent. Van. Mobil Tank, Tube Wag., Dble. Bolster & LMR Guards Van.	B	10d		—	7/57	6/17/6	5/58	6/17/6
G19	Tank Goods Train	80054	SD Cattle Wag., Dble. Bolster Mobil Tank, SD Steel Wagon & W.R. Guards Van.	B		(30019)	—	6/58	6/17/6	12/58	6/17/6
3019	Tank Goods Train	80054	As Above.	—	No box with this number			(4/59)	6/14/-	12/59	6/14/-
EDP20	Passenger Train	7013	D21 Corr. 1st/2nd & Br/2nd	B	10d	30020	—	11/57	7/7/6	5/58	7/7/6
P20	Passenger Train	7013	D21 Corr. 1st/2nd & Br/2nd	B	10d	30020	—	10/58	7/7/6	12/58	7/7/6
3020	Passenger Train	7013	D21 Corr. 1st/2nd & Br/2nd	—	No box with this number			(4/59)	7/3/6	12/59	7/3/6
EDP22	Passenger Train	46232	D22 Corr. 1st/2nd & Br/2nd	B	10d	30022	—	8/57	—	5/58	7/7/6
P22	Passenger Train	46232	D22 Corr. 1st/2nd & Br/2nd	B	10d	30022	—	(6/58)	7/7/6	12/58	7/7/6
3022	Passenger Train	46232	D22 Corr. 1st/2nd & Br/2nd	—	No box with this number			(4/59)	7/3/6	12/59	7/3/6
G25	Freight Train	48158	Refrig. Van, Weltrol, Shell Tank, SD Steel Wag., & LMR Guards Van (Grey)	B	10d	30025	—	(7/58)	7/12/6	12/58	7/12/6
3025	Freight Train	48158	Refrig. Van, Weltrol, Shell etc.	B	No box with this number			(4/59)	7/8/6	12/59	7/8/6

TRACK CODE letters are as follows:

A — 8 curved rails, 1 straight terminal rail and 2 straight half rails.

B — 7 curved rails, 1 curved terminal rail, 1 straight rail, 1 half straight rail and 1 half straight rail with roadway.

C — 7 curved rails, 1 curved terminal rail, 1 half straight, and 1 half straight with roadway.

— Although catalogues show SD Steel Wagon, sets actually come with the SD Open Wagon.

BRITISH RAIL SETS — 2-RAIL

NO.	DESCRIPTION	LOCO	WAGONS/COACHES IN SET	TRACK CODE	BOX TYPE	BOX NO.	BOX CODE	MECC. MAG.	MECC. PRICE	LAST DATE	LAST PRICE
2001	'Ready to Run'	Black	Special Open Wagons & B.R. Guards Van.	D	13a	—	—	4/63	89/6	12/64	4/5/-
2001	'Ready to Run'	Black	Special Open Wagons & B.R. Guards Van.	D	13b	—	—	4/63	89/6	12/64	4/5/-
—	'Ready to Run'	Blue	As Above. Loco has map of Australia on tank sides.			Set not listed in Britain				—	—
2004	'Ready to Run'	Yellow As above. Diesel Shunter.		D	13b	—	—	10/64		5/64	4/5/-
2006	Tank Goods Train	31340	UGB Sand Wag., Open Steel Wag. & W.R. Guards Van.	D	11	30006	—	9/59	63/6	12/64	3/8/6
2007	Tank Passenger Train	31340	S.R. Sub. 1st/2nd & Br/2nd	D	11	30007	—	9/59	75/-	9/62	4/3/9
2008	Tank Goods Train	31337	As 2006 Set.	D	11	30008	—	(10/60)	3/3/6	9/63	3/8/6

NO.	DESCRIPTION	LOCO	WAGONS/COACHES IN SET	TRACK CODE	BOX TYPE	BOX NO.	BOX CODE	MECC. MAG.	MECC. PRICE	LAST DATE	LAST PRICE
2009	Tank Passenger Train	31337	Mar. Sub. 1st/2nd & Br/2nd	D	11	30009	—	(10/60)	3/15/-	9/63	4/3/9
2014	Passenger Train	60030	SD Coaches 4052 & 4053	E	12	30014	—	(5/61)	6/12/6	9/63	7/5/6
2015	Passenger Train	60030	D12 Corr. 1st/2nd & Br/2nd	E	11	30015	—	(2/59)	5/19/6	11/61	6/1/1
2016	Tank Goods Train	69550	Saxa Salt, Mobil Tank, Liverpool Cable, & LMR Guards Van.	E	11	30016	—	11/60	4/15/-	12/61	5/9/6
2016	Tank Goods Train	69550	Now has Alum. Cable & Brown LMR Guards Van.	E	12	30016	—	(1/62)	5/8/-	12/64	4/9/6
2019	Tank Goods Train	80033	Flat Wag. & Tractor, Dble. Bolst. & Load, Flat Wag. & Meat, & LMR Guards Van (Grey)	E	11	30019	—	12/59	5/7/6	12/61	6/9/6
2019	Tank Goods Train	80033	Now shows E.R. Brown Guards	E	12	30019	—	(1/62)	6/7/6	12/64	4/19/6
2020	Passenger Train	7032	D21 Corr. 1st/2nd & Br/2nd	E	11	30020	—	12/59	6/12/6	10/59	6/12/6
2021	Passenger Train	4075	D21 Corr. 1st/2nd & Br/2nd	E	11	30021	—	11/60	6/17/6	10/60	6/17/6
2021	Passenger Train	4075	SD Coaches 4050 & 4051	E	12	30021	—	(5/61)	6/17/6	12/64	5/15/-
2022	Passenger Train	46245	D22 Corr. 1st/2nd & Br/2nd	E	11	30022	—	(2/59)	6/15/-	11/61	6/16/9
2023	Passenger Train	46245	SD Coaches 4052 & 4053	E	11	30023	—	10/61	7/4/4	9/63	7/2/6
2023	Passenger Train	46245	SD Coaches 4052 & 4053	E	12	30023	—	10/61	7/4/4	9/63	7/2/6
2024	Freight Train	48073	Refrig. Van, Weltrol, Shell Tank, Open Wag. & LMR Guards Van (Grey)	E	11	30024	—	10/60	6/17/6	12/61	7/9/6
2024	Freight Train	48073	As Above, but with Brown Guards Van.	E	12	30024	—	(1/62)	7/7/6	9/63	7/7/4
2025	Freight Train	48109	As 2024, with LMR Guards Van (Grey).	E	11	30025	—	12/59	6/12/6	10/59	6/12/6
2030	Freight Train	D8017	Refrig. & Vent. Vans, Grain Wag. & Min. Wag. & LMR Guards Van (Grey).	E	11	30030	—	(2/59)	5/12/6	10/59	5/12/6
2030	Freight Train	D8017	As Above, but with Open Wag.	E	11	30030	—	(10/60)	5/12/6	4/62	5/12/6
2033	Freight Train	D5702	Refrig. & Grain Wags., Vent. Van & LMR Guards Van (Brown)	E	12	30033	—	6/62	6/15/6	1/63	6/15/6
			— Shows loco without yellow front panel.								
2033	Freight Train	D5702	Refrig. & Grain Wags., Vent. Van & LMR Guards Van (Brown)	E	12	30033	—	(3/63)	6/15/6	9/63	6/15/6
			— Shows loco with yellow front panel.								
2034	Passenger Train	D9012	SD Coaches 4052 & 4053	E	12	30034	—	7/62	7/13/-	12/64	5/15/-
2035	Passenger Train	34005	Pullmans 4035, 4036 & 4037	E	11	30035	—	11/61	9/18/1	12/64	7/5/-
2035	Passenger Train	34005	Pullmans 4035, 4036 & 4037	E	12	—	—				
			— with hard polystyrene insert.								
2045	Passenger Train	E3002	— Illustrated Only. Not available	—	(14)	—	—	(1/64)	7/15/-	5/64	—
2049	Breakdown Train	69550	Crane, Packing Van & Coach	E	12	30049	—	4/62	4/19/11	9/63	4/18/6
2050	Suburban Electric		Br/2nd Motor Coach & Br/2nd Dummy	D	12	30050	—	10/62	5/18/-	1/63	5/18/-
			— Shows no yellow panels on loco/Dummy.								
2050	Suburban Electric		As above, but yellow panels now shown for loco/Dummy.	E			—	(4/63)	5/18/-	12/64	3/7/6
2050	Suburban Electric		As above.	E	(14)	Box illus. only.	—	(4/64)	3/7/6	5/64	—
*2051	Suburban Electric		As above.	E		—	—	(1/64)	5/9/6	1/64	5/9/6

* — Price List 1/64 indicates this set having a Hornby 1 Power Control Unit, & therefore different no.

TRACK CODE letters are as follows:

D — Track sufficient for a 3' x 3' space.

E — Track sufficient for a 4' x 3' space.

N.B. Some 2-Rail set boxes do not have number on the box.

NO.	DESCRIPTION /NAME	LOCO NO.	WHEEL ARRANGE.	COLOUR	MOTOR TYPE	LABEL	CPLGS	BOX TYPE	BOX NO.	BOX CODE	MECC. MAG.	MECC. PRICE	LAST DATE	LAST PRICE
(2201)	'Ready to Run' 'B.R.'	—	0-4-0T	Black	Special	—	NPC	—	—	—	—	—	—	Loco not listed separately.
—	'Ready to Run'	—	0-4-0T	Blue	Special	—	NPC	—	—	—	—	—	—	Loco not listed separately.

Yellow Australian map on tank sides.

NO.	DESCRIPTION /NAME	LOCO NO.	WHEEL ARRANGE.	COLOUR	MOTOR TYPE	LABEL	CPLGS	BOX TYPE	BOX NO.	BOX CODE	MECC. MAG.	MECC. PRICE	LAST DATE	LAST PRICE
(2204)	'Ready to Run'	—	0-4-0T	Yell./Orange	Special	—	NPC	—	—	—	—	—	—	Loco not listed separately.

Diesel Shunter

These locos have alloy wheels.

NO.	DESCRIPTION /NAME	LOCO NO.	WHEEL ARRANGE.	COLOUR	MOTOR TYPE	LABEL	CPLGS	BOX TYPE	BOX NO.	BOX CODE	MECC. MAG.	MECC. PRICE	LAST DATE	LAST PRICE
2206	(Export No. 2306)	* 31337	0-6-0T	Black	½-in	—	FMC	9b	31206	3/60	9/59	36/-	10/60	1/16/-

* – Plastic Body, Nickel Silver Wheels and Buffers.

NO.	DESCRIPTION /NAME	LOCO NO.	WHEEL ARRANGE.	COLOUR	MOTOR TYPE	LABEL	CPLGS	BOX TYPE	BOX NO.	BOX CODE	MECC. MAG.	MECC. PRICE	LAST DATE	LAST PRICE
2206		* 31337	0-6-0T	Black	½-in	—	EPC	9b	31206	—	(5/61	1/16/-	9/63	1/18/-
2206		** 31337	0-6-0T	Black	½-in	—	EPC	9b	31206	—	(1/64	1/18/-	12/64	1/18/-

** – Now with Red Plastic Buffers.

NO.	DESCRIPTION /NAME	LOCO NO.	WHEEL ARRANGE.	COLOUR	MOTOR TYPE	LABEL	CPLGS	BOX TYPE	BOX NO.	BOX CODE	MECC. MAG.	MECC. PRICE	LAST DATE	LAST PRICE
2207	(Export No. 2307)	* 31340	0-6-0T	Green	½-in	—	FMC	9b	31207	—	9/59	36/-	10/60	1/16/-

* – Plastic Body, Nickel Silver Wheels and Buffers

NO.	DESCRIPTION /NAME	LOCO NO.	WHEEL ARRANGE.	COLOUR	MOTOR TYPE	LABEL	CPLGS	BOX TYPE	BOX NO.	BOX CODE	MECC. MAG.	MECC. PRICE	LAST DATE	LAST PRICE
2207	(Export No. 2307)	* 31340	0-6-0T	Green	½-in	—	EPC	9b	31207	—	(5/61	1/16/-	12/64	1/18/-
2211	Golden Fleece	60030	4-6-2	Green	½-in	—	—	9c	31211	—	(2/59	3/14/-	10/60	3/14/-
—	Tender for above	—	—	Green	—	Silver	FMC	—	—	—	—	—	—	Lion & Wheel emblems both face loco.
—	Tender for above	—	—	Green	—	Silver	EPC	9c	31211	—	—	—	—	Lion & Wheel emblems face opp. dctns.

* – Loco has Nickel Silver Wheels & Thin Handrails.

NO.	DESCRIPTION /NAME	LOCO NO.	WHEEL ARRANGE.	COLOUR	MOTOR TYPE	LABEL	CPLGS	BOX TYPE	BOX NO.	BOX CODE	MECC. MAG.	MECC. PRICE	LAST DATE	LAST PRICE
2217		* 69550	0-6-2T	Black	½-in	Silver	FMC	9c	31217	—	(5/61	3/19/6	12/64	4/6/6
2217		* 69550	0-6-2T	Black	½-in	Silver	EPC	9c	31217	—	(7/60	2/8/-	10/60	2/8/-

** – Above two locos have small safety valve area. Nickel Silver Wheels.

NO.	DESCRIPTION /NAME	LOCO NO.	WHEEL ARRANGE.	COLOUR	MOTOR TYPE	LABEL	CPLGS	BOX TYPE	BOX NO.	BOX CODE	MECC. MAG.	MECC. PRICE	LAST DATE	LAST PRICE
2217		** 69550	0-6-2T	Black	½-in	Silver	FMC	9c	31217	—	(5/61	2/12/6	1/63	2/16/9
2217		** 69550	0-6-2T	Black	½-in	Silver	EPC	9c	31217	—	(3/63	2/16/9	12/64	2/16/9

* – Above two locos have large safety valve area. Nickel Silver Wheels.

NO.	DESCRIPTION /NAME	LOCO NO.	WHEEL ARRANGE.	COLOUR	MOTOR TYPE	LABEL	CPLGS	BOX TYPE	BOX NO.	BOX CODE	MECC. MAG.	MECC. PRICE	LAST DATE	LAST PRICE
2218		80033	2-6-4T	Black	½-in	Silver	FMC	9c	31217	—	(2/59	3/8/-	12/61	3/19/6
2218		80033	2-6-4T	Black	½-in	Silver	EPC	9c	31217	—	(1/62	3/18/-	12/64	3/18/-
2218		80033	2-6-4T	Black	½-in	Silver	EPC	9c	31218	—	—	—	—	No Hole in Bunker — Unconfirmed.

** – Above two locos have Nickel Silver Wheels & Separate Chimney Casting.

NO.	DESCRIPTION /NAME	LOCO NO.	WHEEL ARRANGE.	COLOUR	MOTOR TYPE	LABEL	CPLGS	BOX TYPE	BOX NO.	BOX CODE	MECC. MAG.	MECC. PRICE	LAST DATE	LAST PRICE
2220	Denbigh Castle	7032	4-6-0	Green	½-in	—	EPC	9a	—	—	(2/59	3/19/-	10/59	3/19/-
—	Tender for above (attached to loco)	—	—	Green	—	—	FMC	—	—	—	—	—	—	Lion & Wheel emblems both face loco.
2221	Cardiff Castle	4075	4-6-0	Green	RF	—	EPC	9c	31221	—	(7/60	4/4/-	12/64	4/8/6
—	Tender for above (attached to loco)	—	—	Green	—	—	—	—	—	—	—	—	—	Lion & Wheel emblems face opposite directions.

(Export No. 2321) – Nickel Silver Wheels.

NO.	DESCRIPTION /NAME	LOCO NO.	WHEEL ARRANGE.	COLOUR	MOTOR TYPE	LABEL	CPLGS	BOX TYPE	BOX NO.	BOX CODE	MECC. MAG.	MECC. PRICE	LAST DATE	LAST PRICE
2224	(Export No. 2324)	48073	2-8-0	Black	RF	—	EPC	9c	31224	—	10/60	—	12/64	4/11/6
—	Tender for above (attached to loco)	—	—	Black	—	—	EPC	—	—	—	—	—	—	Lion & Wheel emblems face opposite directions.

(Export No. 2326) – Nickel Silver Wheels.

NO.	DESCRIPTION /NAME	LOCO NO.	WHEEL ARRANGE.	COLOUR	MOTOR TYPE	LABEL	CPLGS	BOX TYPE	BOX NO.	BOX CODE	MECC. MAG.	MECC. PRICE	LAST DATE	LAST PRICE
2225		48109	2-8-0	Black	½-in	—	FMC	9a	—	—	(2/59	4/1/6	10/59	4/1/6
—	Tender for above (attached to loco)	—	—	Black	—	—	FMC	—	—	—	—	—	—	Lion & Wheel emblems both face loco.

– Nickel Silver Wheels.

NO.	DESCRIPTION /NAME	LOCO NO.	WHEEL ARRANGE.	COLOUR	MOTOR TYPE	LABEL	CPLGS	BOX TYPE	BOX NO.	BOX CODE	MECC. MAG.	MECC. PRICE	LAST DATE	LAST PRICE
2226	City of London	46245	4-6-2	Maroon	½-in	—	EPC	9a	—	—	(2/59	4/1/6	10/60	4/1/6
—	Tender for above	—	—	Maroon	—	—	FMC	—	—	—	—	—	—	Lion & Wheel emblems both face loco.
—	Tender for above	—	—	Maroon	—	—	EPC	9c	31226	—	—	—	—	Lion & Wheel emblems face opposite directions.

(not available separately, although detachable from locomotive).

(Export No. 2326) – Nickel Silver Wheels.

NO.	DESCRIPTION /NAME	LOCO NO.	WHEEL ARRANGE.	COLOUR	MOTOR TYPE	LABEL	CPLGS	BOX TYPE	BOX NO.	BOX CODE	MECC. MAG.	MECC. PRICE	LAST DATE	LAST PRICE
2230		* D8017	Bo-Bo	Green	½-in	—	FMC	9a	—	—	(5/61	4/9/-	12/64	4/16/-
2230		* D8017	Bo-Bo	Green	½-in	—	FMC	9c	31230	—	(2/59	3/1/-	6/62	3/-/9
2230	(Canada)	** D8017	Bo-Bo	Green	½-in	—	FMC	9c	31230	—	(2/59	3/1/-	6/62	3/-/9
2230	(Canada)	** D8017	Bo-Bo	Green	½-in	—	FMC	9c	31230	—	—	—	—	Powered, no buffers. Unlisted.
—	(Canada)													Unpowered, no buffers. Unlisted.

Locos come with either type of emblems, and either thin or thick handrails.

NO.	DESCRIPTION /NAME	LOCO NO.	WHEEL ARRANGE.	COLOUR	MOTOR TYPE	LABEL	CPLGS	BOX TYPE	BOX NO.	BOX CODE	MECC. MAG.	MECC. PRICE	LAST DATE	LAST PRICE
2231	(Export No. 2331)	* D33020	0-6-0T	Green	RF	—	EPC	9c	31231	—	12/60	2/15/6	12/64	3/4/-

* – Loco has single Coupling Rod, Nickel Silver Wheels.

NO.	DESCRIPTION /NAME	LOCO NO.	WHEEL ARRANGE.	COLOUR	MOTOR TYPE	LABEL	CPLGS	BOX TYPE	BOX NO.	BOX CODE	MECC. MAG.	MECC. PRICE	LAST DATE	LAST PRICE
2231		** D33020	0-6-0T	Green	RF	—	EPC	9c	31231	—	12/60	2/15/6	12/64	3/4/-

** – Loco has two Coupling Rods, Nickel Silver Wheels.

NO.	DESCRIPTION /NAME	LOCO. NO.	WHEEL ARRANGE.	COLOUR	MOTOR TYPE	LABEL	CPLGS	BOX TYPE NO.	BOX CODE	MECC. MAG.	MECC. PRICE	LAST DATE	LAST PRICE
2232		—	Co-Co	Green	RF	—	EPC	9c	31232	—	12/60	3/17/6	12/64	4/2/6
	— Nickel Silver Wheels, four with rubber tyres. Metal bogie side frames. Lion & Wheel emblems face opp. direct.												
2233	*	D5702	Co-Bo	Green	RF	—	EPC	9c	31233	—	12/61	4/3/9	1/63	4/6/-
	— Plain green end panels. Nickel Silver Wheels, four with rubber tyres. Metal bogie side frames.												
2233	**	D5702	Co-Bo	Green	RF	—	(NPC)	9c	31233	—	(3/63 | 4/6/-)	12/64	4/6/-
	— Yellow end panels as illustrated. Unconfirmed. Otherwise as above.												
2233	***	D5702	Co-Bo	Green	RF	—	EPC	9c	31233	—	Never Listed.			
	— Plain green end panels, with light at none-motor end of loco. Otherwise as * above.												
	— Also minor differences in body castings and types of numbering.												
2234 Crepello	*	D9012	Co-Co	Green	RF	—	EPC	9d	31234	—	7/62	4/13/6	12/64	4/13/6
	— Nickel Silver Wheels, with four rubber tyres. Metal bogie side frames.												
2234	**	D9012	Co-Co	Green	RF	—	EPC	9d	31234	—	7/62	4/13/6	12/64	4/13/6
	— Plastic bogie side frames. Otherwise as above.												
2235 Barnstaple		34005	4-6-2	Green	RF	—	—	9c	31235	—	11/61	5/16/5	12/64	5/15/-
	— Yellow bands on drive & dummy end. Black inner panels. Lion & Wheel emblems face opposite directions.												
— Tender for above (Export No. 2335)			— Nickel Silver Wheels.										
2245		E3002	Bo-Bo	Blue	RF	—	FPC	9e	32245	—	10/64	3/15/-	12/64	3/15/-
	— Plain green ends for both drive coach and dummy end, as illustrated.												
2250 (Export No. 2350)	*	S65326	Bo-Bo	Green	RF	—	EPC	9d	31250	—	10/62	4/1/6	1/63	4/1/6
2250	**	S65326	Bo-Bo	Green	RF	—	EPC	9d	31250	—	(3/63 | 4/1/6)	12/64	3/4/-
	— Yellow bands on drive & dummy end. Black inner panels.												
2250	***	S65326	Bo-Bo	Green	RF	—	EPC	9d	31250	—	(3/63 | 4/1/6)	12/64	3/4/-
	— As ** above, but inner panels are green. Probably an earlier issue.												
	— All Electric Multiple Units noted above have Nickel Silver Wheels with two rubber tyres, including Bo-Bo Electric loco no. 2245.												

N.B. Export boxes, with the numbers as noted above are of plain red, and with a linen finish to some boxes. There are no differences with the locos themselves, except for the 2250 loco and 4150 dummy trailer coach, which may have nut & bolt fixings for the couplings, instead of the normal rivets.

— Notes about the Lion & Wheel emblems refer to the new B.R. emblem introduced in 1956/7.

POSTWAR LOCOMOTIVES — 3-RAIL

NO.	DESCRIPTION /NAME	LOCO NO.	WHEEL ARRANG.	COLOUR	MOTOR TYPE	LABEL	CPLGS.	BOX TYPE NO.	BOX CODE	MECC. MAG.	MECC. PRICE	LAST DATE	LAST PRICE
EDL1 Sir Nigel Gresley 7		—	4-6-2	Blue	HS	Silver	—	7c	2.5M 6.48	12/47	60/-	4/53	60/-
	— Has pony and bogie frames of light-weight, not prewar. No EDL1 under cab roof, the nameplate has squared ends and the body casting has the chimney tapered at the first boiler band. Maroon wheels. Rear pony connected by split pin.												
EDL1 Sir Nigel Gresley 7		—	4-6-2	Blue	HS	Silver	—	7d	1/51	12/47		4/53	60/-
	— As above, but plate is now rounded off at the ends. Still no EDL1 under cab roof.												
EDL1 Sir Nigel Grelley 7		—	4-6-2	Blue	½-in	Silver	—	7d	5/52	12/47		4/53	60/-
	— Nameplate has rounded corners again, and EDL1 now under cab roof. Pony and bogie are of later type, with pony now secured by screw. The number 7, is much thicker.												
EDL1 Sir Nigel Gresley 7		—	4-6-2	Blue	HS	Silver	—	7d	—	12/47		4/53	60/-
	— Nameplate is squared off and chimney terminates approximately 1/8-in behind boiler band. Otherwise as above.												
EDL1 Sir Nigel Gresley 7		—	4-6-2	Blue	HS	Silver	—	7d	—	12/47		4/53	60/-
	— As above, but with black wheels. These are probably locos returned to Binns Road for repair. Has EDL11 under cab roof. i.e. Silver King bodies painted blue for Sir Nigel Gresley.												
D1 Tender		—	—	Blue	—	None	EMC	1b	DR351 2.5M 4.48	(4/49	7/6	4/53	9/3
	— Plain metal base and plain metal bogie frames. Maroon wheels.												
D1 Tender		—	—	Blue	—	Silver	EMC	1d	32001 6.52	(4/49	7/6	4/53	9/3
	— Plain black base with label. Black bogie frames.												
D1 Tender		—	—	Blue	—	Silver	LMC	1e	32001	(4/49	7/6	4/53	9/3
	— Base is now blue with label.												
D1 Tender		—	—	Blue	—	Silver	LMC	1e	32001	(4/49	7/6	4/53	9/3
	— As above but with black wheels. These are probably repaired tenders.												

NO.	DESCRIPTION /NAME	LOCO NO.	WHEEL ARRANG.	COLOUR	MOTOR TYPE	LABEL	CPLGS.	BOX TYPE	BOX NO.	BOX CODE	MECC. MAG.	MECC. PRICE	LAST DATE	LAST PRICE	Notes
EDL2	Duchess of Atholl	6231	4-6-2	Maroon	HS	None	EMC	7c	—	2.5M 6.48	12/47	—	4/53	62/6	—Fine details such as buffers and boiler bands. Early pony and bogie frames. No EDL2 under cab roof.
EDL2	Duchess of Atholl	6231	4-6-2	Maroon	HS	None	EMC	7c	—	6.49	12/47	—	4/53	62/6	—As above, but nameplate is yellow on maroon background, unlike the normal silver on black, and with strengthened buffers, etc.
EDL2	Duchess of Atholl	6231	4-6-2	Maroon	½-in	None	—	7d	—	3/50	12/47	—	4/53	62/6	—Body has coarser detail and thickened steps etc. Bogie and pony are of later type. Inserts in boiler below both nameplates.
EDL2	Duchess of Atholl	6231	4-6-2	Maroon	½-in	None	—	7d	—	3/51	12/47	—	4/53	62/6	—Identical to above, but only one insert on boiler below left hand nameplate. A projection exists below nameplate on right hand side of boiler.
EDL2	Duchess of Atholl	6231	4-6-2	Maroon	½-in	None	—	7d	—	—	12/47	—	4/53	62/6	—Inserts below both nameplates again. Additional small pad with rivets in front of leading sand box on both sides of boiler.
EDL2	Duchess of Atholl	6231	4-6-2	Maroon	½-in	None	—	7d	—	—	12/47	—	4/53	62/6	—As above but now uses the Duchess of Montrose body, i.e. Has protruding edge along footplate. which is used for lining on the later loco.
EDL2	Duchess of Atholl	6231	4-6-2	Maroon	½-in	None	—	7d	—	—	12/47	—	4/53	62/6	—As above, but body has holes for smoke deflectors. This variation is unconfirmed.
EDL2	Duchess of Atholl	6231	4-6-2	Maroon	½-in	None	FMC	7d	—	—	12/47	—	4/53	62/6	—Has the Montrose body, including smoke deflectors. This item is confirmed, but is an item returned from Binns Road after repair.
D2	Tender	—	—	Maroon	None	None	EMC	1c	DR352	5M 2.50	4/49	8/9	4/53	10/6	—Wheel chassis is not rivetted to the cast metal base, and it has no strengthening corrugations on sides, between the axle holes. Wheels have open spokes.
D2	Tender	—	—	Maroon	None	None	EMC	1d	32002	1/52	(4/49	8/9)	4/53	10/6	—Still no rivetting but has strengthening corrugations on chassis side between axle holes.
D2	Tender	—	—	Maroon	None	None	EMC	1e	32002	—	(4/49	8/9)	4/53	10/6	—Chassis now rivetted to base. Still has open spoked wheels.
D2	Tender	—	—	Maroon	None	None	FMC	1e	32002	—	(4/49	8/9)	4/53	10/6	—As above but with solid wheels having imitation spokes.
EDL2	(Canadian Pacific)	1215	4-6-2	Black	½-in	—	—	No separate box known			(2/58	$11.95)	—	—	—Uses Montrose body, EDL2 under cab roof. Front number straight over headlight, early rear wheels.
EDL2	(Canadian Pacific)	1215	4-6-2	Black	½-in	—	—	No separate box known.			(2/58	$11.95)	—	—	—As above but later wheels in rear pony truck and number curved over headlight.
D2	Tender (CPR)	—	—	Black	HS	—	EMC	No separate box known.			(2/58	$ 1.95)	—	—	—Wheels are early open spoked type.
D2	Tender (CPR)	—	—	Black	—	—	LMC	No separate box known.			(2/58	$ 1.95)	—	—	—Wheels are the later solid type with imitation spokes.
EDL7	(Southern)	2594	0-6-2T	Ol. Green	HS	Gold	EMC	Sets only.			—	—	—	—	—As prewar body but with chamfer in front buffer beam for postwar coupling.
EDL7	(Southern)	2594	0-6-2T	Malachite	HS	Gold	EMC	7c	—	—	6/48	—	4/53	50/-	7c Large Windows.
EDL7	(Southern)	2594	0-6-2T	Green	½-in	Gold	EMC	7c	—	—	6/48	—	4/53	50/-	7c Small Windows.
EDL7	(Southern)	2594	0-6-2T	Green	½-in	Silver	EMC	7d	—	—	6/48	—	4/53	50/-	7d Small Windows.
EDL7	(LMS)	6917	0-6-2T	Black	HS	Gold	FMC	Sets only.			—	—	—	—	—As prewar body but with chamfer in front buffer beam for postwar couplings in front buffer beam. Lettering as prewar.
EDL7	(LMS)	6917	0-6-2T	Black	½-in	Gold	EMC	7c	—	3.5M 5.49	4/49	42/-	4/53	50/-	—No longer has serif lettering. Both large & small window versions.
EDL7	(LMS)	6917	0-6-2T	Black	½-in	Silver	EMC	7d	—	8/50	4/49	42/-	4/53	50/-	—There is a variety of Transfer details.
EDL7	(LNER)	2690	0-6-2T	Black	HS	Gold	EMC	Sets only			—	—	—	—	—As prewar, but with chamfer in front buffer beam for postwar coupling.
EDL7	(LNER)	9596	0-6-2T	Black	HS	Gold	EMC	7c	—	2.5M 6.48	4/49	42/-	4/53	50/-	—Has Large Windows.
EDL7	(LNER)	9596	0-6-2T	Green	½-in	Gold	EMC	7c	—	—	4/49	42/-	4/53	50/-	—Has Large and Small Windows.
EDL7	(LNER)	9596	0-6-2T	Green	½-in	Silver	EMC	7d	—	7/50	4/49	42/-	4/53	50/-	—The above two locos come in slightly varying shades of green, and the numbers vary slightly in size and shape.

NO.	DESCRIPTION /NAME	LOCO NO.	WHEEL ARRANG.	COLOUR	MOTOR TYPE	LABEL	CPLGS.	BOX TYPE	BOX NO.	BOX CODE	MECC. MAG.	MECC. PRICE	LAST DATE	LAST PRICE
EDL7 (GWR)		6699	0-6-2T	Green	HS	Gold	EMC	Sets only?			–	–	–	–
		– This variation is unconfirmed, but would be the postwar version of the prewar loco, with the GWR motif in the form of a circle.												
EDL7 (GWR)		6699	0-6-2T	Green	½-in	Gold	EMC	7c	–	6/48	12/47	–	4/53	50/-
								– Has Large and Small Windows						
EDL7 (GWR)		6699	0-6-2T	Green	½-in	Silver	EMC	7d	–	6/48	12/47	–	4/53	50/-
EDL7 (GWR)		6231	0-6-2T	Green	½-in	Silver	EMC	Originated from sets only.						
		– This obvious error is genuine and at least four are known to exist.												
EDL7 (British Railways)		E9560	0-6-2T	Green	½-in	–	EMC	Set only			–	–	–	–
		– This unusual item is genuine, but only one is known. The boiler has black bands which may not be genuine. It is lettered "British Railways" in yellow on tank sides.												
EDL11	Silver King	60016	4-6-2	Green	½-in	Silver	–	7e	31011	2/53	5/53	–	4/54	59/6
		– Gloss paint. Tender type 1. EDL11 under cab roof.												
EDL11	Silver King	60016	4-6-2	Green	½-in	Silver	–	8a	31011	–	(6/54	59/6)	5/58	3/5/
		– Matt paint. Tender type 2. (Later versions with Double Chimney)												
	Mallard	60022	4-6-2	Green	½-in	Silver	–	7e	31011/1	–	10/58		10/60	3/14/-
		– Has thick hand rails and alloy wheels, both on driving wheels and on pony/bogie trucks. Tender type 3. L11 under cab roof.												
L11	Mallard	60022	4-6-2	Green	½-in	Silver	–	–	–	–	–	–	–	–
3211	"	60022	4-6-2	Green	½-in	Silver	–	8c	34211	–	(5/61	3/19/6)	9/63	4/6/6
					L11 under cab roof									
		– Has thin handrails, nickel silver wheels and plastic bogie and pony wheels. Tender type 4.												
3211	Mallard	60022	4-6-2	Green	½-in	Silver	–	7g	34211	–	(5/61	3/19/6)	9/63	4/6/6
D11	Tender – type 1	–	–	Green	–	Silver	EMC	1f	32005	–	(3/53	9/3)	4/54	9/6
		– Gloss paint. Old totem. Solid metal alloy wheels.												
D11	Tender – type 2	–	–	Green	–	Silver	LMC	2a	32005	4/56	(6/54	8/9)	5/58	10/6
		– Matt paint. Old totem. Solid metal alloy wheels.												
D11	Tender – type 3	–	–	Green	–	Silver	FMC	2a	32005		(6/58	10/6)	12/58	10/6
		– Matt paint. New BR totem, both facing loco. Solid metal alloy wheels.												
D11	Tender – type 4	–	–	Green	–	Silver	EPC	–	–	–	–	–	–	–
		– As above, including totems facing the same direction. Plastic wheels. Came only with loco.												
3212	Duchess of Montrose	46232	4-6-2	Green	½-in	None	–	No box with this number			(2/59	3/18/6)	10/60	3/18/-
		– Nickel silver wheels and plastic bogie/pony wheels. Probably repair items from Binns Road.												
L12	Duchess of Montrose	46232	4-6-2	Green	½-in	None	–	7e	31012/1	2/58	(6/58	3/9/6)	12/58	3/9/6
		– Matt finish and with alloy wheels. Tender type 2. L12 under cab roof.												
EDL12	Duchess of Montrose	46232	4-6-2	Green	½-in	None	–	8a	31012	3/55	(6/54	62/3)	5/58	3/9/6
		– Identical to above, except EDL12 under cab roof.												
EDL12	Duchess of Montrose	46232	4-6-2	Green	½-in	None	–	7e	31012	9/53	(3/53	65/-)	4/54	62/3
		– Gloss finish and with alloy wheels. Tender type 1.												
D12	Tender – type 2	–	–	Green	–	None	FMC	2a	32006	1/56	(6/54	9/11)	12/58	11/6
		– Matt Finish.												
D12	Tender – type 1	–	–	Green	–	None	LMC	1e	32006	12/52	(3/53	10/6)	4/54	9/11
		– Gloss Finish.												
3217		69567	0-6-2T	Black	½-in	Silver	EPC	8c	34217	–	(5/61	2/12/6)	9/63	2/16/9
		– Body has coal in bunker and new BR totem on tank sides. Nickel silver wheels and plastic pony wheels. Body has L17 cast into metal.												
3217		69567	0-6-2T	Black	½-in	Silver	EPC	7g	34217	3/59	(5/61	2/12/6)	9/63	2/16/9
		– As above, but with old BR emblem.												
L17		69567	0-6-2T	Black	½-in	Silver	FMC	8a	31017	–	(6/58	2/9/6)	12/58	2/9/6
		– Alloy wheels, no coal in bunker. Large number and short tail lion.												
EDL17		69567	0-6-2T	Black	½-in	Silver	FMC	7e	31017	–	(6/54	45/-)	5/58	2/9/6
		– As above, but with a long tail lion. EDL17 cast into body.												
EDL17		69567	0-6-2T	Black	½-in	Silver	FMC	7e	31017	–	(6/54	45/-)	5/58	2/9/6
		– Short tail lion and small numbers. Still Matt finish. EDL17 cast into body.												
EDL17		69567	0-6-2T	Black	½-in	Silver	LMC	7e	31017	–	(4/53	47/6)	4/54	45/-
		– As above, but with gloss finish. Early gloss locos also came with unspoked pony wheels.												
3218		80059	2-6-4T	Black	½-in	None	EPC	8c	34218	–	–	–	–	–
		– Has no hole in bunker for magnet. This item is unconfirmed. Nickel silver wheels, plastic wheels.												

NO.	DESCRIPTION /NAME	LOCO. NO.	WHEEL ARRANGE.	COLOUR	MOTOR TYPE	LABEL	CPLGS.	BOX TYPE	BOX NO.	BOX CODE	MECC. MAG.	MECC. PRICE	LAST DATE	LAST PRICE
3218		80059	2-6-4T	Black	½-in	None	EPC	8c	34218		(5/61	3/12/6	9/63	3/18/-
	— Hole in bunker. Has totems facing same direction. Nickel silver and plastic wheels.													
3218		80059	2-6-4T	Black	½-in	None	EPC	8c	34218		(5/61	3/12/6	9/63	3/18/-
	— Hole in bunker. Totems face opposite directions. Nickel silver wheels and plastic wheels.													
3218		80054	2-6-4T	Black	½-in	None	FMC	8a	31018		(2/59	3/8/-	10/60	3/8/-
	— Alloy wheels and old BR emblem. Separate chimney as 80059's.													
L18		80054	2-6-4T	Black	½-in	None	FMC	8a	31018	8/60	(6/58	3/9/6	12/58	3/9/6
	— As above but chimney moulded as part of body. Long tail lion.													
EDL18		80054	2-6-4T	Black	½-in	None	FMC	8a	31018		11/54	(65/-)	5/58	3/9/6
	— As above, but with short tail lion.													
3220	Bristol Castle	7013	4-6-0	Green	½-in	None	FMC	No box with this no.			(2/59	3/19/-	11/61	3/19/11
LT20	Bristol Castle	7013	4-6-0	Green	½-in	None	FMC	8b	31020	2/57	(6/58	4/1/-	12/58	4/1/-
EDLT20	Bristol Castle	7013	4-6-0	Green	½-in	None	FMC	7f	31020		10/57		5/58	4/1/-
	— No loco variations. Tenders come with loco. Totems both face loco. Both have alloy wheels.													
3221	Ludlow Castle	5002	4-6-0	Green	RF	None	EPC	8c	34221		12/61	4/5/2	9/63	4/8/6
	— Loco has nickel silver wheels. Tender comes with loco. Totems face opposite directions.													
3224		48094	2-8-0	Black	RF	None	EPC	8c	34224		12/61	4/7/7	9/63	4/11/6
	— Loco has nickel silver wheels. Totems face opposite directions. EPC on front pony.													
3225		48158	2-8-0	Black	½-in	None	FMC	No box with this no.			(2/59	4/1/6	11/61	4/2/10
LT25		48158	2-8-0	Black	½-in	None	FMC	8b	31025	9/58	8/58	84/-	12/58	4/4/-
LT25		48158	2-8-0	Black	½-in	None	FMC	7f	31025		8/58	84/-	12/58	4/4/-
	— No loco variations. Tenders come with loco. Totems face same direction. All alloy wheels.													
3226	City of Liverpool	46247	4-6-2	Maroon	½-in	None	EPC	8c	34226		11/61	4/10/2	9/63	4/16/-
	— Nickel silver wheels and plastic pony/bogie wheels.													
	— Tender for above —			Maroon			EPC							
3230		D8000	Bo-Bo	Green	½-in	None	FMC	No box with this no.			(2/59	3/1/-	9/62	3/-/9
	— Tender comes with loco but is not permanently attached. Has plastic wheels & totems face opposite directions.													
3230		D8000	Bo-Bo	Green	½-in	None	FMC	8a	31030	2/59	12/58	3/2/6	12/58	3/2/6
	— Nickel silver wheels, two with rubber tyres. Thin hand rails.													
L30		D8000	Bo-Bo	Green	½-in	None	FMC	8a	31030	2/59	12/58	3/2/6	12/58	3/2/6
	— As above, but with thick hand rails.													
	— There are also variations in the totem directions along with the hand rails, but these are not consistent.													
L30 (Canada)		D8000	Bo-Bo	Green	½-in	None	FMC	8a	31030		31030 Powered. No buffers. Unlisted.			
L30 (Canada)		D8000	Bo-Bo	Green	½-in	None	FMC	8a	31030		31030 Unpowered. No buffers. Unlisted.			
3231		D3763	0-6-0	Green	RF	None	EPC	8c	34231		5/61	2/18/6	9/63	3/4/-
	— Nickel silver wheels and single coupling rods.													
3231		D3763	0-6-0	Green	RF	None	EPC	8c	34231		5/61	2/18/6	9/63	3/4/-
	— As above, but with double coupling rods.													
3232		—	Co-Co	Green	RF	None	EPC	8c	34232		5/61	4/2/6	9/63	4/2/6
	— Nickel silver wheels, four with rubber tyres. Metal side frames.													
3233		D5713	Co-Bo	Green	RF	None	EPC	8c	34233		12/61	4/3/9	9/63	4/6/-
	— Nickel silver wheels, four with rubber tyres. Metal side frames.													
3234	St. Paddy	D9001	Co-Co	Green	RF	None	EPC	8d	34234		7/62	4/13/6	9/63	4/13/6
	— Nickel silver wheels, four with rubber tyres. Metal side frames.													
3234	St. Paddy	D9001	Co-Co	Green	RF	None	EPC	8d	34234		7/62	4/13/6	9/63	4/13/6
	— As above, but with plastic bogie side frames.													
3235	Dorchester	34042	4-6-2	Green	RF	None	—	8c	34235		11/61	5/16/5	9/63	5/15/-
	— Nickel silver wheels, and plastic wheels on pony/bogie trucks.													
	— Tender			Green			EPC							
	— Tender comes with loco, but is not permanently attached. Totems face opposite directions.													
3245		E3003	Bo-Bo	Blue	RF	None	FPC							
	— This 3-rail version was never issued.													
3250		S65326	—	Green	RF	None	EPC	8d	34250		10/62	4/1/6	1/63	4/1/6
	— Plain green ends for both dummy and drive unit as illustrated. No confirmation of issue.													
3250		S65326	—	Green	RF	None	EPC	8d	34250		(3/63)	4/1/6	9/63	4/1/6
	— Yellow bands on both dummy and drive units as illustrated later.													
3250		S65326	—	Green	RF	None	EPC	8d	34250		(3/63)	4/1/6	9/63	4/1/6
	— As above, but inner end panels are green, whereas others are black.													
	— All above have nickel silver wheels, of which two have rubber tyres.													

TRACK AND TRACK ACCESSORIES – 2-RAIL

NO.	DESCRIPTION	LENGTH	NO. OF TIES	NO. IN CIRCLE	NO. IN BOX	BOX TYPE	BOX NO.	BOX CODE	MECC. MAG.	MECC. PRICE	LAST DATE	LAST PRICE
2400	TPO Mail Van Set	–	–	–	–	15a	–	–	(2/59	35/6)	12/64	1/18/6
2401	TPO Mail Van 2-rail	–	–	–	–	–	–	–	(2/59)	–	–	–
	–This reference number used only in the 1959 Hornby Book of Trains. See No. 4401 for details.											
2450	Buffer Stop – Nickel Silver Heads		–	–	2	15b	25450	2/60	(2/59	2/-)	12/64	2/3
2450	Buffer Stop – Black covers on Heads of buffers				2	15b	25450	2/60	(2/59	2/-)	12/64	2/3
2451	Buffer Stop – Illuminated, Black Heads			–	2	15b	25451	7/60	(2/59	6/9)	12/64	7/3
2460	Level Crossing – Buff, with rail.	–	–	–	1	15b	32460	–	12/61	7/9	5/61	7/6
2460	Level Crossing – Brown, as illustrated only. Does not exist.					–	–	–	(5/61	7/6)	12/64	7/6
2475	TPO Lineside Apparatus	–	–	–	1	15b	32475	–	(2/59	13/-)	12/64	14/9
2701	Straight Rail	8 5/8"	27	–	12	15b	32701	9/59	10/59	1/5	12/64	1/6
2702	Straight 2/3 Rail	5¾"	18	–	6	15b	32702		3/60	1/3	12/64	1/5
2703	Straight 1/3 Rail	2 7/8"	9	–	6	15b	32703		3/60	1/1	12/64	1/3
2704	Straight Terminal Rail, No. Supp.	8 5/8"	27	–	1	15b	32704		(10/60	3/3)	9/62	3/6
2705	Straight Terminal Rail 1/3"	2 7/8"	9	–	1	15b	32705	–	(10/60	2/11)	11/61	3/3
2706	Straight Short Rail	1 5/16"	4	–	3	15c	–	–	3/60	1/-	12/64	1/1
2707	Straight Terminal Rail & Supp.	8 5/8"	27	–	1	15b	32707	3/61	(5/61	4/-)	5/64	4/4
2708	Straight Terminal Rail 1/3"	2 7/8"	9	–	1	15b	32708	3/61	(5/61	3/9)	12/64	3/9
2709	Curved Rail	–	36	8, 15" rad.	8	15b	32709	–	(1/64	1/6)	1/64	1/6
2710	Curved Rail	–	24	12, 15" rad.	12	15b	32710	–	10/59	1/5	12/64	1/6
2711	Curved Half Rail	–	12	24, 15" rad.	6	15b	32711	5/61	(10/60	1/3)	12/64	1/5
2712	Curved Quarter Rail	–	6	48, 15" rad.	6	15b	32712	–	3/60	1/5	12/64	1/3
2713	Curved Terminal Rail No. Supp.	–	24	12, 15" rad.	1	15b	32713	–	10/59	3/3	11/61	3/6
2714	Curved Terminal Rail & Supp.	–	24	12, 15" rad.	1	15b	32714	–	(5/61	4/-)	5/64	4/4
2719	Curved Rail	–	24	12, 17¼" rad.	12	15b	32719	–	(10/60	1/7)	12/64	1/8
2720	Curved Terminal Rail, No Supp.	–	24	12, 17¼" rad.	1	15b	32720	–	(10/60	3/6)	5/64	4/8
2721	Curved Terminal Rail & Supp.	–	28	12, 17¼" rad.	1	15b	32721	–	(5/61	4/3)	12/64	4/8
2722	Curved Half Rail	–	14	24, 17¼" rad.	6	15b	32722	7/61	(10/60	1/5)	12/64	1/6
2725	Terminal Connector & Supp.	–	–	–	6	22c	32725	–	(1/63	1/9)	12/64	1/9
2728	Switch Point – Right Hand – Manual	5¾"	19	–	1	15b	32728	–	3/60	9/6	12/64	11/3
2729	Switch Point – Left Hand – Manual	5¾"	19	–	1	15b	32729	–	3/60	9/6	12/64	11/3
2731	Switch Point – Right Hand – Electric	5¾"	19	–	1	15b	32731	–	(2/59	15/9)	12/64	19/3
2732	Switch Point – Left Hand – Electric	5¾"	19	–	1	15b	32732	–	(2/59	15/9)	12/64	19/3
2734	Diamond Crossing – Right Hand	5¾"	19	–	1	15b	32734	–	1/62	11/9	12/64	11/9
2735	Diamond Crossing – Left Hand	5¾"	19	–	1	15b	32735	–	1/62	11/9	12/64	11/9
2738	Straight Single Isol. 2/3	5¾"	18	–	3	15b	32738	–	3/60	2/9	12/64	2/-
2739	Straight Double Isol. 2/3	5¾"	18	–	3	15b	32739	–	3/60	1/11	12/64	2/-
2740	Curved Double Isol. 1/2	–	12	24, 15" rad.	3	15b	32740	–	(10/60	1/11)	12/64	2/-
2741	Curved Single Isol. 1/2	–	12	24, 15" rad.	3	15b	32741	9/61	(10/60	2/9)	12/64	2/-
2742	Straight Single Isol. 1/3	2 7/8"	9	–	3	15b	32742	1/61	(10/60	2/7)	12/64	1/11
2743	Curved Double Isol. 1/2	–	14	24, 17¼" rad.	3	15b	32743	-/61	11/61	2/2	12/64	2/2
2745	Uncoupling Rail – Manual	5¾"	18	–	1	15b	32745	–	(10/59	5/6)	12/64	6/-
2746	Uncoupling Rail – Electric	5¾"	18	–	1	15b	32746	–	(10/60	13/11	12/64	16/3
2750	Simplec Switch – Right Hand – Manual	5¾"	19	–	1	15b	32750	–	4/63	7/9	12/64	7/9
2751	Simplec Switch – Left Hand – Manual	5¾"	19	–	1	15b	32751	–	4/63	7/9	12/64	7/9
2752	Simplec Switch – Right Hand – Electric	5¾"	19	–	1	15b	32752	–	10/63	15/-	12/64	15/-
2753	Simplec Switch – Left Hand – Electric	5¾"	19	–	1	15b	32753	–	10/63	15/-	12/64	15/-
2801	Track Pack No. 1 Contains 10 x 2701, 6 x 2702, 3 x 2703, 1 x 2750, 1 x 2751, 2 x 2725.				White label	15e	32801	16/163/2.5	1/64	45/-	12/64	2/5/-
2802	Track Pack No. 2 Contains 12 x 2719, 12 x 2701, 4 x 2702, 2 x 2738, 2 x 2735, 2 x 2750.				Pale Green Label	15e	32802	16/163/2.5	1/64	65/-	12/64	3/5/-

Track (continued)

NO.	DESCRIPTION	LENGTH / CONTENTS	NO. OF TIES	NO. IN CIRCLE	NO. IN BOX	BOX	BOX TYPE	BOX NO.	BOX CODE	MECC. MAG.	MECC. PRICE	LAST DATE	LAST PRICE
2803	Track Pack No. 3	Contains 4 x 2710, 3 x 2712, 13 x 2701, 1 x 2725, 6 x 2702, 6 x 2703, 2 x 2750.					15e	32803	—	1/64	68/6	12/64	3/8/6
2900	Railer	—	—	—	1	Pale Yellow Label	15b	32900	16/163/2.5	9/61	2/11	12/64	2/-

CAT. NO.	DESCRIPTION		NO. IN BOX/PT.	BOX TYPE	BOX NO.	BOX CODE	MECC. MAG.	MECC. PRICE	LAST DATE	LAST PRICE
2905	Connecting Clips	– for 2-rail track	12	19	32905	—	(10/59)	-/9	12/64	-/9
2905	Connecting Clips	– for 2-rail track	12	22a	—	—	(10/59)	-/9	12/64	-/9
2910	Securing Plates and Screws	– for 2-rail track	12	19	32910	—	(10/59)	1/2	12/64	1/2
2910	Securing Plates and Screws	– for 2-rail track	12	22a	—	—	(10/59)	1/2	12/64	1/2
2915	Fishplates	– for 2-rail track	12	22a	32659	—	(10/60)	1/-	12/64	1/-
2915	Fishplates	– for 2-rail track	12	19	—	—	(10/59)	1/-	12/64	1/-

ELEVATED TRACK — Ex Hornby-Acho.

CAT. NO.	DESCRIPTION			MECC. MAG.	MECC. PRICE	LAST DATE	LAST PRICE
6751	Parapet	Straight	No information is known about the packaging of these items.	(3/63)	-/6	12/64	-/6
6752	Parapet	External, Large Radius.	No information is known about the packaging of these items.	(3/63)	-/6	12/64	-/6
6753	Parapet	Internal, Large Radius.	No information is known about the packaging of these items.	(3/63)	-/6	12/64	-/6
6754	Parapet	Internal, Normal Radius.	packaging of these items.	(3/63)	-/6	12/64	-/6
6755	Curved Central Joint		No information is known about the packaging of these items.	(3/63)	-/9	12/64	-/9
6756	Straight Central Joint		No information is known about the packaging of these items.	(3/63)	-/9	12/64	-/9
6757	Straight Element		No information is known about the packaging of these items.	(3/63)	2/6	12/64	2/6
6758	Curved Element	Normal Radius.	No information is known about the packaging of these items.	(3/63)	2/6	12/64	2/6
6759	Curved Element	Large Radius.	No information is known about the packaging of these items.	(3/63)	2/6	12/64	2/6
6760	Approach Element		No information is known about the packaging of these items.	(3/63)	2/6	12/64	2/6
6761	Pillar Base		No information is known about the packaging of these items.	(3/63)	-/6	12/64	-/6
6762	Pillar	One Element.	No information is known about the packaging of these items.	(3/63)	-/9	12/64	-/9
6763	Pillar	Three Element.	No information is known about the packaging of these items.	(3/63)	1/3	12/64	1/3
6764	Pillar	Five Element.	No information is known about the packaging of these items.	(3/63)	1/6	12/64	1/6
6765	Bridge Element		No information is known about the packaging of these items.	(3/63)	1/11	12/64	1/11
6800	Elevated Track Set No. 2		No information is known about the packaging of these items.	(1/64)	2/14/11	12/64	2/14/11
6801	Uncoupling Gradient Set		No information is known about the packaging of these items.	(1/64)	16/11	12/64	16/11

The above 6xxx series was produced in France, but was available for sale in Britain, according to catalogues etc.

TRACK AND TRACK ACCESSORIES — 3-RAIL

CAT. NO.	DESCRIPTION	BOX TYPE NO.	BOX NO.	BOX CODE	COMMENTS	MECC. MAG.	MECC. PRICE	LAST DATE	LAST PRICE
3400	TPO Mail Van Set		(35400)		Box with this number not known to exist.	(2/59)	1/18/6	9/63	2/0/6
32099	TPO Mail Van Set	14f	32099	—	TPO Mail Van, Lineside Apparatus & Switch with green button.	(7/57)	1/18/6	12/58	1/19/6
D1	TPO Mail Van Set	14f	32099	—		3/57	38/6	8/57	1/18/6
3401	TPO Mail Van (See 4401)				This reference number used only in the 1959 Hornby Book of Trains and 1st May 1959 price list. No box with this number.	(2/59)	1/3/-	4/59	1/3/-
3450	Buffer Stop	14g	35450	11/61	Chrome plated heads. 2 per box	(2/59)	2/4	9/63	2/8
32100	Buffer Stop	14f	32100	4/55	Steel Heads. 2 per box	(5/56)	2/1	12/58	2/4
D1	Buffer Stop	14d	32100	8/53	Steel Heads. 2 per box	(4/49)	1/3	4/56	2/1
D1	Buffer Stop	14c	DA 451		Steel Heads. 2 per box.	(4/49)	1/3	4/56	2/1
D1	Buffer Stop	14b	—	7.5M 8.48	Steel Heads. 2 per box	(4/49)	1/3	4/56	2/1
3455	Island Platform - Metal (See 32102)				This reference number used only in the 1959 Hornby Book of Trains and 1st May 1959 price list. No box with this number.	(2/59)	1/4/6	4/59	1/4/6
3456	Island Platform Extension — Metal				Box with this number not known to exist. —	(2/59)	7/3	9/63	7/3
32110	Island Platform Extension — Metal	14f	32110	6/56	1 per box	(5/56)	6/6	12/58	7/6
D1	Island Platform Extension — Metal	14f	32110		1 per box	1/55	5/3	4/56	6/6
3460	Level Crossing — Plastic	14g	35460	2/62	1 per box	(8/61)	7/9	9/63	7/6
3460	Level Crossing — Metal	14g	35460	2/62	1 per box	(2/59)	9/6	5/61	9/11
32104	Level Crossing — Metal	14f	32104	12/53	1 per box	(5/56)	9/6	12/58	9/11
D1	Level Crossing — Metal	14f	32104		1 per box	11/53	9/11	4/56	9/6
3465	Through Station — Metal (See 32170)				This reference number used only in the 1959 Hornby Book of Trains and 1st May 1959 price list. No box with this number.	(2/59)	2/9/-	4/59	2/9/-

CAT. NO.	DESCRIPTION	COMMENTS	LENGTH	RAIL TYPE	TONGUE	NO. IN BOX	BOX TYPE NO.	BOX NO.	BOX CODE	MECC. MAG.	MECC. PRICE	LAST DATE	LAST PRICE
3466	Through Station Extension — Metal (Island Platform with Wall)					1 per box	Box not known to exist.			(2/59)	11/-	9/63	11/-
32172	Through Station Extension — Metal					1 per box	14f	32172	6/56	(5/56)	11/6	12/58	11/6
D1	Through Station Extension — Metal					1 per box	14f	32172	6/56	4/56	11/6	4/56	11/6
3470	Turntable	Box with this number not known to exist.					—	—	—	(2/59)	2/6/-	9/63	2/16/9
32180	Turntable					1 per box	14f	32180	1/57	(5/56)	2/5/-	12/58	2/7/6
D1	Turntable					1 per box	14f	32180	1/57	1/57	2/5/-	8/57	2/5/-
3475	Lineside Apparatus for TPO Mail Van.	Contains Lineside Apparatus and Switch, with green button.					14f	—	—	(2/59)	16/-	9/63	16/3
32198	Lineside Apparatus for TPO Mail Van.	Contains Lineside Apparatus and Switch, with green button.					14f	32198	1/58	(4/57)	16/-	12/58	16/6
D1	Lineside Apparatus for TPO Mail Van.	Contains Lineside Apparatus and Switch, with green button.					14f	32198	1/58	(8/57)	16/-	8/57	16/-
3701	Straight Rail		11½"	A	Wide	6	14g	35701	—	(2/59)	3/3	9/63	3/7
EDB1	Straight Rail		11½"	A	Wide	6	14f	32200 (Square box)	—	(4/57)	3/3	12/58	3/4
EDB1	Straight Rail		11½"	B	Narrow	6	14e	32200 (Square box)	4.53	(7/55)	3/3	1/57	3/3
EDB1	Straight Rail		11½"	C	Narrow	6	14d	32198 (Square box)	71M 12.50	(7/55)	3/3	1/57	3/3
EDB1	Straight Rail		11½"	D	Narrow	6	14c	Rectangular box	16.8M 8.49	(7/55)	3/3	1/57	3/3
EDB1	Straight Rail		11½"	D	Narrow	6	14k	Rectangular box	—	(4/49)	2/8	6/55	3/3
3702	Straight Half Rail		5¾"	A	Wide	6	14g	35702	-/61	(2/59)	2/9	9/63	2/7
EDB1½	Straight Half Rail		5¾"	A	Wide	6	14f	32201	—	(4/57)	2/5	12/58	2/6
EDB1½	Straight Half Rail		5¾"	B	Narrow	6	14e	32201	6.53	(7/55)	2/4	1/57	2/5
EDB1½	Straight Half Rail		5¾"	B	Narrow	6	14d	—	—	(7/55)	2/4	1/57	2/5
EDB1½	Straight Half Rail		5¾"	C	Narrow	6	14c	—	—	(7/55)	2/4	1/57	2/5
EDB1½	Straight Half Rail		5¾"	D	Narrow	6	14k	—	—	(4/49)	2/-	6/55	2/4
3703	Straight Quarter Rail		2 7/8"	A	Wide	6	14g	35703	3/61	(2/59)	2/-	9/63	2/3
EDB1¼	Straight Quarter Rail		2 7/8"	A	Wide	6	14f	—	—	(4/57)	2/-	12/58	2/-
EDB1¼	Straight Quarter Rail		2 7/8"	B	Narrow	6	14e	—	—	(7/55)	2/-	1/57	2/-
EDB1¼	Straight Quarter Rail		2 7/8"	B	Narrow	6	14d	32202	2/52	(7/55)	2/-	1/57	2/-
EDB1¼	Straight Quarter Rail		2 7/8"	C	Narrow	6	14e	—	—	(7/55)	2/-	1/57	2/-
EDB1¼	Straight Quarter Rail		2 7/8"	D	Narrow	6	14k	—	—	(4/49)	1/8	6/55	2/-
EDBT1	Straight Terminal Rail (Capacitor fitted).		11½"	B	Narrow	1	14f	32204	—	—	—	—	—
EDBT1	Straight Terminal Rail (Capacitor fitted).		11½"	B	Narrow	1	14e	32204	3/53	—	—	—	—
EDBT1	Straight Terminal Rail (Capacitor fitted).		11½"	C	Narrow	1	14d	—	—	—	—	—	—
EDBT1	Straight Terminal Rail (No Capacitor)		11½"	D	Narrow	1	14k	—	—	(4/49)	6/3	3/54	4/3
3704	Straight Terminal Half Rail		5¾"	A	Wide	1	14g	35704	—	(2/59)	4/-	9/63	4/11
EDBT1½	Straight Terminal Half Rail		5¾"	A	Wide	1	14f	(32205)	—	(4/57)	4/3	12/58	4/3
EDBT1½	Straight Terminal Half Rail		5¾"	B	Narrow	1	14e	—	—	(7/55)	3/6	1/57	4/3
EDBT1½	Straight Terminal Half Rail		5¾"	B	Narrow	1	14d	—	—	(6/54)	3/3	6/55	3/6
3705	Straight Half Rail, with Roadway.		5¾"	A	Wide	3	14g	—	—	(2/59)	2/10	9/63	3/4
EDBX½	Straight Half Rail, with Roadway.		5¾"	A	Wide	3	14f	32206	—	(4/57)	2/9	12/58	2/11
EDBX½	Straight Half Rail, with Roadway.		5¾"	B	Narrow	3	14e	32206	—	(7/55)	2/9	1/57	2/9
EDBX½	Straight Half Rail, with Roadway.		5¾"	B	Narrow	3	14d	—	—	(6/54)	2/9	6/55	2/9
3706	Straight Short Rail		1 5/16"	A	Wide	3	14g	—	—	(2/59)	2/-	9/63	2/2

TRACK — 3-RAIL

CAT. NO.	DESCRIPTION		LENGTH	RAIL TYPE	TONGUE	NO. IN BOX	BOX TYPE	BOX NO.	BOX CODE	MECC. MAG.	MECC. PRICE	LAST DATE	LAST PRICE
EDBS	Straight Short Rail		1 5/16"	A	Wide	3	14f	32203	3/58	(4/57	1/10)	12/58	2/-
EDBS	Straight Short Rail		1 5/16"	B	Narrow	3	14e	32203	6M 10.52	(7/55	1/9)	1/57	1/10
EDBS	Straight Short Rail		1 5/16"	B	Narrow	3	14d			(7/55	1/9)	1/57	1/10
EDBS	Straight Short Rail		1 5/16"	C	Narrow	3	14c			(7/55	1/9)	1/57	1/10
EDBS	Straight Short Rail		1 5/16"	D	Narrow	3	14k			(4/50	1/6)	6/55	1/9
3710	Curved Rail	8 to circle	—	A	Wide	8	14g	35710	—	(2/59	3/3)	9/63	3/7
EDA1	Curved Rail	15" radius	—	A	Wide	8	14f	32210	—	(4/57	3/3)	12/58	3/4
EDA1	Curved Rail	8 to circle	—	B	Narrow	8	14e	32210	—	(7/55	3/3)	1/57	3/3
EDA1	Curved Rail	15" radius	—	B	Narrow	8	14d			(7/55	3/3)	1/57	3/3
EDA1	Curved Rail	8 to circle	—	C	Narrow	8	14c			(7/55	3/3)	1/57	3/3
EDA1	Curved Rail	15" radius	—	D	Narrow	8	14k			(4/49	2/8)	6/55	3/3
3711	Curved Half Rail	16 to circle	—	A	Wide	6	14g	35711		(2/59	2/5)	9/63	2/7
EDA1½	Curved Half Rail	15" radius	—	A	Wide	6	14f	32211		(4/57	2/5)	12/58	2/6
EDA1½	Curved Half Rail	16 to circle	—	B	Narrow	6	14e	32211	5M 4.53	(7/55	2/4)	1/57	2/5
EDA1½	Curved Half Rail	15" radius	—	B	Narrow	6	14d	—	17M 2.52	(7/55	2/4)	1/57	2/5
EDA1½	Curved Half Rail	16 to circle	—	C	Narrow	6	14c	—	9M 3.50	(7/55	2/4)	1/57	2/5
EDA1½	Curved Half Rail	15" radius	—	D	Narrow	6	14k			(4/49	2/-)	6/55	2/4
						Blue Printing.							
3712	Curved Quarter Rail	32 to circle	—	A	Wide	6	14g	(35712)	-/60	(2/59	2/-)	9/63	2/3
EDA1¼	Curved Quarter Rail	15" radius	—	A	Wide	6	14f	32213	6/56	1/57	—	12/58	2/-
3713	Curved Terminal Rail	8 to circle	—	A	Wide	1	14g	35713	9/61	(2/59	5/3)	9/63	6/-
EDAT1	Curved Terminal Rail	15" radius	—	A	Wide	1	14f	32212	3/5?	(4/57	5/6)	12/58	5/6
EDAT1	Curved Terminal Rail	8 to circle	—	B	Narrow	1	14e			(7/55	4/9)	1/57	5/6
EDAT1	Curved Terminal Rail	15" radius	—	B	Narrow	1	14d			(4/54	4/3)	6/55	4/9
3719	Curved Rail Large Radius	8 to circle		A	Wide	8	14g	(35719)	—	(2/59	3/6)	9/63	3/9
EDA2	Curved Rail Large Radius	17¼" radius		A	Wide	8	14f	(32215)	—	(4/57	3/3)	12/58	3/7
EDA2	Curved Rail Large Radius	8 to circle		B	Narrow	8	14e			(7/55	3/3)	1/57	3/3
EDA2	Curved Rail Large Radius	17¼" radius		B	Narrow	8	14d			10/53	—	6/55	3/3
3720	Curved Terminal Rail	8 to circle	—	A	Wide	1	14a	(35720)	—	(2/59	5/3)	9/63	6/-
EDAT2	Curved Terminal Rail	17¼" radius	—	A	Wide	1	14f	32216	6/58	(4/57	5/6)	12/58	5/6
EDAT2	Curved Terminal Rail	8 to circle	—	B	Narrow	1	14e			(7/55	4/9)	1/57	5/6
EDAT2	Curved Terminal Rail	17¼" radius	—	B	Narrow	1	14d			(6/54	4/3)	6/55	4/9
EDPR	Switch Point Manual	— Right Hand	5¾"	B	Narrow	Pair	14e	32222	7/52	(10/50	10/53) per pair	1/53	10/-
EDPL	Switch Point Manual	— Left Hand	5¾"	B	Narrow								
							Boxes are two-piece type.						
EDPR	Switch Point Manual	— Right Hand	5¾"	B	Narrow	Pair	14d	—	4.50 50M	(10/50	10/3) per pair	1/53	10/-
EDPL	Switch Point Manual	— Left Hand	5¾"	B	Narrow								
							Boxes are one-piece type.						
EDPR	Switch Point Manual	— Right Hand	5¾"	C	Narrow	Pair	14b	—	3.49 60M	(10/50	10/3) per pair	1/53	10/-
EDPL	Switch Point Manual	— Left Hand	5¾"	C	Narrow								
			— Above Points have Silver Labels. Boxes are one-piece.										
EDPR	Switch Point Manual	— Right Hand	5¾"	D	Narrow	Pair	14k	—	11.47	(4/49	9/4½) per pair	4/50	9/6
EDPL	Switch Point Manual	— Left Hand	5¾"	D	Narrow								
			— Above Points have Gold Labels. Boxes also one-piece.										
3728	Isolating Switch Point	— Right Hand	5¾"	A	Wide	1	14g One piece box	35728	12/60	(2/59	11/9)	9/63	13/-
ISPR	Isolating Switch Point	— Right Hand	5¾"	A	Wide	1	14f Two piece box	32247		(4/57	11/9)	12/58	11/11
ISPR	Isolating Switch Point	— Right Hand	5¾"	B	Narrow	1	14e Two piece box	32247	—	6/53	—	1/57	11/9
3729	Isolating Switch Point	— Left Hand	5¾"	A	Wide	1	14g One piece box	35729	-/60	(2/59	11/9)	9/63	13/-
ISPL	Isolating Switch Point	— Left Hand	5¾"	A	Wide	1	14f Two piece box	32248	—	(4/57	11/9)	12/58	11/11
ISPL	Isolating Switch Point	— Left Hand	5¾"	B	Narrow	1	14e Two piece box	32248	—	6/53	— 'each'	1/57	11/9
3731	Switch Point Electric	— Right Hand	5¾"	A	Wide	1	14g One piece box	35731	6/61	(2/59	1/1/-)	9/63	1/4/6

CAT. NO.	DESCRIPTION		LENGTH	RAIL TYPE	TONGUE	NO. IN BOX	BOX TYPE	BOX NO.	BOX CODE	MECC. MAG.	MECC. PRICE	LAST DATE	LAST PRICE
EODPR	Switch Point Electric	– Right Hand	5¾"	A	Wide	1	14f	32225	6/55	(4/57	1/1/6)	12/58	1/1/6
							Two piece box						
EODPR	Switch Point Electric	– Right Hand	5¾"	B	Narrow	1	14e	32225	–	9/52	–	1/57	1/1/6
							Two piece box, red printing on end.						
3732	Switch Point Electric	– Left Hand	5¾"	A	Wide	1	14g	35732	5/62	(2/59	1/1/-)	9/63	1/4/6
							One piece box						
EODPL	Switch Point Electric	– Left Hand	5¾"	A	Wide	1	14f	32226	–	(4/57	1/1/6)	12/58	1/1/6
							Two piece box						
EODPL	Switch Point Electric	– Left Hand	5¾"	B	Narrow	1	14e	32226	–	9/52	–	1/57	1/1/6
							Two piece box, red printing on end.						
3734	Diamond Crossing	– Right Hand	5¾"	A	Wide	1	14g	35734		(2/59	8/6)	9/6	9/11
EDCR	Diamond Crossing	– Right Hand	5¾"	A	Wide	1	14f	32223	6/55	(4/57	8/9)	12/58	8/9
							Two piece box, with red and black printing on end.						
EDCR	Diamond Crossing	– Right Hand	5¾"	B	Narrow	1	14f	32223	3/58	5/54	–	1/57	8/9
							Two piece box, with all red printing on end.						
3735	Diamond Crossing	– Left Hand	5¾"	A	Wide	1	14g	35735	5/62	(2/59	8/6)	9/63	9/11
EDCL	Diamond Crossing	– Left Hand	5¾"	A	Wide	1	14f	32224	11/59	(4/57	8/9)	12/58	8/9
							Two piece box, with red and black printing on end.						
EDCL	Diamond Crossing	– Left Hand	5¾"	B	Narrow	1	14f	32224	–	5/54	–	1/57	8/9
							Two piece box, with all red printing on end.						
3738	Isolating Quarter Rail		2 7/8"	A	Wide	3	14g	32235 & 35738	5/61	(2/59	2/11)	9/63	3/6
IBR¼	Isolating Quarter Rail		2 7/8"	A	Wide	3	14f	32235	5/56 6/57	(4/57	3/-)	12/58	3/-
IBR¼	Isolating Quarter Rail		2 7/8"	B	Narrow	3	14f	32235	5/56	(6/54	2/6)	1/57	3/-
IBR	Isolating Quarter Rail and Switch D2.		2 7/8"	B	Narrow	1	14e	32230	15M 12.52	2/50	–	4/54	6/-
IBR	Isolating Quarter Rail and Switch D2.		2 7/8"	C	Narrow	1	14c	–	5.49 or 28M	(4/49	5/6)	4/54	6/-
							Dark Blue Printing. 4.50						
IBR	Isolating Quarter Rail and Switch D2.		2/78"	D	Narrow	1	14b	–	30M 5.49	(4/49	5/6)	4/54	6/-
				Plated terminals			Mottled Blue.						
IBR	Isolating Quarter Rail and Switch D2.		2 7/8"	D	Narrow	1	14b	–	7M 2.48	(4/49	5/6)	4/54	6/-
				Brass terminals			Light Blue.						
3745	Uncoupling Rail	– Manual	5¾"	A	Wide		No box with this number			(2/59	5/6)	9/63	6/6
UBR	Uncoupling Rail	– Manual	5¾"	A	Wide	1	14f	32240	4/57	(4/57	5/6)	12/58	5/8
UBR	Uncoupling Rail	– Manual	5¾"	B	Narrow	1	14d	–	9.50	(7/55	5/3)	1/57	5/6
				Black base.			Box has white printing.						
UBR	Uncoupling Rail	– Manual	5¾"	C	Narrow	1	14d	–	3.50	(7/55	5/3)	1/57	5/6
				Plain base.			Box has blue printing.						
UBR	Uncoupling Rail	– Manual	5¾"	C	Narrow	1	14b	-	25M 8.49	(7/55	5/3)	1/57	5/6
				Plain base.									
UBR	Uncoupling Rail	– Manual	5¾"	D	Narrow	1	14k	–	25M 11.47	(4/49	4/6)	6/55	5/3
		– All uncoupling rails appear to have solid steel centre rail.											
3746	Uncoupling Rail	– Electric	5¾"	A	Wide		No box with this number.			(2/59	14/6)	9/63	16/-
EUBR	Uncoupling Rail	– Electric	5¾"	A	Wide	1	14f	32239	3/58	(4/57	14/9)	12/58	14/11
EUBR	Uncoupling Rail	– Electric	5¾"	B	Narrow	1	14e	32239	9/54	1/55	–	1/57	14/9
3747	Isolating Tabs	Blue	–	–	–	–	No package with this number			(2/59	-/7)	9/63	-/7
32231	Isolating Tabs	Blue	–	–	-	12	23a	32231	–				
		Blue	–	–	–	12	23a	57510	–	2/52	–	7/58	-/7
							Large Envelope with blue printing.						
IT	Isolating Tabs	Blue	–	–	–	4	23a	57509	–	(10/51	-/6)	12/58	-/7
							Small Envelope with either blue or mauve printing.						
–	Isolating Tabs	Green – Unconfirmed.			–	–	–	–	–	–	–	–	–
3900	Railer		–	–	–	–	No box with this number			(2/59	2/4)	9/63	2/4
32241	Railer		–	–	–	–	14f	32241	–	(5/56	2/5)	12/58	2/5
D1	Railer		–	–	–	–	14e	32241	–	10/52	2/2)	4/56	2/5
3905	Terminal Screws		–	–	–	12	22a	35412	–	Never listed for retail sale.			

Track 'RAIL TYPES':–

A – Tinned brass rails including centre rail.
B – Tinned brass centre rail and steel outer rails.
C – Tinned brass outer rails and steel centre rail.
D – All rails are steel. Early postwar.

A fifth type would be:
E Tinned brass outer rails, with steel centre rail, but with prewar base. i.e. The Meccano Ltd. label is in the centre of the base close to the centre insulation and support piece. These are prewar rails, included

POSTWAR ROLLING STOCK — COACHES

CAT. NO.	DESCRIPTION	COMPANY /REGION	COACH NO.	BOGIE TYPE	WHEEL TYPE	CPLGS.	BOX TYPE	BOX NO.	BOX CODE	MECC. MAG.	MECC. LAST PRICE DATE	LAST PRICE
D2	Articulated Set,	LNER	LNER 45401	SGb	EPW	EMC	4b	D252	4.48	11/48		

(Never Listed for Sale after war in UK, but listed outside).

All 3rd & Br/3rd   & 45402 — two piece box.

Special Artic. Set Comprising 2 x Br/3rd's and All 3rd exists. Was specially made up in the Liverpool factory for Canada.

CAT. NO.	DESCRIPTION	COMPANY /REGION	COACH NO.	BOGIE TYPE	WHEEL TYPE	CPLGS.	BOX TYPE	BOX NO.	BOX CODE	MECC. MAG.	MECC. LAST PRICE DATE	LAST PRICE
D1	Corr. Cch. 1st/3rd	LNER	LNER 42759	SGb	EPW	EMC	4b	—	4M 7.48	(4/49 7/6)	1/53	9/6
D1	Corr. Cch. 1st/3rd	LNER	LNER 42759	SGb	EPW	EMC	4d	32010	4.51	4/49 7/6	1/53	9/6
D1	Corr. Cch. Br/3rd	LNER	LNER 45402	SGb	EPW	EMC	4b	(DR361)	4M 7.48	4/49 7/6	1/53	9/6

— All above have brown coach ends.

| D1 | Corr. Cch. Br/3rd | LNER | LNER 45402 | SGb | EPW | EMC | 4d | 32011 | 4.51 | (4/49   7/6) | 1/53 | 9/6 |

— The above has plain (teak) ends.

| D1 | Corr. Cch. All 3rd | LNER | LNER 45401 | SGb | EPW | EMC | 4b | (DR361) | 4M 7.48 | 4/53   9/- | 3/55 | 9/- |
| D1 | Corr. Cch. All 3rd | LNER | LNER 45401 | SGb | EPW | EMC | 4g | 32012 | 11/53 | (4/53   9/- | 3/55 | 9/- |

— The above two coaches have brown ends. All above coaches have white roofs.

| 32012 | Corr. Cch. All 3rd | LNER | LNER 45401 | SGb | EPW | EMC | 4g | 32012 | 8/54 | 4/53   9/- | 3/55 | 9/- |
| D1 | Corr. Cch. Br/3rd | LNER | LNER 45401 | SGb | EPW | EMC | 4g | 32012 | 2/52 | (4/53   9/- | 3/55 | 9/- |

— The above two coaches have plain (teak) ends and a grey roof.

— All LNER coaches have teak finish.

D1	Corr. Cch. All 3rd	LNER	LNER 45401	SGb	FPW	EMC	4f	32012	12/52	4/53 9/-	3/55	9/-
32013	Corr. Cch. 1st/3rd	B.R. (E)	E42759E	SB	FPW	FMC	5a	32013	5/55	5/56 9/3	10/57	9/3
D11	Corr. Cch. 1st/3rd	B.R. (E)	E42759E	SGb	FPW	LMC	4d	32013	11/53	3/53 9/6	4/56	9/3
D11	Corr. Cch. 1st/3rd	B.R. (E)	E42759E	SGb	FPW	EMC	4e	32013	6.25M 12.52	3/53 9/6	4/56	9/3
32014	Corr. Cch. Br/3rd	B.R. (E)	E45402E	SB	FPW	FMC	5a	32014	7/54	5/56 9/3	10/57	9/3
D11	Corr. Cch. Br/3rd	B.R. (E)	E45402E	SGb	FPW	LMC	4d	32014	—	3/53 9/6	4/56	9/3
D11	Corr. Cch. Br/3rd	B.R. (E)	E45402E	SGb	FPW	EMC	4e	32014	5M 11.53	3/53 9/6	4/56	9/3

— Above have BR red and cream finish, grey roofs and tinplate windows.

| 32015 | Corr. Cch. 1st/3rd | LMS | LMS 4183 | LMS | FPW | LMC | 4d | 32015 | 4.51 | Not listed under this number. | | |
| D3 | Corr. Cch. 1st/3rd | LMS | LMS 4183 | LMS | EPW | EMC | 4d | 32015 | 4.51 | (4/49   12/6) | 1/53 | 13/6 |

— Above have grey roofs.

| D3 | Corr. Cch. 1st/3rd | LMS | LMS 4183 | LMS | EPW | EMC | 4c | DR363 | 2.50 | 4/49   12/6 | 1/53 | 13/6 |
| D3 | Corr. Cch. 1st/3rd | LMS | LMS 4183 | LMS | EPW | EMC | 4b | DR363 | 6.49 | 4/49   12/6 | 1/53 | 13/6 |

— Above have early silver-grey roofs. All coaches are Maroon, which can vary in shade.

| 32016 | Corr. Cch. Br/3rd | LMS | LMS 26133 | LMS | FPW | LMC | 4d | 32016 | 4.51 | Not listed under this number. | | |
| D3 | Corr. Cch. Br/3rd | LMS | LMS 26133 | LMS | LPW | EMC | 4d | 32016 | 4.51 | (4/49   12/6) | 1/53 | 13/6 |

— Above have grey roofs.

| D3 | Corr. Cch. Br/3rd | LMS | LMS 26133 | LMS | EPW | EMC | 4c | DR363 | 2.50 | 4/49   12/6 | 1/53 | 13/6 |
| D3 | Corr. Cch. Br/3rd | LMS | LMS 26133 | LMS | EPW | EMC | 4b | DR363 | 3.5M 6.49 | 4/49   12/6 | 1/53 | 13/6 |

— Above coaches are Maroon, which can vary in shade.

4005	Corr. Cch. 1st/3rd	B.R. (M)	M4183	SB	SO	EPC	6a	(36005)	—	This item never illustrated.	4/56	13/3
4005	Corr. Cch. 1st/2nd	B.R. (M)	M4183	SB	SO	FMC	6a	(36005)	—	2/59 13/9	11/61	13/10
32017	Corr. Cch. 1st/2nd	B.R. (M)	M4183	SB	SO	FMC	5c	32017	—	8/58 13/11	12/58	13/11
32017	Corr. Cch. 1st/2nd	B.R. (M)	M4183	SB	SO	FMC	5a	32017	12.5M 6.53	—	7/58	13/3
32017	Corr. Cch. 1st/2nd	B.R. (M)	M4183	SB	FPW	FMC	5a	32017	7/58	9/56 13/3	7/58	13/11

— Above coach differs in that it has plain black ends, whereas they are normally lined out.

— Above boxes marked 1st/2nd

D12	Corr. Cch. 1st/3rd	B.R. (M)	M4183	LMS	FPW	LMC	4e	32017	6/53	5/53 13/3	4/56	13/3
4006	Corr. Cch. Br/2nd	B.R. (M)	M26143	SB	SO	EPC	6a	(36006)	—	This item never illustrated.	4/56	13/3
4006	Corr. Cch. Br/2nd	B.R. (M)	M26143	SB	SO	FMC	6a	(36006)	—	2/59 13/9	11/61	13/10
32018	Corr. Cch. Br/2nd	B.R. (M)	M26143	SB	SO	FMC	5c	32018	—	8/58 13/11	12/58	13/11
32018	Corr. Cch. Br/2nd	B.R. (M)	M26143	LMS	SO	FMC	5a	32018	—	—	7/58	13/3
32018	Corr. Cch. Br/2nd	B.R. (M)	M26143	SB	FPW	FMC	5a	32018	7/58	9/56 13/3	7/58	13/11

— Above coach differs in that it has plain black ends, whereas they are normally lined out.

— Above boxes marked 1st/2nd.

| 32018 | Corr. Cch. Br/3rd | B.R. (M) | M26143 | SB | FPW | FMC | 5a | 32018 | 1/54 | 5/56   13/3 | 7/56 | 13/3 |
| 32018 | Corr. Cch. Br/3rd | B.R. (M) | M26143 | SB | FPW | FMC | 5a | 32018 | — | 5/56   13/3 | 7/56 | 13/3 |

CAT. NO.	DESCRIPTION	COMPANY /REGION	COACH NO.	BOGIE TYPE	WHEEL TYPE	CPLGS.	BOX TYPE	BOX NO.	BOX CODE	MECC. MAG.	MECC. PRICE	LAST DATE	LAST PRICE
D12	Corr.Cch.Br/3rd	B.R. (M)	M26143	LMS	FPW	LMC	4e	32018	6.53	5/53	—	4/56	13/3
	— Above coaches are Red & Cream with Grey roofs, and plastic windows.												
32090	Sub'n.Cch.1st/2nd	B.R.	—	SB	FPW	FMC	Box with '1st/2nd' unknown			9/56	8/9	10/57	8/9
32090	Sub'n.Cch.1st/3rd	B.R.	—	SB	FPW	FMC	5a	32090	—	6/56	8/9	6/56	8/9
D13	Sub'n.Cch.1st/3rd	B.R.	—	SB	FPW	LMC	5a	32090	—	1/55	9/-	4/56	8/9
32091	Sub'n.Cch.Br/2nd	B.R.	—	SB	FPW	FMC	Box with 'Br/2nd' unknown.			9/56	8/9	10/57	8/9
32091	Sub'n.Cch.Br/3rd	B.R.	—	SB	FPW	FMC	5a	32091	8/55	6/56	8/9	6/56	8/9
D13	Sub'n.Cch.Br/3rd	B.R.	—	SB	FPW	LMC	5a	32091	8/55	6/54	9/-	4/56	8/9
	— Above coaches are Maroon with Grey roofs, with tinplate windows.												
								This item never illustrated.					
4009	Corr. Cch. 1st/2nd	B.R. (W)	W15862	SB	SO	EPC	6a	(36009)	—	2/59	13/9	11/61	13/10
4009	Corr. Cch. 1st/2nd	B.R. (W)	W15862	SB	SO	FMC	6a	(36009)	—	8/58	13/11	12/58	13/11
32094	Corr. Cch. 1st/2nd	B.R. (W)	W15862	SB	SO	FMC	5c	32094	12/57	7/57	13/11	7/58	13/11
32094	Corr. Cch. 1st/2nd	B.R. (W)	W15862	SB	FPW	FMC	5a	32094	9/57	10/57	13/11	8/57	13/11
D21	Corr. Cch. 1st/2nd	B.R. (W)	W15862	SB	FPW	FMC	5a	32094	9/57		—	8/57	13/11
								This item never illustrated.					
4010	Corr. Cch.Br/2nd	B.R. (W)	W34481	SB	SO	EPC	6a	(36010)	—	2/59	13/9	11/61	13/10
4010	Corr. Cch.Br/2nd	B.R. (W)	W34481	SB	SO	FMC	6a	(36010)	—	8/58	13/11	12/58	13/11
32095	Corr. Cch.Br/2nd	B.R. (W)	W34481	SB	SO	FMC	5c	32095	12/57	8/58	13/11	12/58	13/11
32095	Corr. Cch.Br/2nd	B.R. (W)	W34481	SB	FPW	FMC	5a	32095	3/58	7/57	13/11	7/58	13/11
D21	Corr. Cch.Br/2nd	B.R. (W)	W34481	SB	FPW	FMC	5a	32095	3/58	10/57	—	8/57	13/11
	— The above coaches are Brown & Cream with Grey roofs and plastic windows.												
								This item never illustrated.					
4013	Corr. Cch. 1st/2nd	B.R. (M)	M4193	SB	SO	EPC	6a	(36013)	—	2/59	13/9	9/62	13/9
4013	Corr. Cch. 1st/2nd	B.R. (M)	M4193	SB	SO	FMC	6a	(36013)	—	8/58	13/11	12/58	13/11
32022	Corr. Cch. 1st/2nd	B.R. (M)	M4193	SB	SO	FMC	5c	32022	12/57	7/57	13/11	7/58	13/11
32022	Corr. Cch. 1st/2nd	B.R. (M)	M4193	SB	FPW	FMC	5a	32022	12/57	8/57	13/11	8/57	13/11
D22	Corr. Cch. 1st/2nd	B.R. (M)	M4193	SB	FPW	FMC	5a	32022	12/57		—	8/57	13/11
								This item never illustrated.					
4014	Corr. Cch.Br/2nd	B.R. (M)	M26143	SB	SO	EPC	6a	(36014)	—	2/59	13/9	11/61	13/10
4014	Corr. Cch.Br/2nd	B.R. (M)	M26143	SB	SO	FMC	6a	(36014)	—	8/58	13/11	12/58	13/11
32023	Corr. Cch.Br/2nd	B.R. (M)	M26143	SB	SO	FMC	5c	32023	8/57	7/57	13/11	7/58	13/11
32023	Corr. Cch.Br/2nd	B.R. (M)	M26143	SB	FPW	FMC	5a	32023	8/57	8/57	13/11	8/57	13/11
D22	Corr. Cch.Br/2nd	B.R. (M)	M26143	SB	FPW	FMC	5a	32023	8/57		—	8/57	13/11
	— The above coaches are Maroon with Grey roofs and plastic windows.												
4021	Sub'n. Cch. 1st/2nd	B.R.	—	SB	SO	EPC	6a	(36021)	—	5/61	12/-	12/64	9/6
4021	Sub'n. Cch. 1st/2nd	B.R.	—	SB	SO	FMC	6a	(36021)	—	2/59	10/3	10/60	10/3
32092	Sub'n. Cch. 1st/2nd	B.R.	—	SB	SO	FMC	5c	32092	—	8/58	10/6	12/58	10/6
32092	Sub'n. Cch. 1st/2nd	B.R.	—	SB	FPW	FMC	5a	32092	8/56	9/56	10/-	7/58	10/6
D14	Sub'n. Cch. 1st/3rd	B.R.	—	SB	FPW	FMC	5a	32092	7/56	5/56	10/-	7/56	10/-
							Box now says Br/3rd.						
	— The above coach differs in having windows at one end, like a Brake/End.												
4022	Sub'n. Cch.Br/2nd	B.R.	—	SB	SO	EPC	6a	(36022)	—	5/61	12/-	12/64	9/6
4022	Sub'n. Cch.Br/2nd	B.R.	—	SB	SO	FMC	6a	(36022)	—	2/59	10/3	10/60	10/3
32093	Sub'n. Cch.Br/2nd	B.R.	—	SB	SO	FMC	5c	32093	2/57	8/58	10/6	12/58	10/6
32093	Sub'n. Cch.Br/2nd	B.R.	—	SB	FPW	FMC	5a	32093	—	9/56	10/-	7/58	10/6
D14	Sub'n. Cch.Br/3rd	B.R.	—	SB	FPW	FMC	5a	32093	7/56	5/56	10/-	7/56	10/-
							Box now says Br/3rd.						
	— The above coaches are Maroon with Grey roofs and plastic windows.												
4025	Sub'n. Cch. 1st/2nd	B.R. (S)	S41060	SB	SO	EPC	6a	(36025)	—	5/61	12/-	12/64	9/6
4025	Sub'n. Cch. 1st/2nd	B.R. (S)	S41060	SB	SO	FMC	6a	(36025)	—	4/59	10/3	10/60	10/3
4026	Sub'n. Cch.Br/2nd	B.R. (S)	S43374	SB	SO	EPC	6a	(36026)	—	5/61	12/-	12/64	9/6
4026	Sub'n. Cch.Br/2nd	B.R. (S)	S43374	SB	SO	FMC	6a	(36026)	—	4/59	10/3	10/60	10/3
	— The above coaches are Green with Grey roofs and plastic windows.												
4035	Pullman Cch. First	B.R.	ARIES	CG	SO	EPC	6b	(36035)	—	3/61	18/10	12/64	14/11
4035	Pullman Cch. First	B.R.	ARIES	CG	SO	EPC	6b	(36035)	—	10/60	17/6	1/64	14/11
4035	Pullman Cch. First	B.R.	ARIES	CSB			*As illustrated only, no actual items.*			6/62	18/6	6/62	18/6

— Export No. 4185

CAT. NO.	DESCRIPTION	COMPANY/REGION	COACH NO.	BOGIE TYPE	WHEEL TYPE	CPLGS.	BOX TYPE	BOX NO.	BOX CODE	MECC. MAG.	MECC. PRICE DATE	LAST DATE	LAST PRICE
4036	Pullman Coach Second	B.R.	Car 74	CG	SO	EPC	6b	(36036)	—	—	3/61	18/10	12/64	14/11
4036	Pullman Coach Second	B.R.	Car 74	SB	SO	EPC	6b	(36036)	—	(10/60)	17/6	1/64	14/11
4036	Pullman Coach Second	B.R.	Car 74	CSB	—		—			6/62	18/6	6/62	18/6
	— Export No. 4186 — As illustrated, no actual items.												
	— The above coaches are Brown and Cream, with super detail roofs in Grey, and plastic windows.												
4037	Pullman Coach Br/2nd	B.R.	Car 79	CG	SO	WPC	6b	(36037)	—	—	3/61	18/10	12/64	14/11
4037	Pullman Coach Br/2nd	B.R.	Car 79	SB	SO	EPC	6b	(36037)	—	(10/60)	17/6	1/64	14/11
4037	Pullman Coach Br/2nd	B.R.	Car 79	CSB	—		—			6/62	18/6	6/62	18/6
	— Export No. 4187 — As illustrated only, no actual items.												
	— The above coaches are Brown and Cream, with super detail roofs in Grey, and plastic windows.												
4047	Restaurant Car	B.R. (W)	W9572	SB	SO	EPC	6b			(5/61	16/-)	12/64	12/6
4047	Restaurant Car	B.R. (W)	W9572	SB	SO	FMC	6a	(36047)	5/62	2/59	15/6	10/60	15/6
32096	Restaurant Car	B.R. (W)	W9572	SB	SO	FMC	5c	32096	—	8/58	15/11	12/58	15/11
32096	Restaurant Car	B.R. (W)	W9572	SB	SO	FPW	5a	32096	10/57	7/57	15/11	7/58	15/11
D20	Restaurant Car	B.R. (W)	W9572	SB	SO	FPW	5a	32096	10/57	11/57	15/11	8/57	15/11
	— The above coaches are Brown and Cream, with Grey metal roofs and plastic windows.												
4048	Restaurant Car	B.R. (W)	W9562	SB	SO	EPC	6b			(5/61	16/-)	12/64	15/11
4048	Restaurant Car	B.R. (W)	W9562	SB	SO	FMC	6a	(36048)	7/61	2/59	15/6	10/60	15/6
32097	Restaurant Car	B.R. (W)	W9562	SB	SO	FMC	5c	32097	—	8/58	15/11	12/58	15/11
32097	Restaurant Car	B.R. (W)	W9562	SB	SO	FPW	5a	32097	—	7/57	15/11	7/58	15/11
D20	Restaurant Car	B.R. (W)	W9562	SB	SO	FPW	5a	32097	—	11/57	15/11	8/57	15/11
	— The above coaches are Red and Cream, with Grey metal roofs and plastic windows.												
4049	Restaurant Car	B.R. (W)	W9566W	SB	SO	EPC	6b			(7/61	16/2)	7/61	16/2
	— Red window frames.												
4049	Restaurant Car	B.R. (W)	W9566W	SB	SO	EPC	6b			(5/61	16/-)	12/64	12/6
	— White window frames.												
4049	Restaurant Car	B.R. (W)	W9566W	SB	SO	FMC	6a			4/59	—	—	
	— White window frames.												
4049	Restaurant Car	B.R. (W)	W9566W	SB	SO	FMC	6a			(2/59	15/6)	10/60	15/6
	— Red window frames.												
4050	Corr. Coach 1st/2nd	B.R. (W)	W15870	CSB	SO	EPC	6b	(36050)	11/60	12/60	14/11	Not illustrated.	14/11
4050	Corr. Coach 1st/2nd	B.R. (W)	W15870	SB	SO	EPC	6b	(36050)	11/60	(10/60)	14/11	12/64	12/6
	— The above coaches are Brown and Cream with plastic roofs and windows.												
4051	Corr. Coach Br/2nd	B.R. (W)	W34290	CSB	SO	EPC	6b	(36051)	11/60	12/60	14/11	Not illustrated	14/11
4051	Corr. Coach Br/2nd	B.R. (W)	W34290	SB	SO	EPC	6b	(36051)	11/60	(10/60)	14/11	12/64	12/6
	— The above coaches are Brown and Cream, with super detail plastic roofs and windows.												
4052	Corr. Coach 1st/2nd	B.R. (E)	E15770	CSB	SO	EPC	6b	(36052)	12/60	12/60	14/11	Not illustrated	14/11
4052	Corr. Coach 1st/2nd	B.R. (E)	E15770	SB	SO	EPC	6b	(36052)	12/60	(10/60)	14/11	12/64	12/6
	— The above coaches are Brown and Cream, with super detail plastic roofs and windows.												
4053	Corr. Coach Br/2nd	B.R. (E)	E35173	CSB	SO	EPC	6b	(36053)	12/60	12/60	14/11	Not illustrated	14/11
4053	Corr. Coach Br/2nd	B.R. (E)	E35173	SB	SO	EPC	6b	(36053)	12/60	(10/60)	14/11	12/64	12/6
	— The above coaches are Maroon, with super detail Grey roofs and windows.												
4054	Corr. Coach 1st/2nd	B.R. (S)	S15573	SB	SO	EPC	6b	—		5/62	16/11	12/64	12/6
4055	Corr. Coach Br/2nd	B.R. (S)	S35001	SB	SO	EPC	6b	—		5/62	16/11	12/64	12/6
	— The above two coaches are Green, with super detail Grey roofs and plastic windows.												
4060	Coach, Open First	B.R. (W)	W3085	CSB	SO	EPC	6b	36060	10/61	12/61	16/2	1/64	12/6
4060	Coach, Open First	B.R. (W)	W3085	SB	SO	EPC	6b	36060	10/61	(5/61	16/-)	12/64	12/6
	— The above coaches are Brown and Cream, with super detail Grey roofs and plastic windows.												
4061	Coach, Open Second	B.R. (W)	W3984	CSB	SO	EPC	6b	36061	11/61	12/61	16/2	1/64	12/6
4061	Coach, Open Second	B.R. (W)	W3984	SB	SO	EPC	6b	36061	11/61	(5/61	16/-)	12/64	12/6
	— The above coaches are Brown and Cream, with super detail plastic Grey roofs and windows.												
4062	Coach, Open First	B.R. (M)	M3002	CSB	SO	EPC	6b	36062	12/62	12/61	16/2	1/64	12/6
4062	Coach, Open First	B.R. (M)	M3002	SB	SO	EPC	6b	36062	12/62	(5/61	16/-)	12/64	12/6
	— The above coaches are Maroon, with super detail Grey roofs and windows.												
4063	Coach, Open Second	B.R. (M)	M3716	CSB	SO	EPC	6b	36063	2/61	12/61	16/2	1/64	12/6
4063	Coach, Open Second	B.R. (M)	M3716	SB	SO	EPC	6b	36063	2/61	(5/61	16/-)	12/64	12/6
	— The above coaches are Maroon, with super detail plastic Grey roofs and windows.												

Table I — Passenger Rolling Stock (continued)

CAT. DESCRIPTION NO.	COMPANY /REGION	COACH NO.	BOGIE TYPE	WHEEL TYPE	CPLGS.	BOX TYPE	BOX NO.	BOX CODE	MECC. MAG.	MECC. PRICE	LAST DATE	LAST PRICE
4070 Restaurant Car	B.R. (W)	W1910	SB	SO	NPC	6c	34070			16/9	4/63	—
4070 Restaurant Car	B.R. (W)	W1910	SB	SO	EPC	6c	34070		(1/63	16/9)	12/64	12/6
— Export No. 4220												
— The above coach is Brown and Cream, with super detail plastic Grey roof and windows.												
4071 Restaurant Car	B.R. (E)	E1939	SB	SO	NPC	6c	34071			16/9	4/63	—
4071 Restaurant Car	B.R. (E)	E1939	SB	SO	EPC	6c	34071		(1/63	16/9)	12/64	12/6
— Export No. 4221												
— The above coach is Maroon, with super detail plastic Grey roof and windows.												
4075 Passenger Brake Van (Full Brake)	B.R. (E)	E81312	CSB	SO	EPC	6b	(36075)	7/61	(10/60	14/11)	12/64	12/6
— Export No. 4225												
— The above coach is Maroon, with super detail plastic Grey roof and windows.												
4076 6-wheel Passenger Brake	B.R. (M)	M32958	Base Type 22		NPC	6c	34076			13/-	10/63	12/6
— Export No. 4228												
— The above coach is Maroon, with super detail plastic Grey roof and windows.												
4078 Sleeping Car	B.R. (W)	W2402	CSB	SO	EPC	6b	(36078)	1/61	(10/60	14/11)	12/64	12/6
— Export No. 4231												
— The above coach is Maroon, with super detail plastic Grey roof and windows.												
4081 Sub'n. Coach 1st/2nd	B.R. (S)	S46291	SB	SO	EPC	6b	(36081)	4/62		15/-	12/64	10/6
— Export No. 4231												
4082 Sub'n. Coach Br/2nd	B.R. (S)	S43381	SB	SO	EPC	6b	(36082)	4/62		15/-	12/64	10/6
4082 Sub'n. Coach Br/2nd	B.R. (S)	543381	SB	SO	EPC	6b	(36082)					
— Most coaches have this 'incorrect' number. The correct numbered one is rare.												
— Export No. 4232												
— The above coaches are Green, with super detail plastic Grey roofs and windows.												
4083 Sub'n. Coach 1st/2nd	B.R. (M)	M41012	SB	SO	EPC	6b	(36083)			15/-	12/64	10/6
— Export No. 4233												
4084 Sub'n. Coach Br/2nd	B.R. (M)	M43277	SB	SO	EPC	6b	(36084)	4/62		15/-	12/64	10/6
— Export No. 4234												
— The above coaches are Maroon, with super detail plastic Grey roofs and windows.												
4150 Elec. Driving Trailer Coach	B.R. (S)	S77511	SB	SO	EPC	6b	32045	10/62		1/1/-	12/64	10/6
— With yellow band on drive end, and black rear panel.												
4150 Elec. Driving Trailer Coach	B.R. (S)	S77511	SB	SO	EPC	6b	32045	10/62		1/1/-	12/64	10/6
— As above, but inner rear panel is green.												
— Export No. 4250												
4150 Elec. Driving Trailer Coach	B.R. (S)	S77511	SB	SO	EPC	6b	32045	10/62	(1/62	1/1/-)	1/63	1/1/-
— As illustrated, without yellow panel on drive end. This item is unconfirmed.												
— The above coaches are Green, with super detail plastic Grey roof. Goes with locos 2250 & 3250.												

POSTWAR ROLLING STOCK — PRENATIONALISED WAGONS & VANS ETC.

CAT. DESCRIPTION NO.	COMPANY & WAGON NO.	BODY COLOUR	WHEELS	CPLGS.	BOX TYPE	BOX NO.	BOX CODE	FIRST DATE	FIRST PRICE	LAST DATE	LAST PRICE
D1 Goods Brake Van	SR 55975	Brown	EPW	EMC	1b	32045		9/48	7/3	1/53	7/-
D1 Goods Brake Van	SR 55975	Brown	EPW	EMC	1c	DR376	1250 6.50	9/48	7/3	1/53	7/-
— Single window on end.											
D1 Goods Brake Van	SR 55975	Brown	FPW	EMC	(1d)	32045		9/48	7/3	1/53	7/-
— Two windows on end, one each side of door.											
D1 Goods Brake Van	GWR W68796	Grey-Green	EPW	EMC	1b	—	2M 5.48	9/48	7/3	1/53	7/-
D1 Goods Brake Van	GWR W68796	Grey-Green	EPW	EMC	1c	DR376		9/48	7/3	1/53	7/-
D1 Goods Brake Van	GWR W68796	Grey-Green	FPW	EMC	(1d)	32045		9/48	7/3	1/53	7/-
D1 Goods Brake Van	LNER NE20T 178717	Brown	EPW	EMC	1b	—	5.48	9/48	7/3	1/53	7/-
D1 Goods Brake Van	LNER NE20T 178717	Brown	EPW	EMC	1c	DR376	6.50	9/48	7/3	1/53	7/-
D1 Goods Brake Van	LNER NE20T 178717	Brown	FPW	EMC	(1d)	32045		9/48	7/3	1/53	7/-
— The above Goods Brake Vans have White roofs.											
D1 Goods Brake Van	LMS 730026	Brown	EPW	EMC	1b	—	5.48	9/48	7/3	1/53	7/-
— Silver-Grey roof											
D1 Goods Brake Van	LMS 730026	Brown	EPW	EMC	1c	DR376	6.50	9/48	7/3	1/53	7/-
— Grey roof											
D1 Goods Brake Van	LMS 730026	Brown	FPW	EMC	1d	32045	4.51	9/48	7/3	1/53	7/-
— Grey roof											
— All Goods Brake Vans have type 1d bases.											
— The above Goods Brake Vans come in slightly varying shades of brown, from deep chocolate to red-brown.											
D1 Open Wagon (5 plank)	SR 12T 19260	Brown	EPW	EMC	1b	—	3.48	9/48	4/6	1/53	4/6
D1 Open Wagon (5 plank)	SR 12T 19260	Brown	EPW	EMC	1c	DR382	4.50	9/48	4/6	1/53	4/6
D1 Open Wagon (5 plank)	SR 12T 19260	Brown	FPW	EMC	1d	32075		9/48	4/6	1/53	4/6
D1 Open Wagon	GWR GW 12T 109458	Grey	EPW	EMC	1b	—	3.48	9/48	4/6	1/53	4/6
D1 Open Wagon	GWR GW 12T 109458	Grey	EPW	EMC	1c	DR382	4.50	9/48	4/6	1/53	4/6
D1 Open Wagon	GWR GW 12T 109458	Grey	FPW	EMC	1d	32075		9/48	4/6	1/53	4/6
D1 Open Wagon	LNER NE 12T 404844	Grey-Green	EPW	EMC	1b	—	3.48	9/48	4/6	1/53	4/6
D1 Open Wagon	LNER NE 12T 404844	Grey	EPW	EMC	1c	DR382	4.50	9/48	4/6	1/53	4/6
D1 Open Wagon	LNER NE 12T 404844	Grey	FPW	EMC	1d	32075		9/48	4/6	1/53	4/6

CAT. DESCRIPTION	COMPANY & WAGON NO.	BODY COLOUR	WHEELS	CPLGS.	BOX TYPE	BOX NO.	BOX CODE	FIRST DATE	FIRST PRICE	LAST DATE	LAST PRICE
D1 Open Wagon	LMS 12T 210112	Brown	EPW	EMC	1b	—	3.48	9/48	4/6	1/53	4/6
D1 Open Wagon	LMS 12T 210112	Brown	EPW	EMC	1c	DR382	4.50	9/48	4/6	1/53	4/6
D1 Open Wagon	LMS 12T 210112	Brown	FPW	EMC	1d	32075	6.52	9/48	4/6	1/53	4/6
— Open Wagons have type 1b bases.											
D1 Coal Wagon (5 plank)	SR 12T 19260	Brown	EPW	EMC	1b	—	9.48	9/48	5/-	1/53	5/6
D1 Coal Wagon (5 plank)	SR 12T 19260	Brown	EPW	EMC	1c	DR372		9/48	5/-	1/63	5/6
D1 Coal Wagon (5 plank)	SR 12T 19260	Brown	FPW	EMC	(1d)	32025		9/48	5/-	1/53	5/6
D1 Coal Wagon	GWR GW 12T 109458	Grey	EPW	EMC	1b	—		9/48	5/-	1/53	5/6
D1 Coal Wagon	GWR GW 12T 109458	Grey	EPW	EMC	1c	DR372	10.50	9/48	5/-	1/53	5/6
D1 Coal Wagon	GWR GW 12T 109458	Grey	FPW	EMC	(1d)	32025		9/48	5/-	1/53	5/6
D1 Coal Wagon	LNER NE 12T 404844	Grey	EPW	EMC	1b	—		9/48	5/-	1/53	5/6
D1 Coal Wagon	LNER NE 12T 404844	Grey-Green	EPW	EMC	1c	DR372		9/48	5/-	1/53	5/6
D1 Coal Wagon	LNER NE 12T 404844	Grey-Green	FPW	EMC	1d	32025		9/48	5/-	1/53	5/6
D1 Coal Wagon	LMS 12T 210112	Brown	EPW	EMC	1b	—		9/48	5/-	1/53	5/6
D1 Coal Wagon	LMS 12T 210112	Brown	EPW	EMC	1c	DR372	10.50	9/48	5/-	1/53	5/6
D1 Coal Wagon	LMS 12T 210112	Brown	FPW	EMC	1d	32025	4.51	9/48	5/-	1/53	5/6
— Coal Wagons have type 1b bases. Wagon identical to Open Wagons, but with plastic imitation coal.											
D2 High Sided Wagon (7 plank)	LNER NE 12T 91508	Grey	EPW	EMC	1b	—	3.48	9/48	5/-	1/53	4/9
D2 High Sided Wagon (7 plank)	LNER NE 12T 91508	Grey-Green	EPW	EMC	1c	DR378	7.50	9/48	5/-	1/53	4/9
D2 High Sided Wagon (7 plank)	LNER NE 12T 91508	Grey-Green	FPW	EMC	1d	32055	—	9/48	5/-	1/53	4/9
D2 High Sided Wagon	LMS 12T 608344	Brown	EPW	EMC	1b	—	3.48	9/48	5/-	1/53	4/9
D2 High Sided Wagon	LMS 12T 608344	Brown	EPW	EMC	1c	DR378	4.50	9/48	5/-	1/53	4/9
D2 High Sided Wagon	LMS 12T 608344	Brown	FPW	EMC	1d	32055	10.51	9/48	5/-	1/53	4/9
— High Sided Wagons have type 1b bases.											
D2 High Sided Coal Wagon (7 plank)	LNER NE 12T 91508	Grey	EPW	EMC	(1b)	—		9/48	5/6	1/53	5/9
D2 High Sided Coal Wagon (7 plank)	LNER NE 12T 91508	Grey-Green	EPW	EMC	1c	DR373	7.50	9/48	5/6	1/53	5/9
D2 High Sided Coal Wagon (7 plank)	LNER NE 12T 91508	Grey-Green	FPW	EMC	1d	32030	10.52	9/48	5/6	1/53	5/9
D2 High Sided Cl. Wag.	LMS 12T 608344	Brown	EPW	EMC	(1b)	—		9/48	5/6	1/53	5/9
D2 High Sided Cl. Wag.	LMS 12T 608344	Brown	EPW	EMC	1c	DR373	7.50	9/48	5/6	1/53	5/9
D2 High Sided Cl. Wag.	LMS 12T 608344	Brown	FPW	EMC	1d	32030	10.51	9/48	5/6	1/53	5/9
— High Sided Coal Wagons are identical to High Sided Wagons, but with imitation coal.											
— Bases are type 1b.											
D1 Goods Van	SR 12T 48277	Brown	EPW	EMC	1b	—		9/48	5/-	1/53	5/3
D1 Goods Van	SR 12T 48277	Brown	EPW	EMC	1c	DR375		9/48	5/-	1/53	5/3
D1 Goods Van	SR 12T 48277	Brown	FPW	EMC	1d	32040	4.51	9/48	5/-	1/53	5/3
— White Roof.											
D1 Goods Van	GWR GW 12T 112699	Grey	EPW	EMC	1b	—	9.48	9/48	5/-	1/53	5/3
D1 Goods Van	GWR GW 12T 112699	Grey	EPW	EMC	1c	DR375		9/48	5/-	1/53	5/3
D1 Goods Van	GWR GW 12T 112699	Grey	FPW	EMC	(1d)	32040		9/48	5/-	1/53	5/3
— White Roof											
D1 Goods Van	LNER NE 12T N182153	Brown	EPW	EMC	1b	—	3.48	9/48	5/-	1/53	5/3
D1 Goods Van	LNER NE 12T N182153	Brown	EPW	EMC	1c	DR375	6.50	9/48	5/-	1/53	5/3
D1 Goods Van	LNER NE 12T N182153	Brown	FPW	EMC	1d	32040	4.51	9/48	5/-	1/53	5/3
— White Roof											
D1 Goods Van	LMS 12T 508194	Brown	EPW	EMC	1b	—	9.48	9/48	5/-	1/53	5/3
— Silver-Grey Roof											
D1 Goods Van	LMS 12T 508194	Brown	EPW	EMC	1c	DR375	6.50	9/48	5/-	1/53	5/3
— Grey Roof											
D1 Goods Van	LMS 12T 508194	Brown	FPW	EMC	1d	32040	4.51	9/48	5/-	1/53	5/3
— Grey Roof											
— Goods Vans have type 1b bases.											

CAT. NO.	DESCRIPTION	COMPANY & WAGON NO.	BODY COLOUR	WHEELS	CPLGS.	BOX TYPE	BOX NO.	BOX CODE	FIRST DATE	FIRST PRICE	LAST DATE	LAST PRICE
D1	Fish Van	LNER NE 10T 168975	Brown	EPW	EMC	1b	—	3.48	9/48	5/-	1/53	5/3
D1	Fish Van	LNER NE 10T 168975	Brown	EPW	EMC	1c	DR374	6.50	9/48	5/-	1/53	5/3
D1	Fish Van	LNER NE 10T 168975	Brown	FPW	EMC	1d	32035	10.51	9/48	5/-	1/53	5/3

— Fish Vans have type 1b bases.

— White Roof

CAT. NO.	DESCRIPTION	COMPANY & WAGON NO.	BODY COLOUR	WHEELS	CPLGS.	BOX TYPE	BOX NO.	BOX CODE	FIRST DATE	FIRST PRICE	LAST DATE	LAST PRICE
D1	Meat Van	SR 10T 51298	Buff	EPW	EMC	1b	—	3.48	9/48	5/-	1/53	5/3

— Silver-Grey Roof

| D1 | Meat Van | SR 10T 51298 | Buff | EPW | EMC | 1c | DR380 | 4.50 | 9/48 | 5/- | 1/53 | 5/3 |

— White Roof

| D1 | Meat Van | SR 10T 51298 | Buff | FPW | EMC | 1d | 32065 | 10.51 | 9/48 | 5/- | 1/53 | 5/3 |
| D1 | Meat Van | LMS 6T N19631 | Brown | EPW | EMC | 1b | — | 3.48 | 9/48 | 5/- | 1/53 | 5/3 |

— Silver-Grey Roof

| D1 | Meat Van | LMS 6T N19631 | Brown | EPW | EMC | 1c | DR380 | 10.50 | 9/48 | 5/- | 1/53 | 5/3 |

— Grey Roof

| D1 | Meat Van | LMS 6T N19631 | Brown | FPW | EMC | 1d | 32065 | 8.52 | 9/48 | 5/- | 1/53 | 5/3 |

— Grey Roof

— Meat Vans have type 1b bases.

D1	Horse Box	LNER NE 2337	Teak	EPW	EMC	1b	—		9/48	5/-	1/53	5/3
D1	Horse Box	LNER NE 2337	Teak	EPW	EMC	1c	DR379	10.50	9/48	5/-	1/53	5/3
D1	Horse Box	LNER NE 2337	Teak	FPW	EMC	1d	32060	6.52	9/48	5/-	1/53	5/3

— Horse Boxes have type 1b bases.

— White Roof

| D1 | Cattle Truck | GWR GW 8T 106324 | Grey-Green | EPW | EMC | 1b | — | 3.48 | 9/48 | 5/- | 1/53 | 5/3 |

— Cream interior finish, two small square windows. White Roof.

| D1 | Cattle Truck | GWR GW 8T 106324 | Grey | FPW | EMC | 1c | DR371 | 7.50 | 9/48 | 5/- | 1/53 | 5/3 |

— White interior finish, two small square windows. White Roof.

| D1 | Cattle Truck | GWR GW 8T 106324 | Grey | FPW | EMC | 1d | 32020 | 10.51 | 9/48 | 5/- | 1/53 | 5/3 |

— White interior finish, one rectangular window. White Roof.

| D1 | Cattle Truck | LMS 710018 | Brown | EPW | EMC | 1b | — | 3.48 | 9/48 | 5/- | 1/53 | 5/3 |

— Cream interior finish, two small square windows. Silver-Grey Roof.

| D1 | Cattle Truck | LMS 710018 | Brown | FPW | EMC | 1c | DR371 | 7.50 | 9/48 | 5/- | 1/53 | 5/3 |

— Cream interior finish, two small square windows. Silver-Grey Roof.

| D1 | Cattle Truck | LMS 710018 | Brown | FPW | EMC | 1d | 32020 | 8.52 | 9/48 | 5/- | 1/53 | 5/3 |

— Cattle Trucks have type 1b bases.

— One rectangular window and Grey Roof. THIS ITEM IS UNCONFIRMED.

| D1 | High Cap. Wagon (Brick Wagon) | LNER NE 50T N163535 | Brown | EPW | EMC | (1b) | — | 3.48 | 4/49 | 6/6 | 1/53 | 8/- |

— (Painted black wheels)

| D1 | High Cap. Wagon "Return to Fletton" | LNER NE 50T N163535 | Brown | FPW | EMC | 1c | DR377 | 12.49 | 4/49 | 6/6 | 1/53 | 8/- |
| D1 | " | LNER NE 50T N163535 | Brown | FPW | EMC | 1d | 32050 | 10.51 9M | 4/49 | 6/6 | 1/53 | 8/- |

— High Capacity Wagons have type 11a bases with type DBb bogie frames. Chassis is brown.

| D1 | High Cap. Wagon | LNER NE 50T N163535 | Brown | FPW | EMC | 1d | 32050 | 10.51 9M | 4/49 | 6/6 | 1/53 | 8/- |

— Usual brown base, but inside is not painted black.

POSTWAR ROLLING STOCK – TANK WAGONS

CAT. NO.	DESCRIPTION	COMPANY & WAGON NO.	BODY COLOUR	WHEELS	CPLGS.	BOX TYPE	BOX NO.	BOX CODE	FIRST DATE	FIRST PRICE	LAST DATE	LAST PRICE
D1	Oil Tank Wagon	'Royal Daylight'	Red	EPW	EMC	1b	—		9/48	6/-	1/53	5/6
D1	Oil Tank Wagon	'Royal Daylight'	Red	EPW	EMC	1c	DR381	11.49	9/48	6/-	1/53	5/6
D1	Oil Tank Wagon	'Royal Daylight'	Red	FPW	EMC	1d	32070	4.51	9/48	6/-	1/53	5/6

— No 'Esso' or 'Paraffin' on sides of tank.

D1	Petrol Tank Wagon	'Esso'	Buff	EPW	EMC	1b	—	3.48	9/48	6/-	1/53	5/6
D1	Petrol Tank Wagon	'Esso'	Buff	EPW	EMC	1c	DR383	11.49	9/48	6/-	1/53	5/6
D1	Petrol Tank Wagon	'Esso'	Buff	FPW	EMC	1d	32081	4.51	9/48	6/-	1/53	5/6

— Has light orange band, with the word 'Esso' in blue on tank sides.

D1	Petrol Tank Wagon	'Power Ethyl'	Green	EPW	EMC	1b	—		9/48	6/-	1/53	5/6
D1	Petrol Tank Wagon	'Power Ethyl'	Green	EPW	EMC	1c	DR383		9/48	6/-	1/53	5/6
D1	Petrol Tank Wagon	'Power Ethyl'	Green	FPW	EMC	1d	32080	4.51 20M	9/48	6/-	1/53	5/6
D1	Petrol Tank Wagon	'Power Ethyl'	Green	FPW	EMC	1d	32080	4/54	9/48	6/-	1/53	5/6

— Box has no date code on side.

| D1 | Petrol Tank Wagon | 'Power Ethyl' | Green | FPW | EMC | 2a | 32080 | 8/54 | 9/48 | 6/- | 1/53 | 5/6 |

— Box says 'Power Ethyl', whereas later boxes say 'Power'.

— Has the word 'Power' in silver, and the word 'Ethyl' in red on tank sides. Earlier types have a bright 'Power' and later types have a dull 'Power'.

— There is no confirmation that this item continued into 1954, only that boxes continued with the word 'Ethyl'.

— Tank wagons have type 1b bases.

— Unlike prewar tank wagons, the cap on top of each wagon is black, whereas the prewar tanks had the caps in the same colour as the tank.

CAT. NO.	DESCRIPTION	WAGON NO.	BODY COLOUR	ROOF COLOUR	BASE TYPE	WHEEL TYPE	CPLGS.	BOX TYPE NO.	BOX NO.	BOX CODE	MECC. MAG. PRICE	MECC. MAG. DATE	LAST DATE	LAST PRICE
4300	Blue Spot Fish Van	12T E87231	White	Grey	24	SO	EPC	3a	36300	12/61	6/9	11/61	12/64	5/11
	— Export No. 4450													
4300	Blue Spot Fish Van	12T E87231	Cream	Grey	24	SO	EPC	3a	36300	12/61	6/9	11/61	12/64	5/11
	— Export No. 4450													
32035	Fish Van	10T E168975	Brown	Grey	3a	FPW	FMC	2a	32035	5/56	5/-	(5/56)	12/58	5/-
D1	Fish Van	10T E168975	Brown	Grey	3a	FPW	LMC	2a	32035	1/55	5/3	(3/53)	4/56	5/-
D1	Fish Van	10T E168975	Brown	Grey	1b	FPW	LMC	1e	32035	10M 5.53	5/3	(3/53)	4/56	5/-
D1	Fish Van	10T E168975	Brown	Grey	1b	FPW	EMC	1d	32035	—	5/3	(3/53)	4/56	5/-
4301	Banana Van	12T B881967	Brown	Grey	6	SP	EPC	3b	(36301)	7/62	7/-	4/62	12/64	4/11
	— Export No. 4451													
4301	Banana Van	12T B881967	Brown	Grey	4b	SP	EPC	3b	(36301)	7/62	—	(5/61)	—	—
4305	Passenger Fruit Van	10T W2910	Maroon	Grey	9	SO	EPC	3a	36305	8/60	7/-	—	12/64	5/11
	— Export No. 4455													
4305	Passenger Fruit Van	10T W2910	Maroon	Grey	9	SO	EMC	3a	36305	8/60	6/8	11/60	10/60	6/8
4305	Passenger Fruit Van	10T W2910	Maroon	Black	9	SO	FMC	3a	36305	8/60	6/8	11/60	10/60	6/8
4310	Goods Brake Van M.R.	20T M730973	Brown	Grey	3d	SO	NPC	3a	(36310)	—	As per Hornby Book of Trains			
	— Export No. 4460													
4310	Goods Brake Van M.R.	20T M73093	Brown	Grey	3d	SO	EPC	3a	(36310)	—	6/6	(1/62)	12/64	4/11
4310	Goods Brake Van M.R.	20T M730973	Brown	Grey	3d	SO	EPC	3a	(36310)	—	With grey internal partitions			
4310	Goods Brake Van M.R.	20T M730012	Grey	Grey	3d	SO	EPC	3a	(36310)	—	6/6	(5/61)	12/61	6/6
4310	Goods Brake Van M.R.	20T M730012	Grey	Grey	3c	SO	EPC	3a	(36310)	—	6/6	(5/61)	12/61	6/6
4310	Goods Brake Van M.R.	20T M730012	Grey	Grey	3d	SO	FMC	3a	(36310)	—	5/11	(2/59)	10/60	5/11
4310	Goods Brake Van M.R.	20T M730012	Grey	Grey	3c	SO	FMC	3a	(36310)	—	5/11	(2/59)	10/60	5/11
32044	Goods Brake Van M.R.	20T M730012	Grey	Grey	3c	SO	FMC	2b	32044	—	6/-	(7/58)	12/58	6/-
SD6	Goods Brake Van M.R.	20T M730973	Grey	Grey	3c	SO	FMC	2b	32044	—	6/-	10/58	12/58	6/-
	— Export No. 4460													
32045	Goods Brake Van	20T M730026	Grey	Grey	3c	FPW	FMC	2a	32045	5/53	7/-	(5/56)	5/58	7/-
32045	Goods Brake Van	20T M730026	Grey	Grey	3b	FPW	FMC	2a	32045	5/53	7/-	(5/56)	5/58	7/-
D1	Goods Brake Van	20T M730026	Grey	Grey	1d	FPW	LMC	2a	32045	5/53	6/9	(7/54)	4/56	7/-
D1	Goods Brake Van	20T M730026	Grey	Grey	1d	FPW	LMC	1e	32045	14M 6.53	—	5/53	6/54	6/9
	Roof has no rain gutters or chimney													
D1	Goods Brake Van	20T M730026	Grey	Grey	1d	FPW	EMC	1d	32045	—	7/-	(3/53)	6/54	6/9
	Roof has no rain gutters or chimney													
4311	Goods Brake Van	20T B950350	Brown	Grey	3d	SO	NPC	3a	32043	7/62	—	—	—	—
	— Export No. 4461													
4311	Goods Brake Van	20T B950350	Brown	Grey	3d	SO	EPC	3a	32043	7/62	6/9	(5/61)	12/64	5/11
4311	Goods Brake Van	20T B950350	Brown	Grey	3d	SO	FMC	2d	32043	12/59	5/11	(2/59)	10/60	5/11
SD6	Goods Brake Van	20T B950350	Brown	Grey	3c	SO	FMC	2d	32043	12/59	6/-	1/59	10/60	5/11
32046	Goods Brake Van	20T E178717	Brown	Grey	3b	FPW	FMC	2a	32046	12/55	7/-	(5/56)	5/58	7/-
32046	Goods Brake Van	20T E178717	Brown	Grey	3b	FPW	LMC	2a	32046	12/55	7/-	(5/56)	5/58	7/-
D1	Goods Brake Van	20T E178717	Brown	Grey	3b	FPW	EMC	2a	32046	12/55	6/9	(10/53)	4/56	7/-
D1	Goods Brake Van	20T E178717	Brown	Grey	1d	FPW	LMC	1f	32046	3/55	6/9	(10/53)	4/56	7/-
D1	Goods Brake Van	20T E178717	Brown	Grey	1d	FPW	EMC	1f	32046	3/55	7/-	(3/53)	9/53	6/9
D1	Goods Brake Van	20T E178717	White	Grey	1d	FPW	EMC	1f	32046	—	—	—	6/54	6/9
	Roof has no rain gutters or chimney													
4312	Goods Brake Van	20T W35247	Brown	Grey	3d	SO	NPC	3a	(36312)	7/62	Although illustrated, the 'Brown' plastic Brake Van was not issued.			
	— Export No. 4462													
4312	Goods Brake Van	20T W56421	Grey	Grey	3d	SO	EPC	3a	(36312)	7/62	6/6	(1/62)	12/64	4/11
	(Illustrated as Brown)													
4312	Goods Brake Van	20T W56421	Grey	Grey	3d	SO	EPC	3a	(36312)	7/62	6/6	(5/61)	10/60	5/11
	(Illustrated as Grey)													
4312	Goods Brake Van	20T W56421	Grey	Grey	3b	SO	FMC	3a	(36312)	7/62	5/11	(2/59)	10/60	5/11
4312	Goods Brake Van	20T W56421	Grey	Grey	3b	SO	FMC	3a	(36312)	7/62	5/11	(2/59)	10/60	5/11
32048	Goods Brake Van	20T W56421	Grey	Grey	3d	SO	FMC	2b	32048	3/58	6/-	(7/58)	12/58	6/-
SD6	Goods Brake Van	20T W56421	Grey	Grey	3d	SO	FMC	2b	32048	3/58	6/-	9/58	12/58	6/-
32047	Goods Brake Van	14T W68796	Grey	Grey	3b	FPW	FMC	2a	32047	4/56	7/-	(5/56)	5/58	7/-
D1	Goods Brake Van	14T W68796	Grey	Grey	3b	FPW	LMC	2a	32047	4/56	7/-	4/56	8/57	7/-
32049	Caboose - C.P.R.	437270	Black	Black	3b	FPW	LMC	1e	32049	—	$1.55	(2/58)	2/58	$1.55
32049	Caboose - C.P.R.	437270	Black	Black	3b	SO	LMC	1e	32049	—	$1.55	(2/58)	2/58	$1.55

CAT. NO.	DESCRIPTION	WAGON NO.	BODY COLOUR	ROOF COLOUR	BASE TYPE	WHEEL TYPE	CPLGS.	BOX TYPE NO.	BOX NO.	BOX CODE	MECC. MAG.	MECC. PRICE	LAST DATE	LAST PRICE
D1	Caboose - C.P.R.	437270	Black	Black	1d	FPW	LMC	1e	32049	—	(2/58	$1.55)		
4313	Gunpowder Van	11T B887002	Brown	Grey	6	SO	EPC	3a	(36313)	6/62	4/62	7/-	12/64	4/11
	— Export No. 4463													
4315	Horse Box (BR)	E96435	Maroon	Grey	9	SO	EPC	3a	36315	7/60	(5/61	10/6)	12/64	8/11
	— Export No. 4465													
4315	Horse Box (BR)	E96435	Maroon	Grey	9	SO	FMC	3a	36315	7/60	3/60	9/6	10/60	9/6
4316	Horse Box (SR)	S96412	Green	Grey	9	SO	EPC	3a	36316	6/60	(5/61	10/6)	12/64	8/11
	— Export No. 4466													
4316	Horse Box (SR)	S96412	Green	Grey	9	SO	FMC	3a	36316	6/60	9/60	9/6	10/60	9/6
32060	Horse Box	E2337	Red	Grey	3a	FPW	FMC	2a	32060		(5/56	5/-)	8/58	5/-
D1	Horse Box	E2337	Red	Grey	3a	FPW	LMC	2a	32060		(3/53	5/3)	4/56	5/-
D1	Horse Box	E2337	Red	Grey	1b	FPW	LMC	2a	32060		(3/53	5/3)	4/56	5/-
D1	Horse Box	E2337	Red	Grey	1b	FPW	EMC	1e	32060	1OM 5.53	(3/53	5/3)	4/56	5/-
D1	Horse Box	E2337	Red	Grey	1b	FPW	EMC	1d	32060		(3/53	5/3)	4/56	5/-
	Windows are at opposite ends of van, as opposed to normal windows both at same end of van.													
4318	Packing Van	12T DE545523	Red	Grey	6	SP	EPC	3b	(36318)	7/62	5/62	5/7	12/64	3/11
	— Export No. 4468													
4318	Packing Van	12T DE545523	Red	Grey	4b	SP	FMC	3b	(36318)	7/62	—			
4320	Refrigerator Van	6T W59850	White	Grey	6	SP	EPC	3b	(36320)	7/62	(5/61	5/6)	12/64	4/11
	— Export No. 4470													
4320	Refrigerator Van	6T W59850	Cream	Grey	4b	SP	EPC	3a	(36320)		—			
4320	Refrigerator Van	6T W59850	White	Grey	4b	SP	EPC	3a	(36320)		—			
4320	Refrigerator Van	6T W59850	Cream	Grey	4b	SP	FMC	3a	(36320)		(2/59	5/3)	10/60	5/3
4320	Refrigerator Van	6T W59850	White	Grey	4b	SP	FMC	3a	(36320)		(2/59	5/3)	10/60	5/3
32062	Refrigerator Van	6T W59850	Cream	Grey	4b	SP	FMC	2b	32062	5/58	(6/58	5/5)	12/58	5/5
SD6	Refrigerator Van	6T W59850	Cream	Grey	4b	SP	FMC	2b	32062	5/58	7/58	5/5	12/58	5/5
32065	Meat Van	10T S50494	White	Grey	3a	FPW	FMC	2a	32065	12/56	(5/56	5/-)	12/58	5/-
D1	Meat Van	10T S50494	White	Grey	3a	FPW	LMC	2a	32065	3/54	(3/53	5/3)	4/56	5/-
D1	Meat Van	10T S50494	White	Grey	1b	FPW	LMC	2a	32065		(3/53	5/3)	4/56	5/-
D1	Meat Van	10T S50494	White	Grey	1b	FPW	EMC	1e	32065		(3/53	5/3)	4/56	5/-
D1	Meat Van	10T S50494	White	Grey	1b	FPW	EMC	1d	32065		(3/53	5/3)	4/56	5/-
4323	Utility Van - S.R.	S2380S	Green	Grey	19	SO	EPC	3a	36323	12/61	12/61	12/8	12/64	11/6
	— Export No. 4473													
4325	Ventilated Van	12T B757051	Brown	White	6	SP	EPC	3a	(36625)	/62	(5/61	5/6)	12/64	3/11
	— Long Wheelbase / Export No. 4475													
4325	Ventilated Van	12T B757051	Brown	White	4b	SP	EPC	3a	(36625)	/62	—			
4325	Ventilated Van	12T B757051	Brown	White	2b	SP	EPC	3a	(36625)	/62	—			
4325	Ventilated Van	12T B757051	Brown	White	4b	SP	FMC	2b	32401	6/58	(2/59	5/3)	10/60	4/8
4325	Ventilated Van	12T B757051	Brown	White	2b	SP	FMC	2b	32401	6/58	(2/59	5/3)	10/60	4/8
32041	Ventilated Van	12T B757051	Brown	White	2b	SP	FMC	2b	32041	6/58	(6/58	4/9)	12/58	4/9
SD6	Ventilated Van	12T B757051	Brown	White	2b	SP	FMC	2b	23401	6/58	8/58	4/9	12/58	4/9
32040	Goods Van	12T B755414	Brown	Grey	3a	FPW	FMC	2a	32040		(8/57	5/-)	12/58	5/-
D1	Goods Van	12T B755414	Brown	Grey	3a	FPW	LMC	2a	32040		(3/53	5/3)	4/56	5/-
D1	Goods Van	12T B755414	Brown	Grey	3a	FPW	LMC	2a	32040		(3/53	5/3)	4/56	5/-
D1	Goods Van	12T B755414	Brown	Grey	1b	FPW	EMC	1e	32040	12.52-20M	(3/53	5/3)	4/56	5/-
D1	Goods Van	12T B755414	Brown	Grey	1b	FPW	EMC	1d	32040	6.52	(3/53	5/3)	4/56	5/-
4326	Ventilated Van	10T W29798	Brown	Grey	—	—	—	No box with this number exists		B. R. Sticker	(4/59	5/3)	12/59	5/3
32058	Ventilated Van	10T W29798	Brown	Grey	9	SP	FMC	2a	32058	11/56	(7/58	7/6)	12/58	7/6
32058	Ventilated Van	10T W29798	Brown	Grey	9	FPW	FMC	2a	32058	11/56	(6/56	6/9)	6/58	7/6
D1	Ventilated Van	10T W29798	Brown	Grey	9	FPW	FMC	2a	32058	11/56	11/56	6/9	8/57	7/6
4401	TPO Mail Van	W807	Maroon	Grey	(SB)	SO/EPW	EPC	6b	36401	6/61	(5/61	1/3/6)	12/64	1/4/9
4401	TPO Mail Van	*W807	Maroon	Grey	(SB)	SO/EPW	FMC	5a	32098		(	1/3/-)	10/60	1/3/-
4401	TPO Mail Van	W807	Maroon	Grey	(SB)	SO/EPW	FMC	5a	32098		(9/59	1/3/-)	10/60	1/3/-
32098	TPO Mail Van	*W807	Maroon	Grey	(SB)	FPW	FMC	5a	32098		(7/58	1/3/6)	12/58	1/3/6
32098	TPO Mail Van	W807	Maroon	Grey	(SB)	FPW	FMC	5a	32098		(4/57	1/3/-)	6/58	1/3/6
D1	TPO Mail Van	W807	Maroon	Grey	(SB)	FPW	FMC	5a	32098		(8/57	1/3/-)	8/57	1/3/-

*These two items are identical, except for the reference numbers.

— As above, but corridor connection on wrong side of coach.

CAT. NO.	DESCRIPTION	WAGON NO.	BODY COLOUR	ROOF COLOUR	BASE TYPE	WHEEL TYPE	CPLGS.	BOX TYPE	BOX NO.	BOX CODE	MECC. MAG.	MECC. PRICE	MECC. LAST DATE	LAST PRICE
4605	Bogie Well Wagon	4OT B901006	Grey	—	15(PB)	SO	NPC	3a	36605	—	—	7/6	12/64	7/11
4605	Bogie Well Wagon	4OT B901006	Grey	—	15(PB)	SO	EPC	3a	36605	—	(5/61	7/6	12/64	7/11
4605	Bogie Well Wagon	4OT B901006	Grey	—	15(DB)	SO	EPC	3a	36605	—	—	—	—	—
4605	Bogie Well Wagon	4OT B901006	Grey	—	15(PB)	SO	FMC	3a	36605	—	(2/59	7/6	10/60	7/6
4605	Bogie Well Wagon	4OT B901006	Grey	—	15(DB)	SO	FMC	3a	36605	—	—	—	—	—
32053	Bogie Well Wagon	4OT B901006	Grey	—	15(PB)	FPW	FMC	2a	32053	10/55	(10/55	7/9	12/58	7/9
32053	Bogie Well Wagon	4OT B901006	Grey	—	15(DB)	FPW	FMC	2a	32053	10/55	(10/55	7/9	12/58	7/9
32053	Bogie Well Wagon	4OT B901006	Grey	—	15(DB)	FPW	LMC	2a	32053	10/55	11/55	7/6	12/58	7/9
D1	Bogie Well Wagon	4OT B901006	Grey	—	15(DB)	FPW	LMC	2a	32053	10/55	11/55	7/6	12/58	7/9
32050	High Capacity Wagon 'Empty to Fletton'	5OT E163535	Brown/Black Base	—	11d	SO	FMC	2a	32050	3/58	(7/58	7/9	12/58	7/9
32050	High Capacity Wagon	5OT E163535	Brown/Black Base	—	11d	FPW	FMC	2a	32050	3/57	7/57	7/9	6/58	7/9
32050	High Capacity Wagon	5OT E163535	Brown/Black Base	—	11d	FPW	LMC	2a	32050	3/55	7/57	7/9	6/58	7/9
D1	High Capacity Wagon	5OT E163535	Brown/Black Base	—	11c	FPW	LMC	2a	32050	3/55	7/54	7/6	4/56	7/6
D1	High Capacity Wagon	5OT E163535	Brown/Black Base	—	11b	FPW	LMC	2a	32050	3/55	7/54	7/6	4/56	7/6
D1	High Capacity Wagon	5OT E163535	Brown/Black Base	—	11b	FPW	EMC	1f	32050	9/53	5/53	—	4/56	7/6
D1	High Capacity Wagon	5OT E163535	Brown/Black Base	—	11b	FPW	EMC	1e	32050	12.52	(3/53	8/-	6/54	7/6

— N.B. All have DBb bogie side frames.

CAT. NO.	DESCRIPTION	WAGON NO.	BODY COLOUR	ROOF COLOUR	BASE TYPE	WHEEL TYPE	CPLGS.	BOX TYPE	BOX NO.	BOX CODE	MECC. MAG.	MECC. PRICE	MECC. LAST DATE	LAST PRICE
4610	Bogie Bolster Wagon	3OT M720550	Grey/Black	Grey/Black	14	SO(PB)	EPC	3a	32051	9/61	(5/61	8/6	12/64	6/11
4610	Bogie Bolster Wagon	3OT M720550	Grey/Black	Grey/Black	14	SO(DB)	EPC	3a	32051	9/61	(5/61	8/6	12/64	6/11
4610	Bogie Bolster Wagon	3OT M720550	Grey/Black	Grey/Black	14	SO(PB)	FMC	2c	32051	—	(2/59	8/3	10/60	8/3
4610	Bogie Bolster Wagon	3OT M720550	Grey/Black	Grey/Black	14	SO(DB)	FMC	2c	32051	—	(2/59	8/3	10/60	8/6
32051	Bogie Bolster Wagon	3OT M720550	Grey/Black	Grey/Black	14	FPW(PB)	FMC	2a	32051	8/57	(7/58	8/6	12/58	8/6
32051	Bogie Bolster Wagon	3OT M720550	Grey/Black	Grey/Black	14	FPW(DB)	FMC	2a	32051	3/58	(7/58	8/6	12/58	8/6
32051	Bogie Bolster Wagon	3OT M720550	Grey/Black	Grey/Black	14	FPW(DB)	LMC	2a	32051	7/56	(5/56	7/9	6/58	8/6
D1	Bogie Bolster Wagon	3OT M720550	Grey/Black	Grey/Black	14	FPW(DB)	EMC	1f	32051	1/54	(4/53	7/6	4/56	7/9
D1	Bogie Bolster Wagon	3OT M720550	Grey/Black	Grey/Black	14	FPW(DB)	EMC	1e	32051	7/53	(4/53	7/6	4/56	7/9
4612	Bogie Wagon with Timber Load	—	—	—	—	—	—	—	—	—	(1/63	—	11/63	—

Although listed on price lists and in dealer's literature, this item was never issued.

CAT. NO.	DESCRIPTION	WAGON NO.	BODY COLOUR	ROOF COLOUR	BASE TYPE	WHEEL TYPE	CPLGS.	BOX TYPE	BOX NO.	BOX CODE	MECC. MAG.	MECC. PRICE	MECC. LAST DATE	LAST PRICE
4615	Double Bolster, with load	21T B920022	Grey/Black	Grey/Black	13	SP	EPC	3a	(36615)	—	(5/61	7/-	12/64	6/11
4615	Double Bolster — Export No.4815	21T B920022	Grey/Black	Grey/Black	13	SP	FMC	2a	32052	1/62	1/60	6/8	10/60	6/8

— box has red and white label, and no.4615.

CAT. NO.	DESCRIPTION	WAGON NO.	BODY COLOUR	ROOF COLOUR	BASE TYPE	WHEEL TYPE	CPLGS.	BOX TYPE	BOX NO.	BOX CODE	MECC. MAG.	MECC. PRICE	MECC. LAST DATE	LAST PRICE
32052	Double Bolster (No load).	21T B920022	Grey/Black	Grey/Black	13	SP	FMC	2a	32052	6/6	7/58	6/6	12/58	6/6
4620	Breakdown Crane	DE 961665 & No. 133	Red Gloss	Grey	13	FPW	FMC	2a	32052	10/56	(6/56	6/3	6/58	6/6
4620	Breakdown Crane — Export No.4820	DE 961665 & No. 133	Red Gloss	Grey	13	FPW	FMC	2a	32052	10/56	12/56	6/3	8/58	6/6
4620	Breakdown Crane	DE 961665 & No. 133	Red Matt	Grey	Spec.	SO	NPC	17	36620	—	—	—	—	—
4620	Breakdown Crane	DE 961665 & No. 133	Red Matt	Grey	Spec.	SO	EPC	17	36620	—	(5/61	1/14/-	12/64	1/14/-
4620	Breakdown Crane	DE 961665 & No. 133	Red	Grey	Spec.	SO	EPC	16	36620	—	(2/59	1/12/6	10/60	1/12/6
4620	Breakdown Crane	DE 961665 & No. 133	Red	Grey	Spec.	SO	FMC	16	36620	—	(2/59	1/12/6	10/60	1/12/6
4625	Bulk Grain Wagon	2OT B885040	Grey	Grey	10	SP	EPC	3a	(36625)	4/62	(5/61	7/-	12/64	5/11
4625	Bulk Grain Wagon — Export No.4825	2OT B885040	Grey	Grey	10	SP	FMC	3a	(36625)	4/62	(2/59	6/8	10/60	6/8
32067	Bulk Grain Wagon	2OT B885040	Grey	Grey	10	SP	FMC	2b	32067	2/59	1/58	6/9	12/58	6/9
SD6	Bulk Grain Wagon	2OT B885040	Grey	Grey	10	SP	FMC	2b	32067	2/59	2/58	6/9	12/58	6/9
4626	Presflo Bulk Cement — Export No.4826	—	Brown	Brown	12	SO	EPC	3b	36626	5/62	11/61	7/1	12/64	5/11
4627	I.C.I. Bulk Salt — Export No.4827	—	Blue	Blue	12	SO	EPC	3b	36627	5/62	11/61	7/1	12/64	5/11
4630	Cattle Wagon — Export No.4830	8T B893344	Brown	Grey	10	SP	EPC	3a	(36630)	2/61	(5/61	6/-	12/64	5/11
4630	Cattle Wagon	8T B893344	Grey	Grey	10	SP	FMC	3a	(36630)	2/61	(2/59	5/3	10/60	5/3
32021	Cattle Wagon	8T B893344	Grey	Grey	10	SP	FMC	2b	32021	3/58	5/58	5/5	12/58	5/5
SD6	Cattle Wagon	8T B893344	Grey	Grey	10	SP	FMC	2b	32021	3/58	4/58	5/5	12/58	5/5
32020	Cattle Truck	8T B893344	Brown	Grey	3a	FPW	FMC	2a	32020	4/57	5/56	5/-	9/58	5/-
D1	Cattle Truck	8T B893344	Brown	Grey	3a	FPW	LMC	2a	32020	4/57	3/53	5/3	4/56	5/-
D1	Cattle Truck	8T B893344	Brown	Grey	1b	FPW	LMC	1f	32020	—	3/53	5/3	4/56	5/-

CAT. NO.	DESCRIPTION	WAGON NO.	BODY COLOUR	ROOF COLOUR	BASE TYPE	WHEEL TYPE	CPLGS.	BOX TYPE	BOX NO.	BOX CODE	MECC. MAG.	MECC. PRICE	LAST DATE	LAST PRICE
D1	Cattle Truck	8T B893344	Brown	Grey	1b	FPW	EMC	1e	32020		(3/53	5/3)	4/56	5/-
D1	Cattle Truck	8T B893344	Brown	Grey	1b	FPW	EMC	1d	32020		5/53	—	4/56	5/-
4635	Coal Wagon	13T B477015	Grey	—	7	SP	EPC	3a	(36635)	2/61	(5/61	6/-)	12/64	5/11
4635	Coal Wagon	13T B477015	Grey	—	4a	SP	EPC	3a	(36635)		—	—	—	—
4635	Coal Wagon	13T B477015	Grey	—	2a	SP	EPC	3a	(36635)		—	—	—	—
4635	Coal Wagon	13T B477015	Grey	—	4a	SP	FMC	3a	(36635)		(2/59	5/3)	10/60	5/3
4635	Coal Wagon	13T B477015	Grey	—	2a	SP	FMC	3a	(36635)		(2/59	5/3)	10/60	5/3
32026	Coal Wagon	13T B477015	Grey	—	2a	SP	FMC	2b	32026	11/58	(12/58	5/6)	12/58	5/6
SD6	Coal Wagon	13T B477015	Grey	—	2a	SP	FMC	2b	32026	11/58	12/58	5/6		
32025	Coal Wagon	12T E404844	Grey	—	3a	FPW	FMC	2a	32025	4/54	(5/56	5/3)	8/58	5/6
32025	Coal Wagon	12T E404844	Grey	—	3a	FPW	LMC	2a	32025		(5/56	5/3)	8/58	5/6
D1	Coal Wagon	12T E404844	Grey	—	1b	FPW	LMC	1f	32025		(3/53	5/6)	4/56	5/3
D1	Coal Wagon	12T E404844	Grey	—	1b	FPW	EMC	1e	32025	3.53	(3/53	5/6)	4/56	5/3
D1	Coal Wagon	12T E404844	Grey	—	1b	FPW	EMC	1d	32025		(3/53	5/6)	4/56	5/3
32030	High Sided Coal Wagon	12T M608344	Grey	—	3a	FPW	FMC	2a	32030	2/56	(5/56	5/6)	12/58	5/9
32030	High Sided Coal Wagon	12T M608344	Grey	—	3a	FPW	LMC	2a	32030		(5/56	5/6)	12/58	5/9
D2	High Sided Coal Wagon	12T M608344	Grey	—	1b	FPW	LMC	1f	32030	1/54	(3/53	5/9)	4/56	5/6
D2	High Sided Coal Wagon	12T M608344	Grey	—	1b	FPW	EMC	1e	32030	9/53	5/53	—	4/56	5/6
D2	High Sided Coal Wagon	12T M608344	Grey	—	1b	FPW	EMC	1d	32030	12/52	5/53	—	4/56	5/6
4640	Goods Wagon —Steel Type	12T B486865	Brown	—	6	SP	EPC	3a	36640	6/62	(5/61	4/4)	12/64	3/11
4640	Goods Wagon	12T B486865	Brown	—	4a	SP	EPC	3a	36640		—	—	—	—
4640	Goods Wagon	12T B486865	Brown	—	2a	SP	EPC	3a	36640		—	—	—	—
4640	Goods Wagon	12T B486865	Brown	—	4a	SP	FMC	3a	36640		(2/59	4/4)	10/60	4/4
4640	Goods Wagon	12T B486865	Brown	—	2a	SP	FMC	3a	36640		(2/59	4/4)	10/60	4/4
32071	Goods Wagon	12T B486865	Brown	—	2a	SP	FMC	2b	32071	5/58	(5/58	4/6)	12/58	4/6
SD6	Goods Wagon	12T B486865	Brown	—	2a	SP	FMC	2b	32071	5/58	5/58	4/6	12/58	4/6
4644	Hopper Wagon	21T B414029	Grey	—	20	SO	NPC	3c	34644	—	10/63	6/6	12/64	6/11
4645	Low Sided Wagon — Export No. 4845	13T B459325	Brown/Black		3e	SP	EPC	3b	(36645)	1/61	(5/61	5/-)	12/64	4/11
4645	Low Sided Wagon	13T B459325	Brown/Black		3e	SP	FMC	3b	(36645)		(2/59	4/4)	10/60	4/4
32085	Low Sided Wagon	13T B459325	Brown/Black		3e	SP	FMC	2c	32085	2/59	(7/58	4/6)	12/58	4/6
32085	Low Sided Wagon	13T B459325	Brown/Black		3e	FPW	FMC	2a	32085	8/56	(5/56	4/3)	6/58	4/6
D1	Low Sided Wagon	13T B459325	Brown/Black		3e	FPW	LMC	2a	32085		(4/53	4/-)	4/56	4/3
D1	Low Sided Wagon	13T B459325	Brown/Black		3e	FPW	EMC	2a	32085		4/54		4/56	4/3
4646	Low Sided Wagon — with Cable Drums	M486 — 'Aluminium Cables' in plastic.	Grey/Black		3f	SP	EPC	3a	(36646)	—	(11/61	6/6)	12/64	5/11
4646	— Export No. 4846	M486 — 'Liverpool Cables' in wood.	Grey/Black		3f	SP	EPC	3a	(36646)	—	(5/61	6/6)	6/62	6/6
4646	Low Sided Wagon	M486	Grey/Black		3f	SP	FMC	3a	(36646)	—	(2/59	5/11)	10/60	5/11
32086	Low Sided Wagon	M486	Grey/Black		3f	SP	FMC	2c	32086		(7/58	6/-)	12/58	6/-
32086	Low Sided Wagon	M486	Grey/Black		3f	FPW	FMC	2a	32086		(5/56	5/9)	6/58	6/-
32086	Low Sided Wagon	M486	Grey/Black		3f	FPW	LMC	2a	32086		(5/56	5/9)	6/58	6/-
D1	Low Sided Wagon	M486	Grey/Black		3f	FPW	LMC	2a	32086	4/54	(4/53	4/11)	4/56	5/9
D1	Low Sided Wagon	M486	Grey/Black		3f	FPW	EMC	2a	32086	6/53	4/54	—	4/56	5/9
4647	Low Sided Wagon — with Furniture Container	13T B459325	Brown/Black		3e	SP	EPC	3a	(36647)	3/61	(5/61	6/6)	12/64	5/11
4647	— Export No. 4847	13T B459325	Brown/Black		3e	SP	FMC	3a	(36647)	4/59	(2/59	5/11)	10/60	5/11
32087	Low Sided Wagon	13T B459325	Brown/Black		3e	SP	FMC	2c	32087		(7/58	6/-)	12/58	6/-
32087	Low Sided Wagon	13T B459325	Brown/Black		3e	FPW	FMC	2a	32087	4/56	(5/56	5/9)	6/58	6/-
D1	Low Sided Wagon	13T B459325	Brown/Black		3e	FPW	LMC	2a	32087	4/56	5/56	5/9	12/56	5/9
4648	Low Sided Wagon — with Meat Container	13T B459325	Brown/Black		3e	SP	EPC	3a	(36648)		(5/61	6/6)	12/64	5/11
4648	— Export No. 4848	13T B459325	Brown/Black		3e	SP	FMC	3a	(36648)		(2/59	5/11)	10/60	5/11
32088	Low Sided Wagon	13T B459325	Brown/Black		3e	SP	FMC	2c	32088	2/59	(7/58	6/-)	12/58	6/-
32088	Low Sided Wagon	13T B459325	Brown/Black		3e	FPW	FMC	2a	32088	5/56	(5/56	5/9)	6/58	6/-
D1	Low Sided Wagon	13T B459325	Brown/Black		3e	FPW	LMC	2a	32088	—	6/56	5/9	12/56	5/9
4649	Low Sided Wagon — with Dublo Dinky Tractor	13T B459325	Brown/Black		3e	SP	EPC	3b	36649	—	(5/61	6/6)	12/64	4/11
4649	— Export No. 4849	13T B459325	Brown/Black		3e	SP	FMC	3b	36649	—	4/59	—	10/60	5/10
4652	Machine Wagon — 'Lowmac' —Export No. 4852	25T B904631	Brown	—	23	SO	EPC	3b	36652	—	11/61	7/1	12/64	4/11

The weights beneath wagon come in both

Cat. No.	Description	Wagon No.	Colour					No.			
4654	Rail Cleaning Wagon	—	Black	21	SP	NPC	3a	(36654)	—	12/64 —	12/64 5/11
4655	Mineral Wagon (Plastic)	16T B54884	Grey	7	SO	EPC	3a	(36655)	9/62	5/61 6/-	12/64 4/11
4655	Mineral Wagon	16T B54884	Grey	4a	SO	EPC	3a	(36655)	9/58	7/61 6/-	12/61 6/-
4655	Mineral Wagon	16T B54884	Grey	4a	SO	FMC	3a	(36655)	9/58	2/59 5/3	10/60 5/3
32057	Mineral Wagon	16T B54884	Grey	4a	SO	FMC	2b	32057	9/58	7/58 5/6	12/58 5/6
SD6	Mineral Wagon	16T B54884	Grey	4a	SO	FMC	2b	32057	9/58	10/58 5/6	12/58 5/6
32056	Mineral Wagon (Metal)	16T B54884	Grey/Black	3a	FPW	FMC	2a	32056	1/56	5/56 5/-	9/58 5/6
32056	Mineral Wagon	16T B54884	Grey/Black	3a	FPW	LMC	2a	32056	1/56	5/56 5/-	9/58 5/6
D2	Mineral Wagon	16T B54884	Grey/Black	3a	FPW	LMC	2a	32056	6/53	9/53 4/11	4/56 5/-
D2	Mineral Wagon	16T B54884	Grey/Black	1b	FPW	LMC	1f	32056	6/53	9/53 4/11	4/56 5/-
D2	Mineral Wagon	16T B54884	Grey/Black	1b	FPW	EMC	1e	32056	—	8/53 4/11	4/56 5/-
D2	Mineral Wagon	16T B54884	Grey/Black	1b	FPW	EMC	1e	32056	—	8/53 4/11	4/56 5/-
4656	Mineral Wagon (Plastic)	16T B550200	Brown	7	SO	EPC	3b	36656	—	8/62 5/9	12/64 4/11
4657	'United Dairies' Milk Tank Wagon — Export No. 4857		White	18	SO	EPC	3b	(36657)	—	8/62 11/-	12/64 9/11
4657	'United Dairies' Milk Tank Wagon		Off-White (Tank supports as above)	18	SO	EPC	3b	(36657)	—	(12/61) 11/-	12/64 9/11
4657	'United Dairies' Milk Tank Wagon		Off-White (Tank supports all at high level)	18	SO	EPC	3b	(36657)	—	—	—
4657	'United Dairies' Milk Tank Wagon		Off-White (Tank supports all at low level)	18	SO	EPC	3b	(36657)	—	—	—
4657	'United Dairies' Milk Tank Wagon		Cream (Tank supports all at high level)	18	SO	EPC	3b	(36657)	—	—	—
4657	'United Dairies' Milk Tank Wagon		Cream (Tank supports all at high level)	18	SO	EPC	3b	(36657)	—	—	—
4658	Prestwin Silo Wagon — Export No. 4858	20T B873000	Brown (Tank supports both high and low)	6	SO	EPC	3b	(36658)	6/62	8/62 8/6	12/64 6/11
4660	U.G.B. Sand Wagon 'United Glass Limited'		Yellow	7	SP	NPC	3a	(36660)	—	—	—
4660	U.G.B. Sand Wagon		Yellow	7	SP	EPC	3a	(36660)	—	1/62 4/9	12/64 3/11
4660	'United Glass Bottle Co.'		Yellow	4a	SP	EPC	3b	36660	—	5/61 4/8	6/62 4/9
4660	'United Glass Bottle Co.'		Yellow	2b	SP	EPC	3b	36660	9/62	—	—
4660	'United Glass Bottle Co.'		Yellow	4b	SP	FMC	3b	36660	9/62	2/59 4/8	10/60 4/8
4660	'United Glass Bottle Co.'		Yellow	2b	SP	FMC	3b	36660	9/62	2/59 4/8	10/60 4/8
32069	'United Glass Bottle Co.'		Yellow	2b	SP	FMC	2b	32069	10/58	9/58 4/9	12/58 4/9
SD6	'United Glass Bottle Co.'		Yellow	2a	SP	FMC	2b	32069	10/58	11/58 4/9	12/58 4/9
4665	Saxa Salt Wagon — Export No. 4865		Yellow	7	SP	NPC	3b	36665	—	—	—
4665	Saxa Salt Wagon		Yellow	7	SP	EPC	3b	36665	—	5/61 6/-	12/64 4/11
4665	Saxa Salt Wagon		Yellow	4b	SP	EPC	3b	36665	—	—	—
4665	Saxa Salt Wagon		Yellow	2b	SP	EPC	3b	36665	2/59	2/59 5/6	10/60 5/6
4665	Saxa Salt Wagon		Yellow	4b	SP	FMC	3b	36665	2/59	2/59 5/6	10/60 5/6
32068	Saxa Salt Wagon		Yellow	2b	SP	FMC	2b	32068	11/58	12/58 5/9	12/58 5/9
SD6	Saxa Salt Wagon		Yellow	2b	SP	FMC	2b	32068	11/58	11/58 5/9	12/58 5/9
4670	Standard Wagon	13T B477015	Grey	7	SP	EPC	3b	36670	—	5/61 4/8	12/64 4/11
4670	Standard Wagon	13T B477015	Grey	4a	SP	EPC	3a	36670	—	—	—
4670	Standard Wagon	13T B477015	Grey	2a	SP	EPC	3a	36670	—	—	—
4670	Standard Wagon	13T B477015	Grey	4a	SP	FMC	3a	36670	2/59	2/59 4/8	10/60 4/8
4670	Standard Wagon	13T B477015	Grey	2a	SP	FMC	3a	36670	2/59	2/59 4/8	10/60 4/8
32074	Standard Wagon	13T B477015	Grey	2a	SP	FMC	2b	32074	4/58	7/58 4/9	12/58 4/9
SD6	Standard Wagon	13T B477015	Grey	2a	SP	FMC	2b	32074	4/58	6/58 4/9	6/58 4/9
32075	Open Wagon	12T E404844	Grey/Black	3a	FPW	FMC	2a	32075	1/58	5/56 4/6	12/58 4/9
32075	Open Wagon	12T E404844	Grey/Black	3a	FPW	LMC	2a	32075	3/56	5/56 4/6	12/58 4/9
D1	Open Wagon	12T E404844	Grey/Black	1b	FPW	LMC	1f	2075	—	3/53 4/6	4/56 4/6
D1	Open Wagon	12T E404844	Grey/Black	1b	FPW	EMC	1e	32075	—	3/53 4/6	4/56 4/6
32055	High Sided Wagon	12T M608344	Grey/Black	3a	FPW	FMC	2a	32055	5/56	5/56 4/9	9/58 5/-
32055	High Sided Wagon	12T M608344	Grey/Black	3a	FPW	LMC	2a	32055	5/56	5/56 4/9	9/58 5/-
D2	High Sided Wagon	12T M608344	Grey/Black	1b	FPW	LMC	1f	32055	1/54	3/53 4/9	4/56 4/9
D2	High Sided Wagon	12T M608344	Grey/Black	1b	FPW	EMC	1e	32055	10.52	3/53 4/9	4/56 4/9

4654 — Comes with 6 cleaning cotton wool plugs, and written instruction sheet in red and white, no. 57087 (A suitable replacement for these are the blank cigarette filter ends)

First items were issued with wagon no. labels on opposite side.

CAT. NO.	DESCRIPTION	WAGON NO.	BODY COLOUR	ROOF COLOUR	BASE TYPE	WHEEL TYPE	CPLGS.	BOX TYPE	BOX TYPE NO.	BOX CODE	MECC. PRICE	MECC. MAG. DATE	MECC. LAST DATE	LAST PRICE
4675	I.C.I. Chlorine Tank Wagon	—	White	—	17	SO	EPC	3b	36675	1/62	9/6	5/61	12/64	7/11
— Export No. 4875														
32070	I.C.I. Chlorine Tank Wagon		White	—	17	SO	FMC	3b	36675	5/61	9/-	2/60	10/60	9/-
	This item never listed under this number, although on box.													
D1	Tank Wagon	'Royal Daylight'	Red	—	3a	FPW	LMC	1e	32070	6/53	5/6	3/53	5/55	5/3
D1	Tank Wagon	'Royal Daylight'	Red	—	1b	FPW	LMC	1e	32070	1.53	5/6	3/53	5/55	5/3
D1	Tank Wagon	'Royal Daylight'	Red	—	1b	FPW	EMC	1e	32070	—	5/6	3/53	5/55	5/3
4676	Tank Wagon	'Esso'	Grey	—	5	SP	EPC	3b	36676	6/61	6/6	5/61	12/64	5/11
— Export No. 4876														
4676	Tank Wagon	'Esso'	Grey	—	4a	SP	EPC	3a	(36676)	—	—	—	—	—
4676	Tank Wagon	'Esso'	Grey	—	2a	SP	EPC	3a	(36676)	—	—	—	—	—
4676	Tank Wagon	'Esso'	Grey	—	4a	SP	FMC	3a	(36676)	—	5/11	2/59	10/60	5/11
4676	Tank Wagon	'Esso'	Grey	—	2a	SP	FMC	3a	(36676)	—	5/11	2/59	10/60	5/11
32081	Tank Wagon	'Esso'	Grey	—	3a	SP	FMC	2a	32081	—	6/-	7/58	12/58	6/-
32081	Tank Wagon	'Esso'	Grey	—	3a	FPW	FMC	2a	32081	2/56	5/9	5/56	6/58	6/-
D1	Tank Wagon	'Esso'	Grey	—	3a	FPW	LMC	2a	32081	—	5/6	3/53	4/56	5/9
D1	Tank Wagon	'Esso'	Grey	—	1b	FPW	LMC	2a	32081	4/51	5/6	3/53	4/56	5/9
D1	Tank Wagon	'Esso'	Grey	—	1b	FPW	EMC	1e	32081	10.52	5/6	3/53	4/56	5/9
32083	Tank Wagon	'Vacuum'	Red	—	3a	FPW	FMC	2a	32083	8/55	5/9	5/56	10/57	6/-
D1	Tank Wagon	'Vacuum'	Red	—	3a	FPW	LMC	2a	32083	5/54	5/3	5/55	4/56	5/9
D1	Tank Wagon	'Vacuum'	Red	—	1b	FPW	LMC	2a	32083	—	5/3	7/55	4/56	5/9
32080	Tank Wagon	'Power'	Green	—	3a	FPW	LMC	2a	32080	8/55	5/9	6/56	9/56	5/9
D1	Tank Wagon	'Power'	Green	—	1b	FPW	LMC	2a	32080	5/54	5/3	6/54	4/56	5/9
D1	Tank Wagon	'Power'	Green	—	1b	FPW	EMC	2a	32080	—	5/3	1/55	4/56	5/9
4677	Tank Wagon	'Mobil'	Red	—	5	SP	EPC	3b	(No change from 'Mobil' box).	—	6/6	5/61	12/64	5/11
— Export No. 4877														
4677	Tank Wagon	'Mobil'	Red	—	4a	SP	EPC	3a	(36677)	—	—	—	—	—
4677	Tank Wagon	'Mobil'	Red	—	2a	SP	EPC	3a	(36677)	—	—	—	—	—
4677	Tank Wagon	'Mobil'	Red	—	4a	SP	FMC	3a	(36677)	—	5/11	2/59	10/60	5/11
4677	Tank Wagon	'Mobil'	Red	—	2a	SP	FMC	3a	(36677)	—	5/11	2/59	10/60	5/11
32084	Tank Wagon	'Mobil'	Red	—	3a	SP	FMC	2a	32084	—	6/-	7/58	12/58	6/-
32084	Tank Wagon	'Mobil'	Red	—	3a	FPW	FMC	2a	32084	2/57	6/-	7/57	6/58	6/-
D1	Tank Wagon	'Mobil'	Red	—	3a	FPW	FMC	2a	32084	2/57	6/-	8/57	8/57	6/-
D1	Tank Wagon	'Mobil'	Red	—	3a	FPW	FMC	2a	32084	—	6/-	8/57	4/57	6/-
32084	Tank Wagon	'Mobil Oil Co.,'	Red	—	3a	FPW	FMC	2a	32084	7/56	5/9	5/56	5/56	5/9
D1	Tank Wagon	'Mobil Oil Co.,'	Red	—	1b	FPW	LMC	2a	32084	7/56	5/9	12/56	12/56	5/9
D1	Tank Wagon	'Mobil Oil Co.,'	Red	—	1b	FPW	EMC	2a	32084	—	5/9	7/56	12/56	5/9
4678	Tank Wagon	'Shell'	Yellow	—	5	SP	EPC	3b	36678	5/61	6/6	5/61	12/64	5/11
— Export No. 4878														
4678	Tank Wagon	'Shell'	Yellow	—	4a	SP	EPC	3a	(36678)	—	—	—	—	—
4678	Tank Wagon	'Shell'	Yellow	—	2a	SP	EPC	3a	(36678)	—	—	—	—	—
4678	Tank Wagon	'Shell'	Yellow	—	4a	SP	FMC	3a	(36678)	—	5/11	2/59	10/60	5/11
4678	Tank Wagon	'Shell'	Yellow	—	2a	SP	FMC	3a	(36678)	—	5/11	2/59	10/60	5/11
32082	Tank Wagon	'Shell'	Yellow	—	3a	SP	FMC	2a	32082	—	6/-	7/58	12/58	6/-
32082	Tank Wagon	'Shell'	Yellow	—	3a	FPW	FMC	2a	32082	—	6/-	7/57	6/58	6/-
D1	Tank Wagon	'Shell'	Yellow	—	3a	FPW	LMC	2a	32082	—	5/9	5/56	5/56	5/9
D1	Tank Wagon	'Shell'	Yellow	—	3a	FPW	LMC	2a	32082	—	5/3	5/55	4/56	5/9
4679	Tank Wagon	'Traffic Services'	Grey	—	16	SO	EPC	3b	36679	1/61	10/6	5/61	12/64	9/11
4679	Tank Wagon	'Traffic Services'	Grey	—	16	SO	FMC	3b	36679	5/61	9/6	3/60	10/60	9/6
4680	Tank Wagon	'Esso Fuel Oil'	Black	—	5	SP	EPC	3b	36680	5/61	6/6	5/61	12/64	5/11
— Export No. 4880														
4680	Tank Wagon	'Esso Fuel Oil'	Black	—	4a	SP	EPC	3b	36680	—	—	—	—	—
4680	Tank Wagon	'Esso Fuel Oil'	Black	—	2a	SP	EPC	3b	36680	—	—	—	—	—
4680	Tank Wagon	'Esso Fuel Oil'	Black	—	4a	SP	FMC	3b	36680	—	5/11	2/59	10/60	5/11
4680	Tank Wagon	'Esso Fuel Oil'	Black	—	2a	SP	FMC	3b	36680	—	5/11	2/59	10/60	5/11
4685	Bogie Tank Wagon	'I.C.I. Caustic Liquor'	Blue	—	25(DB)	SO	EPC	3b	(36685)	6/62	12/6	8/62	12/64	11/6
4685	Bogie Tank Wagon	'I.C.I. Caustic Liquor'	Blue	—	25(PB)	SO	EPC	3b	(36685)	6/62	—	—	—	—
4685	Bogie Tank Wagon	'I.C.I. Caustic Liquor'	Blue	—	25(PB)	SO	FMC	3b	(36685)	6/62	—	—	—	—
4690	Tube Wagon	2OT W73349	Brown/Black	—	9	SP	FMC		No box with this number.	—	4/4	4/59	10/60	4/4
32076	Tube Wagon	2OT W73349	Brown/Black	—	9	FPW	FMC		32076	10/56	6/-	6/56	12/58	6/-

Tank has no star on sides.

CAT. NO.	DESCRIPTION	TYPE	COMMENTS	COLOUR	FPW	FMC	BOX TYPE	BOX NO.	BOX CODE	MECC. MAG.	MECC. MAG. PRICE	LAST DATE	LAST PRICE
D1	Tube Wagon		2OT W73349	Brown/Black	9	Spec.	2a	32076	10/56	11/56	6/-	8/57	6/-
—	Open Wagon (Standard Wagon type moulding)			Yellow		Spec.							
—	Open Wagon (Steel Wagon type moulding)			Buff	Spec.	SP		NPC					
—	Goods Brake Van (E.R. Goods Brake Van type moulding)			Red	Spec.	SP		NPC					

— The above items are those in the ready-to-run sets. Bases are plastic, and not metal.
As the above items were not available separately, there are no boxes.

POSTWAR ACCESSORIES

CAT. NO.	DESCRIPTION	TYPE	COMMENTS	COLOUR	FPW	FMC	BOX TYPE	BOX NO.	BOX CODE	MECC. MAG.	MECC. MAG. PRICE	LAST DATE	LAST PRICE
5055	Engine Shed – 2 road	Plastic Kit		Buff/Grey			17	37005	—	9/59	17/9	12/64	19/6
5005	Engine Shed – 2 road	Plastic Kit		Buff/Grey			16	37005	—	9/59	17/9	12/64	19/6
5006	Engine Shed Extension	Plastic Kit		Buff/Grey			17	37006	—	9/59	12/6	12/64	14/3
5006	Engine Shed Extension	Plastic Kit		Buff/Grey			16	37006	—	9/59	12/6	12/64	14/3
5010	Footbridge	Metal	Stairs have triangular shaped supports below	Buff			15b	37010	7/60	(2/59	11/-	12/64	12/6
32101	Footbridge	Metal	top of stairs. No trian-	Buff			14f	32101	3/56	(5/56	10/3	12/58	11/6
D1	Footbridge	Metal	gular pieces. Has lugs	Buff			14d	—	—	6/50	—	4/56	10/3
D1	Footbridge	Metal	which slip into slots	Buff			14c	DA454	2/54	(4/49	9/9	4/56	10/3
D1	Footbridge	Metal	in bridge.	Buff			14b	(DA454)	—	(4/49	9/9	4/56	10/3
5015	Girder Bridge	Plastic		Red/Grey			15b	37015	11/61	(3/63	11/9	12/64	11/9
5015	Girder Bridge	Metal		Orange/Green			15b	37015	10/61	(2/59	17/6	1/63	19/3
32141	Girder Bridge	Metal		Orange/Green			14f	32141	—	(5/56	17/11)	12/58	17/11
D1	Girder Bridge (Viaduct)	Metal		Orange/Green			14f	32141	—	(2/57	17/11	4/57	17/11
5020	Goods Depot	Plastic Kit		Buff/Orange			17	37020	—	(1/60	25/-	12/64	1/9/-
5020	Goods Depot	Plastic Kit		Buff/Orange			16	37020	—	(1/60	25/-	12/64	1/9/-
5025	Gradient & Mile Posts	Plastic	8 Gradient &	White			15b	(37025)	—	11/61	2/11	12/64	2/9
5025	Gradient & Mile Posts	Plastic	4 Mile Posts	White			20	—	—	(2/59	2/11)	12/64	2/9
5030	Island Platform	Plastic Kit	No white to	Buff/Orange			17	37030	—	(1/60	9/11	12/64	11/3
5030	Island Platform	Plastic Kit	platform edges	Buff/Orange			16	37030	—	(1/60	9/11	12/64	11/3
32012	Island Platform	Metal	No white to	Buff/Orange			14f	32102	5/55	(5/56	1/3/6	12/58	1/5/-
D1	Island Platform	Metal	platform edges	Buff/Orange			14d	32102	2/53	(4/49	15/9)	4/56	1/3/6
D1	Island Platform	Metal	White edges to platform	Buff/Orange			14c	DA456 (or D456)	3/52	9/50	16/6	4/56	1/3/6
5035	Loading Gauge	Metal	Small base	Black/White			15b	37035	11/61	(2/8)	2/9	12/64	2/11
32150	Loading Gauge	Metal	Small base	Black/White			14f	32150	10/55	(7/57	2/9	12/58	2/9
D1	Loading Gauge	Metal	Small base	Black/White			14f	32150	10/55	(8/57	2/9	8/57	2/9
32150	Loading Gauge	Metal	Base fits under	Black/White			14f	32150	11/55	(5/56	2/6)	4/57	2/9
D1	Loading Gauge	Metal	track – old type	Black/White			14e	32150	9/52	1/55	2/4	4/56	2/6
D1	Loading Gauge	Metal	Base fits under	Black/White			14d	—	10M 12.52	(10/49	2/3)	4/56	2/6
D1	Loading Gauge	Metal	track – old type	Black/White			14c	32150	10M 1.54	(10/49	2/3)	4/56	2/6
D1	Loading Gauge	Metal	Base fits under track – old type	Black/White			14b	DA459	50M 10.49	(10/49	2/3)	4/56	2/6
5037	Lineside Notices	Plastic	6 in container	Black			20	—	—	6/62	1/9	12/64	1/9
5040	Platelayer's Hut	Plastic	6 in box	Buff/Orange			15b	37040	9/61	7/59	1/-	12/64	1/-
5045	Colour Light Signal	Home	Type 2T lamps (noted inside base)				15b	Type of box unknown		(2/59	10/3)	12/64	11/3
5045	Colour Light Signal	Home					14f	37047	—	(2/59	10/3)	12/64	11/3
32115	Colour Light Signal	Home	Old type lamps				14f	32115	7/59	(7/58	10/6)	12/58	10/6
ES6	Colour Light Signal	Home	Old Type Lamps				14e	—	11/58	11/58	10/6	12/58	10/6

Box is dark blue with picture of signal in light blue oval on lid.

CAT. NO.	DESCRIPTION	TYPE	COMMENTS	COLOUR	FPW	FMC	BOX TYPE	BOX NO.	BOX CODE	MECC. MAG.	MECC. MAG. PRICE	LAST DATE	LAST PRICE
5046	Colour Light Signal	Distant	Type 2T lamps (noted inside base)				15b	Type of box unknown		(2/59	10/3)	12/64	11/3
5046	Colour Light Signal	Distant					14f	37046	2/64	(2/59	10/3)	12/64	11/3
32116	Colour Light Signal	Distant	Old type lamps				14f	32116	8/59	(7/58	10/6)	12/58	10/6
ES6	Colour Light Signal	Distant	Old type lamps				14e	—	11/58	11/58	10/6	12/58	10/6

Box is dark blue with picture of signal in light blue oval on lid.

CAT. NO.	DESCRIPTION	TYPE	COMMENTS	COLOUR	FPW	FMC	BOX TYPE	BOX NO.	BOX CODE	MECC. MAG.	MECC. MAG. PRICE	LAST DATE	LAST PRICE
5047	Colour Light Signal	Junction-Home	Type 2T lamps (noted inside base)				15b	Type of box unknown		(2/59	16/11)	12/64	19/6
5047	Colour Light Signal	Junction-Home	Type 2T lamps				14f	37045	—	(2/59	16/11)	12/64	19/6
32117	Colour Light Signal	Junction-Home	Old type lamps				14f	32117	11/58	(7/58	17/6)	12/58	17/6
ES7	Colour Light Signal	Junction-Home	Old type lamps				14e	Unlike above items, this type of box not known for junction signal.		12/58	17/6	12/58	17/6
5050	Signal Manual	Home	2 in box, large counter weights				15b	37050	—	(2/59	2/8)	12/64	3/3

CAT. NO.	DESCRIPTION	TYPE	COMMENTS	COLOUR	BOX TYPE NO.	BOX NO.	BOX CODE	MECC. MAG.	MECC. PRICE	LAST DATE	LAST PRICE
32128	Signal Manual	Home	2 in box, large etc.	—	14f	32128	10/58	(5/58	2/9	12/58	2/9
32130	Signal Manual	Home	2 in box, large etc.	—	14f	32130	—	(5/56	2/6	1/58	2/9
						Box has sticker noting '2 Home'					
D1	Signal Manual	Home	2 in box, large etc.	—	14f	32130	—	(8/52	2/2	4/56	2/6
D1	Signal Manual	Home	Small counter weights	—	14f	For earlier boxes, see below.	7/50	—	—	4/52	2/2
						Base painted either black or white.					
5051	Signal Manual	Distant	2 in box, large counter weights	—	15b	37051	—	(2/59	2/8	12/64	3/3
32129	Signal Manual	Distant	2 in box, large etc.	—	14f	32129	—	(5/58	2/9	12/58	2/9
32130	Signal Manual	Distant	2 in box, large etc.	—	14f	32130	—	(5/56	2/6	1/58	2/9
						Box has sticker noting '2 Distant'					
D1	Signal Manual	Distant	2 in box, large etc.	—	14f	32130	—	(8/52	2/2	4/56	2/6
D1	Signal Manual	Distant	Small counter weights	—	14f	For earlier boxes, see below.	7/50	—	—	4/52	2/2
						Base painted either black or white.					
—	Signal Manual	One distant & home in same box	Large counter weights	—	14f	32130	—/54	—	—	—	—
—	Signal Manual	One distant & home in same box	Large counter weights	—	14e	32130	2.51	—	—	—	—
—	Signal Manual		Large counter weights	—	14d	Type of box unconfirmed	—	—	—	—	—
—	Signal Manual		Small counter weights	—	14c	DA452	—	—	—	—	—
—	Signal Manual		Small counter weights	—	14b	DA452	12M 11.49	—	—	—	—
—	Signal Manual		Small counter weights	—	14b	—	12.5M 2.49	—	—	—	—
5055	Signal Manual	Double Arm	Large counter weights / 2 in box	—	15b	37055	7/61	(2/59	3/6	12/64	4/3
32131	Signal Manual	Double Arm	Large counter weights etc.	—	14f	32131	1/57	(5/56	3/-	12/58	3/6
32131	Signal Manual	Double Arm	Large counter weights etc.	—	14e	32131	3/53	(8/52	2/9	4/56	3/-
—	Signal Manual	Double Arm	Large counter weights etc.	—	14d	Type of box unconfirmed		(8/52	2/9	4/56	3/-
D2	Signal Manual	Double Arm	Small counter weights	—	14c	DA453	—	7/50	—	4/52	2/9
D2	Signal Manual	Double Arm	Small counter weights	—	14b	DA453	11.49	7/50	—	4/52	2/9
D2	Signal Manual	Double Arm	Small counter weights	—	14b	—	—	7/50	—	4/52	2/9
5060	Signal Manual – Junction Home	Junction Home	Large counter weights / 2 in box	—	15b	37060	4/61	(2/59	3/10	12/64	4/11
32133	Signal Manual – Junction Home	Junction Home	Large counter weights etc.	—	14f	32133	12/58	(5/58	3/11	12/58	3/11
32132	Signal Manual – Junction Home	Junction Home	Large counter weights etc.	—	14f	32132	1/58	(5/56	3/6	1/58	3/11
						Box has sticker noting '2 Home'.					
D3	Signal Manual – Junction Home	Junction Home	Large counter weights etc.	—	14f	32132	1/58	(7/53	3/9	4/56	3/6
D3	Signal Manual – Junction Home	Junction Home	Small counter weights	—	—	— This type is not known to exist					
						For other boxes, see below.					
5061	Signal Manual – Junction Distant	Junction Distant	Large counter weights / 2 in box	—	15b	37061	1/62	(2/59	3/10	12/64	4/11
32134	Signal Manual – Junction Distant	Junction Distant	Large counter weights etc.	—	14f	32134	5/58	(5/58	3/11	12/58	3/11
32132	Signal Manual – Junction Distant	Junction Distant	Large counter weights etc.	—	14f	32132	10/58	(5/56	3/6	1/58	3/11
						Box has sticker noting '2 Distant'					
D3	Signal Manual – Junction Distant	Junction Distant	Large counter weights etc.	—	14f	32132	10/58	(7/53	3/9	4/56	3/6
D3	Signal Manual – Junction Distant	Junction Distant	Small counter weights	—	—	— This type is not known to exist					
						For other boxes, see below.					
—	Signal Manual – Junction	One distant & one home Large counter weights in same box	Large counter weights	—	14f	32132	1/55	—	—	—	—
—	Signal Manual – Junction	One distant & one home in same box	Large counter weights	—	14e	32132	6/53	—	—	—	—
5065	Signal Electric	Home	Large counter weights	—	16	(37065)	—	(2/59	9/6	12/64	11/9
			Rectangular yellow end label with black printing.								
32135	Signal Electric	Home	Large counter weights	—	14f	32135	—	(5/56	9/3	12/58	9/11
ED1	Signal Electric	Home	Large counter weights	—	14e	32135	—	(8/52	9/-	4/56	9/3
			Light blue label with red printing, and sticker 'Home'								
ED1	Signal Electric	Home	Large counter weights	—	14e	32135	—	11/52	—	4/56	9/3
5066	Signal Electric	Distant	Large counter weights	—	16	(37066)	—	(2/59	9/6	12/64	11/9
			Rectangular yellow label on ends with black printing.								
32135	Signal Electric	Distant	Large counter weights	—	14f	32135	—	(5/56	9/3	12/58	9/11
ED1	Signal Electric	Distant	Large counter weights	—	14f	32135	—	(8/52	9/-	4/56	9/3
			Light blue label with red printing, and sticker 'Distant'								
ED1	Signal Electric	Distant	Large counter weights	—	14e	32135	—	11/52	—	4/56	9/3
			Light blue label with blue printing, and sticker 'Distant'								

Hornby Dublo accessories — catalogue listing (continued)

No.	Description	Type	Model note	Box colour	Box code	Box no.						Label / notes
5070	Signal Electric	Double Arm	Large counter weights		16	(37070)	—	2/59	14/6	12/64	17/3	Rectangular yellow end label with black printing.
32136	Signal Electric	Double Arm	Large counter weights		14f	32136	9/56	(5/56	13/6)	12/58	14/11	
ED2	Signal Electric	Double Arm	Large counter weights		14e	32136	—	(8/52	13/11)	4/56	13/6	Light blue label with red printing.
ED2	Signal Electric	Double Arm	Large counter weights		14e	32136	8/54	11/52	—	4/56	13/6	Light blue label with red printing.
5075	Signal Electric – Junction Home		Large counter weights		16	(37075)	—	(2/59	15/-)	12/64	17/9	
32137	Signal Electric – Junction Home		Large counter weights		14f	32137	—	(5/56	14/-)	12/58	15/6	
ED3	Signal Electric – Junction Home		Large counter weights		14e	32137	—	7/53	14/3	4/56	14/-	Light blue label with blue printing, and sticker 'Home'
5076	Signal Electric – Junction Distant		Large counter weights		16	(37076)	—	(2/59	15/-)	12/64	17/9	
32137	Signal Electric – Junction Distant		Large counter weights		14f	32137	—	(5/56	14/-)	12/58	15/6	
ED3	Signal Electric – Junction Distant		Large counter weights		14e	32137	8/54	7/53	14/3	4/56	14/-	Light blue label with blue printing, and sticker 'Distant'
5080	Signal Cabin	Metal	Buff and Green roof	Buff	15b							Box of this type unknown
5080	Signal Cabin	Metal	Buff and Green roof	Buff	16	37080	6/62					Green roof never illustrated
5080	Signal Cabin	Metal	Buff and Orange roof	Buff	16	37080	—	2/59	15/-	12/64	17/9	
32160	Signal Cabin	Metal	Buff and Orange roof	Buff	14f	32160	6/56	5/56	13/9	12/58	15/6	
D1	Signal Cabin	Metal	Buff and Orange roof	Buff	14e	32160	—	(5/56	13/9)	12/58	15/6	14e Type of box unconfirmed
D1	Signal Cabin	Metal	Buff and Orange roof	Buff	14d	DA458	1/53	9/50	11/3	4/56	13/9	
D1	Signal Cabin	Metal	Buff and Orange roof	Buff	14c	(or D458)	—	4/49		4/46	13/9	
5083	Terminal Station	Plastic Kit		Buff	18	37083	—	11/61	69/6	12/64	2/19/11	
5084	Canopy Extension	Plastic Kit		Buff	—		—	4/62	1/2/-	12/64	1/2/-	White, with red and yellow lettering.
5085	Suburban Station	Plastic Kit		Buff/Orange	17	37085	—	1/60	22/6	12/64	1/3/3	
5085	Suburban Station	Plastic Kit		Buff/Orange	16	37085	—	1/60	22/6	12/64	1/3/3	
32170	Through Station	Metal	No white edges to platform	Buff/Orange	14f	32170	—	5/56	2/5/-	12/58	2/10/-	
D1	Through Station	Metal	No white edges to platform	Buff/Orange	14d	32170	—	9/50	37/6	4/56	2/5/-	
D1	Through Station	Metal	No white edges to platform	Buff/Orange	14c	DA455	11/48	4/49	33/6	4/46	2/5/-	
D1	Through Station	Metal	White edges to platform	Buff/Orange	14c	DA455	—	4/49	33/6	4/46	2/5/-	
5086	Platform Extension	Plastic	6 in box	Buff	15b	37086	4/61	2/59	2/9	12/64	2/11	—Early stations were rivetted, later ones were fixed by screws.
5087	Fence for Platform Extension	Plastic	6 in box	Buff	15b	37087	—	2/59	1/6	12/64	1/7	
5089	Side Platform Extensions for Terminal Station	Plastic	?	Buff	15b	37089	—	(11/61)	2/6	12/64	2/6	
5090	Telegraph Pole	Plastic – Polypropylene	6 in box	Brown	15b	(37090)	—	4/59	—	12/64	3/9	
5090	Telegraph Pole	Plastic – Nylon	6 in box	Brown	15b	(37090)	—	2/59	3/6	12/64	3/9	
5091	Tunnel – Single Track	Plastic	Black liner	Buff/Green	24	37091	—	9/59	9/11	12/64	10/9	
5091	Tunnel – Single Track	Plastic	Green liner	Buff/Green	24	37091	—	9/59	9/11	12/64	10/9	
5092	Tunnel – Double Track	Plastic	Black liner	Buff/Green	24	36092	—	2/59	23/11	12/64	1/5/6	
5092	Tunnel – Double Track	Plastic	Green liner	Buff/Green	24	37092	—	2/59	23/11	12/64	1/5/6	
5094	Tunnel Portal – Double Track	Plastic	Smoke over portal	Buff	—		—	(10/60	2/9	12/64	2/11	
5094	Tunnel Portal etc.	Plastic	No smoke over portal	Buff	15b		—	10/60	2/9	12/64	2/11	
5095	Water Crane	Metal	Black base with no. 2 on underside.	Buff	15b	37095	—	1/62	1/9	12/64	1/9	
5095	Water Crane	Metal	Black base etc.	Brown	15b	37095	—	2/59	1/9	6/62	1/9	
5095	Water Crane	Metal	Black base with no. 1 on underside.	Brown	14f	37095	—	2/59	1/9	6/62	1/9	
5095	Water Crane	Metal	Black base etc.	Brown	14f	(37095)	—	2/59	1/9	6/62	1/9	
32140	Water Crane	Metal	Black base with no. 2 on underside.	Brown	14f	32140	8/57	5/56	1/9	12/58	1/9	Box has sticker with no. 5095
D1	Water Crane	Metal	Black base without any number	Brown	14e	32140	6.25M 7.53	3/50	—	4/56	2/6	
D1	Water Crane	Metal	Brown base underside without and number	Brown	14c	DA457	5.5M 2.50	4/49	2/6	4/56	1/9	

HORNBY-ACHO PRODUCTS AVAILABLE IN BRITAIN

CAT. NO.	DESCRIPTION	COMMENTS	COLOUR	BOX COLOUR	FIRST DATE	FIRST PRICE	LAST DATE	LAST PRICE
SETS								
610	Passenger Train	'L'Aquilon'	—	—	4/62	8/12/9	1/63	8/12/9
611	Suburban Passenger Train		—	—	4/62	9/7/6	12/64	9/7/6
615	Passenger Train	'Le Vendeen'	—	—	4/62	10/17/-	12/64	10/17/-
620	Goods Train	'Le Picard'	—	—	4/62	8/10/-	1/63	8/10/-
LOCOMOTIVES								
634	Co-Co Diesel		Blue-Purple	—	4/62	7/15/-	1/63	7/15/-
635	0-6-0 Diesel Shunter		Green	—	Undated Catalogue Only			
636	2-6-2 Tank		Black	—	4/62	6/5/6	1/63	6/5/6
636	Bo-Bo Electric		Blue-Green	—	8/61	5/10/-	12/64	5/8/6
ACCESSORIES								
657	Connecting Board			—	4/62	10/9	12/64	10/9
658	Lighting Kit for Accessories			—	4/62	10/9	12/64	10/9
661	Buffer Stop including 1/6-th rail			—	Undated Catalogue Only			
662	Colour Light Signal			—	4/62	1/7/-	12/64	1/7/-
663	Directional Signal for Points			—	Undated Catalogue Only			
664	Speed Reducer			—	4/62	1/2/-	12/64	1/2/-
665	2-Light Gantry Signal			—	Undated Catalogue Only			
690	Station Kit – Plastic		Grey	—	8/61	1/17/6	1/63	1/17/-
691	Island Platform – Plastic		Grey	—	8/61	7/11	1/63	7/11
692	Signal Cabin – Plastic		Grey	—	8/61	11/6	1/63	11/3
695	Crossing for Tracks		Grey	—	4/62	17/9	12/64	17/9
699	Railer		Grey	—	4/62	3/6	12/64	3/6
783	Switch for Points & Uncoupling Rail		Grey	—	4/62	9/6	1/63	9/6
784	Switch for Colour Light Signal		Grey	—	4/62	9/6	1/63	9/6
785	Switch – Permanent Contact		Grey	—	Undated Catalogue Only			
786	Switch – Impulse Contact		Grey	—	Undated Catalogue Only			
ROLLING STOCK								
700	Brake Van		Brown	Green & White	Undated Catalogue Only			
701	Goods Wagon with Lattice		Brown	Green & White	4/62	8/6	1/63	8/6
702	'Primagaz' Tank Wagon		Grey	Green & White	4/62	15/9	1/63	15/9
703	Bulk Cement Transporter		Grey	Green & White	4/62	13/6	12/64	13/6
704	Goods Van with sliding doors	Items have special	Brown	Green & White	4/62	15/9	1/63	15/9
705	Refrigerator Van 'STEF'	bases of plastic.	White	Green & White	8/61	11/9	1/63	11/9
706	'C.T.C.' Bulk Grain Wagon	with Hornby-Dublo	Grey	Green & White	4/62	13/6	1/63	13/6
707	Chemical Wagon	style couplings, but	Grey	Green & White	Undated Catalogue Only			
708	Goods Wagon	mounting is different	Dark Grey	Green & White	8/61	8/11	12/64	8/9
709	'Simotra' Mineral Wagon	to British items.	Grey	Green & White	4/62	12/3	1/63	12/3
712	Milk Insulated Tank Wagon	Plastic wheels on.	Yellow	Green & White	Undated Catalogue Only.			
716	Axle Transporter Wagon – with axle load	metal axles.	Brown	Green & White	4/62	11/9	1/63	11/9
717	Flat Wagon – with removable stake sides		Brown	Green & White	4/62	9/6	1/63	9/6
718	Low Sided Wagon	After 1964, items	Brown	Green & White	8/61	8/3	12/64	8/3
726	Bogie 'Arbel' Coal Wagon	had European type	Dark Grey	Green & White	Undated Catalogue Only			
727	Bogie Low Sided Wagon	couplings, and came	Brown	Green & White	Undated Catalogue Only			
728	Bogie Goods Wagon	in Blue & White	Brown	Green & White	Undated Catalogue Only			
729	Bogie Coal Wagon	boxes.	Dark Grey	Green & White	4/62	1/1/3	1/63	1/1/3
COACHES								
733	Passenger Coach 2nd Class		Green	Green & White	8/61	16/6	12/64	16/3
734	Passenger Coach 1st Class		Green	Green & White	8/61	16/6	12/64	16/3
735	Suburban Passenger Coach 2nd Class		Green	Green & White	4/62	1/3/6	1/63	1/3/6
736	Suburban Passenger Coach 1st Class		Green	Green & White	4/62	1/3/6	1/63	1/3/6
737	Inox Passenger Coach 1st Class		Silver	Green & White	4/62	1/4/9	1/63	1/4/9
739	Dining Car (Wagon Lits)		Blue	Green & White	Undated Catalogue Only			
742	Mail Van with windows		Maroon	Green & White	Undated Catalogue Only			

* Some reference literature uses the above coach numbers with an added '1' at the end. i.e. 7331, 7341 etc. (Undated Catalogue has code 72881/02 & 57.B.16.273, and is probably 1962).

(For additional items not listed for import by Meccano Limited, but possibly available through other importers, see pages 277–284).

Appendices

Leaflet No.

1. Hornby-Dublo ½" Motor 2 and 3 rail.
2. Hornby-Dublo 5/8" Motor 2 and 3 rail – Type A and B – Old and New.
3. Nos. 2206 and 2207 0-6-0 Tank Locomotive – 2 rail.
4. Nos. 2211 and 3211 4-6-2 Streamlined Locomotive – 2 and 3 Rail.
5. No. 3212 4-6-2 Locomotive 'Duchess of Montrose' – 3 rail.
6. Nos. 2217 and 3217 0-6-2 Tank Locomotive – 2 and 3 rail.
7. Nos. 2218 and 3218 2-6-4 Tank Locomotive – 2 and 3 rail.
8. Nos. 3220 and 3221 4-6-0 Castle Class Locomotive & Tender – 3 rail (3220 - Old, 3221 - New).
9. Nos. 2220 and 2221 4-6-0 Castle Class Locomotive & Tender – 2 rail (2220 - Old, 2221 - New).
10. Nos. 2225 and 2224 2-8-0 Freight Locomotive & Tender – 2 rail (2225 - Old, 2224 - New).
11. Nos. 3225 and 3224 2-8-0 Freight Locomotive & Tender – 3 rail (3225 - Old, 3224 - New).
12. Nos. 2226 and 3226 4-6-2 City Class Locomotive & Tender – 2 and 3 rail.
13. Nos. 2230 and 3230 Bo-Bo Diesel Electric Locomotive – 2 and 3 rail.
14. Nos. 2231 and 3231 0-6-0 Diesel Shunting Locomotive – 2 and 3 rail.
15. Nos. 2232 and 2234, 3232 and 3234 Co-Co and Deltic Diesel Electric Locomotives 2 & 3 rail.
16. Nos. 2233 and 3233 Co-Bo Diesel Electric Locomotive – 2 and 3 rail.
17. Nos. 2235 and 3235 4-6-2 West Country Class Locomotive & Tender – 2 and 3 rail.
18. No. 20 Clockwork Locomotive. ('0' Gauge – not included)
19. No. 30 Clockwork Locomotive. ('0' Gauge – not included)
20. No. 40 Clockwork Tank Locomotive. ('0' Gauge – not included)
21. No. 50 Clockwork Locomotive. ('0' Gauge – not included)
22. Nos. 2250 and 3250 Electric Motor Coach – 2 and 3 rail.
24. Meccano Matic Clockwork Motor. (Not included)
25. Meccano No. 1 Clockwork Motor. (Not included)
26. Meccano 'Emebo' Electric Motor. (Not included)

HORNBY-DUBLO ½" MOTOR   2 AND 3-RAIL

LOCOMOTIVES Nos. 2206 AND 2207 2-RAIL — LOCOMOTIVES Nos. 3220 AND 3225 3-RAIL

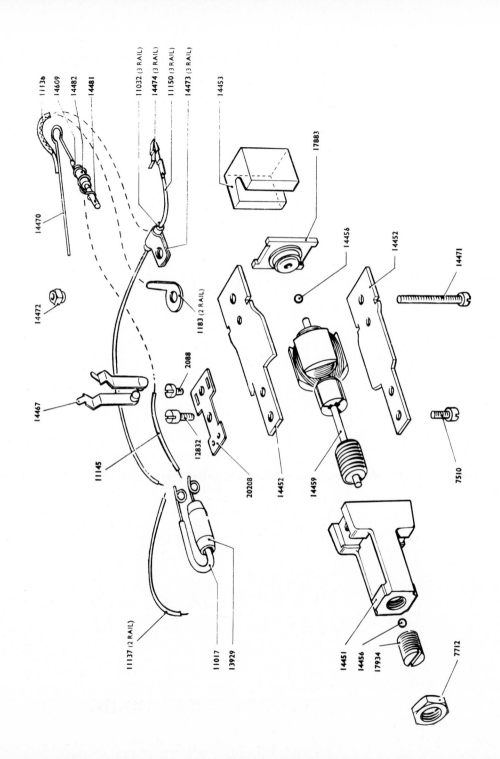

2088	Screw
7510	Screw
7712	Locking Nut
11017	P.V.C. Sleeve
11136	Tinned Copper Braid
11145	Connecting Wire
12832	Screw
13929	Choke
14451	Bearing Casting
14452	Pole Piece
14453	Magnet
14456	Ball Bearing
14459	Armature Shaft Assembly
14467	Brush Arm Assembly
14470	Brush Spring
14471	Screw
14472	Nut
14481	Copper Strip
14482	Condenser
14609	Cambric Sleeve
17883	Fixed Bearing Support Assembly
17934	Adjustable Bearing Housing Assembly
20208	Insulator for Brush Arms

2-RAIL

| 1183 | Soldering Tag |
| 11137 | Connecting Wire |

3-RAIL

11032	P.V.C. Sleeve
11150	Connecting Wire
14473	Clamp for Wire
14474	Plug

2

SERVICING LEAFLET

HORNBY DUBLO 5/8" MOTOR 2 & 3-RAIL—TYPE A. & B. OLD TYPE & NEW

LOCOMOTIVES Nos. 2221, 2224, 2235 2-RAIL—LOCOMOTIVES Nos. 3221, 3224, 3235 3-RAIL

7501	Screw
7712	Locking Nut
11009	P.V.C. Sleeve
11541	Ball Bearing
17942	Adjustable Bearing Housing Assembly
20746	Screw
21451	Main Casting (Type 'A')
21452	End Casting ⎫ End Casting Assembly
21462	Brush Holder ⎬ (Accommodates Bearing
21463	Brush Holder ⎭ Assembly 17942)
	Insulator Job No. 18421
21453	Armature Shaft Assembly—Type 'A'
21458	Ring Magnet
21461	Brush
21464	Brush Spring L.H.
21465	Brush Spring R.H.
21466	Spring Mounting Plate ⎫ Spring Mounting
21467	Spring Retaining Pin ⎬ Plate Assembly
21468	Contact Piece ⎬ Job No.
21471	Soldering Tag ⎭ 18353
21476	Fixed Bearing Housing Assembly
21481	Main Casting—Type 'B'
21482	Armature Shaft Assembly—Type 'B'

ON ORIGINAL TYPE MOTORS:—

18422	End Casting Assembly. Was Fitted Instead of 18421
21469	Grub Screw ⎫ Was Fitted
21474	Adjustable Bearing ⎬ Instead of
	Housing Assembly ⎭ 21476
21460	Fixed Bearing. Was fitted Instead of 17942

2-RAIL

11005	P.V.C. Sleeve ⎫
11032	P.V.C. Sleeve ⎬
13929	Choke ⎬ Suppression
14482	Condenser ⎬ Assembly
14782	Connecting Wire ⎬ Job No. 18373
18353	Spring Mounting ⎬
	Plate Assembly ⎭

3-RAIL

11005	P.V.C. Sleeve ⎫
11032	P.V.C. Sleeve ⎬
11150	Connecting Wire ⎬ Suppression
13929	Choke ⎬ Assembly
14482	Condenser ⎬ Job 18374
18353	Spring Mounting ⎬
	Plate Assembly ⎭
14474	Plug

LOCOMOTIVE	**MOTOR No.**
2-RAIL	
2221 (Castle)	21472 ('A')
2224 (2-8-0)	21473 ('B')
2235 (West Country)	21473 ('B')
3-RAIL	
3221 (Castle)	21450 ('A')
3224 (2-8-0)	21480 ('B')
3235 (West Country)	21473 ('B')

21451 ("A" TYPE 2 13/32" LONG)
21481 ("B" TYPE 2 1/8" LONG)
RED SPOT (3 RAIL)
RED SPOT (2 RAIL)
21469
21474
11541
21476
11541
21453 ("A" TYPE 2 7/8" LONG)
21482 ("B" TYPE 2 19/32" LONG)

11005   21471   14482
13929   11009   21467
11032   21465
                7501
21463   21464
21460   21468
11541   21456
21458   14474
               20746
               11150 (3 RAIL)
21462   14782 (2 RAIL)
21461
7712
17942
11541

FOR 2 RAIL LOCOS 14474 IS OMITTED AND WIRE SOLDERED TO COLLECTOR

Hornby DUBLO

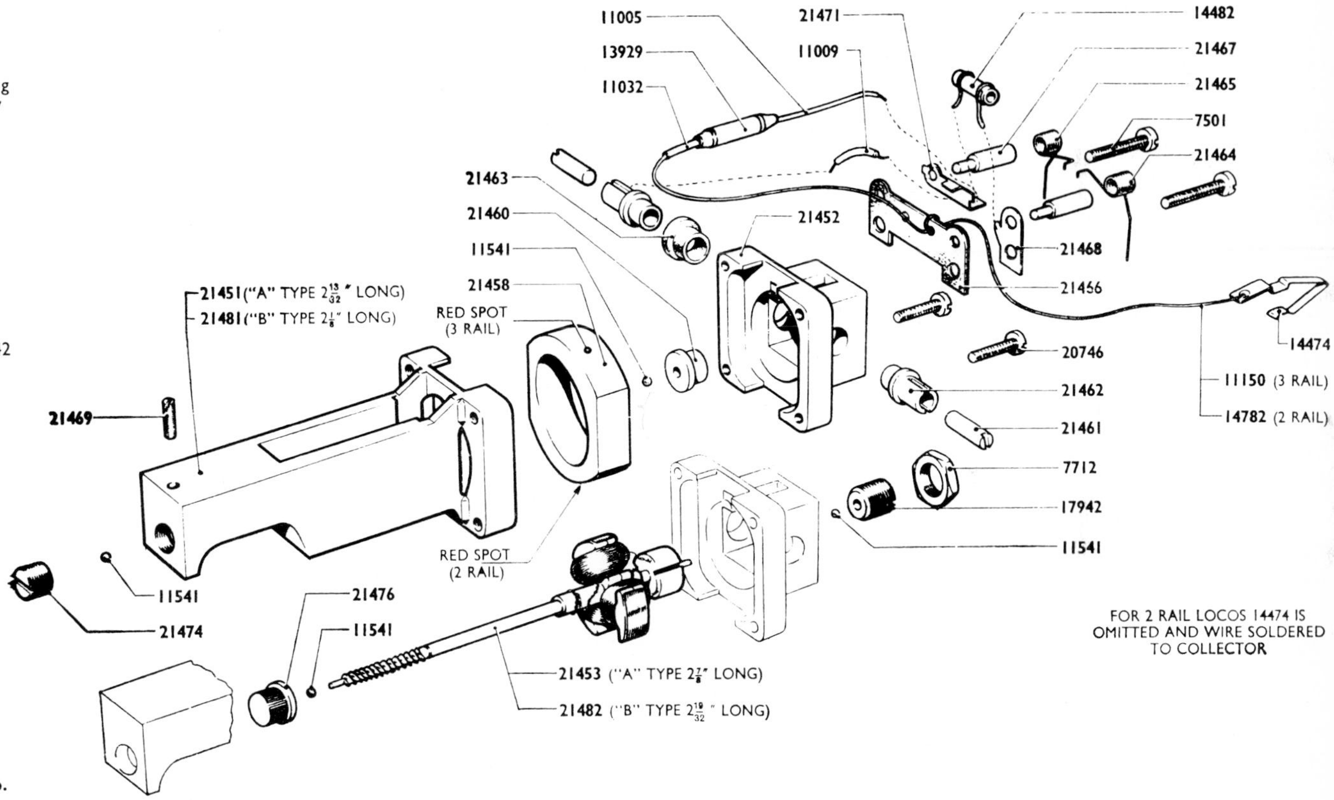

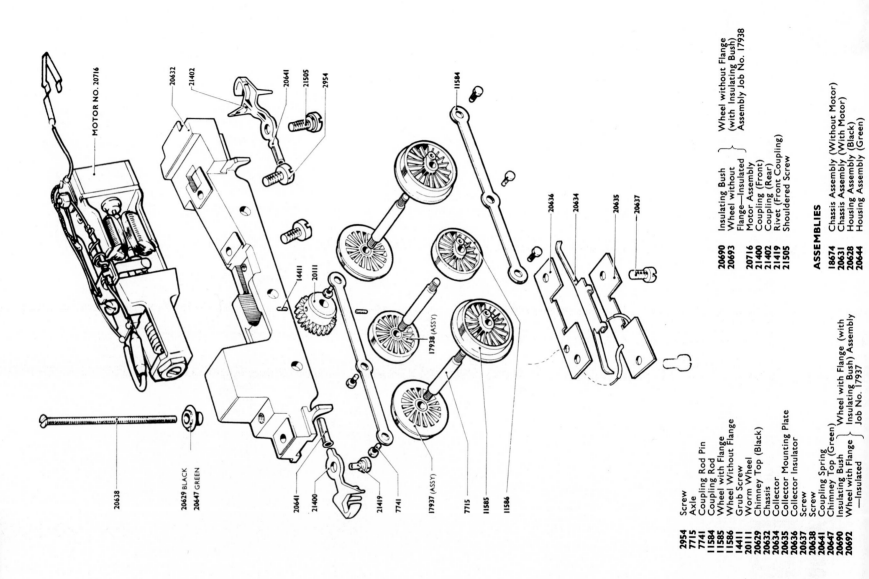

SERVICING LEAFLET **3**

ISSUED DECEMBER 1962

0-6-0 TANK LOCOMOTIVE 2-RAIL

No. 2206 and No. 2207

MOTOR NO. 20716

20638

20629 BLACK
20647 GREEN

1411

20111

20641

21400

21419

7741

17937 (ASSY)

17938 (ASSY)

7715

11585

11586

20632

21402

20641

21505

2954

11584

20636

20634

20635

20637

2954	Screw
7715	Axle
7741	Coupling Rod Pin
11584	Coupling Rod
11585	Wheel with Flange
11586	Wheel Without Flange
14411	Grub Screw
20111	Worm Wheel
20629	Chimney Top (Black)
20632	Chassis
20634	Collector Mounting Plate
20635	Collector
20636	Collector Insulator
20637	Screw
20638	Screw
20641	Coupling Spring
20647	Chimney Top (Green)
20690	Insulating Bush
20692	Wheel with Flange—Insulated

Wheel with Flange (with Insulating Bush) Assembly Job No. 17937

20690	Insulating Bush
20693	Wheel without Flange—Insulated
20716	Motor Assembly
21400	Coupling (Front)
21402	Coupling (Rear)
21419	Rivet (Front Coupling)
21505	Shouldered Screw

Wheel without Flange (with Insulating Bush) Assembly Job No. 17938

ASSEMBLIES

18674	Chassis Assembly (Without Motor)
20631	Chassis Assembly (With Motor)
20628	Housing Assembly (Black)
20644	Housing Assembly (Green)

Hornby DUBLO

ISSUED
DECEMBER
1962

SERVICING LEAFLET

4

4-6-2 STREAMLINED LOCOMOTIVE 2-RAIL & 3-RAIL

No. 2211 2-RAIL   No. 3211 3-RAIL

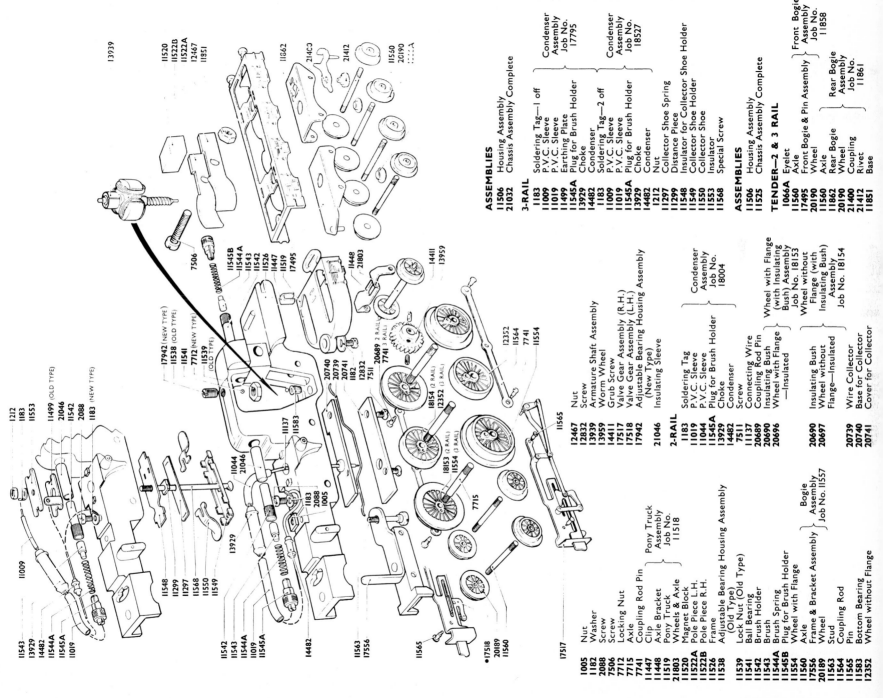

1005	Nut
1182	Washer
2088	Screw
7506	Screw
7712	Locking Nut
7715	Axle
7741	Coupling Rod Pin
11447	Clip
11448	Axle Bracket
11519	Pony Truck
21803	Wheels & Axle
11520	Magnet Block
11522A	Pole Piece L.H.
11522B	Pole Piece R.H.
11526	Frame
11538	Adjustable Bearing Housing Assembly (Old Type)
11539	Lock Nut (Old Type)
11541	Ball Bearing
11542	Brush Holder
11543	Brush
11544A	Brush Spring
11545A	Plug for Brush Holder
11545B	Wheel with Flange
11554	Axle
11560	Frame & Bracket Assembly
20189	Wheel
11563	Stud
11564	Coupling Rod
11565	Pin
11583	Bottom Bearing
12352	Wheel without Flange

12467	Nut
12832	Screw
13939	Armature Shaft Assembly
13959	Worm Wheel
14411	Grub Screw
17517	Valve Gear Assembly (R.H.)
17518	Valve Gear Assembly (L.H.)
17942	Adjustable Bearing Housing Assembly (New Type)
13929	Insulating Sleeve
21046	

2-RAIL

1183	Soldering Tag
11019	P.V.C. Sleeve
11044	P.V.C. Sleeve
11545A	Plug for Brush Holder
13929	Choke
14482	Condenser
7511	Screw
11137	Connecting Wire
20689	Coupling Rod Pin
20690	Insulating Bush
20696	Wheel with Flange —Insulated
20690	Insulating Bush
20697	Wheel without Flange—Insulated
20739	Wire Collector
20740	Base for Collector
20741	Cover for Collector

ASSEMBLIES

11506	Housing Assembly
21032	Chassis Assembly Complete

3-RAIL

1183	Soldering Tag—1 off
11009	P.V.C. Sleeve
11019	P.V.C. Sleeve
1499	Earthing Plate
11545A	Plug for Brush Holder
13929	Choke
14482	Condenser
1183	Soldering Tag—2 off
11009	P.V.C. Sleeve
11019	P.V.C. Sleeve
11545A	Plug for Brush Holder
13929	Choke
14482	Condenser
1212	Nut
1297	Collector Shoe Spring
1299	Distance Piece
1548	Insulator for Collector Shoe Holder
1549	Collector Shoe Holder
1550	Collector Shoe
1553	Insulator
1568	Special Screw

ASSEMBLIES

11506	Housing Assembly
11525	Chassis Assembly Complete

TENDER—2 & 3 RAIL

1066A	Eyelet
11560	Axle
17495	Front Bogie & Pin Assembly
20190	Wheel
11560	Axle
11862	Rear Bogie
20190	Wheel
21400	Coupling
21412	Rivet
11851	Base

Hornby DUBLO

4-6-2 "DUCHESS OF MONTROSE" LOCOMOTIVE 3-RAIL

No. 3212 3-RAIL

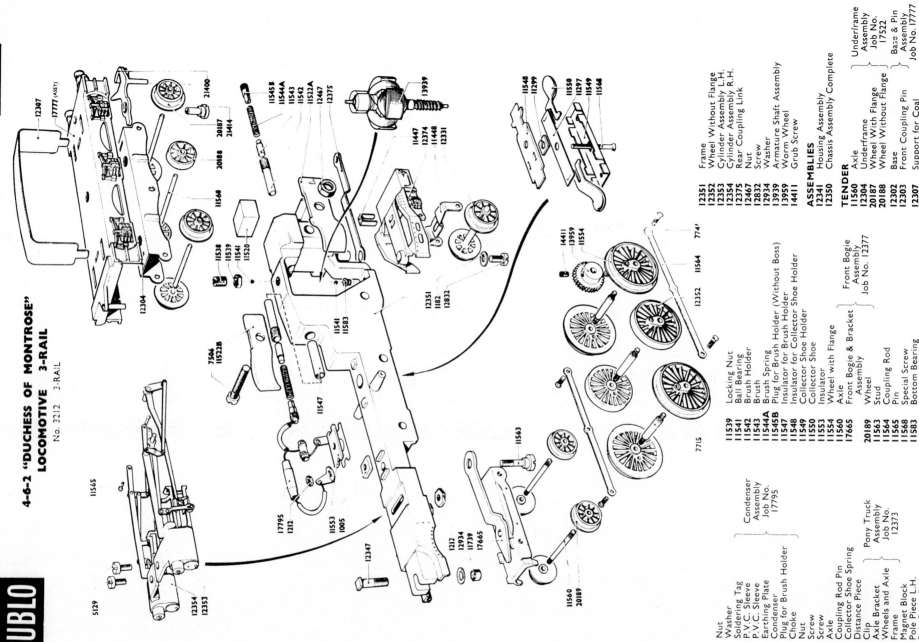

1005	Nut
1182	Washer
1183	Soldering Tag
1009	P.V.C. Sleeve
1019	P.V.C. Sleeve
1499	Earthing Plate
4482	Condenser
11545A	Plug for Brush Holder
13929	Choke
1212	Nut
5129	Screw
7506	Screw
7715	Axle
7741	Coupling Rod Pin
11297	Collector Shoe Spring
11299	Distance Piece
11447	Clip
11448	Axle Bracket
12331	Wheels and Axle
12374	Frame
11520	Magnet Block
11522A	Pole Piece L.H.
11522B	Pole Piece R.H.
11538	Adjustable Bearing Housing Assembly

11539	Locking Nut
11541	Ball Bearing
11542	Brush Holder
11543	Brush
11544A	Brush Spring
11545B	Plug for Brush Holder (Without Boss)
11547	Insulator for Brush Holder
11548	Insulator for Collector Shoe Holder
11549	Collector Shoe Holder
11550	Collector Shoe
11553	Insulator
11554	Wheel with Flange
11560	Axle
17665	Front Bogie & Bracket Assembly
20189	Wheel
11563	Stud
11564	Coupling Rod
11565	Pin
11568	Special Screw
11583	Bottom Bearing
11739	Nut
12347	Front Stud

12351	Frame
12352	Wheel Without Flange
12353	Cylinder Assembly L.H.
12354	Cylinder Assembly R.H.
12375	Rear Coupling Link
12467	Nut
12832	Screw
12934	Washer
13939	Armature Shaft Assembly
13959	Worm Wheel
11411	Grub Screw

ASSEMBLIES

12341	Housing Assembly
12350	Chassis Assembly Complete

TENDER

11560	Axle
12304	Underframe
20187	Wheel With Flange
20188	Wheel Without Flange
12302	Base
12303	Front Coupling Pin
12307	Support for Coal
21400	Coupling

Condenser Assembly Job No. 17795

Pony Truck Assembly Job No. 12373

Front Bogie & Bracket Assembly Job No. 12377

Underframe Assembly Job No. 17522

Base & Pin Assembly Job No. 17777

SERVICING LEAFLET

ISSUED DECEMBER 1962

6

0-6-2 TANK LOCOMOTIVE 2-RAIL AND 3-RAIL
No. 2217 2-RAIL AND No. 3217 3-RAIL

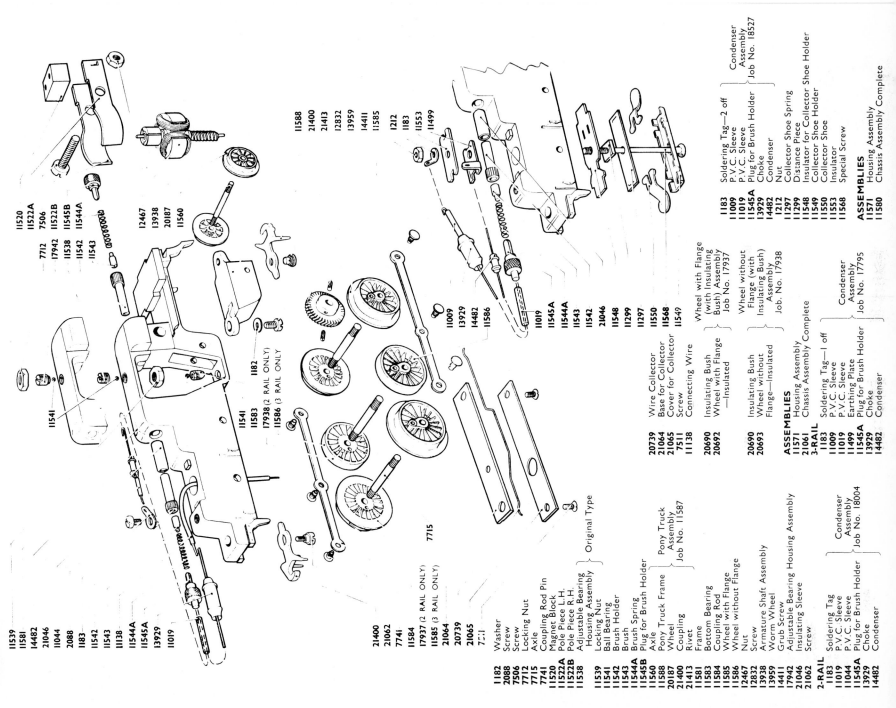

1182		Washer
2088		Screw
7506		Screw
7712		Locking Nut
7715		Axle
7741		Coupling Rod Pin
11520		Magnet Block
11522A		Pole Piece L.H.
11522B		Pole Piece R.H.
11538		Adjustable Bearing Housing Assembly
11539		Locking Nut
11541		Ball Bearing
11542		Brush Holder
11543		Brush
11544A		Brush Spring
11545A		Plug for Brush Holder
11545B		Axle
11560		Pony Truck Frame
11588		Wheel
20187		Coupling
21400		Rivet
21413		Frame
12467		Bottom Bearing
12832		Coupling Rod
13938		Wheel with Flange
13959		Wheel without Flange
14411		Nut
11942		Screw
21046		Armature Shaft Assembly
21062		Worm Wheel
		Grub Screw
		Adjustable Bearing Housing Assembly
		Insulating Sleeve
		Screw
2-RAIL		
11183		Soldering Tag
11019		P.V.C. Sleeve
11044		P.V.C. Sleeve
11545A		Plug for Brush Holder
13929		Choke
14482		Condenser

APPENDIX I   391

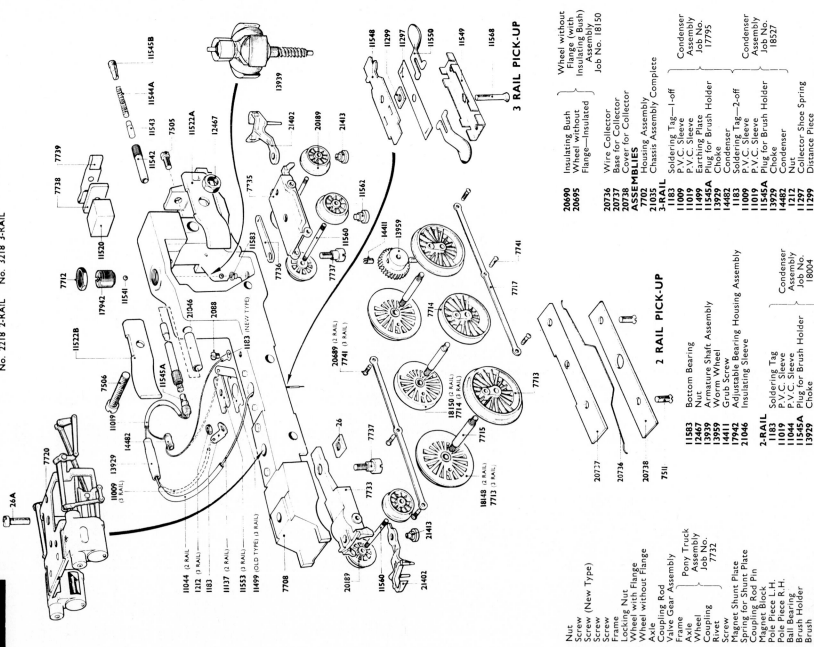

3 RAIL PICK-UP

2 RAIL PICK-UP

20690	Insulating Bush	
20695	Wheel without Flange—Insulated	
20736	Wire Collector	
20737	Base for Collector	
20738	Cover for Collector	
ASSEMBLIES		
7702	Housing Assembly	
21035	Chassis Assembly Complete	
3-RAIL		
1183	Soldering Tag—1-off	
11009	P.V.C. Sleeve	
11019	P.V.C. Sleeve	
11499	Earthing Plate	
11545A	Plug for Brush Holder	Condenser Assembly Job No. 17795
13929	Choke	
14482	Condenser	
1183	Soldering Tag—2-off	
11009	P.V.C. Sleeve	
11019	P.V.C. Sleeve	
11545A	Plug for Brush Holder	Condenser Assembly Job No. 18527
13929	Choke	
14482	Condenser	
1212	Nut	
11297	Collector Shoe Spring	
11299	Distance Piece	
11548	Insulator for Collector Shoe Holder	
11549	Collector Shoe Holder	
11550	Collector Shoe	
11553	Insulator	
11568	Special Screw	
ASSEMBLIES		
7702	Housing Assembly	
7703	Chassis Assembly Complete	

11583	Bottom Bearing	
12467	Nut	
13939	Armature Shaft Assembly	
13959	Worm Wheel	
14411	Grub Screw	
17942	Adjustable Bearing Housing Assembly	
21046	Insulating Sleeve	
2-RAIL		
1183	Soldering Tag	
11019	P.V.C. Sleeve	
11044	P.V.C. Sleeve	
11545A	Plug for Brush Holder	Condenser Assembly Job No. 18004
13929	Choke	
14482	Condenser	
7511	Screw	
11137	Connecting Wire	
20689	Coupling Rod Pin	
20690	Insulating Bush	Wheel with Flange (with Insulating Bush) Assembly Job No. 18148
20694	Wheel with Flange—Insulated	

26	Nut	
26A	Screw (New Type)	
2088	Screw	
7505	Screw	
7506	Screw	
7708	Frame	
7712	Locking Nut	
7713	Wheel with Flange	
7714	Wheel without Flange	
7715	Axle	
7717	Coupling Rod	
7720	Valve Gear Assembly	
7733	Frame	Pony Truck Assembly Job No. 7732
11560	Axle	
20189	Wheel	
21402	Coupling	
21413	Rivet	
7737	Screw	
7738	Magnet Shunt Plate	
7739	Spring for Shunt Plate	
7741	Coupling Rod Pin	
11520	Magnet Block	
11522A	Pole Piece L.H.	
11522B	Pole Piece R.H.	
11541	Ball Bearing	
11542	Brush Holder	
11543	Brush	
11544A	Brush Spring	
11545B	Plug for Brush Holder	
11560	Axle	
17670	Frame & Bracket Assembly	Rear Bogie Assembly Job No. 7734
20189	Wheel	
21402	Coupling	
21413	Rivet	

11044	Wheel with Flange (2 RAIL)	
1212	Wheel with Flange (3 RAIL)	
1183	Wheel without Flange	
11137	Axle (2 RAIL)	
11553	Coupling Rod (3 RAIL)	
11499	Coupling Rod (OLD TYPE) (3 rail)	

4-6-0 CASTLE CLASS LOCOMOTIVE AND TENDER 3-RAIL

No. 3220 ORIGINAL TYPE WITH ½" MOTOR — No. 3221 MODIFIED TYPE WITH ⅝" MOTOR

Hornby DUBLO

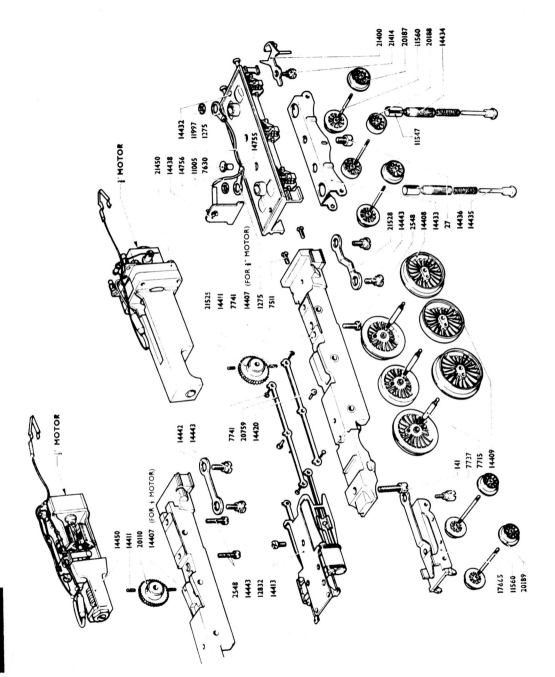

141	Screw
2548	Screw
7511	Screw
7715	Axle
7737	Screw
7741	Coupling Rod Pin
11560	Axle
17665	Bogie & Bracket Assembly
20189	Wheel

Front Bogie Assembly Job No. 12377

12832	Screw
14407	Chassis (for Motor Job No. 21450)
14408	Wheel with Flange
14409	Wheel without Flange
14411	Grub Screw
14413	Cylinder Assembly
14420	Connecting Rod Pin
14443	Screw
20759	Coupling Rod
21450	Motor Assembly
21525	Worm Wheel

TENDER

27	Screw
1275	Soldering Tag
7630	Rivet
11005	P.V.C. Sleeve
11547	Insulator

11560	Axle
14433	Underframe
20187	Wheel with Flange
20188	Wheel without Flange
11997	Washer
14432	Chassis
14434	Collector Shoe Holder
14435	Collector Shoe
14436	Spring
14439	Insulator
14440	Eyelet
14443	Screw
14755	Connecting Wire
14756	Connecting Wire
21400	Coupling
21414	Rivet
21528	Drawbar

Underframe Assembly Job No. 17833

Insulator Assembly Job No. 14438

For ⅝" MOTOR—ITEMS AS STATED, EXCEPT FOR:—

14407	Chassis (For Motor Job No. 14450)
14442	Drawbar
14450	Motor Assembly
20110	Worm Wheel

ASSEMBLIES

14392	Housing Assembly
14406	Chassis Assembly (with motor)
18667	Chassis Assembly (without motor)

4-6-0 CASTLE CLASS LOCOMOTIVE AND TENDER 2-RAIL

No. 2220 ORIGINAL TYPE WITH ½" MOTOR—No. 2221 MODIFIED TYPE WITH ⅝" MOTOR

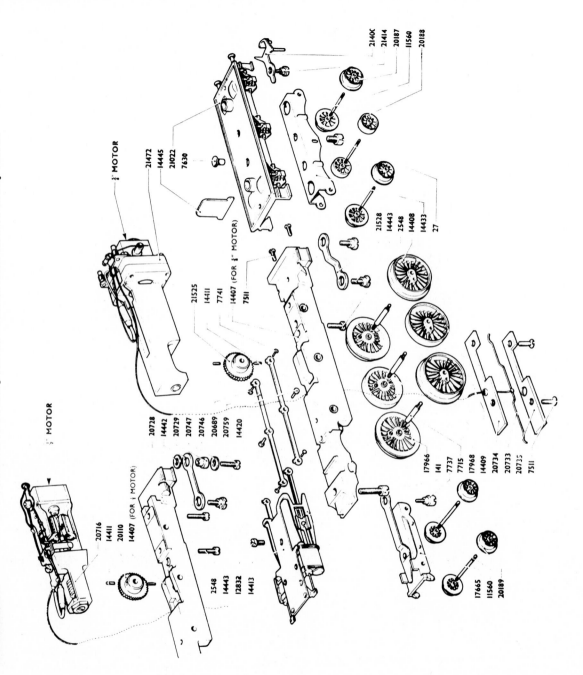

141	Screw	
2548	Screw	
7511	Screw	
7715	Axle	
7737	Screw	
7741	Coupling Rod Pin	
11560	Axle	
17665	Bogie & Bracket Assembly	Front Bogie Assembly Job. No. 12377
20189	Wheel	
12832	Screw	
14407	Chassis (For motor job No. 21472)	
14408	Wheel with Flange	
14409	Wheel without Flange	
14411	Grub Screw	
14413	Cylinder Assembly	
14420	Connecting Rod Pin	
20689	Coupling Rod Pin (Insulated Wheels)	
20690	Insulating Bush	
20698	Wheel with Flange —Insulated	Wheel with Flange (with Insulating Bush) Assembly Job No. 17966
20690	Insulating Bush	
20699	Wheel without Flange—Insulated	Wheel without Flange (with Insulating Bush) Assembly Job No. 17968
20733	Wire Collector	
20734	Base for Collector	
20735	Cover for Collector	
20759	Coupling Rod	
21472	Motor Assembly	
21525	Worm Wheel	

TENDER

27	Screw	
7630	Rivet	
11560	Axle	
14433	Underframe	Underframe Assembly Job No. 17833
20187	Wheel with Flange	
20188	Wheel Without Flange	

14443	Screw
14445	Front Plate
21022	Chassis
21400	Coupling
21414	Rivet
21528	Drawbar

FOR ⅝" MOTOR—ITEMS AS STATED, EXCEPT FOR:—

14407	Chassis (For Motor Job No. 20716)
14442	Drawbar
20110	Worm Wheel
20716	Motor Assembly
20728	Washer
20729	Insulating Bush
20746	Screw
20747	Washer

ASSEMBLIES

14392	Housing Assembly
18666	Chassis Assembly (without motor)
21023	Chassis Assembly (with motor)

2548	Screw
7502	Screw
7511	Screw
14909B	Chassis
21473	Motor Assembly – ⅝″
21526	Worm Wheel
21528	Drawbar
7513	Screw
7715	Axle
7733	Frame
11560	Axle
20189	Wheel
21402	Coupling
21413	Rivet
7737	Screw
7741	Coupling Rod Pin
14411	Grub Screw
14442	Drawbar
14909A	Chassis (Obsolete)
20111	Worm Wheel
20716	Motor Assembly (½″)
20728	Washer
20729	Insulating Bush
20746	Screw
20747	Washer
14443	Screw
14910	Wheel with Flange
14911	Wheel without Flange
14912	Coupling Rod
14913	Cylinder Assembly
20689	Coupling Rod Pin (insulated wheels)
20690	Insulating Bush
20700	Wheel with Flange —Insulated
20690	Insulating Bush
20701	Wheel without Flange—Insulated
20730	Wire Collector
20731	Base for Collector
20732	Cover for Collector

Modified Type Only

Front Pony Truck Assembly Job No. 7732

Original Type Only

Wheel with Flange (with Insulating Bush) Assembly Job No. 18177

Wheel without Flange (with Insulating Bush) Assembly Job No. 18175

TENDER

27	Screw
7630	Rivet
11560	Axle
14433	Underframe
20187	Wheel with Flange
20188	Wheel without Flange
14445	Front Plate
21027	Chassis
21400	Coupling
21419	Rivet

Underframe Assembly Job No. 17833

ASSEMBLIES

14902	Housing Assembly
18668	Chassis Assembly (without Motor)
21028	Chassis Assembly (with Motor)

½″ MOTOR
20716
14913 (ASSY)
21473 (ASSY)
7513
7502
7511
14445
7630
21027
14411
20111
14909A
14411
21526
7511
14433
21400
14909 B
2548
20728
14442
20729
20747
20746
20731
20730
20732
7511
21528 14443
27
21419
2548
14443
21402
21413
7733
7737
20689
18175 (ASSY)
18177 (ASSY)
7715
14911
14910
21402
21413
20189
11560
11560
20187
20188
14912
7741

2548	Screw	
7502	Screw	
7511	Screw	
14909	Chassis	
21480	Motor Assembly (⅝)	Modified Type Only
21526	Worm Wheel	
21528	Drawbar	
7513	Screw	
7715	Axle	
7733	Frame	
11560	Axle	Front Pony Truck Assembly Job No. 7732
20189	Wheel	
21402	Coupling	
21413	Rivet	
7737	Screw	
7741	Coupling Rod Pin	
14411	Grub Screw	
14442	Drawbar	
14450	Motor Assembly (½")	Original Type Only
14909	Chassis (obsolete)	
20111	Worm Wheel	
14443	Screw	
14910	Wheel with Flange	
14911	Wheel without Flange	
14912	Coupling Rod	
14913	Cylinder Assembly	

TENDER

27	Screw	
1275	Soldering Tag	
7630	Rivet	
11005	P.V.C. Sleeve	
11547	Insulator	
11560	Axle	Underframe Assembly Job No. 17833
14433	Underframe	
20187	Wheel with Flange	
20188	Wheel without Flange	
11997	Washer	
14434	Collector Shoe Holder	
14435	Collector Shoe	
14436	Spring	
14439	Insulator	Insulator Assembly Job No. 14438
14440	Eyelet	
14443	Screw	
14755	Connecting Wire	
14756	Connecting Wire	
14931	Chassis	
21400	Coupling	
21419	Rivet	

ASSEMBLIES

14902	Housing Assembly
14908	Chassis Assembly (with Motor)
18669	Chassis Assembly (without Motor)

⅝" MOTOR

½" MOTOR

26A	Screw
7502	Screw
7506	Screw
7712	Locking Nut
7715	Axle
7737	Screw
7741	Coupling Rod Pin
11447	Clip — Pony Truck
11448	Axle Bracket — Assembly
12331	Wheel & Axle — Job No.
12374	Frame — 12373
11520	Magnet Block
11522A	Pole Piece (L.H.)
11522B	Pole Piece (R.H.)
11541	Ball Bearing
11542	Brush Holder
11543	Brush
11544A	Brush Spring
11545B	Plug for Brush Holder
11554	Wheel with Flange — Front
11560	Axle — Bogie
17665	Bogie & Bracket Assembly — Assembly
20189	Wheel — Job No. 12377
11583	Bottom Bearing
12352	Wheel without Flange
12467	Nut
13939	Armature Shaft Assembly
13959	Worm Wheel
14411	Grub Screw
17942	Adjustable Bearing Housing Assembly
20758	Chassis Casting
20759	Coupling Rod
20762	Screw
20763	Drawbar
20764	Cylinder Assembly
21046	Insulating Sleeve

2-RAIL

1183	Soldering Tag—1 off
11019	P.V.C. Sleeve
11044	P.V.C. Sleeve — Condenser
11545A	Plug for Brush Holder — Assembly
13929	Choke — Job No. 18004
14482	Condenser
7511	Screw
11137	Connecting Wire
20689	Coupling Rod Pin

20690	Insulating Bush	Wheel with Flange
20696	Wheel with Flange —Insulated	(with Insulating Bush) Assembly Job No. 18153

20690	Insulating Bush	Wheel without Flange (with Insulating Bush) Assembly Job No. 18154
20697	Wheel without Flange—Insulated	

20737	Base for Collector
20738	Cover for Collector
20739	Wire Collector

ASSEMBLIES

20751	Housing Assembly
20767	Chassis Assembly Complete

3-RAIL

1183	Soldering Tag—1 off
11009	P.V.C. Sleeve
11019	P.V.C. Sleeve — Condenser
11499	Earthing Plate — Assembly
11545A	Plug for Brush Holder — Job No. 17795
13929	Choke — (Old Type)
14482	Condenser

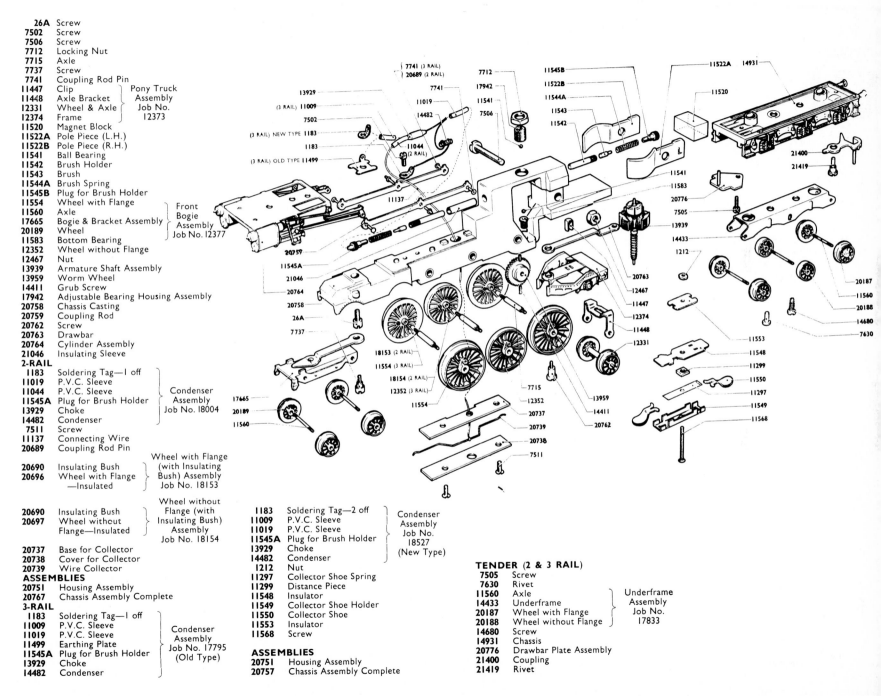

1183	Soldering Tag—2 off
11009	P.V.C. Sleeve — Condenser
11019	P.V.C. Sleeve — Assembly
11545A	Plug for Brush Holder — Job No.
13929	Choke — 18527
14482	Condenser — (New Type)
1212	Nut
11297	Collector Shoe Spring
11299	Distance Piece
11548	Insulator
11549	Collector Shoe Holder
11550	Collector Shoe
11553	Insulator
11568	Screw

ASSEMBLIES

20751	Housing Assembly
20757	Chassis Assembly Complete

TENDER (2 & 3 RAIL)

7505	Screw
7630	Rivet
11560	Axle
14433	Underframe — Underframe
20187	Wheel with Flange — Assembly
20188	Wheel without Flange — Job No. 17833
14680	Screw
14931	Chassis
20776	Drawbar Plate Assembly
21400	Coupling
21419	Rivet

Hornby DUBLO

13

SERVICING LEAFLET

BO-BO DIESEL ELECTRIC LOCOMOTIVE 2-RAIL & 3-RAIL

No. 2230 2-RAIL   No. 3230 3-RAIL

Hornby DUBLO

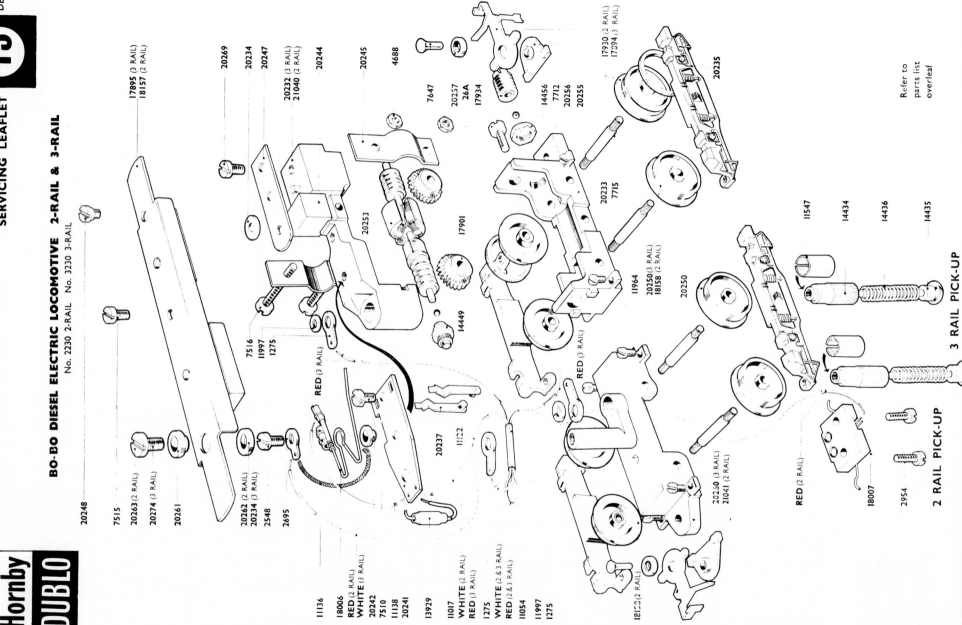

Refer to
parts list
overleaf

2 RAIL PICK-UP

3 RAIL PICK-UP

BO-BO DIESEL ELECTRIC LOCOMOTIVE 2-RAIL AND 3-RAIL

26A	Screw
1275	Soldering Tag
2548	Screw
2695	Soldering Tag
4688	Nut
7510	Screw
7515	Screw
7516	Screw
7647	Rivet
7712	Locking Nut
7715	Axle
11017	P.V.C. Sleeve
11054	P.V.C. Sleeve
11122	Connecting Wire
11136	Copper Braid
11138	Connecting Wire
11964	Screw
13929	Choke
14449	Fixed Bearing Assembly
14456	Ball Bearing
14481	Copper Strip
14482	Condenser } Condenser Assembly Job No. 18006
14609	Cambric Sleeve
20239	Brush Spring
17934	Adjustable Bearing Housing Assembly
20233	Bottom Casting
20234	Washer
20235	Sideframe
20237	Brush Arm Assembly
20241	Insulator
20242	Bush
20243	Worm Wheel } Worm Wheel Assembly Job No. 17901
20249	Grub Screw
20244	Magnet
20245	Pole Piece
20247	Swivel Plate
20248	Pivot Screw
20250	Wheel
20251	Wheel with tyre groove } Wheel (with Tyre) Assembly Job No. 17894
20252	Tyre
20253	Armature Shaft Assembly
20255	Coupling
20256	Coupling Insulating Piece
20257	Coupling Insulating Washer
20269	Screw

2-RAIL

2954	Screw
7093	Rivet
7621	Rivet } Mounting Plate Assembly Job No. 18157
20230	Mounting Plate
20270	Weight (3 off)
20252	Tyre
20703	Wheel (tyre groove) insulated } Wheel (tyre groove) Insulated Assembly Job No. 17930
20690	Insulating Bush
20261	Insulating Bush
20262	Washer
20263	Pivot Screw (9 32″ Long)
20690	Insulating Bush
20702	Wheel (insulated) } Wheel (insulated) Assembly Job No. 18158
20742	Wire Collector (L.H.)
20743	Wire Collector (R.H.) } Collector Assembly Job No. 18007
20744	Base for Collector
20745	Collector Retaining Pin
21040	Top Casting
21041	Casting for Bogie

ASSEMBLIES

21037	Housing Assembly
21038	Motor Bogie Assembly
21039	Front Bogie Assembly

3-RAIL

7621	Rivet
20230	Mounting Plate } Mounting Plate Assembly Job No. 17895
20270	Weight—1 off
11547	Collector Shoe Insulator
11997	Washer
14434	Collector Shoe Holder
14435	Collector Shoe
14436	Collector Shoe Spring
20232	Top Casting
20260	Casting for Bogie
20274	Screw (3 16 Long)

ASSEMBLIES

20221	Housing Assembly
20231	Motor Bogie Assembly
20259	Front Bogie Assembly

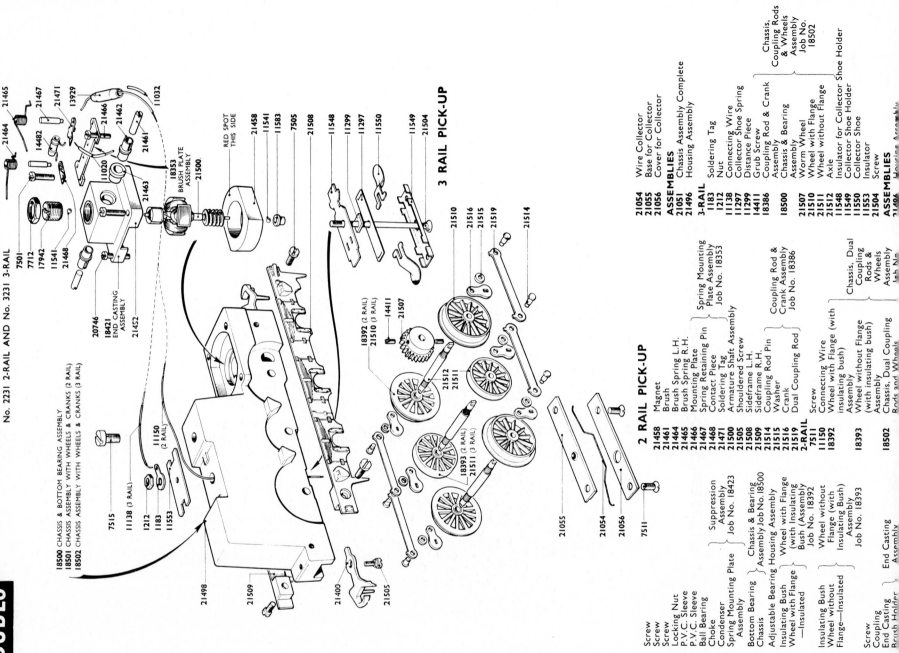

18500 CHASSIS & BOTTOM BEARING ASSEMBLY
18501 CHASSIS ASSEMBLY WITH WHEELS & CRANKS (2 RAIL)
18502 CHASSIS ASSEMBLY WITH WHEELS & CRANKS (3 RAIL)

RED SPOT THIS SIDE

18353 BRUSH PLATE ASSEMBLY

21452 END CASTING ASSEMBLY

2 RAIL PICK-UP

3 RAIL PICK-UP

7501	Screw
7505	Screw
7515	Screw
7712	Locking Nut
11020	P.V.C. Sleeve
11032	P.V.C. Sleeve
11541	Ball Bearing
13929	Choke
14482	Condenser
18353	Spring Mounting Plate Assembly
11583	Bottom Bearing
21498	Chassis
17942	Adjustable Bearing Housing Assembly
20690	Insulating Bush
21052	Wheel with Flange (with Insulating Bush (Assembly) Job No. 18392 —Insulated
20690	Insulating Bush
21053	Wheel without Flange—Insulated
20746	Screw
21400	Coupling
21452	End Casting Assembly
21467	Brush Holder

2-RAIL

21458	Magnet
21461	Brush
21464	Brush Spring L.H.
21465	Brush Spring R.H.
21466	Mounting Plate
21467	Spring Retaining Pin
21468	Contact Piece
21471	Soldering Tag
21500	Armature Shaft Assembly
21505	Shouldered Screw
21508	Sideframe L.H.
21509	Sideframe R.H.
21514	Coupling Rod Pin
21515	Washer
21516	Crank
21519	Dual Coupling Rod

2-RAIL

7501	Screw
11150	Connecting Wire
18392	Wheel with Flange (with insulating bush) Assembly
18393	Wheel without Flange (with insulating bush) Assembly Job No. 18393
18502	Chassis, Dual Coupling Rods and Wheels

21054	Wire Collector
21055	Base for Collector
21056	Cover for Collector

ASSEMBLIES

21051	Chassis Assembly Complete
21496	Housing Assembly

3-RAIL

1183	Soldering Tag
1212	Nut
11138	Connecting Wire
11297	Collector Shoe Spring
11299	Distance Piece
14411	Grub Screw
18386	Coupling Rod & Crank Assembly
18500	Chassis & Bearing Assembly
21507	Worm Wheel
21510	Wheel with Flange
21511	Wheel without Flange
21512	Axle
21548	Insulator for Collector Shoe Holder
21549	Collector Shoe Holder
21550	Collector Shoe
21553	Insulator
21504	Screw

ASSEMBLIES

CO-CO DIESEL LOCOMOTIVE   2-RAIL AND 3-RAIL

Nos. 2232 and 2234 2-RAIL — Nos. 3232 and 3234 3-RAIL

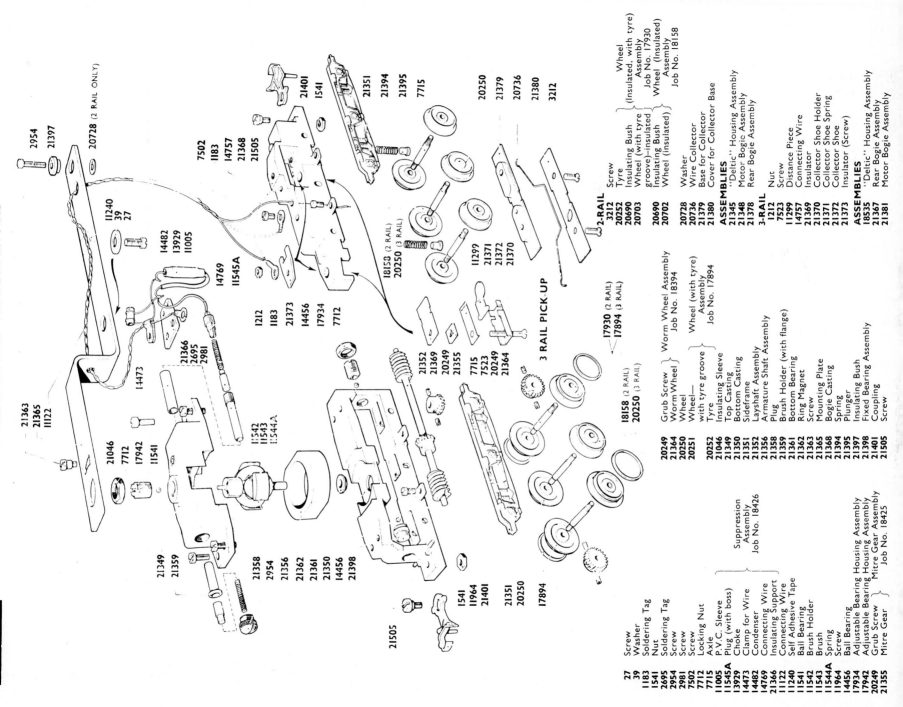

27	Screw
39	Washer
1183	Soldering Tag
1541	Nut
2695	Soldering Tag
2954	Screw
2981	Screw
7502	Screw
7712	Locking Nut
7715	Axle
11005	P.V.C. Sleeve
11545A	Plug (with boss)
13929	Choke
14473	Clamp for Wire
14482	Condenser
14769	Connecting Wire
21366	Insulating Support
11122	Connecting Wire
11541	Self Adhesive Tape
11542	Ball Bearing
11543	Brush Holder
11544A	Brush
11964	Spring
14456	Screw
17934	Ball Bearing
17942	Adjustable Bearing Housing Assembly
20249	Adjustable Bearing Housing Assembly
21355	Mitre Gear

20249	Grub Screw
21364	Worm Wheel
20250	Wheel—
20251	with tyre groove
20252	Tyre
21046	Insulating Sleeve
21349	Top Casting
21350	Bottom Casting
21351	Sideframe
21352	Layshaft Assembly
21356	Armature Shaft Assembly
21358	Plug
21359	Brush Holder (with flange)
21361	Bottom Bearing
21362	Ring Magnet
21363	Screw
21365	Mounting Plate
21368	Bogie Casting
21394	Spring
21395	Screw
21397	Plunger
21398	Insulating Bush
21401	Fixed Bearing Assembly
21505	Coupling
	Screw

2-RAIL	
3212	Screw
20252	Tyre
20690	Insulating Bush
20703	Wheel (with tyre groove)—insulated
20690	Insulating Bush
20702	Wheel (insulated)
20728	Washer
20736	Wire Collector
21379	Base for Collector
21380	Cover for Collector Base

ASSEMBLIES

21345	"Deltic" Housing Assembly
21348	Motor Bogie Assembly
21378	Rear Bogie Assembly

3-RAIL	
1212	Nut
7523	Screw
11299	Distance Piece
14757	Connecting Wire
21369	Insulator
21370	Collector Shoe Holder
21371	Collector Shoe Spring
21372	Collector Shoe
21373	Insulator (Screw)

ASSEMBLIES

18535	"Deltic" Housing Assembly
21367	Rear Bogie Assembly
21381	Motor Bogie Assembly

Wheel (Insulated, with tyre) Assembly Job No. 17930
Wheel (Insulated) Assembly Job No. 18158

3 RAIL PICK-UP

18153 (2 RAIL)
20250 (3 RAIL)

18158 (2 RAIL)
20250 (3 RAIL)

Grub Screw } Worm Wheel Assembly Job No. 18394
Worm Wheel }

Wheel (with tyre) Assembly Job No. 17894

17930 (2 RAIL)
17894 (3 RAIL)

Suppression Assembly Job No. 18426

Mitre Gear Assembly Job No. 18425

Hornby DUBLO

CO-BO DIESEL ELECTRIC LOCOMOTIVE 2-RAIL AND 3-RAIL

No. 2233 2-RAIL — No. 3233 3-RAIL

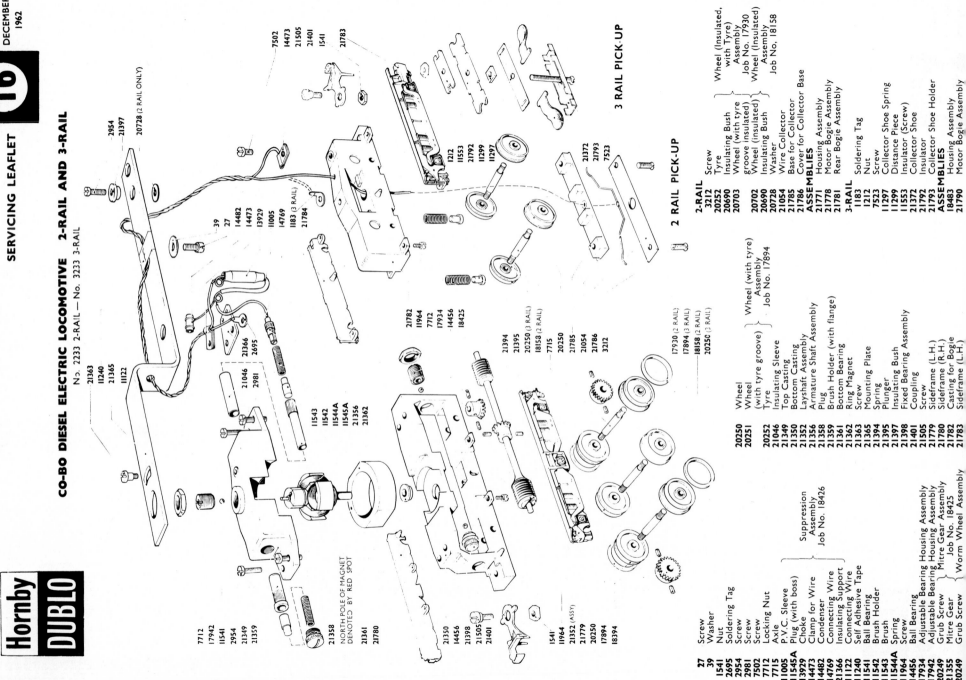

NORTH POLE OF MAGNET
DENOTED BY RED SPOT

3 RAIL PICK-UP

2 RAIL PICK-UP

2-RAIL	
3212	Screw
20252	Tyre
20690	Insulating Bush
20703	Wheel (with tyre groove insulated)
20702	Wheel (insulated)
20690	Insulating Bush
20728	Washer
21054	Wire Collector
21785	Base for Collector
21786	Cover for Collector Base
ASSEMBLIES	
21771	Housing Assembly
21778	Motor Bogie Assembly
21781	Rear Bogie Assembly
3-RAIL	
1183	Soldering Tag
1212	Nut
7523	Screw
11297	Collector Shoe Spring
11299	Distance Piece
11553	Insulator (Screw)
21372	Insulator
21792	Collector Shoe
21793	Collector Shoe Holder
ASSEMBLIES	
18483	Housing Assembly
21790	Motor Bogie Assembly

Wheel (Insulated, with Tyre) Assembly Job No. 17930
Wheel (Insulated) Assembly Job No. 18158

7502		
14473		
21505		
21401		
1541		
21783		
2954		
21397		
20728 (2 RAIL ONLY)		

1212	
11553	
21792	
11299	
11297	

21372	
21793	
7523	

39	
27	
14482	
14473	
13929	
11005	
14769	
1183 (3 RAIL)	
21784	

1363	
11240	
21365	
11122	

| 21046 | |
| 2981 | |

| 21366 | |
| 2695 | |

11543	
11542	
11544A	
11545A	
21356	
21362	

Suppression Assembly Job No. 18426

21782	
11964	
7712	
17934	
14456	
18425	

21394	
21395	
20250 (3 RAIL)	
18158 (2 RAIL)	
7715	
20250	
21785	
21054	
21786	
3212	

21350	
14456	
21398	
21401	

1541	
11964	
21352 (ASSY.)	
21779	
20250	
17894	
18394	

7712	
17942	
11541	
2954	
21349	
21359	

21358

21361
21780

Wheel — 20250
Wheel (with tyre groove) — 20251
Tyre — 20252
Insulating Sleeve — 21046
Top Casting — 21349
Bottom Casting — 21350
Layshaft Assembly — 21352
Armature Shaft Assembly — 21356
Plug — 21358
Brush Holder (with flange) — 21359
Bottom Bearing — 21361
Ring Magnet — 21362
Screw — 21363
Mounting Plate — 21365
Spring — 21394
Plunger — 21395
Insulating Bush — 21397
Fixed Bearing Assembly — 21398
Coupling — 21401
Screw — 21505
Sideframe (L.H.) — 21779
Sideframe (R.H.) — 21780
Casting for Bogie Job No. 18425 — 21782
Sideframe (L.H.) — 21783

Wheel (with tyre groove) — 17930 (2 RAIL)
17894 (2 RAIL)
Wheel (with tyre) Assembly Job No. 17894
18158 (2 RAIL)
20250 (3 RAIL)

27	Screw
39	Washer
1541	Nut
2695	Soldering Tag
2954	Screw
2981	Screw
7502	Screw
7712	Locking Nut
7715	Axle
11005	P.V.C. Sleeve
11545A	Plug (with boss)
13929	Choke
14473	Clamp for Wire
14482	Condenser
14769	Connecting Wire
21366	Insulating Support
11122	Connecting Wire
11240	Self Adhesive Tape
11541	Ball Bearing
11542	Brush Holder
11543	Brush Holder
11544A	Brush
11964	Spring
14456	Screw
17934	Ball Bearing
17942	Adjustable Bearing Housing Assembly
20249	Adjustable Bearing Housing Assembly
20249	Mitre Gear Assembly
21355	Mitre Gear Job No. 18425
20249	Worm Wheel Assembly

ISSUED
DECEMBER
1962

17

SERVICING LEAFLET 17 2 AND 3-RAIL

4-6-2 WEST COUNTRY CLASS LOCOMOTIVE AND TENDER

No. 2235 2-RAIL — No. 3235 3-RAIL

2548	Screw
3212	Screw
7510	Screw
7516	Screw
7715	Axle
7737	Screw
7741	Coupling Rod Pin
11560	Axle
18441	Frame & Bracket Assembly
21717	Wheel

Front Bogie
Assembly
Job No.
21728

14411	Grub Screw
21741	Worm Wheel

Worm Wheel Assembly
Job No. 18443

20638	Screw
20759	Coupling Rod
21394	Spring
21395	Plunger
21473	⅝″ Motor (Type B)
21706	Drawbar Guide Bracket
21712	Chassis
21715	Wheel with Flange
21716	Wheel without Flange
21718	Cylinder Assembly
21730	Spring
21732	Ballast Piece
21734	Pony Truck Frame
21736	Axle Plate
21803	Wheel and Axle
21738	Screw
21740	Drawbar Assembly

Pony Truck
Assembly
Job No. 21733

2-RAIL

7511	Screw
20689	Coupling Rod Pin
20690	Insulating Bushes (2)
21713	Wheel with Flange —Insulated

Wheel with Flange
(with Insulating
Bushes) Assembly
Job No. 18438

20690	Insulating Bushes (2)
21714	Wheel without Flange—Insulated

Wheel without
Flange (with
Insulating Bushes)
Assembly
Job No. 18440

20737	Base for Collector
20738	Cover for Collector
20739	Wire Collector

ASSEMBLIES

21701	Housing Assembly
21711	Chassis Assembly (with Motor)
18645	Chassis Assembly (without Motor)

3-RAIL

1183	Soldering Tag
1212	Nut
11297	Collector Shoe Spring
11299	Distance Piece
11548	Insulator for Collector Shoe Holder
11549	Collector Shoe Holder
11550	Collector Shoe
11553	Insulator
21504	Special Screw

ASSEMBLIES

18447	Housing Assembly
18646	Chassis Assembly (without Motor)
21747	Chassis Assembly (with Motor)

TENDER (2 & 3-RAIL)

11560	Axle
20187	Wheel with Flange
20188	Wheel without Flange
21691	Underframe
14680	Screw
21400	Coupling
21419	Rivet
21691	Underframe
12303	Coupling Pin

Underframe
Assembly
Job No.
18444

Underframe & Coupling
Pin Assembly
Job No. 18485

21694	Ladder

Hornby DUBLO

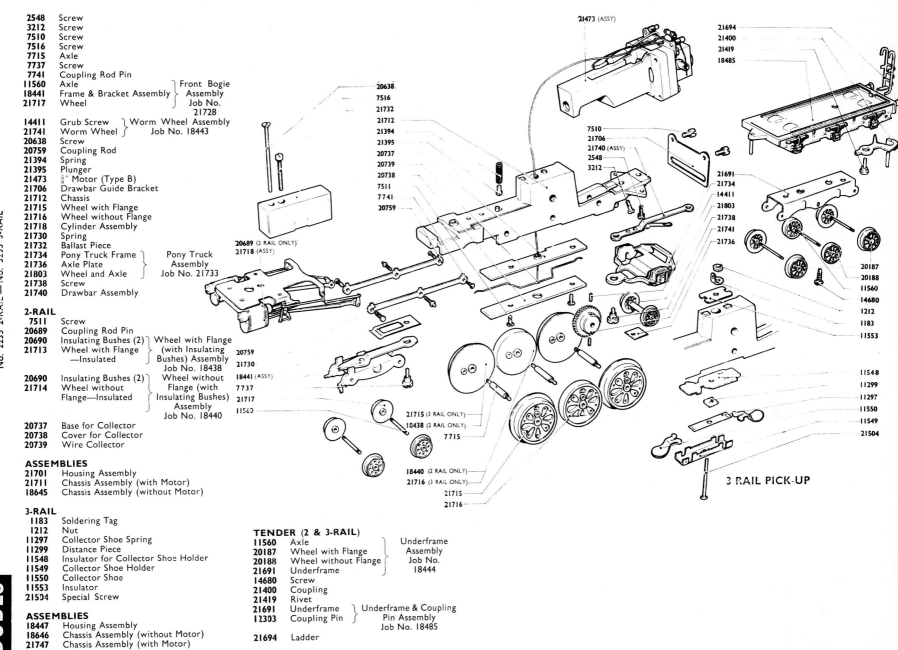

21473 (ASSY)

21694
21400
21419
18485

20638
7516
21732
21712
21394
21395
20737
20739
20738
7511
7741
20759

7510
21706
21740 (ASSY)
2548
3212

21691
21734
14411
21803
21738
21741
21736

20689 (2 RAIL ONLY)
21718 (ASSY)

20759
21730
18441 (ASSY)
7737
21717
11560

20187
20188
11560
14680
1212
1183
11553

11548
11299
11297
11550
11549
21504

21715 (3 RAIL ONLY)
18438 (2 RAIL ONLY)
7715

18440 (2 RAIL ONLY)
21716 (3 RAIL ONLY)
21715
21716

3 RAIL PICK-UP

SERVICING LEAFLET

ELECTRIC MOTOR COACH 2 AND 3-RAIL

No. 2250 2-RAIL — No. 3250 3-RAIL

22

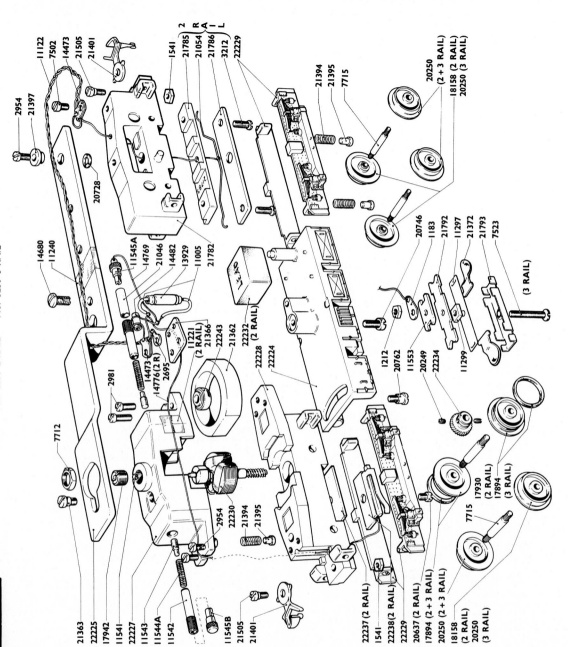

1541	Nut
2695	Soldering Tag
2954	Screw
2981	Screw
7502	Screw
7712	Locking Nut
7715	Axle
11005	P.V.C. Sleeve
11545A	Plug (with boss)
13929	Choke
14473	Clamp for Wire
14482	Condenser
14769	Connecting Wire
21366	Insulating Support
11122	Connecting Wire
11240	Self Adhesive Tape
11541	Ball Bearing
11542	Brush Holder
11543	Brush
11544A	Spring
11545B	Plug
14680	Adjustable Bearing Housing Assembly
17942	Grub Screw
20249	Wheel
20250	Wheel (with tyre groove)
20251	Tyre
20252	Washer
20728	Screw
25746	Screw
20762	Insulating Sleeve
21046	

21362	Ring Magnet
21363	Screw
21394	Spring
21395	Plunger
21397	Insulating Bush
21401	Coupling
21505	Screw
21782	Casting for Bogie
22224	Underframe
22225	Mounting Plate
22227	Top Casting
22228	Bottom Casting
22229	Sideframe
22230	Armature Shaft Assembly
22234	Worm Wheel
22243	Ball Bearing Complete

ASSEMBLY

22214	Body Assembly
3212	Screw
11221	Self Adhesive Tape
14776	Connecting Wire
20252	Tyre
20690	Insulating Bush
20703	Wheel (with tyre groove) Insulated
20637	Screw
20690	Insulating Bush
20702	Wheel (insulated)

Wheel (with tyre groove) Assembly Job No. 17894

Wheel (Insulated, with tyre groove) Insulated Job No. 17930

21054	Wire Collector
21785	Base for Collector
21786	Cover for Collector
22232	Weight
22237	Collector Insulator
22238	Collector Assembly

ASSEMBLIES

22226	Motor Bogie Assembly
22239	Rear Bogie Assembly

3 RAIL

1183	Soldering Tag
1212	Nut
7523	Screw
11297	Collector Shoe Spring
11299	Distance Piece
11553	Insulator
21372	Collector Shoe
21792	Insulator
21793	Collector Shoe Holder

ASSEMBLIES

22241	Motor Bogie Assembly
22242	Rear Bogie Assembly

ISSUED DECEMBER 1962

MECCANO LTD.

| ARTICLE | PERFORMANCE DATA FOR DUBLO LOCOMOTIVES. | MEMO. Nº 20689 |

USED ON	REFER ALSO TO

NOTES: TEST TRACK TO CONSIST OF 8 CURVES & 2 STRAIGHTS (3 RAIL) OR 12 CURVES & 2 STRAIGHTS AND 2-1/3 STRAIGHTS (2 RAIL). MAINS VOLTAGE SUPPLIED TO POWER UNIT TO BE 240 VOLTS.

REPAIR TESTING :- ALL LOCOS UNDER GUARANTEE, PERFORMANCE AS STATED. OTHER REPAIRED LOCOS MAY BE ONE SECOND SLOWER IN EITHER DIRECTION.

FOR 2 RAIL TRACK THE INNER RAIL IS TO BE POSITIVE WHEN LOCOS ARE RUNNING FORWARDS IN A CLOCKWISE DIRECTION.

2 RAIL	3 RAIL	LOCOMOTIVE	MAX. TIME FOR 5 LAPS		MAX. CURRENT	LOAD
			FORWARD	REVERSE		
2211	3211	STREAMLINED LOCO & TENDER.	25 SECS	27 SECS	·65 AMPS	FOUR SD6 COACHES
	3212	"DUCHESS" & TENDER.	25 "	27 "	·65 "	" " "
2218	3218	2-6-4 TANK.	25 "	27 "	·65 "	" " "
2221	3221	"CASTLE" CLASS & TENDER (5/8" MOTOR)	25 "	27 "	·65 "	" " "
2220	3220	" " " " (1/2" MOTOR)	30 "	32 "	·65 "	" " "
2224	3224	2-8-0 FREIGHT & TENDER (5/8" MOTOR)	28 "	28 "	·65 "	" " "
2225	3225	" " " " (1/2" MOTOR)	33 "	35 "	·65 "	" " "
2230	3230	BO-BO DIESEL 1000 B.H.P.	30 "	32 "	·65 "	" " "
2226	3226	"CITY" CLASS & TENDER.	25 "	27 "	·65 "	" " "
2206/7		0-6-0 TANK.	30 "	32 "	·55 "	" " "
2231	3231	0-6-0 DIESEL SHUNTER.	30 "	32 "	·65 "	" " "
2232	3232	CO-CO DIESEL ELECTRIC.	25 "	27 "	·65 "	" " "
2235	3235	4-6-2 WEST COUNTRY & TENDER.	25 "	27 "	·65 "	" " "
2233	3233	CO-BO DIESEL.	25 "	27 "	·65 "	" " "
2217	3217	0-6-2 TANK.	30 "	32 "	·65 "	" " "

					LIMITS ON DIMENSIONS	DRAWN R.W.
					FRACTIONS :— ± ·008"	TRACED I.M.D.
					DECIMALS :— ± ·003"	CHECKED
					SPECIAL LIMITS AS SHOWN	APPROVED
5	REDRAWN & REVISED. 2 RAIL ADDED.		6219	11-4-61 K.R.M.	DISTRIBUTION	
ISSUE	DESCRIPTION OF CHANGE		C.O. No.	DATE SIG.		SCALE
MATERIAL						DATE 1-10-57

MECCANO L^TD.

TITLE	DUBLO DIMENSIONS			MEMO. No. 20537
				SHEET 1.

SALES No	DESCRIPTION	DIMENSIONS. INCHES	DIMENSIONS. CENTIMETRES	REMARKS.
3212	DUCHESS LOCO & TENDER	OVERALL LENGTH 12¼	31·1	
2206/7	0-6-0 TANK LOCO.	" " 5½	13·9	
2211/3211	STREAMLINED LOCO. & TENDER.	" " 11⅜	28·8	
2217/3217	0-6-2 TANK LOCO.	" " 6 3/16	15·7	
2218/3218	2-6-4 " "	" " 7 13/16	19·8	
2221/3221	CASTLE LOCO & TENDER.	" " 10 13/16	27·4	
2224/3224	FREIGHT " " "	" " 10¾	27·3	
2226/3226	4-6-2 CITY CLASS LOCO. & TENDER.	" " 12¼	31·1	
2230/3230	1000 B.H.P DIESEL ELECTRIC LOCO.	" " 7 13/16	19·8	
2231/3231	0-6-0 SHUNTING "	" " 5⅛	13·0	
2232/3232	CO-CO DIESEL LOCO.	" " 9 15/16	25·2	
2233/3233	CO-BO " "	" " 9 9/16	24·2	
2235/3235	WEST COUNTRY CLASS LOCO. & TENDER.	" " 11⅛	28·2	
2250/3250	SUBURBAN ELECTRIC MOTOR COACH.	" " 9¾	24·7	
4005	CORRIDOR COACH 1st/2nd B.R.	" " 9⅛	23·2	
4006	" " BRAKE/2nd B.R.	" " 9⅛	23·2	
4009	" " 1st/2nd W.R.	" " 9⅛	23·2	
4010	" " BRAKE/2nd W.R.	" " 9⅛	23·2	
4013	" " 1st/2nd B.R.	" " 9⅛	23·2	
4014	" " BRAKE/2nd B.R.	" " 9⅛	23·2	
4021	SUBURBAN COACH 1st/2nd B.R.	" " 8	20·3	
4022	" " BRAKE/2nd B.R.	" " 8	20·3	
4025	" " 1st/2nd S.R.	" " 8	20·3	
4026	" " BRAKE/2nd S.R.	" " 8	20·3	
4047	COMPOSITE RESTAURANT CAR W.R.	" " 9⅛	23·2	
4048	" " CAR B.R. (CREAM & RED)	" " 9⅛	23·2	
4049	" " " B.R. (MAROON)	" " 9⅛	23·2	
2400	T.P.O. LINESIDE APPARATUS 2 RAIL.	LENGTH 9 3/32 WIDTH 2 7/16	23·1 × 6·2	
3400	T.P.O " " 3 RAIL.	" 12⅛ " 3¼	30·8 × 8·2	
4401	T.P.O. MAIL VAN 2 OR 3 RAIL.	OVERALL LENGTH 9⅛	23·2	
4050	1st/2nd CORRIDOR COACH W.R. BROWN & CREAM.	OVERALL LENGTH 9¾	24·7	
4051	BRAKE/2nd " " " " " "	" " 9¾	24·7	
4052	1st/2nd " " B.R. MAROON	" " 9¾	24·7	
4053	BRAKE/2nd " " " "	" " 9¾	24·7	
4054	1st/2nd " " S.R. GREEN.	" " 9¾	24·7	
4055	BRAKE/2nd. " " " "	" " 9¾	24·7	
4060	1st. OPEN COACH W.R. BROWN & CREAM.	" " 9¾	24·7	
4061	2nd. " " " "	" " 9¾	24·7	
4062	1st " " B.R. MAROON,	" " 9¾	24·7	
4063	2nd. " " " "	" " 9¾	24·7	
4070	RESTAURANT CAR. W.R. BROWN & CREAM.	" " 9¾	24·7	
4071	" " B.R. MAROON.	" " 9¾	24·7	
4072	BUFFET RESTAURANT CAR S.R. GREEN.	" " 9¾	24·7	
4074	PASSENGER BRAKE VAN W.R. BROWN & CREAM.	" " 9¾	24·7	
4075	" " " B.R. MAROON.	" " 9¾	24·7	
4078	1st/2nd SLEEPING CAR B.R. "	" " 9¾	24·7	
4081	SUBURBAN 1st/2nd COACH S.R. GREEN.	" " 9¾	24·7	

DRAWN BY M.C.	TRACED BY I.M.D.	CHECKED BY J.C.M.	DATE 1-6-61	MEMO No 20537 SHT. 1.

MECCANO L^TD^

TITLE	DUBLO DIMENSIONS	Memo No. 20537
		SHEET 2.

Sales No	DESCRIPTION	DIMENSIONS INCHES		DIMENSIONS CENTIMETRES.	REMARKS.
4082	SUBURBAN BRAKE - 2nd COACH S.R. GREEN.	OVERALL LENGTH	9 3/4	24·7	
4083	.. 1st./2nd. .. B.R. MAROON	.. ..	9 3/4	24·7	
4084	.. BRAKE - 2nd	.. ..	9 3/4	24·7	
4150	ELECTRIC DRIVING TRAILER	.. ..	9 3/4	24·7	
4035	PULLMAN CAR - ARIES	.. ..	9 3/4	24·7	
4036	.. .. - 2nd PARLOUR.	.. ..	9 3/4	24·7	
4037	.. .. - BRAKE 2nd	.. ..	9 3/4	24·7	
4318	PACKING VAN FOR BREAKDOWN CRANE	.. ..	3 5/8	9·2	
4076	6 WHEELED PASSENGER BRAKE VAN.	.. ..	5 13/16	14·7	
4300	'BLUE SPOT' FISH VAN.	.. ..	4 3/16	10·6	
4301	BANANA VAN	.. ..	3 5/8	9·2	
4305	PASSENGER FRUIT VAN (W.R.)	.. ..	5 5/16	13·5	
4310	GOODS BRAKE VAN (L.M.R.)	.. ..	4 3/8	11·2	
4311	GOODS BRAKE VAN (B.R.)	.. ..	4 3/8	11·2	
4312	GOODS BRAKE VAN (W.R.)	.. ..	4 3/8	11·2	
4313	GUNPOWDER VAN.	.. ..	3 5/8	9·2	
4315	HORSE BOX (B.R.)	.. ..	5 5/16	13·5	
4316	HORSE BOX (S.R.)	.. ..	5 5/16	13·5	
4320	REFRIGERATOR VAN (W.R.)	.. ..	3 5/8	9·2	
4323	4 WHEELED UTILITY VAN.	.. ..	5 15/16	15·0	
4325	VENTILATED VAN - 12 ton.	.. ..	3 5/8	9·2	
4605	BOGIE WELL WAGON.	.. ..	6 7/8	17·5	
4610	BOGIE BOLSTER WAGON.	.. ..	6 1/2	16·5	
4615	DOUBLE BOLSTER WAGON (WITH TIMBER LOAD)	.. ..	5 1/8	13·0	
4620	BREAKDOWN CRANE - COMPLETE.	.. ..	13 5/16	33·8	
4625	BULK GRAIN WAGON (20 ton)	.. ..	3 15/16	10·0	
4626	PRESFLO BULK CEMENT WAGON (B.R)	.. ..	3 1/2	8·9	
4627	I.C.I. 20 ton BULK SALT WAGON.	.. ..	3 1/2	8·9	
4630	CATTLE WAGON (8 ton)	.. ..	3 15/16	10·0	
4635	COAL WAGON.	.. ..	3 5/8	9·2	
4638	'CONFLAT P' WAGON WITH 2 CONTAINERS.	.. ..	5 3/16	13·1	
4639	OPEN FERRY WAGON S.R.	.. ..	4 5/8	11·7	
4640	GOODS WAGON (STEEL TYPE)	.. ..	3 5/8	9·2	
4644	21 ton HOPPER WAGON.	.. ..	4 1/4	10·8	
4645	LOW SIDED WAGON	.. ..	3 15/16	10·0	
4646	.. .. .. with CABLE DRUMS	.. ..	3 15/16	10·0	
4647	.. .. .. with FURNITURE CONTAINER	.. ..	3 15/16	10·0	
4648	.. .. .. INSULATED MEAT ..	.. ..	3 15/16	10·0	
4649	.. .. TRACTOR	.. ..	3 15/16	10·0	
4652	LOWMAC MACHINE WAGON.	.. ..	5 9/16	14·2	
4655	16 ton MINERAL WAGON (GREY)	.. ..	3 5/8	9·2	
4656	.. .. .. (RED)	.. ..	3 5/8	9·2	
4657	UNITED DAIRIES MILK TANK WAGON (6 WHEEL)	.. ..	4 1/8	10·5	
4658	PRESTWIN SILO WAGON.	.. ..	3 5/8	9·2	
4660	U.G.B. SAND WAGON.	.. ..	3 5/8	9·2	
4665	SAXA SALT WAGON.	.. ..	3 5/8	9·2	
4667	12 ton SHOCK ABSORBING WAGON.	.. ..	3 5/8	9·2	
4670	13 ton STANDARD WAGON.	.. ..	3 5/8	9·2	
4675	I.C.I. CHLORINE TANK WAGON.	.. ..	4 1/4	10·8	
4676	ESSO TANK WAGON.	.. ..	3 5/8	9·2	
4677	MOBIL TANK WAGON.	.. ..	3 5/8	9·2	
4678	SHELL TANK WAGON.	.. ..	3 5/8	9·2	

DRAWN BY M.C.	TRACED BY I.M.D.	CHECKED BY J.C.M.	DATE 1-6-61	MEMO. No 20537 SHT. 2.

MECCANO LTD.

TITLE	DUBLO DIMENSIONS			MEMO. No. 20537
				SHEET 3.
Sales No.	DESCRIPTION	DIMENSIONS INCHES	DIMENSIONS CENTIMETRES	REMARKS.
4679	TRAFFIC SERVICES LTD TANK WAGON	OVERALL LENGTH 4 5/8	11·7	
4680	ESSO FUEL OIL TANK WAGON.	" " 3 5/8	9·2	
4685	I.C.I. CAUSTIC LIQUOR BOGIE WAGON.	" " 5 11/16	14·4	
1041	HORNBY CONTROLLER.	5 1/16 × 5 × 2 1/2	12·8 × 12·7 × 6·3	
1080	" BATTERY "	4 3/16 × 4 3/16 × 1	10·6 × 10·6 × 2·5	
1100	HORNBY II POWER CONTROL UNIT.	7 1/16 × 4 3/8 × 2 7/8	17·9 × 11·1 × 7·3	
1120	HORNBY III " " "	6 7/8 × 6 1/4 × 4 1/4	17·4 × 15·9 × 10·8	
1613	SWITCH FOR POINTS & SIGNALS	LENGTH 2 1/4 WIDTH 7/16	5·7 × 1·1	
1614	SWITCH for POINTS & SIGNALS	LENGTH 2 1/4 WIDTH 7/16	5·7 × 1·1	
1616	" " ISOLATING RAILS.	" " " "	" " "	
1620	" " COLOUR LIGHT SIGNALS	" " " "	" "	
2450	BUFFER STOP	LENGTH 2 WIDTH 1 5/16	5·1 × 3·3	
2451	" " with LIGHT	" " " "	" "	
2460	LEVEL CROSSING (2 RAIL)	" 6 " 5 3/4	15·2 × 14·6	
2701	STRAIGHT RAIL – FULL 2 RAIL	LENGTH 8 5/8	21·9	
2702	2/3	5 3/4	14·6	
2703	1/3	2 7/8	7·3	
2704	FULL TERMINAL RAIL	8 5/8	21·9	
2705	1/3 " "	2 7/8	7·3	
2706	SHORT	1 5/16	3·3	
2710	CURVED RAIL FULL 15in RADIUS	RADIUS TO CENTRE LINE		
2711	1/2 " "	OF TRACK = 15"	38·0	
2712	1/4 " "	12 FULL CURVES IN A		
2713	FULL TERM! 15in "	COMPLETE CIRCLE.		
2719	FULL-LARGE RADIUS	RADIUS TO CENTRE LINE		
2720	FULL TERM! LGE. "	OF TRACK = 17·284	43·9	
2722	1/2 LARGE RADIUS.	12 LARGE RAD. CURVES IN COMP. CIRCLE		
2728	SWITCH POINTS (H.O.) R.H.	5 3/4 LONG & HALF CURVE	14·6	
2729	" " " L.H.	" " " " " "	"	
2731	ELECT. OPERATED POINTS R.H.	" " " " "	"	
2732	" " " L.H.	" " " " "	"	
2734	DIAMOND CROSSING R.H.	5 3/4 LONG.	14·6	
2735	" " L.H.	" "	"	
2738	STRAIGHT ISOLATING RAIL – 2/3 SINGLE	" "	"	
2739	" " " – 2/3 DOUBLE	" "	"	
2740	CURVED ISOLATING 1/2 RAIL – DOUBLE	15 RADIUS	38·0	
2741	" " " " – SINGLE	" "	" "	
2742	STRAIGHT ISOLATING 1/3 RAIL – SINGLE	LENGTH 2 7/8	7·3	
2743	CURVED ISOLATING 1/2 RAIL – DOUBLE LARGE RADIUS	17·284 RADIUS	43·9	
2745	UNCOUPLING RAIL (H.O.)	LENGTH 5 3/4	14·6	
2746	ELEC. OPERATED UNCOUPLING RAIL.	" "	14·6	
2900	RAILER (2 RAIL)	" 12	30·4	
3450	BUFFER STOP (3 RAIL)	LENGTH 2"	5·1	
346	LEVEL CROSSING (3 RAIL)	LENGTH 6 WIDTH 5	15·2 × 12·7	
3701	STRAIGHT RAIL – FULL (3 RAIL)	" 11 1/2	29·2	

DRAWN BY M.C. TRACED BY I.M.D. CHECKED BY J.C.M. DATE 1·6·61 MEMO No 20537 SHT. 3.

MECCANO LTD.

TITLE	DUBLO DIMENSIONS.	Memo No. 20537
		SHEET 4.

Sales Nº	DESCRIPTION.	DIMENSIONS INCHES	DIMENSIONS CENTIMETRES	REMARKS.
3702	STRAIGHT RAIL - HALF	LENGTH 5 3/4	14·6	
3703	- QUARTER.	2 7/8	7·3	
3704	- HALF TERMINAL	5 3/4	14·6	
3705	- HALF RAIL with ROADWAY.	5 3/4	14·6	
3706	- SHORT	15/16	3·3	
3710	CURVED RAIL - FULL	RADIUS TO CENTRE		
3711	- HALF	RAIL OF TRACK = 15"	38·0	
3712	- QUARTER	8 RAILS IN A COMPLETE		
3713	- FULL TERMINAL.	CIRCLE.		
3719	- FULL LARGE RADIUS	RADIUS TO CENTRE RAIL = 17·284	43·9	
3720	- FULL LARGE RADIUS TERM.	8 CURVES IN A COMPLETE CIRCLE.		
3728	ISOLATING SWITCH POINTS - R.H.	5 3/4 LONG & HALF CURVE.	14·6 & HALF CURVE.	
3729	" " " - L.H.	5 3/4 " " " "	" " " "	
3731	ELECTRICALLY OPERATED POINTS - R.H.	5 3/4 " " " "	" " " "	
3732	" " " - L.H.	5 3/4 " " " "	" " " "	
3734	DIAMOND CROSSING - R.H.	LENGTH 5 3/4	14·6	
3735	" " - L.H.	" 5 3/4	14·6	
3738	ISOLATING RAIL	" 2 7/8	7·3	
3470	TURNTABLE (3 RAIL ONLY.)	14 5/8 DIA.	37·2	
3745	UNCOUPLING RAIL (HAND OPERATED)	LENGTH 5 3/4	14·6	
3746	UNCOUPLING RAIL (ELECTRICALLY OPERATED)	" "	14·6	
3900	RAILER (3 RAIL)	" 12	30·4	
5005	ENGINE SHED KIT.	LENGTH 12 13/16 WIDTH 5 3/16	32·5 × 13·2	
5006	" " EXTENSION	" " " 5	32·5 × 12·7	
5010	FOOTBRIDGE.	LENGTH 7 3/8 × WIDTH 5	18·7 × 12·7	
5015	GIRDER BRIDGE.	" 11 1/2 " 3	29·2 × 7·6	
5020	GOODS DEPOT KIT.	" 11 1/2 " 4 11/16	29·2 × 11·9	
5025	GRADIENT & MILE POSTS	HEIGHT 5/8	1·6	
5030	ISLAND PLATFORM (KIT)	LENGTH 23 WIDTH 2 1/2	58·4 × 6·3	
5035	LOADING GAUGE.	HEIGHT 3 5/8	9·2	
5040	PLATELAYER'S HUT.	LENGTH 1 9/16 WIDTH 1 1/16	3·9 × 2·7	
5045/6	SINGLE HEAD COLOUR LIGHT SIGNAL	HEIGHT 2 3/4	7·0	
5047	JUNCTION " " " 'HOME'	" 2 7/8	7·3	
5081	SIGNAL - SINGLE ARM 'DISTANT'	" 4 7/16 BASE 1" SQ.	11·3 × 2·5	
5055	" - DOUBLE ARM.	" " " "	11·3 × 2·5	
5061	" - JUNCTION 'DISTANT'	" " " "	11·3 × 2·5	
5065	" - SINGLE ARM. (ELEC. OP.) 'HOME'	" " BASE 1 1/2 SQ.	11·3 × 3·8	
5070	" - DOUBLE ARM. (ELEC. OPERATED)	" " " "	11·3 × 3·8	
5075	" - JUNCTION (ELEC. OP.) 'HOME'	" " " "	11·3 × 3·8	
5080	SIGNAL CABIN	" 6 3/8 WIDTH 2 1/2	16·2 × 6·3	
5083	DUBLO TERMINAL STATION (KIT)	LENGTH 21 3/4 × " 11 1/2	55·3 × 29·2	
5083	DUBLO THROUGH STATION (KIT)	" 23 " 16	58·5 × 40·5	
5085	SUBURBAN STATION (KIT)	" 23 " 5 1/2	58·4 × 14·0	
5086	PLATFORM EXTENSION.	LENGTH 11 1/2 WIDTH 2 1/2	29·2 × 6·3	
5087	FENCE for PLATFORM EXTENSION.	" "	"	
5090	TELEGRAPH POLE.	HEIGHT 3 15/16 BASE 1 1/8 DIA.	10·0 × 2·8	
5091	TUNNEL - SINGLE TRACK.	LENGTH 8 7/16 WIDTH 5 1/2	21·4 × 14	
5092	" - DOUBLE TRACK.	" 16 3/8 " 13	41·5 × 33	
5095	WATER CRANE.	HEIGHT 2 7/8	7·3.	

DRAWN BY M.C.	TRACED BY I.M.D.	CHECKED BY J.E.M.	DATE 1-6-61	MEMO. No 20537 SHT. 4.

APPENDIX IV   BRUSH IDENTIFICATION FOR HORNBY DUBLO LOCOMOTIVES

1505	Brush	2211	A4— 2-rail 'Golden Fleece'
1506	Brush spring	2217	0-62T 2-rail No. 69550
		2218	2-6-4T 2-rail BR 80033
		2226	4-6-2 LMR 'City of London'
		2232	Co-Co loco 2-rail
		2234	Co-Co Deltic 'Crepello'
		3211	A4 3-rail 'Mallard'
		3212	4-6-2 'Duchess of Montrose'
		3217	0-6-2T 3-rail 69567
		3218	2-6-4T 3-rail 80259 and 80054
		3226	4-6-2 'City of Liverpool' 3-rail
		3232	Co-Co 3-rail
		3233	Co-Bo 3-rail
		2250	Electric Motor Coach 2-rail
		3234	Co-Co Deltic 'St. Paddy'
		3250	Electric Motor Coach 3-rail
1507	Brush	2221	'Castle' Class loco — 'Cardiff Castle'
1508	Brush spring	2224	2-8-0 8F 2-rail BR 48073
		2231	0-6-0 Shunter 2-rail D3302
		2235	4-6-2 'Barnstaple' Class West Country
		3221	'Castle' Class Loco 'Ludlow Castle'
		3224	2-8-0 8F 3-rail BR 48094
		3231	0-6-0 Shunter 3-rail D3763
		3235	4-6-2 'Dorchester' Class West Country
1510	Brush Arm	2206	0-6-0 Tank Black
		2207	0-6-0 Tank Green
		2220	'Castle' Class Loco 'Denbigh Castle'
		2225	8F 2-8-0 BR 48109
1511	Brush Arm	3220	'Castle' Class loco 'Bristol Castle'
		2230	Bo-Bo 2-rail
		3230	Bo-Bo 3-rail

APPENDIX V   SUPER DETAIL WAGONS
SALE — STOCK FIGURES FOR 1964 ONLY
Taken from the Triang Official Stock Figures kindly forwarded by Mr. Richard Lines

Item	Model	Part No.	Introduced	Sold in 1964	Stock 1964
1	Bulk Grain Wagon	4625	2/58	700	4100
2	Cattle Wagon	4630	4/58	800	2400
3	Steel Goods Wagon	4640	5/58	1900	3600
4	Goods Wagon	4670	6/58	1300	400
5	Refrigerator van	4320	7/58	800	3600
6	Ventilated van	4235	8/58	1300	2700
7	WR goods brake	4312	9/58	1250	2800
8	16 ton grey mineral	4655	10/58	1300	900
9	LMR brown goods brake	4310	11/58	1300	1800
10	United Glass Sand Wagon	4660	11/58	800	3900
11	13 Ton Coal Wagon	4635	12/58	1400	400
12	Saxa Salt Van	4665	12/58	1400	1800
13	ER goods brake	4311	1/59	1500	1200
14	Esso Fuel Oil Tanker (black)	4680	1/60	700	1400
15	Horsebox BR maroon	4315	3/60	1260	Nil
16	Horsebox SR green	4316	3/60	1100	2000
17	ICI Chlorine Tanker	4675	4/60	400	9300
18	Traffic Services Tanker	4679	5/60	650	3150
19	WR Passenger Fruit Van	4305	11/60	850	3500
20	Prestflo Bulk Cement	4626	11/61	500	9500
21	ICI Bulk Salt Wagon	4627	11/61	600	7700
22	Lowmac Machine Wagon	4652	11/61	1300	4500
23	Blue Spot Fish Van	4300	11/61	750	2100
24	SR 4-wheel Utility Van	4323	12/61	700	1100
25	Gunpowder Van	4313	4/62	375	8600
26	Banana Van	4301	4/62	650	7400

Item	Model	Part No.	Introduced	Sold in 1964	Stock 1964
27	Packing Van	4318	5/62	600	7450
28	16 ton brown Mineral	4656	8/62	Nil no figures recorded	Nil
29	6-wheel United Dairies	4657	8/62	750	4150
30	Prestwin Silo Wagon	4658	8/62	850	5200
31	ICI Bogie liquor tanker	4685	8/62	950	1500
32	21 ton hopper Wagon	4644	10/63	2500	400
33	Rail Cleaning Wagon	4654	12/64	839	1700
34	Lowsided Wagon	4645		900	800
35	Lowsided with cable drums	4646		1350	1850
36	Lowsided furniture container	4647		500	2400
37	Lowsided Wagon Insulated container	4648		400	2600
38	Lowsided Wagon with tractor	4649		1500	600
39	Bogie Bolster Wagon	4610		1300	1300
40	Bogie Well Wagon	4605		1650	1600
41	Double Bolster Wagon	4615		800	700
42	Esso (silver) tanker	4676		1150	1600
43	Mobil red Tanker	4677		1100	1700
44	Shell yellow Tanker	4678		1100	2800

Total Wagons Sold in 1964   43,824

Total Wagons remaining in stock   128,200

APPENDIX VI   SUPER DETAIL COACHES
SALE — STOCK FIGURES FOR 1964 ONLY

Item	Model	Part No.	Introduced	Sold in 1964	Stock 1964
1	WR Corridor 1st 2nd coach	4050	12/60	360	6000
2	WR Corridor Brake 2nd coach	4051	12/60	400	5000
3	BR Corridor 1st 2nd coach	4052	12/60	600	4300
4	BR Corridor Brake 2nd coach	4053	12/60	450	3250
5	BR Passenger Brake van	4075	3/61	450	9500
6	BR Composite sleeping car	4078	3/61	300	10650
7	Pullman Car 1st Class Aries	4035	3/61	850	3800
8	Pullman Car 2nd Class No. 74	4036	3/61	850	5000
9	Pullman Car Brake /2nd No. 79	4037	3/61	750	5400
10	WR Open First Class coach	4060	12/61	150	6750
11	WR Open Second Class coach	4061	12/61	250	7700
12	BR open First Class coach	4062	12/61	300	5150
13	BR open Second Class coach	4063	12/61	250	6750
14	BR Southern Suburban 1st/2nd coach	4081	4/62	300	5100
15	BR Southern Suburban Brake 2nd	4082	4/62	200	1950
16	BR Maroon suburban 1st/2nd coach	4083	4/62	250	2300
17	BR Maroon suburban Brake/2nd	4084	4/62	200	2400
18	Southern Mainline corridor 1st/2nd	4054	4/62	250	6850
19	Southern Mainline corridor Brake/2nd	4055	4/62	250	5900
20	Electric Driving Trailer coach	4150	10/62	350	1200
21	WR Restaurant car	4070	4/63	300	2700
22	BR Restaurant car	4071	4/63	500	300
23	6-wheel Passenger Brake	4076	10/63	1750	2100

Total sold in 1964   10,310

Total left in stock in 1964   110,050

ALSO INCLUDED IN THE 1964 CATALOGUE:

Item	Model	Part No.	Introduced	Sold in 1964	Stock 1964
24	BR Tinplate Suburban 1st/2nd coach	4021		— no figures recorded	
25	BR Tinplate Suburban Brake/2nd	4022		300	650
26	SR Tinplate Suburban 1st/2nd coach	4025		350	350
27	SR Tinplate Suburban Brake/2nd	4026		225	1300
28	Composite Restaurant car WR	4047		250	2250
29	Composite Restaurant car BR	4048		250	1850
30	Composite Restaurant car BR Maroon	4049		250	1000
				1625	7400

APPENDIX VII   BUILDINGS AND ACCESSORIES
SALE – STOCK FIGURES FOR 1964 ONLY

		Sold in 1964	Stock left
5083	Terminal/through station	450	400
5084	Canopy extension	200	100
5085	Suburban station	—	—
5030	Island Platform	1850	2000
5020	Goods Depot	600	3500
5080	Signal Cabin	—	—
5010	Footbridge	2000	1400
5005	Engine Shed	900	7700
5006	Engine Shed Extension	100	7500
5091	Single Track Tunnel	—	—
5092	Double Track Tunnel	350	4150
5015	Girder Bridge	500	1000
2460	Level Crossing 2 rail	3000	4650
5086	Box of six Platform extensions	250	3000
5087	Box of six platform fences	200	1300
5040	Box of six platelayers huts.	480	400
5090	Telegraph pole	—	—
5095	Water Crane	1100	900
5035	Loading gauge	1000	2500
5037	Lineside notices	1100	6800
5089	Side platform extensions	250	600
5025	Gradient and mile posts	500	4000

APPENDIX VIII   SIGNALS
SALE – STOCK FIGURES FOR 1964 ONLY

		Sold in 1964	Stock left
Colour Aspect Signals			
5045	Single head – home	None	None
5046	Single head – distant	1300	2800
5047	Double head – home	1300	750
Semaphore Signals Manual			
5050	Single Arm – home	1400	3000
5057	Single Arm – distant	—	—
5055	Double Arm Signal	1250	2000
5060	Junction Signal – home	—	—
5061	Junction Signal – distant	750	1100
Semaphore Signals (electrically operated)			
5065	Single Arm – home	480	200
5066	Single Arm – distant	300	200
5070	Double Arm Signal	300	500
5075	Junction Signal – home	300	100
5076	Junction Signal – distant	150	550
Switches			
1612	Switch link handle connecting two switches	—	—
1613	Red, for points and semaphore signals	11000	2500
1616	Black, for isolating rails	2500	800
1620	Green, for colour aspect signals only	3500	1700

NOTE: FOR COMPARATIVE FIGURES ON LOCOMOTIVES –
SEE INDIVIDUAL MODEL HISTORIES – PAGES 83 TO 173

Source Material

Literature from the Meccano Co. Ltd. including trade and model leaflets, catalogues, bulletins, drawings, photographs and original artwork, not least the Meccano Magazine and the Hornby Railway Company articles.
The Railway Modeller magazine.
The Model Railway Constructor magazine.
The Model Railway News magazine.
Bassett-Lowke catalogue – 'The 6.30 Down'.
Edward Beal's 'Scale Railway Modelling Today', (1939).
Cecil Gibson's 'History of British Dinky Toys'.
Eric Treacy's 'Steam Up' 1948.
The Beetle Bulletin of British Industrial Plastics Ltd.
'Engineering' – The Design Council's magazine for Engineers.
Triang and Triang Hornby catalogues of the Rovex Co. Ltd.
Official British Railways photographs, from old Meccano files.
Pullman Car Company drawings and photographs, from old Meccano files.
The John Griffiths drawings of the pre-war wooden buildings.
The Chris Willis re-drawing of the 0-6-2 tank housing.
A photograph of the Wills Finecast Co. Ltd.

Index